lonely planet

D0254815

Mauritius,
Réunion
& Seychelles

Tom Masters
Jean-Bernard Carillet

MAURITIUS

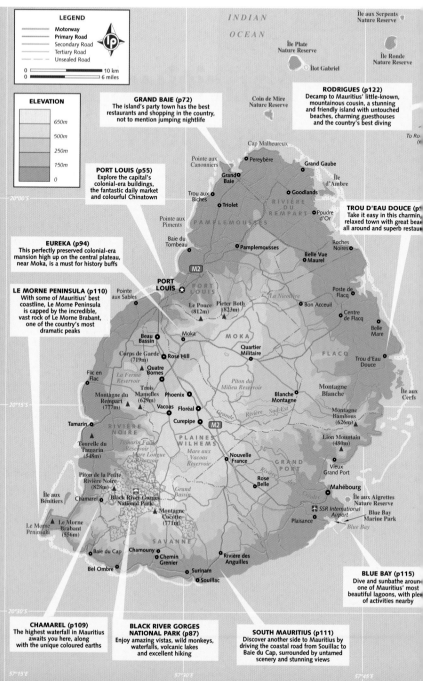

LEGEND
- Motorway
- Primary Road
- Secondary Road
- Tertiary Road
- Unsealed Road

0 — 10 km
0 — 6 miles

ELEVATION
- 650m
- 500m
- 250m
- 150m
- 0

INDIAN OCEAN

Île aux Serpents Nature Reserve

Île Plate Nature Reserve

Île Ronde Nature Reserve

Îlot Gabriel

GRAND BAIE (p72)
The island's party town has the best restaurants and shopping in the country, not to mention jumping nightlife

RODRIGUES (p122)
Decamp to Mauritius' little-known, mountainous cousin, a stunning and friendly island with untouched beaches, charming guesthouses and the country's best diving

To Ro...

Coin de Mire Nature Reserve

Cap Malheureux

PORT LOUIS (p55)
Explore the capital's colonial-era buildings, the fantastic daily market and colourful Chinatown

Pointe aux Canonniers

Pereybère

Grand Gaube

Grand Baie

Île d'Ambre

Trou aux Biches

Triolet

Goodlands

RIVIÈRE DU REMPART

TROU D'EAU DOUCE (p...)
Take it easy in this charming relaxed town with great bea... all around and superb restau...

Pointe aux Piments

PAMPLEMOUSSES

Poudre d'Or

EUREKA (p94)
This perfectly preserved colonial-era mansion high up on the central plateau, near Moka, is a must for history buffs

Baie du Tombeau

Pamplemousses

Belle Vue Maurel

Roches Noires

LE MORNE PENINSULA (p110)
With some of Mauritius' best coastline, Le Morne Peninsula is capped by the incredible, vast rock of Le Morne Brabant, one of the country's most dramatic peaks

Pointe aux Sables

PORT LOUIS

PORT LOUIS

Le Pouce (812m)

Pieter Both (823m)

La Nicolière

Poste de Flacq

Bon Acceuil

Centre de Flacq

Belle Mare

Beau Bassin

Moka

MOKA

Corps de Garde (719m)

Rose Hill

Quartier Militaire

FLACQ

Flic en Flac

La Ferme Reservoir

Quatre Bornes

Piton du Milieu Reservoir

Trou d'Eau Douce

Île aux Cerfs

Montagne du Rempart (777m)

Trois Mamelles (629m)

Phoenix

Vacoas

Floréal

Blanche Montagne

Montagne Blanche

Tamarin

Curepipe

Montagne Bambous (626m)

RIVIÈRE NOIRE

Tourelle du Tamarin (548m)

Tamarin Falls Reservoir

Mare Longue Reservoir

PLAINES WILHEMS

Mare aux Vacoas Reservoir

Nouvelle France

Lion Mountain (480m)

Piton de la Petite Rivière Noire (828m)

Grand Bassin

GRAND PORT

Vieux Grand Port

Île aux Bénitiers

Chamarel

Black River Gorges National Park

Montagne Cocotte (771m)

Rose Belle

Mahébourg

Île aux Aigrettes Nature Reserve

Le Morne Peninsula

Le Morne Brabant (556m)

SAVANNE

Plaisance

SSR International Airport

Blue Bay Marine Park

Blue Bay

Baie du Cap

Chamouny

Chemin Grenier

Rivière des Anguilles

BLUE BAY (p115)
Dive and sunbathe around one of Mauritius' most beautiful lagoons, with ple... of activities nearby

Bel Ombre

Surinam

Souillac

CHAMAREL (p109)
The highest waterfall in Mauritius awaits you here, along with the unique coloured earths

BLACK RIVER GORGES NATIONAL PARK (p87)
Enjoy amazing vistas, wild monkeys, waterfalls, volcanic lakes and excellent hiking

SOUTH MAURITIUS (p111)
Discover another side to Mauritius by driving the coastal road from Souillac to Baie du Cap, surrounded by untamed scenery and stunning views

20°00'S

20°15'S

20°30'S

57°15'E

57°30'E

57°45'E

RÉUNION

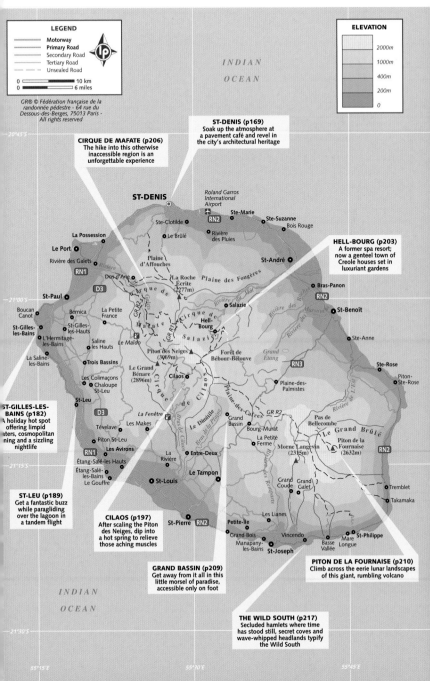

LEGEND

Motorway
Primary Road
Secondary Road
Tertiary Road
Unsealed Road

0   10 km
0   6 miles

ELEVATION

2000m
1000m
400m
200m
0

INDIAN OCEAN

CIRQUE DE MAFATE (p206)
The hike into this otherwise inaccessible region is an unforgettable experience

ST-DENIS (p169)
Soak up the atmosphere at a pavement café and revel in the city's architectural heritage

HELL-BOURG (p203)
A former spa resort; now a genteel town of Creole houses set in luxuriant gardens

ST-GILLES-LES-BAINS (p182)
A holiday hot spot offering limpid waters, cosmopolitan dining and a sizzling nightlife

ST-LEU (p189)
Get a fantastic buzz while paragliding over the lagoon in a tandem flight

CILAOS (p197)
After scaling the Piton des Neiges, dip into a hot spring to relieve those aching muscles

GRAND BASSIN (p209)
Get away from it all in this little morsel of paradise, accessible only on foot

PITON DE LA FOURNAISE (p210)
Climb across the eerie lunar landscapes of this giant, rumbling volcano

THE WILD SOUTH (p217)
Secluded hamlets where time has stood still, secret coves and wave-whipped headlands typify the Wild South

ST-DENIS

Roland Garros International Airport

Ste-Clotilde
Ste-Marie
Ste-Suzanne
Bois Rouge
Le Brûlé
Rivière des Pluies
St-André

La Possession
Le Port
Rivière des Galets
RN1
St-Paul
Plaine d'Affouches
Dos-d'Ane
D3
La Roche Écrite (2277m)
Plaine des Fougères
Bras-Panon
RN2
Salazie
St-Benoît

Boucan Canot
Bernica
La Petite France
St-Gilles-les-Hauts
Hell-Bourg
Ste-Anne
St-Gilles-les-Bains
L'Hermitage-les-Bains
Saline les Hauts
Le Maïdo
Piton des Neiges (3069m)
Forêt de Bébour-Bélouve
Grand Étang
RN3
Ste-Rose
Piton-Ste-Rose
La Saline-les-Bains
Trois Bassins
Le Grand Bénare (2896m)
Cilaos
Plaine-des-Palmistes

Les Colimaçons
Chaloupe St-Leu
St-Leu
D3
La Fenêtre
Les Makes
Grand Bassin
Bourg-Murat
La Petite Ferme
Pas de Bellecombe
Le Grand Brûlé
Piton de la Fournaise (2632m)
RN2

Tévelave
Piton St-Leu
Les Avirons
RN1
Étang-Salé-les-Hauts
La Rivière
Entre-Deux
Morne Langevin (2385m)
Étang-Salé-les-Bains
Le Gouffre
Le Tampon
St-Louis
Grand Coude
Grand Galet
Tremblet
Takamaka

St-Pierre
RN2
Petite-Île
Les Lianes
St-Philippe
Grand Bois
Manapany-les-Bains
Vincendo
St-Joseph
Basse Vallée
Mare Longue

INDIAN OCEAN

20°45'S
21°00'S
21°15'S
21°30'S
55°15'E
55°30'E
55°45'E

SEYCHELLES

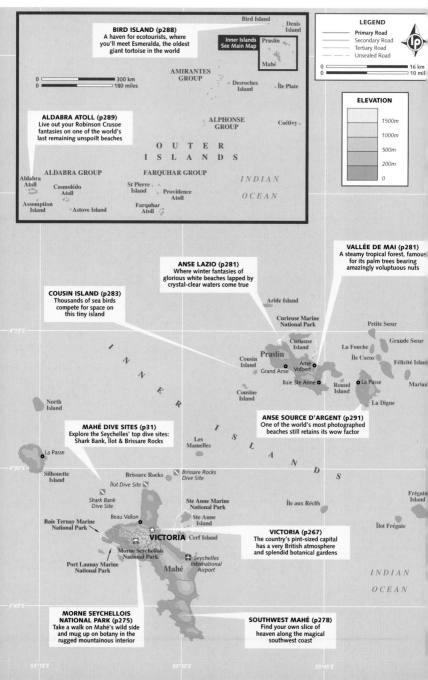

BIRD ISLAND (p288)
A haven for ecotourists, where you'll meet Esmeralda, the oldest giant tortoise in the world

ALDABRA ATOLL (p289)
Live out your Robinson Crusoe fantasies on one of the world's last remaining unspoilt beaches

VALLÉE DE MAI (p281)
A steamy tropical forest, famous for its palm trees bearing amazingly voluptuous nuts

ANSE LAZIO (p281)
Where winter fantasies of glorious white beaches lapped by crystal-clear waters come true

COUSIN ISLAND (p283)
Thousands of sea birds compete for space on this tiny island

ANSE SOURCE D'ARGENT (p291)
One of the world's most photographed beaches still retains its wow factor

MAHÉ DIVE SITES (p31)
Explore the Seychelles' top dive sites: Shark Bank, Îlot & Brissare Rocks

VICTORIA (p267)
The country's pint-sized capital has a very British atmosphere and splendid botanical gardens

MORNE SEYCHELLOIS NATIONAL PARK (p275)
Take a walk on Mahé's wild side and mug up on botany in the rugged mountainous interior

SOUTHWEST MAHÉ (p278)
Find your own slice of heaven along the magical southwest coast

LEGEND

Primary Road
Secondary Road
Tertiary Road
Unsealed Road

ELEVATION

1500m
1000m
500m
200m
0

On the Road

TOM MASTERS COORDINATING AUTHOR

Few days in Mauritius rivalled this one, when after a long day of research we arrived at the beautiful colonial-era estate of Eureka (p94), set beneath towering peaks and amid thick forest, for an overnight stay. A short hike down the hillside took us to a series of fantastic waterfalls for a cold shower and swim, which was a blissful release from the afternoon heat. We were back in time to watch sunset from the terrace with a rum punch – magical.

JEAN-BERNARD CARILLET

Scratching the leathery neck of a giant tortoise in the Seychelles is an experience I won't forget – I was utterly fascinated by these animals that seem to come straight off the set of *Jurassic Park*. They can easily be seen on Curieuse Island (p283) and Bird Island (p288). On Bird Island, I even paid my respects to Esmeralda – a 300kg, two-centuries-old monster of a specimen. My tip: bring the kids!

See full author bios page 324

Mauritius, Réunion & Seychelles

Three unique island destinations cast adrift in the warm azure waters of the Indian Ocean; Mauritius, Réunion and Seychelles can all stake a convincing claim to being a piece of paradise, rightly attracting those seeking romance, pampering and the perfect white-sand beach. Few who come here ever leave disappointed, although the lively and warm people, the relaxed vibes and the music of everyday life are likely to leave an even greater impression on any visitor than even the most sumptuous palm-fringed beaches, luxurious hotels and crystal-clear waters.

Indeed, the biggest mistake anyone could make would be to assume that these islands are for beach holidays only – while you'll probably see some of the best beaches you've ever come across, there's so much more to each destination that any trip will be an unforgettable and exciting experience, whether it be trekking in the lush volcanic landscape of Réunion's steamy interior, exploring Mauritius' fascinating colonial past in its myriad mansions, museums and factories or just island hopping between deserted islands and picturesque villages in the Seychelles.

Despite the British being the last colonial power to dominate the region, it's actually the French influence that permeates and informs the experience of Mauritius, Réunion and Seychelles today. While Réunion remains a part of France, independent Mauritius and Seychelles retain so much of their French past (mixed in with their equally beguiling Afro-Asian cultural influences) that even the most cosmopolitan traveller will be impressed by the cultural palimpsests that have come to define the region. Go, enjoy and remember – paradise doesn't come much better than this.

Take the plunge into one of Réunion's natural spas – Cascade de la Grande Ravine (p222)

JEAN-BERNARD CARILLET

INTERVIEW 1:

Homemade Hotels

NAME	Josette Marchal-Vexlard
AGE	48
OCCUPATION	Hotelier
RESIDENCE	La Preneuse, Rivière Noire, Mauritius

'I was brought up in the rainy Central Plateau town of Phoenix, where they make Mauritius' famous beer, and I always dreamed of living by the sea and decided to move as soon as I was an adult. I bought my house by the beach in Rivière Noire 24 years ago – these days I could never afford to buy such a house – only millionaires seem to live on the sea these days. For much of my career I was a businesswoman – one of the first in Mauritius in fact. I sold spices to big companies in Europe and the US and it was while travelling for work that I first discovered the *chambre d'hôte* or homestay. I found it so much better than a cold, impersonal hotel and a unique chance to get to know locals and see how they lived. In 1994 a terrible cyclone here wiped out all my crops, so I was forced to shut my factory and had no idea what to do. I decided to open my own *chambre d'hôte* (p108), the real deal, just like in France. It gives me great pleasure to run a place that people come back to time and time again.'

AS RELATED TO TOM MASTERS

'I decided to open my own *chambre d'hôte,* the real deal, just like in France. It gives me great pleasure to run a place that people come back to time and time again.'

Cast adrift your plans in the sleepy coastal village of Grande Rivière Noire (p108), Mauritius

JEAN ROBERT

INTERVIEW 2:
Creole Cuisine

NAME	Françoise Baptiste
AGE	44
OCCUPATION	Cookery author
RESIDENCE	Grande Montagne, Rodrigues, Mauritius

'Rodrigues' cuisine is different from that in Mauritius – ours is far less spicy, based around lots of freshly caught fish, and freshly picked fruit, herbs and beans.'

'I've been passionate about food since childhood thanks to my great-uncle who was a wonderful cook. He taught me all his traditional recipes, and most importantly that one should never cook from duty, but only for pleasure. I've always believed it important to keep our traditions and local identity as islanders, so a few years ago I decided to collect together recipes from throughout Rodrigues and publish them all in one volume. Rodrigues' cuisine is different from that in Mauritius – ours is far less spicy, based around lots of freshly caught fish, and freshly picked papaya, pineapple, bananas, wild strawberries, herbs and red and white beans. Few people leave uninspired by what they taste here. Life is simple on Rodrigues; there are no social classes, we get up early, we go to bed early, we leave our doors unlocked at night. More than anything I love the quiet joy of life here, the good-natured Rodriguans and the beauty that surrounds us all.'

AS RELATED TO TOM MASTERS

Catch of the day, Mauritius

JOHN HAY

Pep up your palate with the spicy delights of Mauritian cuisine (p47)

JOHN HAY

BEST EATING EXPERIENCES IN MAURITIUS

Le Pescatore (p71) Book an outside table overlooking the sea for the perfect romantic dinner and some stunningly prepared fresh fish and seafood.

Eureka (p94) Enjoy lunch on the veranda of a perfectly preserved colonial mansion, or – even better – overnight in one of the charming garden houses and enjoy a delicious home-cooked meal on your own porch.

Panoramour (p118) For a real splurge, head to this thrillingly located hilltop restaurant where the venison and boar actually live up to the superb views across the Domaine du Chasseur private estate.

Recover from last night's rum cocktails with some tropical antioxidants at Port Louis' Central Market (p57), Mauritius

JEAN-BERNARD CARILLET

INTERVIEW 3:
Reinventing the Past

NAME	Jean-Michel Furia
AGE	32
OCCUPATION	Specialised guide
RESIDENCE	Ste-Marie, Réunion

'I'm a Kaf Malbar, which means I'm a mix from Indian and Malagasy descent – the archetypal Réunionnais combo! Sadly, the multicultural facets of our island are underrated. Visitors tend to favour the heavily promoted west coast, the Cirques and the volcano. It's understandable, but there's much more to do in Réunion than lazing on a beach or trekking the interior. Few visitors have heard about our fascinating Creole and Indian heritage. There's a wealth of religious buildings on this island – mosques, churches, temples – that testify to our rich past, of which I'm very proud. My tip? Try to make your trip coincide with fire walks (December and January; p227), and don't overlook the east coast (p224), which is less commercialised than the west. And take time to discover Creole architecture in St-Denis, St-Pierre, Entre-Deux, St-Joseph and Hell-Bourg, where you'll find a flurry of well-preserved *cases créoles* (traditional Creole houses). This is my Réunion!'

AS RELATED TO JEAN-BERNARD CARILLET

'Few visitors have heard about our fascinating Creole and Indian heritage.'

Soak up the good vibrations and rich Indian cultural heritage of St-Louis (p193), Réunion

JEAN-BERNARD CARILLET

INTERVIEW 4:
Creole Melodies

NAME	Christine Salem
AGE	35
OCCUPATION	Singer
RESIDENCE	St-Denis, Réunion

'From my father's side, I'm Breton. From my mother's side, I'm African. In my songs, I'm Réunionnais. I'm talking about everyday life, and the hardships of the people, such as housing and the impact of modernity on traditional life. I'm also talking about slavery, which is still a taboo in Réunion. How am I doing it? I'm using *maloya* music (p162). *Maloya* is a music for rebels, it's our blues music. *Maloya* was forbidden until 1980, it was considered a 'dirty' music. After many years of struggle, *maloya* is now totally recognised as part of the Creole culture. I use African instruments, including the *roulèr*. There are many places in Réunion where visitors can listen to my music and that of other Réunionnais singers. I recommend Le Séchoir (p192) in St-Leu and the Bato Fou (p217) in St-Pierre. The Sakifo Festival (p191) in St-Leu in August is also a good place to take the pulse of the island. And if you're invited to a *kabar* (p162), don't miss it! Some people even go into a trance.'

AS RELATED TO JEAN-BERNARD CARILLET

'Maloya is a music for rebels, it's our blues music.'

The stirring rhythms of *séga* and *maloya* (p162) echo the struggles of Réunion's past and present

JEAN-BERNARD CARILLET

INTERVIEW 5:

Beneath the Surface

NAME	Michel Gardette
AGE	52
OCCUPATION	Dive instructor & underwater treasure hunter
RESIDENCE:	Praslin, Seychelles

'I've pioneered diving in the Seychelles. I was one of the first to dive the Aldabra Atoll, in 1990, and I've dived all over the Indian Ocean. As compared with, say, the Maldives, the Seychelles have fewer fish but the species here are bigger. The main highlight is the dramatic seascape, with a wealth of granite formations and a contoured topography, which gives the sites a peculiarly sculpted look.

'The good news is that you don't have to be a strong diver to enjoy the Seychelles (p31). Most sites are accessible to novices, and conditions are very safe year-round. Beginners love it! And there's a huge potential for discovery, especially around Aldabra, Cosmoledo and Astove (p33). I saw giant clams that could contain two divers! It was unbelievable! Not to mention sea turtles – thousands of them. My advice: stay tuned, because these atolls are going to open up soon to diving. It's a new frontier.'

AS RELATED TO JEAN-BERNARD CARILLET

'Seychelles' main highlight is the dramatic seascape, with a wealth of granite formations and a contoured topography'

Spot parrotfish, moray eels and sea turtles while diving the crystalline waters of Seychelles (p31)

MICHAEL AW

Contents

Getting Started

Even in our globalised, media-savvy world it still seems odd that any of these Indian Ocean gems needs a PR machine to promote them – each destination is so self-evidently lovely (just say their names out loud and savour the images that immediately spring to mind) – that marketing seems utterly unnecessary. Tell a friend where you're going and their reaction will say it all.

As if you needed another reason to go, travel to Mauritius, Réunion and Seychelles is exceptionally safe and easy. There are superb tourism infrastructures in each country, excellent planning resources online, a good level of English is spoken everywhere and the choice of activities, hotels and eating is hard to rival anywhere. Of course islands this beautiful are rarely free of crowds and development, so it's important to read up on specific destinations to see if they'll provide the kind of holiday you're looking for – divers looking for social life and entertainment should avoid honeymooner magnets (and vice versa), while those looking to get away from crowds should steer clear of big resorts and head off the beaten path. Of course the main disadvantage to travel here is the distance most people will need to travel. Flights are not cheap, and are environmentally harmful, although once you're in the region it's relatively inexpensive to travel about and accommodation can be tailored to almost any budget.

WHEN TO GO

Nestled between the Tropic of Capricorn and the equator, all three countries offer year-round heat and there's almost no time in any country when travel isn't advised. However, there are of course nuances, and depending on what you're interested in doing there are considerations to take into account. For example, if you're planning a hiking trip to Réunion, the best time is during the dry season, which runs from late April until October. Likewise, diving in Mauritius is best from October to December and March to April.

The time of year perhaps best avoided is January to February when it's the peak of the cyclone season. Although direct hits are rare, cyclones way offshore can still bring grey days and strong winds, even to the Seychelles, which technically lies outside the cyclone belt.

For climate charts for Mauritius see p135, Réunion p249, Seychelles p297.

The climate in all three destinations is broadly similar: a hot, rainy summer from December to April (October to April in the Seychelles) is followed by a cooler, drier winter from May to November (May to September in the Seychelles). Rainfall levels are much higher in the mountains, particularly in Réunion, which boasts a number of world records. Cilaos holds the world record for most rain in a single day – a total of 1870mm fell on 16 March 1952.

Coastal temperatures rarely drop below 20°C in Mauritius and Réunion, or below 24°C in the Seychelles, making these islands a truly year-round destination.

For all three destinations you are advised to plan your travel well in advance, especially during the French holidays when hotels can be booked up months before. Ask your travel agent for advice on the dates of school holidays in France, which vary slightly from year to year. The Christmas to New Year period is also particularly busy. Airline reservations may be difficult to get at this time, so book well ahead to avoid disappointment. Keep in mind that many hotels hike up their room rates during the peak seasons.

For more information on the best times to travel, see p55 for Mauritius, p169 for Réunion, and p267 for the Seychelles.

DON'T LEAVE HOME WITHOUT...

- Getting any necessary vaccinations and visas.
- Non-beach clothing: some of the best restaurants in all three countries are smart affairs and shorts or bikini tops simply won't do – think lightweight but smart clothing, decent shoes and non-denim trousers for men. Also if you plan to go into the mountains, bring a long-sleeved top for the cool night air.
- Plenty of sun cream, after-sun lotion and bug repellent. Since the Chikungunya epidemic (see p309) most hotels will provide free electronic mosquito repellents to put on at night, but an extra layer of protection is always good, especially for evening dining outside or for long walks.
- Walkers should bring binoculars, walking boots, a lightweight waterproof jacket, a compass and a basic medical kit.
- Divers should bring their certification and log, as well as any equipment they want to use for diving.
- Even non-divers will save money and time bringing their own mask, snorkel and flippers so they can dive right in and start exploring.
- Everyone should bring flip flops, a sun hat, good sunglasses with UV protection, a driving licence if you want to hire a car and travel insurance details to know what activities are and aren't included in your policy.

COSTS & MONEY

None of these destinations are ever going to be bargains, the main expense being the flights needed to cover the huge distances most visitors have to travel to get here. However, despite enjoying a reputation for opulence and exclusivity, it's perfectly possible to visit all three countries on a limited budget.

Seychelles has traditionally been the most expensive of the lot, and while it remains the most exclusive today, its tourist board has recently been involved in promoting cheaper accommodation options such as guesthouses; as a result the country has become a far better destination for independent travellers. Réunion is the next most expensive, while Mauritius is a very budget-friendly option for those who want to backpack, although five-star hotels also proliferate, making the huge choice of accommodation options part of the island's attraction.

You can keep accommodation costs down by staying in self-catering apartments or small guesthouses and by basing yourself in one place; the longer you stay (and the more of you there are), the cheaper it becomes. It helps to travel off-season as well: prices are generally discounted and there's more chance of being able to bargain.

On the positive side, it's possible to eat reasonably cheaply, even in the Seychelles, by patronising snack stands and getting takeaway meals – or, of course, by self-catering. Restaurants cover a huge scope of price ranges, from barely more expensive than takeaways to almost as expensive as those in London or Paris. In four- and five-star resorts and hotels, restaurants tend to be very pricey, although as most guests are on half or full-board packages, the costs are reduced. Buses in all three destinations provide a cheap method of getting around, although car hire is reasonably priced everywhere too.

It's also worth investigating package holidays, including flights and accommodation, since these can often work out cheaper than travelling independently.

HOW MUCH IN MAURITIUS?

Scuba dive Rs 1000

Meal in an upmarket restaurant Rs 500

Bottle of Phoenix beer Rs 50

Short taxi ride Rs 100

Packet of Bois Chéri vanilla tea Rs 75

Mauritius

As far as a daily budget is concerned, backpackers staying in the cheapest guesthouses and eating meals at street stands can expect to spend in the region of €25 to €30 per person. Opting for a midrange hotel and smarter restaurants will push it up to at least €50. These costs are calculated on the basis of two people sharing a room; single travellers will need to budget extra. As soon as you jump to four- and five-star accommodation you're looking at €175 per person at the very minimum.

Réunion

Prices in Réunion are roughly similar to those found in mainland France. The absolute minimum daily budget, possible if you're staying in youth hostels and the cheapest guesthouses and eating takeaway meals or self-catering, will be €40 per person on the basis of two people sharing a room. For a reasonably comfortable midrange hotel, with a light lunch and dinner in a decent restaurant, you're looking at around €80 to €100 per person.

Seychelles

Visitors to the Seychelles on a tight budget will struggle to get by on less than €70 per person per day (on the basis of two people sharing a room in a guesthouse or self-contained bungalow). A more realistic budget, allowing you to stay at a moderately priced hotel and treat yourself to a few good restaurants, will come in at around €100 to €150 per person per day. Living it up in a top-end resort will usually cost at least €250 per person per day, but will shoot up very quickly with meals and activities. Island hopping and indulging in excursions and other activities also jacks costs up considerably.

TRAVEL LITERATURE

There's a surprisingly small amount of literature about each island, although there are definitely some interesting writings available if you persevere. Bernardin de St-Pierre's 1773 *Journey to Mauritius* describes Mauritius in its early colonial period, complete with a horrendous account of the treatment of slaves, the experience of which would inform Bernardin de St-Pierre's later works, including his classic *Paul and Virginie* (1787), the now deeply unfashionable love story of two young French émigrés brought up in Mauritius (see the boxed text, p83).

A more recent addition to the writing about the island is Patrick O'Brian's enjoyable historical novel *The Mauritius Command* (1977), a swashbuckling adventure in the Aubrey-Maturin series, which sees Captain Jack Aubrey sent on a mission to rid Mauritius and Réunion of the French during the Napoleonic Wars. It's considered by some to be the best of the entire Aubrey-Maturin series.

In his funny and informative book *Golden Bats & Pink Pigeons,* naturalist Gerald Durrell tells of his time spent rescuing a number of Mauritian species from the brink of extinction. Durrell was too late for the dodo, but Errol Fuller does the bird proud with his comprehensive and quirky *Dodo: From Extinction to Icon,* which covers the history and the myths surrounding this endearing creature.

An unusual book about Réunion's social history is Françoise Verges' *Monsters and Revolutionaries,* which looks at the complex relationship between the colonisers and colonised on the island through a number of different prisms.

Seychelles travel lit is best represented by Athol Thomas' *Forgotten Eden.* Though written in the 1960s and now out of print, it still paints a vivid picture of the beauty and magic of these islands.

HOW MUCH IN RÉUNION?

Tandem flight paragliding in St-Leu €60

Car hire per week €200

Stodgy *carri* €9

One night in a *chambres d'hôte* (double) €45

Glass of local rum €3

HOW MUCH IN SEYCHELLES?

One night in a swish resort – the sky's the limit

Local bus ride €0.25

Boat excursion €90

One dive €50

Bottle of beer €1.20

TOP FIVE...

Beaches in the Region

- Trou d'Argent, Rodrigues, Mauritius (p128) – this remote stunner on the island of Rodrigues is well deserving of its cult status.
- Île aux Cerfs, Mauritius (p98) – sadly no longer a secret, but the white sand and shallow cobalt-blue water of this beautiful offshore island are unforgettable.
- Anse Source d'Argent, La Digue, Seychelles (p291) – one of the most famous tropical beaches in the world, this beauty is something out of pure fantasy.
- Anse Lazio, Praslin, Seychelles (p281) – Praslin's loveliest beach boasts great sand and an unbelievably blue lagoon.
- Anse Intendance, Mahé, Seychelles (p278) – in the south of the main island of Mahé, this beautiful stretch of sand will not disappoint.

Festivals & Events

- Divali (Dipavali) – processions and dance displays mark the festival of light in Réunion (p227) and Mauritius (p137); late October or early November.
- Festival Kreol – Seychellois celebrate Creole culture with a week of music, dance and other jollifications (p298); last week in October.
- Maha Shivaratri – Mauritian Hindus turn out in force to make offerings at the holy lake of Grand Bassin (p89); February or March.
- Teemeedee – Hindus and Tamils brave the heat during fire-walking ceremonies in Mauritius (p136) and Réunion (p227); December and January.
- Grand Raid – in the aptly named 'cross-country for crazies', participants run across Réunion in just 18 hours (p248); October or November.

Beyond the Reefs by William Travis takes a look back at the Seychelles of the 1970s, before conservation issues came to the fore, when Travis saw plenty of action as a shark fisher and latter-day adventurer.

Empires of the Monsoon by Richard Hall is the most informative and entertaining history of the Indian Ocean. It only touches briefly on Mauritius, Réunion and the Seychelles, but it does place them in a broader context.

INTERNET RESOURCES

Mauritius Government Portal (www.gov.mu) This huge and multifaceted site contains all the information you could ever need about Mauritius including a huge selection of links.

Mauritius Tourism Promotion Authority (www.tourism-mauritius.mu) The official site of Mauritius on the web has a great selection of hotels, activities and other useful information including plenty of ecotourism suggestions.

Reunion Tourisme (www.la-reunion-tourisme.com) Reunion's official tourist website (in French only) is an encyclopaedia of things to see and do.

Seychelles.net (www.seychelles.net) Official home of the Seychelles Tourism Board, this website overflows with great tips and ideas.

Virtual Seychelles (www.virtualseychelles.sc) An excellent resource for background about Seychelles, including webcams and links to specialist websites for all interests.

RESPONSIBLE TRAVEL

As well as creating much of the region's wealth, tourism has cost local people and, most particularly, the local environment dearly. Worst affected are the coasts and particularly the fringing lagoon, where areas of the coral reef and the fragile marine environment are seriously degraded. The sheer

TIPS FOR RESPONSIBLE TRAVEL

- Be careful not to damage coral reefs when diving or snorkelling.
- Never buy souvenirs made from materials such as turtleshell, seashells or coral.
- Never drop litter anywhere and bring a bag to pick up any litter left by less considerate people.
- Buy locally made produce, souvenirs and other day-to-day objects whenever possible.
- Don't light fires and be very careful when disposing of cigarette butts, particularly during droughts or the dry season.

number of tourists also makes extra demands on water supplies, electricity and other resources; creates problems of waste management; and puts more vehicles on the roads.

The good news is that all three countries are now taking these problems seriously and generally as a result development has been curtailed to a more considered pace. Ecotourism has been expanded enormously too, although in many places it is more of a buzzword than anything particularly beneficial to the environment.

Not that tourism can be blamed for all of the region's environmental woes of course, but there are positive steps that we as individual travellers can take to lessen our impact on the environment (see the boxed text, above).

For further guidelines regarding the underwater world see the boxed text, p32; for tips on low-impact hiking, see the boxed text, p235.

Itineraries
CLASSIC ROUTES

JAUNT AROUND MAURITIUS   Two Weeks
A fortnight is ideal to sample the many facets of Mauritian life. Because Mauritius is so small, it's possible to base yourself in one place and make day trips by bus, taxi or hire car.

Start with discovering the markets and museums of **Port Louis** (p55), then head north to **Trou aux Biches** (p68) or **Pereybère** (p79). Possible excursions include **Pamplemousses** (p83), **Grand Baie** (p72) and the **northern islands** (p78).

Admire the views at **Cap Malheureux** (p81), before heading south to laze on the beaches at **Belle Mare** (p98), which stretch in long, white, sandy arcs south to **Trou d'Eau Douce** (p95). Make this your base for day trips to the **Île aux Cerfs** (p98) and the **Domaine du Chasseur** (p117).

After a few days, decamp to the laid-back town of **Mahébourg** (p111) or the sparkling azure lagoon of **Blue Bay** (p115); eco-explore **Île aux Aigrettes** (p116).

Drive south along the glorious coast road via **Souillac** (p119) and **Baie du Cap** (p121) to make your next stop **Flic en Flac** (p103). Here you can delight in the underwater world, go hiking in the **Black River Gorges** (p87) and rummage for clothes around **Curepipe** (p90) and **Quatre Bornes** (p92) before heading back to Port Louis.

The two-week circuit of Mauritius will take you to sun-drenched beaches, botanical gardens, idyllic islands and lively market towns, all packed into just 300km.

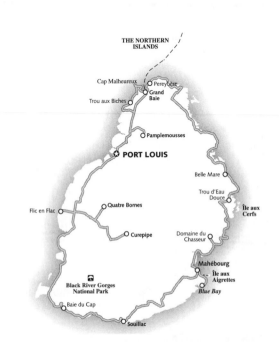

TOUR OF RÉUNION
Two Weeks

In two weeks, you can loop around the island, take a couple of jaunts into the interior and even visit a bubbling volcano.

Spend the first day sampling the infamous nightlife of **St-Gilles-les-Bains** (p182) before heading to the beach to recover at **L'Hermitage-les-Bains** (p182). Allow three days to make the most of the area's botanical gardens, museums and water sports.

Head next to the **Cirque de Cilaos** (p197), where you should allow at least two days to soak up the rugged mountain scenery and the laid-back atmosphere.

The volcano awaits at **Piton de la Fournaise** (p210). Base yourself at the Gîte du Volcan, ready to make a dawn ascent for stunning views.

Next make for the bright lights of **St-Pierre** (p212) – if possible, get here for the huge Saturday market and stay the night near **St-Joseph** (p220). Don't miss **Ste-Rose** (p229), where lava laps at the door of a church and narrowly misses the Virgin Mary.

As you head back to the north of the island, go inland and stay at least two nights in **Hell-Bourg** (p203), exploring the **Cirque de Salazie** (p202). Finally, set off towards the capital via the Indian-influenced **St-André** (p225) and end your trip sampling café-culture and Creole architecture in the capital, **St-Denis** (p169).

From sophisticated beach resorts to mountain villages, art galleries to volcanoes, two weeks is perfect to sample the variety Réunion has to offer. Get hooked on the hiking, and you could easily fill a month. This tour covers around 400km.

ESSENTIAL SEYCHELLES   **Two Weeks**

Two weeks is fine for a taster of the Seychelles' islands – allowing plenty of time for enjoying the very best of the country's superb beaches.

On the first day, tune into island life in the capital, **Victoria** (p267), checking out the market and strolling among the palm trees in the botanical gardens. Move on to **Beau Vallon** (p272), where three days can easily be spent messing around in and on the water – schedule in a day's diving or a boat trip to **Ste Anne Marine National Park** (p273). Devote the next two days to the beaches and byways of **Mahé** (p267), and walking in the **Morne Seychellois National Park** (p275).

Next, cruise over to **Praslin** (p280). Ogle curvaceous coco de mer nuts in the **Vallée de Mai** (p281), before flaking out on the perfect, sugar-white sands at **Anse Lazio** (p281). Fill the next four days with snorkelling, diving and swimming off **Anse Volbert** (p283), getting up close and personal with giant tortoises on **Curieuse Island** (p283) and walking among cacophonous clouds of sea birds on **Cousin Island** (p283).

From Praslin, make sail for **La Digue** (p289). Three days is the perfect amount of time to lapse into La Digue's slow vibe. Visit **Anse Source d'Argent** (p291) – the archetypal paradise beach. Get there late afternoon for the best atmosphere. Take a snorkelling trip around nearby islands, then find solitude on the beaches of **Grand Anse** (p291) and **Petite Anse** (p291). All too soon, it will be time to tear yourself away for the trip back to Victoria.

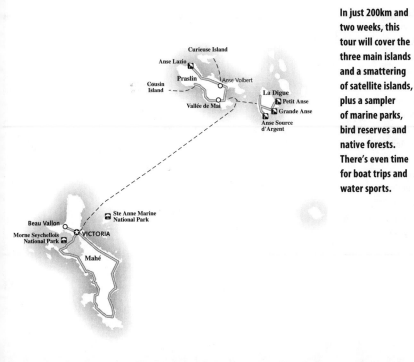

In just 200km and two weeks, this tour will cover the three main islands and a smattering of satellite islands, plus a sampler of marine parks, bird reserves and native forests. There's even time for boat trips and water sports.

ROADS LESS TRAVELLED

RODRIGUES – THE OTHER MAURITIUS   One Week

Some call Rodrigues a mini-Mauritius, even though it's different in almost every way. What they really mean is that this is the closest you can get to Mauritius before tourism took off , with an almost total lack of development compared to the mainland, and few tourists who make it out this far, on the 1½-hour flight into the Indian Ocean. A week is ample time to discover the delights of this small, mountainous island. Depending on the weather you can divide the days between walking, diving and taking boat trips to nearby islands.

First, though, spend half a day strolling the streets of **Port Mathurin** (p125). The island's endearingly sleepy 'capital' springs into life on Saturday morning when it seems the entire population descends for the weekly market.

The classic coastal hike starts at **St François** (p128), then heads south via a gem of a beach at **Trou d'Argent** (p128) to **Gravier** (p128), from where there are buses back to Port Mathurin. On a separate outing, climb **Mt Limon** (p129) for island-wide views.

You're spoilt for choice when it comes to diving. Top spots include the channel off St François, **La Passe St François** (p29), on the edge of the lagoon, with more options beyond the reefs. As for boat trips, first choice should be **Île aux Cocos** (p131) for its wealth of birdlife. There's good snorkelling around the little-visited **Île aux Chats** and **Île Hermitage** (p131) off the south coast.

On your last day, treat yourself to a seafood feast at one of the great family-run restaurants scattered around the island.

Leave behind the commercialism of Mauritius' main island for a week to discover a more traditional way of life among the fishing and agricultural communities of Rodrigues. Divers are in for a treat, too, exploring the underwater world of the massive, encircling lagoon.

RÉUNION'S SUD SAUVAGE   One Week

Réunion's 'Wild South' offers volcanic landscapes, massive ravines, wave-lashed cliffs and sensational hiking trails. You can discover the best of the region in a reasonably leisurely week.

Start at **Ste-Rose** (p229) and head south to find the first tongues of lava tumbling down to the sea. Pay a quick visit to the **Vierge au Parasol** (p230) before crossing the threatening lava fields of **Le Grand Brûlé** (p224), to spend a night or two near **St-Philippe** (p223) or **St-Joseph** (p220); stay up in the hills for a real taste of rural life. From here you can visit a spice garden, learn about vanilla and local crafts or hike the spectacular **Rivière des Remparts** (p221).

Pass quickly through **St-Pierre** (p212) en route to the high plateau of **Plaine-des-Cafres** (p208) to visit the **Maison du Volcan** (p208). Take the magnificent forest road up to **Piton de la Fournaise** (p210), Réunion's restless volcano. Climb to the top at the crack of dawn; circuit the crater rim to leave the crowds behind.

Now drop back down to Plaine-des-Cafres, where you could spend a couple of days hiking to **Grand Bassin** (p209), a village at the end of the world. Finally, head for **Plaine-des-Palmistes** (p211), where the hikes through the **Forêt de Bébour-Bélouve** (p212) and to **Trou de Fer** (p212) provide unforgettable experiences.

This one-week tour of southern Réunion takes you across lava fields, past breathtaking coastal scenery and up a volcano to gaze into the jaws of the giant. It ends 200km later among the quiet rural villages of the high plains.

TAILORED TRIPS

THE ADRENALIN RUSH

Réunion rightly markets itself as the 'intense isle'; almost every conceivable stomach-churning, heart-pumping activity is on offer. With a bit of planning – and a fair amount of cash – adventure-sports enthusiasts can test their stamina in an action-packed week. Check your insurance policy, take a deep breath and go for it!

Kick off day one in **St-Gilles-les-Bains** (p206) with an ear-popping helicopter ride, ducking and weaving around the three Cirques. On landing, hotfoot it up to **Le Maïdo** (p180), grab a mountain bike and hurtle down to the coast again along vertiginous biking trails.

Later that day push on to **Cilaos** (p197). Make a crack-of-dawn start to scale the almost vertical **Piton des Neiges** (p199); to really enjoy the experience, spread the climb over two days. On day four, there's a choice between slithering down canyons, bouncing down rivers on a raft or galloping amid forests and pastures in the Hautes Plaines in Reunion's heartland.

At the end of day four, up sticks for **St-Leu** (p189). Spend days five and six swooping high above the lagoon by paraglider, plunging off the reef to scuba dive with sharks, or surfing the world-famous left-hander – La Gauche de St-Leu – at the mouth of the **Ravine des Colimaçons** (p190); less-experienced surfers will find thrills and spills aplenty riding the area's quieter waves.

Day seven? Definitely the day of rest!

DIVER'S & SNORKELLER'S DELIGHT

You could spend a lifetime diving the reefs and granite outcrops of the Seychelles, but a week is enough time to sample a range of sites, including some of the very best in the Indian Ocean.

Jump in at the deep end at **Shark Bank** (p31) off the northwest coast of **Mahé** (p31). No prizes for guessing what's in store here: sharks aplenty with their stingray sidekicks, barracuda and other bruisers. Off Mahé's north tip, **Îlot** (p32) offers an unbelievable variety of smaller fish in shimmering shoals. Nearby, **Brissare Rocks** (p32) is ablaze with fire coral.

On day four, head over to **Praslin** (p32) for a change of scene. The waters around **Curieuse Island** (p283) are teeming with fish life in dazzling, dizzying displays.

Spend your last day exploring the islands northwest of **La Digue** (p32). The rock formations around **Île Cocos** (p291), **Marianne** (p32) and the sisters, **Petite** and **Grande Sœur** (p291), are out of this world. Marine turtles are common, while stingrays, eagle rays and reef sharks add a touch of spice. Even the odd manta and whale shark cruise through from time to time.

Diving in Mauritius, Réunion & Seychelles

A growing number of travellers come to the Indian Ocean for the mother lode of dive sites, and justifiably so. Though largely overshadowed by the iconic Maldives, scuba diving is increasingly popular in Mauritius, Réunion and Seychelles. Beneath the clear turquoise waters is a trove of unbelievable riches: rainbow-coloured fish and large pelagic species (and yes, sharks are part of the package!), a dramatic seascape, a few wrecks and a host of drop-offs and reefs. It's not the cheapest place on earth to dive (Thailand or the Red Sea it ain't) but it's a great place to learn, and in turn love, scuba diving. Good news: bar a few areas, the dive sites are never crowded.

The dive sites presented (see the relevant regional maps for their location) are only a sampling of hundreds of sites available.

HOW MUCH?

Introductory dive: €40-60

Single dive: €40-60 (including equipment rental)

Open Water certification course: €300-400

MAURITIUS

So, you want variety? Abundant marine life, dramatic seascapes, atmospheric wrecks – Mauritius has it all, not to mention well-established, high-quality dive operators. Mauritius is almost entirely surrounded by a barrier reef, within which turquoise lagoons provide great possibilities for snorkellers, swimmers and novice divers. And there is the *pièce de résistance*: Rodrigues, which has virgin sites and outstanding fish life.

Dive Sites
EAST MAURITIUS
There is a fantastic parade of pelagic and reef fish to be observed in the **Passe de Belle Mare**. Strong tidal currents push the deep water back and forth through the passage, providing nutrients for a staggering array of species. The seascape is another draw; the passage is peppered with numerous chasms, gullies, coral canyons and sandy valleys. Sharks, especially bull sharks and grey sharks, regularly patrol the area. There are at least five different sites in the Passe.

Towards the south, off Trou d'Eau Douce, the **Passe de Trou d'Eau Douce** is another worthwhile site, though it's less spectacular than Passe de Belle Mare. It's usually done as a drift dive.

See under Activities headings in the East Mauritius section (p95) for local dive centres.

SOUTHEAST MAURITIUS
Off the southeast coast it's the dramatic underwater terrain that impresses more than anything, making for unique profiles. You'll be rewarded with a profusion of caves, tunnels and giant arches – it's very scenic – as well as large numbers of pelagics thrown in for good measure. The hitch? From June to August, most sites are exposed to the prevailing winds – expect choppy seas in rough weather.

Colorado is the magic mantra. As befits its name, this site looks like an underwater version of the famous American valley. This 400m-long canyon is peppered with chasms, tunnels, crevices and boulders where masses of lobsters, jacks, groupers and barracudas seek shelter. Another must-see dive is **Roches Zozo**, close to Colorado. It features a huge rock that rises from the sea bed to about 12m, pocked with crevices where lobsters hide. To the south, **Grotte Langouste** is a cave brimming with lobsters.

Don't worry too much about the effects of the 2004 tsunami – most sites in Mauritius, Réunion and Seychelles are not coral dives.

Wreck buffs will explore the **Sirius**, a 19th-century vessel that rests in the 20m range off Mahébourg, but it's not in good shape.

For beginners, **Blue Bay** is a safe, lovely spot to learn to dive, with a parade of reef fish to be observed on the sprawling reef. Blue Bay is the only place in Mauritius where you'll find patches of thriving coral.

See p115 for local dive centres.

NORTH MAURITIUS

The north coast is a magnet for divers of all levels, and it's no wonder – there's a good balance of thrilling dives, wrecks, drop-offs and easy dives.

The islands off the coast (Île Plate, Coin de Mire) are the main highlights, with splendid sites and diverse fish life – not to mention a sense of wilderness. **La Fosse aux Requins** will make your spine tingle. On the northwestern side of Île Plate, a bowl-shaped basin carved into the cliff is home to an eerie concentration of blacktip sharks (from five to about 30 certain days) that keep swirling around. Why? Possibly because the waters here are rich in oxygen thanks to the swell. Good news for novice divers in search of excitement: this shallow dive (12m) is accessible with an Open Water certificate, though the current can be a bit tricky. One proviso: the encounter with the sharks is probable but cannot be guaranteed.

Coin de Mire Island is another diver's treat, with a few stunning drop-offs – we recommend **Carpenters** and the aptly named **The Wall**. Both have fairly good coral formations and tons of fish life. Near The Wall, the shipwreck **Djabeda** is a former Japanese freighter that was scuttled in 1998 in 30m. It's more atmospheric than fishy.

To the northwest, Trou aux Biches is the main jumping-off point to a variety of superb dives. Be sure to fill your logbook with **Holt's Rock** (also known as Stenopus), which features two rocky domes and big boulders; **Lobster Rock**, in about 20m, geared to novice divers; and **Tombant de la Pointe aux Canonniers**, between Holt's Rock and Lobster Rock, suitable for experienced divers, with an exhilarating drop-off that tumbles from 32m to about 60m. Other reputable walls in the area: **Caravelle**, **Corsaire Wall** and **Kingfish**, all embellished with black coral and seafans. In the mood for wrecks? Make a beeline for **Waterlily** and **Emily**, as well as the photogenic, 45m-long **Stella Maru**, all of which are accessible to novice divers.

See under Activities headings in the North Mauritius section (p66) for local dive centres.

WEST MAURITIUS

The Flic en Flac area ranks among the best in Mauritius when it comes to diving. Conditions are optimal year round – it's protected from the prevailing winds – and visibility is usually excellent. We can't gush enough about **Rempart Serpent** (Snake Rampart), possibly the quirkiest dive in Mauritius. Located a 15-minute boat trip from Flic en Flac, it takes its name from the sinuous rock lying about 25m below the surface, which attracts perhaps the greatest concentration in the world of weird and wonderful scorpion fish, stonefish, moray eels and lion-fish. Another fave is **La Cathédrale**, with a memorable seascape – think a warren of cavelets, stipples, passages and ledges. It's full of reef species, including fusiliers, surgeonfish, groupers, snappers, angelfish and lobsters. One downside: it's so popular that it's fairly congested. **Couline Bambou** and **Manioc** are less crowded but no less attractive.

Wreck fans will be spoiled here too, with a handful of atmospheric wrecks, including the **Kei Sei 113**, scuttled in the 1980s. Resting at about 35m, it's accessible to seasoned divers only. Beginners might try the **Tug II**, a 20m-long tugboat scuttled in 1981 that sits on the sand in about 20m. She's now

Before embarking on a scuba-diving trip, be sure to obtain reliable information about the physical and environmental conditions of the dive site and dive only at sites within your realm of experience.

In Mauritius, look out for the *Field Guide to Corals of Mauritius* by Ruby Moothien Pillay, Hiroaki Terashima, Atmanun Venkatasami and Hiro'omi Uchida. In Réunion, look out for *Fonds Sous-Marins de l'Île de la Réunion* by Eric Dutrieux (in French).

home to thousands of colourful fish. Hint: lie without moving on the sandy bottom and you'll see swaying conger eels slip down into their burrows.

And the southwest coast? The area between Le Morne Peninsula and Rivière Noire has a few diving hotspots, including the fishy **Passe St Jacques** and **Casiers**. The weak points are the average visibility and the fairly dull topography.

See under Activities headings in the West Mauritius section (p101) for local dive centres.

RODRIGUES
This is the Indian Ocean at its best. A true gem, Rodrigues boasts numerous untouched sites for those willing to experience something different. There's a profusion of coral that you won't see anywhere else in Mauritius, and the density of fish life is astounding. The underwater scenery is another pull, with a smorgasbord of canyons, arches and caves.

Rodrigues' signature dives include **La Passe St François** and **Le Canyon**, off the east coast. La Passe St François is a kilometre-long channel teeming with tuna, unicorn fish, groupers, turtles, rays and jacks (of the *Caranx ignobilis* variety) the size of a small car. Le Canyon is a truly atmospheric dive site – you'll dive in a canyon that runs under the reef, with openings that allow beams of sunlight to pass through. If you're after Tolkienesque scenery, ask for **La Basilique**, which is like an underwater medieval castle carved into the reef, full of galleries, faults and archways (but no coral). **Karlanne** is another hot favourite, offering dense marine life and healthy coral formations, especially those of the *Acropora* and *Porites* genuses.

The south coast has its fair share of thrilling dives too. Most sites are in the area of **La Grande Passe**. To say it's fishy is an understatement, and you don't need to go below 20m of water to admire the full gamut of reef species.

See p129 for local dive centres.

Practicalities
DIVING CONDITIONS
Although Mauritius is diveable year-round, the most favourable periods are October to December, March and April (January and February are peak months for cyclone activity). During July and August, when the southeast trade winds are at their strongest, the seas are too rough and murky for diving all along the east coast and around Rodrigues. Visibility is heavily weather dependent and thus varies a lot – from a low of 10m at certain sites at certain periods of the year to 40m at others.

Current conditions vary a lot, from imperceptible to powerful. Water temperatures range from a low of 22°C in August to a high of 28°C between December and February.

DIVE OPERATORS
There are at least 40 professional dive centres in Mauritius. Most belong to the **Mauritius Scuba Diving Association** (MSDA; ☎ 454 0011; www.msda-cmas.org), which is affiliated with CMAS and makes regular and rigorous checks. Most dive centres are also affiliated with one or more of the internationally recognised certifying agencies, usually PADI or CMAS. Many dive centres in Mauritius are hotel-based, but they all welcome walk-in clients. In general, you can expect well-maintained equipment, good facilities and professional staff, but standards may vary from one centre to another, so it pays off to shop around.

RÉUNION
Who said that diving in Réunion wasn't interesting? OK, it lacks the underwater charisma of the Seychelles or Mauritius, and it's mostly famous for its

For identification of tropical fish and corals, refer to *Reef Fishes & Corals* and *More Reef Fishes & Nudibranchs* by Dennis King, or the *Indian Ocean Reef Guide* by Helmut Debelius.

SNORKELLING

If the idea of total immersion doesn't appeal to you, snorkelling is possible in the three countries. It's a great way to explore the underwater world with minimal equipment and without the costs associated with diving. Even the shallowest reefs are home to many colourful critters. In all three destinations, rental gear is widely available from dive centres.

In Mauritius, top spots include the marine park at Blue Bay and along the west coast off Flic en Flac and Trou aux Biches, not forgetting the lagoon around Rodrigues. Companies running trips on glass-bottomed boats will often include snorkelling in the deal.

In Réunion, the lagoon along the west coast between St-Gilles-les-Bains and La Saline-les-Bains offers great snorkelling, with particularly good marine life off L'Hermitage-les-Bains. Take advice before leaping in as the currents can be dangerous.

In the Seychelles, the sheltered lagoons provide safe havens for swimming and snorkelling. The Ste Anne and Port Launay Marine National Parks are firm favourites in the waters around Mahé. Around Praslin, try off Anse Lazio and Anse Volbert beaches, or take a boat trip from Anse Volbert to St-Pierre islet. Close to La Digue, the submerged granite boulders around Coco, Grande Sœur and Marianne islands are teeming with fish life.

---

trekking options, but it shouldn't be sneezed at. You'll be positively surprised; there's a wide choice of shallow dives inside the lagoon for novices and deeper dives (mostly 25m to 40m) just outside for more experienced divers, as well as a few purpose-sunk wrecks thrown in for good measure.

Dive Sites

Most dive sites are located off the west coast between Boucan Canot and Grand Bois.

ST-GILLES-LES-BAINS

If you want relaxed diving, St-Gilles will appeal to you. Diving here is focused on the reefs, which slope gently away in a series of valleys to a sandy bottom in about 25m – very reassuring. Pelagics are rare, but small reef species are prolific.

Colourful sites such as **La Tour de Boucan** and **Le Pain de Sucre**, none of which are deeper than 20m, offer great opportunities off Boucan Canot. The setting is the strong point, with a contoured terrain and lots of small critters in the recesses (damselfish, parrotfish, triggerfish, lobsters), as well as a few seafans. On **Petites Gorgones** (also known as Saliba), keep an eye out for leaf scorpionfishes and turtles. Straight off L'Hermitage-les-Bains, **La Passe de L'Hermitage** is an exciting dive. The terrain is nicely sculpted, with little canyons and large boulders that act as magnets for a wealth of species. Sadly, visibility is often reduced.

If you have a hankering for wrecks, the **Haï Siang** (maximum depth 55m) and the **Navarra** (maximum depth 55m) will keep you entertained, though at such depths they are accessible to very experienced divers only. Novice divers will head to **La Barge**, off St-Paul, a relaxing wreck dive in less than 22m.

See p184 for local dive centres.

ST-LEU

St-Leu features splendid wall diving and good coral fields. Here walls tumble steeply to several dozen metres. Be sure to bookmark **Tombant de la Pointe au Sel**, south of St-Leu, which is widely regarded as Réunion's best all-round dive site. In addition to great scenery, this stunning drop-off offers a fabulous array of fish life and seldom fails to produce good sightings of pelagics, especially tuna, barracuda and jacks, as well as hammerhead sharks between October and November.

Coral bleaching is triggered by unnaturally high temperatures that cause the polyps to expel the symbiotic algae that give them their colour. If the temperature does not drop quickly enough, the coral eventually dies from the loss of the protective algae.

Les Pyramides is another stunner, with two seamounts rising from 70m to 38m. For novices, nothing can beat the very secure yet atmospheric **Le Jardin des Kiosques**, with a depth ranging from 3m to 18m. It's all about little canyons and grooves. Another relaxing site, **La Maison Verte** is blessed with good coral formations.

Wreck enthusiasts will enjoy the **Antonio Lorenzo**, a well-preserved vessel that rests in about 35m on a sandy bottom off Pointe des Chateaux. Fish life is not dynamic – it's the ambience that's the pull.

Whales can be seen cruising past the area from October to November.

See p190 for local dive centres.

ST-PIERRE

Savvy divers, this area is for you. Absolutely no crowds and only one dive boat (yours): this is diving near St-Pierre. It's unhyped and that's why we enjoy it so much. There are a host of untouched sites between St-Pierre and Grand Bois. The main drawcard here is the topography, with numerous ridges, canyons and drop-offs. Sites well worth bookmarking include **Petit Tombant Tres Poissonneux**, **Japonicus**, **Demotel** and **Cap Thérèse**, to name a few.

See p214 for local dive centres.

Practicalities

DIVING CONDITIONS

While it is possible to dive all year, the best time is October to April, when the water is at its warmest (about 28°C). However, you might want to avoid February through March, which is the cyclone season. Water temperatures can drop to about 21°C in August.

DIVE OPERATORS

The dive centres are concentrated around St-Gilles-les-Bains, St-Leu and St-Pierre. The standard of diving facilities is high. You'll find professional dive centres staffed with qualified instructors catering to divers of all levels. Staff members usually speak English. Most dive centres are affiliated with PADI, SSI or CMAS – all internationally recognised dive organisations.

Take note that a simple medical certificate stating you are fit enough to dive is compulsory for diving in France. You can get one from your doctor in your home country or have it faxed or emailed to the dive centre. Otherwise, you can get one from any doctor in Réunion (€21).

'this stunning drop-off offers a fabulous array of fish life and seldom fails to produce good sightings of pelagics'

SEYCHELLES

The Seychelles is sure to elicit strong emotions. Billed as one of the Indian Ocean's great diving destinations, it almost rivals the Maldives, though it's much less hyped – all the better for you. Good news: you don't need to be a strong diver – there are sites for all levels.

There's excellent diving off Mahé, Praslin and La Digue, the three main islands. The strong point is the underwater scenery, complete with big granite boulders and seamounts – it's as atmospheric as on land. If you have the chance to embark on a live-aboard, you'll dive the outer islands and Aldabra. Here you'll feel like Cousteau exploring unchartered territory – simply unforgettable.

Dive Sites

MAHÉ

If you are based in the north, whet your appetite with **Shark Bank**, Mahé's signature dive, for experienced divers only. As the name suggests, sharks are a fairly common sight around this 30m-tall granite pillar 9km off Beau

Vallon (Mahé) – they're generally reef sharks, but you will also see whale sharks between February and November. Expect to encounter brissant rays the size of Mini Mokes, eagle rays, barracuda, batfish and teeming yellow snapper and big-eyes. The pillar is covered with bright orange sponges and white gorgonians. There is nearly always a strong current at this site. **Îlot** is a granite outcrop just off north Mahé which consists of several large boulders topped by a tuft of palm trees. The current in the channel can be quite strong, but the cluster of boulders yields one of the highest densities of fish life in the Seychelles. Golden cup coral festoons the canyons and gullies, and gorgonians and other soft corals abound. You're sure to see yellow-spotted burr fish, turtles, anemones and clownfish, peppered moray eels, Spanish dancer nudibranchs and thousands of hingeback shrimps. Îlot is about a 15-minute boat ride from Beau Vallon. It's suitable for all levels of divers. About 5km north of Mahé, and accessed from Beau Vallon, **Brissare Rocks** is another granite pinnacle. The site features abundant fire coral and great concentrations of yellow snapper, wrasse, parrotfish and fusiliers, as well as groupers and eagle rays. Reef sharks and whale sharks are also known to visit the area. The Baie Ternay Marine National Park and the Ste Anne Marine National Park also offer great opportunities for experienced divers and novices alike.

> Make sure you allow 24 hours between diving and taking a flight, to minimise the risk of residual nitrogen in the blood that can cause decompression injury.

If you need a break from offshore dives, a few shipwrecks will keep you happy, including the **Twin Barges**, which sit upright on the seabed in about 20m in Beau Vallon bay. The hot favourite is the **Ennerdale**, to the northeast. This massive 216m-long vessel sunk in 1970 on a sandbank after hitting an uncharted rock. She's broken up, but very scenic.

If you're based in the southwest, you'll probably explore **Alice in Wonderland**, famous for its healthy coral formations, **Shark Point**, **Intendance Rock** and **Jailhouse Rock**.

See p272 and p278 for local dive centres.

PRASLIN & LA DIGUE

There are superb dive sites off Aride Island, including **Aride Bank**, which can be accessed from Praslin if you don't mind the tedious 30-minute boat trip to get to the sites. Closer to Praslin, approximately halfway between Aride and Praslin, **Booby Islet** is an exposed seamount which consistently sizzles with fish action.

Local divemasters also recommend **South Cousine Island**, **Cousin**, **Ave Maria Rocks** (noted for its shark sightings), **Marianne Island**, **White Bank** and **Anse Sévère**.

See p283 for local dive centres.

DIVING WITH A CONSCIENCE

Please consider the following tips when diving, to help preserve the ecology and beauty of reefs:

- Encourage dive operators to establish permanent moorings at appropriate dive sites.
- Practise and maintain proper buoyancy control.
- Avoid touching living marine organisms with your body and equipment.
- Take great care in underwater caves, as your air bubbles can damage fragile organisms.
- Minimise your disturbance of marine animals.
- Take home all your trash, and any litter you may find as well.
- Never stand on corals, even if they look solid and robust.
- Do not buy or collect seashells, or buy any seashell or turtleshell products.
- Dive with a local dive operator that follows high safety, ethical and professional standards.

THE FIRST TIME

You've always fancied venturing underwater on scuba? Now's your chance. Mauritius, Réunion and Seychelles are perfect starting points for new divers, as the warm waters and the shallow reefs are a forgiving training environment. Most dive centres offer courses for beginners and employ experienced instructors.

Just about anyone in reasonably good health can sign up for an introductory dive (from €40), including children aged eight and over. It typically takes place in shallow (3m to 5m) water and lasts about 30 minutes. It's escorted by a divemaster.

If you choose to enrol in an Open Water course, count on it taking about four days, including a few classroom lectures and open-water training. Once you're certified, your C-card is valid permanently and recognised all over the world.

OUTER ISLANDS

Now we're talking. Adventurous (and wealthy) divers will be sure to visit some of the outer islands, which open up a whole new world of diving. Desroches, Frégate, North, Silhouette and Denis Islands offer fantastic diving options, with absolutely pristine sites. One step beyond, you'll find Aldabra, Cosmoledo and Astove, which are the stuff of legend. They feature the best sites in the eastern Indian Ocean, with electric fish action in a totally virgin territory and high-voltage drift dives. The catch? It will cost you a king's ransom to access theses sites – they are only served by one live-aboard, the **Indian Ocean Explorer** (www.ioexpl.com). The dives of a lifetime are well worth the splurge.

Practicalities
DIVING CONDITIONS

Diving in the Seychelles heavily hinges on the weather conditions, currents and direction of the wind, but it can be sampled over all of the seasons as there are always sheltered conditions. Dive sites are chosen according to the prevailing winds. The calmest seas are from April to May and October to November. Due to currents and wind, visibility is temperamental and can drop to 5m. But in normal conditions you can expect 25m.

DIVE OPERATORS

The Seychelles' 15-odd diving centres have first-rate personnel and facilities. You'll find dive centres in Mahé, Praslin, La Digue, Ste Anne, Silhouette, Frégate, Denis, North and Desroches. Most centres are affiliated with PADI.

MARINE LIFE

Let's be honest: the western Indian Ocean is not the richest marine realm in the world – some parts of the Caribbean, the South Pacific and the Red Sea boast more prolific fish life. But it's far from being poor – in fact, it has everything from tiny nudibranchs (sea slugs) to huge whale sharks. It's just a matter of quantities, not diversity.

Like Technicolour critters? You'll encounter a dizzying array of reef species darting around the reef, including clownfish, parrotfish, angelfish, emperor-fish, butterfly-fish and various types of grouper. Moray eels are also frequently encountered.

Pelagic fish – larger beasts that live in the open sea, such as tuna and barracuda – sometimes cruise quite close to the reef in search of prey. Of the shark species inhabiting these waters, the most common are the white-tipped reef shark, the hammerhead shark and the reasonably docile nurse shark.

The most common species of ray found around the Seychelles and Mauritius is the manta ray. One of the larger stingray species, often encountered

> If you're a certified diver, don't forget to bring your C-card from a recognised scuba-diving instructional agency and your logbook with you.

at Shark Bank off Mahé, is the brissant (or round ribbon-tailed) ray. It can grow up to 2m across. The blue-spotted stingray is quite common in the sandy areas between the granite boulders of the Seychelles.

The best place to see turtles in the wild is the Seychelles, where there are a number of important breeding grounds for hawksbill and green turtles.

And coral? It's not the strongest point. The Indian Ocean's shallow-water reefs were badly hit by 'coral bleaching' in 1997 and 1998. In parts of the Seychelles, up to 90% of hard corals (the reef-building corals) were wiped out. They are still struggling, but there are encouraging signs of new growth. Fortunately, the fish and other reef creatures don't appear to have been affected.

MARINE CONSERVATION

The main pressures on the marine environment are pollution, over-exploitation and inappropriate activities such as the use of drag anchors, and explosives for fishing. In recent years Mauritius, Réunion and the Seychelles have introduced laws banning destructive practices, such as shell and coral collection, shark finning and spear-fishing. Each has also established marine reserves to protect at least some of their coral reefs. If you're willing to help, there are good volunteering opportunities, especially in Mauritius and the Seychelles.

Mauritius

The most active groups are the **Mauritius Marine Conservation Society** (MMCS; ☎ 696 5368; http://pages.intnet.mu/mmcs in French) and the **Mauritius Underwater Group** (MUG; ☎ 696 5368; http://pages.intnet.mu/mug), both of which were founded by concerned local divers. They run education, research and monitoring programmes, campaign for the control of water pollution and reef destruction and the installation of pavement mooring buoys, and have created artificial reefs (the wrecks along the west coast) to enhance the marine environment. Both groups are also pushing for more marine parks.

In Rodrigues, **Shoals** (☎ 831 1225; www.shoals-rodrigues.org) is campaigning for the installation of 'environmentally friendly' mooring buoys and working with local authorities to establish marine reserves as part of a sustainable fisheries project. It also runs volunteering programmes.

Supported by the **Mauritius Scuba Diving Association** (MSDA; ☎ 454 0011; www .msda-cmas.org), an increasing number of dive operators now regularly clean 'their' stretch of lagoon. If you find an operator polluting or destroying the reef, report it to the MSDA.

Réunion

The **Association Parc Marin de la Réunion** (☎ 0262 34 64 44; http://perso.wanadoo.fr/parcmarin .reunion in French) is charged with managing and protecting the lagoon. After many years campaigning for the park to be upgraded to a nature reserve, it succeeded in early 2007 – the park's now a fully fledged nature reserve.

Seychelles

The **Marine Conservation Society Seychelles** (MCSS; ☎ 713500; www.mcss.sc) monitors and promotes marine habitats and biodiversity. Current projects include whale-shark, turtle and coral reef monitoring. Visitors are welcome to participate in the monitoring programmes (see the website). To add to the fun, you can also adopt a whale shark or a turtle through MCSS.

Nature Seychelles (☎ 601100; www.nature.org.sc) also works to improve biodiversity. Its conservation projects include the restoration of island ecosystems and a recent wide-reaching project to study the effects of coral bleaching on fish life.

Seychelles Island Foundation (☎ 321735; www.sif.sc) concentrates its efforts on studying and protecting Aldabra, a marine biodiversity hot spot.

According to the Convention on International Trade in Endangered Species (CITES), marine turtles are among the world's most endangered species, threatened by pollution and human exploitation. Their downfall has been their edible flesh and eggs, as well as their shell, which is used for jewellery and ornaments.

Mauritius

JEAN-BERNARD CARILLET

Mauritius Snapshots

Despite a serious recession following the millennium, Mauritius is today squaring up to be one of the Indian Ocean's most progressive and dynamic nations, with an increasingly impressive economic model and a liberal democratic political culture many of its African neighbours are sorely in need of.

With its traditional industries of sugar, tea, tobacco and textiles at the end of a long decline, Mauritius is in the process of reorienting itself towards IT, banking and tourism to ensure its long-term economic viability. With its close relationships to the two economic and political powerhouses of the region, South Africa and India, and its unique position both culturally and geographically between Africa and Asia, Mauritius continues to punch well above its weight internationally, and has continued to be an investment-friendly market place, with enviable stability by regional standards.

Despite this positive outlook, Mauritius is not a place without problems. Racial conflict still simmers in some urban areas, particularly between Hindu and Muslim populations, creating an atmosphere of tension in and around Port Louis which, while unnoticeable to most visitors, rather goes against the culture of tolerance and mutual respect that underpins Mauritian society – officially at least.

Internationally as well, tensions still continue between Mauritius and its former colonial masters, Britain, over the shabby British treatment of both Mauritius and the Chagos Islanders in the dispute about ownership of the Chagos Archipelago. The British-owned islands are leased until 2016 to the US, which uses the main island, Diego Garcia, as one of its major air bases (see p42). Mauritius claims the archipelago as its own territory, and the British, who have removed some 2000 Chagossians to Mauritius and Seychelles (despite several international legal cases that have deemed this illegal) are refusing to budge an inch. Following a new ruling by the UK's Court of Appeal in 2007, however, they may be forced to – the judge described Britain's acts as unlawful and ruled that the Chagossians had the right of return to all islands save Diego Garcia itself with immediate effect.

Domestically corruption remains a big issue in all walks of life – it brought down the first government of current Prime Minister Navin Ramgoolam in 2000 when two of his senior ministers were accused of taking huge backhanders. Ramgoolam was back in power at the time of writing, however, after a brief hiatus when Paul Bérenger, the first non-Hindu prime minister of Mauritius, led the country. The same names conspicuously crop up again and again in Mauritian politics – Navin Ramgoolam is, after all, the son of Sir Seewoosagur Ramgoolam, Mauritius' independence leader and the island's first prime minister – and politics is definitely a family affair here, although this is something shrugged off by locals on the whole.

Another recent problem was the Chikungunya epidemic (see p309), which afflicted many countries across the Indian Ocean, and resulted in a sharp drop in hotel reservations and visitor numbers in 2005 to 2006. Numbers bounced back by the end of 2006, however, and although Chikungunya is still present in Mauritius, there's no longer the epidemic there was in 2005. In general Mauritius came off far better than Réunion, where deaths and infections were both much higher.

Despite Mauritius making great economic progress in recent years, this isn't felt at all levels of society. Patches of extreme poverty still exist throughout the island (particularly in Port Louis, some shanty towns

FAST FACTS

Population: 1,250,000

Area: 2040 sq km

Total coastline: 177km

Highest point: Mt Piton (828m)

Literacy rate: 85.6%

Unemployment rate: 9.4%

Life expectancy: 72.88 years

Annual GDP: US$16.7 billion

Population living below the poverty line: 10%

Languages: English, Creole, Bhojpuri & French

around the country and – most pronouncedly – in Rodrigues) although most visitors are unlikely to witness this first hand.

All in all, things look rosy today for this buoyant and ambitious island nation, aware of its problems but fiercely proud of its multiculturalism, tolerance and stability, just off the coast of a continent where these traits are in all too short a supply.

HISTORY

Mauritius had no native population predating the European colonisers (unless you count the ill-fated dodo), and so unlike many other small islands for which colonisation resulted in the savage destruction of the native inhabitants a short period later, Mauritius' initial history is pleasantly guilt-free (again, unless you count the dodo). This historical point is vastly important to understanding the country's inclusive culture of tolerance and easy acceptance of all people: there's nobody in the ethnic melting pot able to claim precedence over the others. Broadly speaking Mauritius experienced four distinct historical periods in its colonisation leading up to full independence from the UK in 1968.

The Dodo: From Extinction to Icon is a fascinating history of how the demise of this one species due to human behaviour has become such a powerful worldwide metaphor for the dangers humans pose to their environment.

THE FIRST COLONISERS

Although Arab traders knew of Mauritius – which they rather unfairly called Dina Arobi (Isle of Desolation) – perhaps as early as the 10th century, the first Europeans to discover these uninhabited islands were the Portuguese, around 1507. They, too, were more interested in trade and never attempted to settle.

In 1598, a group of Dutch sailors landed on the southeast coast of the island and claimed it for the Netherlands. For the next 40 years the Dutch used Mauritius as a supply base for Batavia (Java), before deciding to settle near their original landing spot. Settlement ruins can still be seen at Vieux Grand Port, near Mahébourg.

The colony never really flourished, however, and the Dutch abandoned it in 1710. Nevertheless, they left their mark: the Dutch were responsible for the extinction of the dodo and for introducing slaves from Africa, deer from Java, wild boar, tobacco and, above all, sugar cane.

Mauritius was originally named in honour of the Dutch prince Maurits van Nassau by the Dutch explorers who first settled the island in the 17th century.

ÎLE DE FRANCE

Five years later it was the turn of the French, when Captain Guillaume Dufresne d'Arsel sailed across from what is now Réunion and claimed Mauritius for France. The island was rechristened Île de France, but nothing much happened until the arrival in 1735 of the dynamic governor, Bertrand François Mahé de Labourdonnais, Mauritius' first hero. He not only transformed Port Louis into a thriving seaport, but also built the first sugar mill and established a road network.

It was around this time that Mauritius' best-known historic event occurred when the *St Géran* went down during a storm off the northeast coast in 1744. The shipwreck inspired Bernardin de St-Pierre's romantic novel *Paul et Virginie*, an early bestseller (for more details of the event see the boxed text, p83).

As the English gained the upper hand in the Indian Ocean in the late 18th century, Port Louis became a haven for pirates and slightly more respectable corsairs – mercenary marines paid by a country to prey on enemy ships. The most famous Franco-Mauritian corsair was Robert Surcouf, who wrought havoc on British shipping.

During the early colonial periods before they were made extinct, the indigenous Mauritian giant tortoise was so large that two adult men could comfortably sit on its back and enjoy a (slow) ride.

In 1789, French settlers in Mauritius recognised the revolution in France and got rid of their governor. But they refused to free their slaves when the abolition of slavery was decreed in Paris in 1794.

BRITISH RULE

In 1810, during the Napoleonic Wars, the British moved in on Mauritius as part of their grand plan to control the Indian Ocean. Things started badly when they were defeated at the Battle of Vieux Grand Port, the only French naval victory inscribed on the Arc de Triomphe in Paris. Just a few months later, however, British forces landed at Cap Malheureux on the north coast and took over the island.

The new British rulers renamed the island Mauritius, but allowed the Franco-Mauritians to retain their language, religion, legal system and the all-important sugar-cane plantations, on which the economy depended. The slaves were finally freed in 1835, by which time there were over 70,000 on the island. They were replaced or supplemented by labour imported from India and China. As many as 500,000 Indians took up the promise of a better life in Mauritius, often to find themselves living and working in appalling conditions on minimum pay.

By sheer weight of numbers, the Indian workforce gradually achieved a greater say in the running of the country. Their struggle was given extra impetus when Indian political and spiritual leader Mahatma Gandhi visited Mauritius in 1901 to push for civil rights. However, the key event was the introduction of universal suffrage in 1959, and the key personality Dr (later Sir) Seewoosagur Ramgoolam. Founder of the Labour Party in 1936, Seewoosagur Ramgoolam led the fight for independence, which was finally granted in 1968.

INDEPENDENCE

The prime minister of newly independent Mauritius was, not surprisingly, Sir Seewoosagur Ramgoolam. He remained in office for the next 13 years and continued to command great reverence until his death in 1986, since when a host of public buildings has been named in his honour.

Since then the political landscape has largely been dominated by the trio of Anerood Jugnauth, the Indian leader of the Mouvement Socialiste Mauricien (MSM), the Franco-Mauritian Paul Bérenger with his leftist Mouvement Militant Mauricien (MMM) and Navin Ramgoolam, son of Sir Seewoosagur and leader of the Mauritian Labour Party. The former two parties formed their first coalition government in 1982, with Jugnauth as prime minister and Bérenger as finance minister. In the years that followed, the two men were in and out of government, sometimes power-sharing, at other times in opposition to each other, according to the complex and shifting web of allegiances which enlivens Mauritian politics. In 1995 and again in 2005, Navin Ramgoolam beat the MSM-MMM coalition with his Alliance Sociale coalition.

On the economic front meanwhile, Mauritius was undergoing a minor miracle. Up until the 1970s the Mauritian economy could be summed up in one word – sugar. Sugar represented more than 90% of the country's exports, covered most of its fertile land and was its largest employer by far. Every so often, a cyclone would devastate the cane crop, or a world drop in sugar prices would have bitter consequences.

From the 1970s the government went all out to promote textiles, tourism and financial services, much of it based on foreign investment. Soon Mauritius was one of the world's largest exporters of textiles, with Ralph Lauren, Pierre Cardin, Lacoste and other famous brands all manufactured

Slaves, Freedmen and Indentured Laborers in Colonial Mauritius is a newly published collection of academic essays about the various social classes in Mauritius throughout the colonial era, and fascinating reading for anyone interested in the brutal history of slavery.

During the Napoleonic Wars, Port Louis was renamed Port Napoleon until the British took the capital and rechristened it after the French king.

Helen Morgan's fascinating look at the birth of philately, Blue Mauritius: The Hunt for the World's Most Valuable Stamps includes very atmospheric descriptions of the circumstances under which the Mauritius Blue became the world's most valuable stamp.

on the island. Income from tourism also grew by leaps and bounds as the government targeted the luxury end of the market.

The strategy paid off. The 1980s and 1990s saw the Mauritian economy grow by a remarkable 5% a year. Unemployment fell from a whopping 42% in 1980 to less than 6% by 2000 and overall standards of living improved. Even so, rates of unemployment and poverty remained high among the Creole population, many of whom also felt frustrated at their lack of political power in the face of the Indian majority. These tensions spilled out on to the streets of Port Louis in 1999, triggered by the death in police custody of the singer Kaya, an ardent campaigner for the rights of the disadvantaged Creole population, people of mixed Afro-European origin. The riots brought the country to a standstill for four days and forced the government to make political concessions.

'Respect for others and tolerance are deeply engrained in all sectors of society'

THE CULTURE

Mauritius is often cited as an example of racial and religious harmony, and compared with most other countries it is. On the surface, there are few signs of conflict. However, racial divisions are still apparent, more so than in the Seychelles or Réunion. Tensions between the Hindu majority and Muslim and Creole minorities persist despite the general respect for constitutional prohibitions against discrimination, and constitute one of the country's few potential political flash points.

THE NATIONAL IDENTITY

Despite being a relatively young country (less than 40 years old) with a diverse population, there is a surprisingly strong sense of national identity in Mauritius that transcends racial and cultural ties. Of the various forces binding Mauritians together, the most important is language. Not the official language of English, but Creole, which is the first language of 70% of the population and understood by virtually all Mauritians. Another common bond is that everyone is an immigrant or descended from immigrants. Food and music are also unifiers, as is the importance placed on family life. Mauritius is a small, close-knit community. Living in such close proximity breaks down barriers and increases understanding between the different groups. Respect for others and tolerance are deeply engrained in all sectors of society, despite the occasional flare up of racial tension.

KAYA

It was a black day for Mauritius, and a blacker one still for the Creole community. On 21 February 1999, the singer Joseph Topize (aka Kaya) was found dead in his police cell, seemingly a victim of police brutality, after being arrested for smoking cannabis at a prolegalisation rally.

As the pioneer of *seggae*, a unique combination of reggae and traditional *séga* beats, Kaya provided a voice for disadvantaged Creoles across the country. His death in the custody of Indian police split Mauritian society along racial lines, triggering four days of violent riots that left several people dead and brought the country to a standstill.

An autopsy cleared the police of wrongdoing, but the events have forced the Indian-dominated government to acknowledge *la malaise Créole*, Creoles' anger at their impoverished status in a country that has been dominated by Indians since independence.

In contrast to these violent scenes, Kaya's music is full of positive energy. The classic album *Seggae Experience* is a tribute to the singer's unique vision.

Mauritians place great importance on education – not just to get a better job, but as a goal in its own right. Lawyers, doctors and teachers are regarded with tremendous respect. The pinnacle of success for many is to work in the civil service, though this is beginning to change as salaries rise among artisans and businesspeople.

As individuals, Mauritians live up to their reputation of being friendly, laid-back, hospitable and generous. Many go out of their way to help strangers, and there's nothing a Mauritian likes more than a good chat. They are gentle people, more likely to make a joke about something than get angry. Cultural differences do occur, however: the Chinese tend to be more reserved than the happy-go-lucky Creoles, who work hard but do love a good party.

LIFESTYLE

In general, each ethnic group maintains a way of life similar to that found in their countries of origin, even if they are second- or third-generation Mauritian. Several generations typically live together under one roof and the main social unit is the extended family – as witnessed by the size of family parties on a Sunday picnic. Mauritians are usually married by the age of 25. The majority of wives stay home to raise the family, while the husband earns the daily bread. Arranged marriages are still the norm among Indian families, while the Hindu caste system has also been replicated to some degree. Among all groups, religion and religious institutions continue to play a central role in community life.

'the main social unit is the extended family – as witnessed by the size of family parties on a Sunday picnic'

As with elsewhere, this very traditional pattern is starting to break down as the younger generation grows more individualistic and more Western-ised. They are far more likely to socialise with people from other communities, and intermarriage is on the rise. Other forces for change are the rise in consumerism and the emergence of a largely Indian and Chinese middle class. Middle-class couples are more likely to set up their own home and to have fewer children, while the wife may even go out to work. Statistics also show a slight decline in the number of marriages, while the divorce rate has doubled over the last decade.

Women's equality still has a long way to go in Mauritius. Many women have to accept low-paid, unskilled jobs, typically in a textile factory or as a cleaner. Even highly qualified women can find it hard to get promotions in the private sector, though they do better in the public service. This may be set to change, however, as in 2003 the government passed a Sex Discrimination Act and set up an independent unit to investigate sex discrimination cases, including sexual harassment at work. The unit's also charged with raising awareness levels and educating employers about equal opportunities.

There is little evidence of premeditated discrimination against gays and lesbians in Mauritius. Nevertheless, it's a very macho society, and gays and especially lesbians tend to keep a low profile. At the time of writing the Attorney General and Minister of Justice and Human Rights, Rama Valyden, was planning to introduce comprehensive anti-discriminatory legislation protecting sexual minorities.

Despite the fact that all forms of discrimination are illegal under the Mauritian constitution, it is widely recognised that the Creole minority has been socially, economically and politically marginalised. It's a vicious circle. Creoles find it harder to get work, partly because of low levels of literacy, but few Creole children complete secondary school because they're needed to help support the family. Expectations are also lower – and so it goes on. Creole poverty is particularly noticeable in the almost exclusively Creole island of Rodrigues.

RESPONSIBLE TRAVEL

The people of Mauritius have a well-deserved reputation for being exceptionally tolerant. That said, there are a few 'rules' of behaviour to abide by.

Although beachwear is fine for the beaches, you will cause offence and may invite pestering if you dress skimpily elsewhere. Nude bathing is forbidden, while women going topless is tolerated around some hotel pools, but not on the beaches.

Mauritius has many temples and mosques. You are welcome to visit, but should dress and behave with respect: miniskirts and singlet tops are a no-no, and it is normal to remove your shoes – there's usually a sign indicating where to leave them. Many temples and mosques also ask you not to take photos, while some Hindu temples request that you remove all leather items, such as belts. At mosques, you may be required to cover your head in certain areas, so remember to take along a scarf. Never touch a carving or statue of a deity. If at any time you're unsure about protocol, the best thing to do is ask.

As a result of the economic boom, overall living standards have improved in recent years and the majority of houses now have piped water and electricity. However, the gap between rich and poor is widening. It is estimated that the top 20% of the population earns 44% of the total income and that 10% lives below the poverty mark. A labourer's wage is just Rs 6000 per month, while a teacher might earn Rs 12,000. There is minimal social-security provision in Mauritius; people rely on their family in times of need. You'll find a few beggars around the markets and mosques, but the visible presence of poverty on the streets is relatively discreet.

Crime levels also remain relatively low, though petty crime is on the rise. It mostly involves burglaries, but tourists can be a target for thieves (see p135). While drug use is even less of a problem, it too is increasing. Small amounts of heroin are smuggled in from South Africa en route to Réunion and elsewhere and some is consumed locally.

One thing that is rife is corruption, though the only form likely to affect tourists is the commission system prevalent among taxi drivers (see p135). Local drivers fume about police 'fines'; connections are used to the maximum; and newspapers are full of financial scandals in the cosy, closed world of the Hindu-dominated administration. But after years of inaction, the present government seems serious about tackling the problem. In 2002 it set up the Independent Commission Against Corruption, which has unearthed some pretty dirty dealings. Among a number of high-profile cases, two senior bank officials were arrested for embezzling Rs 866 million and a former cabinet minister for accepting Rs 4.5 million in bribes.

Culture Shock Mauritius is a useful read for anyone wanting to know the dos and don'ts on the island.

ECONOMY

Former Prime Minister Paul Bérenger envisaged Mauritius enjoying a 'quantum leap' to a 'knowledge island' during his brief premiership, making Mauritius the Indian Ocean's internet hub, and while progress continues to be made along these lines, traditional agricultural activities, tourism and textiles continue to provide most of the jobs in the country.

But Mauritius has effectively run out of space to develop its tourism industry significantly further, with all the best beaches having been taken. The last major expansion, the building of four huge hotels on the southern coast on the former Bel Ombre Sugar Estate, was surely the last of its kind. Meanwhile the sugar industry is being downsized; vast work forces are being laid off because of increased mechanisation or factory closures. In light of these developments it's clear that Mauritius needs a sound economic vision for the future to stave off mass unemployment and crippling recession as the 21st century gets underway. You can expect to see lots more call centres here (with much of the population speaking fluent Hindu or Mandarin, there's lots of scope for service industries for both China and India being based here) as well as IT free-trade zones.

The banking industry – Mauritius' shady little secret world of massive international money transfers – continues to see huge benefits for the economy, although not as obviously at street level.

For the moment Mauritius still hums along nicely. Its people, many of them naturally mercantile traders by heritage, love to barter, haggle and hawk – and if a stroll through Port Louis or Curepipe can be seen as a microcosm of the country in general, then it's clear than Mauritians are eager workers who highly value material success.

'Mauritians, many of them naturally mercantile traders by heritage, love to barter, haggle and hawk'

POPULATION

Mauritius is made up of four ethnic groups: Indo-Mauritian (68%), Creole (27%), Sino-Mauritian (3%) and Franco-Mauritian (2%). Another small group you might come across are the Chagos Islanders (see the boxed text, below).

Although the population growth rate (currently 0.9%) is quite low, a quarter of Mauritians are under 15 years of age. The country also has one of the world's highest population densities, with an average of nearly 600 people per sq km, rising to a staggering 3000 per sq km in urban areas. Worst are Port Louis and the Central Plateau towns, which developed in the wake of the malaria epidemics that hit the coast in the 1860s (p90). Even more people are drifting to urban areas in search of work as the sugar factories mechanise and close down altogether. The vast majority of Mauritians now work in construction, industry and the service sector – all very urban activities.

THE CHAGOS ISLANDERS

One of the most prolonged betrayals in British colonial history is that surrounding the secret exile of the Chagos Islanders from their homeland in the 1960s and 1970s, in order to lease the main island, Diego Garcia, to the United States for use as a military base.

The islanders were 'resettled' in Mauritius and the Seychelles between 1965 and 1973. Some 5000 now live in abject poverty in the slums of Port Louis, where they continue to fight for their right to return home. The islanders won derisory compensation of £4 million from the British in 1982, which was paid out to the poverty-stricken islanders in return for them signing away their rights – many of them not realising at the time what the legal documents they were signing meant.

In 2000 the High Court in London ruled that the Chagossians had been evicted illegally and upheld their right to be repatriated. Nothing happened, so the Chagossians went back to court. In October 2003 the judge rejected their claim for further compensation, though he acknowledged that the British government had treated the islanders 'shamefully' and that the compensation had been inadequate. In May 2007 the Chagossians won a further case at the Court of Appeal in London, in which the government's behaviour was condemned as unlawful and an abuse of power. The judges in the case also refused to place a stay on the ruling, meaning the Chagossians were free to return to all islands (with the exception of Diego Garcia itself) with immediate effect. The British government is likely to appeal the decision with Britain's supreme court, the Law Lords, although what will happen between the two cases is anything but clear.

John Pilger's superb 2004 documentary is essential viewing for anyone who wants to learn the truth behind the British government's claims to respect human rights. You can watch it online here: www.jonhs.net/freemovies/stealing_a_nation.htm. Further information and ways to help the Chagossians can be found here: www.chagossupport.org.uk.

The Indian population (the majority of which is Hindu) is descended from the labourers who were brought to the island to work the cane fields. Nowadays, Indians form the backbone of the labouring and agricultural community and own many of the island's small- and medium-sized businesses, typically in manufacturing and the retail trade. The Central Plateau towns such as Rose Hill have a strong Indian flavour.

Indians also tend to be prominent in civic life. Because they are in the majority, Hindus always win elections. The prime minister between 2003 and 2005, Franco-Mauritian Paul Bérenger, was the first non-Indian at the helm in the country's history, and he only managed that through a deal struck with his predecessor, Indian Anerood Jugnauth (see p38).

After the Indo-Mauritians, the next largest group is the Creoles, descendants of African slaves, with varying amounts of European ancestry. Creoles as a whole form the most disadvantaged sector of society. The majority work in low-paid jobs or eke out a living from fishing or subsistence farming, most notably on Rodrigues, where Creoles make up 98% of the population.

Mauritius' 30,000 Sino-Mauritians are involved mostly in commerce. Despite their small numbers, the Chinese community plays a disproportionate role in the country's economy, though they tend to avoid politics. Most came to the country as self-employed entrepreneurs and settled in the towns (particularly Port Louis), though most villages have at least one Chinese store.

Franco-Mauritians, the descendants of the *grands blancs* (rich whites), have their hands on Mauritius' purse strings. Most of the sugar mills, banks and other big businesses are still owned by Franco-Mauritians, who tend to screen themselves off from their former labourers in palatial private residences in the hills around Curepipe, and own almost all the luxurious holiday homes along the coast. Many others have decamped completely to live in South Africa and France.

Grand Bassin in southern Mauritius is the largest Hindu pilgrimage outside India. Believed to have been created when Shiva spilled some water from the Ganges that he was carrying on his head, the lake is visited by half a million pilgrims each year.

RELIGION

There is a close link between religion and race in Mauritius and a remarkable degree of religious tolerance. Mosques, churches and Hindu temples can be found within a stone's throw of each other in many parts of the country.

Over half the population is Hindu, all of whom are of Indian origin. Festivals play a central role in the Hindu faith and the calendar's packed with colourful celebrations. See p136 for a rundown of the most important ones.

There's a certain amount of resentment against the Hindus in Mauritius, not for religious reasons but because the Hindu majority dominates the country's political life and its administration. Up until now, with the economy in full swing, this has merely resulted in grumbling about discrimination and 'jobs for the boys', but there's a fear this might change if the economy really begins to falter.

Nearly a third of the population is Roman Catholic. Catholicism is practised by most Creoles, and it has picked up a few voodoo overtones over the years. Most Franco-Mauritians are also Catholic and a few Chinese and Indians have converted, largely through intermarriage.

Muslims make up roughly a fifth of the population. Like the Hindus, Mauritian Muslims originally came from India. In Mauritius, where Islam coexists in close proximity to other religions, it tends to be fairly liberal, though attendance at mosque is high and many Muslim women wear hijab.

Sino-Mauritians are the least conspicuous in their worship. The one big exception is Chinese New Year, which is celebrated in Port Louis with great gusto. There are a few Chinese temples in Port Louis.

ARTS

Mauritian architecture, literature and fine arts are all firmly based in the French tradition. The country's music, however, is African in origin and is very much alive and kicking.

Literature

Mauritius' most famous contribution to world literature – one that has become entangled in the island's history – is the romantic novel *Paul et Virginie* by Bernardin de St-Pierre, which was first published in 1788 (see the boxed text, p83). An English translation of the novel is widely available in Mauritius. The author captures the landscapes beautifully, though his ultramoralistic tear-jerker is less likely to appeal to modern tastes.

Joseph Conrad's oblique love story *A Smile of Fortune*, collected in '*Twixt Land and Sea* (1912) is set in Mauritius, although it's hardly very flattering about the place. Set in the late 19th century it does, however, give a taste of the mercantile activity of the time and the curious mix of 'negroes', Creoles, 'coolies' and marooned Frenchmen who populated the island then. Visitors to the island will certainly identify with Conrad's description of Mauritius as the '"Pearl of the Ocean"… a pearl distilling sweetness on the world', but will undoubtedly find the current inhabitants far more pleasant to deal with than the characters described in the story.

> 'Visitors to the island will certainly identify with Conrad's description of Mauritius as the "Pearl of the Ocean"'

Those who want to read a 20th-century Mauritian novel should try something by Malcolm de Chazal, whose most famous works are *Sens Plastique*, available in translation, and *Petrusmok*. Chazal was an eccentric recluse, but he inspired a whole generation of local writers. His works are a highly original blend of poetry and philosophy, and are peppered with pithy statements, such as 'Avoid clean people who have a dirty stare'.

Of living writers, perhaps the best-known internationally is Carl de Souza. In his novel *Le Sang de l'Anglais* he looks at the often ambivalent relationship between Mauritians and their countries of origin, while *La Maison qui Marchait Vers le Large*, set in Port Louis, takes intercommunity conflict as its theme. *Les Jours Kaya* is a coming-of-age book set against the violence following Kaya's death (see p39).

Other contemporary novelists to look out for include Ananda Devi, Shenaz Patel and Natacha Appanah-Mouriquand. Unfortunately, their works as yet are only available in French, regarded as the language of culture.

In more recent times, the French author JMG Clézio, whose father was Mauritian, has also set a number of novels in Mauritius, of which *Le Chercheur d'Or* (The Prospector) has been translated into English.

Music & Dance

You'll hear *séga* everywhere nowadays, but in the early 20th century it fell seriously out of fashion. Its revival in the early 1950s is credited to the Creole

---

RECOMMENDED RHYTHMS

- *Île Maurice*, Ti-Frère (Ocora; 1991) The best of Ti-Frère, with lyrics translated into English.
- *Île Maurice: Séga Ravanne*, Fanfan (Ocora; 1999) *Séga* taken from the oral tradition.
- *Album d'Or*, Cassiya (Cassiya Productions; 2000) Modern *séga* interpretations.
- *Makoutia: Chants et Danses de Rodrigues*, Racines. Good introduction to Rodriguan music, with English text.
- *Seggae Experience*, Kaya (Meli-Mela; 1999) Kaya's classic album is still widely available in Mauritius.

SÉGA!

Séga is the powerful combination of music and dance originally conceived by African slaves as a diversion from the injustice of their daily existence. At the end of a hard day in the cane fields, couples danced the *séga* around campfires on the beach to the accompaniment of drums.

Because of the sand (some say because of the shackles), there could be no fancy footwork. So today, when dancing the *séga*, the feet never leave the ground. The rest of the body makes up for it and the result, when the fire is hot, can be extremely erotic. In the rhythm and beat of *séga*, you can see or hear connections with the Latin American salsa, the Caribbean calypso, and the African origins of the people. It's a personal, visceral dance where the dancers let the music take over and abandon themselves to the beat.

The dance is traditionally accompanied by the beat of the *ravanne*, a primitive goatskin drum. The beat starts slowly and builds into a pulsating rhythm which normally carries away performers and onlookers alike. You may be lucky enough to see the dance being performed spontaneously at beach parties or family barbecues. Otherwise, you'll have to make do with the less authentic *séga* soirees offered by some bars and restaurants and most of the big hotels, often in combination with a Mauritian buffet. Nonresidents are usually welcome, though may have to pay (generally around Rs 200/100 per adult/child, which is then deducted from your food or drink bill).

---

singer Ti-Frère, whose song 'Anita' has become a classic. Though he died in 1992, Ti-Frère is still the country's most popular *séga* star. More recent Creole groups and singers with a wide following include Cassiya, Fanfan and the prolific Jean-Claude Gaspard.

Séga evolved slightly differently in Rodrigues. Here the drum plays a more prominent role in what's known as *séga tambour*. The island's accordion bands are also famous for their surprising repertoire, which includes waltzes, polkas, quadrilles and Scottish reels. Over the years these were learned from passing European sailors and gradually absorbed into the local folk music. They're now an essential part of any Rodriguan knees-up.

A new Mauritian musical form was invented by Creole musician Kaya in *seggae*, which blends elements of *séga* and reggae. With his band Racine Tatane, Kaya gave a voice to dissatisfied Creoles around the island. Tragically, the singer died in police custody in February 1999. Following in Kaya's footsteps, Ras Natty Baby and his Natty Rebels are one of most popular *seggae* groups; sales gained an extra boost when Ras Natty Baby was imprisoned for heroin trafficking in 2003.

Recently, *ragga*, a blend of house music, traditional Indian music and reggae, has been gaining a following. Mauritian *ragga* groups include Black Ayou and the Authentic Steel Brothers.

> The website www.sega.mu is devoted entirely to Mauritius' much loved national music, which developed from the songs and dances of slaves. You can listen to *séga* here as well as read a very detailed history.

Architecture

Caught up in the need to develop its economy, Mauritius paid little attention to its architectural heritage until recently. As a result many splendid colonial mansions and more humble dwellings have been lost under the sea of concrete. Those still standing may be luckier. In 2003 the government set up a National Heritage Fund charged with preserving the country's historic buildings.

Those which have fared best are the plantation houses dating from the 18th and 19th centuries, which you'll still see standing in glorious isolation amid the cane fields. Many are privately owned and closed to the public, such as Le Réduit (p94), near Moka, which is now the President's official residence. Others have been converted into museums and restaurants, including Eureka (p94), a beautifully restored mansion also near Moka. But rescuing these houses is expensive and time-consuming. Many of the

> Another great music site is www.radiomoris.com, where you can listen to the radio station live and hear lots of great *séga*, *ragga* and *seggae*.

THE ARCHITECTURAL HERITAGE

The first French settlers naturally brought with them building styles from home. Over the years the architecture gradually evolved until it became supremely well suited to the hot, humid tropics. It's for this reason that so many of the grand plantation houses have survived the ravages of time.

Flourishes that appear to be ornamental – vaulted roofs and decorative pierced screens, for example – all serve to keep the occupants cool and dry. The most distinctive feature is the shingled roof with ornamental turrets and rows of attic windows. These wedding-cake touches conceal a vaulted roof, which allows the air to circulate. Another characteristic element is the wide, airy *varangue* (veranda), where raffia blinds, fans and pot plants create a cooling humidity.

The roofs, windows and overhangs are usually lined with delicate, lace-like *lambrequins* (decorative wooden borders), which are purely ornamental. They vary from simple, repetitive floral patterns to elaborate pierced friezes; in all cases a botanical theme predominates.

Lambrequins, shingle roofs and verandas or wrought-iron balconies are also found in colonial-era town houses. The more prestigious buildings were constructed of brick, or even stone, and so are better able to withstand cyclones and termites. In Port Louis, Government House and other buildings lining Place S Bissoondoyal are all fine examples.

At the other end of the scale, traditional labourers' houses typically consist of two rooms (one for sleeping, one for eating) and a veranda; because of the fire risk the kitchen is usually separate. Nowadays they are built of corrugated iron rather than termite-resistant hardwood, but are still painted in eye-catching colours that offset the white *lambrequins*. The garden overflowing with edible and ornamental plants is almost as important as the house itself.

raw materials, such as tamarind wood, are in short supply. It's easier and cheaper to rip down the old timber frames, and throw up brand new concrete blocks on the sturdy foundations beneath.

The majority of Mauritians now live in nondescript concrete apartment blocks in the towns and cities. Middle-class families might possibly afford a seaside apartment or villa. The coast around Trou aux Biches and Flic en Flac is lined with these uninspiring boxes, all cheek by jowl. A few more enlightened developers are beginning to add traditional flourishes, such as *lambrequins* (decorative wooden borders) and bright paintwork. Hotels and restaurants are also getting better at incorporating a bit of local colour.

As for major civic projects, the most prestigious in recent times has been Port Louis' Caudan Waterfront development. Given its location at the very heart of the capital, the architects decided to incorporate elements of the traditional architecture found around nearby Place S Bissoondoyal. Further inspiration came from the nearby stone-and-steel dockyard buildings to provide another link with the past.

Mauritius Style: Life on the Verandah is a beautiful coffee table book depicting the many different Mauritian interiors that have so artfully combined French, Asian and African aesthetics.

Visual Arts

Historically, Mauritian artists took their lead from what was happening in Europe and, in particular, France. Some of the 18th- and 19th-century engravings and oils of Mauritian landscapes you see could almost be mistaken for Europe. The classical statue of Paul and Virginie in Port Louis' Blue Penny Museum and the one of King Edward VII in the city's Champ de Mars were both created by Mauritius' best-known sculptor, Prosper d'Épinay.

In the 20th century, the surrealist writer and painter Malcolm de Chazal injected a bit of local colour into the scene. Inspired by the island's prolific nature, his paintings are full of light and energy. You'll see numerous copies of the *Blue Dodo* and other Chazal works around, but originals are extremely rare.

Contemporary Mauritian art tends to be driven by the tourist market. One artist you'll find reproduced everywhere is Vaco Baissac, instantly recognisable from the blocks of colour outlined in black, like a stained-glass window. His gallery is in Grand Baie (p77).

Other commercially successful artists include Danielle Hitié, who produces minutely detailed renderings of markets as well as rural scenes, and Françoise Vrot, known for her very expressive portraits of women field-workers. Both artists are exhibited in galleries in Grand Baie, where Vrot also has her studio (p77).

Keep an eye out for exhibitions by more innovative contemporary artists such as Hervé Masson, Serge Constantin, Henri Koombes and Khalid Nazroo. All have had some success on the international scene, though are less visible locally.

FOOD & DRINK

The rich and diverse heritage of Mauritius makes for some good reading on restaurant menus, with Indian, Chinese, French and African cuisine all having a 'greatest hits'–like showing in most places you'll visit. Mauritian, or Creole, cuisine takes various elements from each when preparing the fish and seafood dishes that are the national staple. For food-related vocabulary and expressions, see p316.

STAPLES & SPECIALITIES

Mauritian cuisine is very similar across the island, a rich and delicious mix of Indian spices and local fresh seafood and fish prepared with strong influences from Chinese, French and African cuisine. The cuisine of Rodrigues is quite different, less spicy but with more fresh fruit and beans used as ingredients.

In Mauritius, rice, noodles, fish and seafood are the staples of everyday life, although to a great extent what people eat depends on their ethnic background. A Sino-Mauritian may well start the day with tea and noodles, a Franco-Mauritian with a *café au lait* and croissant, and an Indo-Mauritian with a chapati. However, come lunchtime nearly everyone enjoys a hot meal – whether it be a spicy seafood *carri* (curry) or *mines* (noodles) and a cooling beer. Dinner is the main meal of the day and is usually eaten *en famille* (with family). The Mauritians love their cocktail hour, and so you'll nearly always have an *apéro* (apéritif) or a *petit punch* – usually a rum-based fruit cocktail. While meat is widely eaten (especially in Chinese and French cuisine), the most common mainstays are fish and seafood. Marlin is a big favourite, as are mussels, octopi and calmari.

DRINKS

Unsurprisingly the national drink is rum, and although most agree that Mauritian rum isn't up to the standard of the Caribbean equivalent, there are still some excellent brands produced, particularly Green Island – the dark variety of which is superb. Despite a long history of rum production in Mauritius, the socially preferred spirit tends to be whiskey – a hangover from the 150-year British rule.

The national beer is Phoenix, an excellent pilsner produced at the Phoenix Brewery since the 1960s and a regular prizewinner at festivals around the world. The other premium brand of the brewery, Blue Marlin, is also very good.

Unlikely to be at your local multiplex any time soon is Mauritius' first ever film, *Benares,* made on the island in 2005. It's a touching portrait of two friends from the country travelling to Port Louis to find wives.

Genuine Cuisine of Mauritius (Éditions de L'Océan Indien; eoibooks@intnet .mu; 1998), by Guy Félix, is a great Mauritian recipe book.

To make a 'millionaire's salad' you must cut down a whole palm tree, just to use the edible heart of palm. Once the heart of palm is removed, the plant dies.

The Mauritians are also great tea drinkers and you shouldn't miss trying the range of Bois Chéri teas on sale throughout the country. The vanilla tea is the most famous and is quite delicious and refreshing even in the heat of the day, and you'll have a chance to see it being made and to taste it at the Bois Chéri Factory in southern Mauritius (p119).

During Hindu and Muslim festivals, deliciously flavoured drinks such as *lassi* (Indian yoghurt drink) and almond milk (almond- and cardamom-flavoured milk) are prepared.

WHERE TO EAT & DRINK

There tends to be quite a bit of segregation between 'tourist' restaurants and 'local' ones, particularly around bigger resort areas. In places such as Port Louis and the central highlands this is a lot less pronounced, and most places have a mixed clientele.

Throughout this chapter we've tried to avoid including solely tourist eateries unless they are very special or the only things on offer. Nearly all restaurants have menus in English, or at least staff who speak English, so communication difficulties are kept to a minimum.

Most restaurants have several cuisines served up cheek by jowl, although they're nearly always separated from each other on the menu. While in better restaurants this will mean each cuisine is prepared by a different expert chef, on the whole most chefs are decent at cooking one cuisine and prepare the remaining dishes with something approaching indifference. The rule is a fairly obvious one – don't go to a Chinese restaurant for a good curry.

The best places to eat throughout the country tend to be *tables d'hôte*, private hosted meals often given by people who run guesthouses as well, but just as often offered alone. These give you a unique insight into local life, as you'll usually dine with the host couple and often their children, plus any other travellers who've arranged to come by (or people staying in the guesthouse). It's nearly always necessary to book a *table d'hôte*, preferably a day in advance, although it's always worth asking – bigger operations will sometimes be able to accommodate last-minute additions.

Opening hours tend to be quite flexible (and unpredictable in smaller places!) although as a rule it's good not to leave eating too late – even though many places are officially open until 11pm, if they're empty by 10pm then there's a chance they'll shut early. Port Louis is a ghost town for everything including eating in the evening as the middle classes tend to live out of town, so it's usually the Caudan Waterfront or nothing after dark.

Quick Eats

Places to enjoy quick eats on the run are in plentiful supply in Mauritius. Street vendors are at every bus station and town square, and takeaway shops can be found in numerous shopping centres and markets; both offer inexpensive local treats, including Indian, French and Chinese delicacies. Almost all restaurants, except the most upmarket, will do takeaway. In Mauritius, roadside food stalls serving dinner dishes such as *biryani* (curried rice), Indian rotis and *farattas* (unleavened flaky flour pancakes) are popular.

The atmospheric markets are worth visiting for the popular *gâteaux piments* (deep-fried balls of lentils and chilli), which are cooked on the spot. You should also try the delicious *dhal puris,* rotis, samosas and *bhajas* (fried balls of *besan* dough with herbs or onion).

Indian and Chinese restaurants offer quick and inexpensive meals and snacks. Remember to buy some Indian savouries such as *caca pigeon* (an Indian nibble) or the famous Chinese *char siu* (barbecue pork).

Look out for delicious, thirst-quenching almond-based drink *alouda* while visiting Mauritius. Topped with ice cream, it's the perfect antidote to the midday heat or after enjoying a particularly hot curry…

Bat Curry is a specialty in some restaurants in Mauritius, although you won't see it on the menu; it tends to be a specialty the islanders keep to themselves.

Try cooking some delicious recipes for yourself by visiting Madeleine Phillipe's excellent website at www.ile-maurice.tripod.com

VEGETARIANS & VEGANS

Vegetarians will fare well in Mauritius, although they may be disappointed by the lack of variety. Indian restaurants tend to offer the best choice, but often this is limited to a variation on the theme of *carri de légumes* (vegetable curry). Chinese restaurants are also good for vegetarians, while Creole and French places are much more limiting, although almost everywhere has a vegetable curry on the menu. Pescatarians will be spoiled for choice as almost every eatery in the country offers fresh seafood and freshly caught fish cooked to perfection.

Vegans will find things harder, but not unassailably so – most resorts will be able to offer vegan options with advance warning, and again Indian restaurants will offer the most choice.

HABITS & CUSTOMS

Eating habits vary across ethnic groups. Some groups eat with their fingers, others don't eat meat on Fridays and some abstain from eating pork – it's hard to generalise across the community.

Breakfasts are normally very quick and informal. Lunch is also a fairly casual affair, although at the weekend it tends to be more formal, when family and friends gather to share the pleasures of the table. In restaurants, special menus are offered for weekend lunches. Before dinner, which is a very formal occasion, *gajacks* (predinner snacks) and predinner drinks (*un apéro* or *un petit punch*) are commonly served; during the meal, wine or beer is usually served.

As eating and drinking are important social activities, behaviour at the table should be respectful. Locals can be strict about table manners, and it's considered rude to pick at your food or mix it together. You are also expected to be reasonably well dressed. Unless you are in a beach environment, wearing beachwear or other skimpy clothing won't be well received – casual but neat clothing is the norm. When invited to dine with locals, bring a small gift; perhaps some flowers or a bottle of wine.

If you are attending a traditional Indian or Chinese meal or a dinner associated with a religious celebration, follow what the locals do. Generally, your hosts will make you feel comfortable, but if you are unsure, ask about the serving customs and the order of dishes. Definitely attend an Indian or a Chinese wedding if you get the opportunity – these celebrations are true culinary feasts.

Les Délices de Rodrigues (in French), by Françoise Baptiste, presents recipes from Rodrigues. Madame Baptiste also arranges bespoke Rodrigues cookery courses at her guesthouse in Grande Montagne, Rodrigues. Contact her for details (see p130).

ENVIRONMENT

THE LAND

Mauritius is the peak of an enormous volcanic chain that also includes Réunion, though it is much older and therefore less rugged than Réunion.

The island's highest mountains are found in the southwest, from where the land drops slightly to a Central Plateau before climbing again to the chain of oddly shaped mountains behind Port Louis and the Montagne Bambous range to the east. Beyond these mountains a plain slopes gently down to the north coast.

Unlike Réunion, Mauritius has no active volcanoes, although remnants of volcanic activity abound. Extinct craters and volcanic lakes, such as the Trou aux Cerfs crater in Curepipe and the Grand Bassin holy lake, are good examples. Over the aeons, the volcanoes generated millions of lava boulders, much to the chagrin of the indentured farm labourers, who had to clear the land for sugar cane. Heaps of boulders dot the landscape. Some that have been piled into tidy pyramids are listed monuments!

Mauritius also includes a number of widely scattered inhabited islands, of which the most important is Rodrigues, 600km to the northeast. Rodrigues is another ancient volcanic peak and is surrounded by a lagoon twice the size of the island itself. Mauritius also owns the sparsely inhabited islands of Cargados Carajos northeast of the mainland and the Agalega Islands, two islands adjacent to the Seychelles.

Mauritius also stakes territorial claim to the Chagos Archipelago, officially part of the British Indian Ocean Territory and controversially ceded to the US military until 2016 (see p42).

WILDLIFE

Mauritius is a haven for botanists, zoologists, ornithologists and all sorts of other 'ologists'. To experience some of what's on offer in the way of flora and fauna, visitors must go to the botanical gardens at Pamplemousses and Curepipe, to Casela Nature Park and the Black River Gorges National Park in the southwest, and to Île aux Aigrettes, La Vanille and the Domaine du Chasseur in the south.

The best source of information is the **Mauritian Wildlife Foundation** (MWF; ☎ 631 2396; www.ile-aux-aigrettes.com/pages/mwf.htm), which was founded in 1984 to protect and manage the country's many rare species. The MWF vigorously supports the creation of national parks and reserves, and the monitoring of whales, dolphins and turtles. It has had significant success in restoring the populations of several endangered bird species and in conserving endemic vegetation. Nevertheless, there is still a long way to go.

For information on marine life, see p33.

Animals

Mauritius has only one native mammal, the wonderful fruit bat – a common sight at twilight each evening as they come to life and begin their night's foraging. All other mammals present on the island were introduced with varying degrees of success by successive colonists. Mongooses are typical of the slapdash ecological management of the past – they were introduced from India in the late 19th century to control plague-carrying rats. The intention was to import only males, but some females slipped through and soon there were mongooses everywhere. They remain fairly common, as are the bands of macaque monkeys that hang out around Grand Bassin and the Black River Gorges. Java deer, imported by the Dutch for fresh meat, and wild pigs also roam the more remote forests.

Native reptiles include the beautiful turquoise-and-red Ornate Day gecko and Telfair's skink, a clawed lizard, both of which can be seen on Île aux Aigrettes. You can rest easy if you see a slithering critter – there are no dangerous reptiles in Mauritius.

As for bird life, the best-known representative was the dodo, the super-sized pigeon that found its docility rewarded with extinction (see the boxed text, p78). The dodo was only the first of the many now extinct victims of Mauritius' colonisation. Several other local bird species looked doomed until a few years back, although thanks to phenomenal conservation efforts, some now have a chance of survival.

The Mauritius kestrel was the victim of pesticide poisoning, habitat destruction and hunting. By 1974 just six birds remained: four in the wild and two in captivity. A captive breeding programme established in 1973 has led to an amazing recovery, with numbers now over 800. With luck,

All the indigenous giant tortoises of Mauritius and Rodrigues are extinct, but similar Aldabra giant tortoises from Madagascar have been reintroduced in captivity to the islands in recent decades.

For a full lowdown on the excellent conservation work undertaken by the Mauritian Wildlife Fund and for details of how to volunteer, check out www.mauritian-wildlife .org.

you might see kestrels in the Black River Gorges and at the Domaine du Chasseur, north of Mahébourg.

The lovely pink pigeon has also been pulled back from the brink thanks to captive breeding. From a mere 10 or so individuals in 1990 there are now around 400. A colony has now been established on Île aux Aigrettes, off Mahébourg, safe from egg-stealing rats and monkeys and human poachers.

Similar captive breeding programmes are helping to preserve the echo parakeet, found mainly in the Black River Gorges, and the Rodrigues fruit bat (see p124), among other endangered species.

The birds you're most likely to see, however, are the introduced songbirds, such as the little red Madagascar fody, the Indian mynah (its yellow beak and feet giving it a cartoon-character appearance) and the most common bird of all on Mauritius – the red-whiskered bulbul. Between October and May the Terre Rouge estuary north of Port Louis provides an important wintering ground for migratory water birds such as the whimbrel, the grey plover and the common and curlew sandpipers.

Plants

Almost one-third of the 900 plant species found in Mauritius are unique to these islands. Many of these endemic plants have fared poorly in competition with introduced plants such as guava and privet, and have been depleted by introduced deer, pigs and monkeys. General forest clearance and the establishment of crop monocultures have exacerbated the problem, so that less than 1% of Mauritius' original forest is intact.

Mauritius' forests originally included the tambalacoque tree, which is also known as the dodo tree and is not far from extinction itself. It's a tall tree with a silver trunk and a large, tough seed that supposedly only germinates after being eaten by, and passing through the stomach of, a dodo. Scientists are sceptical about this rumour, but there's no denying the tree is extremely difficult to propagate. The easiest place to find this and other rare plant species is in the botanical gardens at Pamplemousses.

For a tropical island, Mauritius is not big on coconut palms. Instead, casuarinas (also known as *filaos*) fringe most of the beaches. These tall, wispy trees act as useful windbreaks and grow well in sandy soil. Along with casuarinas, eucalyptus trees have been widely planted to help stop erosion.

Other impressive and highly visible trees are the giant Indian banyan and the brilliant red flowering flamboyant, or royal poinciana.

Staying with shades of red, one flower you will see in abundance is anthurium, with its single, glossy petal and protruding yellow spadix. The plant originated in South America and was introduced to Mauritius in the late 19th century. The flower, which at first sight you'd swear was plastic, can last up to three weeks after being cut and is therefore a popular display plant. Now grown in commercial quantities for export, it is used to spruce up hotels and public meeting places.

Mangroves are enjoying a renaissance in Mauritius today. Originally cut down to reduce swamp areas where malarial mosquitos could breed, they've been discovered to be an important part of the food chain for tropical fish, and thus large projects to develop mangrove areas have been undertaken, particularly on the east coast.

NATIONAL PARKS

Since 1988, several international organisations have been working with the government to set up conservation areas in Mauritius. About 3.5% of the

Gerald Durrell's highly readable account of his adventures in Mauritius, *Golden Bats and Pink Pigeons*, remains a great companion to any trip, especially given that many of the species Durrell describes are extremely rare and even extinct today.

IMPORTANT NATIONAL PARKS

Park	Features	Activities	Best time to visit
Balaclava Marine Park (p66)	lagoon, coral reef, turtle breeding grounds	snorkelling, diving, glass-bottomed boat tours	all year
Black River Gorges National Park (p87)	forested mountains, Mauritius kestrel, black ebony trees, macaque monkeys	hiking, bird-watching	Sep-Jan for flowers
Blue Bay Marine Park (p115)	lagoon, corals, fish life	snorkelling, diving, glass-bottomed boat tours	all year
Île aux Aigrettes Nature Reserve (p116)	coral island, coastal forests, pink pigeons, giant Aldabra tortoises	ecotours	all year

land area is now protected either as national parks, managed mainly for ecosystem preservation and for recreation, or as nature reserves.

The largest park is the Black River Gorges National Park, established in 1994 in the southwest of the island. It covers some 68 sq km and preserves a wide variety of forest environments, from pine forest to tropical scrub, and includes the country's largest area of native forest. Two of the most important nature reserves are Île aux Aigrettes and Île Ronde, both of which are being restored to their natural state by replacing introduced plants and animals with native species.

In 1997 two marine parks were proclaimed at Blue Bay, near Mahébourg, and Balaclava on the west coast, but the number of visitors to the area makes it difficult to establish rigorous controls and there is a need to encourage local fishermen to use less destructive techniques.

'the Black River Gorges National Park preserves a wide variety of forest environments, from pine forest to tropical scrub'

ENVIRONMENTAL ISSUES

The environment of Mauritius has paid a heavy price for the country's rapid economic development. Tourist arrivals have been increasing at a rate of 9% a year for the last 20 years and, despite the set backs of the Chikungunya virus, there's little sign of a slow down. If anything, the government is keen to encourage even more tourists – at least, the rich ones – to plug the gap left by a declining sugar industry. However, the expansion of tourist facilities is straining the island's infrastructure and causing problems such as environmental degradation and excessive demand on services such as electricity, water and transport.

For many species it is already too late, but there is a growing awareness of the need for conservation among decision makers and the general public. The difficulty is to achieve a balance between protecting the immensely fragile island ecosystems and easing the ever-increasing pressure on land and other natural resources.

One area of particular concern is the amount of new development along the coast, much of it tourist related. Luckily, Mauritians are very keen to put environmental concerns first: a proposal for a hotel on Île des Deux Cocos in Blue Bay, for example, met with such fierce resistance that it has been abandoned.

The government now requires an environmental impact assessment for all new building projects, including coastal hotels, marinas and golf courses, and even for activities such as undersea walks. Planning regulations for hotel developments on Rodrigues are particularly strict: they must be small, single storey, built in traditional style and stand at least 30m back from the high-tide mark. Since water shortages are a problem on Rodrigues, new hotels must also recycle their water.

To combat littering and other forms of environmental degradation, the government has established a special environmental police force charged with enforcing the legislation and educating the local population. To report wrongdoers, there is even a **hotline** (☎ 210 5151).

If anything, the marine environment is suffering even more from over-exploitation. The coast off Grand Baie is particularly affected by too many divers and boats concentrated in a few specific locations. In addition, silting and chemical pollution are resulting in extensive coral damage and falling fish populations. For more information on marine conservation in Mauritius, see p34.

The Mauritian Wildlife Foundation is heavily involved in raising awareness of conservation issues among the local population and tourists. A visit to see MWF's work on Île aux Aigrettes (p116) is highly recommended.

MAURITIUS

Mauritius

Mauritius is a fascinating, world-in-one-island slice of paradise, the very name of which conjures up images of tropical luxury and stupendous extravagance. While in many places famed for cobalt-blue seas, white sandy beaches and luxury hotels you may eventually find yourself wishing for something other than sunbathing and swimming to do, in Mauritius it's often hard to know what to do next, so full is it of historic sights, cultural diversity, geographic variation and almost limitless activities to distract you from the daily grind of beach and pool. Despite all this, perhaps the island's single biggest asset is the relaxed charm of its warm and welcoming people.

Mauritius is the most developed of the Mascarene Islands, but with a bit of effort and resourcefulness you can escape the crowds and find your own patch of this most diverse of destinations. The smells, noises and bustle of the mercantile capital Port Louis, Africa's wealthiest city, are never far away, while the busy garment markets in the Central Plateau towns of Quatre Bornes and Curepipe and the dramatic virgin forests of the Black River Gorges National Park give the lie to Mauritius being just another beach destination. But what beaches though – from the stunning sand-rimmed lagoons and popular wide public beaches to the picturesque islands off the country's coastline, there's truly something for everyone here. Add to this the joys of Chinese, Indian, French and African cuisine, the rousing beat of *séga* music and the infectious party spirit of the locals, and you soon understand why Mauritius really is so many people's idea of paradise on earth.

HIGHLIGHTS

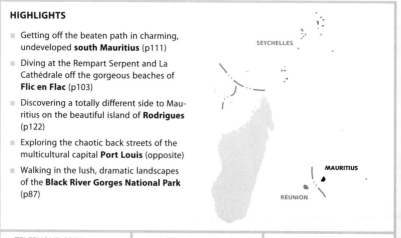

- Getting off the beaten path in charming, undeveloped **south Mauritius** (p111)
- Diving at the Rempart Serpent and La Cathédrale off the gorgeous beaches of **Flic en Flac** (p103)
- Discovering a totally different side to Mauritius on the beautiful island of **Rodrigues** (p122)
- Exploring the chaotic back streets of the multicultural capital **Port Louis** (opposite)
- Walking in the lush, dramatic landscapes of the **Black River Gorges National Park** (p87)

SEYCHELLES

MAURITIUS

RÉUNION

| ▪ TELEPHONE CODE: 230 | ▪ POPULATION: 1.25 MILLION | ▪ AREA: 2040 SQ KM |

CLIMATE & WHEN TO GO

Mauritius enjoys a typically tropical climate with year-round heat, although the southeast trade winds help it never to feel too muggy. The summer months are from December to April, when it can nevertheless be extremely humid, and the winter, such as it is, runs from May to November, and is cooler and drier.

The best months to visit Mauritius are May to early December. January and February, the peak cyclone months, are best avoided by water-sports enthusiasts and divers. Cyclones rarely hit Mauritius (although Rodrigues has suffered far more regularly than the mainland) but cyclones way out at sea can bring days of squally rain.

Coastal temperatures range between 25°C and 33°C in summer and between 18°C and 24°C in winter. On the plateau it will be some 5°C cooler. The highlands are also the wettest part of the island – it can rain here at any time of year, and even when it's not raining the area can be cloaked in low-lying cloud.

When the winds are at their strongest in July and August it can be blustery on the east coast, though the breeze brings welcome relief in summer.

Apart from the Christmas-New Year peak, Mauritius doesn't really have high and low seasons. The situation is more dependent on outside factors (such as the French school holidays, which cause a big increase in demand and prices in August).

PORT LOUIS

pop 172,000

With its spectacular setting beneath the impressive mountain peaks of Le Pouce and Pieter Both, Port Louis makes an impression on anyone arriving on the main road from the airport – descending from the Central Plateau into the hectic city centre with the Indian Ocean spread out in a perspective-defying frieze above the city is a wonderful experience.

Despite being the national capital, the main economic hub and the biggest city in the country, Port Louis occupies a rather strange place in the psyche of modern Mauritius. Its low-lying position has historically made it an undesirable locale, with disease in the 18th and 19th centuries frequently

devastating it, meaning that the professional classes have traditionally lived outside the city, particularly in the Central Plateau towns of Rose Hill, Moka, Vacoas and Quatre Bornes. This trend continues today, to the extent that Port Louis (the final s is usually silent, although many Mauritians pronounce it when speaking English) can sometimes seem like a city without a middle class, without a centre and a ghost town after dark.

This impression is totally false, however – Port Louis has plenty going for it, but it's a city that profits from exploration: those who only visit the fantastically Disneyesque Caudan Waterfront will get a very bland impression of the national capital. The bustle and chaos of the streets, the city's famous market, Chinatown, the collection of museums and some wonderfully preserved colonial buildings make Port Louis far more than a place to come for some pricey shopping away from the beach.

HISTORY

Port Louis was first settled in the 17th century by the Dutch, who called it Noordt Wester Haven. It was the French governor Bertrand François Mahé de Labourdonnais, however, who took the initiative and developed it into a busy capital and port after 1736. Labourdonnais is commemorated with a much-photographed statue at the seaward end of Place S Bissoondoyal (formerly Place d'Armes), the square that marks the city centre.

Few cities have bounced back from as many natural disasters as Port Louis, or Port Napoleon as it was known briefly in the early 19th century before the British took the island. Between 1773 and 1892 a series of fires, plagues and tropical storms all tried, and failed, to level the town. In 1819 cholera arrived from Manila on the frigate *Topaz,* killing an estimated 700 Port Louis residents. Things quietened down until 1866, when malaria suddenly appeared on the scene, causing a further 3700 fatalities. Around this time people started heading for the cooler (and healthier) Central Plateau, so the town's population was mercifully small when the 1892 cyclone whipped through, and destroyed 3000 homes.

The 20th century has seen Port Louis become one of Africa's most important financial centres and ports – to which the ever-growing number of high-rise glass-fronted banks in the city centre attest.

ORIENTATION

Port Louis is divided by Mauritius' only motorway, which runs just by the harbour area and the development of the Caudan Waterfront. On the Caudan side there's the sanitised city with smart shops and bars but with little atmosphere, while the vast majority of the city is on the other side of the road – dirty, colourful, chaotic and much more fun.

The centre of the city is hard to pin down exactly – the natural centre is Place S Bissoondoyal, a picturesque palm-lined avenue that runs from the harbour to Government House. From here nearly all the sites of interest are within easy walking distance. The main banks have their offices around this square or along nearby Sir William Newton St, while Royal St, which runs northeast through Chinatown, is also of interest to travellers.

Port Louis' two main bus stations are located either side of the city centre, each a few minutes' walk from Place S Bissoondoyal. Arriving from the airport, you'll be dropped at the more southerly Victoria Square bus station.

INFORMATION
Bookshops
Bookcourt (☎ 211 9262; Caudan Waterfront) The country's best bookshop sells a broad range of English and French books, including guidebooks.
Editions de L'Ocean Indien (☎ 211 1310; Jules Koenig St) A good selection of titles about Mauritius.
Librairie Allot Ltd (☎ 212 7132; 1st fl, Happy World House, Sir William Newton St) Usually stocks the IGN map of Mauritius and a good selection of literature.
Librairie du Trèfle (☎ 212 1106; 5 Royal St) An atmospheric place catering for the local market.

Emergency
Ambulance (☎ 114)
Fire services (☎ 995)
Police (☎ emergency 999, headquarters 203 1212; Line Barracks, Lord Kitchener St)

Internet Access
Cyber Café (☎ 210 6978; Dumat St; ◷ 9am-4pm Mon-Fri) A small place near the Victoria Sq bus station.
Smart Net Café (☎ 210 2177; Ramphul Bldg, Chausée St; ◷ 9am-4pm Mon-Fri, 9am-noon Sat) Small but centrally located.

Zenith Internet Café (Astrolabe, Port Louis Waterfront; ◷ 10am-8pm Mon-Thu, 10am-10pm Fri & Sat, 10am-4pm Sun) The best in town, with plug-in for laptops possible.

Medical Services
Dr Jeetoo Hospital (☎ 212 3201; Volcy Pougnet St) Provides 24-hour medical and dental treatment and has a 24-hour pharmacy. Staff speak English and French.
Medical Trading Pharmacy (☎ 294 0440; Chausée St) One of the best pharmacies in the city, just by Company Gardens.

Money
You'll find ATMs throughout Port Louis, while all the main banks are concentrated around Sir William Newton St. Standard banking hours are 9am to 3.15pm Monday to Thursday, 9am to 3.30pm Friday. Some banks are open on Saturday mornings, while those at the airport are open whenever flights arrive.
Barclays (☎ 207 1800; Sir William Newton St)
HSBC (☎ 203 8333; Pl S Bissoondoyal)
Mauritius Commercial Bank (MCB; ☎ 202 5000; 9-15 Sir William Newton St)
State Bank of Mauritius (☎ 202 1111; State Bank Tower, Pl S Bissoondoyal)

Post
Central post office (☎ 208 2851; Place du Quai; ◷ 8.15am-4pm Mon-Fri, 8.15-11.45am Sat) The last 45 minutes before closing are for stamp sales only.

Tourist Information
Mauritius Tourism Promotion Authority (MTPA; ☎ 210 1545; www.mauritius.net; Air Mauritius Centre, President John Kennedy St; ◷ 9am-4pm Mon-Fri, 9am-noon Sat) Distributes maps of Port Louis and Mauritius and can advise on car hire, excursions and hotels throughout the country.

DANGERS & ANNOYANCES

Port Louis is a city with a big underclass and as such is not safe at night. After dark all travellers should stick to well-lit main streets and avoid Company Gardens, favoured hang out of pimps and drug dealers. If you don't know your exact route, take a taxi. During the daytime it's a very safe city but beware of pickpockets anywhere, although particularly in the market and around the bus stations.

SIGHTS & ACTIVITIES

Most of Port Louis' sights are scattered around the waterfront and southeast along Poudrière St and Intendance St. Although some, such as

Fort Adelaide, are slightly further out, the distances are small and you can easily hop around the shops, museums and the market in a day.

Central Market

Port Louis' rightly famous **Central Market** (5.30am-5.30pm Mon-Sat, 5.30am-11.30pm Sun), the centre of the local economy since Victorian times, was cleaned up considerably in a 2004 renovation. Many comment that it's lost much of its dirty charm and atmosphere (you're far less likely to see rats, although it's still quite possible!), but it's still a good place to get a feel for the everyday life of many locals, watch the hawkers at work and buy some souvenirs. Most authentic are the wonderful fruit and vegetable sections (including herbal medicines and aphrodisiacs) and the meat, fish and seafood market.

If you're looking for souvenirs, a wide variety of Malagasy handicrafts are available, along with souvenir T-shirts of varying quality. The level of hustling here can be tiresome, however, and you'll have to bargain hard; start by slashing the price quoted by about 30%.

Blue Penny Museum

Whether or not you fully understand the philatelic obsession with the Mauritian one penny and two-pence stamps of 1847, the **Blue Penny Museum** (210 8176; www.bluepenny museum.com; Caudan Waterfront; adult/child/family Rs 150/80/350; 10am-5pm Mon-Sat) is far more wide ranging than its name suggests, taking in the history of the island's exploration, settlement and colonial period. It's Port Louis' best museum, well lit and designed, with a fantastic selection of maps, photographs and engravings from different periods in history, as well as a gallery for temporary exhibitions and a good shop.

The pride of the museum's collection is two of the world's rarest stamps: the red one-penny and blue two-pence 'Post Office' stamps issued in 1847 (see the boxed text, below). To preserve the colours, they are only lit up for 10 minutes at a time: every hour, on the half-hour. They were purchased by a group of Mauritian companies as a national treasure and are probably the most valuable objects on the entire island!

On the ground floor you'll see the country's most famous work of art: a superbly lifelike statue by the Mauritian sculptor Prosper d'Épinay, carved in 1884. Based on Bernardin de St-Pierre's novel *Paul et Virginie* (see the boxed text, p83), it shows the young hero carrying his sweetheart across a raging torrent.

Natural History Museum

There's only one real attraction at this small but proud **museum** (212 0639; Chaussée St; admission free; 9am-4pm Mon, Tue, Thu & Fri, 9am-noon Sat) and that's to see the famous – though somewhat grubby – reconstruction of a dodo. Scottish scientists assembled the curious-looking bird in the late 19th century, using the only complete dodo skeleton in existence (see p78). The rest of the museum's three halls get marks for trying, but the majority of the other exhibits are a sad testimony to the fact that fish don't readily lend themselves to the process of taxidermy. Look out, however, for the stuffed birds, including the solitaire and red rail, both also now extinct.

Chinatown

The Chinese have traditionally occupied a quietly industrious position in the life of Port Louis. The region between the two 'friendship gates' on Royal St forms the centre of Port Louis' Chinatown. Here you'll see the rich

---

STAMP OF APPROVAL

Philatelists (stamp collectors to the rest of us) go weak at the knees at the mention of the Mauritian 'Post Office' one-penny and two-pence stamps. Issued in 1847, these stamps were incorrectly printed with the words 'Post Office' rather than 'Post Paid'. They were recalled upon discovery of the error, but not before the wife of the British governor had mailed out a few dozen on invitations to one of her famous balls!

These stamps now rank among the most valuable in the world. The 'Bordeaux cover', a letter bearing both stamps which was mailed to France, was last sold for a staggering US$3.8 million. In 1993 a consortium of Mauritian companies paid US$2.2 million for the pair of unused one-penny and two-pence stamps now on display in Port Louis' Blue Penny Museum (above). This is the only place in the world where the two can be seen together on public view.

PORT LOUIS

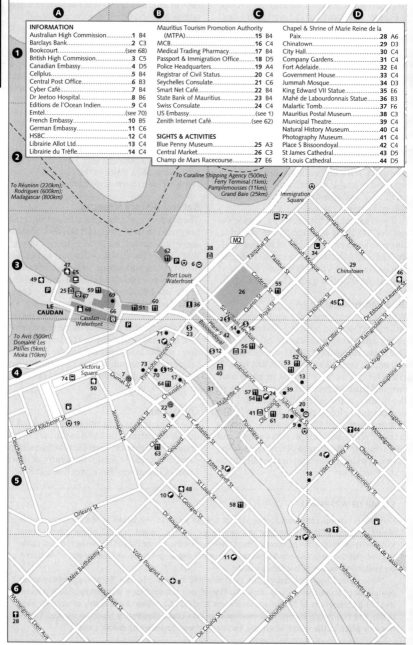

INFORMATION
Australian High Commission	1 B4
Barclays Bank	2 C3
Bookcourt	(see 68)
British High Commission	3 C5
Canadian Embassy	4 D5
Cellplus	5 B4
Central Post Office	6 B3
Cyber Café	7 B4
Dr Jeetoo Hospital	8 B6
Editions de l'Ocean Indien	9 C4
Emtel	(see 70)
French Embassy	10 B5
German Embassy	11 C6
HSBC	12 C4
Librairie Allot Ltd	13 C4
Librairie du Trèfle	14 C4

Mauritius Tourism Promotion Authority (MTPA)	15 B4
MCB	16 C4
Medical Trading Pharmacy	17 B4
Passport & Immigration Office	18 D5
Police Headquarters	19 A4
Registrar of Civil Status	20 C4
Seychelles Consulate	21 C6
Smart Net Café	22 B4
State Bank of Mauritius	23 B4
Swiss Consulate	24 C4
US Embassy	(see 1)
Zenith Internet Café	(see 62)

SIGHTS & ACTIVITIES
Blue Penny Museum	25 A3
Central Market	26 C3
Champ de Mars Racecourse	27 E6

Chapel & Shrine of Marie Reine de la Paix	28 A6
Chinatown	29 D3
City Hall	30 C4
Company Gardens	31 C4
Fort Adelaide	32 E4
Government House	33 C4
King Edward VII Statue	35 E6
Mahé de Labourdonnais Statue	36 B3
Malartic Tomb	37 F6
Mauritius Postal Museum	38 C3
Municipal Theatre	39 C4
Natural History Museum	40 C4
Photography Museum	41 C4
Place S Bissoondoyal	42 C4
St James Cathedral	43 D5
St Louis Cathedral	44 D5

To Réunion (220km);
Rodrigues (600km);
Madagascar (800km)

To Coraline Shipping Agency (500m);
Ferry Terminal (1km);
Pamplemousses (11km);
Grand Baie (25km)

Immigration
Square

Port Louis
Waterfront

LE
CAUDAN

Caudan
Waterfront

To Avis (500m);
Domaine Les
Pailles (5km);
Moka (10km)

Victoria
Square

M2

Chinatown

Jummah Mosque

Place S
Bissoondoyal

Lord Kitchener St

Jennings St

Barracks St

Chevreau St

Brown Sequard St

Sir William Newton St

Corderie St

Queen St

Royal St

L'Homme St

Rémy Ollier St

Sir Seewoosagur Ramgoolam St

Bourbon St

Jules Koenig St

Intendance St

Mallefille St

Poudière St

Sir Virgil Naz St

Dauphine St

Eugène St

Church St

Monseigneur St

Frère Felix de Valois St

Pope Hennessy St

Lislet Geoffroy St

St Denis St

Vishnu Kchetra St

Labourdonnais St

De Coucy St

Raoul Rivet St

Volcy Pougnet St

Marie Barthelemy St

Orleans St

St Georges St

St Louis St

Du Rouget St

Dr Cavell St

Edith Cavell St

Sir C Antelme St

Chaussée St

Dr John Kennedy St

Dumas St

Deschartres St

Emmanuel Anquetil St

Rivière St

Pasteur St

Farquhar St

Old Council St

Sir Edouard Laurent St

MAURITIUS

```
   0                        400 m
   0                        0.2 miles
```

To SSR Memorial
Centre for
Culture (100m);
Père Laval's
Shrine (2.5km)

Keneevassen St

Arsenal St

32 🏛

Suffren St

Laurent St

Conin St

D'Estaing St

Shakespeare St

27
Champ de Mars
Racecourse

🛈 35

To Le Pouce
(4km)

● 37

mercantile life of the hard-working Chinese community, the busy Chinese restaurants and groceries and the streets echoing with the unmistakable clatter of mah jong tiles.

Place S Bissoondoyal

Port Louis' most imposing boulevard is named after Sookdeo Bissoondoyal, a senior Mauritian politician, independence leader and, eventually, opposition leader against Ramgoolam, who died in 1977. The road that bears his name is lined with royal palms and leads up to **Government House**, a beautiful French colonial structure dating from 1738, although it was added to later. Outside it stands a typically solemn statue of Queen Victoria in full 'we are not amused' mode, while the statue of **Mahé de Labourdonnais** at the quayside end of the avenue is the best-loved in the city and has become its emblem throughout Mauritius.

Photography Museum

This small but engaging **museum** (☎ 211 1705; Old Council St; admission Rs 100; ☽ 10am-noon & 1-3.30pm Mon-Fri), down a lane opposite the Municipal Theatre, is the labour of love of local photographer Tristan Bréville. He's amassed a treasure trove of old cameras and prints, including several daguerreotypes (the forerunner of photographs) produced in Mauritius in 1840, just a few months after the technique was discovered in France. The museum also contains a vast archive of historical photos of the island, only a tiny fraction of which are on display.

Jummah Mosque

The **Jummah Mosque** (Royal St; ☽ 8am-noon & 2-4pm Mon-Thu, Sat & Sun), the most important mosque in Mauritius, was built in the 1850s, and is a delightful blend of Indian, Creole and Islamic architecture – it would look equally at home in Istanbul, Delhi or New Orleans! Visitors are welcome in the peaceful inner courtyard except on Fridays and during the month of Ramadan.

Company Gardens

It's a real pity that Company Gardens has such a sleazy atmosphere as it's by far the most attractive park in the city, with its vast banyan trees, huge number of statues, quiet benches and fountains. During the day it's perfectly safe (though keep your wits about you), but you should avoid it at night when it's a flash point for muggings, drug deals and pimps. Once the vegetable patch of the French East India Company in early colonial times, it's now best known for its statues of local sculptor Prosper d'Épinay and the much-loved musician Ti-Frère (see p44).

Municipal Theatre

This appealing theatre on Jules Koenig St has changed little since it was built in 1822, making it the oldest theatre in the Indian Ocean region. Decorated in the style of the classic London theatres, it seats about 600 over three levels, and has an exquisitely painted dome ceiling with cherubs and chandeliers. Photos of Margot Fonteyn, who danced here in 1975, adorn the foyer. Performances are in the evenings – usually at 8pm. Unless you get lucky and someone lets you glimpse inside, you'll need to buy tickets for a performance to visit.

Mauritius Postal Museum

This rather lacklustre two-room **museum** (☎ 213 4812; Pl du Quai; admission free; ✆ 9am-3.45pm Mon-Fri, 9-11.30am Sat) beside the central post office houses a mishmash of commemorative stamps and other postal paraphernalia from around the world. These include copies of the famous 'Post Office' stamps of 1847 (see the boxed text, p57), though you can now see the originals in the Blue Penny Museum. There's also a decent display of 19th-century and early-20th-century communication devices. The museum shop sells replica first-day covers of the famous stamps, which make unusual souvenirs.

Cathedrals & Churches

Notable places of worship include the **St James Cathedral** (Poudrière St) and **St Louis Cathedral** (Sir William Newton St). Inaugurated in 1850, St James has a peaceful, wood-panelled interior with plaques commemorating local worthies. The more austere, but also busier, St Louis Cathedral dates from 1932 and is popular with the Chinese community.

The modern **chapel and shrine of Marie Reine de la Paix** (Monseigneur Leen Ave) is a popular spot for prayers, and the ornamental gardens offer views over the city. The most important place of pilgrimage for Mauritian Christians is the shrine of Père Laval on the city's northern outskirts (p66).

SSR Memorial Centre for Culture

This simple **house museum** (☎ 242 0053; Sir Seewoosagur Ramgoolam St; admission free; ✆ 9am-4pm Mon-Fri, 9am-noon Sat) near the Jardin Plaine Verte was home to Mauritius' father of independence, Sir Seewoosagur Ramgoolam, from 1935 until 1968. It's an interesting exhibit on his life, with some fascinating photographs, a collection of his personal belongings and even films about the great man, beloved by all Mauritians.

Fort Adelaide

Fort Adelaide, also known as the Citadel, resembles a Moorish fortress. Built by the British, the fort sits high on the crown of the hill, offering splendid views over the city and its harbour. The quickest route up is via Suffren St. Allow around 10 minutes for the climb.

Champ de Mars Racecourse

This racecourse was a military training ground until the **Mauritius Turf Club** (☎ 211 2147; www.mauritiusturfclub.com) was founded in 1812, making it the second-oldest racecourse in the world. Mauritian independence was proclaimed here in 1968. Within the racecourse stands a statue of **King Edward VII** by the sculptor Prosper d'Épinay, and the **Malartic Tomb**, an obelisk to a French governor.

The racing season lasts from May to late November, with meetings usually held on a Saturday. The biggest race of all is the Maiden Cup in September. If you're here on a race day, it's well worth joining the throng of betting-crazy locals. Tickets for the stands cost Rs 150, but admission to the rest of the ground is usually free. For dates of meetings, contact the Mauritius Turf Club or check the local press.

WALKING TOUR

Begin your exploration on **Victoria Sq (1)**, one of the capital's main bus stations and a chaotic hub of activity from dawn till dusk. Watch the street hawkers, the food sellers and busy locals out shopping as you wander down **President John Kennedy St (2)** and join the city's grandest colonial avenue, **Place S Bissoondoyal (3**; p59), then walk inland towards **Government House (4**; p59), in front of which a decidedly imperious statue of Queen Victoria still stands guard. Turn right along Chaussée St to pay a quick visit to the dodo in the **Natural History Museum (5**; p57), then cut up through lovely **Company Gardens (6**; p59),

PORT LOUIS WALKING TOUR

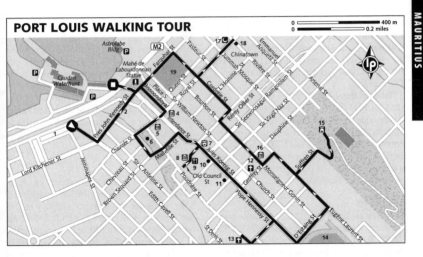

which provides a rare patch of green in the city centre, with huge banyan trees and other tropical delights (prostitutes and drug dealers notwithstanding). Head up Mallefille St and turn right on Intendance St. Here you'll see the charming **Municipal Theatre** (**7**; opposite) pretty perfectly preserved from British colonial times. On the other side of the road, stroll down Old Council St, a charming cobbled lane leading gently uphill to one of Port Louis' most attractive corners. Here you'll find a clutch of colonial buildings, one of which contains the **Photography Museum** (**8**; p59) while the **Restaurant du Vieux Conseil** (**9**; p63) occupies the courtyard of another and makes a great place for lunch.

Retracing your steps back to busy Jules Koenig St and turning right will take you past the modern and unprepossessing **City Hall** (**10**) and the more appealing **Supreme Court** (**11**), built in 1780, with its ornate gates and shady courtyard. A little further on, **St Louis Cathedral** (**12**; opposite) lies off to your left (visible across an open square). You're now on Pope Hennessy St, from where you could take a short detour south along Labourdonnais St to **St James Cathedral** (**13**; opposite).

A row of striking, colonial-era bungalows and a grey-stone secondary school, built in 1893, mark the top end of Pope Hennessy St. Beyond lies the **Champs de Mars racecourse** (**14**; opposite), though outside the race season there's nothing in particular to see. Better to save your energy for the climb to **Fort Adelaide** (**15**; opposite) for expansive views.

From the fort, drop back down to Monseigneur Gonin St to see the grand, colonnaded **archbishop's residence (16)**, then head northwest along Corderie St, lined with cloth merchants, to Royal St. A right turn here brings you to the delightful **Jummah Mosque** (**17**; p59) and then to the first of the 'friendship gates' that marks the entrance to **Chinatown** (**18**; p57). When you've had your fill of exploring, head down Jummah Mosque St to Farquhar St, turn left and you'll soon find yourself caught up in the pell-mell of the **Central Market** (**19**; p57). Finally, take one of the underpasses to the waterfront for some well-earned refreshment.

SLEEPING

There's not a huge choice of accommodation in Port Louis – there are three business hotels (two of which are very smart and part of the Caudan Waterfront complex), while the rest cater to budget travellers and are all fairly mediocre.

Budget

Hotel Le Grand Carnot (☎ 240 3054; 17 Dr Edouard Laurent St; s/d incl breakfast Rs 500/600) This is an atmospheric, slightly noisy place for backpackers, but the best of the budget gang. The rooms are rather makeshift but pleasant enough; some have big balconies overlooking the busy daily clothes market outside.

Bourbon Tourist Hotel (☎ 240 4407; fax 242 2087; 36 Jummah Mosque St; s/d/t incl breakfast Rs 770/880/1200; ✷) Slap-bang in the middle of Chinatown, this idiosyncratic 16-room place feels more like a student hall of residence than a hotel. The bathrooms are pretty horrible, although all rooms have air-con, TVs and phones. It's on the 1st floor (go through the tunnel from the street).

Tandoori Hotel (☎ 212 0031; Jemmapes St; s/d Rs 600/1200; 🗭) While it's extremely noisy during the day due to its location next to the main bus station, it's perfectly quiet at night here. The rooms are comfortable, but there's no natural daylight in any of the rooms, which lends it a depressing air. The price goes up by Rs 200 per person for air-con.

Midrange

Le St Georges Hotel (☎ 211 2581; www.blue-season -hotels.com; 19 St Georges St; s/d incl breakfast Rs 1500/1950; 🗭 🖵 🏊) Towering above the surrounding residential neighbourhood, Le St Georges is excellent value for money. The rooms are fairly unexciting but they are clean and equipped with all the necessary comforts. There's a decent breakfast and a pool for relaxing by as well as a pleasant bar and restaurant. The location is also good, just a five-minute walk from the centre of town.

Le Suffren Hotel & Marina (☎ 202 4900; www.le suffrenhotel.com; Caudan Waterfront; s/d Rs 3600/4600; 🗙 🗭 🖵 🏊) The newest addition to Port Louis' hotel scene, Le Suffren is the trendier, less stuffy sister hotel to the Labourdonnais, just a short complimentary boat ride away. For better or for worse you feel like you're almost out of the city despite being just a couple of minutes from the waterfront. The rooms are smaller than the Labourdonnais but the place has a very pleasant, convivial feel with an excellent bar and restaurant.

Labourdonnais Waterfront Hotel (☎ 202 4000; www.labourdonnais.com; Caudan Waterfront; s/d incl breakfast Rs 5200/6200; 🗙 🗭 🖵 🏊) Definitely the best in town, the Labourdonnais is an ultra-smart business hotel on the Caudan Waterfront. The rooms are excellent – even the standards are huge. All are bathed in light, have cavernous bathrooms and most have excellent views of the city and harbour, particularly the so-called 'turret rooms' at each top corner. Facilities include a gym, pool and business centre.

EATING

Port Louis has a great eating scene where the ethnic diversity of the city again comes up trumps. Chinatown is packed with good little Chinese options, while European cafés, smart restaurants on the waterfront and endless snackbars give you plenty of choice. As the middle classes tend to reside outside the city many places are only open for lunch. In the evening and at weekends head to the waterfront for any degree of choice. Another option is to head out of town to Domaine Les Pailles (p65) for a choice of expensive but excellent options.

Restaurants
BUDGET

Mystic Masala (Port Louis Waterfront; set menus Rs 60-110 🕑 lunch & dinner) Tasty Indian snacks and light meals are the order of the day at this harbourfront kiosk with its handful of trestle tables. Portions aren't huge but a side order of samosas or a *dosa masala* (pancake-like bread with a spicy potato filling) and a glass of *lassi* (yoghurt drink) or *alouda* (sweet, milky drink) will round things off nicely.

Le Calife (☎ 203 4561; Edith Cavell St; mains Rs 100; 🕑 lunch Mon-Fri) This attractive place is one of the best spots for lunch in town, teeming with locals and full of atmosphere. The homemade halal biryani is the speciality here, and most who try come back for more. Other Creole and Indian specialties are also on the menu.

First Restaurant (☎ 212 0685; cnr Royal & Corderie Sts; mains from Rs 120; 🕑 lunch & dinner Tue-Sun) If the age-old rule that a good Chinese restaurant is full of Chinese diners applies, then First is a winner. Packed with large family groups enjoying vast feasts of delicious Cantonese cooking, this is Chinatown's finest and prices are surprisingly reasonable for the quality of the fare.

Debonairs Pizza (☎ 210 9203; Intendance St; sandwiches from Rs 80, pizzas from Rs 180; 🕑 lunch & dinner) The pizza at this fast-spreading South African chain is nothing special, but it's a good place for a quick, cheap lunch. There are tables inside, but takeaway and delivery are available ('we deliver smartly' is the restaurant's slightly odd tagline), as are a number of non-pizza options.

Tandoori Express (☎ 210 9898; Astrolabe Bldg, Port Louis Waterfront; mains Rs 75-200, set menus Rs 100-175; 🕑 lunch & dinner, closed Sun & dinner Mon) Popular with local families day and night, this great canteen serves up delicious curries and thalis, superb naan bread and a range of other Indian dishes to suit all tastes. Order and pay inside and your food will be brought out to your waterside table.

MIDRANGE

La Bonne Marmite (☎ 212 4406; 18 Sir William Newton St; set menus Rs 150; ⏰ lunch only Mon-Fri; ✖) This quaint establishment is one to savour away from the glitzy waterfront gang. Its unfussy menu of Creole, Indian and Chinese dishes is excellent value and the welcome is always friendly.

Black Steer (☎ 211 9147; Caudan Waterfront; burgers Rs 150-200, grills from Rs 250; ⏰ lunch & dinner; ✖) This popular steakhouse overlooks the harbour and offers great steaks, mixed grills, combos and the like. It's now added a few dishes for non-carnivores, such as baked spuds and vegetable curries, but its stock in trade are the excellent hamburgers and rump steaks.

La Flore Mauricienne (☎ 212 2200; 10 Intendance St; mains Rs 150-450; ⏰ 7.30am-5pm Mon-Fri, 8.30am-1pm Sat; ✖) There's something rather Parisian about the bustle and brusque service here, but then this is a long-standing favourite lunchtime haunt of the local business and political elite as well as tourists. The daily specials are always good value, and there's a big selection of dishes including a good vegetarian choice. Inside it's a more formal setting, whereas the terrace is a great place to people-watch.

Restaurant du Vieux Conseil (☎ 211 0393; Old Council St; mains Rs 200; ⏰ lunch Mon-Sat) Down a charming side street, this lunchtime institution must have the most delightful location of any restaurant in Port Louis. The food is nothing spectacular, and somewhat pricey, but there's a good choice from crepes and salads to octopus curry and smoked marlin, and the charming setting is worth making a diversion for.

Namaste (☎ 211 6710; Caudan Waterfront; mains from Rs 200; ⏰ lunch & dinner, closed lunch Sun; ✖) One of the best Indian restaurants in town, Namaste manages to be atmospheric despite its location in the sanitised Caudan Waterfront. The specialities here are North Indian (and not huge either), but it's a classy place with excellent service. Book ahead to get a table on the balcony outside as they're always in demand.

TOP END

L'Escale (☎ 202 4000; Labourdonnais Waterfront Hotel, Caudan Waterfront; mains from Rs 250; ⏰ 6.30am-11pm; ✖) The main restaurant of the Labourdonnais Waterfront Hotel, this refined and elegant spot is one of the best in town. The broad menu includes an excellent vegetarian selection, as well as superb local creations such as prawn stew and pan-fried red snapper.

Le Capitaine (☎ 213 0038; Caudan Waterfront; mains Rs 250-500; ⏰ lunch & dinner; ✖) Given its location and standards of service, this surprisingly reasonable restaurant specialises in seafood and also offers classic French dishes such as duck confit. It's in a great location with lots of tables on the terrace overlooking the harbour and has a stylish interior décor.

The Courtyard (☎ 210 0810; Chevreau St; mains from Rs 400; ⏰ lunch Mon-Fri; ✖) Built around an eponymous courtyard, this newly opened European-style restaurant also features a stylish, understated indoor dining space. The meaty menu includes Australian beef and fresh local seafood dishes realised with flair. A good spot to impress.

La Rose des Vents (☎ 202 4000; Labourdonnais Waterfront Hotel, Caudan Waterfront; mains Rs 300-800; ⏰ lunch & dinner, closed Sat lunch & Sun; ✖) The Labourdonnais Waterfront Hotel boasts this upmarket seafood restaurant, famed for its lobster dishes.

Quick Eats

Port Louis is a snackers' paradise. The Central Market and bus stations provide happy hunting grounds, but you'll find stalls all over town peddling samosas and *gâteaux piments* (deep-fried balls of lentils and chilli), sandwiches or more substantial curries. To spot the best just look for the queues from mid-morning onwards. A perennial favourite is the *dhal puris* **stall** (cnr Sir William Newton & Rémy Ollier Sts). Nearby, **Bombay Sweets Mart** (7 Rémy Ollier St) is famous for the Indian nibbles colourfully known as *caca pigeon* (literally, 'pigeon droppings'). It also sells other sweet and savoury snacks. If you'd rather sit down to eat, head for Tandoori Express or Mystic Masala (see opposite).

Self-Catering

Self-caterers should head for the Central Market. There's also the handy **Winner's Supermarket** (Sir Célicourt Antelme St). Most restaurants, apart from the expensive ones, do takeaway.

DRINKING

Port Louis is not exactly a happening place at night and come sunset the city is virtually silent as the commuters retire to the Central Plateau towns. What evening life there is tends to be concentrated on the Caudan Waterfront.

Keg & Marlin (☎ 211 6821; Caudan Waterfront; ⊙ noon-midnight Mon-Thu, to 3am Fri, to 1am Sat & Sun; ⊗) The location makes this a great place to enjoy a sundowner while watching the world go by. While its outdoor seating is as Mauritian as can be, inside it's a garish imitation of an English pub. There's live music here at weekends and it's unquestionably the main bar in the city, enjoying popularity with expats, locals and visitors alike.

Beer & Spice (☎ 210 5376; Astrolabe Bldg, Port Louis Waterfront; ⊙ 9am-11pm; ⊗) On the other side of the waterfront complex, this quiet and friendly café-bar is a popular place with locals, serving a wide variety of drinks, good sandwiches and decent coffee.

Latitude 20 (☎ 202 4000; Labourdonnais Waterfront Hotel, Caudan Waterfront; ⊙ 9am-midnight; ⊗) Despite being a hotel bar this is probably still Port Louis' best spot for a cocktail. The nautical theme may not scream good taste, but the drinks are very well made and there's usually a pianist doing his thing in the corner.

Sunset Café (☎ 211 9137; Caudan Waterfront; ⊙ 9am-10pm Mon-Thu, to midnight Fri & Sat, to 11pm Sun; ⊗) Usually a place where parched day-trippers end up taking refuge in cold beer, this is an over-priced spot, but not unpleasant, with views over the harbour.

ENTERTAINMENT

Port Louis offers very little in the way of evening entertainment. A movie, a cocktail or a gamble are about all that's available; for nightlife you'll be better off in Grand Baie or Flic en Flac.

Casino

Port Louis Casino (☎ 210 4203; Caudan Waterfront; ⊙ 10am-4am, gaming tables 8pm-4am; ⊗) The mighty popular city casino is about the liveliest place in town after midnight – its salient feature externally is its ship-shaped design, crowned at its prow by the campest lion imaginable. Meow. There are slot machines downstairs and blackjack and American roulette on the 1st floor. Smart-casual dress is required.

Cinemas

Star Cinema (☎ 211 5361; Caudan Waterfront; tickets Rs 150; ⊗) This is Port Louis' biggest and best cinema, with three screens offering mainstream international releases. Films are generally dubbed in French and there are usually four or five screenings a day.

Cinemaxx (☎ 210 7416; Caudan Waterfront; tickets Rs 100; ⊗) The two-screen Cinemaxx usually shows one Hindi or Tamil film and one international release daily. Again, most films are dubbed in French, though occasionally you'll find one with English subtitles.

Live Music

Keg & Marlin (☎ 211 6821; Caudan Waterfront; ⊙ noon-midnight Mon-Thu, to 3am Fri, to 1am Sat & Sun; ⊗) At the weekends the Keg & Marlin transforms into Port Louis' only live-music venue. Standards vary enormously from rock outfits to *séga*.

Theatre

Municipal Theatre (Jules Koenig St) There are frequent plays – in French, English and Creole – as well as jazz and classical music recitals at Port Louis' principal theatre. Ticket prices vary, but most events cost around Rs 100. Look for announcements in the local press or call the tourist office to find out what's on. Theatre tickets can be purchased at the box office in the theatre itself.

SHOPPING

Central Market (⊙ 5.30am-5.30pm Mon-Sat, 5.30am-11.30pm Sun) Port Louis' main market has a wide selection of T-shirts, basketry, spices and souvenirs; bargain to get a decent price.

Craft Market (☎ 210 0139) Based in the Caudan Waterfront, this market is less fun but also less hassle than central market. You'll find more upmarket souvenirs, such as Mauritius glass and essential oils from the Domaine de l'Ylang Ylang. The model ship manufacturer **MAST** (☎ 211 7170) also has an outlet here.

The Caudan Waterfront is also the place to go for trendy knick-knacks and designer boutiques, including Floreal, Maille St, Shibani, IV Pl@y and Habit. **Power Music** (☎ 211 9143) stocks a good selection of CDs by local artists.

GETTING THERE & AWAY
Air

All of the main airlines serving Mauritius have offices near the waterfront.

Air Austral (☎ 202 6677; Rogers House, 5 President John Kennedy St, Port Louis)

Air France (☎ 202 6747; Rogers House, 5 President John Kennedy St, Port Louis)

Air Madagascar (☎ 203 2150; IBL House, Caudan Waterfront, Port Louis)

Air Mauritius (☎ 207 7212; Air Mauritius Centre, President John Kennedy St, Port Louis)

Air Seychelles (☎ 202 6655; Rogers House, 5 President John Kennedy St, Port Louis)

British Airways (☎ 202 8000; IBL House, Caudan Waterfront, Port Louis)

Emirates (☎ 213 9100; Harbour Front Bldg, Place d'Armes, Port Louis)

Singapore Airlines (☎ 208 7695; 3 President John Kennedy Street, Port Louis)

South African Airways (☎ 202 6737; Rogers House, 5 President John Kennedy St, Port Louis)

Bus

Port Louis' two bus stations are both located in the city centre. Buses for northern and eastern destinations, such as Trou aux Biches, Grand Baie and Pamplemousses, leave from Immigration Square, northeast of the Central Market.

Buses for southern and western destinations, such as Mahébourg, Curepipe and Quatre Bornes, use the Victoria Square terminus just south of the centre.

The first departure on most routes is at about 6am; the last leaves at around 6pm.

Car

Car rental is expensive in Port Louis. You'll find better rates in major tourist centres such as Grand Baie, Flic en Flac or Mahébourg. Given the size of the island, all car-rental agencies will deliver a car to your hotel anywhere on the island – therefore it makes sense to contact agencies outside the capital such as Beau Bassin's **Exodus Car Hire** (☎ 454 4396; www.exoduscarhire.com) who will charge a small fee to bring the car to you.

Ferry

Ferries to Rodrigues and Réunion dock beside the passenger terminal on Quai D of Port Louis harbour, 1km northwest of town. For more information about boats to and from Rodrigues see p125, and p306 for Réunion.

GETTING AROUND
To/From the Airport

There are no special airport buses, but regular services between Port Louis and Mahébourg call at the airport; the stop is near the roundabout, roughly 300m from the terminal buildings. Heading to the airport from Port Louis, allow two hours to be on the safe side and make sure the conductor knows where you're going, as drivers occasionally skip the detour down to the airport.

Expect to pay around Rs 700 to Rs 900 for a taxi ride from Port Louis to the airport.

Car

Given the number of traffic snarls, it's not worth trying to drive around Port Louis. Day-trippers are advised to leave their car in one of the car parks in the waterfront complex. These are open from 7am to 11pm and cost Rs 25 for the first four hours plus Rs 25 for each additional hour.

Cars can be parked on the street for a maximum of two hours at a time in any one place and the appropriate number of parking coupons, available at any filling station, must be displayed on the dashboard. See p153 for more about street parking.

Taxi

Expect to pay around Rs 50 to Rs 100 for a short taxi ride across town, and slightly more at night. As usual, always agree to a price beforehand. It's best to avoid using taxis during morning and evening rush hours, when you'll probably end up just sitting in a traffic jam. See p153 for more information on taxis.

AROUND PORT LOUIS
Domaine Les Pailles

Just a few miles outside of the capital the strange sugar-estate-turned-theme-park **Domaine Les Pailles** (Map p86; ☎ 286 4225; www .domainelespailles.net; ☯ 10am-5pm) has been transformed into a cultural and heritage centre that makes for an enjoyable day or half-day excursion. The facilities include rides in horse-drawn carriages, a miniature railway, a working replica of a traditional ox-driven sugar mill, a rum distillery producing the estate's own brew, a spice garden, a quad-biking circuit and a children's playground.

Visitors can choose to tour the site by train, horse carriage or jeep, with the cost of entry varying accordingly. The cheapest options are one-hour tours by train at Rs 100/80 per adult/child and by horse-drawn carriage at Rs 110/90. A jeep safari costs Rs 450/250 and more expensive packages including lunch are also available. Quad biking costs from Rs 350 for 30 minutes.

On weekdays it's also possible to horse ride around the estate. Call the riding centre, **Les Écuries du Domaine** (☎ 286 4240; ☯ 8am-5.30pm Mon-Fri, 8am-noon Sat), to make a reservation. An hour's riding costs Rs 700 per person.

The Domaine also has a selection of up-market restaurants. Best of the bunch are the **Clos St Louis** (mains Rs 280-450; ☺ lunch Mon-Sat, dinner Fri & Sat), in a replica colonial villa, which offers top-notch Creole and French cuisine, and **Indra** (mains from Rs 250; ☺ lunch & dinner Mon-Sat), which serves excellent Indian fare. Also on offer is Fu Xiao for Chinese and La Dolce Vita for Italian.

To get to the Domaine, take any bus running between Port Louis and Curepipe and ask to be let off at the turning for Domaine Les Pailles (it's clearly signposted). From the main road it takes less than half an hour on foot to the reception. Alternatively, it's a 10-minute taxi ride from Port Louis or Moka.

Père Laval's Shrine

The **shrine** (Map p86; ☎ 242 2129; ☺ 8.30am-noon & 1-4.45pm Mon-Sat, 10am-noon & 1-4pm Sun) of the French Catholic priest and missionary Père Jacques Désiré Laval is something of a Lourdes of the Indian Ocean, with many miracles attributed to visits to the priest's grave. The padre died in 1864 and was beatified in 1979 during a visit by Pope John Paul II. He is credited with converting 67,000 people to Christianity during his 23 years in Mauritius.

Today Père Laval is a popular figure for Mauritians of all religions. Pilgrims come here from as far afield as South Africa, Britain and France to commemorate the anniversary of his death on 9 September. The coloured plaster effigy of the priest that lies on top of the tomb has been rubbed smooth in places by pilgrims touching it in the hope of miracle cures.

At other times of year the shrine is fairly quiet, though the services held on Friday at 1pm and 5pm attract a reasonable crowd. In the same complex is a large modern church and a shop with a permanent exhibition of Père Laval's robe, mitre, letters and photographs.

To get to the shrine, take a bus signed 'Cité La Cure' or 'Père Laval' from the Immigration Square bus station in Port Louis.

NORTH MAURITIUS

Northern Mauritius offers a huge amount to visitors; while its spectacular beaches have inevitably lead to heavy development it's never hard to get away from it all and dis-cover areas that remain largely untouched by mass tourism. Grand Baie is the centre of the country's travel industry (although it's increasingly finding itself challenged for that status by Flic en Flac) and boasts Mauritius' best nightlife, some of its most excellent restaurants and shopping. The small villages around Grand Baie, Trou aux Biches, Mont Choisy and Pereybère are growing at an incredible pace and all have wonderful beaches to enjoy, making them other obvious attractions in the region. The lagoon, sheltered from the prevailing winds, offers a host of water sports and is particularly good for snorkelling and diving.

Cap Malheureux, the island's most northerly point, marks the current end of the coast's development. Save a few resorts in Grande Gaube, there are no hotels until halfway down the east coast. The lack of beaches and remote location mean that you're truly in the wild.

Inland a plain of sugar-cane fields, pocked with piles of volcanic boulders stacked by slaves and indentured labourers, slopes gently down to the sea. Here you'll find the wonderful SSR Botanical Gardens and the rightly popular L'Aventure du Sucre – a museum dedicated to Mauritius' traditional colonial export.

Getting There & Around

The most useful bus routes in and around this area are those running from Port Louis' Immigration Square bus station up the coast to Trou aux Biches, Grand Baie, Pereybère and Cap Malheureux. There are also express services direct from Port Louis to Grand Baie. Port Louis is also the starting point for buses via Pamplemousses to Grand Gaube.

To reach this area from the airport you'll need to change buses in Port Louis. Alternatively, a taxi to towns along the northwest coast should cost in the region of Rs 800. Count on around Rs 1000 to Grand Gaube.

Many hotels and guesthouses have bikes for rent and can help organise car rental. Otherwise, you can approach the rental agencies directly. The largest concentration is in Grand Baie, and there are a smattering of outlets in and around Trou aux Biches and Pereybère.

BALACLAVA & BAIE DE L'ARSENAL

Balaclava is named after the region's black-lava rocks, rather than the Crimean battle-field. It is an attractive wild area overlooking

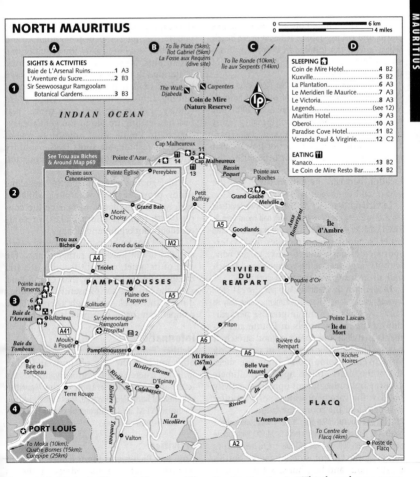

NORTH MAURITIUS

SIGHTS & ACTIVITIES
Baie de L'Arsenal Ruins............1 A3
L'Aventure du Sucre................2 B3
Sir Seewoosagur Ramgoolam
  Botanical Gardens................3 B3

SLEEPING
Coin de Mire Hotel.................4 B2
Kuxville...............................5 B2
La Plantation.........................6 A3
Le Meridien Ile Maurice...........7 A3
Le Victoria...........................8 A3
Legends........................(see 12)
Maritim Hotel.........................9 A3
Oberoi...............................10 A3
Paradise Cove Hotel................11 B2
Veranda Paul & Virginie...........12 C2

EATING
Kanaco...............................13 B2
Le Coin de Mire Resto Bar........14 B2

To Île Plate (5km);
Îlot Gabriel (5km);
La Fosse aux Requins
(dive site)

To Île Ronde (10km);
Île aux Serpents (14km)

The Wall;
Djabeda

Carpenters

Coin de Mire
(Nature Reserve)

INDIAN OCEAN

See Trou aux Biches
& Around Map p69

Pointe aux
Canonniers

Pointe d'Azur

Pointe Église

Pereybère

Cap Malheureux

Pointe aux
Roches

Bassin
Paquet

Petit
Raffray

Grand Gaube

Melville

Mont
Choisy

Grand Baie

Anse Bonavergent

Trou aux
Biches

Fond du Sac

Goodlands

Île
d'Ambre

Triolet

PAMPLEMOUSSES

RIVIÈRE
DU
REMPART

Poudre d'Or

Pointe aux
Piments

Plaine des
Papayes

Pointe Lascars

Baie de
l'Arsenal

Balaclava

Solitude

Sir Seewoosagur
Ramgoolam
Hospital

Piton

Île du
Mort

Baie du
Tombeau

Moulin
à Poudre

Pamplemousses

Rivière du
Rempart

Roches
Noires

Baie du
Tombeau

Terre Rouge

Rivière Citrons

D'Epinay

Mt Piton
(267m)

Belle Vue
Maurel

FLACQ

La
Nicolière

Rivière

L'Aventure

PORT LOUIS

Valton

To Moka (10km);
Quatre Bornes (15km);
Curepipe (25km)

To Centre de
Flacq (4km)

Poste de
Flacq

the secluded Baie de l'Arsenal. You can still see the **ruins** of the French arsenal, along with a flourmill and a lime kiln, within the grounds of the Maritim Hotel, one of the more sympathetic of several big hotels along here. Non-residents can obtain permission to visit the ruins from the security guard at the hotel entrance; the track begins about 30m inside the gate to the right.

There are no bus services to Balaclava or Baie de l'Arsenal. A taxi from Port Louis will cost Rs 300 to Rs 350.

Sights

Mauritius Aquarium (Map p69; ☎ 261 4561; www .mauritiusaquarium.com; Coastal Rd, Pointe aux Piments; adults/children/family Rs 195/95/525; ☺ 9.30am-5pm Mon-Sat, 10am-4pm Sun) This brand new enterprise is Mauritius' first aquarium and fills a much-needed niche for non-divers and children to see the incredible marine life of the Indian Ocean up close. The five buildings contain various types of environment, including 'the deep,' an impressive 15m-long slice of reef life. There's daily fish feeding at 11am, which makes for great viewing.

Sleeping & Eating

Maritim Hotel (Map p67; ☎ 204 1000; www.maritim .de; Balaclava; s/d incl breakfast from Rs 5860/8820; ⊠ ⊠ ⊠ ☒) The Maritim is a well-established German-owned hotel with an enviable position out of the wind on Turtle Bay. Its main plus points are a 25-hectare park, complete with a nine-hole golf course, tennis courts and riding stables. It has a great beach where guests can indulge in everything from snorkelling to water-skiing, and a choice of three restaurants.

La Plantation (Map p67; ☎ 204 3000; www.apavou -hotels.com; Baie des Tortues; s/d with half board Rs 9000/13,500; ✂ ✂ 🖳 🖵) Open since 2000, this huge complex is an all-encompassing resort built in an impressive colonial style (particularly striking is the pool of flowers that greets you in reception, not to mention the 1000-sq-metre pool below). It's got a great location between the Citron River and the ocean, and the beach is lovely.

Le Victoria (Map p67; ☎ 204 2000; www.levictoria -hotel.com; Pointe aux Piments; s/d with half board from Rs 9300/13,300 ✂ ✂ 🖳 🖵) This relaxed four-star hotel is popular with families and watersports enthusiasts and it's easy to see why, with its large sea-facing rooms, good beach and all-inclusive water-sports activities.

Le Meridien Ile Maurice (Map p67; ☎ 204 3333; www.lemeridien.com; Pointe aux Piments; room only Rs 15,000; ✂ ✂ 🖳 🖵) This impressive new edition to the luxury hotels in Pointe aux Piments is stylish and enjoys a good stretch of beach. The building itself is not particularly attractive and some won't enjoy the sheer size of the place – this is not for an intimate getaway but rather for an upmarket activity holiday: the variety of water sports on offer is superb and the rooms are huge.

our pick **Oberoi** (Map p67; ☎ 204 3600; www.oberoi hotels.com; Pointe aux Piments; r from Rs 34,500, with private pool from Rs 68,000; ✂ ✂ 🖳 🖵) Quite simply stunning, the Oberoi is definitely the north's most famous and best hotel. Set in copious gardens, the hotel boasts a gorgeous beach and stunningly set out grounds including a high-flowing waterfall that dominates the ensemble. The best villas here have their own pools and gardens enjoying total privacy and making them perfect for honeymooners. Inside it's all understated luxury, an inventive mix of African and Asian design, making the most of natural light. The two pools can easily lay claim to being the most beautiful in all Mauritius and other features include wonderfully chic public areas, superb restaurants and a world-class spa.

TROU AUX BICHES & AROUND

Relaxed Trou aux Biches and the neighbouring village of Mont Choisy are fast-

developing tourist destinations full of people seeking better beaches than Grand Baie while staying nearby for activities and restaurants. Trou aux Biches (The Does' Wateringhole) enjoys gorgeous white-sand beaches shaded by casuarina trees, continuing almost unbroken to sleepy Mont Choisy, a charming spot with more great beaches leading up along the gently curving bay to Pointe aux Canonniers, one of the most fashionable spots in the country with a great selection of accommodation and dining options.

The lagoon, sheltered from the prevailing winds, provides great swimming, while the variety and abundance of marine life coupled with good visibility makes for some excellent snorkelling and diving.

There's no doubt that the ongoing development boom here has rather robbed the area of its quiet, unspoilt feel, but it's still cheaper and far less hectic than Grand Baie. Even the beaches are pleasantly uncrowded during the week, although there's fierce competition for picnic spots at weekends.

Information
Neither Trou aux Biches nor Mont Choisy offer much in the way of shops and other facilities. There are a few grocery stores scattered around and a branch of the **Mauritius Commercial Bank** (MCB; Royal Rd, Mont Choisy), with a 24-hour ATM and a **bureau de change** (🕑 9am-5pm Mon-Fri, 9am-noon Sat).

Activities
Trou aux Biches and Mont Choisy are both important water-sports centres. Activities on offer range from touring the lagoon in a glass-bottomed boat to parasailing, water-skiing, deep-sea fishing and diving.

Snorkelling equipment (Rs 150 per day) can be rented at the **boat house** (☎ 728 4335; 🕑 9am-5pm) on Trou aux Biches' public beach. They also rent out pedalos and kayaks (Rs 400 per hour) and offer a variety of other activities, including glass-bottomed boat tours (Rs 450 per hour per person), water-skiing (Rs 550 for 12 minutes) and parasailing (Rs 1000 for 10 minutes).

Prices are similar at the **Casuarina Hotel boat house** (☎ 759 1127; Mont Choisy; 🕑 9am-5pm). In addition, they also offer windsurfing (Rs 300 per hour) and catamaran outings to the northern islands (p78).

MAURITIUS

DEEP-SEA FISHING

Deep-sea anglers should head for the **Corsaire Club** (☎ 265 5209; fax 265 6267; ☼ 9am-5pm) beside Le Pescatore restaurant in Mont Choisy. A half-day's boat charter costs around Rs 13,000, and a full day will set you back Rs 16,000.

DIVING

Dive centres that are consistently recommended for their professional and friendly service include **Nautilus Diving** (☎ 265 5495; www.nautilusdivers.com; ☼ 10am-4pm Mon-Sat), at the Trou aux Biches Hotel, and **Atlantis Diving** (☎ 265 7172; www.atlantis.freewebspace.com; ☼ 8am-5pm), located further south along the main road.

Other good options in the area include **Prodive** (☎ 265 6552; www.geocities.com/padgraphics /prodive; ☼ 8.30am-6.30pm Mon-Sat) at the Casuarina Hotel, **Dive Dream** (☎ 265 5367; www.dive dream.org; Trou aux Biches; ☼ 9am-5pm Tue-Sun) and **Blue Water Diving** (☎ 265 7186; www.bluewaterdiving center.com; Trou aux Biches; ☼ 8am-4.30pm). Dives start at around Rs 1000 to Rs 1200, rising to Rs 1500 or so for a night dive.

GOLF

The nine-hole **golf course** (☎ 204 6565; ☼ 7am-6pm; green fee Rs 800, club hire Rs 400) at the Trou aux Biches Hotel is one of the few public-access courses in Mauritius. There's a helipad for those in a real hurry.

HORSE RIDING

There's an excellent riding school, **Horse Riding Delights** (☎ 265 6159; Mont Choisy Sugar Estate; ☼ daily by reservation) on the edge of Mont Choisy, just after the junction by the Tarisa Resort. Here you can ride in over 200 hectares of land, populated with deer and giant tortoises.

SUBMARINE RIDES

If you fancy diving but don't want to get wet, **Blue Safari Submarine** (☎ 263 3333; www.blue -safari.com; Mont Choisy; adult/child Rs 3200/1800; ☼ 9am-4pm) takes you down among the coral and fishes to a depth of 35m. The ride lasts roughly two hours, of which 40 minutes are spent underwater, with departures every hour according to demand. Reservations are recommended at least a day in advance.

TROU AUX BICHES & AROUND

Sleeping

It seems almost every building along this stretch of coast is available for rent in some shape or form. Much of the accommodation is in the midrange bracket and consists of self-catering apartments, villas and bungalows, often with terraces or balconies for viewing the sunset. A few of the best are listed here.

For a wider choice, contact **Nick Tour** (☎ 265 5279; nicktour@intnet.mu; Trou aux Biches) and **Grand Baie Travel & Tours** (GBTT; ☎ 265 5261; www.gbtt.com; Beach Villas, Mont Choisy); both manage a range of well-maintained accommodation in the area. You should try to book in advance for the best options, but there's nearly always something available at late notice.

BUDGET

Rocksheen Villa (☎ 265 5043; www.rocksheenvilla.com; 161 Morcellement Jhuboo, Trou aux Biches; s/d incl breakfast Rs 550/650, studio from Rs 650; ❄) Down a quiet side street about 300m back from the beach (coming from the sea turn left after passing La Marmite Mauricienne) is this homely guesthouse run by a charming Scottish-Mauritian couple. In fact, it has proven so popular that they've built an extension. Well run and spotlessly clean, the place receives consistently good reports from travellers.

Hotel Villa Kissen (☎ 265 5523; www.villa-kissen.com; Trou aux Biches; s/d incl breakfast Rs 850, studio Rs 1000; ❄ ☎) This friendly guesthouse recently relocated to smarter premises near the beach. It's now a great option; each room comes with air-con, a private balcony, TV and safe. The studios have their own kitchens.

MIDRANGE

Beach Villas (☎ 265 5261; www.gbtt.com; Mont Choisy; studio/apt from Rs 2125/3150; ❄ ☎) Grand Baie Travel & Tours have eight different properties in the area, all let from the office here. The accommodation is comfy, if a little sterile, consisting of self-catering studios (for two persons) and apartments (for up to four). The small beach is a bit rocky, although there's sand just 50m down.

Résidences C'est Ici (☎ 265 5231; www.cest-ici.com; Trou aux Biches; studio/apt from Rs 3000/3300; ❄) This hotel has spruce, well-equipped self-catering accommodation at very reasonable prices. The two-person studios through to the apartments for up to five all have their own terrace. It's set among coconut palms right on the beach.

Colonial Beach Hotel (☎ 261 5187; cbeach@intnet.mu; Trou aux Biches; s/d with half board Rs 4000/5500; ⓟ ❄ ☎) This small and intimate hotel on the beach offers decent accommodation in white two-storey blocks. There are two pools and good snorkelling right in front of the beach.

our pick Le Sakoa (☎ 265 5242; www.lesakoa.com; Trou aux Biches; s/d incl breakfast from Rs 4700; ❄ ☎) Deservedly popular, the Sakoa needs to be booked well in advance as it's a great deal. This spacious accommodation is in wonderful two-storey thatched blocks radiating out from the fantastic beach. The whole place oozes style and carefree charm.

Tarisa Resort (☎ 265 6600; www.tarisa-hotel.com; Mont Choisy; s/d Rs 4700; ⓟ ❄ ☎ ☎) Mont Choisy's most-luxurious hotel, the attractive Tarisa is block booked by tour operators, mainly the French Look Voyages group, and isn't usually accessible to independent travellers; however, it's worth a try as it's well located and has great rooms.

Coralia Mont Choisy (☎ 265 6070; mont_choisy@intnet.mu; Mont Choisy; s/d incl breakfast Rs 4968/6625, with half board Rs 5685/8065; ❄ ☎ ☎) The rooms here may be fairly charmless, but there's a decent if rather small beach with a large range of water sports available and a good pool, plus the welcome is at least friendly.

Casuarina Hotel (☎ 204 5000; www.hotel-casuarina.com; Trou aux Biches; s/d with half board from Rs 6500/9000, apt room only from Rs 8000; ❄ ☎) Definitely one of the more interesting midrange places, the Moorish style found externally here is matched by equally inventive apartment layouts. It's also pleasantly small and so feels very relaxed. The only minus is having to cross the road to the beach, but otherwise this place is great.

TOP END

Le Canonnier (☎ 263 7000; www.lecanonnier-hotel.com; Pointe aux Canonniers; s/d with half board from Rs 8000/11,500; ⓟ ❄ ☎ ☎) The location here is one of the best in the country: the beachy head of a peninsula with attractive beaches on all sides and even a ruined lighthouse (now rather sacrilegiously housing a kids club) on the grounds. It's a pity then that the accommodation is in rather uninspiring beige blocks. Inside the rooms are spacious (and equally beige) but the guests seem delighted with the experience. Oh, and check out that banyan tree – surely the largest in Mauritius?

Trou aux Biches Hotel (☎ 204 6565; www.trouaux biches-hotel.com; Trou aux Biches; s/d with half board from Rs 12,650/18,000; P ✕ 🖳 🐾) This classic beach hotel is on a great open stretch of bay that's superb for swimming. It boasts a huge pool and considerable style, although doesn't always feel five star. The huge grounds, comfortable accommodation and big range of activities make it particularly attractive to families.

Eating

As ever more restaurants set up along here, there is an increasingly broad selection of outlets catering for most tastes. Self-caterers should head for the well-stocked **Chez Popo Supermarket** (Royal Rd) in Trou aux Biches. Around Mont Choisy, **Persand Royal Supermarket** (Royal Rd) is your best bet.

BUDGET & MIDRANGE

Souvenir Restaurant (☎ 265 7047; Trou aux Biches; mains Rs 45-125; ❤ 7am-9pm Mon-Sat, 7am-2pm Sun) Always busy, this unfussy and friendly place sees locals and tourists enjoying quality food at low prices. As well as the restaurant there's a shop inside, giving it the feel of a local hub.

L'Assiette du Nord (☎ 265 7040; Trou aux Biches; mains Rs 125-200; ❤ lunch & dinner) A popular option where you can opt for the terrace or a slightly smarter dining area behind the fish tank partition. Seafood features strongly, served in Chinese, Indian and Creole style. Try fish cooked in banana leaf with madras sauce or perhaps prawns in garlic butter.

La Marmite Mauricienne (☎ 265 7604; Trou aux Biches; mains from Rs 150; ❤ lunch & dinner) This basic but sweet place down the road beyond L'Assiette du Nord has a pleasant outdoor feel, with lots of tables on the terrace (although sadly on a rather busy road). The menu is Mauritian, featuring mostly seafood, noodles and curries.

Coco de Mer (☎ 265 7316; Trou aux Biches; mains Rs 180; ❤ lunch & dinner Tue-Sun; ✕) This excellent Seychellois restaurant serves up top-notch fish dishes, curries and all manner of seafood. Each meal is accompanied by a delicious selection of salads and a lentil soup, so you're unlikely to leave empty. The Saturday evening buffet (Rs 300) is excellent value.

Hidden Reef (☎ 263 0567; Pointe aux Canonniers; mains Rs 250; ❤ dinner; ✕) This convivial, smart little addition to a great stretch of restaurants on the main road to Grand Baie has a beautifully lit courtyard for romantic al fresco dining and

a sumptuous menu of freshly sourced seafood and fish. The chocolate brownies are unbelievably good. One of our favourites.

Pizza & Pasta (☎ 265 7000; Mont Choisy; mains Rs 250; ❤ lunch & dinner) Advertised for miles around, this large garden complex just next to the Mont Choisy public beach looks great from the outside and is pretty charmingly set out inside, but the food is sadly mediocre, overpriced and not particularly authentic either.

TOP END

La Cravache d'Or (☎ 265 7021; Trou aux Biches; mains Rs 500; ❤ lunch & dinner Mon-Sat) One of the best restaurants in Mauritius, La Cravache d'Or enjoys an absolutely gorgeous setting right on the beach, making it perfect for a romantic meal. The small daily-changing menu features meat and fish dishes, although vegetarians can be catered for. Reserve in advance at weekends, and at any time you'd like to sure of sitting at one of the sea-view tables.

ourpick **Le Pescatore** (☎ 265 6337; Mont Choisy; mains Rs 700, set menu Rs 2200; ❤ lunch & dinner) For sheer style and charm Le Pescatore has to be our favourite restaurant in northern Mauritius. Wonderfully chic, light décor and a great terrace overlooking the fishing boats in the sea below set the scene for a truly superior eating experience. Dishes such as lobster in ginger and saké sauce, and St Brandon Berry fish with carrot juice and cardamom give you an idea of what to expect.

Drinking

The best bar this side of Grand Baie is **Latina** (☎ 491 5338; Pointe aux Canonniers; ❤ 3pm-2am), a great little roadside DJ bar with friendly staff and dark-red décor. For clubs, you have to head into Grand Baie.

Getting There & Around

Trou aux Biches and Mont Choisy are served by nonexpress buses running between Port Louis' Immigration Square bus station and Cap Malheureux via Grand Baie. There are bus stops about every 500m along the coastal highway.

A taxi to Grand Baie costs around Rs 200, to Port Louis Rs 300 and to the airport Rs 900. A return trip to Pamplemousses, including waiting time, should be in the region of Rs 500.

To hire a car, contact **Flambeau** (☎ 262 6357; Trou aux Biches) or the slightly more expensive **Winkworth** (☎ 263 4789; persand@intnet.mu), beside

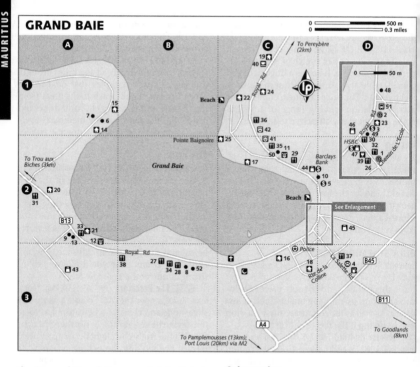

GRAND BAIE

the Persand Royal Supermarket in Pointe aux Canonniers.

GRAND BAIE
pop 2800

Grand Baie was once called De Bogt Zonder Eyndt (Bay Without End) by the Dutch in the 17th century. Now frequently referred to as a resort and famous for its nightlife, Grand Baie is actually a surprisingly cosmopolitan and classy town, and although it's the centre of northern Mauritius' tourism industry, it can hardly be written off as a mere resort. Indeed, its beach is mediocre and its eponymous bay crowded with fishing boats. But despite this, many people prefer to eat, shop and go out in Grand Baie itself for the variety and quality on offer, and make day trips instead to the surrounding villages to enjoy good beaches.

Granted it's popular, but Grand Baie is not a bad place to base yourself. It's the main departure point for cruises to the northern islands (p78). Public transport connections are also good and there's a wide choice of accommodation from cheap apartments to top-notch luxury resorts.

Orientation

Orientation in Grand Baie is easy, as almost everything is strung out along the coastal highway. The centre point of the town is the Sunset Boulevard shopping complex (including the jetty) at the junction of the coastal highway (known here as Royal Rd), with the road inland to Goodlands and the M2 motorway via the Super U Hypermarket.

The terminus for express buses to and from Port Louis is on Royal Rd about 100m north of the town centre. Nonexpress services via Trou aux Biches stop every few hundred metres along the coast road.

Information
BOOKSHOPS

Papyrus (☎ 263 0012; Richmond Hill Bldg, La Salette Rd; ⊗ 9am-7pm Mon-Sat, 9.30am-noon Sun) A reasonably well-stocked bookshop with a range of mainly French-language books and magazines.

INTERNET ACCESS

Cyber Escales (La Salette Rd; ⊗ 10am-8pm Mon-Sat)
Cyber Pirate (Galeries Espace Ocean; ⊗ 9.30am-8pm Mon-Sat, 10am-noon Sun) The best in town.

Internet Café (☎ 263 2478, Super U Hypermarket, La Salette Rd; ☀ 9am-8.30pm Mon-Thu, 9am-9pm Fri & Sat, 9am-1.30pm Sun) Next to the checkouts.

MONEY
Mauritius Commercial Bank (MCB; Royal Rd; ☀ exchange bureau 8am-6pm Mon-Sat, 9am-noon Sun)
State Bank (Royal Rd; ☀ exchange bureau 8am-6pm Mon-Sat, 9am-noon Sun)
Thomas Cook Exchange Bureau (☀ 8am-8pm)

POST
Post office (Richmond Hill Bldg; ☀ 8.15am-4pm Mon-Fri, 8.15am-11.45pm Sat) Out near the Super U Hypermarket; the last 45 minutes before closing are for stamp sales only.

Sights & Activities
Grand Baie's prime attraction is the range of water-based activities on offer. Otherwise, the only specific sights are a couple of vividly colourful Tamil temples: **Surya Oudaya Sangam** (☀ 8am-5pm Mon-Sat) at the west end of town, and the older **Shiv Kalyan Vath Mandir** towards Pereybère. Both are dedicated to Shiva. Visitors are welcome but shoes should be removed before entering.

CRUISES
Cruises are a popular activity in Grand Baie. Perhaps the most interesting is that offered by **Yacht Charters** (☎ 263 8395; www.isla-mauritia .com; Royal Rd; ☀ 8am-7pm). Its magnificent sailing ship, the *Isla Mauritia*, was built in 1852 and is claimed to be the world's oldest active schooner. Today the *Isla Mauritia* offers two day-cruises per week on a Wednesday and Saturday, with snorkelling, lunch at Baie du Tombeau and traditional music for Rs 1950, or Rs 975 for under 10s. It's best to book at least a day in advance.

Other companies offer cruises on modern catamarans. The most popular options are the day trips around the northern islands (p78), including a barbecue lunch and stops for swimming and snorkelling. You can also take a sunset cruise, with the option of dinner on board. Prices start at around Rs 1400 per adult (Rs 600 for children under 12) for a day trip around the northern islands, and Rs 600 per person for a sunset cruise (excluding dinner).

One of the biggest operators is **Croisières Australes** (☎ 670 4301; www.mttb-mautourco.com), which owns the two luxury 'Harris Wilson' boats; bookings can be made through MauriTours or any other Grand Baie tour agent (see p74).

MAURITIUS

DEEP-SEA FISHING
Based beside the Sunset Boulevard jetty, **Sportfisher** (☎ 263 8358; www.sportfisher.com; Royal Rd; half-/full day from Rs 9500/12,500 per boat; ⊗ 6am-6pm) has four boats, each taking up to six people (three anglers and three companions). Most tour agents can also arrange trips.

DIVING
The local diving industry has emphatically moved down the coast to less built-up Mont Choisy and Trou aux Biches, but a number of operators still maintain a base in Grand Baie. Among these, **Neptune Diving** (☎ 263 3768; neptunediving@intent.mu; Royal Rd; ⊗ 8.30am-4.30pm Mon-Sat), gets consistently good reports. A dive costs around Rs 1200. **Prodive** (☎ 265 6552; www .geocities.com/padgraphics/prodive; ⊗ 8.30am-6.30pm Mon-Sat), based at the Casuarina Hotel in Trou aux Biches also has an office in Grand Baie outside the Grand Bay Beach Hotel.

UNDERSEA WALKS
For nondivers, **Captain Nemo's Undersea Walk** (☎ 263 7819; www.captainemo-underseawalk.com; Royal Rd; per person Rs 1000; ⊗ 8.30am-5pm) provides the unique experience of walking underwater wearing a diver's helmet and weight belt. Solar-powered pumps on the boat above feed oxygen to you during the 25-minute 'walk on the wet side'. Walks are available to everyone over the age of seven. There are trips every few hours from 9am to 3pm. In peak season it's advisable to book a day in advance.

SEMISUBMERSIBLES
A number of semisubmersible vessels offer coral-viewing tours. *Le Nessee* (adult/child Rs 800/450) is a distinctive yellow semi-submarine run by Croisières Australes (p73). It departs from Grand Baie's Sunset Boulevard jetty several times daily and the trip lasts just under two hours, with 30 minutes of snorkelling for those who wish. Tickets are available from hotels and tour agents.

SWIMMING & SPAS
The beach at Grand Baie is nothing special and the bay here is congested with boats. Instead, you're better off heading for La Cuvette public beach beside the Veranda Hotel on the bay's north side. It's not huge, but the sand is good and the water clean.

Another option is to visit **Grand Baie Gym & Hydro Spa** (☎ 263 4891; www.grandbaiegym.com; 3 X Club

Rd; day membership Rs 650) where as well as enjoying the fabulous pool and gym, you can indulge in a huge range of spa treatments, steam yourself in the hammam and enjoy low-fat dishes at the café. The gym is located in a building across the road from the spa.

Tours
Grand Baie's numerous tour agents can provide information on things to do in the area with the aim, naturally, of signing you up for this cruise package or that coach trip. While prices tend to be similar, the details may vary, so make sure you know exactly what is included. All agents sell tickets for glass-bottomed boat trips, undersea walks, *Le Nessee* (left) and the Blue Safari Submarine (p69). Many also offer car-hire services and airport transfers and can organise accommodation.

Tour agents with a reliable reputation:

Ebrahim Travel & Tours (☎ 263 7845; www.gbccar .mu; Ebrahim Flats, Royal Rd)

Grand Baie Travel & Tours (GBTT; ☎ 263 8771; www.gbtt.com; Royal Rd) This office mainly sells air tickets; its accommodation office is in Mont Choisy.

La Colombe Tourist Bureau (☎ 283 9262; www .mauritiuslacolombe.com; Royal Rd)

Maurisun Adventure & Tours (☎ 263 0192; www .maurisun.com; Royal Rd) A cut above the competition with its range of adventure tours, including sea kayaking.

MauriTours (☎ 263 6056; www.mauritours.net; Sunset Boulevard, Royal Rd) Upmarket all-round travel agency selling air tickets, excursions, accommodation, island tours and cruises.

Northview Tours (☎ 263 5023; http://pages.intnet.mu/nor tours; Royal Rd)

Prodive Tours (☎ 263 0632; prodive@hotmail.com; Royal Rd)

Sleeping
Much of the budget and midrange accommodation in Grand Baie takes the form of self-catering studios and apartments. There are some excellent deals around, especially if you arrive at a quiet time of the year and with three friends in tow. A clutch of smart hotels occupies the east side of the bay, but Grand Baie is not a centre for luxury.

BUDGET
Residence Peramal (☎ 263 8109; residenceperamal@intnet .mu; Royal Rd; studio Rs 1075, apt Rs 1350-1720) Excellent-value self-catering accommodation on a little promontory plum in the centre of Grand Baie. The fan-cooled units (for up to

four people) are modern, spacious and well maintained. Not surprisingly, it gets booked up well in advance.

Filao Village Hotel (☎ 263 7482; www.filaosvillage.8k.com; Pointe aux Canonniers; studio incl breakfast from Rs 1250; 🔀 🖳) This is a superb place; pretty thatched blocks house just 12 rooms organised around a decent pool and look onto the bay with access to a little beach. It's out of the way without being remote – a perfect spot for relaxation.

MIDRANGE

Ventura Hotel (☎ 263 6030; www.hotelventura.com; Royal Rd; s/d incl breakfast Rs 1600/2500; 🅿 🔀 🖳) It may look virtually deserted but this is a decent central option with a surprisingly pleasant pool and public area once you get through the indifferent exterior. You have a choice of double rooms and family rooms, which sleep four. All have TV, air-con, phone and a view onto the pool.

Grand Bay Beach Hotel (☎ 263 4984; www.grandbaybeachhotel.com; Royal Rd; s/d/t incl breakfast Rs 1700/2200/2600, apt from Rs 3200; 🔀 🖳) This well-located hotel in the very centre of town has clean, bright rooms that are great value for money. Rooms come with a balcony, TV, phone and kitchen and there's a cool roof terrace featuring a small pool and some excellent views. You'll pay an Rs 250 supplement for a sea view.

Ti Fleur Soleil (☎ 563 0380; www.tifleursoleil.com; Royal Rd; s/d incl breakfast from Rs 1800/2400, apt 4300; 🔀) The 'little sunflower' is a sweet, friendly hotel that can't be beaten for its location right in the heart of Grand Baie. The glowing reviews in the guestbook attest to the hotel's popularity although some have moaned about the quality of breakfast. The rooms – all with terrace – are clean and simple. There's a choice of fan-cooled or air-con rooms.

Ocean Villas (☎ 263 1000; www.ocean.mu; Royal Rd; r incl breakfast from Rs 2200, apt from Rs 3700; 🅿 🔀 🖳 🔀) Recommended for its broad range of accommodation, from straightforward hotel rooms to self-catering units for up to eight people and sleek honeymoon suites remodelled in 2006 with sunken baths. Facilities include an excellent new pool plus a small strip of beach (with limited water sports on offer), a restaurant and the love nest – a private house on the beach.

our pick Chez Vaco (☎ 263 4391; www.papillonhotelsandvillas.com; Pointe aux Canonniers; s/d Rs 2100/3100; 🔀 🖳) A welcome addition to Grand Baie's accommodation scene, this stylish yet budget guesthouse is a real find. Whether it's the charming little garden decorated with local art and comfortable furniture or the small but delightful rooms, all of which successfully create an atmosphere of warm minimalism, this is an innovative place. Rooms 7 and 12 are the largest and have closed-off bathrooms. There's also a free speedboat transfer across the lagoon to Grand Baie from a small beach up the road.

Les Orchidées (☎ 263 8780; www.mauritius-island.com/orchidees; Route de la Colline; r incl breakfast from Rs 2500; 🔀 🔀) Highly recommended and extremely popular (book ahead), this small hotel is set back from the coast in a quiet location just a short walk from the centre of town. Sweet, simple, brightly coloured rooms and a charming pool area make this a great option.

Veranda Hotel (☎ 209 8000; www.verandagroup.com; Royal Rd; s/d/t with half board from Rs 5500/7900/10,500; 🅿 🔀 🖳 🔀) The rather elegant public areas here give the Veranda a sense of exclusivity unusual for the price. The two pools, good facilities and a recent refit of the rooms also help. The beach is fine, but no great shakes, although the location is handy for town and there's a new Seven Colours spa here to help with relaxation.

TOP END

Merville Beach Hotel (☎ 209 2200; www.naiade.com; s/d with half board from Rs 7600/11,500; 🔀 🖳 🔀) The Merville enjoys a friendly atmosphere, very pleasant gardens, a sweet little stretch of beach and pleasant rooms in well-maintained yellow thatched blocks. There are also good sports facilities to match, including a dive centre.

Le Mauricia (☎ 209 1100; www.lemauricia-hotel.com; s/d with half board from Rs 7500/10,500; 🔀 🔀) One of the more affordable four-stars, Le Mauricia sits in spacious grounds on a prime stretch of palm-fringed beach. It's big and efficient, and has two good-sized pools and all the activities you'd expect: everything from a kids club to a raft of water and land sports. Cheerful and airy rooms come with sea-view terraces.

Royal Palm (☎ 209 8300; www.royalpalm-hotel.com; s/d with half board from Rs 35,500/51,000; 🔀 🔀 🖳 🔀) The flagship hotel of the Beachcomber group and a member of Leading Hotels of the World, the Royal Palm is nothing short of stunning. Suites are impeccable (for there are no mere rooms here), with a huge number of categories from junior to royal, and the service and

MAURITIUS

facilities are top-notch. The health spa even boasts its own restaurant serving low-calorie cuisine so you can jump into your private pool (or the sea) with confidence.

Eating

While the centre of town is packed with eateries, the very best tend to be slightly outside the heart of Grand Baie, particularly toward Le Canonnier and Pereybère. You'll have no end of choice though; the following are just the best of a good bunch.

BUDGET

Café Müller (☎ 263 5230; Royal Rd; salads & sandwiches from Rs 100; ⏰ 9.30am-5pm Mon-Sat) This charming addition to Grand Baie's café scene is a great place for breakfast or a light lunch. As the name suggests, it's a German-run café and bakery that rustles up great sandwiches in a lovely grassy garden.

Crok Chaud (☎ 269 1313; Royal Rd; salads & sandwiches Rs 120; ⏰ 7am-5pm Mon-Sat, 7am-noon Sun) The best coffee in town, hands down, and a damn fine little patisserie, this roadside gem is a great place to start the day, indulge in a mid-morning cake or have a nice lunch.

La Vieille Rouge (☎ 518 0579; La Salette Rd; mains Rs 150; ⏰ 10am-midnight) The Red Snapper isn't exactly a find, but it's one of Grand Baie's more reliable budget eateries. You'll find a standard selection of Creole curries, Chinese dishes, fresh fish and so forth. It's all tasty and comes in decent portions, although the set menu at Rs 450 seems a little steep.

MIDRANGE

Don Camillo (☎ 263 8540; Royal Rd; pizzas Rs 170-290, pasta Rs 150-220; ⏰ dinner daily, lunch Mon-Sat; ⏹) Despite its unpromising location beside the Caltex petrol station, Don Camillo is a great place to taste real pizza. In the evening it's positively buzzing – either get there early or reserve.

Luigi's (☎ 269 1125; Royal Rd; pizzas & pasta Rs 170-280; ⏰ lunch & dinner Tue-Sun) Classic little trattoria serving authentic pizza and pasta dishes plus a range of daily specials, such as seafood gnocchi. Make sure you leave room for one of the scrumptious deserts.

Le Tandoor (☎ 263 1378; Royal Rd; www.letandoor .com; mains Rs 200; ⏰ lunch & dinner) Excellent Indian cooking makes Le Tandoor stand out amid some stiff competition in Grand Baie. Even though it's located on the main road, there's quite a buzz each evening (reserva-

tions advised) as the place hums to hungry travellers enjoying excellent curries, naans and tandoori dishes.

Thai Foon (☎ 269 1169; Royal Rd; mains Rs 230; ⏰ lunch & dinner; ⏹) Newly opened in 2006 by the original team behind Pereybère's Wang Thai, authenticity is the watchword at Thai Foon. This means fresh ingredients imported from Bangkok, a Thai chef and some excellent Thai cocktails. The eating space is stylish but relaxed, with outside seating available.

Alchemy (☎ 269 1137; mains Rs 250; La Salette Rd; ⏰ lunch & dinner) This friendly place set back from the coastal road is a great mix of bar and grill. The pizzas are cooked in a traditional wood-fired oven and are excellent, plus there's a big range of steaks and seafood, and imaginative daily specials.

TOP END

Le Capitaine (☎ 263 6867; Royal Rd; mains from Rs 280; ⏰ lunch & dinner) This is a popular place serving good standard seafood and fish dishes in a pleasant convivial space that combines style with informality and great bay views. Fresh lobster is the pick of the menu, while other delicious mains include whole crab cooked in white wine, and lobster ravioli with fresh mushroom and cucumber quenelle. Reservations are essential in the evening.

Paparazzi (☎ 263 8836; Sunset Boulevard; pizzas from Rs 200, mains from Rs 300; ⏰ lunch & dinner) This smart pizza restaurant on the second floor of Sunset Boulevard (on the non-bay side) is a winner. It's far pricier than any other pizzeria in Mauritius, but the quality suggests why. There's free delivery if you're feeling lazy.

our pick **Iguana Lounge** (☎ 263 5758; Royal Rd; mains from Rs 350; ⏰ lunch & dinner) Next to Fusion (see below) and incongruously situated facing an Esso garage, Iguana Lounge is one of our favourite places in town. For upscale Mexican – excellent burritos and chili con carne – look no further. Reserve a table in the charming back garden as they're hard to come by.

Fusion (☎ 269 1338; Royal Rd; mains Rs 400; ⏰ dinner) Possibly the most self-consciously fashionable dining option in Grand Baie, Fusion looks just as it sounds – flash, minimalist, sleek and a little intimidating. You'll see the smart set out for dinner here, sampling fusion-flavoured Mauritian-Asian cooking.

Ebisu (☎ 263 1035; Royal Rd; mains from Rs 400; ⏰ lunch & dinner) Sharing the same site and management as La Langouste Grisée (see

below), Ebisu offers a sushi bar as well as
more substantial teppanyaki theatrics. Reservations are advised in the evenings.

La Langouste Grisée (☎ 263 1035; www.lalangouste
grisee.com; Royal Rd; mains Rs 450; ⏲ lunch & dinner)
This is a restaurant frequented by the great
and the good of Grand Baie, offering very
stylish dining in an attractive garden overlooking a pond as well as charming indoor
tables. As a winner of the Fourchette d'Or in
2005, 'the Tipsy Lobster' is generally recognised as one of the best restaurants on the
island. Sample dishes from its imaginative
Franco-Mauritian menu include Dorado
fillet with peanut sauce and banana slices.
Lobster is obviously the speciality and vegetarians really shouldn't bother coming.

SELF-CATERING
The **Super U Hypermarket** (La Salette Rd; ⏲ 9am-
4.30pm Mon-Sat, 9am-1.30pm Sun) sells almost everything self-caterers could want. You can also
buy groceries and other essentials at **Grand
Baie Store** (Royal Rd) and **Store 2000** (Royal Rd), and
there's a good **vegetable shop** (Royal Rd) at the
west end of town.

For a real treat, **L'Épicerie Gourmand** (Royal
Rd; ⏲ 9.30am-7pm Mon-Sat, 9am-noon Sun) is a treasure-trove of imported delicacies including
cheese, ham and pâté. It also sells luscious
cakes and pastries and ice cream.

Drinking
Alchemy (☎ 269 1137; La Salette Rd; ⏲ 8am-midnight)
A convivial little bar attracting a mixed
crowd of locals and tourists with its cheap
prices and retro soundtrack. Saturday is usually *séga* night – this is a good place to catch
a performance outside the big hotels.

B52 (☎ 263 0214; La Salette Rd; ⏲ 10am-midnight
Mon-Sat) This large, popular spot serves up
great cocktails all day long in its al fresco
setting back from the main coastal road.

Lotus on the Square (☎ 263 3251; Royal Rd;
⏲ 9.30am-5pm Mon-Sat) The garden of this small,
arty café on the road to Pereybère makes a
nice place to linger over a latte or cappuccino. It also does refreshing fruit juices and
homemade sorbets in unusual flavours such
as tamarind, basil and cinnamon.

La Rhumerie (☎ 263 7664; ⏲ 7am-midnight)
Friendly bar with a lethal selection of *rhum
arrangés* (flavoured rums); Rs 70 a shot or
Rs 300 for five.

Sunset Café (☎ 263 9602; Sunset Boulevard, Royal Rd;
⏲ 8.30am-7.30pm Mon-Sat, 8.30am-6pm Sun) Inside the
Sunset Boulevard complex overlooking the
water, this is a pleasant place for coffee.

Entertainment
NIGHT CLUBS
Buddha Club (☎ 263 7664; Royal Rd; Wed admission free,
Fri & Sat Rs 250; ⏲ 11.30pm-5am Wed-Sat; ✖) Grand
Baie's top nightspot positively sizzles on a
Friday and Saturday night when all three
dance floors are packed. Smart-casual dress
is required.

Star Dance (☎ 263 6388; Royal Rd; Tue-Thu & Sun
admission free, Fri admission free for women, Fri & Sat Rs
250; ⏲ Tue-Sun 11pm-5am; ✖) Next door to Buddha Bar, its rival also has three dance floors
with a choice of techno, tropical and '60s to
'80s music. It's slightly more relaxed and less
selective as well.

Zanzibar (☎ 263 3265; Royal Rd; admission Rs 100;
⏲ 11.30pm-5am Mon-Sat) There's a nicely intimate,
clubby atmosphere to this small bar-disco
decked out with sofas and African artefacts.
The most relaxed place in town.

Shopping
Sunset Boulevard (Royal Rd) This shopping complex is home to chic boutiques including
knitwear specialists Floreal, Maille St and
Shibani; Harris Wilson for menswear; and
Hémisphère Sud for fabulous leather goods.
Cheaper clothing stores, such as Red Snapper
and IV Pl@y, are concentrated in and around
the Super U Hypermarket.

Grand Baie Bazaar (⏲ 9.30am-4.30pm Mon-Sat, 9am-
noon Sun) This craft market off Royal Rd has a
broad range of Mauritian and Malagasy crafts.
Prices aren't fixed, but it's not expensive and
there's minimal hassling from vendors.

To purchase some original art, visit the
studio of **Françoise Vrot** (☎ 263 5118; www.tropic
scope.com; Reservoir Rd; ⏲ 10am-1pm & 3-6.30pm) to
see her expressive portraits of women fieldworkers; or head to **Galerie Vaco Baissac** (☎ 263
3106; Dodo Square, Royal Rd, Grand Baie; ⏲ 9.30am-7pm
Mon-Sat) to buy one of Vaco Baissac's instantly
recognisable works.

Getting There & Away
There are no direct buses to Grand Baie from
the airport, so it's necessary to change in Port
Louis and you have to transfer between two
bus stations to do so. Almost all people will
have a transfer provided by their hotel and

DEAD AS A DODO

Illustrations from the logbooks of the first ships to reach Mauritius show hundreds of plump flightless birds running down to the beach to investigate the newcomers. Lacking natural predators, these giant relatives of the pigeon were easy prey for hungry sailors, who named the bird *dodo*, meaning 'stupid'. It took just 30 years for passing sailors and their pets or pests – dogs, monkeys, pigs and rats – to drive the dodo to extinction; the last confirmed sighting was in the 1660s.

Just as surprising as the speed of the dodo's demise is how little evidence remains that the bird ever existed. A few relics made it back to Europe during the 18th century – a dried beak ended up at the University of Copenhagen in Denmark, while the University of Oxford in England managed to get hold of a whole head and a foot – but until recently our knowledge of the dodo was mainly based on sketches by 17th-century seamen.

However, in 1865 local schoolteacher George Clark discovered a dodo skeleton in a marshy area on the site of what is now the international airport. The skeleton was reassembled by scientists in Edinburgh, and has formed the basis of all subsequent dodo reconstructions, one of which is on display in the Natural History Museum in Port Louis.

For the full story of the dodo's demise, read Errol Fuller's fascinating book *Dodo: From Extinction to Icon*.

for others arriving after a 12-hour flight, we definitely suggest taking a cab – or better still, ordering one in advance via the hotel.

Express buses run directly between Immigration Square in Port Louis and Grand Baie every half-hour, terminating near Cyber Pirate on Royal Rd. Nonexpress buses en route to Cap Malheureux will also drop you in Grand Baie. Buses between Pamplemousses and Grand Baie leave roughly every hour.

For taxi rides from Grand Baie, expect to pay around Rs 200 to Trou aux Biches, Rs 500 to Port Louis and Rs 800 to the airport. A return trip to Pamplemousses, including waiting time, should set you back Rs 500 or so.

Getting Around
CAR

There are numerous car-rental companies in Grand Baie, so you should be able to bargain, especially if you're renting for several days. Prices generally start at around Rs 1200 per day for a small hatchback. Find out whether the management of your hotel or guesthouse has a special discount agreement with a local company. Otherwise, try one of the agents listed here. Motorbikes of 50cc and 100cc are widely available in Grand Baie; rental charges hover at around Rs 500 per day, less if you rent for several days.

Europcar (☎ 263 7948; www.europcar.mu; Royal Rd)
GBC Car Rental (☎ 263 7845; www.gbccar.mu; Royal Rd)
Keiffel Tours (☎ 263 8226; keiffeltour@intnet.mu; Royal Rd)

BICYCLE

Many hotels and guesthouses can arrange bicycle hire. Rates vary, but expect to pay between Rs 100 and Rs 150 per day, or less if you hire for several days. Most of the local tour operators have bikes for rent; just walk down Royal Rd and see what's on offer.

NORTHERN ISLANDS
Coin de Mire, Île Plate & Îlot Gabriel

The islands closest to the northern tip of Mauritius – Coin de Mire, Île Plate and Îlot Gabriel - are popular day trips from Grand Baie.

The distinctive Coin de Mire (Gunner's Quoin), 4km off the coast, was so named because it resembles the quoin or wedge used to steady the aim of a cannon. The island is now a nature reserve and home to a number of rare species, such as the red-tailed tropicbird and Bojer's skink. It's hard to get here a landing is often difficult. You'll need to visit on an organised tour, and even then you may have to be content with visiting another island if the weather changes. Despite its striking shape there's not much to see here anyway – it's the kind of place that looks far better from far away.

Most operators take you to Île Plate, 7km further north, which offers good snorkelling.

Îlot Gabriel is a pretty island lying within the coral reef just east of Île Plate and is a popular lunch stop for day cruises.

Boats to the islands depart from Grand Baie. You can book through almost any of the local tour agents or directly with the cruise companies (p73). Prices start at Rs 1000 per person, including lunch. Dive centres in Grand Baie (p74) also offer dive trips around these islands.

Île Ronde & Île aux Serpents

Île Ronde (Round Island) and Île aux Serpents (Snake Island) are two significant nature reserves about 20km and 24km respectively from Mauritius. It is not possible to land on them. Ironically, Île Ronde is not round and has snakes, while Île aux Serpents is round and has no snakes; the theory is that an early cartographer simply made a mistake.

Île Ronde covers roughly 170 hectares and scientists believe it has more endangered species per square kilometre than anywhere else in the world. Many of the plants, such as the hurricane palm (of which one lonely tree remains) and the bottle palm, are unique to the island.

The endemic fauna includes the keel-scaled boa and the burrowing boa (possibly extinct), three types of skink and three types of gecko. Among the sea birds that breed on the island are the wedge-tailed shearwater, the red-tailed tropicbird and the gadfly (or Round Island) petrel. Naturalist Gerald Durrell gives a very graphic description of the island in his book *Golden Bats and Pink Pigeons*.

The smaller Île aux Serpents (42 hectares) is a renowned bird sanctuary. The birds residing on the island include the sooty tern, the lesser noddy, the common noddy and the masked (blue-footed) booby. Nactus

geckos and Bojer's skinks are also found here.

PEREYBÈRE

The rapidly developing northern neighbour of Grand Baie, Pereybère (peu-ray-bear) enjoys a relaxed pace and old-world simplicity you won't find in many places on the north coast. This, however, is set to change as development continues apace. Unlike Grand Baie there's a great beach here, which is why it's a popular place to base a trip from. With the recent addition of Pereybère's first boutique hotel and the growing number of restaurants, watch this space, as the town is clearly set for big things.

Information

Pereybère boasts an efficient internet café, the **Hard Drive Café** (☎ 263 1076; Royal Rd; per min Rs 2; ⏰ 8am-9.30pm). The **Mauritius Commercial Bank** (MCB; Royal Rd) has an **exchange bureau** (⏰ 8am-6pm Mon-Sat, 9am-noon Sun) open outside regular banking hours.

Activities

Most people come to Pereybère simply to unwind beside the beautiful azure lagoon. The swimming is good here and the roped-off area is particularly safe for children. When the weekend crowds get too much, there are quieter beaches a short stroll away at Pointe d'Azur.

There's also good snorkelling offshore. The best coral can be found directly off the public

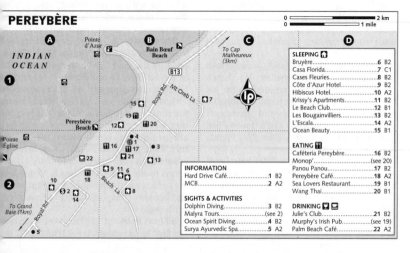

PEREYBÈRE

SLEEPING 🛏	
Bruyère.....................................**6** B2	
Casa Florida............................**7** C1	
Cases Fleuries.........................**8** B2	
Côte d'Azur Hotel...................**9** B2	
Hibiscus Hotel.......................**10** A2	
Krissy's Apartments..............**11** B2	
Le Beach Club.......................**12** B1	
Les Bougainvilliers...............**13** B2	
L'Escala..................................**14** A2	
Ocean Beauty........................**15** B1	

EATING 🍴	
Cafétéria Pereybère...............**16** B2	
Monop'.............................(see 20)	
Panou Panou.........................**17** B2	
Pereybère Café......................**18** A2	
Sea Lovers Restaurant...........**19** B1	
Wang Thai..............................**20** B1	

INFORMATION	
Hard Drive Café.......................**1** B2	
MCB...**2** A2	

SIGHTS & ACTIVITIES	
Dolphin Diving.........................**3** B2	
Malyra Tours....................(see 2)	
Ocean Spirit Diving.................**4** B2	
Surya Ayurvedic Spa................**5** A2	

DRINKING 🍷 🍸	
Julie's Club.............................**21** B2	
Murphy's Irish Pub............(see 19)	
Palm Beach Café....................**22** A2	

0 ━━━━━━━ 2 km
0 ━━━━━━━ 1 mile

beach (but watch out for glass-bottomed boats and water-skiers).

Divers can organise expeditions through **Ocean Spirit Diving** (☎ 563 0376; Royal Rd; gringo spirit@yahoo.mu; ☺ 8am-8pm Mon-Sat, 8am-noon Sun) and **Dolphin Diving** (☎ 263 9428; gurrobyj@hotmail .com; Stephen Rd; ☺ 8am-3pm Mon-Sat).

Further activities and tours can be booked through **Malyra Tours** (☎ 263 6274; www.villamalyra .com; Royal Rd).

For some indulgent relaxation, head to the very smart **Surya Ayurvedic Spa** (☎ 263 1637; www .spasurya.com; Royal Rd; ☺ 9am-8pm) to treat yourself to some Indian massage or a steam in the hammam.

Sleeping

While there are a few larger hotels on the beach side of the main road, the majority of accommodation here is made up of charming guesthouses and little hotels in the back streets, a short walk from the town centre and public beach.

BUDGET

L'Escala (☎ 263 7379; lescala@intnet.mu; Royal Rd; studio Rs 500-800, apt from Rs 1000; ☒) The pleasant atmosphere here somewhat compensates for very basic rooms, with almost nothing save the very barest of essentials in them. However, it's cheap and the owners mean well.

Bruyère (☎ 263 7316; dod.chettiar@intnet.mu; Beach Lane; 1/2 r apt from Rs 700/900; ☒) There are just three delightful apartments in this family home of a charming Scottish-Mauritian couple; all are simply but tastefully furnished with kitchenettes and TVs. It's in a quiet residential area close to the beach and town centre, the last, unmarked house on a no-through road.

Cases Fleuries (☎ 263 8868, casefle@intnet.mu; Beach Lane; studio from Rs 1000, apt from Rs 1300; ☒) There's something surprisingly rarefied in the air here considering the perfectly reasonable prices. A variety of studios and apartments for up to six people are set in a flower-filled garden, and the crowd is a wealthy French one for the most part.

Krissy's Apartments (☎ 263 8859, limfat@intnet .mu; Beach Lane; studio/apt from Rs 1050/1600; ☒) This secure, well-run budget complex consists of three studios and eight apartments, all with self-catering facilities. A cleaner comes once every three days, but the whole place is clean and good value.

Les Bougainvilliers (☎ /fax 263 8807; studio/apt Rs 1100/1200; ☒) Swathed in bougainvillea flowers, this homely place offers a broad range of clean (if slightly oddly furnished) studios and apartments with up to three bedrooms. Currently only half have air-con, but nearly all have kitchens. The management was building a restaurant at the time of our last visit.

Casa Florida (☎ 263 7371; www.casaflorida.net; Mon Oreb Lane; s/d incl breakfast Rs 1040/1270, apt from Rs 1630 ☒ ☒ ☒) This place is great value for money with huge, attractive grounds and a selection of sweet, spacious rooms, all very basically furnished but comfortable with balconies and TV. There's a bar and restaurant, with *séga* on Saturday nights.

MIDRANGE

Le Beach Club (☎ 263 5104; www.le-beachclub.com; Royal Rd; studio from Rs 2000, apt from Rs 3500; ☒) This complex of studios and two-bedroom apartments is one of the few places on the seafront and has a great little beach, perfect for swimming. The units are furnished in bright tropical colours. It's worth paying a bit extra for a balcony and sea views. Be aware that reception closes at 5pm during the week, at 2pm on Saturday and all day Sunday, so arrange your arrival with them in advance if you're coming in outside these times.

Côte d'Azur Hotel (☎ 263 8320; www.hotelcotedazu .net; Royal Rd; d/studio/apt from Rs 2200/2600/3000; ☒) A choice of extremely well-equipped hotel-style rooms and one- and two-bedroom apartments in a modern block on the main road. All come with air-con, private safe, satellite TV and phone, while some boast a CD player, Jacuzzi and a washing machine.

Ocean Beauty (☎ 263 6000; www.ocean.mu; Point d'Azur; r incl breakfast from Rs 5000; ☒ ☐ ☒) Developed by the people who own Ocean Villa in Grand Baie, Ocean Beauty is a boutique hotel aimed squarely at honeymooners. This is boutique basic though, which means the rooms are stylish and atmospheric, but there's very little else to the hotel – even staff are hard to come across sometimes. Despite this, it's a great spot for romance; breakfast is served on your balcony and there's direct access to the lovely town beach. Come here for romance and fun rather than pampering, and beware of the pool that plays Enya at you while you swim.

Hibiscus Hotel (☎ 263 8554; www.hibiscushote com; Royal Rd; s/d with half board from Rs 5850/8600; ☒ ☒

The recently refitted Hibiscus boasts thickly vegetated gardens, a super pool and private beach of sorts (although there's quite a bit of rock to negotiate). Accommodation is in clean, comfortable rooms in three-storey blocks.

Eating

Pereybère Café (☎ 263 8700; Royal Rd; mains Rs 90-150, set menus from Rs 320; ☾ lunch & dinner) This popular restaurant across the road from the public beach offers outdoor and indoor dining amid Chinese décor and serves up excellent-value Chinese fare. Reservations are a must for dinner.

Panou Panou (☎ 269 1457; Royal Rd; mains Rs 150-200; ☾ lunch & dinner Mon-Sat) This friendly place serves up seafood and grills in an open bar space on the main road opposite the public beach.

Caféteria Pereybère (☎ 263 8539; Royal Rd; mains Rs 180-260; ☾ 10.30am-10pm) This friendly all-day café-restaurant behind the public beach offers grilled fish, octopus curry, and steak and chips from an extensive menu. Portions are on the small side.

Wang Thai (☎ 263 4050; Royal Rd; mains Rs 180; ☾ dinner daily, lunch Tue-Sun; ✺) Long the best restaurant in town and a pioneer of authentic Thai food in Mauritius, Wang Thai is a sophisticated, airy place with Buddha statues and raw silks setting the scene for surprisingly affordable Thai cuisine. Treat your tastebuds to such classics as *tom yum thalay* (lemongrass-laced seafood soup), green curries and *phad thai* (mixed fried noodles).

Sea Lovers Restaurant (☎ 263 6299; restosealovers@ yahoo.com; mains Rs 300-600; ☾ lunch & dinner; ✺) This is by far the smartest restaurant in Pereybère, with its gorgeous terrace overlooking the public beach and stylish wooden furniture and décor, but when we ate here the service was almost comedically messy. While the food was excellent – rich seafood and delicious fish imaginatively cooked – the long waits between courses, the regular arrival at our table of another table's order and the fact that not once did the same waiter come to our table made for a disappointing dining experience. On a different night with better service this could be a superb place.

Self-caterers should head for **Monop'** (Royal Rd; ☾ 9am-7pm Mon-Sat, 7.30am-noon Sun) situated beneath Wang Thai.

Drinking & Entertainment

Pereybère is far quieter than neighbouring Grand Baie (where you should head if you're seeking some nightlife), though there are a few options for a quiet drink or two.

Julie's Club (☎ 269 0320; Royal Rd; ☾ 11am-midnight) Relaxed and friendly bar with live music or some other event most Friday and Saturday nights (including live *séga*).

Murphy's Irish Pub (☎ 263 6299; Royal Rd; ☾ 11am-midnight) What were the odds that Mauritius' first Irish pub would land in tiny Pereybère? Perhaps more suited to Grand Baie, Murphy's makes an unusual bedfellow for the swanky Sea Lovers Restaurant, run by the same team. In true Irish-pubs-abroad style, it looks nothing like an Irish pub, but has cold beer and big-screen sports.

Palm Beach Café (☎ 263 5821; Royal Rd; ☾ 11.30am-8pm Tue-Sun) The place to sip a coffee or fresh juice lulled by the sound of the waves. It also serves snacks and light meals.

Getting There & Around

Buses between Port Louis and Cap Malheureux stop in Pereybère as well as Grand Baie. Services run roughly every 30 minutes.

You can rent cars, motorbikes and bicycles through the local tour agents. Cars start at Rs 600 per day and motorbikes at Rs 400 for a 50cc or 100cc bike. Pedal bikes cost upwards of Rs 100 per day. Most of Grand Baie's car-hire companies will also drop off and pick up cars in Pereybère.

CAP MALHEUREUX

The northern edge of Mauritius has stunning views out to the islands off the coast beyond, most obviously of the dramatic slopes of Coin de Mire. Although it feels like rather a backwater today, 'Cape Misfortune' (thus named for the number of ships that foundered on the rocks here) is a place of great historical importance for Mauritius: it was here that the British invasion force finally defeated the French in 1810 and took over the island.

A little further on lies the minuscule fishing village also known as Cap Malheureux, with its much-photographed church, the red-roofed Notre Dame Auxiliatrice. It's worth a quick peek inside for its intricate woodwork and a holy-water basin fashioned out of a giant clamshell. A sign strictly prohibits newly-weds 'faking' a church wedding for the photographers here – really, some people, eh? You can attend mass here at 6pm on Saturday and 9am on Sunday.

Heading around the coast the landscape becomes wilder and more rugged. In between the rocky coves and muddy tidal creeks a clutch of hotels occupy the few decent beaches. They offer a perfect hideaway for those who want to get away from it all.

Sleeping

Kuxville (Map p67; ☎ 262 7913; www.kuxville.de; studios from Rs 2600, apt from Rs 4200) There's a huge choice of accommodation on offer at this perennially popular German-run apartment complex about 1.5km west of Cap Malheureux village. Accommodation is in impeccably clean studios or apartments sleeping up to four people; 'gardenside' units are in a newer compound across the road. There's a fine little beach and a small dive centre as well as various other water sports.

Coin de Mire Hotel (Map p67; ☎ 262 7302; www.coindemire-hotel.com; s/d with half board from Rs 3000/4800, superior rooms Rs 4600/6000; ☒ ☒) This charming place is affordable and relatively comfortable. The gardens are pleasant and the rooms are fine, although there's only air-con and TVs in the superior rooms. There are two pools, a restaurant, a bar (with live entertainment, including *séga*) and a range of water activities. The small rather unimpressive beach is just the other side of the main road but transport to Pereybère and Grand Baie is simple: the bus stops outside the hotel. Now part of the Veranda Group, you'll need to book in advance to stay here.

Paradise Cove Hotel (Map p67; ☎ 204 4000; www.paradisecovehotel.com; s/d with half board from Rs 17,000/22,500; ☒ ☒ ☒ ☒) Fully renovated in 2003, Paradise Cove is a five-star boutique resort aimed at honeymooners. Terribly understated but as utterly luxurious as its name suggests, it's built on an attractive small cove – the beach is at the end of an inlet from the sea, which gives it remarkable privacy. Other great touches include a golf course, tennis courts, free water sports, a dive centre, brightly painted and delightful rooms and 'love nests' on the promontory overlooking the northern islands. With three restaurants, a Cinq Mondes spa and award-winning gardens, this stylish place is a great destination for couples.

Eating

Outside the hotel restaurants there's just a few eating options in the area.

Kanaco (Map p67; ☎ 262 8378; mains from Rs 120-150; ☺ lunch & dinner) Opposite a Tamil temple, Kanaco is a very friendly, clean, and welcoming family-run place specialising in Mauritian cuisine and seafood.

Le Coin de Mire Resto Bar (Map p67; ☎ 262 8070; mains from Rs 180; ☺ lunch & dinner) Opposite the church in Cap Malheureux village, this place offers a huge range of dishes, from omelettes and fried rice to wild-boar curry. The food is simple but decent, and service and the view from the upstairs dining room are other good reasons to come.

Getting There & Away

Buses run roughly every half hour between Port Louis' Immigration Square bus station and Cap Malheureux, via Grand Baie. A taxi to Port Louis will cost at least Rs 600, to the airport Rs 1000.

GRAND GAUBE

Grand Gaube is where the development of northern Mauritius currently ends, although it has itself become the latest flash point for hotel building in recent years. Despite this it remains a tiny fishing village with a good beach about 6km east of Cap Malheureux. Beyond the small rocky bays of Grande Gaube there are almost no beaches until a long way down the east coast, making any trip beyond here an illuminating glimpse into traditional Mauritian life without the tourists. In 1744 the *St Géran* foundered off Grand Gaube in a storm, inspiring the famous love story *Paul et Virginie*, by Bernardin de St-Pierre (see the boxed text opposite).

Inland from Grand Gaube, the landscape is open and windswept, the cane fields rapidly being built over with modern housing estates. There's nothing specific to see in the area, but it has a distinctly Mauritian atmosphere, a world away from the tourist developments on the west coast.

Sleeping & Eating

Veranda Paul & Virginie (Map p67; ☎ 266 9700; http://paul-et-virginie-hotel.com; s/d with half board from Rs 3600/4800; ☒ ☒ ☒ ☒) The longest established hotel in Grande Gaube is a pleasant surprise. It's small enough not to be overwhelming, yet offers all the services and comforts required for luxury: two pools, a couple of restaurants, a Seven Colour's 'wellness' spa, plenty of entertainment and activities, and a kids club. The style is colonial, although the atmosphere is very relaxed. The rooms are stylishly fitted out and spacious, all with sea views, and there's a small but attractive beach.

Legends (Map p67; ☎ 698 9800; www.naiade.com; s/d with half board from Rs 13,000/18,500; ⓟ ⓧ ⓛ ⓡ) This very large, stylish newer establishment enjoys an idyllic location miles from the mass tourism found further down the coast. Guests here are welcomed with a drum-banging ceremony, and have the run of the pretty bay and the hotel's well-appointed surroundings. The hotel is Feng Shui themed (God help us), but don't be distracted by the waffle about metal elements, Chi flow or the mirror being a 'reflection of serenity' – at the end of the day Legends is a smart beach hotel whose marketing people have just got a little bit over-excited.

Getting There & Away

Buses run every 15 minutes or so between Port Louis' Immigration Sq bus station and Grand Gaube.

A taxi to Port Louis will cost around Rs 500, to Grand Baie Rs 300 and to the airport Rs 1000.

PAMPLEMOUSSES

Most visitors to northern Mauritius take the time to visit Pamplemousses for its famous botanical gardens, which are worth a diversion if you fancy an afternoon away from the beach. Officially known as the Sir Seewoosagur Ramgoolam Botanical Gardens (occasionally referred to as the Royal Botanical Gardens), they feature a stunning variety of endemic and foreign plant species. The nearby decommissioned Beau Plan sugar factory has also been converted into a fascinating museum.

The town itself was named for the grapefruit-like citrus trees that the Dutch introduced to Mauritius from Java. It has a typically Mauritian feel and is a million miles away from Grand Baie or Trou aux Biches, although there are no other sights.

Sir Seewoosagur Ramgoolam Botanical Gardens

Don't be put off if you've never been particularly interested in botany before coming here – along with London's Kew Gardens the **SSR Botanical Gardens** (Map p67; admission free; ⏰ 8.30am-5.30pm) are one of the best places in the world to be introduced to a huge variety of plants, trees and flowers. It's also one of the most popular tourist attractions in Mauritius and easily reached from almost anywhere on the island.

Named after Sir Seewoosagur Ramgoolam, the first prime minister of independent

---

PAUL & VIRGINIE

Mauritius' most popular folk tale tells the story of two lovers, Paul and Virginie, who encounter tragedy when the ship that is carrying Virginie founders on the reef. Although Paul swims out to the wreck to save her, Virginie modestly refuses to remove her clothes to swim ashore, and drowns; Paul dies of a broken heart shortly after.

The story was written by Bernardin de St-Pierre in the 18th century, but was inspired by a real-life tragedy that took place some years earlier. In 1744, the ship *St Géran* was wrecked during a storm off Île d'Ambre, to the southeast of Grand Gaube, with almost 200 lives lost. Among them were two female passengers who refused to undress to swim ashore and were dragged down by the weight of their clothes. The true story is more a tragedy of social mores than one of romance!

The *St Géran* was carrying a horde of Spanish money and machinery from France for the island's first sugar refinery. A French dive expedition explored the wreck in 1966 and many of their finds are on display in Mahébourg's National History Museum and the Blue Penny Museum in Port Louis.

You'll run into Paul and Virginie everywhere in Mauritius. The statue by Prosper d'Épinay is perhaps the most famous memorial. The original is in the Blue Penny Museum and there's a copy near the town hall in Curepipe.

Mauritius, the gardens also house the funerary platform where he was cremated. His ashes were scattered on the Ganges in India.

The plants are gradually being labelled and map-boards installed, but this is still very patchy and thus the gardens are really best seen with a guide (up to four people/10 people Rs 50/Rs 40 per person for an hour's tour), as you'll miss many of the most interesting species if you go alone. Alternatively, you can buy an excellent guidebook (Rs 225) at the **booths** (8.30am-5.30pm Tue-Sun) located just inside the two entrances, or from tourist shops all over the island before you come.

The gardens were started by Mahé de Labourdonnais in 1735 as a vegetable plot for his Mon Plaisir Château, but came into their own in 1768 under the auspices of the French horticulturist Pierre Poivre. Like Kew Gardens in England, the gardens played a significant role in the horticultural espionage of the day. Poivre imported spice plants from around the world in a bid to end France's dependence on Asian spices. The gardens were neglected between 1810 and 1849 until British horticulturalist James Duncan transformed them into an arboretum for palms and other tropical trees.

Palms still constitute the most important part of the horticultural display, and they come in an astonishing variety of shapes and forms. Some of the more prominent are the stubby bottle palms, the tall royal palms and the talipot palms, which flower once after about 40 years and then die. Other varieties include the raffia, sugar, toddy, fever, fan and even sealing-wax palms. There are many other curious tree species on display, including the marmalade box tree, the fish poison tree and the sausage tree.

The centrepiece of the gardens is a pond filled with giant Victoria amazonica water lilies, native to the Amazon region. Young leaves emerge as wrinkled balls and unfold into the classic tea-tray shape up to 2m across in a matter of hours. The flowers in the centre of the huge leaves open white one day and close red the next. The lilies are at their biggest and best in the warm summer months, notably January.

Various international dignitaries have planted trees in the gardens, including Nelson Mandela, Indira Gandhi and a host of British royals.

The gardens have two entrances, both on the west side. The main gate (supposedly sent all the way from Crystal Palace in London) is the more southerly, opposite the church. The second is in the northwest corner beside the car park.

Labourdonnais' old mansion **Mon Plaisir** (closed Monday) contains a free exhibition of photographs and is well worth a look. To complete the picture there are some animals in open pens including giant tortoises and deer.

L'Aventure du Sucre

Just across the motorway from the botanical gardens, the former Beau Plan sugar factory now houses this excellent **museum** (Map p67; ☎ 243 0660; www.aventuredusucre.com; adult/child Rs 300/150; 9am-5pm). It not only tells the story of sugar in fascinating detail, but also along the way covers the history of Mauritius, slavery, the rum trade and much, much more. Allow at least a couple of hours to do it justice.

The original factory was founded in 1797 and only ceased working in 1999. Most of the machinery is still in place and former workers are on hand to answer questions about the factory and the complicated process of turning sugar cane into crystals. There are also videos and interactive displays as well as quizzes for children. At the end of the visit you can taste four of the fifteen different varieties of unrefined sugar, two of which were invented in Mauritius.

If all that's set your taste buds working, you could sup a glass of sugar cane juice at **Le Fangourin** (☎ 243 0660; mains Rs 150-550; 9am-5pm), a stylish café-restaurant in the grounds of the museum. It specialises in sophisticated Creole cuisine and all sorts of sugary delights.

Getting There & Away

Pamplemousses can be reached by bus from Grand Baie, Trou aux Biches, Grand Gaube and Port Louis. Services from Grand Baie and Trou aux Biches run approximately every hour and stop near the sugar museum on the way to the botanical gardens.

Buses from Port Louis' Immigration Square bus station and Grand Gaube operate every 10 to 15 minutes. These buses only stop at the botanical gardens, from where it takes about 10 minutes to walk to the museum.

CENTRAL MAURITIUS

The island's mountainous centre is often overlooked by visitors seeking a quick fix of sun and sand, which is a shame as the magical mountains, the Black River Gorges National Park and the bustling towns of the Central Plateau all make for very worthwhile visits. As you can drive anywhere in Mauritius in under an hour, it's well worth hiring a car and exploring the country's interior for a day or two. Walkers and birdwatchers will love the Black River Gorges National Park, climbers and hikers will love the idiosyncratic, almost whimsical nature of Mauritius' volcanic mountains and anyone who likes bargain hunting will enjoy a trip to Curepipe or Quatre Bornes for the shopping and markets or to Floréal's textile museum. There's very little else to see in the corridor of towns that runs almost unbroken from Curepipe to Port Louis, but over half the population dwells here (drawn by the cool highland air) and it's about as unlike picture-postcard Mauritius as can be imagined, with busy streets, factories, bustling shops and traffic everywhere. This is modern Mauritius, whether you like it or not.

Southwest of Curepipe lies a more appealing region of lakes and natural parkland. The Mare aux Vacoas reservoir is the island's largest lake. It is flanked to the west by the Mare Longue and Tamarin Falls reservoirs – the latter named after a spectacular series of seven waterfalls immediately north of the lake – and to the south by Grand Bassin. This crater lake, sacred to Hindus, is one of the most important pilgrimage sites in the country.

Getting There & Around

The Central Plateau towns are served by frequent bus connections with Port Louis. Other useful routes include the direct services between Quatre Bornes and Flic en Flac, on the west coast, and between Curepipe and Mahébourg, to the southeast; the latter service passes via the airport.

If you don't have your own transport, the easiest way to get around is by taxi.

There are no bike or motorbike rental outlets in the area. As for cars, companies elsewhere on the island will always deliver to your hotel.

HIKING THE CENTRAL PLATEAU & BLACK RIVER GORGES

The mountain ranges fringing the Central Plateau offer a variety of rambles and longer hikes. One of the most popular is the excellent but steep ascent of Le Pouce, on the plateau's northern edge. To the west near Rose Hill, Corps de Garde is more of a challenge but equally rewarding.

The most varied hiking, however, is to be found in the beautiful highland area southwest of Curepipe, where the Black River Gorges National Park offers a range of environments from dry lowlands to the wet, forest-cloaked peaks. Surrounded by casuarina and conifer trees and tumbling waterfalls, it is like no other part of Mauritius. Of several hikes traversing the park, the classic route follows the Macchabée Trail down the Black River Valley to emerge on the west coast.

While Le Pouce and Corps de Garde can be reached by bus either from the plateau towns or Port Louis, accessing the trailheads within the national park will require private transport or a taxi ride.

Information

In general, hiking information is thin on the ground. Your best option is to seek advice from local people before setting out. The exception is the national park, where wardens at the two information centres (see p88) can give some advice on the trails, sell decent maps and organise local guides.

Maps

The two visitor centres sell an excellent national park map for Rs 5, which has all the main trails and landmarks marked on it. The IGN map (p138) isn't completely up to date but shows most of the tracks and footpaths. Roads marked in yellow on this map are generally just rough tracks, sometimes passable only to 4WD vehicles, but perfectly acceptable as footpaths. They're all easy enough to follow, but smaller tracks (shown on the IGN map as dashed lines) are more difficult and may be overgrown, requiring a little bushbashing.

Central Plateau

On the northern edge of the Central Plateau, the prominent thumb-shaped peak known as Le Pouce makes a great introduction to walking in Mauritius. It's an easy hike,

MAURITIUS

CENTRAL MAURITIUS

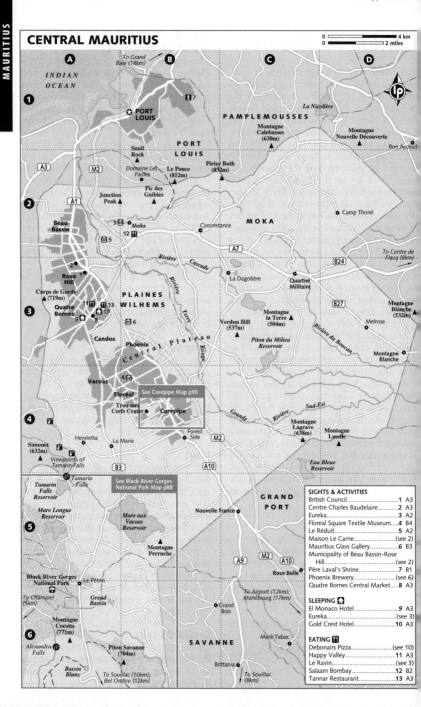

0 — 4 km
0 — 2 miles

INDIAN OCEAN

To Grand Baie (18km)

PORT LOUIS

PAMPLEMOUSSES

La Nicolière

Montagne Calebasses (630m)

Montagne Nouvelle Découverte

Bon Acceuil

PORT LOUIS

Snail Rock

Domaine Les Pailles

Le Pouce (812m)

Pieter Both (832m)

Junction Peak

Pic des Guibies

Camp Thorel

MOKA

Moka

Circonstance

To Centre de Flacq (8km)

Beau Bassin

Rivière Cascade

Rose Hill

Corps de Garde (719m)

La Dagotière

Quartier Militaire

Montagne Blanche (532m)

Quatre Bornes

PLAINES WILHEMS

Verdun Hill (537m)

Montagne la Terre (504m)

Melrose

Montagne Blanche

Candos

Phoenix

Central Plateau

Piton du Milieu Reservoir

Rivière du Boucan

Vacoas

Floréal

Trou aux Cerfs Crater

See Curepipe Map p90

Curepipe

Grande Rivière Sud-Est

Montagne Lagrave (638m)

Montagne Laselle

Simonet (632m)

Henrietta

La Marie

Forest Side

Eau Bleue Reservoir

Viewpoints of Tamarin Falls

See Black River Gorges National Park Map p88

Tamarin Falls Reservoir

Tamarin Falls

Mare Longue Reservoir

Mare aux Vacoas Reservoir

GRAND PORT

Nouvelle France

Black River Gorges National Park

Le Pétrin

Grand Bassin

Montagne Perruche

To Chamarel (5km)

Montagne Cocotte (771m)

Rose Belle

To Airport (12km); Mahébourg (17km)

Alexandra Falls

Piton Savanne (704m)

Grand Bois

SAVANNE

Bassin Blanc

To Souillac (10km); Bel Ombre (12km)

Mare Tabac

Brittania

To Souillac (8km)

SIGHTS & ACTIVITIES

British Council	1 A3
Centre Charles Baudelaire	2 A3
Eureka	3 A2
Floreal Square Textile Museum	4 B4
Le Réduit	5 A2
Maison Le Carne	(see 2)
Mauritius Glass Gallery	6 B3
Municipality of Beau Bassin-Rose Hill	(see 2)
Père Laval's Shrine	7 B1
Phoenix Brewery	(see 6)
Quatre Bornes Central Market	8 A3

SLEEPING

El Monaco Hotel	9 A3
Eureka	(see 3)
Gold Crest Hotel	10 A3

EATING

Debonairs Pizza	(see 10)
Happy Valley	11 A3
Le Ravin	(see 3)
Salaam Bombay	12 B2
Tannar Restaurant	13 A3

offering a splendid half-day outing with stunning views over the plateau, and north to Port Louis and the coast. Corps de Garde, to the southwest of Rose Hill, is an impressive peak that also makes for an exhilarating half-day hike.

LE POUCE

The ascent of Le Pouce (812m) is best tackled from the south, near the town of Moka (p94).

The path starts northeast of Moka. To get there by public transport, hop on a bus heading to Nouvelle Découverte from Curepipe, Rose Hill or Port Louis' Victoria Square bus station and ask the driver to drop you off at the trailhead; services run roughly every half hour. Travelling by car, follow signs for Eureka from the motorway, then take the right turn signed to Le Pouce. After roughly 3km, where the road bends sharply to the right, a dirt track (also signed to Le Pouce) heads off east through the sugarcane fields and marks the beginning of the track.

After about 700m the path starts zigzagging steeply uphill. A 30-minute climb brings you out on a saddle, from where you get your first views over Port Louis. From there it takes another 20 minutes or so walking east along the ridge to reach the base of the 'thumb'. The final ascent is almost vertical in places; if you don't feel up to it, never mind – even from the base you get sweeping views over the whole island.

Rather than returning the same way, you can head down to Port Louis, emerging into the southeastern suburbs of the city. The path leads steeply down the north side of the ridge from the saddle. Allow about an hour for the descent.

CORPS DE GARDE

The wedge-shaped massif dominating Rose Hill (p93) offers a very rewarding ascent, though it's not for anyone with vertigo.

To reach the start of the trail from central Rose Hill, follow Dr Maurice Curé St northeast from the junction with Royal Rd. After about 1km, take a right turn into Surverswarnath St (you'll pass a Tamil temple on your left) and continue until you hit a staggered junction with the main road. On the far side, follow St Anne St up to a second staggered junction near the Hart de Keating stadium and follow Cretin Ave, which leads out into the fields.

The easiest trail to follow begins just beyond the football ground and Hindu crematorium. It runs straight up to the red-and-white radar antenna at the top of the ridge. From here, the main track follows the ridge south, passing a huge perched boulder before reaching a tricky cliff over which you'll need to scramble. There are several more hair-raising sections to test your courage before you reach the nose (719m), which offers amazing views over the plains.

Allow about three hours for the walk if you're starting from the centre of Rose Hill; 1½ hours if you drive up to the trailhead.

TAMARIN FALLS

These falls, roughly 8km southwest of Curepipe (p90), are awkward to reach but it's worth the effort for a beautiful, deep, cool bathe at the bottom of the series of seven falls. They are only accessible via a challenging trail that begins near the Tamarin Falls reservoir, south of the village of Henrietta, but you will have to explore to find it. It's best to take one of the local guides usually waiting around Henrietta bus station.

There are buses to Henrietta from Curepipe every 20 minutes or so and from Port Louis roughly every hour. From Henrietta, it's about a 2km walk to the falls.

Black River Gorges National Park

Mauritius' sole national park is a spectacularly wild expanse of thick forest covering 3.5% of the island's surface and home to over 300 species of flowering plants and nine species of bird unique to Mauritius, including the famous pink pigeon which is staging a very gradual comeback from the brink of extinction.

It's possible to drive or take a bus through the park and stop for great views along the way (although you'll be far from alone), but the best way to see the park is of course on foot. A network of hiking trails crisscross the wild and empty Black River Gorges National Park. While the markings have improved in recent years and there are good maps available, you should check the route and the current state of the trails at the information centres before setting off. Alternatively, you

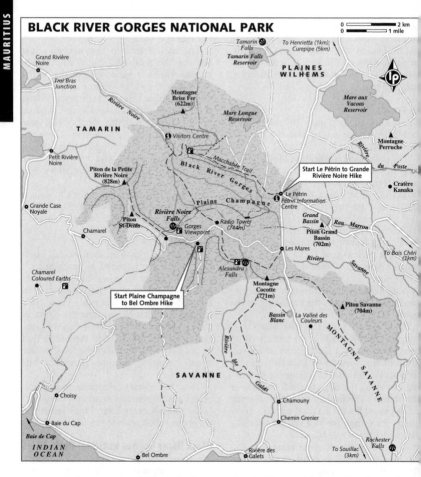

BLACK RIVER GORGES NATIONAL PARK

may want to hire a guide, which can be done via the visitors centre.

The main **visitors centre** (⏰ 9am-3pm Mon-Fri, 9am-4pm Sat & Sun) is at the park's western entrance, about 5km southeast of Grande Rivière Noire (p108). From here it's possible to proceed only on foot into the park proper. The alternative is the **Pétrin Information Centre** (☎ 507 0128; ⏰ 8am-3pm Mon-Fri, 8am-11am Sat) at the eastern entrance to the park. Staff at both can advise on the different trails and hand out fairly sketchy maps. They also sometimes act as guides. You should make the arrangements at least a day or two in advance. Rates start at Rs 1200 a day.

There are numerous trails that crisscross the park and nine of the best are detailed in

the official map. All the trailheads are clearly marked and are accessed from one of the two roads running through the park. The main road runs north–south along the park's eastern boundary, past the Pétrin Information Centre, then swings westward at Les Mares to climb up onto the Plaine Champagne. There's a newly constructed viewing point at Alexandra Falls, from where you get a sweeping view over the south coast. Sadly though, there's no view of the falls themselves and you have to make do with the sound alone. About 2km further west is the Gorges viewpoint, affording spectacular views and the company of wild monkeys. After another 10km the road drops to the coast at Grande Case Noyale.

The second road branches south at the Les Mares junction. After 3km it passes Bassin Blanc, a classic crater lake surrounded by forest. Beyond the lake the road zigzags down the valley to Chamouny and Chemin Grenier.

Getting to the trailheads is difficult without your own transport. The best option is to get a taxi to drop you off and then pick up a bus at the lower end; the coast road is well covered by buses travelling between the main towns.

There is nowhere to buy food or drinks in the park, even at the visitor centres. Make sure you bring plenty of water and energy-boosting snacks. You'll also need insect repellent, binoculars for bird-watching, wet-weather gear, and shoes with a good grip.

The best time to visit the park is during the flowering season between September and January. Look for the rare tambalacoque or dodo tree, the black ebony trees and the wild guavas (see the boxed text, p101). Bird-watchers should keep an eye out for the Mauritius kestrel, pink pigeon, echo parakeet and Mauritius cuckoo-shrike, among other rarities; park wardens can indicate the most likely viewing spots. For a full list of hikes see the official map – below are two of our favourites.

LE PÉTRIN TO GRANDE RIVIÈRE NOIRE
This is a superb 15km hike that takes you through some of the finest and most scenic countryside in Mauritius. It begins beside the Pétrin Information Centre and traverses the national park, passing tiny pockets of indigenous vegetation dispersed through acacia and other introduced forest. Though steep in parts, it's moderately easy and reasonably fit walkers should be able to do it in four to five hours.

The first part of the walk follows the Macchabée Trail, a forestry track heading west from Le Pétrin along the ridge to a viewpoint overlooking the Grande Rivière Noire Valley. From here the route descends precipitously along a steep and devilishly slippery track for about 1km, emerging on a wider path that continues down to the river and, eventually, to the visitors centre.

Most people arrange for a taxi to meet them at the visitors centre. If not, the last 5km is a less interesting but easy stroll along a sealed road that brings you out on the coast beside the Jade Pavilion restaurant and supermarket at the Trois Bras junction in Grande Rivière Noire. From here you can pick up buses to Quatre Bornes and Port Louis.

PLAINE CHAMPAGNE TO BEL OMBRE
The trailhead for this 16km walk is on the Curepipe–Chamarel Rd, just under 1km west of the radio tower that marks the road's highest point. The trail heads due south to Bel Ombre, passing through lovely mixed forests and plantations. After 10km you leave the park and start to cross private land. The last

---

GRAND BASSIN

According to legend, Shiva and his wife Parvati were circling the earth on a contraption made from flowers when they were dazzled by an island set in an emerald sea. Shiva, who was carrying the Ganges River on his head to protect the world from floods, decided to land. As he did so a couple of drops of water sprayed from his head and landed in a crater to form a lake. The Ganges expressed unhappiness about its water being left on an uninhabited island, but Shiva replied that dwellers from the banks of the Ganges would one day settle there and perform an annual pilgrimage, during which water from the lake would be presented as an offering.

The dazzling island is, of course, Mauritius; the legendary crater lake is known as Grand Bassin (or Ganga Talao). It is a renowned pilgrimage site, to which up to 500,000 of the island's Hindu community come each year to pay homage to Shiva during the Maha Shivaratri celebrations. This vast festival takes place over three days in February or March (depending on the lunar cycle) and is the largest Hindu celebration outside India.

The most devoted pilgrims walk from their village to the sacred lake carrying a *kanvar*, a light wooden frame or arch decorated with paper flowers. Others make their way by coach or car. Once there they perform a *puja*, burning incense and camphor at the lake shore and offering food and flowers.

Visitors are welcome to attend Maha Shivaratri, but should do so with respect: dress modestly, and remove your shoes before entering temples and holy places.

stretch meanders along some rather confusing tracks, but a reasonably good sense of direction will get you to the coast road without too much difficulty. From Bel Ombre, there are buses to Curepipe and Rivière des Galets.

Allow about four hours for this moderately easy walk.

CUREPIPE
pop 80,000

Effectively Mauritius' second city, Curepipe is a bustling highland commercial centre famous for its rainy weather and clothes shopping. Its strange name reputedly stems from the malaria epidemic of 1867 when people fleeing from lowland Port Louis would 'cure' their pipes of malarial bacteria by smoking them here, although in fact it's more likely to be named after a fondly remembered town in France.

While it will be of limited interest to most visitors, it makes a pleasant half-day excursion inland from the beach. Shoppers looking for bargain clothes will fare well here and there are a couple of interesting sights, including a perfectly formed mini volcanic crater.

Curepipe is the highest of the plateau towns. At 550m above sea level, temperatures are refreshingly cool in summer, but the town is often swathed in cloud. The damp climate gives the buildings an ageing, mildewed quality. Bring an umbrella, as it can rain without warning at any time of year. According to lowlanders, Curepipe has two seasons: the little season of big rains and the big season of little rains.

Orientation

Curepipe is bisected by Royal Rd, which runs approximately north–south. Most of the banks, shops and restaurants are on this street around the junction with Châteauneuf St. Head east along Châteauneuf St for the bus station. Most of the sights, such as the Trou aux Cerfs crater and the botanical gardens, are within easy walking distance of the centre.

Information

The major banks, most with ATMs, are located on Royal Rd.

Digit@l C@ffeine (☎ 670 5335; Sunsheel Centre, Royal Rd; ☼ 9.30am-7pm Mon-Sat, 10am-noon Sun) Offers plenty of PCs with access at Rs 1 per minute.

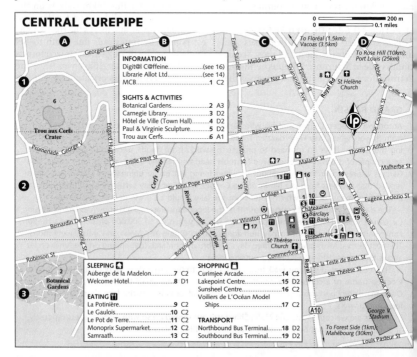

CENTRAL CUREPIPE

0 ———— 200 m
0 ———— 0.1 miles

INFORMATION
Digit@l C@ffeine..................(see 16)
Librarie Allot Ltd..................(see 14)
MCB...1 C2

SIGHTS & ACTIVITIES
Botanical Gardens....................2 A3
Carnegie Library........................3 D2
Hôtel de Ville (Town Hall)........4 D2
Paul & Virginie Sculpture........5 D2
Trou aux Cerfs...........................6 A1

SLEEPING
Auberge de la Madelon............7 C2
Welcome Hotel...........................8 D1

EATING
La Potinière................................9 C2
Le Gaulois.................................10 C2
Le Pot de Terre.........................11 C2
Monoprix Supermarket...........12 C2
Samraath...................................13 C2

SHOPPING
Curimjee Arcade......................14 C2
Lakepoint Centre.....................15 D2
Sunsheel Centre.......................16 C2
Voiliers de L'Océan Model
Ships.......................................17 C2

TRANSPORT
Northbound Bus Terminal.......18 D2
Southbound Bus Terminal.......19 D2

Librairie Allot Ltd (☎ 676 1253; Curimjee Arcade, Royal Rd) There's an excellent range of books, papers and magazines in French and English here, hidden away inside the arcade.

Mauritius Commercial Bank (MCB; Cnr Châteauneuf St & Royal Rd; ✆ 9am-5pm Mon-Sat) Exchange Bureau.

Sights

TOWN CENTRE

Overlooking a small park in the centre of Curepipe, the **Hôtel de Ville** (town hall) is one of Mauritius' best surviving examples of colonial-era architecture. Its gable windows, veranda and the decorative wooden friezes known as *dentelles* are typical of the style (see p45). The building was moved here from Moka in 1903.

The park's main draw is a copy in bronze of the famous statue of the fictitious lovers Paul and Virginie by Mauritian sculptor Prosper d'Épinay (see the boxed text, p83). The original is on display in Port Louis' Blue Penny Museum (p57).

Next to the town hall, the stone building with the distinctive neoclassical porch houses the municipal **Carnegie Library** (☎ 674 2278; ✆ 9.30am-6pm Mon-Fri, 9.30am-3pm Sat). Its collection includes rare books on Mauritius dating back to the 18th century.

TROU AUX CERFS

About 1km west of central Curepipe, the **Trou aux Cerfs** is an extinct volcanic crater some 100m deep and 1km in circumference. The bowl is heavily wooded, but from the road around the rim – a favourite spot for joggers and walkers – you get lovely views of the plateau. There are benches for rest and reflection, and a radar station for keeping an electronic eye on cyclone activity.

BOTANICAL GARDENS

These well-kept and informal **gardens** (admission free; ✆ 8am-6pm May-Sep, 7am-7pm Oct-Apr), with their lakes and lawns, provide another pleasant spot for some quiet contemplation. They were created in 1870 to grow plants in need of a more temperate climate than exists at the Sir Seewoosagur Ramgoolam Botanical Gardens in Pamplemousses (p83).

Sleeping

Unless you're on business here, it's hard to imagine why you'd need to stay in Curepipe, although it's perfectly possible and won't break the bank.

Welcome Hotel (☎ 675 3265; fax 674 7292; 196 Royal Rd; d incl breakfast Rs 550, without toilet Rs 450) This very basic place is friendly enough and the fan-cooled rooms are clean and functional, with iron bedsteads. It's a 10-minute walk from the centre of town.

Auberge de la Madelon (☎ 670 1885; www.aub ergemadelon.ltd.mu; 10 Sir John Pope Hennessy St; s/d incl breakfast Rs 600/750; ❄ 🖥 🏊) Excellent value and centrally located, this well-run place is simple and small, with 15 comfy en-suite rooms and a proactive and helpful management. Free wi-fi and a small pool area are the latest bonuses for guests.

Eating

Le Pot de Terre (☎ 676 2204; Pot de Terre Lane; mains Rs 50-125; ✆ 7.30am-8pm Mon-Sat, 7.30am-2pm Sun) This local favourite is a great place to meet locals and a world away from the tourist-oriented restaurants you'll find on the coast. Clouds of smoke and the sound of animated conversations characterise the joint, with a simple and tasty menu of sandwiches, grills and noodles.

Samraath (☎ 793 1413; Petit Bateau Bldg, 2nd fl, Royal Rd; mains Rs 100; ✆ lunch & dinner Mon-Sat, dinner Sun; ❄) You really need to know this place is here, but luckily now you do. Down a tiny side street next to the college, this almost-hidden restaurant is a surprise – delightfully painted in bright orange and yellow, the Indian food is superb and the atmosphere and décor are the best in town. Vegetarians will be in heaven here and Chinese cuisine is also served for those who don't fancy a curry.

La Potinière (☎ 676 2648; Sir Winston Churchill St; mains from Rs 200, crepes Rs 100-200; ✆ lunch Mon-Sat; ❄) Curepipe's most obviously upmarket restaurant hides in an unassuming concrete block, but inside all is starched linen and gleaming tableware. It serves predominantly French cuisine, with a choice of sweet and savoury crepes as well as more substantial dishes, and excellent homemade deserts.

Le Gaulois (☎ 675 5674; Dr Ferrière St; mains Rs 300-400; ✆ lunch Mon-Sat) This family-run place is a tiny and unfussy affair, which serves predominantly Franco-Mauritian cuisine – grilled lobster, Creole-style bouillabaisse, prawns in garlic sauce – at rather premium prices just off the main drag.

For self-caterers, there's the **Monoprix Supermarket** (Royal Rd) in the centre of town.

Shopping

Most people come to Curepipe to shop and few leave without some bargains. Try busy Châteauneuf St for bargain clothing outlets. There are several shopping malls around the central crossroads. Of these, the **Curimjee Arcade** (Royal Rd) contains a collection of upmarket duty-free shops selling clothes and souvenirs. Further north, the glitzy new **Sunsheel Centre** (Royal Rd) is also worth a look. There's a lovely Indian fabric shop on the ground floor and outlets of Habit and Café Cotton. The new **Lakepoint Centre** (Elizabeth Ave) is the latest arrival and has the pricier clothes shops in it.

Curepipe is a centre for model-ship showrooms and workshops. One such place is **Voiliers de L'Océan** (☎ 676 6986; voiliers@intneta.mu; Sir Winston Churchill St; 🕙 9am-6pm), which has a good selection. You can see the ships being made between 8am and 5pm Monday to Friday.

Getting There & Away

Curepipe is an important transport hub, with frequent bus services to Port Louis (Victoria Square), Mahébourg, Centre de Flacq, Moka and surrounding towns such as Floréal, Phoenix, Quatre Bornes and Rose Hill. There are two terminals – the northbound and the southbound. Most services go from the northbound (Port Louis, Rose Hill, Quatre Bornes), while Mahébourg is served from the southbound terminal. The terminals lie on either side of Châteauneuf St, at the junction with Victoria Ave.

Expect to pay around Rs 600 for a taxi ride from Curepipe to the airport and Rs 500 to Port Louis.

AROUND CUREPIPE

The Black River Gorges National Park, some 10km southwest of Curepipe, is a favourite haunt of hikers, but it also provides two spectacular drives. Perhaps the more stunning road, but only by a whisker, is that cutting west across Plaine Champagne before corkscrewing down to the coast; at each bend the view seems better than the last. The other road takes you plunging steeply down to the south. If you are feeling more energetic, you might try one of the hiking trails; for more information, see p87.

Floréal

This rather posh suburb northwest of Curepipe has become synonymous with the high-quality knitwear produced by the Floreal Knitwear Company. Of particular interest is the **Floreal Square Textile Museum** (Map p86; ☎ 698 8011; Swami Sivananda Ave; adults/children Rs 100/50; 🕙 9.30am-5.30pm Mon-Fri, 9.30am-4pm Sat) and shopping mall on the main road from Curepipe. Some of the workers who painstakingly put the clothes together will take you step by step through the commercial knitwear business. There's also a short video presentation and displays outlining the history not only of knitwear but of clothes and textiles in general.

You can buy Floreal knitwear in the shop below the museum; prices are good and there's a wider choice than in Floreal's other outlets around the island. The mall contains several equally upmarket clothes boutiques, and there's even a café on hand should you need sustenance. It serves slightly pricey but good quality cakes and light lunches such as salads and homemade quiche.

Phoenix

This industrial centre is the home of the **Phoenix Brewery** (Map p86), located beside the M2 motorway, which brews Phoenix Beer and Blue Marlin. While Phoenix doesn't hold much of interest for visitors (sadly the brewery is not open to the public), the **Mauritius Glass Gallery** (Map p86; ☎ 698 8007; adults/children Rs 50/25; 🕙 8am-4pm Mon-Fri, 8am-noon Sat), beside the brewery, produces unusual – and environmentally sound – souvenirs made from recycled glass. You can see them being made using traditional methods in the workshop, which also doubles as a small museum.

QUATRE BORNES
pop 78,000

For many people Quatre Bornes is nothing more than a big conurbation built up around the tediously busy road linking Flic en Flac to the M1. Its main street, St Jean Rd, is always choked with traffic, but despite this the town is pleasantly lively with lots of shopping. The twice-weekly **clothes market** on Thursday and Sunday is well worth a visit. Locals flock here from miles around to rummage the stalls, where it's possible to find top-quality garments with almost imperceptible flaws selling at low prices; check carefully though, since quality varies enormously. There's nothing much else to bring you here, however. There's an internet centre on the 2nd floor of the Orchard Centre on St Jean Rd.

Sleeping

El Monaco Hotel (Map p86; ☎ 425 2608; elmo@bow .intnet.mu; St Jean Rd; s/d/t incl breakfast Rs 1200/1400/2000; P ✿) Just off the main drag in a quiet courtyard with a pool and attractive garden, the Monaco offers functional but perfectly decent rooms with fan, bathroom, TV and telephone.

Gold Crest Hotel (Map p86; ☎ 454 5945; www.gold cresthotel.com; St Jean Rd; s/d incl breakfast Rs 1520/1855; ✿ ▣) Definitely the best hotel in town and probably worth the slight price hike from the Monaco, the spanking new Gold Crest offers all the usual amenities of a business hotel, from smart, comfortable rooms to a good restaurant.

Eating

Debonairs Pizza (Map p86; ☎ 425 2608; St Jean Rd; pizzas from Rs 120; ⏲ lunch & dinner) Next door to the Gold Crest Hotel is another outlet of the South African pizza and sub pedlars, Debonairs – a great place for a quick lunch.

Tannar Restaurant (Map p86; ☎ 465 3140; St Jean Rd; mains Rs 150-200; ⏲ lunch & dinner) This smart oasis amid the chaos of St Jean Rd is definitely the place to go for a high-quality Indian meal. The décor is modern, the whole place a lovely shade of orange and there's an excellent-value range of curries too.

Happy Valley (Map p86; ☎ 454 6065; St Jean Rd; mains Rs 160-350; ⏲ lunch & dinner, closed Wed; ✿) Far more down to earth than Tannar is long-standing local favourite Happy Valley. House specials include Peking duck, spicy squid and the aptly named Three Marvels Hot Pot, a seafood and vegetable steamboat. At Sunday lunchtime it's packed with local Chinese families tucking into dim sum (four pieces of dim sum from Rs 50).

Getting There & Away

Frequent bus services operate between Rose Hill, Port Louis and the bus station in Quatre Bornes beside the town hall. Buses for Curepipe, Floréal and Flic en Flac stop at regular intervals along St Jean Rd.

ROSE HILL

pop 106,000

Rose Hill, wedged between Beau Bassin and Quatre Bornes in the middle of the Central Plateau conurbation, is virtually a suburb of Port Louis and a major cultural centre for Mauritius. The town sits at the foot of the impressive Corps de Garde mountain (see p87 for more about tackling this peak) and retains a few interesting old buildings from the colonial era. It also has a reputation as a cheap place to shop, particularly for imported Indian textiles.

Most places of interest are strung out along St Jean Rd, which is Rose Hill's main thoroughfare. The intersection of St Jean Rd and Vandermeersch St marks the town centre, where you'll find the bus station and the main shopping malls as well as numerous basic restaurants and food stalls. For tiptop Indian snacks, you can't beat the *dhal puris* sold by **Dewa & Sons** (Arab Town market, Royal Rd) to the south of the centre; they're reputed to be the best on the island.

Sights

Two of the most important cultural centres in Mauritius are located in Rose Hill. The **British Council** (☎ 403 0200; general.enquiries@mu .britishcouncil.org; St Jean Rd; ⏲ 11am-5pm Tue-Fri, 9am-2.30pm Sat) is across the main road from the bus station. It has a regular programme of events in English and a good library.

Behind Maison Le Carne is the **Centre Charles Baudelaire** (Map p86; ☎ 454 7929; ccb@intnet .mu; 15/17 Gordon St; ⏲ 10am-5.30pm Tue-Fri, 9am-3pm Sat), which puts on an impressive schedule of plays, concerts and other events promoting French culture.

There are also several impressive Creole buildings in the centre of Rose Hill. The **Municipality of Beau Bassin-Rose Hill** (Map p86) on St Jean Rd is housed in an unusual Creole building that was constructed in 1933 as a theatre. Next door, **Maison Le Carne** (Map p86) is a more attractive old Creole mansion. It now houses the Mauritius Research Council.

Getting There & Away

There are regular buses from Port Louis and Curepipe to Rose Hill, and from Rose Hill to Centre de Flacq on the east coast.

MAURITIUS

MOKA & AROUND
pop 8500

The most charming of the Central Plateau towns, the country's academic centre and official home to the President of Mauritius, picturesque Moka is a great place to visit for a taste of Mauritian history. The scenery is dramatic here too, with waterfalls, valleys and the towering Le Pouce Mountain (812m) in the background, which provides stunning views over the Central Plateau and north to Port Louis (see p87 for more about climbing Le Pouce). The undoubted attraction here, though, is the beautiful colonial mansion of Eureka, which is a fascinating place to visit. Almost perfectly preserved from the mid-19th century, it provides some of the most unique accommodation in the country.

Eureka

A highlight of any visit to Mauritius is **Eureka** (Map p86; ☎ 433 8477; www.maisoneureka.com; house only Rs 175, house & garden Rs 300; ☻ 9am-5pm Mon-Sat, 9am-3.30pm Sun), a more or less perfectly preserved Creole mansion built in the 1830s, which stands in woodland on the northwest edge of Moka. A masterpiece of tropical construction, the house boasts 109 doors, which keep the interior deliciously cool during the hot summers and, unless you're unlucky and bump into a tour group, you're also likely to have the place virtually to yourself. The unusual name is believed to have been the reaction to its second owner, Eugène Le Clézio, when his bid to purchase the house at auction in 1856 was successful.

Coming here instantly transports you into the colonial world, with the fine, expansive gardens, the impeccably preserved collection of period furniture imported by the French East India Company and the day-to-day items such as the toilet, which bring the colonial experience to life. There's also a Chinese room and a music room and, the height of sophistication in those days, a colonial shower contraption. Lining the staircase are some fine antique maps of Asia and Africa and a very tatty globe.

The courtyard behind the house is surrounded by stone cottages, which were once the staff quarters and kitchen, and beyond the main house are a number of cottages that function as one of Mauritius' most atmospheric accommodation options (see right). The gorgeous grounds extend to a se-

ries of beautiful waterfalls about a 15-minute walk away on a trail from the main house (swimming is great here in the large pools four or five cascades down).

To get to Eureka, take a bus from Curepipe or Victoria Square in Port Louis and get off at Moka. Eureka is signed about 1km north of the bus stop.

Le Réduit

Close to the university is Le Réduit (Map p86), a superb mansion surrounded by an extensive park. It was built in 1778 for the French governor Barthélémy David, who succeeded Mahé de Labourdonnais. Now the President's official residence, it is sadly closed to the public.

Sleeping & Eating

Eureka (Map p86; ☎ 433 8477; www.maisoneureka.com; r incl breakfast Rs 3450; ☻ lunch) You can both eat and sleep at Eureka, and while the decent food served on the terrace at lunch (set menu Rs 750) is a delightful but rather overpriced experience, the fantastic group of bungalows to one side of the main mansion are perfect for a romantic retreat. Much of the time you'll be the only people staying here, and it's hard to imagine a more blissful spot. Each bungalow is individually furnished (Simone is our favourite) with ensuite facilities and a double bed. There's even a main house you can rent with three bedrooms (also available individually), which is just as stylish. Watching the sunset here by the small pool is about as good as it gets.

ourpick Salaam Bombay (Map p86; ☎ 433 1003; Royal Rd; dishes Rs 140-340; ☻ lunch & dinner) This friendly place, rather unfortunately located on the side of a busy roundabout, is nevertheless superb. There's a delicious range of tandoor and tikka dishes as well as plenty of choices for vegetarians. You can also eat pizza here, courtesy of the next-door pizza delivery company run by the same management.

Le Ravin (Map p86; ☎ 433 4501; mains Rs 300-600; ☻ lunch, dinner by reservation) Next door to Eureka on the main road is this charming French-Creole restaurant on the banks of the river. It's owned and run by the Eureka management, so it's squarely aimed at tourists, although it is a lovely spot and a great place to treat yourself to a long lunch.

EAST MAURITIUS

Lacking a Flic en Flac or a Grand Baie around which infinite numbers of postcard stands, takeaways and souvenir shops can grow up, the east coast of Mauritius feels enviably untouched by mass tourism, which is fantastic as the island's very best beaches are to be found here – both long stretches of deserted public beach and equally impressive sands behind the elegant gates of five-star hotels. East Mauritius is definitely the most exclusive side of the island and the congregation of luxury hotels around Belle Mare attracts the kind of crowd likely to take a helicopter transfer from the airport when they arrive. However, relaxed Trou d'Eau Douce has retained the feel of a sleepy fishing village despite rubbing shoulders with grand hotels and being the starting point for the country's favourite boat excursion – the Île aux Cerfs. Trou d'Eau Douce also provides the only good source of budget accommodation in the area, and is a good place to base yourself, with plenty of eating, sleeping and activity options.

Inland from the coast, fields of sugar cane interspersed with vegetable gardens slope gently up towards the mountains. The main town, Centre de Flacq, has a good market and is also useful for its banks, shops and transport connections.

Getting There & Around

The main transport hub for east Mauritius is Centre de Flacq. You'll have to change here coming by bus from Port Louis, the Central Plateau towns or from Mahébourg in the south. There are onward connections from Centre de Flacq to villages along the east coast, although some services are pretty infrequent.

Most hotels and guesthouses have bikes for rent. Otherwise, you can rent bikes in Trou d'Eau Douce. Car rental can either be arranged through your hotel or through one of the big agencies (see p152).

TROU D'EAU DOUCE
pop 5400

'Sweet water hole' is the major crossroads on the east coast and its unwitting tourism capital as a result. It's a thoroughly lovely place, large and rambling along a wonderful bit of coast and just a short boat jour-

ney away from the massively popular Île aux Cerfs, a favoured weekend picnic excursion for Mauritians. Indeed, as soon as you get to the town centre you'll have 'Île aux Cerfs?' shouted at you by hopeful touts who line the road. Despite this, the town makes a great base for exploring the east coast, with plenty of good accommodation and eating options. The town beach is lovely, although the bay is busy with fishing and speedboats, so be aware. It's pretty much a one-road town, with almost everything strung out along the coast-hugging Royal Rd. The centre is marked by a church, near which you'll find the post office, police station and a small petrol station.

Information

Les Hollandais Cybercafé (Map p96; ☎ 480 0138; Le Maho; 9am-7pm Mon-Sat) Down a side street between Chez Tino and Soleil des Z'Iles, this cyber café also doubles as a patisserie.

Mauritius Tourism Promotion Authority (MTPA; Map p96; ☎ 480 0925; Royal Rd; 9am-5pm Mon-Sat) Provides information and can help with accommodation booking, car hire and excursions to the Île aux Cerfs.

Sous le Manguier (Map p96; ☎ 419 3855; Royal Rd; 10am-2.30pm) This restaurant has internet access at lunchtime.

Activities

The town's only diving centre, **Easy Divers** (Map p96; ☎ 911 4103/782 0186; Royal Rd; 8am-4pm), can be found opposite the public beach.

Sleeping

There's more choice here than anywhere else on the east coast, and you'll find a decent range of budget and midrange accommodation. For luxury, head either way along the coast.

BUDGET & MIDRANGE

Sous le Manguier (Map p96; ☎ 419 3855; slm@intnet.mu; Royal Rd; studio Rs 400, apt Rs 600-1100;) The owners of this restaurant rent out two tidy self-catering apartments (for up to four people) and a small studio.

Auberge Etiennette (☎ 480 0497; etienet@bow.intnet.mu; Royal Rd; d/studio Rs 500/600) A very small family-run guesthouse with extremely basic facilities. Fan-cooled rooms have TVs and mosquito nets. While there's an extension planned, at the moment it's rather too basic to be much fun.

EAST MAURITIUS

0 — 5 km
0 — 3 miles

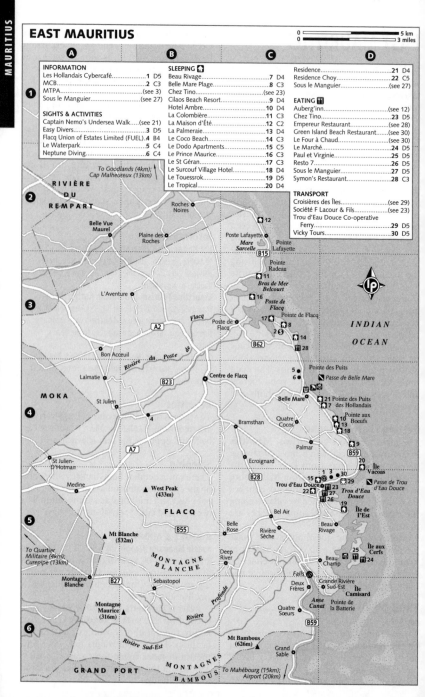

Residence Choy (Map p96; ☎ 480 0144; Royal Rd; studio with/without air-con Rs 850/650; ✗) A large complex of small studio apartments a short distance from the centre of town, the Residence Choy is very comfortable, providing a good standard of accommodation including self-catering facilities.

Le Dodo Apartments (Map p96; ☎ 480 0034; Royal Rd; apt from Rs 700) Four neat and very spacious apartments in a modern block set back from the main road, a short stroll from the town beach. All have a fan, TV and balcony or terrace. Bike hire is available for Rs 100 per day.

Chez Tino (Map p96; ☎ 480 2769; Royal Rd; r incl breakfast from Rs 700; ✗) The charming Chez Tino restaurant also has three en suite doubles on its top floor. They're a little cramped but comfortable. An excellent breakfast in the downstairs restaurant is included.

Cilaos Beach Resort (Map p96; ☎ 480 2985; www .beach-bungalows.mu; Royal Rd; studio/apt from Rs 1300/2000) This small complex of apartments and studios is right on the beach just north of Trou d'Eau Douce. It's a bit of a hike into town unless you have a car, but it's very friendly and relaxed – rooms are comfy and clean, and although simple they include kitchens for self-catering. There's also a stable on the site and horse-riding excursions can be arranged.

TOP END

our pick **Le Touessrok** (Map p96; ☎ 402 7400; www .oneandonlyletouessrok.com; s/d incl breakfast from Rs 22,500/30,000, ste from Rs 35,000; Ⓟ ✗ ✗ 🖳 🖵) Already a classic hotel known for the favour of royalty and celebrities, Le Touessrok was given a sublime multi-million dollar refit in 2003 when it became the One & Only Le Touessrok, part of the global luxury chain owned by Sol Kerzner. This partnership ended in 2007, and it's now just Le Touessrok again, but the hotel is so impeccably run and so beautifully designed that even without the One & Only name, it's bound to retain its cachet. Where to begin? The hotel is designed over two islands on a peninsula, so it has several beaches, all of which are superb. The whole place has a Moorish style to it, although the public areas are more minimalist while still beautiful and calming. The rooms are equally tasteful, with vast bathrooms, a personal butler and every possible convenience from free wi-fi to espresso machines, DVD players and remote-control everything. The hotel owns not only Île aux Cerfs (p98), but also the tot-

ally exclusive, Robinson Crusoe–style hide-away, Îlot Mangénie. If you have the money or you're on a honeymoon, this is never going to be a bad choice.

Eating

Resto 7 (Map p96; ☎ 480 2766; Sept Croisées; mains Rs 120-350; ⏲ lunch & dinner) Signed 1km south of town, this friendly, family-run place specialises in seafood and local dishes such as lobster and octopus curry as well as more snacky options, like baguettes, all served in an attractive al fresco setting. Don't get the owner started about Sunderland FC. It also offers well-priced boat trips to Île aux Cerfs.

Chez Tino (Map p96; ☎ 480 2769; Royal Rd; mains Rs 150-400; ⏲ lunch daily, dinner Mon-Sat) Pufferfish hanging in vast numbers from the ceiling characterise this brilliant, quirky little place. Reserve a table on the wonderful terrace for the best views and enjoy a superb meal of Mauritian cooking with a heavy focus on seafood.

Sous le Manguier (Map p96; ☎ 419 3855; Royal Rd; lunch Rs 250, dinner incl drinks Rs 450; ⏲ lunch, dinner on reservation only) Opposite the church, this excellent *table d'hôte* (where you eat with the family) is, as its name suggests, 'under the mango tree' and you'll get some fantastic home-cooked food. The downstairs restaurant is open during the day, while in the evening the owners invite you to join them for a veritable feast of local specialities on their upstairs terrace.

Green Island Beach Restaurant (Map p96; ☎ 515 0240; Royal Rd; mains Rs 250; ⏲ lunch & dinner Tue-Sun) It's hard to miss this place with its bright-orange exterior. Here you'll find Sino-Franco-Mauritian cuisine and seafood on offer at slightly higher prices than most other eateries but with a great position overlooking the sea to compensate.

Le Four à Chaud (Map p96; ☎ 480 1036; Royal Rd; mains Rs 300; ⏲ lunch & dinner Sun-Fri, dinner Sat) This is the smartest place in town and where you should head for a romantic evening of feasting on *fruits de mer* while enjoying a fantastic wine list. Reserve ahead to get one of the few balcony tables with sea views, and note that the menu is exclusively seafood. The name is a play on words (it's opposite the old lime kiln, or *four à chaux*).

Getting There & Around

There are no direct buses from Port Louis to Trou d'Eau Douce. You'll need to change at

WEDDING BELLS

If you have ever fantasised about walking out of your wedding reception onto a tropical beach, Mauritius could be the venue you've been searching for. Most of the luxury hotels on the island offer special wedding and honeymoon packages, with perks including tropical flowers, champagne and special romantic meals for newlyweds. For that extra something, the local civil status officer can perform the ceremony on the hotel beach, or even underwater courtesy of Blue Safari Submarine (see p69).

Under Mauritian law, civil weddings can be celebrated by nonresidents upon production of a certificate of nonresidency, which can be obtained from the **Registrar of Civil Status** (Map pp58-9; ☎ 201 1727; civstat@intnet.mu; Emmanuel Anquetil Bldg, Jules Koenig St, Port Louis). The application process takes at least 10 days, and requires two copies of the birth certificates and passports of both parties. Alternatively, you can let someone else do the work and book a complete wedding package from abroad direct with the hotel or through a travel agent.

Centre de Flacq, from where onward services to Trou d'Eau Douce run every half-hour. Taxis cost around Rs 300 from Centre de Flacq and Rs 1000 from the airport.

Vicky Tours (☎ 760 0254; Royal Rd; ☺ 9am-7pm), at the north end of town, rents bicycles for Rs 125 a day.

ÎLE AUX CERFS

This stunning island off the east coast of Mauritius is one of the most popular day trips in the country for both foreigners and Mauritians alike. In fact it's rather become a victim of its own success, inasmuch as it's now hard to find the deserted beaches that were once the main draw in the first place. While the island was once populated by *cerfs* or stags (imported for hunting from Java) you'll find only touts and tourists there today. However, the further you go from the boat jetty, the more likely you are to find a patch of sand between the sunbronzed bodies. At low tide you can also wade across to the smaller and quieter Île de l'Est, which is joined to Île aux Cerfs by a picturesque sand bar. In winter, the beaches on the island's west side provide sheltered sunbathing spots.

Much of the Île aux Cerfs belongs to the plush Le Touessrok hotel (p97). The majority of water sports on offer are reserved for hotel guests, although the magnificent 18-hole golf course is also open to outsiders as long as they book in advance.

Many visitors bring picnics to the island, but there are two restaurants on Île aux Cerfs. The **Paul et Virginie restaurant** (Map p96; mains from Rs 250; ☺ noon-3pm) on the beach offers not inexpensive seafood while **Le Marché**

(Map p96; mains from Rs 200; ☺ noon-3pm) serves up Mauritian fare.

Getting There & Away

Despite what the signs say, there is no public ferry to Île aux Cerfs. Guests of Le Touessrok get whisked over to the island for free on the hotel launch. Lesser mortals have to use one of the private operators in Trou d'Eau Douce. Those with a reliable reputation include **Vicky Tours** (Map p96; ☎ 754 5597; Royal Rd; ☺ 9am-5pm), **Trou d'Eau Douce Co-operative Ferry** (Map p96; ☎ 519 0452; Royal Rd; ☺ 8.15am-5pm), **Croisières des Îles** (Map p96; ☎ 519 0876; Royal Rd; ☺ 8am-5pm), and **Société F.Lacour & Fils** (Map p96; ☎ 480 2311; Royal Rd; ☺ 8am-5pm), all at the north end of town. You can also arrange boats through Resto 7 and Chez Tino (see p97) or through your hotel or guesthouse.

Prices tend to be fairly standard, at around Rs 300 per person for the return trip by ordinary boat (15 minutes each way) and Rs 500 by speedboat (five minutes). Depending how busy it is, boats leave roughly every 30 minutes between 9am and 4pm, with the last boat back at 5pm at the latest.

Most operators also offer various combinations of Île aux Cerfs with glass-bottomed boat trips, snorkelling and a barbecue lunch.

BELLE MARE & AROUND

North from Trou d'Eau Douce as far as Pointe de Flacq, a 10km-long beach includes some of the best white sand and azure ocean in Mauritius, unsurprisingly also home to the largest stretch of luxury hotels in the country. The beach around Belle Mare is generally regarded as one of the island's finest; Palmar beach, just to the south, is not far behind.

Belle Mare itself is a small, nondescript kind of place with little to recommend it. However, there are several currency exchanges here and two supermarkets.

Information

Mauritius Commercial Bank (MCB; ☑ 9am-5pm Mon-Sat, 9am-noon Sun) has a useful branch with exchange facilities and an ATM near the Belle Mare Plage hotel. You'll find a few supermarkets in Belle Mare, but for other services the closest town is Centre de Flacq.

Activities

The east coast's most famous dive site, 'the Pass', is located off Belle Mare. To explore this and other local sites, contact **Neptune Diving** (Map p96; ☎ 515 0936 or 251 4152; ☑ 8.30am-4.30pm Mon-Sat) at the Emeraude Hotel.

Captain Nemo's Undersea Walk (Map p96; ☎ 263 7819; www.captainemo-underseawalk.com; Rs 870; ☑ 8.30am-5pm), the long-established Grand Baie operation, operates from beside the Residence hotel for nondivers – see p134 for more information about this activity. For a fun half-day out **Le Waterpark** (Map p96; ☎ 415 2626; Coastal Rd; adult/child Rs 350/185; ☑ 10am-5.30pm) offers rides, slides and thrills aplenty.

Sleeping

Despite being achingly exclusive for the most part, there are a couple of midrange options on the Belle Mare coast. Those seeking solitude should head north along the road towards Poste Lafayette.

MIDRANGE

La Colombière (Map p96; ☎ 410 5282; www.colombiere -sur-mer.com; Poste Lafayette; studio/apt from Rs 1200/3200; P ⌧ ⌧) This sweet, low-key establishment faces the Prince Maurice hotel across the lagoon – the truly audacious could probably swim across and have a dip in their pool – although it's hard to imagine an establishment more different. People come here for carefree beach fun and to kitesurf. Most units are in a rather unattractive block and are a bit cramped at the cheaper end, but clean and well equipped. There are two small pools and a tennis court.

La Maison d'Été (Map p96; ☎ 410 5039; www.lamais ondete.com; Poste Lafayette; studio Rs 2500/3000; ⌧) This was, until recently, Coral Beach Bungalows, but has been transformed by a lovely Franco-Mauritian couple into La Maison d'Été, one of the most charming and relaxed guesthouses in the country. Six simple but beautifully appointed self-catering studios are arranged around a good pool and are just a few metres from the beach where there's great snorkelling to be had. Jean Claude is an excellent chef and runs a fantastic little restaurant, Auberg'inn, where eating is a treat.

Le Surcouf Village Hotel (Map p96; ☎ 415 1800; www.lesurcouf.net; s/d with half board from Rs 2500/4500; P ⌧ ⌧) This delightful place oozes relaxed charm and unpretentious fun, a world away from its stuffier neighbours. All the bungalows face the lagoon, and there are free glass-bottom boat trips and non-motorised water sports. The white-sand beach is on a peaceful bay and despite not being very wide is still delightful.

Le Tropical (Map p96; ☎ 480 1300; www.naiade.com; Royal Rd; s/d full board from Rs 3390/5100; ⌧ ⌧) There's little to complain about at this well-run and affordable three-star place a little way out of Trou d'Eau Douce. It's pleasantly small with just 60 rooms, and has a good stretch of beach right on the lagoon, which even features some 19th-century canons. Accommodation is in two-storey blocks facing the sea.

Le Coco Beach (Map p96; ☎ 415 1010; www.lecoco beach.com; Poste de Flacq; s/d with half board from Rs 4500/6600; P ⌧ ⌧) This unforgettable place thinks it's Disney Land, but in reality is just one gigantic mistake. The theme is circus – as seen in the big top–style main building, the staff on rollerskates or the accommodation blocks, which all look like clowns' dressing rooms. Altogether it's huge, but unrelentingly colourful, and walking about is like constantly trying to shake off a hangover. The beaches are good, though, and facilities are extensive. Management clearly realises how awful the theme here is, and a total renovation has been mooted.

TOP END

`our pick` **La Palmeraie** (Map p96; ☎ 401 8500; www .palmeraie-hotel.com; s/d with half board from Rs 9000/12,500; P ⌧ ⌧ ⌧) This brand new Moroccan-style hotel is the first four-star boutique hotel in Mauritius and offers a brilliant fusion of tradition and modernity. The rooms are simple and colourful, with bathrooms open to the main room and a private toilet, while the public areas are stunning. The clever design stands out, from the Moorish turrets of the orange building down to the gorgeous pool overlooked by the Oasis Beach Bar. With a choice of two restaurants, a superb Moroccan spa and a great stretch of beach popular with kitesurfers, this is one of the most exciting new additions to the Mauritian hotel scene.

Hotel Ambre (Map p96; ☎ 401 8000; www.apavou-hotels.com; Palmar; s/d incl breakfast from Rs 8500/12,500; ✕ ✕ ▯ ▮) This well-run hotel operated by the French Apavou group is one of the more affordable four-stars. There is a large pool, a beautiful, wide and sandy beach and good water-sports facilities are available. Rooms are spacious if a little spartan in some cases.

Beau Rivage (Map p96; ☎ 402 2000; www.naiade.com; Belle Mare; s/d with half board from Rs 15,000/22,000; ▯ ✕ ✕ ▯ ▮) This is the jewel in the crown of the Naiade group; its most glamorous and stylish hotel. The three-storey thatched villas, grouped around a huge pool, blend seamlessly with the palm trees. Inside, imaginative use of sophisticated, tropical colours gives the rooms character and style. A sumptuous place for romance and relaxation.

Belle Mare Plage (Map p96; ☎ 402 2600; www.belle mareplagehotel.com; Poste de Flacq; s/d with half board from Rs 16,000/22,800; ▯ ✕ ✕ ▯ ▮) One of Mauritius' most delightful and exclusive hotels, the Belle Mare Plage quite simply ticks every box. Whether you love golf (with no less than two championship-level courses and a well-respected golf academy, this is a golfer's dream), being pampered in the exceptional spa, enjoying the superb beach and pool, eating in the several restaurants (including the superb Blue Penny Café) or just soaking up the incredible design and style (the entire reception is scented with vanilla and ylang-ylang with water features everywhere), then this is the place for you.

Residence (Map p96; ☎ 401 8888; www.theresidence.com; Belle Mare; s/d with half board from Rs 16,000/23,000; ✕ ✕ ▯ ▯ ▮) A minimalist dark-wood, high-ceilinged reception area filled with miniature palms, orchids and the odd Asian antique provides a suitably remarkable entrance for this grand, old-world hotel. The beautifully proportioned, multi-level pool means you'll never have to suffer sharing the water with unruly kids again. The beach is spectacular with a huge swimming area – the rest of the hotel is not as stunning as its public areas would suggest, but this is still a sumptuous place for relaxation in style.

Le St Géran (Map p96; ☎ 401 1688; www.oneandon lylesaintgeran.com; Poste de Flacq; s/d with half board from Rs 31,500/41,500; ✕ ✕ ▯ ▮) Now the One & Only group's only property in Mauritius after losing Le Touessrok in a divorce with its local partners, this classic hotel will be the focus of the luxury group's efforts and thus will probably only get better and better in the next few years. As it is, it's superb, with a wide choice of beaches, a nine-hole golf course, an excellent water-sports centre, five tennis courts, a kids club and selection of three world-class restaurants including an outlet of Alain Ducasse's famously innovative Spoon. The rooms are large, with butler service, DVD players and gorgeous décor. Regulars here have included Nelson Mandela and John Travolta.

Le Prince Maurice (Map p96; ☎ 413 9130; www .princemaurice.com; Poste de Flacq; s/d incl breakfast from Rs 32,500/43,500; ✕ ✕ ▯ ▮) One of the *grande dames* of Mauritian tourism, Le Prince Maurice is still comfortably one of the best hotels in the country. Its location, as the furthest north by some way of the luxury hotels on the east coast, means it feels pleasantly remote. Set in immense grounds the hotel is all about peace, calm and some serious style. The wonderful wooden reception area opens directly onto a huge infinity pool, which merges perfectly with the sea beyond. Its two fabulous beaches are lined with suites, which open directly onto them. A wonderful, classic hotel for a seriously glamorous experience.

Eating

As the hotels here are so all encompassing, few people leave them to eat out, so eating options are limited. However, all hotels welcome nonguests to dine at their à la carte restaurants and the choice is superb, although prices are consummately high. Particular notice should go to the Blue Penny Café at the Belle Mare Plage and Alan Ducasse's Spoon at Le St Géran. The following are more affordable options.

Symon's Restaurant (Map p96; ☎ 415 1135; Belle Mare; mains Rs 150-250; ☉ 10am-10pm; ✕) This is our choice of the two restaurants next to each other on the main coastal road north of Belle Mare. The Indian food is of quite absurdly good quality, even if the views are ho-hum. A great option.

Auberg'inn (Map p96; ☎ 410 5039; Postes Lafayette; mains Rs 200; ☉ 8am-10pm Mon-Sat; ✕) This superb place is run as a restaurant open to the public despite also functioning as the hotel restaurant for the charming La Maison d'Été. Chef and owner Jean-Claude serves up an enticing menu of pizzas, pasta, fusion and seafood. Sample dishes include Bouillabaisse Lafayette, beef carpaccio, and octopus and green papaya curry. Takeaway pizza is also available.

Empereur Restaurant (Map p96; ☎ 415 1254; Belle Mare; mains Rs 250; ☺ lunch & dinner Thu-Tue; ☒) Next door to Symon's, this somewhat cavernous but pleasantly cool restaurant offers Mauritian and Chinese food at slightly inflated prices. It's no great shakes, but absolutely fine none the less.

Getting There & Around

There are very occasional buses to Palmar from Centre de Flacq, but none to Belle Mare. At least one bus an hour runs from Centre de Flacq north via Poste Lafayette to Rivière du Rempart.

A taxi from Centre de Flacq to Belle Mare or Palmar costs about Rs 300.

CENTRE DE FLACQ
pop 16,700

Centre de Flacq is a world away from picture-postcard Belle Mare and the coast. Here there's the chaotic bustle you'd expect to find in the east coast's main settlement, and while there's nothing much to see or do, it's well worth an excursion if you're bored of the beach.

Five kilometres west of Centre de Flacq along the road to Quartier Militaire, the **Flacq Union of Estates Limited** (Map p96; FUEL; ☎ 413 2583) sugar mill is the largest and most modern on the island. Tours of the plant take place during the cane harvest (July to early November); phone ahead to find out when they run.

GUAVAS

During the guava season, from February to June, you will see hundreds of Mauritian families scrumping the fruit from wild guava trees all over Mauritius. The small red fruits resemble tiny apples and have a tart skin but a delicious soft interior with hard seeds; they taste like fresh strawberries! In case you are worried about picking the wrong thing, you'll see vendors selling bags of the fruit throughout the season for next to nothing. Try them the Indian way, with salt and chilli.

Getting There & Away

Centre de Flacq is a regional gateway and gets direct buses from Port Louis' Immigration Square bus station and Rose Hill, Curepipe, Mahébourg (via the coast road), Trou d'Eau Douce, Palmar and Poste Lafayette.

Taxis leave from near the market in Centre de Flacq and charge around Rs 300 to go to Belle Mare or Trou d'Eau Douce.

WEST MAURITIUS

The dramatic mountain outcrops that suddenly shoot up along the otherwise flat landscape as you head south along the western coast of Mauritius are home to one of the fastest-growing regions for tourism in the country. Flic en Flac, which is currently experiencing the biggest building boom of anywhere on the island, will be giving Grand Baie a run for its money very soon as Mauritius' tourism capital.

However, the west coast is far more than just Flic en Flac; there are some superlative beaches on and off all the way down to the extraordinary-looking Le Morne Peninsula at the island's southwestern tip. Along the way there's some excellent diving to be experienced, a small surfing scene in Tamarin, and Grande Rivière Noire is a centre for big-game fishing and dolphin watching. Inland too there's plenty to draw people here; the most visited sight in the southwest is Chamarel's famous coloured earths, in the hills east of Le Morne. There's also Casela Nature Park, near Flic en Flac, and an old watchtower – now a museum – at La Preneuse, north of Grande Rivière Noire. The Black River Gorges National Park (p87) is also within easy striking distance; the park's western entrance is only a few kilometres inland from Grande Rivière Noire.

Getting Around

The main bus routes in west Mauritius are those from Port Louis down to Grande Rivière Noire, and from Quatre Bornes to Baie du Cap. There is also a regular service between Quatre Bornes and Chamarel.

Your hotel or guesthouse should be able to arrange bike and car hire. Otherwise, one of the outlets in Flic en Flac or La Gaulette should be able to help.

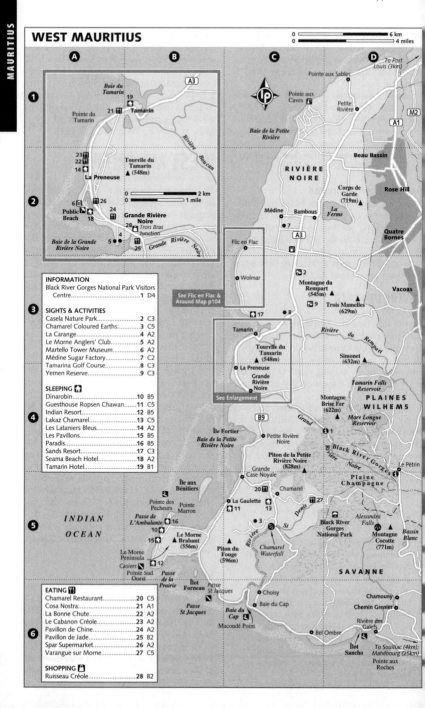

WEST MAURITIUS

INFORMATION

Black River Gorges National Park Visitors
  Centre..**1** D4

SIGHTS & ACTIVITIES

Casela Nature Park............................**2** C3
Chamarel Coloured Earths..............**3** C5
La Carange...**4** A2
Le Morne Anglers' Club....................**5** A2
Martello Tower Museum...................**6** A2
Médine Sugar Factory.......................**7** C2
Tamarina Golf Course.......................**8** C3
Yemen Reserve...................................**9** C3

SLEEPING

Dinarobin..**10** B5
Guesthouse Ropsen Chawan.........**11** C5
Indian Resort....................................**12** B5
Lakaz Chamarel...............................**13** C5
Les Lataniers Bleus..........................**14** A2
Les Pavillons.....................................**15** B5
Paradis...**16** B5
Sands Resort.....................................**17** C3
Seama Beach Hotel..........................**18** A2
Tamarin Hotel...................................**19** B1

EATING

Chamarel Restaurant.......................**20** C5
Cosa Nostra.......................................**21** A1
La Bonne Chute................................**22** A2
Le Cabanon Créole...........................**23** A2
Pavillon de Chine..............................**24** A2
Pavillon de Jade...............................**25** B2
Spar Supermarket............................**26** A2
Varangue sur Morne........................**27** C5

SHOPPING

Ruisseau Créole................................**28** B2

FLIC EN FLAC & AROUND
pop 3000

The wonderfully named town of Flic en Flac marks the beginning of a superb stretch of beachy coastline that runs down on and off to the very southern Le Morne Peninsula. However, unless you're staying in one of the many high-end hotels, you may feel a little cheated of the tropical paradise promised by the postcards. Development here is in overdrive with the result today being that Flic en Flac has lost its charming village feel and is threatening to become one long strip of hotels, expensive restaurants and souvenir shops. The beach, while gorgeous, can be litter-strewn in places and heaving at weekends when it plays host to throngs of locals from the central highlands who descend en masse for picnics by the sea.

That said, if you stay at any of the resorts outside the town, which includes all the high-end options, Flic en Flac offers some wonderful spots, great diving and a good selection of eating and drinking. Another advantage is that Flic en Flac is located a long drive away from the main coastal road, so you don't have the constant stream of fast-flowing traffic that plagues other towns on the west coast.

Flic en Flac is thought to be a corruption of the old Dutch name Fried Landt Flaak (meaning 'Free and Flat Land'), and it's easy to imagine how magical the place must have looked to explorers arriving in the 18th century.

Orientation

The centre of Flic en Flac is dominated by Pasadena Village, which is basically a large Spar supermarket with a small shopping centre and a few eateries attached. If you follow the road around here you're parallel to the immense public beach, and it's along here that development is most apparent. However, at the end of the stretch of concrete apartment blocks and ever-changing restaurants you'll enter far more refined Wolmar, a suburb of Flic en Flac where all the luxury hotels congregate.

Information

The police station and post office are both on Royal Rd near Pasadena Village. The MTPA has a **tourist office** (☎ 453 8860; ⏰ 9am-5pm Mon-Sat) inside Pasadena Village where you can get information and organise car hire, excursions and accommodation.

Flic en Flac Tourist Agency (☎ 453 9389; www.ff tourist.com; ⏰ 8.30am-5pm Mon-Sat, 8.30am-1pm Sun)

Offers tours and cruises, car, bike and motorbike rental and can help find accommodation.

Mauritius Commercial Bank (MCB; ⏰ 8am-6pm Mon-Sat, 9am-noon Sun) Exchange bureau.

Smartnet Café (⏰ 8.30am-8pm Mon-Sat, 8.30am-5pm Sun) You'll find this cramped and rather unpleasant internet café inside the Spar supermarket.

Zub Express (☎ 434 8868; Coastal Rd; ⏰ 10am-6pm) This new cybercafé and general store is at the Wolmar end of Flic en Flac but is a much more pleasant place to go online.

Sights & Activities
CASELA NATURE PARK

This 14-hectare **nature park** (Map p102; ☎ 452 0693; www.caselayemen.mu; adult/child Rs 150/50; ⏰ 9am-5pm May-Sep, 9am-6pm Oct-Apr) is on the main road 1km south of the turn to Flic en Flac. It is beautifully landscaped and has sweeping views over the coastal plain. The park houses some 1500 birds, representing species from around the world – some in rather small cages – including rare pink pigeons. There are also tigers, zebras, monkeys and deer living in a semi-reserve, and giant tortoises, one of which is 180 years old. Children are well catered for with a petting zoo, playground and mini golf (Rs 45).

Casela also offers 'safaris' by jeep, mountain bike or on foot around the nearby 45-sq-km **Yemen Reserve** (Map p102; ☎ 452 0693), where deer, wild pigs, fruit bats and monkeys can be seen in their natural habitat; prices vary according to the different packages. Quad biking (around Rs 1700 per hour) and rock climbing (half/full day Rs 1800/2200) are also on offer.

The park has a pleasant **restaurant** (mains Rs 200-350; ⏰ 10am-4pm) serving drinks, snacks and more substantial meals to visitors.

DIVING

The lagoon off Flic en Flac is good for swimming and snorkelling, and some of the best and most varied diving in Mauritius is to be found off the coast here; for more information see p28. The Rempart Serpent and the Cathedral are both outstanding sights.

The two main dive centres in town are **Exploration Sous-Marine** (☎ 453 8450; www.pierre-szalay .com; ⏰ 8.30am-4pm Mon-Fri, 8.30am-2pm Sat), based at Villas Caroline, and the cheaper **Sea Urchin Diving Centre** (☎ 752 5307; www.sea-urchin-diving.com; ⏰ 9am-4pm Mon-Sat). Nearly all the big hotels in Wolmar have their own dive centres.

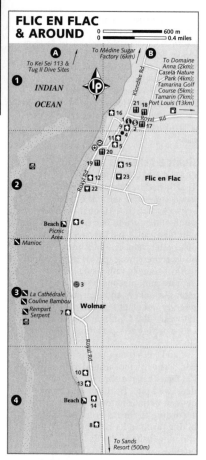

GOLF

The newly opened **Tamarina Golf Course** (Map p102; ☎ 423 8595; Tamarin Bay) is an 18-hole Wright-designed course with some great ocean and mountain views – your hotel can usually organise a visit.

Sleeping

As a rule, budget accommodation as well as guesthouses and apartments are mainly located in Flic en Flac itself, while the luxury options are further down the coast in Wolmar.

BUDGET

Little Acorn (☎ 453 5277; studio Rs 650) These extremely cheap apartments are fan-cooled and so basic you'd hardly remember you were on holiday. However, they are centrally located and are one of the lowest priced options around.

MÉDINE SUGAR FACTORY

Rather unattractively spewing out smoke into the countryside around Flic en Flac is the **Médine Sugar Factory** (Map p102; ☎ 452 0401; adult/child Rs 150/75; ⏲ tours 9am, 10.30am, 12.30pm & 2pm Mon, Wed, Fri Jul-early Nov), one of the country's biggest. If you get stuck behind a sugar-cane lorry overburdened by harvested crops somewhere in the region, you can bet it's heading here. During the cutting season (July to early November) it's possible to take a guided tour (one hour) of the factory. The guide takes you around the mill, explaining the whole complicated production process, and also the distillery, where the 'waste' molasses are turned into rum. The visit ends with a tasting session. The factory's 6km north of Flic en Flac.

Résidence Art (☎ 453 5277; fax 453 5278; s/d/apt Rs 550/675/1100) These self-catering studios and apartments offer decent value for money in the very centre of town, a short walk from the beach and in easy reach of other amenities.

La Désirade (☎ 453 8520; apt from Rs 1000; 🏠) Two large, homely and well-equipped apartments for up to four people hidden from the main road behind a small, flowery garden. The upstairs apartment has air-con and is slightly more expensive.

Easy World Hotel (☎ 453 8557; fax 464 5233; r Rs 700, apt from Rs 1200) These decent, clean but basic apartments are set back a little from the main road. All doubles and apartments (which sleep four) are self-catering, although ask to see several since standards vary.

MIDRANGE

Escale Vacances (☎ 453 9389; www.fftourist.com; apt Rs 2150; 🏠 🛏) A justifiably popular modern apartment complex across the road from Flic en Flac beach. The fully equipped, one-bedroom duplexes represent excellent value for money; those on the front get sea views, though cop some road noise. It's well run and friendly.

Manisa Hotel (☎ 453 8558; manisa@intent.mu; Coastal Rd; s/d incl breakfast Rs 2100/2350; 🏠 🛏) Right in the thick of things, the Manisa is at one of the main crossroads at the heart of modern Flic en Flac. Although not the best place for a quiet stay, this is a good deal if you want to be right on the beach and with a younger, party crowd.

Villa Paul & Virginie (☎ 453 8537; paulet virginie@email.com; s/d/t incl breakfast Rs 2200/3300/4000; 🏠) This eccentric, 14-room hotel has the advantage of being in the centre of town while remaining quiet. Each room has a name and decorative theme, such as yin and yang (Japanese simplicity) or Africa (zebra-skin patterns and native art). Some of the décor won't be to all tastes, but at least you can be sure of individuality – no tour groups to be found here.

Villas Caroline (☎ 453 8411; www.carolinegroup.com; s/d with half board from Rs 3300/4000, self-catering apt Rs 5700; 🏠 🛏) This hotel has a fantastic location facing directly onto Flic en Flac beach at its widest point. There's a decent infinity pool, live *séga* at the weekends and a great restaurant, the Indian Moti Mahal. Rooms are nothing fancy, but the apartments offer more space and better value.

Golden Beach Resort (☎ 453 8235; www.golden beachhotel.com; Coastal Rd; s/d with half board Rs 2500/4400;

🏠 🖥 🛏) This small and friendly place offers comfortable accommodation to the south of the main strip, just as Flic en Flac gives way to smarter Wolmar. Rooms are comfortable, all equipped with TV and phone. There's a good size pool and a pleasant stretch of beach to which there is direct access.

TOP END

Sands Resort (Map p102; ☎ 403 1200; www.thesands .info; Wolmar; s/d with half board from Rs 9300/13,300; ✗ 🏠 🖥 🛏) With gorgeous views from the pool and beach out into Tamarin Bay and towards Le Morne, this sophisticated but unpretentious hotel enjoys an airy, tropical elegance, from the open, timber-frame lobby to the bedrooms with their subtle, earthy tones, generous bathrooms and sea-view balconies or terraces. There are two restaurants, a spa and plenty of sports activities, including a dive centre.

Sugar Beach Resort (☎ 453 9090; www.sugarbeach resort.mu; Wolmar; s/d with half board from Rs 10,500/15,500; ✗ 🏠 🖥 🛏) With its mock-plantation mansion look and its wonderfully colonial lawns, Sugar Bay is a well-run resort catering to a huge number of people coming to enjoy the smart settings and great beach. It's a very family-friendly resort (think lots of kids in the pool and live entertainment at dinner) and shares facilities with La Pirogue next door. Stylish and smart.

La Pirogue (☎ 453 8441; www.lapirogue.com; Wolmar; r full board Rs 14,500; ✗ 🏠 🖥 🛏) Next door to Sugar Beach, La Pirogue ('the fishing boat') shares the same management but has a totally different feel. While its neighbour is a plantation mansion, La Pirogue is a fishing village–style settlement, all thatched roofs and laid-back charm. It's a delightful place, with spacious rooms, an excellent range of activities and a beautiful beach.

Hilton (☎ 403 1000; www.mauritius.hilton.com; Wolmar; s/d with half board from Rs 25,500/30,500; ✗ 🏠 🖥 🛏) With water everywhere and quite sublime gardens, the Hilton is unsurprisingly going for an exotic tropical paradise feel here. Frankly, once you're here there'll be no reason to leave, with four excellent restaurants (including the acclaimed Ginger Thai), an enormous wending pool, fabulous beach, vast spa and an evening torch ceremony to accompany sunset. Sadly though, even at this price you still have to pay for wi-fi access and, while certainly comfy, the rooms lack inspiration.

our pick **Taj Exotica Resort & Spa** (☎ 403 1500; www.tajhotels.com; Wolmar; s/d Rs 26,660/43,000; ✗ ✗ ☐ ☐) Easily the most luxurious hotel on Mauritius' east coast, the Taj Exotica has re-defined the top level of accommodation here since it was built in 2004. The accommoda-tion consists entirely of villas – some 65 in three different categories are scattered around the huge grounds. Calm is the overwhelm-ing impression given by the spacious public areas, stunning pool and magnificent, award-winning Jiva Spa. The villas themselves are huge, all equipped with indoor and outdoor showers, private plunge pool and – naturally – a butler.

Eating

While there are a few decent restaurants in Flic en Flac, you need to know where to look. Most are average, no bargain and cater exclusively to tourists. For the very best (and extremely expensive) options, head to some of the better hotel restaurants, such as Ginger Thai at the Hilton or Cilantro at the Taj Exotica, although nonguests should reserve in advance.

BUDGET

Leslie Restaurant (☎ 453 8172; Royal Rd; mains Rs 100-150; ☽ lunch & dinner Tue-Sun) This sweet little Cre-ole place at the north end of town is on the main road; it's friendly, and serves tasty cur-ries and Chinese dishes in decent portions.

Le Papayou (☎ 453 9826; Royal Rd; mains Rs 100-200; ☽ 9am-10pm) Service can come with a smile or a scowl at this tiny place opposite Leslie Restau-rant, but that's all just part of the charm. Lo-cals and tourists both flock here for the cheap prices and eclectic menu. This is also the best place in town to come for breakfast (served from 9am to 11.30am) and good coffee.

Spar supermarket (Royal Rd; ☽ 8am-8pm Mon-Sat, 8am-5pm Sun) This huge supermarket will sort out self-caterers.

MIDRANGE & TOP END

Sunset Garden (☎ 453 8614; Klondike Rd; mains Rs 150-280; ☽ lunch & dinner, Wed-Mon) Don't be put off by the rather garish exterior or the cheesy name. Step into the delightful garden of this newly opened restaurant and you'll be shown to a charming table amid the bushes and trees. Food is of very good quality, encom-passing Thai, Mauritian and Chinese, all in very stylish surroundings. There's cabaret on Saturday.

Restaurant de L'Ouest (☎ 453 8726; Royal Rd; main Rs 160; ☽ lunch & dinner) Right in the thick o things, this is a fine place for a meal. Whil the crowd is almost exclusively foreign and the nightly entertainment (including *séga* on Sundays) is sometimes unwelcome, the Mauritian food is imaginatively prepared and beautifully presented.

Moti Mahal (☎ 435 8411; Villas Caroline; mains Rs 300 ☽ dinner only Tue-Sun) It's such a pity that such excellent cooking is served up in what is very much a hotel restaurant. While we can't fault the delicious northern Indian tandoors (the *murg makhani* is sublime), around you it's business as usual for the Villas Caroline hotel, complete with truly soulless live 'entertainment'. Still for our money, it's the best place in town.

Domaine Anna (☎ 453 9650; Médine; mains Rs 150-300; ☽ lunch & dinner Tue-Sun) You'll need to cab or drive it out here, but the Domaine Anna is one of Flic en Flac's most refined dining expe-riences. The impressive colonial-style build-ing has space for hundreds of diners, but it's not usually too busy, making it a great place for an intimate meal. The speciality on the wide-ranging menu is lobster, and be aware that vegetarians are almost entirely ignored – veggies should call ahead and ask for non-meat options if they plan to come.

Drinking & Entertainment

While you're always welcome as a nonguest to visit a hotel and take in the evening's enter-tainment, there's far more moderately priced fun to be had in the town's bars.

Kenzibar (☎ 453 5259; ☽ 6.30pm-midnight Tue-Sat) Beside Villa Paul & Virginie, this is the best in town. It has flaming torches, live music and African ambience, not to mention a mean *rhum arrangé*.

There's also a nameless bar opposite the Manisa Hotel facing the public beach. It's regularly overflowing by 10pm and knocks out a mean cocktail.

Getting There & Away

There is a bus from Port Louis to Flic en Flac and Wolmar every 20 minutes or so. A taxi from Port Louis to Flic en Flac will cost you Rs 400, and Rs 1000 to the airport.

Getting Around

The big hotels usually offer bicycle and car hire. However, you'll probably find cheaper prices at the switched-on **Flic en Flac Tourist**

gency (☎ 453 9389; www.fftourist.com) in the centre of Flic en Flac. Count on Rs 150 to Rs 200 per day for bikes and upwards of Rs 1200 for the smallest car. The agency also rents out 100cc motorbikes from Rs 500 a day.

Other car-rental outlets include the following:

asy Drive Rent a Car (☎ 453 8557; easyworld@ ntent.mu)

Sixt (☎ 453 8475; sixtcar@intnet.mu)

TAMARIN

pop 3500

Tamarin is pleasantly dead-end. Despite having a great beach and being within a short drive of some interesting sights, it's hard to imagine anywhere less likely to see a development frenzy the likes of its nearby neighbour Flic en Flac. If anything, Tamarin's time in the sun (metaphorically at least) has been and gone: it was here that people flocked when surfing suddenly took off in Mauritius in the 1970s. People still do come here for the surf from May to September, as witnessed by a couple of surfing shops on the main road, but frankly it otherwise feels like a forgotten town. Tamarin's most notable building is the Shree Sathya Saj Semelan Centre, painted an incredible bright pink and orange.

Around Tamarin the surrounding landscape is drier and harsher than elsewhere in Mauritius. Salt production is a major industry in the area and the town is encircled by salt evaporation ponds, which give a rather barren feel to the outskirts.

Sleeping & Eating

There are a couple of budget guesthouses on the road down to the beach from the church although none are really worth recommending. Ask for a room from any of the locals if you specifically want to stay here.

Tamarin Hotel (Map p102; ☎ 483 6927; www.blue -season-hotels.com; s/d with half board from Rs 3900/5500; P ✗ ⌨ ⌂) This wonderful place should be in all film location scouts' address books, as nowhere does retro '70s like the Tamarin Hotel. Despite a total refit in 2002, the management decided to retain the colours the hotel was originally painted with in the early 1970s. It's definitely one of the country's most unique hotels as a result, and the colour scheme (matched inside the rooms as well) surprisingly works. There's a great

pool, the beach is just metres away and the atmosphere is extremely friendly.

Cosa Nostra (Map p102; ☎ 483 6169; Royal Rd; pizzas Rs 280; ✆ lunch & dinner Tue-Sun) A real unexpected gem here is this great pizza restaurant on the main road. It's clearly a smart place, but it has a great garden out the back as well. The pizzas are delicious, although service is very slow. Come here when you aren't in a hurry.

Getting There & Around

Buses headed for Tamarin leave Port Louis roughly every hour and Quatre Bornes every 20 minutes.

A taxi from Port Louis or from Curepipe costs around Rs 600; from the airport it's about Rs 1000.

LA PRENEUSE

A few kilometres south of Tamarin, the quiet village of La Preneuse makes an interesting stop for a quick visit to the Martello Tower, which formed part of the old coastal fortifications and now houses an informative museum. La Preneuse was named after a French ship involved in a naval battle with the English in the area in the late 18th century.

Martello Tower Museum

In the 1830s the British built five Martello towers – copies of the tower at Mortella Point in Corsica (the order of the vowels was obviously not a priority for the British, hence the slight name change) – to protect their young colony. The coastal defences were built as a precaution in case the French navy came to support a feared rebellion: the British were at the time trying to abolish slavery on the island in the face of fierce opposition from local French planters, who believed the lack of cheap labour would destroy the sugar-cane industry.

While the other towers have either disappeared or are in ruins, the one at La Preneuse has been opened as a **museum** (Map p102; ☎ 583 0178; adult/child Rs 50/10; ✆ 9.30am-5pm Tue-Fri, 9.30am-1.30pm Sun & Sun). After a short video presentation, the guide points out the tower's ingenious design. With walls over 3m thick in places and topped by a cannon with a 2km range, it certainly seems impregnable, though in this case it was never put to the test.

Sleeping & Eating

La Preneuse offers a couple of places to stay – one of them excellent – and two interesting

restaurants. Self-caterers can stock up in the
big Spar supermarket on the main road.

Seama Beach Hotel (Map p102; ☎ 483 5506; s/d/tr
incl breakfast Rs 500/800/1200) Reggae plays amid
this sprawling complex a short distance from
the Martello Tower. It's decorated in a fairly
haphazard way, there's only one room with
air-con and rooms are basic with small bathrooms, but it's near the beach and cheap.

ourpick **Les Lataniers Bleus** (Map p102; ☎ 483 6541;
http://leslataniersbleus.com; d incl breakfast from Rs 3500;
P ⊠ 🖳 🖳) Surely one of the most charm-
ing *chambres d'hôte* (family-run B&B) in the
country is this, one of the very first, run by
the formidable Josette Marchal-Vexlard. The
rooms are delightful, whether in the main
block or scattered around the grounds. The
beach is just metres from the main house,
which is beautifully decked out. The stunning
private villa has five bedrooms and a communal kitchen; you can rent one room or
the whole villa. The evening meals (Rs 600;
by reservation only) are highly recommended
and are a great chance to meet fellow travellers and hear about local life from the
impressive hosts.

Le Cabanon Créole (Map p102; ☎ 483 5783; mains
Rs 90; ☯ lunch & dinner) Friendly service and authentic and inexpensive Creole home-cooking make this traditional family-run place a
perennial favourite. It serves a limited range
of daily dishes such as *rougail saucisses* and
chicken curry; specials, like lobster or whole
fresh fish, can be ordered in advance. It's
best to reserve in the evenings as there are
only a handful of tables.

La Bonne Chute (Map p102; ☎ 483 6552; mains Rs
250; ☯ lunch & dinner Mon-Sat) Behind the wall
next to the Caltex petrol station is this attractive garden-style restaurant, which has
recently been refurbished. The food is great
value for the gastronomy on offer: venison
in its own red-wine marinade and roast
boar in spices are typical dishes served in
the large dining area and garden.

Getting There & Away
La Preneuse is on the same bus route as
Tamarin, with services from Port Louis
roughly every hour and Quatre Bornes every
20 minutes. A taxi from Port Louis or the
Central Plateau towns costs in the region of
Rs 600. From the airport count on at least
Rs 1000.

GRANDE RIVIÈRE NOIRE
pop 2200

Two kilometres on from La Preneuse, the
otherwise sleepy community of Grande Rivière Noire is a major centre for big-game
fishing. Just offshore from the mouth of the
estuary, the ocean bottom plunges to 700m
providing the perfect environment for jacks
and other bait fish. These small fry attract big
predators such as tuna, shark and marlin. If
you're after more gentle pursuits, you can also
arrange cruises and dolphin-watching expeditions from here, and one of the two main
entrances to the Black River Gorges National
Park (p87) lies just 5km inland.

Activities
Deep-sea fishing is the main activity here between November and March. A number of
local fishermen offer fully equipped boats.
Many of them congregate at **Le Morne Anglers'
Club** (Map p102; ☎ 483 5801; www.morneanglers.com;
☯ 6.30am-8.30pm), signed off the main road.
You can also arrange trips through **La Carange**
(Map p102; ☎ 729 9497; ☯ 6am-5pm) nearby. Prices
vary between around Rs 6000 and Rs 10,000
for a half-day trip (six hours) and Rs 10,000
to Rs 15,000 for a full nine hours.

Le Morne Anglers' Club also offers boat
charter and catamaran cruises (Rs 1800 per
person) along the coast, for a spot of dolphin
watching combined with snorkelling and a
barbecue lunch.

Eating
There are a couple of decent Chinese restaurants in town, although there's a wider choice
at the touristy Ruisseau Créole just out of
town, where you'll find an Italian restaurant,
a pizzeria, a steak house and a grill house all
serving up high quality but pricey food.

Pavillon de Jade (Map p102; ☎ 483 6630; dishes Rs
70-250; ☯ lunch & dinner; ⊠) You'll find this appealing restaurant, with its bright and breezy
room and views of the mountains, above a
supermarket on the Trois Bras junction just
south of Grande Rivière Noire.

Pavillon de Chine (Map p102; ☎ 483 5787; mains
from Rs 150; ☯ closed Thu) Further north, this
restaurant is more upmarket but opens onto
the highway.

Shopping
Ruisseau Créole (Map p102; ☎ 483 8000; www.ruisseaucre
ole.com; ☯ 9.30am-6.30pm Mon-Sat) This upmarket

shopping centre on the main coastal road is one of the big draws to the area. It boasts four restaurants and a host of other good shopping options. Prices are high, though, and it's aimed almost exclusively at foreigners.

Getting There & Away

The Quatre Bornes to Baie du Cap service covers Grande Rivière Noire, with departures every 20 minutes or so. There are also buses every one to two hours from Port Louis. Taxi fares should be the same as for Tamarin (p107).

LA GAULETTE & AROUND

pop 2000

South of Grande Rivière Noire, the mountains draw ever closer to the coast. There are pine woods and mangroves along the shore, but little in the way of habitation, beyond some extremely poor shanty towns along the road, until you reach the fishing village of La Gaulette 8km or so later. La Gaulette boasts a couple of restaurants and a well-stocked supermarket. The reason most people come to this area, however, is to visit the famous coloured earths of Chamarel, in the hills 9km east of La Gaulette. Chamarel features on almost every tour itinerary, however, you'll find more colours and fewer people at the rival ite near Souillac (p120), although Souillac lacks the beautiful location. From Chamarel, a spectacular mountain road climbs onto the Plaine Champagne in the Black River Gorges National Park, while another, almost as scenic, heads south to Baie du Cap.

Sights & Activities

For some reason the **Chamarel coloured earths** (Map p102; ☎ 483 8298; admission Rs 75; ⏲ 7am-5.30pm), 4km south of the quiet village of Chamarel, have become one of the most famous sights of Mauritius, although they can be quite underwhelming after a long journey. The countryside around Chamarel is beautiful, and so it's well worth an excursion up here, but the coloured earths are more of an interesting curiosity on the side rather than a star attraction. The colours themselves are believed to be the result of uneven cooling of molten rock. In fact, there is a surprising amount of variation, particularly in bright sunlight.

About 3km down the road from the entrance gate to the earths, it's definitely worth stopping off at the viewpoint over the Chamarel

waterfall, which plunges more than 100m in a single drop.

Both sites lie in the grounds of a private estate that once belonged to Charles de Chazal de Chamarel, who entertained Matthew Flinders during Flinders' captivity in Mauritius during the Napoleonic Wars (p121).

To visit the area's other obvious attraction, the nearby Île aux Bénitiers, contact **Ropsen Chawan** (☎ 451 5763; ropsen@intnet.mu), who not only runs a good guesthouse but also offers boat excursions to the island to swim, snorkel and watch the dolphins (Rs 1200 for a half day excursion including a barbeque lunch).

Sleeping

Guesthouse Ropsen Chawan (Map p102; ☎ 451 5763, ropsen@intnet.mu; studio from Rs 700-1800; ☒) The only accommodation in La Gaulette itself is provided by a friendly local taxi driver who has a range of tidy self-catering studios and apartments for up to six people. He also provides evening meals on request (Rs 180 for a main course), organises boat trips and hires out cars (Rs 800 to Rs 1000 per day), mopeds (Rs 500 per day) and bikes (Rs 100 per day).

Lakaz Chamarel (Map p102; ☎ 483 5240; www.lak azchamarel.com; Piton Canot; s/d with half board from Rs 4500/5900; ☐ ☒ ☒) This 'exclusive lodge' in the countryside around Chamarel is a wonderfully conceived collection of seven houses (being extended to 11 at the time of writing) offering a blissful getaway amid gorgeous forests and streams, with a pool and some beautifully decorated rooms. A small spa was also being built at the time of writing.

Eating

La Gaulette Restaurant (☎ 451 5116; La Gaulette; dishes from Rs 100; ⏲ lunch & dinner Tue-Sun; ☒) The pink colour scheme of this Chinese-Creole restaurant just across the road from Pointe Pecheur (following) won't be to everyone's taste, but the food is perfectly acceptable and not expensive.

Pointe Pecheur (☎ 451 5910; La Gaulette; mains Rs 200; ⏲ 10am-10pm; ☒) This fun, busy little haunt is popular with locals and travellers alike. The menu features Chinese and Mauritian fare such as squid in saffron sauce and jugged chicken Mauritius style.

Sirokan Garden (☎ 451 5115; La Gaulette; mains Rs 300; ⏲ lunch & dinner) This charming Creole restaurant on the main road just as you enter

La Gaulette is known locally as the best place in town for lobster. The food is of excellent standard, as is the rustic atmosphere and friendly service.

Chamarel Restaurant (Map p102; ☎ 483 6937; www .chamarel.mu; set menu Rs 665; ⊙ lunch Mon-Sun) Perched on the hillside 1km west of Chamarel, the prime attraction here is the stunning view rather than the pricey food. The views are definitely worth it though, and despite being touristy, the food is good and the service friendly.

Varangue sur Morne (Map p102; ☎ 483 5710; mains from Rs 600; ⊙ 11am-4.30pm) This former hunting lodge is an institution, and it's not too hard to see why. Its stunning location offers great views over the national park towards the ocean and the superb, meaty menu is impressive with typical dishes such as braised wild boar or shrimp flambéed in Île de France Rum. Sadly it's rather expensive and service can be a bit snooty, although it's still a good place to impress a date. Reservations are advised.

Getting There & Around

Buses (every 20 minutes) between Quatre Bornes and Baie du Cap stop in La Gaulette. There are no direct buses from Port Louis. Instead you have to go via Quatre Bornes, or take the bus from Port Louis to Grande Rivière Noire and change.

There are infrequent buses from Quatre Bornes to Chamarel, which drop you by the entrance to the estate. Frankly it's a hassle to do this excursion by bus and you'll save a lot of time and effort doing it by taxi or taking an organised excursion here.

A taxi from Port Louis to La Gaulette will cost around Rs 600; from the airport, Rs 900. Expect to pay Rs 600 or so for the return fare from La Gaulette to Chamarel.

You can rent cars (from Rs 900 per day), bicycles (Rs 100 per day) and 50cc motor-bikes (Rs 500) from Ropsen Chawan in La Gaulette (p109).

LE MORNE PENINSULA

Visible from much of southern Mauritius, Le Morne Brabant (556m) is the stunning, vast rock from which this beautiful peninsula takes its name. The peninsula itself has some of the country's best beaches along its 4km shores and is home to a number of upmarket hotels. Almost totally uninhabited by locals, the peninsula nevertheless has a particular resonance in Mauritian culture – it was apparently to here that a group of escaped slaves fled in the early 19th century, hiding out on top of the mountain to remain free. The story has it that the slaves, ignorant of the fact that slavery had been abolished subsequent to their escape, panicked when they saw a troop of soldiers making their way up the cliffs one day. Believing they were to be recaptured, the slaves flung themselves from the cliff tops to their deaths in huge numbers, which explains the origin of the name Le Morne (Mournful One). Although there are no historical records to substantiate the story, it's an important one for Mauritians as a reminder of the island's brutal history.

Sleeping & Eating

Indian Resort (Map p102; ☎ 401 4200; resa.indian@ apavou-hotels.com; s/d with half board from Rs 10,500/15,000; Ⓟ ⊠ ⊠ 🖳 ⊠) This vast place at the remot-est end of the peninsula is located on a gor-geous stretch of beach and features some lovely gardens and some great antiques scattered around. If anything it suffers from being too large – conferences are common - but for that it has an incredible array of activi-ties on offer, from kitesurfing to four pools, a kids club and huge spa.

Les Pavillons (Map p102; ☎ 401 4000; pavillons@naiade .intnet.mu; s/d with half board from Rs 10,600/15,700; Ⓟ ⊠ 🖳 ⊠) In the midst of the big five-star hotels is this small and friendly member of the Naïade group. The rooms are in attrac-tive plantation-style pavilions and the whole place has a nicely upbeat atmosphere. There are three restaurants, clubs for children and teenagers, and decent sports facilities. Not surprisingly, you'll need to book well ahead.

Paradis (Map p102; ☎ 401 5050; www.paradis-hote .com; s/d with half board from Rs 18,200/26,000; ⊠ ⊠ Ⓟ 🖳 ⊠) The Paradis is a mecca for sport enthusiasts. In addition to all the usual water sports, there's a championship golf course, six floodlit tennis courts and a hi-tech gym, plus kids are equally well looked after. When it all gets too much, you can collapse in the health spa for a sports massage or even a special 'after-golf' massage. The rooms are suitably luxurious and the views arguably the best on the peninsula.

Dinarobin (Map p102; ☎ 401 4900; www.dinarob in-hotel.com; s/d with half board from Rs 21,600/30,800; Ⓟ ⊠ ⊠ 🖳 ⊠) Infused with the smell of vanilla plants, this stunning place remains he best on the peninsula, enjoying a spectacular location at the foot of the mountain. ts sublime public areas incorporate a carp-tuffed water world of classy features, while he rooms are superb and elegant. Golfers ¬ave access to three championship courses ¬earby. Guests also have access to the facilities at the Paradis next door.

Getting There & Away

Buses en route between Quatre Bornes ¬nd Baie du Cap stop on the main road ¬y the junction for Le Morne. These buses ¬un roughly every hour. A taxi from Port ¬ouis to the Le Morne hotels will cost in ¬he region of Rs 1000 and from the airport ¬s 1200.

SOUTH MAURITIUS

A highlight of any visit to Mauritius will be ¬aking in the relatively undeveloped south ¬f the island, which includes some of the ¬ountry's most wonderful scenery and wild-¬st landscapes. While the area around Blue ¬ay has been a long-established favourite ¬ith tourists for its great beaches and crys-¬al-clear waters, the majority of the south ¬oast has no beach, thankfully limiting ¬otel construction for the most part. One ¬ig recent development was the building ¬f three huge luxury hotels on the former ¬ugar estate of Bel Ombre. This was fol-¬owed in 2006 by the opening of another ¬ig luxury hotel in the nearby hamlet of St ¬elix, all of which will of course contribute ¬o the area's economy, but, many fear, will ¬lso mean Mauritius' most unspoiled corner ¬ill gradually become more and more like ¬he rest of the island. For now though, the ¬rea is the most 'Mauritian' in the country ¬nd the drive along the coastal road from ¬ouillac to Le Morne really shouldn't be ¬issed. Other highlights include the typi-¬ally sleepy town of Mahébourg, the won-¬erful nature reserve Île aux Aigrettes and ¬mposing Lion Mountain, which dominates ¬he region.

Getting There & Around

¬ahébourg is the main transport hub in this ¬egion, with buses departing from here for ¬estinations along both the east and south ¬oasts. Mahébourg is also the best place to arrange car hire and about the only one offering bicycles and motorbikes for rent.

Towns along the south coast have slightly better bus connections than those in the east. Useful services include those from Souillac to Curepipe and Port Louis, and from Baie du Cap up the west coast to Quatre Bornes.

MAHÉBOURG

pop 16,000

There's something relentlessly charming about Mahébourg, with its sleepy feel, a mix of old and new and few quirky sights. Budget travellers have a good choice of accommodation here, and it makes a good base for any traveller, with beaches just a short distance out of the town and plenty to see and do in the surrounding area.

Founded in 1805, Mahébourg (pronounced my-bor) was named after the famous French governor Mahé de Labourdonnais. It started life as a busy port, but these days it's something of a backwater, with a small fishing fleet and a relaxed and friendly atmosphere. Lion Mountain stands guard to the north while out to sea a smattering of islands mark the far side of the lagoon, which changes from one intense colour to another at great speed.

Mahébourg's most worthwhile site is its interesting history museum. The church also merits a quick look in passing and, if time allows, it's worth venturing just north of town to visit a delightful old biscuit factory. There are no beaches in the town itself, but Blue Bay is within easy reach as well as Pointe d'Esny, from where boats leave for Île aux Aigrettes.

Orientation

There's a decidedly French air to Mahébourg's grid of tree-lined streets, which spread north and east from the butter-coloured Catholic church. The main commercial area is found to the northeast, focused on the market and nearby bus station. Hotels and guesthouses are scattered among the quiet residential streets lying between Royal Rd and the seafront.

Information

Cybersurf (☎ 631 4247; Rue de Labourdonnais; ☾ 9am-8.30pm Mon-Sat, 9am-noon Sun)
HSBC (☎ 631 9633; Royal Rd)
Man Ramdhayan (☎ 631 5638) Offers minibus tours of the island; prices start at Rs 400 per person. Book by

MAURITIUS

SOUTH MAURITIUS

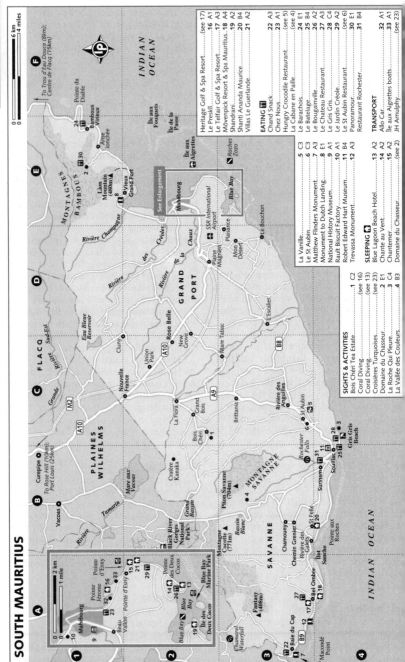

0   6 km
0   4 miles

To Trou d'Eau Douce (8km);
Centre de Flacq (15km)

INDIAN
OCEAN

SIGHTS & ACTIVITIES
Bois Chéri Tea Estate...............................1 C2
Coral Diving..(see 16)
Coral Diving..(see 13)
Croisières Turquoises...........................(see 23)
Domaine du Chasseur...........................2 E1
La Roche Qui Pleure............................3 C4
La Vallée des Couleurs.........................4 B3

SLEEPING
Blue Lagoon Beach Hotel....................13 A2
Chante au Vent....................................14 A2
Chantemer...15 A2
Domaine du Chasseur......................(see 2)

La Vanille..5 C3
Le St Aubin..6 C3
Matthew Flinders Monument................7 A3
Monument to Dutch Landing................8 E1
National History Museum......................9 A1
Rault Biscuit Factory...........................10 A1
Robert Edward Hart Museum.............11 B4
Trevassa Monument.............................12 A3

Heritage Golf & Spa Resort............(see 17)
Le Preskîl..16 A1
Le Telfair Golf & Spa Resort...............17 A3
Mövenpick Resort & Spa Mauritius...18 A4
Shandrani..19 A2
Shanti Ananda Maurice........................20 B4
Villas Le Guerlande.............................21 A2

EATING
Chand Snack.......................................22 A3
Chez Nous...23 A1
Hungry Crocodile Restaurant...........(see 5)
La Cabane en Paille...........................(see 4)
Le Barachois......................................24 E1
Le Batelage..25 B4
Le Bougainville...................................26 A2
Le Chateau Restaurant.......................27 A3
Le Gris Gris..28 C4
Le Jardin Créole................................29 A2
Le St Aubin Restaurant.....................(see 6)
Panoramour..30 E1
Restaurant Rochester.........................31 B4

TRANSPORT
Allo Car...32 A1
Île aux Aigrettes boats........................33 A1
JH Amulphy.......................................(see 23)

hone (there's no office) and he'll come and pick you up
t your hotel.

Iauritius Commercial Bank (MCB; ☎ 631 2879; Rue
es Délices)

'ost office (⊙ 8.15am-4pm Mon-Fri, 8.15am-11.45pm
at) The last 45 minutes before closing are for stamp sales
nly.

tarnet Café (☎ 631 3454; London Way Commercial Centre;
⊙ 10am-7pm Mon-Tue & Thu-Sat, 9.30am-1.30pm Wed &
un)

iights

'ou can easily cover Mahébourg's smatter-
ng of sights in a day, leaving plenty of time
o wander the back streets and take a stroll
along the seafront. Everything can be tackled
on foot, though you might want to hire a bike
o get out to the biscuit factory.

NATIONAL HISTORY MUSEUM

The colonial mansion housing this **museum**
Map p112; ☎ 631 9329; Royal Rd; admission free; ⊙ 9am-
pm daily, closed Tue), just south of the Mahé-
ourg centre, used to belong to the Robillard
amily and played an important part in the
sland's history.

It was here in 1810 that the injured com-
nanders of the French and English fleets were
aken for treatment after the Battle of Vieux
Grand Port, the only naval battle in which the
French got the upper hand over their British
oes. The story of the victory is retold in the
nuseum, along with salvaged items – canons, grapeshot and the all-important wine
ottles – from the British frigate *Magicienne,*
vhich sank in the battle.

The museum contains some fascinating
rtefacts, including early maps of the island
nd renderings of some of the early fauna of
Mauritius that was quickly destroyed by the
Dutch – including, of course, the ubiquitous
lodo. One real curio is a picture of Dutch gen-
lemen riding in pairs on the back of a giant
ortoise, the local variety of which quickly
vent the way of the dodo.

Also on display are the bell and part of the
argo of Spanish coins from the wreck of the
t Géran. The sinking of the ship in 1744, off
he northeast coast of Mauritius, inspired the
amous love story *Paul et Virginie* by Bernar-
lin de St-Pierre (p83).

Other exhibits include early Dutch and
'ortuguese maps of Mauritius; china and
eautiful seafaring instruments from assorted
vrecks; a pistol supposedly belonging to the

legendary corsair Robert Surcouf; the furniture of Mahé de Labourdonnais; and portraits
of these and other figures pivotal in the history
of Mauritius. Don't miss the Mauritian train
carriage in the back yard either.

NOTRE DAME DES ANGES

The butter-coloured tower of Notre Dame
des Anges church provides a focal point in
Mahébourg. The original church was built in
1849, but it has been restored several times
over the years, most recently in 1938. Take a
quick peek inside at the baronial roof timbers.
Local people visit throughout the day to make
offerings to Père Laval (p66), whose statue
stands to your right immediately inside the
door. It's worth a visit just for the priceless
'beware of children' sign outside.

RAULT BISCUIT FACTORY

In 1870 the Rault family started producing manioc biscuits at their little **biscuit
factory** (Map p112; ☎ 631 9559; adult/child Rs 100/75;
⊙ 9am-3pm Mon-Fri) on the northern outskirts
of Mahébourg. It has changed hardly a jot
since. The crispy, square cookies are made
almost entirely by hand, using a secret recipe
passed down the generations, and baked on
hotplates over stoves fuelled with dried sugar
cane leaves. The short guided tour ends
with a chance to sample the end result –
with a nice cup of tea of course. The factory is on the other side of the Cavendish
Bridge; when you cross the bridge take the
left of the three roads, the first right and
then the first left.

Sleeping

Mahébourg has a small number of guesthouses
catering to independent travellers.

Nice Place Guesthouse (☎ 631 1208; niceplace59@
hotmail.com; Rue de Labourdonnais; s/d from Rs 500/600,
studio Rs 700) This place lives up to its name,
and is the best budget option in town. Run
by a lovely Indian couple, it has slightly
faded rooms (with shared showers, toilets
and basic kitchen facilities) and new self-
catering studios and a fantastic roof terrace
perfect for beers at sundown.

Hotel les Aigrettes (☎ 631 9094; saidadhoomun@
hotmail.com; cnr Rue du Chaland & Rue des Hollandais; s/d
600/900, apt Rs 1400; 🖫) Newly refurbished, this
well-located 19-room hotel is decent value
for money. There's some rather questionable
taste in some of the rooms, but they're all

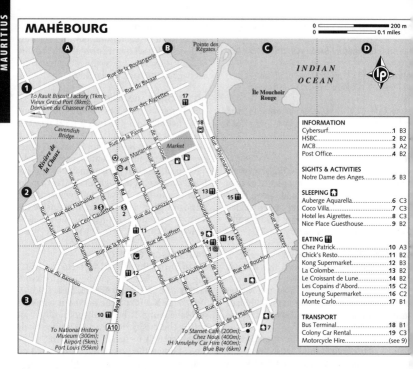

MAHÉBOURG

```
0                    200 m
0                    0.1 miles
```

INDIAN OCEAN

Île Mouchoir Rouge

Pointe des Régates

To Rault Biscuit Factory (1km);
Vieux Grand Port (8km);
Domaine du Chasseur (10km)

Cavendish Bridge

Rivière de la Chaux

Market

To National History Museum (300m); Airport (5km); Port Louis (55km)

To Starnet Café (200m); Chez Nous (400m); JH Arnulphy Car Hire (400m); Blue Bay (6km)

INFORMATION
Cybersurf..................................1 B3
HSBC..2 B2
MCB...3 A2
Post Office................................4 B2

SIGHTS & ACTIVITIES
Notre Dame des Anges.............5 B3

SLEEPING
Auberge Aquarella.....................6 C3
Coco Villa.................................7 C3
Hotel les Aigrettes.....................8 C3
Nice Place Guesthouse...............9 B2

EATING
Chez Patrick.............................10 A3
Chick's Resto............................11 B2
Kong Supermarket....................12 B3
La Colombe.............................13 B2
Le Croissant de Lune...............14 B2
Les Copains d'Abord................15 C2
Loyeung Supermarket...............16 C2
Monte Carlo.............................17 B1

TRANSPORT
Bus Terminal............................18 B2
Colony Car Rental....................19 C3
Motorcycle Hire....................(see 9)

clean and well maintained. There's a decent pool and Jacuzzi, and car and bike hire are also available.

Coco Villa (☎ 631 2346; http://mahecocovilla.net; Rue Shivananda; s/d from Rs 1000/1200;) Next door to Auberge Aquarella, Coco Villa has basic but immaculate rooms, many with sea views and balconies, which make it better value despite not being quite as charming as its neighbour.

Auberge Aquarella (☎ 631 2767; aquarellamu@email .com; 6 Rue Shivananda; s/d/ste incl breakfast from Rs 1380/1610/2500) This excellent hotel is run by a charming couple that take their guests' happiness very seriously. The rooms and bungalows are all stylishly decked out, although you should request one overlooking the sea for the best views. The breakfast is good and evening meals can be provided as well if you request them.

Eating & Drinking

Despite its size, Mahébourg is not a culinary treat and its nightlife is virtually non-existent. The places below are the better options that exist.

BUDGET

Chick's Resto (Royal Rd; pizza Rs 75; 9am-11pm) O it's not the Café de Flore, but Chick's wit its outdoor tables is about the only place i town to kick back with a cold beer and shoo the breeze with the locals. Pizza and chicke is also available.

Le Croissant de Lune (☎ 716 4080; Rue de Labou donnais; sandwiches & pizza from Rs 100; 7.30am-7p Mon-Sat, 7.30am-1pm Sun;) This charming Ger man-run café is a great place for breakfas or a light lunch. It serves up delicious pas tries cooked on the premises, pizza and ver good sandwiches.

Monte Carlo (☎ 631 7449; Rue de la Passe; mains 120; lunch & dinner Fri-Wed;) This rather sorr place has seen better times and is in a fairl uninspiring location facing the bus statior but the food served up is perfectly good. serves reliable Creole, Chinese and mor pricey French cuisine.

MIDRANGE & TOP END

La Colombe (☎ 631 8594; 5 Rue des Hollandais; mains 200; lunch & dinner) Disco lights, kitsch déco and friendly staff await you at Mahébourg iveliest venue, on a side street set back from he promenade. House specials include venion and wild boar with honey. Things liven p a bit on Saturday, which is occasionally *éga* night.

Chez Nous (Map p112; ☎ 631 8906; Barachois; mains Rs 50; ⏰ lunch & dinner, closed Wed & Sat lunch; ✖) On windy bay between Mahébourg and Blue Bay, Chez Nous offers great views across the agoon from its tables (all indoors due to the vind) and a dodgy selection of Athena posters n the wall (check out those adorable three-year-olds getting married…) The mainly eafood menu is good, with smoked marlin he speciality.

Chez Patrick (☎ 631 9298; Royal Rd; mains Rs 275; ⏰ lunch & dinner; ✖) Patrick's is hugely popular vith tourists for its traditional atmosphere nd authentic Creole cooking. Portions are n the small side, however, and when it's busy ervice can be slow. It's advisable to reserve n the evening.

Les Copains d'Abord (☎ 631 9728; Rue Shivananda; mains Rs 300; ⏰ 9am-11pm; ✖) With its good location on the seafront promenade and smart lécor, Les Copains d'Abord is the best restauant in town, owned by the former proprietor f the smart Domaine du Chasseur. The cuiine is mixed Mediterranean and Mauritian vith particularly good seafood.

Getting There & Away
Mahébourg is an important transport hub. There are express buses every half hour to and from Port Louis and at least every 15 minutes from Curepipe. Most but not all these uses stop at the airport en route; check before oarding. The shuttle to Blue Bay runs every 0 minutes.

Buses running north from Mahébourg go o Centre de Flacq via Vieux Grand Port every 0 minutes or so. Heading south, there are ess frequent services to Souillac via Rivière les Anguilles.

A taxi for the 15-minute hop from SSR nternational airport to Mahébourg costs round Rs 350. From Port Louis expect to ay Rs 600.

Getting Around
'or car hire, **Colony Car Rental** (☎ 631 7062; Rue de la olonie) not only offers some of the lowest rates n the island, but the owner is exceptionally elpful. He also does competitively priced airort pick-ups. Otherwise, most guesthouses

can help, or try **JH Arnulphy** (Map p112; ☎ 631 9806; ste.arnulphy@intnet.mu) beside Chez Nous restaurant. Arnulphy can also help with bicycle hire; rates start at Rs 75 per day. Blue Bay makes a leisurely excursion by bicycle.

Nice Place Guesthouse hires out 100cc motorcycles for Rs 500 a day.

AROUND MAHÉBOURG
While Mahébourg itself is short of sand, the beaches begin only a couple of kilometres south at Pointe d'Esny and continue down the coast for 4km to the hugely picturesque Blue Bay, aptly named for its brilliant-blue lagoon. In 1997 the Blue Bay Marine Park was established to protect the relatively unspoilt coral reef. Just offshore, rare endemic animal and plant species are being reintroduced to the Île aux Aigrettes Nature Reserve.

Pointe d'Esny & Blue Bay
The coast from Pointe d'Esny to Blue Bay is lined with holiday villas and expensive houses and is one of Mauritius' most exclusive residential areas. At weekends in particular Blue Bay beach is crowded with picnickers, but during the week it can be blissfully quiet. Gently sloping and protected, the beach is excellent for children. There are a couple of good restaurants and some fine places to stay in the area, and visitors can indulge in the usual array of water sports.

ACTIVITIES
Blue Bay is the main centre for water-based activities in southern Mauritius. Options vary from snorkelling and diving to cruising around the offshore islands. There are a huge number of sea urchins in the sea here – so always be careful where you put your feet (and preferably wear some form of protective shoe).

The main dive operator is **Coral Diving** (Map p112; ☎ Blue Lagoon 631 9501, Le Preskil 604 1000; www .coraldiving.com; ⏰ 9am-5pm Mon-Sat, 9am-1pm Sun) with centres at both the Blue Lagoon Beach Hotel in Blue Bay, and Le Preskil at Pointe d'Esny.

Croisières Turquoises (Map p112; ☎ 631 8347; croistur@intnet.mu; ⏰ 8am-4.30pm Mon-Fri, 8am-noon Sat), near Chez Nous restaurant on the southern outskirts of Mahébourg, specialises in luxury catamaran cruises. Boats sail up to Île aux Cerfs (Rs 2000 per person) several days a week from Pointe Jérome near Le Preskil hotel.

SLEEPING

Blue Bay is a popular place to stay, particularly with families. One slight disadvantage is the rumble of early-morning departures from the nearby airport; there aren't that many, but they can be noisy. Many of the best options here are private lets and *chambres d'hôte*.

our pick Chante au Vent (Map p112; ☎ 631 9614; www.chanteauvent.com; r from Rs 1200, studio from Rs 1700; P) This guesthouse is excellent value for money and you'll usually need to book in advance to stay here. The rooms in the main house are right on the beach, while the spacious apartments are all on the other side of the road. The breakfast here is great, served on the veranda overlooking the sea.

Chantemer (Map p112; ☎ 631 3861; www.chantemer.mu; d incl breakfast from Rs 2200) With only five rooms, you'll need to book well ahead for this attractive and well-run private guesthouse with a lovely garden leading down to the beach. It's all very tastefully decorated with family heirlooms and artworks and the owner goes out of her way to be helpful.

Villas Le Guerlande (Map p112; ☎ 631 9882; www.leguerlande.com; d incl breakfast Rs 3450, s/d apt from Rs 2085/4170;) This is a complex of bright and breezy self-catering one-bedroom studios and bungalow-apartments for up to four people. The cheaper, gardenside bungalows are across a quiet road from the beach.

Blue Lagoon Beach Hotel (Map p112; ☎ 631 9529; www.bluelagoonbeachhotel.com; s/d incl breakfast from Rs 3240/5000; P) This hotel is at the very heart of Blue Bay next to the public beach and enjoys a good range of facilities, its own beach and an excellent diving school. The rooms are fairly basic but perfectly fine.

Le Preskîl (Map p112; ☎ 603 4343; www.lepreskil.com; s/d with half board from Rs 7800/10,500;) Set on its own tiny promontory facing the Île aux Aigrettes across the lagoon, this is Pointe d'Esny's most charming hotel, oozing Creole style with its bright but tasteful colours. There's a gorgeous white beach from which there are great views towards the mountains, and the rooms – while packed rather tightly together – all have charm, housed as they are in brightly painted two-storey blocks.

Shandrani (Map p112; ☎ 603 4343; www.shandrani-hotel.com; s/d with half board from Rs 11,700/16,700;) On the south side of Blue Bay, this relaxed and family-friendly five-star stands in lush gardens on its own private peninsula. It has no fewer than three beaches

and all the facilities you would expect including four restaurants, a golf course, tennis courts, a dive centre and more. The only slight hiccup is the location under the flight path.

EATING

Le Bougainville (Map p112; ☎ 631 8199; mains Rs 170-250, pizzas Rs 120-200; 10am-10pm) In a shady spot behind Blue Bay beach, Le Bougainville attracts a constant stream of customers in search of refreshment. The menu ranges from salads and pizzas to dishes such as chicken with Rodrigues lemon. It's a friendly, relaxed place where locals and foreigners mix and where there's always a good atmosphere.

Le Jardin Créole (Map p112; ☎ 631 5801; mains Rs 250; 10am-10pm;) The plant-filled courtyard of this sophisticated little restaurant at Pointe d'Esny is just the place for a romantic candlelit dinner. The pizzas are excellent, though it's a shame to miss out on luscious Creole mains such as seafood and palm-heart pancake, or grilled tuna with honey, lime and sesame. Reservations are recommended – request a sought-after seat in the garden.

GETTING THERE & AROUND

Buses to and from Mahébourg run every 30 minutes. A taxi there will cost Rs 100.

Car rental is available from **Allo Car** (Map p112; ☎ 631 1810; allocarltd@intnet.mu). The latter also rents bicycles for Rs 100 per day and 50cc motorbikes for Rs 600.

Île aux Aigrettes

This popular ecotourism destination is an island nature reserve roughly 1km off the coast. It preserves very rare remnants of the coastal forests of Mauritius and provides a sanctuary for animal and plant species unique to these islands.

Over most of the island, introduced invasive plants have now been replaced with native species. Rats, shrews and other imported animals, which cause damage to rare plant species and threaten indigenous animal species, are slowly being eradicated. At the same time native species known to have existed on the island in the past – including pink pigeons, giant Aldabra tortoises and Telfair's skinks (a clawed lizard) – are being reintroduced. This is the only place in the world where you are almost certain to see pink pigeons in the wild; the population now numbers over 90 birds.

All this has been achieved by the **Mauritian Wildlife Foundation** (MWF; ☎ 631 2396; www.ile-aux-aigrettes.com; adult/child Rs 800/400), which now manages the reserve and conducts tours of the island; revenues are ploughed back into its conservation work. There are between two and five departures daily from Pointe Jérome, near Le Preskil hotel (Map p112). Bookings should be made a couple of days in advance either by phoning MWF or through a tour agent. The 90-minute tour of the island involves a good deal of walking; wear comfortable shoes and bring a hat, sunscreen, water and insect repellent.

VIEUX GRAND PORT TO BAMBOUS VIRIEUX

North of Mahébourg, the main road hugs the coast as it winds around the base of Lion Mountain and the Montagnes Bambous range. This area was the first settled by the Dutch early in the 17th century, and was one of the first parts of the country to lose its native ebony forest to the burgeoning sugar cane industry. Nevertheless, dense forest still cloaks the mountains. Hunting is a popular activity here, but the vast hunting estates also provide a valuable habitat for many native animal and plant species. One such estate is open to the public and nearby you can visit another where essential oils are distilled using traditional methods. Further north again, nature trails meander through an area of mangrove forest.

There are a few restaurants in the area, but the choice of places to stay is limited. With your own transport, the places described below can easily be covered on a day's outing from Mahébourg or Blue Bay, or from Trou d'Eau Douce to the north. Travelling by bus will involve a fair bit of walking.

Vieux Grand Port

pop 2900

This is the 'cradle of Mauritian history', where the first human inhabitants of the island landed on 9 September 1598 under the command of Wybrandt Van Warwyck. The Dutch later built a fort 3km further north again in what is now the town of Vieux Grand Port, although a monument marks the actual landing point as well (Map p112). It was the local headquarters of the Dutch East India Company until 1710, when the Dutch abandoned the island. The site was then taken over by the French.

The battered ruins of Fort Frederik Hendrik stand in a park near the church at the northern end of Vieux Grand Port and include ruins of an old Dutch church, a bakery, a prison, a forge, a powder magazine and a dispensary. A few clay pipes, wine bottles and other items left behind by the Dutch and French occupants are now on display in the **Frederik Hendrik Museum** (☎ 634 4319; admission free; ⏰ 9am-4pm Mon-Sat, 9am-noon Sun) beside the entrance gate. The museum also outlines the history of the Dutch in Mauritius. Vieux Grand Port is perhaps more famous as the site of the only French naval victory to be inscribed on the Arc de Triomphe in Paris. Relics of the 1810 battle with the English are on display at the National History Museum in Mahébourg.

Lion Mountain

Overlooking Vieux Grand Port is Lion Mountain (480m), immediately recognisable from its sphinx-like profile. The mountain offers a splendid half-day hike with stunning views over the coast. It's a very challenging but rewarding walk that climbs up the lion's 'back' to finish at an impressive viewpoint on the 'head'.

The trail begins beside the police station at the north end of Vieux Grand Port. From there an easy-to-find 4WD track heads inland through the sugar cane; turn right at the first junction and follow the trail up towards the ridge. A set of concrete steps begins on the right just after you reach the start of the forested area. The steps lead to a bunker, from where a footpath climbs through the forest to the top of the lion's back. Once here you can detour to the right for a view out over the coast before heading inland to the peak itself.

The main trail is very obvious and runs straight along the ridge and up over a rocky area to the peak. There are a few hairy scrambles over the rocks before you reach the flat area on the lion's head. From here you can see right across the interior of the island. Return the same way you came up.

Allow around three to four hours for the return trip.

Domaine du Chasseur

One of Mauritius' most famous private estates, **Domaine du Chasseur** (Map p112; Estate of the

Hunter; ☎ 634 5011; domaineduchasseur.mu) is primarily a hunting reserve for wild boar and deer and attracts hunters from around the world. The 950 hectares of forested mountain terrain also act as a reserve for many endemic bird species, including the Mauritius kestrel – one of the world's rarest birds of prey.

If there are no hunters around, visitors can walk up to the restaurant viewpoint or hop on a jeep (Rs 290) for the 1km ride; if you are eating, the entry fees are deducted from your bill. Better still is the guided two-hour forest walk (Rs 290) to a lookout 800m above sea level.

The estate is equally famed for its mountain-top restaurant, **Panoramour** (mains Rs 500, 3-course menu Rs 920; ☺ 8.30am-4.30pm, dinner by reservation), which is perched 500m up on top of a hill with wonderful views to the coast. The helipad that adjoins the restaurant gives you an idea of the kind of people who drop by for lunch – and the food is rightly delicious and probably even worth the prices given the extraordinary views. The restaurant itself is a rambling tree-house affair that looks like the Bambi family's mausoleum, stuffed as it is with hunting trophies from over the years. All the meat is produced on the estate's farm or shot in the park – wild boar kebabs, venison steaks and duck confit all feature on the menu.

Accommodation is provided near the restaurant in thatched **bungalows** (d inc breakfast Rs 4025). However, the feel is resolutely rustic and there are lots of bugs. If you like creature comforts you'll be better off in a hotel on the coast.

Bambous Virieux

This small settlement is the site of a pioneering project to restore the mangroves that were destroyed by the British followin the malaria epidemic of 1866 (see the boxe text, below).

A short nature trail has been create through the mangroves at **Le Barachois** (Ma p112; ☎ 634 5643; r incl breakfast Rs 2600; ☺ 10am 4pm, dinner by reservation), a hotel where you ca stay in simple, rustic rooms with terrace overlooking the water and eat at the excel lent seafood restaurant (mains Rs 200 to R 400).

Getting There & Around

Buses between Mahébourg and Centre d Flacq ply the coast road, passing throug Vieux Grand Port, Anse Jonchée and Bam bous Virieux. There are departures every 2 minutes or so.

A taxi from Mahébourg will cost aroun Rs 1000 for a day trip taking in the Domain du Chasseur.

MAHÉBOURG TO BAIE DU CAP

The south coast of Mauritius, from Mahé bourg west to Baie du Cap, contains som of the country's wildest and most attrac tive scenery. Here you'll find basalt cliff and sheltered sandy coves, waterfalls an traditional fishing villages where fish erfolk sell their catch at roadside stalls Behind the coast, sugar-cane fields an forests clothe the hillside in a patchwork c intense greens.

The region's prime tourist attractions a fascinating crocodile park and a tea plant ation – are concentrated around Rivière de Anguilles and Souillac. Further west there's a area of 'coloured earths' to visit, but in gen eral the scenery is the star attraction. Whil there are a number of beaches, few are suit

---

REPLANTING THE MANGROVES

Following the 1866 malaria epidemic, in which nearly 3700 people died, the British colonial administration correctly identified the mangrove swamps around the coast of Mauritius as the main breeding ground for malaria-carrying mosquitoes. As part of a campaign of eradication, huge tracts of mangrove were uprooted or burned and swamps were filled in with volcanic boulders. Eucalyptus trees were even brought in from Australia to dry up areas of marshy ground.

As an antimalarial strategy, the programme was very successful. It was only later that scientists discovered the important role that mangrove swamps play in the breeding cycles of many of the tropical fish that the islanders depend on for food.

Today the Mauritian government is taking steps to preserve the remaining swamps and to re-establish mangroves, for example, at Bambous Virieux on the southeast coast of Mauritius. Of course, what is good news for tropical fish will also be good news for mosquitoes!

ble for swimming; in most cases the lagoon s too shallow or the current too strong.

This area is also the least developed or tourism, although the international hains have recently moved it with a large development of four properties around Bel Ombre.

Rivière des Anguilles & Around
op 10,000

The town of Rivière des Anguilles, 26km west of Mahébourg, holds no particular interest in ts own right, but there are a number of sights n the countryside around.

LA VANILLE
This fantastic **zoo** (Map p112; ☎ 626 2503; www lavanille-reserve.com; adult/child Mon-Fri Rs 195/75, Sat & Sun Rs 150/60; ☽ 9.30am-5pm), which is part nature reserve and part crocodile farm, makes for a fantastic day out and kids will ove it. It's clearly signed 2km south of Rivère des Anguilles. The park has a success-ul breeding programme for giant Aldabra ortoises, as well as a huge crocodile farm nd a great range of other animals. The enormous Nile crocodiles are particularly impressive (11.30am is feeding time), as vell as the creepy-crawlies on display in he insectarium.

Allow at least an hour for the visit. Should you feel peckish, or curious, try he **Hungry Crocodile Restaurant** (crocodile meat urry Rs 495, fritters Rs 280). It also does more conventional dishes.

BOIS CHÉRI TEA ESTATE
This 250-hectare **tea estate** (Map p112; ☎ 617 109; lesaintaubin@intnet.mu; adult/child Rs 115/230; ☽ 8.30am-3.30pm Mon-Fri, 8.30am-noon Sat) is lo-cated about 12km north of Rivière des Anguilles. Visitors are taken on an hour-long tour of the tea-processing plant, be-fore visiting a rather dusty museum to learn about the history of tea. More appealing is the tea tasting that takes place in the com-pany lodge, in the midst of the plantation with panoramic views of the coast. The es-tate produces seven different sorts of black tea, including the delicious vanilla tea for which it is rightly famous and a coconut-flavoured brew called Dodo tea. It's best to visit in the morning to be sure to see the employees working as things slow down after midday.

LE ST AUBIN
The Bois Chéri tea company also owns **Le St Aubin** (Map p112; ☎ 626 1513; lesaintaubin@intnet.mu; adult/child Rs 180/100; ☽ 8.30am-4pm Mon-Sat), an ele-gant plantation house that dates back to 1819, in the village of St Aubin, 2km west of Rivière des Anguilles. The estate no longer produces sugar, but in the gardens of the house there is a traditional rum distillery and a nursery growing anthurium flowers and vanilla; the guide explains all about the fascinating history of vanilla production.

The best vanilla pods are exported, while the remainder are used in the **restaurant** (ad-mission incl set menu Rs 805; ☽ lunch Mon-Sat) of Le St Aubin, along with palm heart, pineapple, mango, chilli and other produce from the gardens. The traditionally furnished house makes a splendid setting for a meal featuring typical Mauritian dishes, including classics such as palm-heart salad or vanilla chicken. Reservations are recommended.

Souillac & Around
pop 4500

Continuing west along the coast, the next major settlement you come to is Souillac, 7km from Rivière des Anguilles. Again, the town is of little interest, but the coast here is impres-sively rugged and there are a few interesting places dotted around. Souillac is named after the Vicomte de Souillac, the island's French governor from 1779 to 1787.

SIGHTS
Rochester Falls
These are by no means the country's most spectacular falls, but are worth a detour if you're in the area. There are makeshift signs from Souillac that take you on a rather circui-tous but reliable route to the falls (although there are hawkers here and people who want a tip for telling you where to park your car). The falls are a five-minute walk from the hawkers, a beautiful opening in the sugar-cane fields and a dramatic, fast-flowing sight.

Robert Edward Hart Museum
Robert Edward Hart (1891–1954) was a re-nowned Mauritian poet, apparently appre-ciated by the French and the English alike, although we've yet to meet anyone who's heard of him. His rather uninteresting house, Le Nef, is an attractive coral-stone cottage with great views at the end of a one-way

system signed left off the main road as you approach from Rivière des Anguilles, between the bus depot and bus station.

The cottage was opened to the public as a **museum** (Map p112; ☎ 625 6101; admission free; ☉ 9am-4pm Wed-Mon) in 1967. On display are some originals and copies of Hart's letters, plays, speeches and poetry, as well as his fiddle, spectacles and his trusty Britannic toilet. His award from the National Institute of Sciences for services to 'telepathy, hypnotism and personal magnetism' could do with some explanation. Sadly the few explanations on display are only in French. This is definitely rainy-day tourism.

Gris Gris & La Roche qui Pleure

Continue east along the road past the Robert Edward Hart Museum and you come to a grassy cliff top, which affords a view of the black rocky coastline where the reef is broken. A path leads down to the wild and empty Gris Gris beach; a wooden sign warns of the dangers of swimming here. The term *gris gris* traditionally refers to 'black magic', and looking at the tortuous coastline, you can see how the area got its name.

Right at the end of the next headland, 600m further on, La Roche qui Pleure (The Crying Rock; Map p112) resembles a crying man – you'll have to stand there puzzling it out for quite some time, and the waves really have to crash for the 'tears' to come out, but it's oddly satisfying when you finally get it.

La Vallée des Couleurs

The less impressive of the two 'coloured earths' in Mauritius (see p109), **La Vallée des Couleurs** (Map p112; ☎ 622 8686; adult/child Rs 150/75; ☉ 9am-5pm) is nevertheless beautifully situated, with plenty of waterfalls to see, some great flowers and even a collection of giant tortoises to admire, which is good as the coloured earths are by no means stunning, even if there are actually 23 different colours here, as opposed to Chamarel's seven.

A nature trail of sorts leads to the coloured earths past small waterfalls and picnic kiosks with views down to the coast. It takes about an hour to complete the circuit.

There's also a rustic café-restaurant, **La Cabane en Paille** (Map p112; ☎ 723 3115; mains Rs 250; ☉ 10.30am-3pm), serving drinks and slightly pricey but well-prepared local dishes.

EATING

Le Gris Gris (aka Chez Rosy; Map p112; ☎ 625 4179; mains Rs 150-250; ☉ noon-5pm) This smart restaurant beside the Gris Gris car park is a friendly place serving no-nonsense home-cooking.

Restaurant Rochester (Map p112; ☎ 625 4180; mains 275; lunch & dinner, closed dinner Tue) The charming Mme Appadu who ran the Cabane en Paille restaurant at the Vallée des Couleurs for years now runs her own family restaurant in an old colonial building by the bridge to Surinam. The food is traditional Mauritian and it's a popular place for groups.

Le Batelage (Map p112; ☎ 625 6083; mains Rs 400-700; ☉ lunch & dinner) Sadly a bit of a tourist trap (as its location in Le Village des Touristes would suggest), Le Batelage nevertheless enjoys a gorgeous position overlooking the river mouth. The over-attentive staff fuss relentlessly, but the Franco-Creole food is good quality, if unsubtly overpriced.

GETTING THERE & AROUND

There are buses roughly every half hour from Mahébourg to Souillac via the airport and Rivière des Anguilles. From Port Louis, buses run hourly, calling at Rivière des Anguilles en route. There are also frequent services to and from Souillac to Curepipe, with three buses a day taking the coast road via Pointe aux Roches. Buses heading along the coast to Baie du Cap depart hourly.

A taxi from Souillac to Shanti Ananda Maurice costs around Rs 150, Rs 500 to the airport.

Bel Ombre

The latest development in Mauritius' hotel scene is a string of luxury developments in the isolated south of the island, most of which are on the grounds of the former sugar estate of Bel Ombre. You're really miles from the bucket-and-spade atmosphere of Flic en Flac or Grand Baie here, although the hotels are fairly tightly placed together, meaning that despite the general removal from the rest of the country, you don't exactly feel in the middle of nowhere.

The main attraction here is the **Domaine de Bel Ombre** (☎ 623 5615; www.domainedebelombre.mu ☉ daily), a nature reserve set on the old sugar plantation, which was developed by Charles Telfair between 1816 and 1833. Today it's run for birdwatchers, walkers and nature lovers who come here to see the wild stags visit the charming waterfall, quad-bike, putt away on the golf course or eat in one of the superb restaurants. There's even the remains of a chimney from the plantation days.

SLEEPING

Mövenpick Resort & Spa Mauritius (Map p112; ☎ 623 5000; www.movenpick-hotels.com; Bel Ombre; s/d with half board Rs 9200/14,100; P X 🖳 🖭) The most impressive of the three properties built on the Bel Ombre estate and initially known as Le Voile d'Or until it was acquired by the Mövenpick group in 2006. The huge, empty entrance looks like the Temple of Doom at first, but once you're in, it's hard not to be impressed by the stunning central avenue of water between the hotel and the sea. The accommodation is in three-storey buildings facing the sea and the attractions here include the huge spa, which is almost a resort in itself, tennis courts, a diving centre, kids clubs and a great selection of restaurants.

Le Telfair Golf & Spa Resort (Map p112; ☎ 433 5500; www.letelfair.com; Bel Ombre; s/d with half board Rs 13,800/19,700; P X 🖳 🖭) This is a very grand hotel built in the colonial style, albeit with a touch of Disney thrown in for good measure. The site itself is superb, spanning the river leading down to a great stretch of beach and encompassing a huge pool. The rooms are as grand as the rest of the grounds would lead you to expect, housed in white, flouncy buildings with large balconies. There are lovely views back towards the mountains from here too.

Heritage Golf & Spa Resort (Map p112; ☎ 601 1500; www.veranda-resorts.com; Bel Ombre; s/d/tr with half board Rs 13,800/16,800/23,200; P X 🖳 🖭) The heritage in question here is Mauritius' copious African heritage, although the theme is decorative more than anything else, giving rise to stylish interiors, expansive pools, African art on the walls and drums on arrival. It's a very pleasant, smart place with a great beach and a relaxed atmosphere despite five-star standards.

Shanti Ananda Maurice (Map p112; ☎ 603 7200; www.shantiananda.com; St Felix; s/d with half board from Rs 22,600/24,300; P X 🖳 🖭) This property in the village of St Felix opened at the end of 2006 and is brought to you by the owners of the notoriously high-end Ananda in the Himalayas, the exclusive Indian spa resort which is a fixture on the pages of *Condé*

Nast Traveller. Shanti Ananda Maurice is only their second resort in the world and it's suitably spectacular, set in 15 hectares of tropical gardens with a wonderful beach and a huge ESPA spa with a dizzying number of treatments. Although not yet operational when we visited, this promises to be one of Mauritius' most spectacular hotels.

EATING

All the hotels in and around Bel Ombre have several restaurants – all of high standard and at a high price. The pick of the bunch has to be **Le Château Restaurant** (Map p112; ☎ 623 5620; Bel Ombre; mains from Rs 1200; ☉ lunch Mon-Sat, dinner Fri & Sat), a stunning conversion of the old plantation house of the Bel Ombre estate presided over by Dominique Blais, the head chef at Le Telfair. This is a place for an exceptional meal of traditional Franco-Mauritian cuisine with contemporary flourish.

Baie du Cap
pop 2300

The coastline between Baie du Cap and the stunning Le Morne Peninsula is some of the most beautiful in the country, and blissfully free of development. As well as some marvellous stretches of casuarina-lined sand west of Baie du Cap, there's good surf at Macondé Point, on the east side of the bay and some astonishingly dramatic rocky scenery.

The only real sights in the area are a couple of low-key monuments. The first is the **Trevassa Monument** (Map p112), about 1km beyond Bel Ombre village, which commemorates the sinking of the British steamer *Trevassa* in 1923. She went down 2600km off Mauritius. Sixteen survivors were eventually washed ashore at Bel Ombre having survived 25 days in an open lifeboat.

The second is the **Matthew Flinders monument** (Map p112) that stands on the shore 500m west of Baie du Cap. It was erected in 2003 in honour of the arrival here 200 years earlier of the English navigator and cartographer Matthew Flinders. He was less warmly received at the time; the poor bloke didn't know that England and France were at war and he was imprisoned for more than six years. For an interesting read on the subject, take a look at Huguette Ly-Tio-Fane Pineo's book *In the Grips of the Eagle: Matthew Flinders at the Île de France, 1803–1810*.

There are a couple of cheap and cheerful restaurants beside the junction in Baie du Cap village. **Chand Snack** (Map p112; mains around Rs 90; 🕒 7am-10pm; 🗶) is slightly smarter and offers a wider choice.

Bus services along here are limited. Baie du Cap is the terminus for buses from Souillac, and from Quatre Bornes via Tamarin. In both cases buses run approximately every 20 minutes.

RODRIGUES

Rodrigues is one of the most pleasant surprises Mauritius has to offer. Blissfully isolated over 500km northeast of the mainland, this tiny island is a volcanic creation only one million years old, a stunning, mountainous gem where it's hard to feel connected to even Mauritius, let alone the wider world. Often sold rather misleadingly as a 'mini-Mauritius', Rodrigues' differences from its distant master are what actually make people who come here fall for it. Entirely mountainous, far drier than the mainland and with no sugar cane but fruit and vegetables planted everywhere, the vibe is very different indeed. The beaches, while fewer and farther between than on the mainland, are superb and the population, almost entirely African and Creole, is a far cry from Mauritius' ethnic melting pot; most people speak Creole rather than French or English, and over 90% are Roman Catholic.

Rodrigues' unlikely, remote location belies the fact that it's a relatively heavily populated place: although it measures only 8km by 18km, Rodrigues supports a population of about 37,000 people. There's a very autonomous spirit here; while few actually believe independence would be beneficial in the long run, there's a fiercely proud island identity, one no doubt much informed by the population's almost entirely African heritage: most residents are descendents of freed slaves who left Mauritius in the 19th century to enjoy a life free from their former oppressors.

As well as beach holidays and walking, the island offers some of the best diving in Mauritius, being surrounded by extensive coral reefs. Rodrigues is receiving heavy promotion as a back-to-nature destination for holiday-makers from throughout the region. The government seems keen to go the route of sympathetic, small-scale development, with the emphasis on B&B accommodation, and there is much talk of ecotourism. Sadly, it remains the poorest part of the country with people having a far worse quality of life than on the mainland.

History

Rodrigues is named after the Portuguese navigator, Don Diégo Rodriguez, who was the first European to discover the uninhabited island in 1528. Dutch sailors were the next to pay a call, albeit very briefly, in 1601, followed a few years later by the French.

At first Rodrigues was simply a place where ships could take refuge from storms and replenish their supplies of fresh water and meat. Giant tortoises were especially prized since they could be kept alive on board for months. Over the years thousands were taken or killed until they completely died out. Rodrigues also had a big flightless bird, the solitaire, which went the same sorry way as its distant cousin, the dodo.

The first serious attempt at colonisation occurred in 1691 when Frenchman François Leguat and a band of seven Huguenot companions fled religious persecution at home in search of a 'promised land'. They made a good stab at it. Crops grew well and the island's fauna and flora were a source of wonder. Even so, after two years, life on a paradise island began to pall, not least due to the lack of female company. With no boat of their own (the ship they arrived on failed to return as promised), Leguat and his friends built a craft out of driftwood and eventually made it to Mauritius.

The next group to arrive were far more determined. In 1735, the French founded a permanent colony on Rodrigues as part of a European power-struggle to control the Indian Ocean. They established a small settlement at Port Mathurin, but a lack of leadership coupled with the difficult climate meant the colony never really prospered. When the British – who wanted a base from which to attack French-ruled Mauritius – invaded in 1809, they met with little resistance.

One of the more important events under British rule was the arrival of telecommunications in 1901. Rodrigues was one of the staging posts for the undersea cable linking Britain and Australia. The old Cable & Wireless offices are still to be seen at Pointe Canon above Port Mathurin.

Then, in 1967, Rodriguans distinguished themselves by voting against independence

RODRIGUES

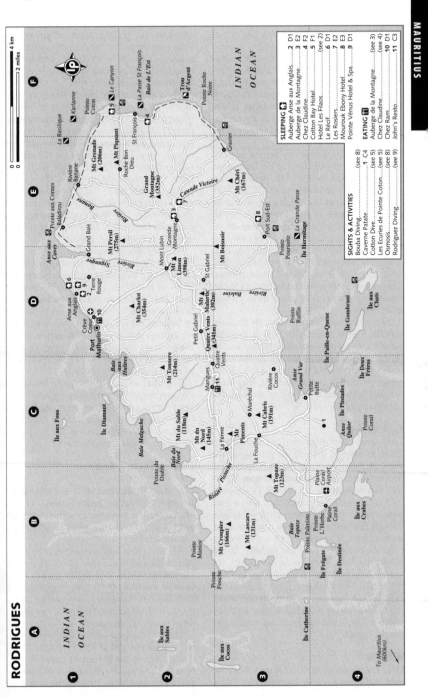

0 _____ 4 km
0 _____ 2 miles

INDIAN OCEAN

Île aux Sables

Île aux Cocos

Île aux Fous

Île Diamant

Baie Malgache

Pointe du Diable

Pointe Manioc

Mt Croupier (166m)

Mt Lascars (131m)

Pointe Fouche

Pointe Palmiste

Pointe L'Herbe

Île Frégate

Île Destinée

Baie Topaze

Baie du Nord

Mt du Sable (118m)

Mt du Nord (145m)

Mt Piments

La Ferme

La Fouche

Mt Cabris (191m)

Mt Topaze (123m)

Rivière Pistache

Plaine Corail Airport

Plaine Corail

Île aux Crabes

Île aux Pintades

Anse Quitor

Pointe Corail

Caverne Patate

Petite Butte

Rivière Cocos

Anse Grand Var

Île Deux Frères

Île Gombrani

Île aux Chats

Pointe Raffin

Rivière Baleine

Baie aux Huitres

Mt Tomere (214m)

Mangues

Quatre Vents

Petit Gabriel

Mt Charlot (354m)

Quatre Vents - Malartic (392m)

Malartic (341m)

St Gabriel

Port Mathurin

Crève Coeur

Anse aux Anglais

Terre Rouge

Mt Persil (275m)

Mt Limon (398m)

Mont Lubin

Sygangue

Grand Baie

Anse aux Cavés

Pointe aux Cornes

Baladirou

Rivière Banane

Rivière Banane

Mt Grenade (206m)

Mt Piquant

Roche Bon Dieu

Grand Montagne (352m)

Grande Montagne

Cascade Victoire

Mt Chéri (167m)

Mt Boisnoir

St François

La Passe St François

Baie de L'Est

Trou d'Argent

Pointe Roche Noire

La Basilique

Karlanne

Pointe Coton

Le Canyon

Rivière Rivière

Graviers

Port Sud-Est

La Grande Passe

Pointe Poursuite

Île Hermitage

Pointe Corail

La Pinsaise

Île Catherine

To Mauritius (600km)

INDIAN OCEAN

INDIAN OCEAN

from Britain by a whopping 90% (the rest of Mauritius voted strongly in favour). It was a dramatic illustration of the difference in outlook between the two islands. Following independence, Rodriguans continued to argue that their needs were significantly different from the rest of the country and that, in any case, they were being neglected by the central government. What they wanted was a greater say in their own future.

The campaign was led by Serge Clair and his Organisation du Peuple de Rodrigues (OPR), founded in 1976. His patience and political skill eventually paid off. In 2001 it was announced that Rodrigues would be allowed a degree of autonomy, notably in socio-economic affairs and in the management of their natural resources. The following year 18 counsellors were elected; the Regional Assembly was formally inaugurated in 2002 with Serge Clair as Chief Commissioner. The assembly is now trying to tackle the overriding problems of population growth and poverty.

Almost as momentous for many islanders was the visit of Pope John-Paul II in 1989. Nearly the entire population turned out to celebrate Mass at La Ferme.

Today the economic mainstays of Rodrigues are fishing and agriculture, with tourism and handicrafts playing an increasingly important role.

Environment

Long-term overfishing coupled with silting (from erosion in the hills) is placing severe stress on the marine ecosystem, with particular concern for the lagoon. **Shoals Rodrigues** (☎ 831 1225; www.shoals-rodrigues.org), an NGO working with local fishing communities, warns that large areas of coral have been damaged, mainly through destructive fishing practices associated with octopus gatherers, who go out on foot to prise the octopus from their shelters. At the same time, fishing with seine nets, which remove young as well as mature fish, is depleting fish stocks. The number of fishing licences has been cut substantially and Shoals is also working to establish a network of marine reserves, which will replenish fish populations throughout the lagoon.

Wildlife

Over the centuries, the thick forest that covered Rodrigues has been destroyed by felling

and intensive grazing. Much of the vegetation you see today consists of introduced species. Of the 38 or so native plant species remaining, all but two are considered endangered, vulnerable or rare.

The government, in collaboration with the MWF, is acting to protect areas of critical importance by clearing them of introduced plants (which grow much more quickly) and replanting native species. It is hoped that these areas will act as refuges for the island's rare endemic fauna, such as the Rodrigues warbler and the Rodrigues fody. The warbler population has made a shaky recovery from near extinction in the 1960s to an estimated 70 pairs today. The fody population has also increased from a low of 60 pairs in 1983 to approximately 300 pairs today.

Another species under threat is the Rodrigues fruit bat. The population of these large, brown bats had reached critically low levels of just 75 in 1974. With the help of strict laws and conservation measures, the population had inched its way up to 5000 or so before Cyclone Kalunde struck in 2003. It's estimated that some 2000 survived, and the numbers are on the rise again. You can see them gliding over Port Mathurin at dusk to reach their feeding grounds.

The small islands surrounding Rodrigues support important colonies of sea birds. Fairy terns and noddies nest on Île aux Cocos and Île aux Sables, off the northwest coast, while a tortoise park is due to open in 2007 near Plaine Corail airport.

Getting There & Away

AIR

The main **Air Mauritius office** (Map p126; ☎ 831 1632; fax 831 1959; ADS Bldg, Rue Max Lucchesi) is in Port Mathurin. There is also an office at the **airport** (☎ 832 7700), which is open for all arrivals and departures.

Air Mauritius has connections between Mauritius and Rodrigues (Rs 5734 return, 1½ hours, two to four flights daily), while **Catovair** (Map p126; ☎ 831 0747; www.catovair.com; Patrico Bldg, Rue François Leguat) also operates on the route (Rs 5290 return, 1½ hours, two flights daily except Wednesday).

There is a luggage limit of 15kg per person, with excess charged at Rs 35 per kilo. When checking in at the Mauritius end, you may be asked how much you weigh. Don't worry, you won't have to go through the indignity of being weighed like a sack of potatoes – an approximation is fine.

All passengers are required to reconfirm their return tickets either immediately on arrival at Rodrigues (there is an Air Mauritius counter in the baggage hall) or at least three days before departure. It's a good idea to phone the airline the day before you leave anyway, just to make sure there's been no change to the schedule.

SEA

The *Mauritius Pride* and the *Mauritius Tro-chetia* make the voyage from Port Louis to Rodrigues four times a month, docking at the passenger terminal on Rue Wolfert Harmensz in Port Mathurin. The outbound trip takes about 36 hours; the return to Mauritius 25 hours, depending on sea conditions. Return fares cost Rs 2450/4900 for a seat/cabin in the *Mauritius Pride* and Rs 3000 for a 2nd-class cabin in the *Mauritius Trochetia*. The boats are popular with locals, so book well ahead.

Information and tickets are available from travel agents or direct from the Mauritius Shipping Corporation. Contact **Coraline Shipping Agency** (Map pp58-9; ☎ 217 2285; msc@coraline intnet.mu; Nova Bldg, Military Rd, Port Louis) and the **Mauritius Shipping Corporation** (Map p126; ☎ 831 0640; www.mauritiusshipping.intnet.mu; Rue François Leguat, Port Mathurin). Tickets should be reconfirmed two days before departure.

Getting Around
TO/FROM THE AIRPORT

Flights arrive at **Plaine Corail Airport** (☎ 831 6301) at the southwest tip of the island. Public bus 206 runs between the airport and Port Mathurin roughly every 40 minutes from 5.30am to 4.30pm. The private **Supercopter bus service** (☎ 831 1859; one-way Rs 150) meets all flights and drops off at hotels in Port Mathurin and Anse aux Anglais; phone ahead to be sure of a seat.

For destinations elsewhere on the island, you can either take the bus to Port Mathurin and then get an onward connection, or arrange for your hotel or a tour operator to pick you up. Prices start at around Rs 300 per person for a round trip.

A taxi to or from Port Mathurin costs Rs 300; to Pointe Coton Rs 600; and to Port Sud-Est Rs 500. Fares are slightly more expensive at night.

BUS

The main bus terminal is in Port Mathurin. In addition to the airport bus, the most useful bus routes are those to Grand Baie and Pointe Coton in the east of the island, and to Gravier, Port Sud-Est and Rivière Cocos on the south coast. All apart from the Grand Baie buses pass through Mont Lubin in the centre of the island. Buses operate every 30 to 45 minutes from about 6am to 5.30pm Monday to Saturday on most routes. The Sunday service is fairly sporadic.

CAR

The road system in Rodrigues has improved enormously and sealed roads now lead to most parts of the island. Though 4WD vehicles are no longer strictly necessary, most hire cars are still sturdy pick-ups.

Car rental can be arranged through most hotels and guesthouses and local tour operators (p126), who will deliver all over the island. There's an **Avis** (☎ 832 8100; www.avismauri tius.com) at the airport although we recommend the cheaper services of **Chou Chou de l'Ile** (☎ 875 2215/831 2410; chouchoudelile@hotmail.com), which is based in Baie aux Huîtres but will deliver pickups and motorbikes anywhere on the island. Expect to pay at least Rs 1200 per day. Most importantly, make sure you have sufficient petrol before setting off for the day – the island's only **petrol station** (Rue Max Lucchesi; ☉ 6am-6.30pm Mon-Sat, 6am-3pm Sun) is in Port Mathurin.

BICYCLE & MOTORCYCLE

If your hotel or guesthouse doesn't offer bike or motorcycle rental, contact one of the outlets in Port Mathurin (below). The going rate is around Rs 200 per day for a bike and Rs 650 for a 125cc motorbike.

TAXI

Most taxis on Rodrigues are 4WD pickups. The fare from Port Mathurin to Pointe Coton costs Rs 400 and to Port Sud-Est Rs 400, slightly more at night. You can also hire taxis by the day for an island tour; expect to pay in the region of Rs 1500.

PORT MATHURIN
pop 6000

This tiny port is the island's hub and, for want of a better word, its capital. The island is run from the local legislative assembly

MAURITIUS

here, although it feels very far from being an administrative centre. It's a friendly, bustling place with a fantastic market, some attractive mosques and an enjoyable atmosphere. Anyone spending any time in Rodrigues will enjoy Port Mathurin, even if just passing through en route to one of the islands' upmarket hotels.

Information

EMERGENCY
Port Mathurin Pharmacy (☎ 831 2279; Rue de la Solidarité; ⌚ 7.30am-4.30pm Mon-Fri, 7.30am-3pm Sat, 7.30am-11am Sun) The only pharmacy on the island.
Queen Elizabeth Hospital (☎ 831 1628) The island's main hospital is at Crève Coeur, immediately east of Port Mathurin.

INTERNET ACCESS
Cyber Logistics (☎ 832 0869; Rue Mamzelle Julia; per min Rs 2; ⌚ 8.30am-4.30pm Mon-Fri, 8.30am-2pm Sat) Offers the cheapest web access in town.
Rodnet Cybercafe (☎ 831 0747; Rue Johnston; per min Rs 3; ⌚ 8.30am-4pm Mon-Fri, 8.30am-noon Sat) Below the Dragon d'Or restaurant.

MONEY
The banks all have offices where you can change money and withdraw cash from the ATMs.
Barclays (☎ 831 1553; Rue de la Solidarité)
Mauritius Commercial Bank (MCB; ☎ 831 1833; Rue Max Lucchesi)
State Bank (☎ 831 1642; Rue Max Lucchesi)

POST
Post office (☎ 831 2098; Rue de la Solidarité; ⌚ 8.15-11.15am & noon-4pm Mon-Fri, 8.15-11.45pm Sat)

TELEPHONE
There are plenty of public phones on Rodrigues and both Mauritian networks have reception here. You can buy phonecards at **Téléshop** (☎ 831 1816; Rue Johnston; ⌚ 8am-8.30pm Mon-Sat), and there is a cardphone outside for international calls.

TRAVEL AGENCIES
There are several excellent travel agencies in town offering a range of activities and tours.
Ecotourisme (☎ 831 2801; www.rodrigues-island.org /ecotourisme.html; Rue Max Lucchesi)

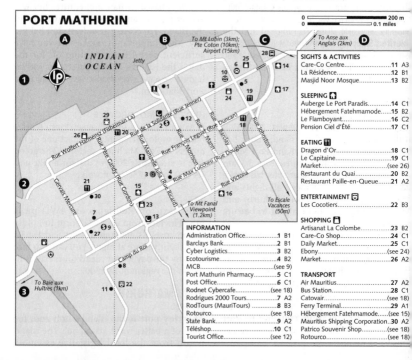

PORT MATHURIN

| 0 | 200 m |
| 0 | 0.1 miles |

INDIAN OCEAN

To Mt Lubin (3km); Pte Coton (10km); Airport (15km)

To Anse aux Anglais (2km)

Jetty

To Mt Fanal Viewpoint (1.2km)

To Escale Vacances (50m)

To Baie aux Huîtres (1km)

Rue Wolfert Hamenez (Fisherman La)
Rue Père Cindy (Rue Cordon)
Rue de la Solidarité (Rue Jennen)
Rue Mamzelle Julia (Rue Ricard)
Rue François Leguat (Rue Duncan)
Rue Max Lucchesi (Rue Douglas)
Rue Morrison
Rue Mann
Rue Barclay
Rue Johnston
Rue Victoria
Gervais Mercure
Camp du Roi

SIGHTS & ACTIVITIES
Care-Co Centre..............................11 A3
La Résidence..................................12 B1
Masjid Noor Mosque.................13 B2

SLEEPING
Auberge Le Port Paradis............14 C1
Hébergement Fatehmamode.....15 B2
Le Flamboyant.............................16 C2
Pension Ciel d'Été......................17 C1

EATING
Dragon d'Or..................................18 C1
Le Capitaine..................................19 C1
Market..(see 26)
Restaurant du Quai...................20 B2
Restaurant Paille-en-Queue......21 A2

ENTERTAINMENT
Les Cocotiers...............................22 B3

SHOPPING
Artisanat La Colombe................23 B2
Care-Co Shop...............................24 C1
Daily Market.................................25 C1
Ebony..(see 24)
Market..26 A2

TRANSPORT
Air Mauritius................................27 A2
Bus Station...................................28 C1
Catovair....................................(see 18)
Ferry Terminal.............................29 A1
Hébergement Fatehmamode...(see 15)
Mauritius Shipping Corporation..30 A2
Patrico Souvenir Shop.............(see 18)
Rotourco...................................(see 18)

INFORMATION
Administration Office...................1 B1
Barclays Bank.................................2 B1
Cyber Logistics.............................3 B2
Ecotourisme...................................4 B2
MCB...(see 9)
Port Mathurin Pharmacy............5 C1
Post Office.......................................6 C1
Rodnet Cybercafe....................(see 18)
Rodrigues 2000 Tours.................7 A2
RodTours (MauriTours) 8 B3
Rotourco...................................(see 18)
State Bank..9 A2
Téléshop..10 C1
Tourist Office............................(see 12)

Rodrigues 2000 Tours (☎ 831 1894; 2000trs@intnet .mu; Rue Max Lucchesi)

RodTours (☎ 831 2249; www.rodrigues-island.org/rod Tours.html; Camp du Roi) Part of MauriTours.

Rotourco (☎ 831 0747; www.rotourco.com; Rue François Leguat)

TOURIST INFORMATION

There's a small but very helpful **tourist of- fice** (☎ 832 0866; www.rodrigues-island.org; Rue de la Solidarité; ☺ 9am-4pm Mon-Fri) in the building of La Résidence. Just walk in through the gate (it looks private but it's quite OK to walk in) and you'll be able to get brochures and advice here from the friendly staff about the vast variety of *chambres* and *tables d'hôte* on the island, plus excursions and hiking.

Sights & Activities

One of the oldest buildings still standing in Port Mathurin, **La Résidence** (Rue de la Solidarité) dates from 1897, when it provided a fairly modest home for the British Chief Commis- sioner. Its facilities are now used as function rooms for the new Regional Assembly.

On the south side of town, **Care-Co** (☎ 831 1766; Camp du Roi; admission free; ☺ 8am-4pm Mon-Fri) is a non-profit association providing train- ing, work and accommodation for people with disabilities and the young unemployed. Around 50 people work at the centre pro- ducing various crafts and some delicious, award-winning honey. Visitors are welcome and are given a guided tour of the work- shops. There's also a small shop here and another on Rue de la Solidarité.

For an island said to be 97% Catholic, there are two surprisingly well-kept mosques in Port Mathurin. The largest of the two, **Masjid Noor Mosque** (☎ 831 2130; Rue Père Gandy) has a sign outside in English proclaiming that visitors are very welcome, although it's not always open.

For fine views over Port Mathurin and the lagoon, there's an easy 1km walk from the end of Rue Mamzelle Julia to a lookout atop Mt Fanal. At dusk this is a good place to see Rodrigues fruit bats.

Sleeping

Port Mathurin makes a convenient base if you are travelling by bus, but frankly it lacks the characterful *chambres d'hôte* you'll find elsewhere on the island. There are plenty of good options though.

Hébergement Fatehmamode (☎ 831 1551; mah mood@intnet.mu; Rue Max Lucchesi; s & d room only from Rs 200, apt from Rs 500) We almost couldn't believe the price when we stayed here – for a tiny sum you get a huge room with access to an even bigger balcony, all spotlessly clean and com- fortable including a kitchenette. Sadly there's no air con and the service leaves something to be desired, but this is hands-down the best bargain in town.

Pension Ciel d'Été (☎ 831 1587; fax 831 2004; Rue François Leguat; s/d incl breakfast Rs 500/800, with half board Rs 750/1200) This charming colonial-style residence is arranged in well-kept gardens. Though it suffers a bit from road noise, it is a popular choice. Fan-cooled rooms are spartan and reli- giously charged with Catholic admonishments to sinners framed on the walls.

Auberge Le Port Paradis (☎ 831 1062; fax 831 2096; Rue François Leguat; s/d Rs 500/1000; 🅿) Near the bus station in a brilliantly located building with some great views of the town, this sprawling place is good value with basic but clean rooms. There's an extra charge of Rs 300 per night for air-con.

Le Flamboyant (☎ 832 0082; www.hotelflamboy ant.com; Rue Victoria; s/d incl breakfast Rs 800/1500, with half board Rs 950/1800; 🅿 🅰) This recently renovated hotel offers slightly boxy rooms with bathroom, TV and minibar. There's a restaurant-bar and a tiny pool squeezed in at the back. It's a friendly place in the town's backstreets.

Escale Vacances (☎ 831 2555; escal.vac@intnet.mu; Rue Johnston; s/d incl breakfast from Rs 2750/4500, with half board Rs 3140/5250; 🅿 🅰) Just outside the cen- tre, but a very short walk from everything nonetheless, this charming conversion of a colonial mansion into a friendly hotel is very successful. The rooms are spacious, well furnished and come with local charm. It's a favourite with groups and is the best stand- ard hotel in town.

Eating

For quick eats, outlets on Rue de la Solidar- ité sell *pain fouré* (filled rolls), noodles and the like for a handful of rupees. There's also a clutch of restaurants offering traditional local cuisine. Specialities are octopus (in cur- ries and salads), succulent ham and chicken, and dishes featuring the famous Rodrigues chillies, lemons and honey.

Dragon d'Or (☎ 831 0541; Rue François Leguat; mains Rs 75-100; ☺ lunch & dinner, closed dinner Wed)

A friendly place serving cheap and cheerful Chinese and Creole fare. Portions are small, but the food is tasty.

Restaurant du Quai (☎ 831 2840; Rue Wolfert Harmensz; mains Rs 100-200; ☒ lunch & dinner Tue-Sun; ☒) This friendly place by the harbour is always full in the evenings with local families and visitors enjoying its fine seafood and lobster dishes. The charming staff are very keen to please and make a damn fine punch cocktail as an aperitif.

Le Capitaine (☎ 831 1581; Rue Johnstone; mains Rs 150; ☒ lunch & dinner Mon-Sat) In the centre of town, Le Capitaine isn't the most romantic place in the world – on our last visit the staff were simultaneously listening to the radio and watching a film that blared out from the TV, seeming uninterested in either – but the food here is good, with an excellent selection of, yes, you've guessed it, seafood.

Restaurant Paille-en-Queue (☎ 831 0561; Rue François Leguat; mains Rs 85-300; ☒ dinner) This rather drably presented place is worth trying for its broad menu of hearty local as well as Chinese fare, including such Rodriguan classics as honey chicken and octopus curry.

Self-caterers will find several small grocery stores on Rue de la Solidarité and Rue Mamzelle Julia. You can buy fresh fruit from stalls near the post office (mornings only from Monday to Saturday). On Saturday there is an excellent **street market** (Rue Wolfert Harmensz) down by the ferry terminal, with a smaller version on Wednesday.

Entertainment

Port Mathurin is no Las Vegas, though occasionally the open-air disco **Les Cocotiers** (☎ 831 1877; Camp du Roi) has something organised on the weekends. Look out for adverts posted around town.

Shopping

Rue de la Solidarité and Rue Mamzelle Julia are the main shopping streets. Here you'll find a number of outlets selling handicrafts, especially baskets and hats made from dried *vacoa* leaves. Items made from coconut fibres and coconut-shell jewellery are also popular souvenirs. Look out, too, for local foodstuffs such as preserved lemons, chillies and honey. The Saturday market is reasonably cheap and a pleasantly relaxed place to shop for fresh produce and some souvenirs. The rest of the week there's a **daily market** (☒ 8am-5pm Mon-Sat)

next to the bridge near the post office which is well worth a visit.

Other recommendations:

Artisanat La Colombe (☎ 831 0430; Rue Max Lucchesi) Specialises in preserved foodstuffs and basketware.

Care-Co (Rue de la Solidarité) Sells coconut-shell items, honey and model boats made by people with disabilities (p127).

Ebony (Rue de la Solidarité) A good range of *vacoa* hats and bags.

Getting There & Away

For information about getting to and from the airport, see p124.

For information about travelling by boat, see p125.

You can rent bikes and motorbikes from **Hébergement Fatehmamode** (☎ 831 1551; mahmood@intnet.mu; Rue Max Lucchesi). Tour agent **Rotourco** (☎ 831 0747; www.rotourco.com; Rue François Leguat) also has a few motorbikes for rent, as does the nearby **Patrico souvenir shop** (☎ 831 2044; Rue François Leguat). Count on Rs 200 per day for a bike and at least Rs 650 for a 125cc motorbike.

Ask your hotel or guesthouse about car hire, or contact a local tour agent. Rates start at around Rs 1200 per day.

Port Mathurin's well-organised bus station (p125) is across the river on the east side of town.

AROUND RODRIGUES

Rodrigues' varied and beautiful landscape demands exploration. Hiring a car is the best way to see the island (although do stop and walk as much as possible). The main attractions are the east-coast beaches and some wonderful home-stays run by local tourism pioneers scattered throughout the island.

The finest beaches are on the east coast from Pointe Coton around to Port Sud-Est. Top of the list is the immaculate beach at **Trou d'Argent**, only accessible by boat or on foot. **St François** and the small cove at **Gravier** are also magical spots. **Anse aux Anglais**, where the first British troops landed, has a decent beach – albeit with grey sand – and is a popular place to stay.

One of the most dramatic roads on the island descends from Mont Lubin to Port Sud-Est, offering great views of the island-spattered lagoon. This south coast is also where you'll find Rodrigues' very own cave system.

While the west of the island has the least to offer tourists, the Île aux Cocos, a nature reserve providing a habitat for a large number of rare birds, is a stand-out attraction and the most popular excursion in Rodrigues.

Last but not least, it's in the beautiful mountainous interior that you'll find Rodrigues at its most traditional.

Sights & Activities
WALKING & RIDING

Rodrigues is perfect for rambling around at your leisure. There are few signposts and the less popular trails are pretty ill-defined, but the landscape is fairly open so it's hard to get too lost.

You can begin the classic coastal walk at Pointe Coton or St François, which takes you south to the gorgeous beach at Trou d'Argent and then around the coast to Gravier. Allow about three hours for the walk, not counting swimming and picnic stops. Both Pointe Coton and Gravier are accessible by bus from Port Mathurin; check the time of the last bus back before you set off.

The walk from Port Mathurin or Anse aux Anglais to Pointe Coton is another good half-day's excursion.

The uplands around Mt Limon and Mt Malartic, which represent the island's highest points, offer great all-round views. The easy way up **Mt Limon** (398m) is to take a bus to the village of Mont Lubin. Then walk east along the road to Grande Montagne for 400m to find the path signposted up to the right; it takes just five minutes to reach the top.

Rodrigues provides some great landscapes for riding in. The island's best stables are **Les Ecuries de Pointe Coton** (Map p123; ☎ 831 8537, 875 5540; Pointe Coton), located adjacent to the Cotton Bay Hotel and whose friendly team can cater to all levels.

WATER SPORTS & FISHING

There are many excellent dive locations around Rodrigues. In general, the marine environment is still remarkably well preserved and there's a tremendous variety of dives on offer. The best sites lie off the east and south coasts (see p29). Rodrigues is also one of the world's best-kept secrets as a place to kitesurf. Devotees have been coming for years and there's a tiny but loyal following in evidence.

The three main dive centres are **Cotton Dive** (Map p123; ☎ 831 8001; diverod@intnet.mu; ☺ 8am-4pm Sun-Fri, closed Jul & Aug) at the Cotton Bay Hotel, **Bouba Diving** (Map p123; ☎ 832 3063; ebony@intnet.mu; ☺ 7am-5pm) at the Mourouk Ebony Hotel and **Rodriguez Diving** (Map p123; ☎ 831 0957; http://rodriguez-diving.tripod.com; ☺ 8am-4pm) at the Pointe Venus Hotel & Spa. In all cases, nonguests should ring ahead to make an appointment. A dive costs from around Rs 1200.

Water sports are available through **Osmosis** (Map p123; ☎ 832 3051; osmosis-rodrigues.com; ☺ 7am-5pm), which is also based at the Mourouk Ebony Hotel. An hour's windsurfing costs Rs 550 or so with all the equipment; kite surfing, Rs 1500 for one descent.

The island's leading deep-sea fishing experts are the **Rod Fishing Club** (Map p123; ☎ 875 0616; www.rodfishingclub.com; Terre Rouge) run by Yann Colas, skipper of the Black Marlin, which makes frequent jigging sorties from Port Mathurin.

CAVERNE PATATE

Caverne Patate, in the southwest corner of the island, is an impressive cave system with a few stalagmite and stalactite formations. The guide points out formations with uncanny resemblances to a dodo, Buckingham Palace and even Winston Churchill!

The requisite permit is issued in the **Administration Office** (Map p126; ☎ 831 2058; Rodrigues Regional Assembly, Rue Morrison, Port Mathurin; ☺ 8am-noon Mon-Fri). It costs Rs 200 for up to 30 people.

There are four guided tours daily, usually at 9.30am, 11.30am, 1.30pm and 3.30pm. You should arrive at the cave entrance on the day and time specified on your permit. The 600m tunnel is an easy walk, but gets slippery in wet weather; wear shoes with a good grip and take a light jacket or pullover.

The track to the caves is signposted off the road from La Ferme to Petite Butte. Buses en route between La Ferme and Rivière Cocos will drop you off at the turn; coming from Port Mathurin, you'll have to change buses at one of these two towns.

Tours

Local tour agents (p126) offer a variety of excursions; the efficient Ecotourisme and Rodrigues 2000 Tours have reliable reputations. Most hotels and guesthouses can also help.

The most popular outing is a day trip to Île aux Cocos (from Rs 800 per person including picnic lunch), followed by various minibus tours of Rodrigues itself (from around Rs 500/1200 for a half/full day). Other options include a boat trip to Île aux Chats (Rs 800 including barbecue lunch) and a variety of guided walks and bike rides.

Sleeping

The main concentration of hotels and guesthouses is found 2km east of Port Mathurin at Anse aux Anglais, although this isn't the best place to truly get away from it all. Other options are scattered along the east and south coasts and in the interior. There are a couple of upmarket hotels, but the nicest choice is a *chambres d'hôte*; as they usually only have a handful of rooms and the best fill up quickly, be sure to book ahead.

Camping is possible just about anywhere on the island. The beaches around Pointe Coton and Grand Baie are good places to start.

NORTH COAST

Le Récif (Map p123; ☎ 831 1804; fax 831 0760; Anse aux Anglais; s/d Rs 600/850, with half board Rs 900/150; 🛇) This unusually stylish place has lots of character in its big, airy rooms decorated in Mauritian style and is looking good after a recent renovation. Perched on the cliff above Anse aux Anglais with access to the small beach below, this is a popular spot. There's a raucous disco on Saturday night in the restaurant.

Hotel Les Filaos (Map p123; ☎ 831 1644; www.filaose travenal-rodrigues.com; Anse aux Anglais; s/d incl breakfast from Rs 1000/1500; 🛋) Smart management has improved this place enormously, making it a great option. There's a large pool and simple, spotless rooms in small blocks arranged around it, next to a small river that runs into the sea.

Auberge Anse aux Anglais (Map p123; ☎ 831 2179; aubergehung@intnet.mu; Anse aux Anglais; s/d with half board from Rs 1150/1840; 🛇 🛋) Tucked off the road in Anse aux Anglais, with a pretty garden, this is a popular choice. Clean, simple rooms come with private bathroom, phone and either fan or, for Rs 300 extra per night, air-con (they're currently in the process of putting air-con in each room). The beach is just a short walk away.

Pointe Vénus Hotel & Spa (Map p123; ☎ 832 0104; resa@otentik.intnet.mu; s/d Rs 7000/10,000; 🛇 🖥 🛋) Definitely Rodrigues' most talked-about recent development, the Pointe Vénus is now considered by most to be the island's most luxurious hotel since it opened in 2004. In fact it's a fairly standard four-star hotel, albeit tastefully designed with a great pool, friendly staff and excellent facilities including a spa, diving centre, two restaurants and a kids club set in extensive grounds. Sadly it's set back from the coast, which makes it less attractive than the other two smart hotels on the island, although another sign that developers now have their sights trained on Rodrigues.

CENTRAL RODRIGUES

Les Rosiers (Map p123; ☎ 831 4703; Grande Montagne; s/d with breakfast Rs 500/1000) If the Auberge de la Montagne is full, you can try this place up the road. Its rather basic rooms and shoddy plumbing make it far less appealing, but the welcome is warm and genuine and you can still organise a *table d'hôte* meal at Auberge de la Montagne.

ourpick Auberge de la Montagne (Map p123; ☎ 831 4607; www.aubergedelamontagne.net.tc; Grande Montagne; s/d with half board from Rs 800/1600) Right at the island's mountainous heart, this long-established, much-loved *chambre d'hôte* is one of our favourites, run by the charming Baptiste family and set overlooking a wonderful fruit orchard. The meals are a real highlight here (see opposite) – Françoise Baptiste is an expert of Rodriguan cookery. The rooms are beautiful, clean and have some excellent views. Book well in advance.

EAST COAST

Chez Claudine (Map p123; ☎ 831 8242; cbmone ret@intnet.mu; St François; s/d with half board Rs 1200/2400) The wonderful Claudine welcomes everyone to her brilliant *chambre d'hôte* overlooking one of Rodrigues' best beaches. Her charmingly furnished white chalet-style house offers a selection of rooms, each with a view of the mountains or the sea. Meals are also delicious and you're well placed for walks along the east coast.

Cotton Bay Hotel (Map p123; ☎ 831 8001; cottonb@ intnet.mu; Pointe Coton; s/d with half board from Rs 7600/10,200; 🛇 🛋) This has long been considered Rodrigues' most luxurious hotel and has a blissfully isolated location on the island's east coast. Rooms are comfortable – if a tad dated – but with the fantastic yellow-sand bay, a great pool and plenty to see and do nearby including the island's best beaches and riding school a short walk away, it's easy to see why it's so enduringly popular.

SOUTH COAST

Mourouk Ebony Hotel (Map p123; ☎ 832 3350; www .mouroukebonyhotel.com; Port Sud-Est; s/d with half board from Rs 5800/8500; 🖳 🖭) This is the other long-established upmarket hotel on Rodrigues, totally isolated at the end of a wiggling mountain road from the mountains and easily recognised from afar by its bright-red roofing. There's a great beach and pool here and a very well-run water-sports and diving centre (it's known for the best kitesurfing on the island), and the staff are extremely friendly.

Eating

It would be a waste to come to Rodrigues and not eat traditional island cuisine at a *table d'hôte.* Outside Port Mathurin these are your best options for a meal out, although there are quite a few other good restaurants scattered about. For self-caterers, most villages have some sort of grocers or general store.

Chez Ram (Map p123; ☎ 832 0736; chezram@intnet .mu; Baie Lascars; mains from Rs 120; 🕑 lunch & dinner Thu-Tue) Just outside Port Mathurin, this pleasant roadside restaurant has a great terrace, sea views and good, reliable local cuisine. It's owned by Yajeswar Ramloll, the owner of Port Mathurin's excellent Restaurant du Quai, so you know you're in safe hands.

John's Resto (Map p123; ☎ 831 6306; Mangue; meals Rs 100-450; 🕑 lunch, dinner by reservation) Rodrigues' best seafood restaurant is up in the hills in the village of Mangue; follow signs for La Ferme. It's a friendly place where they're fanatical about seafood. This is the place to treat yourself to fresh lobster (a bargain at Rs 450 for 500g) or crab.

Auberge de la Montagne (Map p123; ☎ 831 4607; meals Rs 250; 🕑 lunch & dinner by reservation) Françoise Baptiste, the delightful owner of this *chambre d'hôte* and author of a book on Rodriguan cooking, prepares lip-smacking local specialities. You should reserve at least a day in advance.

Chez Claudine (Map p123; ☎ 831 8242; cbmoneret@ intnet.mu; St François; meals from Rs 300; 🕑 lunch & dinner by reservation) If you're walking to Trou d'Argent, phone in advance to reserve lunch at this *chambre d'hôte* at St François. The speciality is seafood grilled on an open wood fire.

Entertainment

Apart from a couple of places in Port Mathurin, nightlife on the island is virtually non-existent. The exception is live folk-music performances. Rodriguans are known as skilled accordionists, who play versions of old colonial ballroom and country dances such as the 'Scottish', the waltz and the mazurka. They also play a distinctive version of the *séga,* known as *séga tambour,* where the drum is unusually prominent. Popular groups include Racines, Cardinal Blanc, Cascavelles and Ambience Tropicale. They often perform at the big hotels, all of which have folk evenings to which nonguests are welcome (it's a good idea to phone ahead).

Le Récif (☎ 831 1804; 🕑 10pm-2am Fri & Sat) In Anse aux Anglais, this is a good place to hear local music. There's often folk music on Friday evenings while Saturday night is all disco, though they play a fair number of local hits.

OFFSHORE ISLANDS

There are many small islands dotted around Rodrigues. Commonly visited islands include Île aux Cocos, to the west, and Île aux Chats and Île Hermitage off the south coast.

Île aux Cocos nature reserve, barely 1km in length, is a nature reserve and bird sanctuary populated by small colonies of noddies and lesser noddies. It is only possible to visit Île aux Cocos on a guided tour (from Rs 600 per person including picnic lunch), which can be arranged through hotels and tour agents. The boat trip takes at least an hour each way; take a jacket as it can be very windy. The birds themselves are interesting, although not spectacular. While birders will love it, the main attraction for non-birdwatchers is the chance to travel to a tiny desert island and to indulge in some good *Lost* fantasies.

Île Hermitage, a tiny island renowned for its beauty (and for its possible hidden treasure), and **Île aux Chats** are both accessible by boat from Port Sud-Est. The latter is an unremarkable island, but is surrounded by a healthy coral reef, which makes it a popular destination for snorkelling and diving.

You can arrange excursions to all these islands through hotels and tour agents. Another option is to try asking local fishermen in Port Sud-Est, who are usually willing to ferry people out to one of the nearby islands and pick them up later.

Mauritius Directory

CONTENTS

ACCOMMODATION

Mauritius is by far the best country of the three destinations covered in this book for variation and choice in accommodation. It's so good, in fact, that it can be overwhelming. Camping is possible in Mauritius, although there are no camp sites as such. You should ask locals where it's acceptable to pitch tents, and perhaps expect some funny looks. The best value and often the most characterful accommodation in Mauritius can usually be found in guesthouses or *chambres d'hôte,* where families rent out one or more of their own rooms to travellers. This is a fantastic way to meet locals and there's usually the option of eating with them as well. *Chambres d'hôte* are particularly popular in Rodrigues (where they're often the only place to stay) while those in Blue Bay are some of the most luxurious and unique in the country.

Private houses for rent are available all over Mauritius. They tend to be holiday homes rented out by their owners through agencies at considerable expense, and of course value for money varies enormously. Most hotels and travel agencies can point you in the direction of private rentals.

Hotels cover the rest of the accommodation range. In Mauritius they range from threadbare, no-star affairs (the capital's non-luxury hotels tend to fit into this category), the like of which you'll find all over Africa, through to five-star luxury complexes each seemingly built to outdo the others. While Mauritius enjoys a very well-to-do and exclusive reputation, its main trade is actually in midrange three-and four-star hotels, although its luxury five-star hotels such as Le Touessrok and the Oberoi are truly world-standard, with jaw-dropping luxury and price tags to match.

Generally speaking, for a double you can expect to pay under Rs 2000 for budget accommodation, between Rs 2000 to Rs 10,000 for midrange, and over Rs 10,000 for top-end accommodation. Recommendations under Sleeping entries are in ascending order of price.

ACTIVITIES

There's way more than sun worship and pampering to be had on Mauritius – you'll find world-class diving, snorkelling and a huge range of water sports, as well as some good hiking to keep you occupied here.

Deep-Sea Fishing

The fisheries around Mauritius support large predators such as marlin, wahoo, tuna and sharks, luring big-game fishermen from around the world. November to April is the prime season for marlin, when the water is

PRACTICALITIES

- Mauritius uses the metric system for weights and measures.

- Electric current is 220V, 50Hz; British-style three-pin sockets are most common, though you'll also find the continental two-pin variety.

- The two most important, widely read dailies are the French language *L'Express* (lexpress.mu) and *Le Mauricien* (lemauricien.com). The *News on Sunday* and the *Mauritius Times* are English-language weeklies.

- There are three free channels in Mauritius run by the state Mauritius Broadcasting Corporation (MBC) – MBC1, MBC2 and MBC3. There are also numerous pay channels. Programming is mainly in Creole but with foreign imports in French, English and numerous Indian languages.

- Radio is a more popular medium, with a huge number of local commercial stations broadcasting in Creole and Hindi, and the BBC World Service and Voice of America, readily available. A couple of the most popular radio stations include Kool FM 89.3 Mhz and Taal FM 94.0 Mhz.

at its warmest. Tuna, wahoo and sharks can be found year-round. Annual fishing competitions are held at Grande Rivière Noire in November and February.

Game fishing has far less environmental impact than commercial fishing, but the weight and the number of fish caught has shown a marked decline since its heyday in the 1970s. It's now rare to catch anything over 400kg. Using the practice of 'tag-and-release' is an option for those who want the thrill without depriving the ocean of these magnificent creatures.

Anglers get to take home a trophy such as the marlin's nose spike, or a couple of fillets, but the day's catch belongs to the operator, who sells it to be served up at local restaurants.

Most of the big hotels run boats, and there are several private operators based at Grande Rivière Noire, Trou aux Biches and Grand Baie. Most outfits have a minimum hire time of around six hours, and each boat can normally take three anglers and three guests. Expect to pay upwards of Rs 12,000 per boat.

Diving & Snorkelling

Diving and snorkelling are very well established in Mauritius and its dive sites compare well to others in the Indian Ocean, although several dive operators during research were keen to point out that Mauritius 'is no Maldives' – a reference to its often lower visibility and less stunning coral. Basically the rule is to choose where you dive carefully and you should have a superb time. The best place

to dive in Mauritius is Rodrigues, where the corals are fantastic and the diver numbers are tiny, so you feel like a pioneer. On the mainland, Blue Bay and Flic-en-Flac have the best diving spots, the particular stand-outs being dive sites Colorado in Blue Bay and Rempart Serpent and La Cathédrale in Flic-en-Flac. Snorkelling can be enjoyed almost anywhere, but again it's particularly fruitful in Rodrigues. Nearly all bigger hotels organise regular snorkelling excursions, often at no charge. For more information on diving in Mauritius, see p27.

Hiking

For those interested in more than the usual beach activities, Mauritius offers some attractive hikes. Most are in the Central Plateau area around the Black River Gorges National Park; see p87 for detailed descriptions. Lion Mountain (north of Mahébourg) is another popular climb, while a day exploring the east coast of Rodrigues is a must for anyone wanting to get away from it all.

As a general rule when hiking, you should pay attention to 'Entrée Interdit' (Entry Prohibited) signs – they may mean you're entering a hunting reserve. 'Chemin Privée' (Private Rd) signs are generally there for the benefit of motorists; most landowners won't object to the odd pedestrian. It's best to ask if you're unsure about where you should and shouldn't walk.

One possibility is to go with a guide. **Yemaya Adventures** (☎ 752 0046; www.yemayaadventures.com) and **Maurisun Adventure & Tours** (☎ 263 0192; www.maurisun.com; Royal Rd) in Grand Baie both offer escorted hikes. On Rodrigues, contact **Osmosis** (☎ 832 3051; osmosis@intnet.mu; Port Sud-Est; ☯ 7am-5pm), based at the Mourouk Ebony Hotel.

Horse Riding
Mauritius has some lovely rambling countryside, which is perfect for riding excursions. There are opportunities for horse and pony riding at Domaine Les Pailles (p65), an estate run as a tourist attraction, at Mon Choisy (p69) and in Rodrigues (p129).

Surfing
A small scene led by Australian and South African surfers built up in the 1970s around Tamarin on the west coast (the surf movie *The Forgotten Island of Santosha* was made here), but the wave crashed during the 1980s.

These days, the scene around Tamarin comprises a small community of local and Réunionnais surfers. You can plug into what's happening and rent surfboards from one of the several surf shops in Tamarin.

The surf at Tamarin itself is fairly tame; better breaks in the area include Le Morne and One Eye's (named after the one-eyed owner of Le Morne estate), both at the northern end of Le Morne Peninsula. There are also good surfing locations near Baie du Cap. Lefts and Rights is further south by Îlot Sancho, and there's a tricky break opposite the public gardens in Souillac. The surfing season lasts from around May to September.

Undersea Walks & Submersibles
One popular but environmentally ruinous way to enjoy the underwater world if you don't dive is to take an 'underwater walk' – available at a number of places but most commonly found in the tourist hub of Grand Baie. Participants don a weight-belt and a diving helmet and stroll along the seabed feeding the fish in a sort of Jules Verne journey beneath the sea way. Oxygen is piped down from the surface – using solar-powered compressors, no less – and divers are on hand in case there are any problems.

Undersea walks carry a greater risk of damaging the sensitive marine environment and they're absolutely no substitute for diving or even snorkelling, so your money is far better spent on enjoying or learning the latter two. Submarine trips are fun and less of an environmental worry, although again they're really only for those who can't or won't dive.

Water Sports
Mauritius is a great place to enjoy water sports, with most bigger hotels offering a dizzying range of activities from sailing to kayaking. Kitesurfing has really taken off recently, with Rodrigues being a superb place to do this, as well as at various spots along the eastern coast of the mainland.

Yacht Cruises
The main centre for cruises is Grand Baie, from where luxury catamarans depart regularly for day trips to the northern islands, sunset cruises and the like. Perhaps the most interesting outing is a trip on the *Isla Mauritia*, a classy old schooner run by Yacht Charters in Grand Baie (p73). On the east coast, a couple of companies offer cruises from Pointe d'Esny (p115) to Île aux Cerfs.

All of these cruises can be booked through tour agents. Most of the big hotels also arrange cruises for their guests. Packages usually include lunch and snorkelling. Whether there's actually enough wind to fill the sails is in the hands of the gods.

BUSINESS HOURS
Banks in Mauritius generally open from 9.30am to 4pm Monday to Friday. Government offices usually open from 9am to 4pm Monday to Friday and 9am to noon Saturday. Restaurants usually open from around 10.30am to 10.30pm Monday to Saturday. Shops typically open from 9am to 5pm Monday to Friday, and 8am to noon on Saturday. Some close on Thursday or Saturday afternoons. However, on Rodrigues in particular, shops and offices close much earlier than 4pm; to be on the safe side it's best to do all your business in the morning.

CHILDREN
Travelling with children in Mauritius presents no particular problems. In fact, kids generally have a ball. The main attraction is undoubtedly the seaside. The beaches at Pereybère, Belle Mare, Blue Bay and Flic en Flac are particularly child-friendly. The domestic and wild animals on display at Casela Nature Park (p103) near Flic en Flac and La Vanille (p119) to the west of Mahébourg should also go down a treat. Older children might be interested in the interactive displays and machinery at L'Aventure du Sucre (p84), the sugar museum at Pamplemousses. Domaine Les Pailles (p65) near Port Louis offers activities to suit

all ages, from pony and train rides for the little ones to quad-biking and full-blown trekking for teenagers.

To put their holiday in context, there's a wonderful series of cartoon books by Henry Koobes (published locally by Editions Vizavi Ltd). The English-language titles include *In Dodoland, SOS Shark* and *Meli-Melo in the Molasses.*

CLIMATE CHARTS

For further information on choosing the best time of the year for visiting Mauritius, see p55.

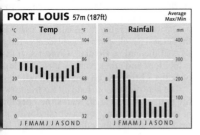

PORT LOUIS 57m (187ft)

CUSTOMS

In Mauritius, visitors aged 16 years and over may import 200 cigarettes or 250g of tobacco; 1L of spirits; 2L of wine, ale or beer; 250mL of *eau de toilette*; and up to 100mL of perfume.

There are restrictions on importing food, plants and animals, for which import permits are required. Other prohibited and restricted articles include spear guns and items made from ivory, shell, turtleshell or other materials banned under the Convention on International Trade in Endangered Species (CITES); it is also illegal to take such items out when you leave.

With regards to currency, visitors to Mauritius may import a maximum of Rs 700 in local currency, and take out Rs 350, but there are no restrictions on foreign currency.

DANGERS & ANNOYANCES

Mauritius is an exceptionally safe country to travel in. Your biggest annoyances are likely to be environmental (mosquitoes in some places, sun burn and the occasional upset stomach), although there are some other things to bear in mind.

Taxi drivers in Mauritius can earn up to 30% commission from certain shops, hotels,

restaurants and other businesses to which they take clients. Keep this in mind if a taxi driver tells you that the place you want to go to is full or closed or more expensive than one he knows. Insist first on going to your chosen destination.

Lying under a coconut palm may seem like a tropical idyll, but there have been some tragic accidents. Take care when walking under coconut trees and don't lie (or park your car) beneath them.

The Indian Ocean is a warm tropical ocean, so there are several aquatic nasties to watch out for. Fortunately, few travellers encounter anything more serious than the odd coral cut. For more information, see p312.

All beaches below the high-tide line are public property, so you are entitled to plop your towel down on the sand, whatever some over-officious security guard might tell you.

Cyclones

Mauritius lies within the cyclone belt. Most cyclones occur between December and March. While direct hits are relatively uncommon, storms miles away can bring very strong winds.

As soon as a cyclone is detected, a system of alerts is used to inform the public of the level of danger. In Mauritius there are four levels of alert. The alerts and then regular bulletins are broadcast on radio and TV.

Theft

Petty theft is not a major problem in this region, but one that you should be aware of. Favourite haunts for thieves are the beaches. Île aux Cerfs is a particular hot spot. The best strategy is not to take any valuables to the beach – and never tempt a passing thief by leaving your belongings unattended.

Be extra careful in crowded places such as markets and avoid walking around with your valuables casually slung over your shoulder. When travelling on public transport, keep your gear near you.

If you hire a car, it's best not to leave anything valuable in it at all. If you must do so, hide everything well out of sight. Wherever possible, park in a secure car park or at least somewhere busy – never park in an isolated spot, especially at night.

Don't leave vital documents, money or valuables lying about in your room. Many hotels provide room safes, which are well worth using. Otherwise, leave your valuables in the safe at reception and get a receipt. While most hotels are reliable, to be extra sure, pack everything in a small, double-zippered bag that can be padlocked, or use a large envelope with a signed seal that will reveal any tampering. Count money and travellers cheques before and after retrieving them from the safe.

If you do have something stolen, report it to the police. The chances of them recovering anything are remote, but you'll need a statement proving you have reported the crime if you want to claim on insurance.

EMBASSIES & CONSULATES
Mauritian Embassies & Consulates
Mauritius has diplomatic representation in the following countries:

Australia (☎ 06-281 1203; mhccan@cyberone.com.au; 2 Beale Crescent, Deakin Canberra, ACT 2600)
France (☎ 01 42 27 30 19; ambassade.maurice@online.fr; 127 Rue de Tocqueville, 75017 Paris)
Germany (☎ 030-263 9360; www.mauritius-embassy.de; Burgraf Centre, 84 Kurfurstenstrasse, 10787 Berlin)
Seychelles (☎ 611100; birdlife@seychelles.net; Conservation Centre, Roche Caiman, PO Box 1310, Mahé)
South Africa (☎ 342 1283/4; 1163 Pretorius St, Hatfield 0083; Pretoria)
UK (☎ 020-7581 0294; mauritius.embassyhomepage.com; 32-33 Elvaston Place, London SW7 5NW)
USA (☎ 202-244 1491; www.maurinet.com/embasydc.html; Suite 441, 4301 Connecticut Ave NW, Washington, DC, 20008)

Embassies & Consulates in Mauritius
Many countries do not have representatives in Mauritius, and usually refer their citizens to the embassy in Pretoria, South Africa. Countries with diplomatic representation in Mauritius include the following:

Australian High Commission (Map pp58-9; ☎ 202 0160; www.mauritius.embassy.gov.au; 2nd fl; Rogers House, 5 President John Kennedy St, Port Louis)
British High Commission (Map pp58-9; ☎ 202 9400; bhc@intnet.mu; 7th fl, Les Cascades Bldg, Edith Cavell St, Port Louis; 8.15am-3.45pm Mon-Thu, 8.15am-1.30pm Fri)
Canada (Map pp58-9; ☎ 212 5500; canada@intnet.mu; 18 Jules Koenig St, Port Louis; 10am-noon Mon-Fri)
France (Map pp58-9; ☎ 202 0100; www.ambafrance-mu.org; 14 St Georges St, Port Louis; 8am-1pm)
Germany (Map pp58-9; ☎ 211 4100; 32 Bis St Georges St, Port Louis; 9am-noon Mon-Fri)
Italy (☎ 211 1427; fax 269 0268; DML Bldg, M1 Motorway, Port Louis)

Seychelles (Map pp58-9; ☎ 211 1688; gfok@intnet.mu; 616 St James Ct, St Denis St, Port Louis)
Switzerland (Map pp58-9; ☎ 208 8763; swiss.consul@intnet.mu; 2 Jules Koenig St, Port Louis; 9am-noon Mon-Fri)
USA (Map pp58-9; ☎ 202 4400; mauritius.usembassy.gov 4th fl, Rogers House, 5 President John Kennedy St, Port Louis; 7.30am-4.45pm Mon-Thu, 7.30am-12.30pm Fri)

FESTIVALS & EVENTS
Given the range of beliefs and customs in Mauritius, hardly a week goes by without some celebration. You can usually find out about the latest *cavadee, teemeedee* or other ceremonies from the Mauritius Tourism Promotion Authority in Port Louis (p56).

On Rodrigues, the main cultural event is the Festival Kréol, which takes place over three days at the end of October. Concerts, crafts exhibitions and other events – including lots of eating – break out all over the island.

The Fête du Poisson, held on Rodrigues in the first week of March, marks the opening of the fishing season. It is celebrated with all sorts of festivities including fishing expeditions – and lots more eating.

Regattas featuring traditional wooden fishing boats are popular in Rodrigues. Most take place in the lagoon off Port Sud-Est between January and December, but the most prestigious event of the year is the regatta held off Pointe de l'Herbe in May.

Hindu Festivals
CAVADEE
One of the more unusual Mauritian festivals, the Thaipoosam Cavadee takes place in January or February each year at most Hindu temples, and features acts of self-mutilation by devotees. Honouring a vow to Subramanya, the second son of Shiva, pilgrims pierce their tongues and cheeks with skewers. They then march from their chosen temple to the banks of a river carrying the *cavadee* (a wooden arch decorated with flowers and palm leaves, with pots of milk suspended from each end of the base) on their shoulders.

The Thaipoosam Cavadee is a public holiday, but other small *cavadees* occur during the rest of the year at selected temples.

TEEMEEDEE
This is a Hindu and Tamil fire-walking ceremony in honour of various gods. The ceremonies occur throughout the year, but

mostly in December and January. After fasting and bathing, the participants walk over red-hot embers scattered along the ground. The Hindu temples in Quatre Bornes, Camp Diable (near Rivière des Anguilles) and The Vale (near Goodlands) are noted for this event. A feat along similar lines is sword climbing, seen mostly between April and June. The best demonstrations occur at Mont Choisy and the towns of Triolet and Solitude (between Port Louis and Trou aux Biches).

OTHER HINDU FESTIVALS
Each year, most of the island's Hindus make a pilgrimage to Grand Bassin, a crater lake in the south of the island, for the festival Maha Shivaratri. For information about the celebration, see the boxed text on p89.

Hindus also celebrate the victory of Rama over the evil deity Ravana during Divali (Dipavali), which falls in late October or early November. To mark this joyous event, countless candles and lamps are lit to show Rama (the seventh incarnation of Vishnu) the way home from his period of exile.

Holi, the festival of colours, is known for the exuberant throwing of coloured powder and water, and tourists are not exempt from the odd dousing. The festival symbolises the victory of divine power over demonic strength. On the night before Holi, bonfires are built to symbolise the destruction of the evil demon Holika. This festival is held in February or March.

Other major public festivals include Pongal (January or February), Ougadi (March or April) and Ganesh Chaturti (August or September). The latter celebrates the birthday of Ganesh, the elephant-headed god of wisdom and prosperity.

Muslim Festivals
Muslims celebrate Eid al-Fitr to mark the end of the fasting month of Ramadan, which is the ninth month of the lunar year. Eid al-Fitr is always a public holiday.

Chinese Festivals
The Chinese New Year is celebrated with the Chinese Spring Festival, which is a public holiday and falls in late January or early February. On New Year's Eve, homes are spring-cleaned and decked in red, the colour of happiness, and firecrackers are let off to ward off evil spirits. On the following day, cakes made of rice flour and honey are given to family and friends. No scissors or knives may be used in case someone is hurt and thus begins the New Year with bad luck.

Christian Festivals
The most important date for many Mauritian Christians is 9 September, Père Laval Feast Day, which marks the anniversary of the priest's death. Pilgrims from around the world come to his shrine at Ste-Croix to pray for miracle cures (p66).

FOOD
Food is likely to be a highlight of any visit with the huge choice of cuisine and some excellent restaurants throughout the country. Be aware that any restaurant aimed at tourists is likely to be anything from 50% to 200% more expensive than a local equivalent and that it pays to plan where you'll eat – many places offer up uninspiring, drab food simply because they're guaranteed customers from big resorts nearby. Choose carefully with the options in this book or ask hotel staff for advice.

In general a budget meal of two courses and some alcohol will cost less than Rs 200. Moving up a notch, you can expect to pay between Rs 200 and Rs 500 in a midrange place, while the bill at a classy, top-of-the-range establishment will be at least Rs 600 per head. For information about just some of the culinary delights in store in Mauritius, see p47.

GAY & LESBIAN TRAVELLERS
Mauritius has a paradoxical relationship to homosexuality. While gay and lesbian rights are legally guaranteed and much of the population is young and progressive, there remains a rigidly conservative streak to the Mauritian character. As a result gay life remains fairly secretive – mainly existing on the internet, in private and at the occasional party. While there were no gay or lesbian bars or clubs on the island at the time of writing, there were one-off club nights and parties organised. A gay rights march in Rose Hill in 2006 was the first ever permitted in the country and a sign that the small, nascent gay movement is gaining in confidence, although there's still a huge way to go.

For gay and lesbian travellers there's little to worry about. Mauritians are generally very

MAURITIUS DIRECTORY

open-minded people and we've never heard of any problems arising from same-sex couples sharing rooms during their holidays. You're still best to avoid public displays of affection outside your hotel and generally to be aware that what might not be abnormal at home may be considered shocking here.

HOLIDAYS

The following public holidays are observed in Mauritius:

New Year 1 & 2 January
Thaipoosam Cavadee January/February
Chinese Spring Festival January/February
Abolition of Slavery 1 February
Maha Shivaratri February/March
Ougadi March/April
National Day 12 March
Labour Day 1 May
Assumption of the Blessed Virgin Mary 15 August
Ganesh Chaturti September
Divali October/November
Arrival of Indentured Labourers 2 November
Eid al-Fitr November/December
Christmas Day 25 December

INSURANCE

A travel-insurance policy to cover theft, loss and medical problems is a good idea. Some policies specifically exclude dangerous activities, which can include scuba diving, motorcycling and even hiking. Always check the small print.

You may prefer a policy that pays doctors or hospitals directly rather than having to pay on the spot and claiming later. If you have to claim later ensure you keep all documentation.

Check that the policy covers ambulances or an emergency flight home.

For more information on health insurance, see p307.

INTERNET ACCESS

Internet access has improved in recent years, with nearly all towns having at least one internet café where you can surf the web. There's a growing trend for hotels to have wi-fi or internet access from the rooms (for those with their own laptop), although sadly even in the five-star hotels these services tend to be charged. We mention in the body of reviews when wi-fi or ADSL line connections are free – otherwise expect to be charged for use.

LEGAL MATTERS

Foreigners are subject to the laws of the country in which they are travelling and will receive no special consideration because they are tourists. If you find yourself in a sticky legal predicament, contact your embassy (see p136). In general travellers have nothing to fear from the police, who rarely harass foreigners and are extremely polite if they do need to stop them. Foreigners are nearly never stopped when driving in Mauritius, unlike locals.

MAPS

The best and most detailed map of Mauritius is that published by the **Institut Géographique Nationale** (IGN; www.ign.fr). The Globetrotter travel map is good for its detailed insets including Port Louis, Curepipe and the botanical gardens at Pamplemousses. Both are available from local bookstores and supermarkets.

There are no decent maps of Rodrigues, but the Ti Boussol, the best one available, is on sale at the airport and tourist shops of Port Mathurin for Rs 80.

MONEY

The Mauritian unit of currency is the rupee (Rs), which is divided into 100 cents. There are coins of 5, 20 and 50 cents, and Rs 1, Rs 5 and Rs 10. The banknote denominations are Rs 25, Rs 50, Rs 100, Rs 200, Rs 500, Rs 1000 and Rs 2000.

ATMs

Armed with your PIN, it's perfectly possible to travel on plastic in Mauritius since ATMs are widespread. Even Rodrigues has a smattering of them. They're mostly located outside banks though you'll also find them at the airports at larger supermarkets and in some shopping malls. The majority of machines accept Visa and MasterCard, or any similar cards in the Cirrus and Plus networks, while Amex now has a tie-in with Mauritius Commercial Bank (MCB).

Credit Cards

Visa and MasterCard are the most useful cards to carry, though Amex is catching up. Nearly all tourist shops and the more upmarket restaurants and hotels accept payment by credit card, as do car-hire companies, tour agents and so forth. Anywhere outside the main tourist haunts and small businesses still expect payment in cash.

A few places add on an extra fee, typically %, to the bill to cover 'bank charges'. The heaper car-hire companies are the worst of-enders. To be on the safe side, always ask. Cash advances on credit cards are available rom most major banks, including MCB, Bar-lays, the State Bank and HSBC. Just remem-er to take your passport.

Moneychangers
Major currencies and travellers cheques can be hanged at the main banks, exchange bureaus nd the larger hotels. Exchange bureaus some-imes offer slightly better rates than banks, ut there's usually little difference. Hotels end to have the worst rates and may add an dditional service commission. As a general ule, travellers cheques bring a better rate than ash. There is no black market in Mauritius.

Banks don't charge commission on chang-ng cash. As for travellers cheques, the system aries. Some banks, such as HSBC, charge 1% f the total, with a minimum of Rs 200, while MCB and the State Bank levy Rs 50 for up to 0 cheques. Don't forget to take along your assport when changing money. And make ure you hang on to the encashment form, vhich will have to be presented if you want o change Mauritian rupees back into foreign urrency at the end of your stay.

Taxes
Most items apart from unprepared food are ubject to 15% VAT. There's no clear rule about vhether this tax is included in prices quoted for neals, rooms and activities. If it's not clear, be ure to ask or you may be in for a nasty shock. Top-end hotels and restaurants sometimes add service charge of about 10% to 15%.

PHOTOGRAPHY
Print and slide film are widely available locally nd there are decent developing studios in Port Louis, Flic en Flac and Grand Baie. For nformation on taking photographs, see the oxed text p140.

POST
The postal service in Mauritius is quick nd reliable. Postcards cost Rs 10 to send to nywhere in the world and most shops sell tamps as well as the local post office. Poste estante is available at central post offices. You usually have to pay a small fee to collect etters and may be asked for your passport.

SHOPPING
If the beaches begin to pall, you can shop till you drop in Mauritius. Given such a wide choice, there is no reason to purchase items made from endangered species – avoid any seashell, coral or turtleshell products.

Bargaining is very much part of life in Mau-ritius. It's usual to bargain in markets and anywhere where prices aren't marked, and sometimes even on marked prices if you're a big spender. As a tourist, however, you'll need well-honed bargaining skills to get much of a discount.

Clothing
The textile industry is one of Mauritius' big-gest earners. Many of the brand-name clothes on sale in Europe, Australia and America are produced in the factories around Curepipe, Floréal and Vacoas. Shoppers can save by buying at the source, and many of the big-ger suppliers have outlet stores where you can snap up items at a fraction of their usual retail price. Those really watching the rupees can opt for convincing – and not-so-convincing – copies of well-known designer brands. One of the best places to pick up genuine seconds is the market at Quatre Bornes (p92). Other vendors tend to congregate on President John Kennedy St in Port Louis, and in the Rose Hill and Cure-pipe markets in central Mauritius. Check care-fully for minor flaws and dodgy stitching.

Floreal Knitwear in Floréal is renowned for its stylish sweaters and other knitted gar-ments. The company supplies Gap, Next and other international outfitters, but you can buy the same items before the branded labels have been added for a fraction of the final cost at their Floréal emporium.

Shibani and Maille St are two other local companies producing high-quality knitwear. Maille St specialises in cashmere sweaters in colours to die for. For kids there's Gecko, while Habit and the fetchingly named IV Pl@y target teens with up-to-the-minute streetwear. You'll find branches of these shops in Port Louis' Cau-dan Waterfront complex, Sunset Blvd in Grand Baie and other upmarket shopping malls.

Handicrafts & Souvenirs
Locally produced basketry, essential oils, sugar, spices, teas and T-shirts all make very portable souvenirs. The Craft Market in Port

(Continued on page 149)

PICTURE PERFECT

The Indian Ocean islands are the very image of paradise, and many photographers strive to capture that image on film. For the most comprehensive guide to taking photographs on the road, get a copy of Lonely Planet's *Travel Photography*.

TECHNICAL TIPS

Take into consideration the heat, humidity, tropical sunlight and equatorial shadows. If you're shooting on beaches, it's important to adjust for glare from water or sand, and to keep sand and salt water well away from your equipment.

Photography

The best times to take photographs on sunny days are the first two hours after sunrise and the last two before sunset. This brings out the best colours. At other times, the harsh sunlight and glare washes everything out, although filters help counter the glare.

Video

As well as filming the obvious things – sunsets, spectacular views – remember to record some of the ordinary details of everyday life. Often the most interesting things occur when you're actually intent on filming something else.

Video cameras have amazingly sensitive microphones, and you might be surprised how much sound they pick up. This can be a problem if there is a lot of ambient noise – filming by the side of a busy road might seem OK when you do it, but you might hear only a deafening cacophony of traffic noise when you view it back home.

RESTRICTIONS

Don't photograph or film airports or anything that looks like police or military equipment or property. Photography is generally not permitted in Hindu temples and mosques – usually there is a sign warning against photography.

It may be insensitive to take photos at certain religious ceremonies, so again, it's best to ask first.

PHOTOGRAPHING PEOPLE

Although there are no cultural taboos about photographing people in this region, you should still ask their permission first as a matter of politeness.

A zoom lens is a relatively unobtrusive means of taking portraits – even if you happened to have obtained permission, a reasonable distance between you and your subject should reduce your subject's discomfort, and result in more natural shots.

UNDERWATER PHOTOGRAPHY

Photographs taken underwater can be startling – at depth, flash photography reveals colours that aren't there for the naked eye. Nowadays, reasonably priced and easy-to-use underwater cameras are available. For souvenir snapshots, disposable underwater cameras are a good option.

If you're serious about underwater photography, it's worth investing in a good flash. As you descend, natural colours are quickly absorbed, starting with the red end of the spectrum. In other words, the deeper you go, the more blue things look. To put the colour back in you need a flash.

In general, 28mm or 35mm lenses work best underwater. Even with these you have to get close to achieve good results, which requires patience when photographing fish. With experience and the right equipment, the results can be superb.

JEAN-BERNARD CARILLET

Fun in the sun by the crystal-clear lagoon of Flic en Flac (p103), Mauritius

OLIVIER CIRENDINI

Île aux Cerfs (p98), Mauritius. Need we say more?

JOHN HAY

Explore the atmospheric back-streets of Port Louis (p55), Mauritius

Take it easy beside the tranquil lagoon of Pereybère (p79), Mauritius

Lobster's just one of the seafood delights of Mauritian cuisine (p47)

Settle in for a sunset drink in Grand Baie (p72), Mauritius

JEAN ROBERT

·elve into Mauritius' past through the
reole architecture and colonial heritage
f Eureka estate (p94)

OLIVIER CIRENDINI

Beach or pool? Snooze or swim? Tough decisions
when staying in Blue Bay (p115), Mauritius

·oak up the views or dive into the deep, cool waters of Tamarin Falls (p87), Mauritius

JEAN ROBERT

JEAN-BERNA

Réunion's iconic Piton de la Fournaise (p210) lets off some steam

ARIADNE VAN ZANDBERGEN

The eerie, ashen landscape of Plaine des Sables
(p211), Réunion

JEAN-BERNA

The Cirque de Salazie surrounds the charmin
hamlet of Hell-Bourg (p203), Réunion

Cascade du Voile de la Mariée (p204), Réunion

Slippery-dip down waterfalls and leap off boulders while canyoning (p199) in Réunion's Cirque de Cilaos

Soar like an eagle from the mountains to the sea while paragliding (p190) above St-Leu, Réunion

RALPH LEE HOPKINS

Soak up the laid-back, tropical vibes of La Digue (p289), Seychelles

HOLGER LEUE

Meet the locals on Curieuse Island (p283), Seychelles

Find your own secret cove cruising the coast of Praslin (p280), Seychelles

HOLGER LEUE

Desert the beach and retreat to the lush, mountainous interior of Mahé (p267), Seychelles

JOHN HAY

RALPH LEE HOPKINS

It doesn't get more idyllic than this: Anse Source d'Argent (p291), La Digue, Seychelles

Indulge your Robinson Crusoe fantasies on Desroches (p289), Amirantes Group, Seychelles

JOHN BORTHWICK

Glide alongside sea turtles while diving off Réunion (p30)

OLIVIER CIRENDINI

JEAN-BERNARD CARILLET

Divers head to Mauritius' Trou aux Biches
(p68) for stunning drop-offs and wrecks

Underwater treasures, Mauritius (p27)

MICHAEL AW

The dancing tentacles of colourful sea
anemones await their next meal

(Continued from page 139)

Louis' Caudan Waterfront complex offers perhaps the widest choice and the quality is high. Other good places to browse are Port Louis' Central Market and the Grand Baie Bazaar. Vendors at both also sell Malagasy handicrafts, including leather belts and bags, embroidery and semiprecious-stone solitaire sets.

From Rodrigues you can take home a very natty vacoas-leaf hat or basket. The island is also famous for its honey and lemon and chilli preserves. Jewellery and other items made from coconut shell by handicapped people are available from Care-Co in Port Mathurin.

Model Ships

Whether or not you could conceive of having one at home, it is difficult not to be impressed by the skill that goes into producing Mauritius' famous model ships. Small-scale shipbuilding has become a huge business and you'll see intricate replicas of famous vessels, such as the *Bounty*, *Victory*, *Endeavour*, *Golden Hind* and even the *Titanic*, for sale all over the island; it's hard to believe that shipbuilding dates back to only 1968, when an unknown Mauritian carved a model ship for fun and launched a whole new industry.

The models are made out of teak or mahogany (cheaper camphor wood is liable to crack), and larger ships take up to 400 hours to complete. Men usually work on the structure and the women do the rigging and sails, which are dipped in tea to give them a weathered look.

If you're thinking of buying, shop around to compare prices, which range from Rs 2400 up to Rs 80,000 or more. One of the best model ship-builders is **Voiliers de L'Océan** (☎ /fax 676 6986; Sir Winston Churchill St, Curepipe; ☻7.30am-6pm); the company also has an outlet, MAST, in the Caudan Waterfront complex. The biggest factory is **Historic Marine** (☎ 283 9404; ☻8am-5pm Mon-Fri, 9am-noon Sat & Sun) in Goodlands, in the north of the island. In both cases the staff will be happy to show you around the workshop (weekdays only) without any pressure to buy.

To get your goods home safely, shops will pack the models for carry-on luggage or in sturdy boxes to go in the hold, and deliver them to your hotel or the airport at no extra charge.

SOLO TRAVELLERS

While Mauritius is very popular with honeymooners and other couples enjoying romantic breaks, there's no taboo about travelling alone and locals are extremely friendly and open, so you'll have plenty of chances to meet people and are unlikely to feel lonely. Single rooms are usually very easy to come by, although at certain midrange and top-end hotels, it's common to charge a flat fee for the room, which can make travelling alone an expensive experience.

TELEPHONE

The telephone service has received massive investment over the last few years. Calls no longer get lost or misrouted and there are public phones on almost every street corner. The state-controlled Mauritius Telecom has a virtual monopoly on landlines, although there's an open market for mobile services – Cellplus (owned by Mauritius Telecom) and Emtel compete with each other for every mobile-phone user in the country.

Coin-operated phones can only be used for calls within Mauritius. You need to feed in a minimum of two Rs 1 coins to make a call, which buys you about two minutes' phone time. They also accept Rs 5 coins.

You can dial abroad using IDD from private phones and public card-phones. Some public phones now accept credit cards, though they're few and far between.

The rate for a call to Australia, Europe or the USA is about Rs 20 per minute. These rates fall by around 25% during off-peak hours (10pm to 6am from Monday to Friday and noon on Saturday to 6am the following Monday).

When phoning Mauritius from abroad, you'll need to dial the international code for Mauritius (230), followed by the local number minus the first 0. There are no area codes in Mauritius.

Mobile Phones

Coverage on Mauritius is generally excellent, and has recently been extended to Rodrigues. If you have a GSM phone and it has been 'unlocked', you can keep costs down by buying a local SIM card from either **Cellplus** (☎ 203 7649, www.cellplus.mu; Mauritius Telecom Tower, Edith Cavell St, Port Louis) or **Emtel** (☎ 212 5400, www.emtel-ltd.com; Air Mauritius Bldg, President John F Kennedy St, Port Louis). A starter pack costs around Rs 600 including Rs 125-worth of calls. To top-up your credit you can buy prepaid cards almost anywhere.

Local calls are charged at between Rs 1.50 and Rs 5 per minute depending if you're calling someone on the same network or not. International calls cost a couple of rupees per minute on top of the standard Mauritius Telecom rates.

Phonecards

Télécartes (phonecards) are on sale at Mauritius Telecom offices, bookstores, news-vendors, supermarkets and the like. They come in denominations of Rs 50, Rs 100, Rs 250 and Rs 500. A Rs 50 card gives you roughly three minutes to Australia, Europe or the USA.

TIME

Mauritius is GMT+4 hours, both on the mainland and on Rodrigues. When it's midday in Port Louis, it's 8am in London, 9am in Paris, 3am in New York and 6pm in Sydney. Mauritius does not operate a system of daylight savings; being equatorial its sunset and sunrise times vary only slightly throughout the year.

TOURIST INFORMATION

Independent travellers remain a proportionally small number in comparison with the package gang, but provision for helping them has improved hugely in recent years, the **Mauritius Tourism Promotion Authority** (MTPA; ☎ 208 6397; www.tourism-mauritius.mu) running a national network of friendly tourist kiosks where you can pick up basic maps and a reasonably useful guide covering the main sights and activities.

MTPA also has a desk in the arrivals hall at the **SSR airport** (☎ 637 3635), though it's only open from the first flight until 1pm. It also operates kiosks in **Flic-en-Flac** (☎ 453 8660), **Ruisseau Créole** (☎ 483 7189), **Pamplemousses** (☎ 243 9900), **Trou d'Eau Douce** (☎ 480 0925) and in **Port Mathurin** (☎ 832 0866). Also useful is Mauritius Telecom's 24-hour phone service, **Tourist Info** (☎ 152). At any time of day or night you can speak to someone (in English) who will at least try to answer your questions.

TRAVELLERS WITH DISABILITIES

Mauritius makes a relatively decent provision for those with mobility problems. Modern buildings conform to international standards for disabled access, although public toilets, pavements and lifts tend not to be as good. Most top-end hotels have wheelchair access, lifts and specially equipped bathrooms. In big hotels, there are always plenty of staff around to help and it is often possible to hire an assistant if you want to go on an excursion or a boat trip. With a bit of extra warning, some riding stables, dive centres and other sports operators can cater for people with disabilities.

None of the public transport systems offer wheelchair access. Anyone using a wheelchair will be reliant on taxis and minibuses.

VISAS

You don't need a visa to enter Mauritius if you are a citizen of the EU, the USA, Australia, Canada, Japan, New Zealand or a number of other countries. You can find more information on the website http://pmo.gov.mu/dha/ministry/novisa.htm. Initial entry is granted for a maximum of one month. If you change your departure plans, make sure you don't exceed your permitted stay.

Extensions for a further three months as a tourist are available from the **Passport & Immigration Office** (Map pp58-9; ☎ 210 9312; fax 210 9322; Sterling House, Lislet Geoffrey St, Port Louis). Applications must be submitted with one form, two passport-size photos, your passport, an onward ticket and proof of finances. Two letters may also be necessary – one from you explaining why you want to stay longer, and one by a local 'sponsor' (it can be someone providing accommodation). Providing you can satisfy these demands there should be no further problems, but since the police are responsible for passport control, and quite a few visitors overstay their entry permits, there are 'get tough' periods.

WOMEN TRAVELLERS

Mauritius is safe for women and you'll not feel out of place travelling solo either. It's still sensible to avoid walking around late at night outside of resorts, particularly as most places have very poor or non-existent street lighting. Port Louis is one extreme example where it really would be foolish to walk about alone after dark. In general men are well-behaved and respectful, but after a few drinks in the evening this can't be taken for granted.

TRANSPORT AROUND MAURITIUS

AIR

Mainland Mauritius has only one airport, the well-run **Sir Seewoosagur Ramgoolam International Airport** (http://mauritius-airport.intnet.mu). There are two domestic airlines, Air Mauritius and Catovair, both of which connect mainland Mauritius with the island of Rodrigues. For more details see p124.

Air Mauritius also offers helicopter tours and charters from SSR International Airport and a number of major hotels. A full one-hour island tour costs Rs 26,000 for up to four passengers; a quick 15-minute jaunt will set you back Rs 10,000. For information and reservations, contact **Air Mauritius Helicopter Services** (☎ 637 3552; helicopter@airmauritius com) or ask your hotel to organise a transfer or trip.

BICYCLE

Cycling isn't really a practical means of long-distance transport in Mauritius – there is simply too much traffic – but bikes are fine for short hops along the coast. Given that the coast is pleasantly flat, it's amazing how much ground you can cover in a day. The coast roads are also quieter than those in the interior, so you can relax and take in the landscape.

In general, the roads are well maintained, but look out for potholes along country lanes. Avoid cycling anywhere at night, as most roads are poorly lit and traffic can be erratic.

You can rent bikes (usually mountain bikes) from most hotels and guesthouses and also from some tour agents and car-rental outlets in the main tourist centres such as Grand Baie, Flic en Flac and Trou d'Eau Douce. The cheapest deals will start at around Rs 100 per day. You'll usually be asked for a deposit of Rs 5000, either in cash or by taking an imprint of your credit card. Most bikes are in pretty reasonable condition, but be sure to check the brakes, gears and saddle (some are mighty uncomfortable) before riding off into the blue-beyond. The bike should have a lock; use it, especially if you leave your bike at the beach and outside shops.

BOAT

The only scheduled domestic passenger services are between Port Louis and Rodrigues. The *Mauritius Trochetia* and the older *Mauritius Pride* between them sail four times a month in each direction; the outward journey takes about 36 hours and the return to Port Louis roughly 25 hours. Tickets and information are available through travel agents or direct from the Mauritius Shipping Corporation: contact **Coraline Shipping Agency** (Map pp58-9; ☎ 217 2285; msc@coraline.intnet.mu; Nova Bldg, 1 Military Rd, Port Louis) or, on Rodrigues, the **Mauritius Shipping Corporation** (Map p126; ☎ 831 0640; www.mauritiusshipping.intnet.mu; Rue François Leguat, Port Mathurin). Return fares cost Rs 2450/4900 for a seat/cabin in the *Mauritius Pride* and Rs 3000 for a 2nd-class cabin in the *Mauritius Trochetia*. These are popular services, so it is advised that you book ahead.

Various private operators offer cruises to offshore islands, or snorkelling and fishing excursions. See p134 and the listings under individual towns for more information about these services.

BUS

Anyone on a budget will fare well using the network of bus routes that criss-cross the island. Bus travel is cheap and fun – you'll usually find yourself chatting to gregarious locals – and although you won't set any land-speed records, it's generally a fairly easy and reliable way to get around.

It's best to stick to express buses whenever possible, as standard buses seem to stop every few metres and can take up to twice as long to reach the same destination. To give an idea of journey times, it takes approximately an hour by standard services from Mahébourg to Curepipe, an hour from Curepipe to Port Louis and an hour from Port Louis to Grand Baie.

Long-distance buses run from around 6am to 6.30pm, though there is a late service between Port Louis and Curepipe until 11pm. Generally there are buses every fifteen minutes or so on the major routes, with less frequent buses on the express services. Buses in country areas can be few and far between.

As an indication, fares range from Rs 12 for a short trip up to a maximum of Rs 30 for the run from Port Louis to Mahébourg. Air-conditioned express buses may be a couple of rupees extra. Tickets are available from the

MAIN BUS COMPANIES IN MAURITIUS

Company	Main routes
Mauritius Bus Transport ☎ 245 2539	Pamplemousses to Crève Coeur
National Transport Corporation (NTC) ☎ 426 1859; cnt.bus@intnet.mu	Port Louis to Centre de Flacq, Curepipe, Flic en Flac, Floréal, Grande Rivière Noire, Pamplemousses, Quatre Bornes, Rose Hill, Souillac; Quatre Bornes to Baie du Cap; Curepipe to Baie du Cap, Floréal, Quatre Bornes, Souillac, Flic en Flac
Rose Hill Transport ☎ 464 1221	Port Louis to Rose Hill
Triolet Bus Service (TBS) ☎ 261 6516	Port Louis to Cap Malheureux, Grand Baie, Mont Choisy, Pereybère, Trou aux Biches; Pamplemousses to Cap Malheureux, Grand Baie, Grande Gaube, Mont Choisy
United Bus Service (UBS) ☎ 212 2026	Port Louis to Curepipe, Mahébourg, Ste-Croix

conductor; keep some small change handy. Retain your tickets, as inspectors often board to check them. Press the buzzer when you want to get off.

The buses are single-deck vehicles bearing dynamic names such as 'Road Warrior', 'Bad Boys' and 'The Street Ruler'. It's perhaps not surprising that some drivers harbour Formula One racing fantasies; fortunately, the frequent stops slow things down a touch. Though the buses are in varying states of disrepair, the fleet is gradually being upgraded.

The buses are almost always packed, especially on the main routes, but turnover is quick at all the stops. If you start the trip standing, you're likely to end up sitting.

Be warned that you could have problems taking large bags or backpacks on a bus. If it takes up a seat, you will probably have to pay for that extra seat. A few travellers have even been refused entry to a full bus if they have a large bag.

There is no country-wide bus service for Mauritius. Instead there are five large regional bus companies (see the table, above) and scores of individual operators. Unfortunately, there are no published timetables available. Your best source of information is to phone the company or the umbrella body, the **National Transport Authority** (☎ 202 2800). Locals also usually know the best way to get from A to B.

CAR & MOTORCYCLE

By far the easiest and quickest way to get around Mauritius and Rodrigues is to hire a car. Prices aren't as low as they could be, considering the numbers of visitors who rent vehicles, but you should be able to negotiate a discount if you're renting for a week or more.

Mauritian roads range from the one stretch of motorway – running from SSR International Airport to Port Louis and Grand Baie – to heavily potholed minor roads. Even on the motorway you'll find people wandering across the road and a generally relaxed attitude. As in most places, the greatest danger comes from other drivers, not the roads. Mauritian drivers tend to have little consideration for each other, let alone for motorbikes. Buses are notorious for overtaking and then pulling in immediately ahead of other vehicles to pick up or drop off passengers; always show extra caution when a bus comes in sight. At night be aware you'll face an assault course of ill-lit oncoming vehicles, totally unlit bikes and weaving pedestrians. Motorcyclists should also be prepared for the elements, as sudden rain showers can come out of clear skies.

Car

Generally, drivers must be more than 23 years of age (some companies require a minimum age of 21) and have held a driving licence for at least one year, and payment must be made in advance. You can pay by credit card (Visa and MasterCard are the most widely accepted), though small companies might add a 3% 'processing fee' for this service. All foreigners are technically required to have an international driving licence. Few rental agencies enforce this, but it's safest to carry one as the police can demand to see it.

Rates for the smallest hatchback start at around Rs 1000 a day (including insurance and unlimited mileage) with one of the independent operators; add Rs 150 or so for air-con. International chains such as Hertz and Sixt charge from Rs 1400 a day. On top of that you will be required to pay a refund-

ble deposit, usually Rs 15,000; most compa-
ies will take an imprint of your credit card
o cover this. Policies usually specify that
drivers are liable for the first Rs 10,000 of
damage in the event of an accident.

While there are dozens of rental outlets in
Mauritius, during the peak Christmas holiday season cars can be hard to come by. It's
est to book several weeks in advance, espe-
ially if you don't want to pay the earth. All
the major international car-rental companies
sted below have airport desks or can deliver
o the airport. Some reliable local companies
re given here too.

DA (☎ 675 2626; www.ada.fr in French)
vis (☎ 208 1624; www.avis.com)
udget (☎ 467 9709; www.budget.com)
xodus (☎ 454 4396; www.exoduscarhire.com)
ertz (☎ 670 4301; www.hertz.com)

Motorcycle

There are only a few places where you can
ent motorbikes, which is a shame as this
s a great way to explore the quiet coastal
oads. While you'll occasionally find a
.25cc bike, most are 100cc or under; the
maller models are sometimes referred to
s scooters.

Whatever the engine size, most places
harge upwards of Rs 450 a day including
a helmet. As with car rental, payment is re-
quested in advance along with a deposit of
Rs 5000 or so.

Most of the bikes are fairly well worn, but
arts are widely available should anything
ail. Beware of 'imitation' parts, which are
opies of genuine manufacturer spares, cast
n inferior metal.

Towns offering motorcycle hire include
Grand Baie, Flic en Flac, Mahébourg and
Port Mathurin. You should be aware that
most motorcycle hire is 'unofficial' so you
may not be covered in case of a collision.

Parking

Parking is free and not a problem in most
of Mauritius, though it's best not to leave
your car in an isolated spot. City parking
equires payment. There are supervised car
parks in Port Louis, but elsewhere you'll
have to park on the street, which involves
buying parking coupons. These are avail-
ble from petrol stations and cost from Rs
50 for 10 coupons, with each coupon valid
for 30 minutes. The same coupons can be

used all over the island. Street parking is
generally free at night and at weekends; the
exact hours, which vary from one town to
another, are indicated on signposts.

Road Rules

Local motorists seem to think they'll save
electricity by not switching on their head-
lights and the police are better at people
control than traffic control. Traffic congestion is heavy in Port Louis. There are many
pedestrian zebra crossings, but cross with
care. Don't expect courtesy and don't expect drivers to be worried about insurance –
you'll get knocked over.

Driving is on the left and the speed
limit varies from 30km/h in town centres
to 80km/h on the open road and is clearly
signed. Even so, not many people stick to
these limits and the island has its fair share
of accidents.

Drivers and passengers are required to
wear seat belts. For lack of sufficient breath-
alysers, the alcohol limit (legally 0.5g/L) is
defined by the police as one glass of beer.

HITCHING

Hitching is never entirely safe in any country in the world, and we don't recommend
it. Travellers who decide to hitch should
understand that they are taking a small but
potentially serious risk. People who choose
to hitch will be safer if they travel in pairs
and let someone know where they are planning to go.

Getting a lift in Mauritius is subject to
pretty much the same quirks of luck and fate
that you experience hitching anywhere. The
only place where it really does come in handy
is Rodrigues. Since few people there own cars,
hitching is a popular way to get around, especially on Sundays, when buses are few and
far between. Those driving in Rodrigues will
make friends by offering lifts to locals who'll
try and flag you down almost anywhere. Obviously, proceed with caution and don't offer
lifts to groups if you're alone.

TAXI

It's sometimes possible to imagine that every
adult male in Mauritius is a taxi driver. Taxi
drivers will often shout out at travellers they see
wandering around Port Louis or Grand Baie,
while ranks outside hotels usually overflow
with drivers. Negotiation is key – meters are

rarely used and you'll usually be ripped off if you get in a taxi without agreeing a price. During the journey most cabbies will also tout for future business; if you aren't careful you may find that you've agreed to an all-day island tour. If you aren't interested, make this very clear, as many drivers won't take no for an answer.

Many guesthouse managers/owners have attempted to mitigate their guests' constant frustration with rip-offs by arranging prices with local taxi drivers. The quotes given under such arrangements, particularly those from small guesthouses, are often acceptable; they can usually arrange competitively priced airport pick-ups as well. Once you've got a feel for the rates, you can venture into independent bargaining.

Taxis charge slightly more at night and may ask for an extra fee if you want the comfort of air-con. It's also worth remembering that some taxis charge around Rs 1 per minute waiting time. It seems minimal, but it adds up if you stop for lunch or do some sightseeing on foot. Your best bet is to negotiate a set fare with the driver that includes waiting time. As a rough bargaining guide, here are some of the fares you can expect to pay for one-way trips.

From	To	Cost
Flic en Flac	Port Louis	Rs 400
Mahébourg	Blue Bay	Rs 100
SSR airport	Mahébourg	Rs 400
SSR airport	Flic en Flac	Rs 1000
SSR airport	Port Louis	Rs 800
SSR airport	Grand Baie	Rs 1000
Trou aux Biches	Grand Baie	Rs 200
Trou aux Biches	Port Louis	Rs 300

HIRING TAXIS

For between Rs 1500 and Rs 2500, you can hire a taxi for a full-day tour of sights around the island (the fare varies with how much ground you intend to cover). You can cut costs by forming a group – the price should *not* be calculated per person. If you want to squeeze a tour of the whole island into one day, keep in mind that this won't leave much time for sightseeing. You're better off splitting the island tour into two days. Once you've agreed to a price and itinerary, it helps to get the details down in writing. Although most drivers can speak both French and English, double-check before setting off to ensure you won't face a day-long communication barrier. If you're lucky, you'll get an excellent and informative guide, but note that most cabbies work on a commission basis with particular restaurants, shops and sights. If you want to go to a restaurant of your choice, you may have to insist on it. Again, small guesthouses can usually recommend a reliable driver.

SHARE TAXI

When individual fares are hard to come by, some cabs will cruise around their area supplementing the bus service. For quick, short-haul trips they pick up passengers waiting at the bus stops and charge just a little more than the bus. Their services are called 'share taxis' or 'taxi trains'. Mind you, if you flag down a share taxi, you'll only be swapping a big sardine can for a small one, and if you flag down an empty cab, you may have to pay the full fare.

Réunion

JEAN-BERNARD CARILLET

Réunion Snapshots

First, the bad news. Réunion faced a major health crisis in 2006, a yea which is considered an 'annus horribilis' in the history of the island. Th mosquito-borne Chikungunya virus (p309) hit this Indian Ocean island i late 2005 and by 2007 had infected about 266,000 people (over one-third c the population). In reality, the whole region was hit, including Mauritius, th Seychelles, Comoros and Madagascar, but not on the same dramatic scale a Réunion. Unsurprisingly, the epidemic had a negative impact on tourism i Réunion. Bookings plummeted by more than 60% in 2006 and early 2007

Now, the good news. Réunion is back on its feet, thanks to a massive ef fort to kill off the mosquito population. Army troops and firefighters wer mobilised and deployed on the island, spraying every potential risk zone with insecticide. Though not exactly environmentally friendly, this strategy paid of By mid-2007 the 'Chik', as it's affectionately (well, almost) dubbed in Réunior was eradicated, and the situation was considered to be back to normal, accord ing to French health officials. The future looks much brighter now.

In 2007 the much-awaited Parc National des Hauts de la Réunion wa created. It encompasses a huge chunk of the rugged interior, and it will g some way to protecting (and promoting) the island's unique cultural and environmental heritage. Local authorities lay emphasis on the island's 'greer image and its fantastic opportunities for ecotourism and outdoor activities Their aim is now to tap into new markets, especially the German and Ang lophone ones, in order to reduce the dependence on the French market.

Paradoxically, one of the greatest immediate concerns is not the envi ronment, but the ever-growing population. Recent estimates suggest tha the population of Réunion will reach one million by 2020. Housing is th main problem. Already there is tremendous pressure on building land Most of the population is concentrated on the coastal strip, where th towns are gradually beginning to merge into one continuous urban 'ring Houses are also spreading slowly up the hillsides and traffic congestion i becoming a major headache.

To relieve some of this pressure, the government has invested in ar ambitious new expressway, the Route des Tamarins, between St-Paul and Étang-Salé-les-Bains, which will open a large swathe of mountainside to new development. Constructions work is well under way.

At the presidential election in April–May 2007, the 500,000 or so Réunion nais voters were wooed by most candidates, who spent a few days campaigning on the island. The results were significantly different from mainland France while Nicolas Sarkozy (right) won over 53% of the votes in mainland France he was massively defeated in Réunion – Ségolène Royal (left) triumphed or the island, winning 64% of the votes. According to analysts, on an islane that's heavily subsidised by mainland France, the social aspects of Royal' programme were considered much more reassuring for most Réunionnais.

FAST FACTS

Population: 800,000 (estimated)

Territory size: 2512 sq km

Languages: French, Creole

Capital: St-Denis

Highest point: Piton des Neiges 3070m

Distance from Réunion to Mauritius: 220km

Unemployment: 30%

Estimated total cars: 340,000

Lychee season: December to February

HISTORY

Réunion has a history similar to that of Mauritius. It was colonised by the French after the mid-17th century but later fell briefly under British rule As in Mauritius, the colonisers introduced plantation crops and African slaves. Later came Indian indentured labourers and Chinese merchants creating an ethnic diversity which is one of these islands' most distinctive haracteristics. While Mauritius gained its independence in 1968, Réunion emains an overseas department of France.

WELCOME TO PARADISE

he first visitors to the uninhabited island were probably Malay, Arab and uropean mariners, none of whom stayed. Then in 1642, the French took the ecision to settle the island, which at the time was called Mascarin. The first ettlers arrived four years later, when the French governor of Fort Dauphin n southern Madagascar banished a dozen mutineers to the island.

On the basis of enthusiastic reports from the mutineers, the King of France .ouis XIV officially claimed the island in 1649 and renamed it Île Bourbon.

However appealing it seemed, there was no great rush to populate and levelop the island. It was not until the beginning of the 18th century that he French East India Company and the French government took control •f the island.

COFFEE, ANYONE?

Coffee was introduced between 1715 and 1730 and soon became the is-and's main cash crop. The island's economy changed dramatically. As offee required intensive labour, African and Malagasy slaves were brought •y the shipload. During this period, cereals, spices and cotton were also ntroduced as cash crops.

Like Mauritius, Réunion came of age under the governorship of the vi-ionary Mahé de Labourdonnais, who served from 1735 to 1746. However, .abourdonnais treated Île de France (Mauritius) as a favoured sibling, and fter the collapse of the French East India Company and the pressure of ongoing rivalry with Britain the governance of Île Bourbon passed directly o the French crown in 1764.

After the French Revolution, the island's name was changed to La Réunion meaning 'Joining' or 'Meeting').

THE BRITISH MOVE IN...

n 1810, during the Napoleonic Wars, Napoleon Bonaparte lost the is-and to the *habits rouges* (redcoats). Under British rule, sugar cane was ntroduced to Réunion and quickly became the primary crop. The vanilla ndustry, introduced in 1819, also grew rapidly.

The British didn't stay long: just five years later, under the Treaty of Paris, the spoils were returned to the French as Île Bourbon. The British, nowever, retained their grip on Mauritius, Rodrigues and the Seychelles.

The most ruthless hunter of runaway slaves was François Mussard, whose name is now remembered only because it has been given to a dank, dark cave near Piton des Neiges.

RÉUNION SNAPSHOTS

For a general introduction to the island, pick up Catherine Lavaux's classic *La Réunion: Du Battant des Lames au Sommet des Montagnes*. It covers everything from the geography and flora of Réunion to its history.

From around 1685, Indian Ocean pirates began using Île Bourbon as a trading base.

BLACK HISTORY

The late-18th century saw a number of slave revolts, and many resourceful Malagasy and African slaves, called *marrons*, escaped from their owners and took refuge in the mountainous interior. Some of them established private Utopias in inaccessible parts of the Cirques, while others grouped together and formed organised communities with democratically elected leaders. These tribal chieftains were the true pioneers of the settlement of Réunion, but most ultimately fell victim to bounty hunters who were employed to hunt them down. The scars of this period of the island's history are still fresh in the population's psyche; perhaps from a sense of shame, there's surprisingly little record of the island's Creole pioneers except the names of several peaks (Dimitile, Enchaing, Mafate, Cimendef) where they were hunted down and killed. The Maison du Peuplement des Hauts in Cilaos (p197) and Hell-Bourg's Écomusée (p203) provide excellent introductions to these sensitive subjects, tracing the history of slavery and '*marronage*' and cele-brating the achievements of these unsung heroes of the Cirques.

... AND THE FRENCH COME BACK TO STAY

In 1848, the Second Republic was proclaimed in France, slavery was abol
ished and Île Bourbon again became La Réunion. Like Mauritius, Réunio
immediately experienced a labour crisis, and like the British in Mauritius
the French 'solved' the problem by importing contract labourers from
India, most of them Hindus, to work the sugar cane.

Réunion's golden age of trade and development lasted until 1870
with the country flourishing on the trade route between Europe, Indi
and the Far East. Competition from Cuba and the European sugar-bee
industry, combined with the opening of the Suez Canal (which short
circuited the journey around the Cape of Good Hope), resulted in a
economic slump.

After WWI, in which 14,000 Réunionnais served, the sugar industr
regained a bit of momentum, but it again suffered badly through th
blockade of the island during WWII.

Réunion became a Département Français d'Outre-Mer (DOM; Frencl
Overseas Department) in 1946 and has representation in the French parlia
ment. Since then there have been feeble independence movements from
time to time but, unlike those in France's Pacific territories, these have
never amounted to much. While the Réunionnais seemed satisfied to re
main totally French, general economic and social discontent surfaced i
dramatic anti-government riots in St-Denis in 1991.

In March 1998, there was a major eruption at the Piton de la Fournaise -
the longest eruption of the volcano in the 20th century, with a total o
196 days of volcanic activity. The turn of the century marked a new er
for Réunion; the local authorities managed to sign a few agreements wit
the French state, which confirmed the launching of subsidised 'grand
chantiers' (big infrastructure works), including the new expressway calle
the Nouvelle Route des Tamarins and the future Route du Littoral. Thes
massive works are expected to sustain growth on the island.

THE CULTURE

THE NATIONAL IDENTITY

The tourist office in
St-Denis has put together
a guide to 12 *créoles*
villages, including
Cilaos, Hell-Bourg and
Entre-Deux, chosen for
their particularly rich
architectural heritage and
traditional way of life.

The physical and cultural distinctions between the various ethnic groups
are far less apparent in Réunion than in Mauritius. In Réunion there ha
been much more interracial mixing over the years. Ask the Réunionnais
how they see themselves and the chances are they'll say 'Creole' – not in
the narrow sense of having Afro-French ancestry, but simply meaning
one of 'the people'. That is, someone who speaks Creole, who was born
and bred on the island and is probably – but not necessarily – of mixed
ancestry. This sense of community is the gel that holds society together.

The Réunionnais are in general more reserved than the Mauritians, bu
within this overall pattern there are local differences: southerners are reck
oned to be more relaxed and friendly, while perhaps not surprisingly the
people living in the Cirques are the most introverted.

While the Réunionnais do also regard themselves as French, they don't
really identify with people from the mainland. There is even a slight un
dercurrent of resentment towards the 100,000 or so mainlanders who
dominate the island's administration and economy. The locals refer to
them very slightly derogatorily as Zoreilles (the Ears); the usual explana
tion is that they are straining to hear what's being said about them in the
local patois.

LIFESTYLE

Contemporary Réunionnais are a thoroughly 21st-century people. The vast majority of children receive a decent standard of education and all islanders have access to the national health system, either in Réunion or in France. There are traffic jams, everyone is on a mobile (cell) phone, and flashy cars are ubiquitous. But beneath this modern veneer, there are many more traditional aspects.

One of the strongest bonds unifying society, after the Creole language, is the importance placed on family life. At the weekend there's nothing the Réunionnais like better than trundling off to the seaside or the mountains for a huge family picnic – think giant-sized rice cookers replete with hearty carris in the company of gramounes (grandparents) and marmailles (children). To get the most sought-after picnic shelters, some members of the family sometimes arrive at 4am to reserve them! Religious occasions and public holidays are also vigorously celebrated, as are more personal, family events, such as baptisms, first communions and weddings.

Though Réunion can't be mistaken for, say, Ibiza, Réunionnais share a zest for the fest. On weekends St-Gilles-les-Bains, L'Hermitage-les-Bains and St-Pierre are a magnet for Réunionnais from all over the island. The towns turn wild on those evenings as flocks of night owls arrive en masse to wiggle their hips and guzzle pints of Dodo beer and glasses of rum.

On a more mundane level, you'll quickly realise that the possession of a brand new car is a sign of wealth and respect. The 'car culture' is a dominant trait. Small wonder that traffic jams are the norm on the coastal roads. Many Réunionnais spend up to two hours daily in their car going to work! One favourite topic of conversation is the state of the roads, especially the tricky Route du Littoral between St-Paul and St-Denis, which is sometimes closed due to fallen rocks.

Another noticeable (though less immediately so) characteristic is the importance of gossip (la di la fé). If you can understand a little bit of French (or Creole), tune in to Radio Free Dom – you'll soon realise that gossip's a national pastime.

A cagier issue is the RMI (see Economy, p160). For the French mainlanders, the Réunionnais are assistés (spoiled children) who get a lot of funds from Paris and from the generous welfare system. For the Réunionnais, it's just resourcefulness, and a way to improve their standard of living.

People are relatively tolerant of homosexuality, though by no means as liberal as in mainland France; open displays of affection may be regarded with disdain, especially outside St-Denis.

There's a refreshingly liberal attitude towards women, and younger Réunionnais women especially are quite outspoken and emancipated. Divorce, abortion and childbirth outside marriage are all fairly uncontentious issues. However, it's not all that rosy: women are poorly represented in local government and politics, and domestic violence is prevalent. This is closely connected to high rates of alcoholism.

Despite the social problems that blight any culture, on the whole it's a society that lives very easily together.

ECONOMY

Réunion is one of the richest islands in the Indian Ocean. The standard of living is fairly high, and it's no surprise. As a French department, the island receives a lot from mainland France (la métropole). However, Réunion faces numerous challenges. The unemployment rate, for example, currently hovers around 30%, way above the national average (about 8% at the time of writing), but at least it's down from the peak of 38% in 1998. It's particularly

It's estimated that 450,000 Réunionnais (almost half of the population living on the island) live in métropole mainland France.

problematic for women and young people without qualifications. Why isn't there any major social outburst? It's simple: the generous French social system, especially the RMI (Revenu Minimum d'Insertion, an allowance that any unemployed person aged over 26 can claim), acts as a lifesaver for many individuals – not to mention the high level of moonlighting *(travail au noir)*, on top of the RMI. You won't see homelessness in Réunion, not simply because of the existence of the RMI but also because of family ties which remain strong.

Réunion imports around 60% of its needs from *la métropole*. In turn, mainland France accounts for some 70% of Réunion's exports. The vast majority is sugar, with other agricultural and marine products coming a distant second.

For the present, Réunion's sugar producers have managed to hang on to their European quotas and guaranteed prices, but following EU enlargement and with the reform of the EU sugar sector that was adopted in 2006, they may not be able to do so for much longer. As a result, the movers and shakers of Réunion's economy are increasingly looking to closer ties with Mauritius and the rest of Africa for their financial future.

Tourism is another major source of income, but it plummeted to 278,000 visitors in 2006 (from 410,000 tourist arrivals in 2005), as a result of the Chikungunya epidemic. The vast majority of visitors are French. It's expected to pick up again in 2008. There's a huge potential for growth, but there are a few hurdles: it's under-promoted in the Anglophone markets; English is not widely spoken on the island (to say the least); and the cost of flights is still prohibitive.

POPULATION

Cultural diversity forms an integral part of the island's social fabric. Réunion has the same population mix of Africans, Europeans, Indians and Chinese as Mauritius, but in different proportions. Creoles (people of Afro-French ancestry) are the largest ethnic group, comprising around 40% of the population. Malabars (Hindu Indians) comprise about 25% of the population, Europeans (ie the French) 6%, the Chinese 3%, and Z'arabes (Muslim Indians) make up about 2%.

The bulk of the island's population lives in coastal zones, with Malabars living predominantly in the east. The rugged interior is sparsely populated. Because the birth rate has remained quite high, a third of the population is under 20 years of age.

Réunion also sees a continual tide of would-be immigrants. With a system of generous welfare payments for the unemployed, the island is seen as a land of milk and honey by those from Mauritius, Seychelles and some mainland African countries. In recent years there has been significant immigration from neighbouring Comoros and Mayotte Islands.

Creoles are called Cafres locally. The mainland French are called Zoreilles or Métro, and the French who have adopted the island's lifestyle and can speak Creole are called Zoréol.

RELIGION

An estimated 70% of the population belongs to the Catholic faith, which dominates the island's religious character. It's evidenced in the many saints' days and holidays, as well as in the names of towns and cities. Religious rituals and rites of passage play an important part in the lives of the people, and baptisms, first communions and church weddings are an integral part of social culture.

About a quarter of Réunionnais are Hindus, which is the dominant faith in the east. Traditional Hindu rites such as *teemeedee,* which features fire-walking, and *cavadee,* which for pilgrims entails piercing the cheeks with skewers, often take place. (For more information on these rites, see (p227.) Muslims make up roughly 2% of the population; as in Mauritius, Islam tends to be fairly liberal, though a number of Muslim women wear the veil.

Interestingly, a great deal of syncretism between Hinduism, Islam and Catholicism has evolved over the years. In fact, many of the Malabar-Réunionnais participate in both Hindu and Catholic rites and rituals.

Apart from celebrating the Chinese New Year, the Sino-Réunionnais community (making up about 3% of the population) is not very conspicuous in its religious or its traditional practices.

As in Mauritius, religious tolerance is the norm. Mosques, churches, Hindu temples and pagodas can be found within a stone's throw of each other in most cities.

ARTS

One of the greatest pleasures of visiting Réunion is experiencing Creole-flavoured French culture or French-flavoured Creole culture, depending on how you look at it. For news of cultural activities on the island, keep an eye on the local press and visit local tourist offices, where you can pick up flyers, theatre programmes and a number of free events guides such as the monthly *Kwélafé* (www.kwelafe.com in French).

Literature

Few Réunionnais novelists are known outside the island and none are translated into English. One of the most widely recognised and prolific contemporary authors is the journalist and historian Daniel Vaxelaire, who has written a number of evocative historical novels. His *Chasseurs des Noires,* an easily accessible tale of a slave-hunter's life-changing encounter with an escaped slave, is probably the best to start with.

Jean-François Sam-Long, a novelist and poet who helped relaunch Creole literature in the 1970s, also takes slavery as his theme. *Madame Desbassyns* was inspired by the remarkable life-story of a sugar baroness. In *La Nuit Cyclone* he explores the gulf between Whites and Blacks in a small village, against a backdrop of black magic and superstition.

Other well-established novelists to look out for are Axel Gauvin *(Train Fou, L'Aimé* and *Cravate et Fils)* and Jules Bénard.

There are several up-and-coming writers who deal with contemporary issues. Joëlle Ecormier spins her first novel, *Plus Léger que l'Air,* around a young islander living in France who returns to Réunion to face her past. *Les Chants des Kayanms* by Agnès Gueneau also revolves around Zoreilles-Réunionnais relationships, in this case a love affair between a local woman

---

THE ODD CULT OF ST-EXPÉDIT

St Expédit is one of Réunion's most popular saints, though some scholars argue there never was a person called Expédit. Whatever the truth, the idea was brought to Réunion in 1931 when a local woman erected a statue of the 'saint' in St-Denis' Notre-Dame de la Délivrance church in thanks for answering her prayer to return to Réunion. Soon there were shrines honouring St Expédit all over the island, where people prayed for his help in the speedy resolution of all sorts of tricky problems.

Over the years, however, worship of the saint has taken on the sinister overtones of a voodoo cult: figurines stuck with pins are left at the saint's feet; beheaded statues of him are perhaps the result of unanswered petitions. The saint has also been adopted into the Hindu faith, which accounts for the brilliant, blood-red colour of many shrines. As a result the Catholic Church has tried to distance itself from the cult, but the number of shrines continues to grow.

REUNION SNAPSHOTS

KABARS

If you're passionate about Creole music (and we're sure you will be), try to attend a *kabar*. A *kabar* is a kind of impromptu concert, or ball, that is usually held in a courtyard or on the beach, where musicians play *maloya*. It's usually organised by associations, informal groups or families, but outsiders are welcome. There's no schedule; *kabars* are usually advertised by means of word of mouth, flyers or small ads in the newspapers. You can also inquire at the bigger tourist offices.

---

and a man from the mainland. It's a lyrical tale, evoking the rhythms of *maloya* (traditional slave music).

Music & Dance

Réunion's music mixes the African rhythms of reggae, *séga* (traditional slave music) and *maloya* with French, British and American rock and folk sounds. Like *séga*, *maloya* is derived from the music of the slaves, but it is slower and more reflective, its rhythms and words heavy with history, somewhat like New Orleans blues; fans say it carries the true spirit of Réunion. *Maloya* songs often carry a political message and up until the 1970s the music was banned for being too subversive.

Instruments used to accompany the *séga* and the *maloya* range from traditional homemade percussion pieces, such as the hide-covered *rouleur* drum and the maraca-like *kayamb*, to the accordion and modern band instruments.

The giants of the local music scene, and increasingly well known in mainland France, are Daniel Waro, Firmin Viry, Gramoun Lélé, Davy Sicard and the group Ziskakan. More recently, women have also emerged on the musical scene, including Christine Salem (see p11) and Nathalie Nathiembé. All are superb practitioners of *maloya*. Favourite subjects for them are slavery, poverty and the search for cultural identity.

As for Creole-flavoured modern grooves, the Réunionnais leave those to their tropical cousins in Martinique and Guadeloupe, although they make popular listening in Réunion. It's all catchy stuff, and you'll hear it in bars, discos and vehicles throughout the islands of the Indian Ocean.

Stay tuned – the website www.runmusic.com (in French) is your chaperone to Réunionnais music.

Architecture

The distinctive 18th-century Creole architecture of Réunion is evident in both the grand villas built by wealthy planters and other *colons* (settlers/ colonists) and in the *ti' cases*, the homes of the common folk.

Local authorities are actively striving to preserve the (few) remaining examples of Creole architecture around the island. You can see a number of beautifully restored houses in St-Denis and in the towns of Cilaos, Entre-Deux, Hell-Bourg and St-Pierre, among other places. They all sport *lambrequins, varangues* and other ornamental features. (For more information about this exotic type of architecture, see Architectural Heritage, p46.)

FOOD & DRINK

Réunionnais like to eat and their food is a pleasure on the palate, with a balanced melange of French cuisine (locally known as *cuisine métro*) and Creole specialities and flavours, not to mention Indian and Chinese influences. A good number of eateries, *chambres d'hôte* (family-run B&Bs) and cafés offer a wide variety of quality food, and not just in the larger towns, with the added bonus of a great choice of drinks.

STAPLES & SPECIALITIES

It's impossible to visit Réunion without coming across *carri* (curry), also spelt *cari* locally, which features on practically every single menu. The sauce comprises tomatoes, onions, garlic, ginger, thyme and saffron (or turmeric) and accompanies various kinds of meat, such as chicken *(carri poulet)*, pork *(carri porc)*, duck *(carri canard)* and guinea fowl *(carri pintade)*. Seafood *carris*, such as *carri thon* (tuna *carri*), *carri espadon* (swordfish *carri*), *carri langouste* (lobster *carri*) and *carri camarons* (freshwater-prawn *carri*), are also excellent. Octopus *carri*, one of the best *carris* you'll eat, is called *civet zourite* in Creole. Local vegetables can also be prepared *carri*-style – try *carri baba figue* (banana-flower *carri*) and *carri ti jaque* (jackfruit *carri*) – but they incorporate fish or meat. *Carris* are invariably served with rice, grains (lentils or haricot beans), *brèdes* (local spinach) and *rougail,* a spicy chutney that mixes tomato, garlic, ginger and chillies; other preparations of *rougail* may include a mixture of green mango and citrus.

The word *rougail* is a bit confusing, though. It's also used for some variations of *carris*. *Rougail saucisses* is in fact sausages cooked in tomato sauce, while *rougail boucané* is a smoked-pork *carri* (without saffron), and *rougail morue* is cod *carri* (also without saffron). You'll also find *civet,* which is another variety of stew. A widespread Tamil stew is *cabri massalé* (goat *carri*). On top of this, you'll find excellent beef meat (usually imported from South Africa), prepared in all its forms (steak, sirloin, rib).

Seafood lovers will be delighted to hear that the warm waters of the Indian Ocean provide an ample net of produce: lobster, prawns, *légine*, swordfish, marlin, tuna and shark, among others. Freshwater prawns, usually served in curry, are highly prized.

Réunionnais love vegetables, eating them in salads or in *gratins* (a baked dish). You'll certainly come across *chou chou* (choko; a speciality in the Cirque de Salazie), *bois de songe* and *vacoa* (a speciality in the Wild South), not to mention *bringelles* (aubergines) and *baba figue* (banana flower).

Snacks include samosas, *beignets* (fritters) and *bonbons piments* (chilli fritters).

Fruits also reign supreme. Two iconic Réunionnais fruits are *litchis* (lychees) and *ananas Victoria* (pineapple of the Victoria variety). Local mangoes, passionfruit and papaya are also fabulously sweet. The local vanilla (see the boxed text, p228) is said to be one of the most flavoured in the world.

Breakfast is decidedly French: *pain-beurre-confiture* (baguette, butter and jam), served with coffee, tea or hot chocolate, is the most common threesome. Added treats may include croissants, *pain au chocolat* (chocolate-filled pastry), brioches and honey.

What about desserts? If you like carb-laden cakes and pies, you'll be happy in Réunion. They might knock five years off your life but they taste so good you won't care. Each family has its own recipe for *gâteaux maison* (homemade cakes), which come in various guises. They are usually made from vanilla, banana, sweet potato, maize, carrot, guava… Our favourite is *macatia* (a variety of bun), which can also be served at breakfast.

DRINKS

Rum, rum, rum! Up in the hills, almost everyone will have their own family recipe for *rhum arrangé,* a heady mixture of local rum and a secret blend of herbs and spices. In fact, not all are that secret. Popular concoctions include *rhum faham,* a blend of rum, sugar and flowers from the faham orchid; *rhum vanille,* made from rum, sugar and fresh vanilla pods; and *rhum bibasse,* made from rum, sugar and tasty *bibasse* (medlar fruit). The family *rhum arrangé* is a source of pride for most Creoles; if you stay in any of the rural *gîtes* or

RÉUNION SNAPSHOTS

For those interested in a simple taste of Réunion cuisine, the *Grand Livre de la Cuisine Réunionnaise* by Marie-France *et al* contains a range of easy-to-follow traditional recipes. *La Cuisine Réunionnaise* by Carole Iva covers similar ground, with the added benefit of colour illustrations.

Unlike *rhum arrangé*, *punch* is made of only one fruit (most commonly banana, vanilla or lychee) and is served as an apéritif. *Rhum arrangé* is usually served as a *digestif* (post-meal drink).

chambres d'hôte you can expect the proprietor to serve up their version with more than a little ceremony.

Réunion being French territory, wine is unsurprisingly taken seriously. Along with French wines, you'll find a good choice of South African reds and whites. The island also has a small but blossoming viniculture in Cilaos, where you can do a tasting (see the boxed text, p199).

The local brand of beer, Bourbon (known as Dodo), is sold everywhere. It is a fairly light, very drinkable beer. Foreign beers are also available. For a refresher, nothing beats a fresh fruit juice or a glass of Cilaos, a high-quality sparkling water from Cirque de Cilaos.

The French take coffee drinking seriously and it's a passion that hasn't disappeared just because they're now in the Indian Ocean. A cup of coffee can take various forms but the most common is a small, black espresso called simply *un café*.

WHERE TO EAT & DRINK

There is a wondrous array of eateries in Réunion, from snack-bar-cum-cafés to high-class restaurants serving fine French cuisine and to *tables d'hôte* (home-cooked meals served at *chambres d'hôte*) and beach restaurants. For self-caterers, there's no shortage of very well-stocked supermarkets, not to mention numerous markets, where you can stock up on delicious, fresh ingredients. On Sunday, most Réunionnais opt for a picnic on the beach or in the Hauts.

On top of *la carte* (menu), most restaurants have *menus* (set courses) and daily specials. You'll also find numerous roadside stalls selling fruits, especially during the lychee season from December to February.

The service charge is included in the bill, and tipping is not necessary. If you want to leave something extra, that's up to you.

HABITS & CUSTOMS

There are relatively few strict rules of dining and etiquette. Though formal restaurants certainly exist, a casual atmosphere and boisterous families are the norm, especially at weekends.

Table manners are more or less the same as those in mainland France. And as in France, lunches are taken seriously in Réunion – long, lingering midday meals are *de rigueur*.

VEGETARIANS & VEGANS

Despite the Indian influence, Réunion is an island of meat lovers. To our knowledge, there aren't any dedicated vegetarian restaurants. That said,

> Drool over your keyboard while checking out the recipes on the following websites (all in French): www.cuisinereunionnaise.com; www.creole.org/cuisine.htm; www.goutanou-cuisine-reunionnaise.org; and www.iledelareunion.net/cuisine-reunion/.

TRAVEL YOUR TASTEBUDS

If you're a gastronomic adventurer, start your culinary odyssey with *salade de palmiste,* a delectable salad made from the bud of the palmiste palm trees, known as the 'heart of palm'. The palm dies once the bud is removed, earning this wasteful salad delicacy the title 'millionaire's salad'. For something a bit more unusual, try *carri bichiques* (a sprat-like delicacy), which is dubbed *le caviar réunionnais* (Réunionnais caviar). You might need to seek out *larves de guêpes* (wasps' larvae), another local delicacy that is available from April to October. Fried and salted, they reputedly increase sexual stamina.

You may also want to learn the terms for *carri pat' cochons* (pig's trotter *carri*) and *carri anguilles* (eel *carri*) so you don't accidentally order them in a restaurant. Réunionnais also drool over *carri tang* (hedgehog *carri*), which you're not likely to find served in restaurants. If you happen to eat it at a private home, let us know if you've survived it…

vegetarians won't go hungry. Salads, rice and fruits are ubiquitous. In Chinese restaurants, menus feature vegetarian dishes, such as chop suey and noodles. Most supermarkets have vegetarian fare too, and *chambres d'hôte* owners will be happy to cook vegetarian dishes if you let them know well in advance. And there's always dessert!

ENVIRONMENT

Réunion lies about 220km southwest of Mauritius, at the southernmost end of the great Mascarene volcanic chain. Réunion's volcano, Piton de la Fournaise, erupts with great regularity, spewing lava down its southern and eastern flanks. The last major eruption occurred in 2007, when lava flows reached the sea and added another few square metres to the island. Since 1998 there have been spectacular eruptions almost every second year – an attraction in its own right. But don't worry: the volcano's perfectly monitored by local authorities and there are strict security measures when it's erupting.

THE LAND

There are two major mountainous areas on Réunion. The older of the two covers most of the western half of the island. The highest mountain is Piton des Neiges (3069m), an alpine-class peak. Surrounding it are three immense and splendid amphitheatres: the Cirques of Cilaos, Mafate and Salazie. These long, wide, deep hollows are sheer-walled canyons filled with convoluted peaks and valleys, the eroded remnants of the ancient volcanic shield that surrounded Piton des Neiges.

The smaller of the two mountainous regions lies in the southeast and is still evolving. It comprises several extinct volcanic cones and one that is still very much alive, Piton de la Fournaise (2632m). This rumbling peak still pops its cork relatively frequently in spectacular fashion, and between eruptions quietly steams and hisses away. No-one lives in the shadow of the volcano, where lava flowing down to the shore has left a remarkable jumbled slope of cooled black volcanic rock, known as Le Grand Brûlé.

These two mountainous areas are separated by a region of high plains, while the coast is defined by a gently sloping plain which varies in width. Numerous rivers wind their way down from the Piton des Neiges range, through the Cirques, cutting deeply into the coastal plains to form spectacular ravines.

WILDLIFE
Animals

Because it was never part of a continental land mass, Réunion has relatively few animal species. The island's only indigenous mammal species are two types of bat, both of which can sometimes be seen around the coast at night. The mammals you're far more likely to see are introduced hares, deer, geckoes, rats and, if you're lucky, chameleons. Tenrecs (called *tang* in Creole), which resemble hedgehogs, were introduced from Madagascar.

The most interesting creepy crawlies are the giant millipedes – some as long as a human foot – which loll around beneath rocks in more humid areas. Another oversized creature is the yellow-and-black *Nephila* spider whose massive webs are a common sight. You'll also find the *Heteropoda venatoria* spider, called *babouk* in Creole.

As far as bird life is concerned, of the original 30 species endemic to the island, only nine remain. The island's rarest birds are the *merle blanc*

Piton de la Fournaise is undoubtedly the island's most iconic attraction and one of the world's most accessible active volcanoes. The website www.fournaise.info (in French) will keep even nonvulcanologists enthralled. Features pictures and even a webcam.

or cuckoo shrike – locals call it the *tuit tuit,* for obvious reasons – and the black petrel. Probably the best chance of seeing – or, more likely, hearing – the *tuit tuit* is directly south of St-Denis, near the foot of La Roche Écrite. Only an estimated 160 pairs remain.

Meet Réunion's feathered creatures in Nicolas Barré and Armand Barau's beautifully illustrated field guide *Oiseaux de la Réunion.*

Bulbuls, which resemble blackbirds (with yellow beaks and legs, but grey feathers), and are locally known as *merles,* are also common. The Mascarene paradise flycatcher is a pretty little bird with a small crest and a long, flowing red tail.

Birds native to the highlands include the *tec-tec* or Réunion stonechat, which inhabits the tamarind forests. There's also the *papangue,* or Maillard buzzard, a protected hawklike bird which begins life as a little brown bird and turns black and white as it grows older. It is Réunion's only surviving bird of prey and may be spotted soaring over the ravines.

The best-known sea bird is the white *paille-en-queue* or white-tailed tropicbird, which sports two long tail plumes. It can often be seen riding the thermals created by the Piton de la Fournaise volcano. Other sea birds include visiting albatrosses, petrels and shearwaters.

Mynahs, introduced at the end of the 18th century to keep the grasshoppers under control, are common all over the island, as are the small, red cardinal-like birds known as fodies.

The best spots to see bird life are the Forêt de Bébour-Bélouve above Hell-Bourg, and the wilderness region of Le Grand Brûlé at the southern tip of the island.

Plants

Now this is Réunion's strong point! Thanks to an abundant rainfall and marked differences in altitude, Réunion boasts some of the most varied plant life in the world. Parts of the island are like a grand botanical garden. Between the coast and the alpine peaks you'll find palms, screw pines (also known as pandanus or *vacoa*), casuarinas *(filaos),* vanilla, spices, other tropical fruit and vegetable crops, rainforest and alpine flora.

Réunion has no less than 700 indigenous plant species, 150 of which are trees. Unlike Mauritius, large areas of natural forest still remain. It's estimated that 30% of the island is covered by native forest; some areas – particularly in the ravines – have never been touched by man.

Find information on local birds and where to spot them on www.seor.fr (in French).

Gnarled and twisted and sporting yellow, mimosa-like flowers, the *tamarin des Hauts* or mountain tamarind tree, is a type of acacia and is endemic to Réunion. Locals compare them to oak trees because the timber is excellent for building. One of the best places to see these ancient trees is in the Forêt de Bébour-Bélouve east of the Cirque de Salazie.

At the other extreme, the lava fields around the volcano exhibit a barren, moonlike surface. Here the various stages of vegetation growth, from a bare new lava base, are evident. The first plant to appear on lava is the heather-like plant the French call *branle vert (Philippia montana).* Much later in the growth cycle come tamarind and other acacia trees.

Afforestation has been carried out mainly with the Japanese cryptomeria, *tamarin des Hauts,* casuarina and various palms.

Like any tropical island, Réunion has a wealth of flowering species, including orchids, hibiscus, bougainvillea, vetiver, geranium, frangipani and jacaranda. Flower-spotters will enjoy the several excellent botanical gardens on the island, including the Conservatoire Botanique National de Mascarin (p192), the Jardin d'Eden (p182) near St-Gilles-les-Bains and the Jardin des Parfums et des Épices (p224) in St-Philippe.

NATIONAL PARKS

It is estimated that nearly a third of the 25km-long lagoon along the west coast from Boucan Canot south to Trois Bassins has already suffered damage from a variety of causes: sedimentation, agricultural and domestic pollution, cyclones, fishermen and divers. To prevent the situation deteriorating even further, a marine park was set up in 1997. In addition to educating local people on the need to keep the beaches and the water clean, the **Association Parc Marin Réunion** (www.chez.com/parcmarin in French) has been working with local fishermen and various water-sports operators to establish protection zones. A fully-fledged nature reserve was created – at last! – in 2007.

There are big plans afoot to protect the interior of the island, too. The **Parc National des Hauts de la Réunion** (www.parc-national-reunion.prd.fr in French) was established in early 2007, resulting in half of Réunion's total land area being now under protection. There's a tightly regulated core area of 1000 sq km, including the volcano, the mountain peaks and the areas around Mafate and Grand Bassin, surrounded by a buffer zone of some 700 sq km to encompass most of the ravines. The plans envisage a totally integrated approach, not only to protect the animal and plant life, but also to preserve traditional ways of life and to encourage sustainable development, including initiatives linked to ecotourism.

ENVIRONMENTAL ISSUES

As in Mauritius, the central problem confronting Réunion is how to reconcile environmental preservation with a fast-growing population in need of additional housing, roads, jobs, electricity, water and recreational space.

Unlike Mauritius, however, the authorities here have access to greater financial resources, backed up by all sorts of European rules and regulations. In general, they have been able to adopt a more coordinated approach, introducing measures to improve water treatment and reduce nitrate use by farmers, for example, at the same time as cleaning up the lagoon.

Despite the establishment of the Parc National des Hauts de la Réunion and the Parc Marin Réunion (see National Parks, above), the island is facing major issues, all related to three massive engineering works that are currently under way.

The 'smaller' is the Route des Tamarins, a 34km expressway that slices across the hills above St-Gilles-les-Bains and requires more than 120 bridges over the ravines; construction work is under way and the road is due for completion sometime in 2009. Local environmentalists have raised objections to the scheme, which cuts across the only remaining savannah habitat on the island and will force displaced farmers onto areas of marginal land.

The second major engineering project is a piece of technical prowess. The idea behind this herculean scheme is to transfer water from the east coast, where supply exceeds demand, to the dry and heavily populated west coast. The solution someone came up with was to drill a tunnel 30km long and 3.5m high right through the island! Tunnelling began in 1989, but needless to say they hit a few hitches along the way. It is reckoned that the project should be completed by 2013.

The third project is the 'Tram-Train', a sort of tramway which will connect major coastal cities, thus avoiding the horrendous traffic jams that plague the west coast. Preliminary studies have started and the first stretch between St-Paul and the airport (via St-Denis) should be completed by 2012.

RÉUNION SNAPSHOTS

A number of traditional distilleries continue to produce essential oils from geranium and vetiver leaves – a great gift for envious friends back home.

Réunion

Oh la la! After a long-haul flight, you step off the plane and you're greeted with a *bonjour*. Then you breakfast on croissants and *chocolat chaud* (hot chocolate). At first glance, Réunion is like a chunk of France teleported to the tropics. But beyond the Gallic panache, you'll soon realise it's a resplendent tapestry, which also blends Indian, African and Chinese influences.

Jutting out of the ocean like a basaltic shield cloaked in green, Réunion is a mini-Hawaii, with astounding geographical diversity. Within an hour or two, the landscape morphs from lava fields to lush primary forest, from jagged peaks to sprawling coastal cities. The *pièce de résistance* is Piton de la Fournaise, one of the world's most accessible active volcanoes. Depending on nature's whims, you might even witness fiery-red molten lava. When the volcano has finished working its magic on you, there are horses to ride, majestic mountains to trek up or paraglide from, drop-offs to dive from, big waves to surf, extinct volcanoes to fly over, and canyons to explore. But it's not all about nature, landscapes and adrenaline – Réunion has its cultural gems as well, with stunning Creole architecture in cute-as-can-be villages, as well as colourful religious buildings and festivals.

We'll be honest, though. Réunion is a tropical island, but one that doesn't fit the cliché of a sun-soaked Edenic paradise. Sure, you'll find appealing palm-ruffled stretches of sand, but none that rivals the super-sexy beaches that are *de rigueur* in the Seychelles or Mauritius. All the better for you: mega-resorts are nonexisaaatent. Open the Pandora's box, and you'll leave the island proclaiming to the world that *La Rénion lé gadiamb* ('Réunion is lovely', in Creole).

HIGHLIGHTS

- Gorging your senses on the Martian landscapes of the **Plaine des Sables** (p211) and the smouldering volcano of **Piton de la Fournaise** (p210)
- Flying high over the mystical, rugged topography of **Cirque de Mafate** (p206), **Cirque de Cilaos** (p197) and **Cirque de Salazie** (p202)
- Going heritage-hunting among the Creole buildings of **Hell-Bourg** (p203), **Entre-Deux** (p194) and **St-Denis** (opposite)
- Quickening your pulse with a rip-roaring mountain-bike descent from **Le Maïdo** (p180), through cryptomeria forests and sugar-cane fields
- Swapping stress for bliss in the perfect valley-village seclusion of **Grand Bassin** (p209)
- Surfing and paragliding by day in **St-Leu** (p190) before diving into **L'Hermitage-les-Bains'** steamy nightlife (p187)

SEYCHELLES

MAURITIUS

RÉUNION

▪ TELEPHONE CODE: 33	▪ POPULATION: 800,000	▪ AREA: 2512 SQ KM

CLIMATE & WHEN TO GO

Because of the high mountains, Réunion's climate varies more than that of Mauritius. It still, however, experiences only two distinct seasons: the hot, rainy summer from December to April and the cool, dry winter from late April to October. The east coast is considerably wetter than the west, but wettest of all are the mountains above the east coast – around Takamaka, Plaine-des-Palmistes and the northern and eastern slopes of the volcano. As with Mauritius, the cyclone season is roughly December to March.

Temperatures on the coast average 22°C during winter and 27°C in summer. In the mountains, they drop to 11°C and 18°C respectively. Clouds generally cover the peaks and high plains from mid-morning. The drier winter months are the most favourable for hiking (see p231 for more information).

The peak tourist seasons are during the French school holidays from late June to early September. From October through to the New Year holidays is also reasonably busy, but after this everything eases down during cyclone-prone February and March. The weather normally changes for the better in April, which isn't a bad time to a visit.

See p249 for the climate chart for St-Denis.

ST-DENIS

pop 140,000

Francophiles will feel comfortable in St-Denis (san-de-*nee*), the capital of Réunion. Except for the palms and flamboyant trees to remind you that you're somewhere sunnier (and hotter), St-Denis could be easily mistaken for a French provincial enclave, with a flurry of trendy shops, brasseries, bistros, and *boulangeries* (bakeries). Mmmmm…those little *pains au chocolat* (chocolate-filled pastries) will linger long on the palate!

With most of Réunion's tourist attractions located elsewhere on the island, most visitors only stay long enough to book *gîtes de montagne* (mountain lodges), pick up a few tourist brochures and rent a car before dashing off to more magnetic locations. But St-Denis warrants more than a fleeting glance. Scratch beneath the French polish and you'll soon realise that the city also boasts an undeniably Creole soul, with a portfolio of delightful colonial and religious buildings and a casual multi-ethnic atmosphere.

If that's not enough, there are always epicurean indulgences. Sip a black coffee at a chic pavement café listening to a *séga* or *maloya* soundtrack or indulge in fine dining at a gourmet restaurant. *Bon appétit*!

HISTORY

St-Denis was founded in 1668 by the governor Regnault, who named the settlement after a ship that ran aground here. But St-Denis didn't really start to develop until the governor Mahé de Labourdonnais moved the capital here from St-Paul in 1738; the harbour was in general more sheltered and easier to defend, and water more abundant.

The 19th century ushered in St-Denis' golden age. As money poured in from the sugar plantations, the town's worthies built themselves fine mansions, some of which can still be seen along Rue de Paris and in the surrounding streets. But in the late 1800s the bottom dropped out of the sugar market and the good times came to a stuttering end. St-Denis' fortunes only began to revive when it became the new departmental capital in 1946. To cope with the influx of civil servants, financiers and office workers, the city expanded rapidly eastwards along the coast and up the mountains behind. Even today the cranes are much in evidence as St-Denis struggles to house its ever-growing population.

ORIENTATION

The centre of St-Denis is built on a grid pattern on a coastal plain dropping gently northwards towards the sea. Life revolves around the seafront Barachois area, and Ave de la Victoire, the main thoroughfare heading inland.

The main shopping area stretches along the semi-pedestrianised Rue Maréchal Leclerc, which strikes east from Ave de la Victoire, and spills over into the surrounding streets.

INFORMATION
Emergency
Ambulance (☎ 15)
Fire services (☎ 18)
Police (☎ emergency 17, headquarters 0262 90 74 74; 133 Rue Jean Chatel)

RÉUNION

ST-DENIS

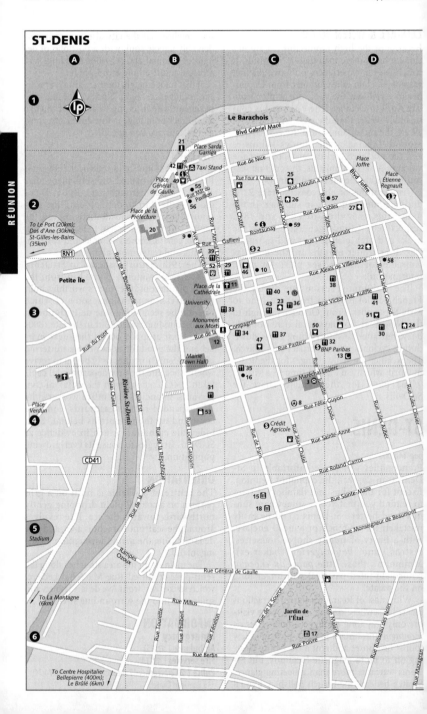

INFORMATION
B@bookcafé..............................**1** C3
Banque de la Réunion..............**2** C2
Central Post Office...................**3** C4
Comité du Tourisme de la Réunion....**4** B2
Fédération Réunionnaise des
  Auberges de Jeunesse.........(see 7)
German Consulate.....................**5** G6
Gîtes de France.........................**6** C2
Maison de la Montagne et
  de la Mer.............................(see 6)
Office du Tourisme...................**7** D2
Police.......................................**8** C4
Service des Étrangers...............**9** B2

SIGHTS & ACTIVITIES
Ancienne Maison des Notaires.......(see 46)
Anciens Magasins Aubinais........**10** C3
Cathédrale de St-Denis.............**11** C3
Former Hôtel de Ville (Town Hall)....**12** B3
Grande Mosquée......................**13** D3
Hindu Temple..........................**14** E4
L'Artothèque...........................**15** C5
Maison Deramond....................**16** C4
Musée d'Histoire Naturelle.......**17** C6
Musée Léon Dierx....................**18** C5
Notre-Dame de la Délivrance....**19** A4
Palais Rontaunay.....................(see 6)
Préfecture...............................**20** B2
Roland Garros Monument.........**21** B1

SLEEPING
Austral Hôtel............................**22** D2
Hôtel Central............................**23** C3
Hôtel Le Mascareignes..............**24** D3
Hôtel Phoenix..........................**25** C2
Le Juliette Dodu.......................**26** C2
Pension des Sables...................**27** D2
Pension Zoulékan Limbada........**28** E3

EATING
B@bookcafé.............................(see 1)
Clos St-Jaques.........................**29** C3
Helios......................................**30** D3
Kim Son...................................**31** B4

La Cardamome.........................**32** D3
La Récré...................................**33** B3
L'Atelier de Ben.......................**34** C3
Le Cadre Noir...........................**35** C4
Le Castel Boulanger.................**36** C3
Le Castel Glacier......................(see 37)
Le Castel Lounge Restaurant....**37** C3
Le DCP....................................**38** D3
Le Labourdonnais....................**39** B2
Le Massalé..............................**40** C3
Le Ness...................................**41** D3
Le Roland Garros.....................**42** B2
L'Igloo....................................**43** C3
Petit Marché............................**44** E4
Reflets des Îles........................**45** E3

DRINKING
Cyclone Café...........................**46** C3
Le Bar a Cas............................**47** C3
Le Boy's..................................**48** E3
Le Rallye.................................**49** B2
Le Zanzibar.............................**50** C3
Moda Bar................................**51** D3

ENTERTAINMENT
Jazzy Bar................................**52** B3

SHOPPING
Grand Marché..........................**53** B4
Petit Marché............................(see 44)
Sorédisc..................................**54** D3

TRANSPORT
Air Austral..............................**55** B2
Air France...............................**56** B2
Air Madagascar.......................**57** D2
Air Mauritius...........................**58** D3
Car Jaune................................(see 60)
Corsairfly...............................**59** C2
L'Océan Bus Terminal...............**60** E3

INDIAN OCEAN

RN2 Cemetery
Blvd Lancastel

To Roland Garros
International
Airport (6km);
Ste-Suzanne
(15km)

Blvd Lancastel
Rue de l'Est
Rue des Limites
Rue de l'Océan
Blvd de l'Océan
Rue Roland Garros
Rue Maréchal Leclerc
Rue Ste-Marie
Rue Sainte-Marie
Rue St-Jacques
Place St-Jacques
Rue de Montreuil
Rue Saint Bernard
Rue Amédée Bédier
Rue Général de Gaulle
Rue Général de Gaulle
Rue d'Après
Rue Jacob
Rue d'Alsace
Rue d'Lorraine
Rue des Lataniers
Rue de Caen
Rue Monthyon
Rue Voltaire
Vauban
Rue Monthyon
Rue Bouvet
Rue Bois de Nèfles
To Hôtel Mercure
Créolia (1.5km)
To Madagascar
Consulate (2km)
Ave André Malraux
Blvd Vauban
Canal du Butor
Le Butor
Rue Jean Cocteau

0 — 500 m
0 — 0.3 miles

Internet Access

B@bookcafé (☎ 0262 90 90 65; 82-88 Rue Juliette
Dodu; per hr €6; ⏰ 8.30am-6.30pm Mon-Fri, 8.30am-7pm
Sat) Pleasant atmosphere upstairs in the Librairie
Autrement.

Medical Services

Centre Hospitalier Bellepierre (☎ 0262 90 50 50;
Allées des Topazes, Bellepierre) Réunion's main hospital
has 24-hour medical and dental treatment, a pharmacy
open round the clock and English-speaking staff.

Money

Bring your credit card or stock up with euros
beforehand! There's no moneychanging
service – it has been superseded in favour
of ATMs. You'll find a cluster of banks with
ATMs near the junction of Rue Jean Chatel
and Rue Labourdonnais; all the main banks
and the central post office have ATMs.
Banque de la Réunion (☎ 0262 40 01 23; 27 Rue
Jean Chatel; ⏰ 9am-4pm Mon-Fri)

Post

Central post office (60 Rue Maréchal Leclerc;
⏰ 7.30am-6pm Mon-Fri, 7.30am-noon Sat)

Tourist Offices

Gîtes de France (☎ 0262 90 78 90; www.reunion
-nature.com in French; 5 Rue Rontaunay; ⏰ 9am-5pm
Mon-Thu, 9am-4pm Fri) Information on *chambres d'hôtes*
(family-run B&Bs) and *gîtes d'étape* (walkers lodges).
Maison de la Montagne et de la Mer (☎ 0262 90
78 78; www.reunion-nature.com in French; 5 Rue Rontaunay; ⏰ 9am-5pm Mon-Thu, 9am-4pm Fri) Same location
as Gîtes de France. For hiking information and booking
gîtes de montagne.
Office du Tourisme (☎ 0262 41 83 00;
otinord@wanadoo.fr; 2 Pl Étienne Regnault; ⏰ 9am-6pm
Mon-Sat) Housed in a former railway station, the St-Denis
tourist office has English-speaking staff and can provide
plenty of information, maps and brochures. You can also
book *gîtes de montagne* here. Also runs tours (in French
only) of St-Denis that take in historic sights such as the
mansions of Rue de Paris (€8).

SIGHTS

St-Denis' most important sights are concentrated along the main road running
from Le Barachois in the north to the Jardin de l'État (botanical gardens) a couple of
kilometres inland.

There is a variety of impressive **Creole mansions** in St-Denis, a number of which have
now been declared historic monuments and

are being slowly restored. See the boxed text
(opposite) for further information.

The place to promenade in St-Denis is **Le
Barachois**. This seafront park, lined by can-
nons facing out to sea, has an area set aside
for *pétanque* (a game similar to bowls), cafés
and a **monument** to the Réunion-born aviator
Roland Garros, leaning nonchalantly on a
propeller. Garros was the first pilot to cross
the Mediterranean. Shady Pl Sarda Garriga,
across the road, was named after the governor
who abolished slavery in Réunion in 1848.

St-Denis is home to a smattering of attractive religious buildings, including **Notre-Dame
de la Délivrance** church (1893), which sits on
the hillside across the usually dry Rivière St-
Denis. It's noteworthy for the statue of St Expédit just inside the door, dressed as a young
Roman soldier. For more information about
this unusual saint see the boxed text, p161.

Smack bang in the centre, it's impossible
to miss the **Grande Mosquée** (121 Rue Maréchal Leclerc;
⏰ 9am-noon & 2-4pm), also known as the Noor-
E-Islam mosque. The cool white-and-green
interior is a haven of peace. The Islamic community in St-Denis is very traditional, so if you
wish to visit, dress and behave with respect.
Also worth a peek is the fairly unassuming,
Tuscan-style **Cathédrale de St-Denis**.

St-Denis' small but wildly colourful **Hindu
temple** (Rue Maréchal Leclerc) stands out among the
shops east of the centre. If you wish to visit, remember to remove your shoes and any leather
items. Photography is not allowed.

St-Denis' strong point is its buildings,
rather than its museums, but it's worth pop-
ping your head into the rewarding **Musée Léon
Dierx** (☎ 0262 20 24 82; 28 Rue de Paris; admission €2;
⏰ 9.30am-5pm Tue-Sun). Housed in the former
bishop's palace, built in 1845, it hosts Réunion's most important collection of modern
art. The more high-profile works include
paintings, sculptures and ceramics by Picasso,
Renoir, Gauguin and Vlaminck, but the majority are by local artists such as the poet and
painter Léon Dierx (1838–1912). The handsome pale-yellow villa next door to the Musée
Léon Dierx contains **L'Artothèque** (☎ 0262 41
75 50; 26 Rue de Paris; admission free; ⏰ 9.30am-5.30pm
Tue-Sun). This contemporary art gallery hosts
changing exhibitions of works by local artists
and those from neighbouring countries.

If you're in search of a shady haven where
you can flake out, head to the attractive **Jardin
de l'État** (botanical gardens; admission free; ⏰ 7am-6pm),

ARCHITECTURAL HEIRLOOMS

St-Denis is devoid of beach, but it boasts a gaggle of well-preserved colonial buildings harking back to the city's heyday in the 19th century. The larger colonial piles are mainly strung out along Rue de Paris. Since few are open to the public, you'll have to content yourself with peering through the railings. This saunter covers the not-to-be-missed buildings in the centre.

One of the grandest is the **Préfecture** (Blvd Gabriel Macé), which stands proudly on the seafront. It began life as a coffee warehouse in 1734 and later served as the headquarters of the French East India Company. Many, however, consider the neoclassical **Former Hôtel de Ville (Town Hall)**, at the north end of Rue de Paris, to be the city's most beautiful building; it's certainly more imposing, with its regimented columns, balustrades and jaunty clock tower. By contrast, the Tuscan-style **Cathédrale de St-Denis** (Rue de Paris) standing nearby is a much more sober affair.

Also of interest are **Palais Rontaunay** (Rue Rontaunay), built in 1854, and **Maison Deramond** (15 Rue de Paris), which was the family home of former French prime minister Raymond Barre and the birthplace of the poet and painter Léon Dierx. On Rue Jean Chatel, you'll stumble across **Anciens Magasins Aubinais** (37 Rue Jean Chatel), a former warehouse, and the **Ancienne Maison des Notaires** (18 Rue Jean Chatel).

Many of these palatial residences feature elaborate verandas and intricate *lambrequins* (ornamental window and door borders). The roof shingles are traditionally made from the wood of the *tamarin des Hauts* (mountain tamarind tree). For more on traditional architecture, see p46.

RÉUNION

at the southern end of Rue de Paris. It features numerous plants used in the manufacture of perfume, tropical oddities from around the world and lots of orchids. At the far end of the gardens stands the somewhat austere Palais Législatif, dating from 1834, which houses the **Musée d'Histoire Naturelle** (☎ 0262 20 02 19; admission €2; ⏰ 10am-5.30pm Tue-Sun). Very little of Réunion's natural history survived long enough to make it into the museum, but there are a few displays of extinct and nearly extinct native species, including the Réunion owl, kestrel, parrot and ibis.

SLEEPING

There's a good choice of midrange hotels scattered around the city but surprisingly little in the way of upmarket accommodation. Advance booking is highly recommended.

Budget

Pension Zoulékan Limbada (☎ 0262 41 05 00; 35 Rue de l'Est; dm €10, d €20) Increasingly popular with travellers, this Indian-run guesthouse occupying a virginal-white building has a quiet location. The four smart but low-key rooms tick all the right boxes, but party animals take note that guests are asked to be quiet at all times and respect prayer times.

Pension des Sables (☎ 0262 40 91 03, 0692 27 72 77; 28 Rue des Sables; d with shared bathroom €28) Quite a snip at these rates: despite its joyless façade, this guesthouse supplies just the right kind of

simple budget accommodation, and you could hardly get a better central location. Transfers to the airport can be arranged.

Midrange

Hôtel Le Mascareignes (☎ 0262 21 15 28; www.hotel mascareignes.com; 3 Rue Laferriere; s €32-38, d €37-43, incl breakfast; ❄) A small block, albeit with some value squeezed in. All rooms are enlivened by murals featuring local critters. Be sure to ask for the more luminous rooms at the front (Nos 6, 7 and 8). Good English is spoken.

Hôtel Phoenix (☎ 0262 41 51 81; fax 0262 40 99 51; 1 Rue du Moulin à Vent; s/d incl breakfast €40/45; ❄) A well-run little number with a central location, the Phoenix offers neat rooms, sparkling bathrooms and a small, flower-filled garden. The air-con is on from 7pm to 7am only, but that's about the worst surprise you'll get. With only eight rooms, advance reservation is recommended.

Austral Hôtel (☎ 0262 94 45 67; hotel-austral@ wanadoo.fr; 20 Rue Charles Gounod; s €70-75, d €80-85; P ❄ 🖥 🗻) Distinctly unimpressive for the price, the Austral is not quite the three-star heavyweight it thinks it is, but the rooms have the requisite comforts and location is tip-top.

Top End

Le Juliette Dodu (☎ 0262 20 91 20; www.hotel-jdodu .com; 31 Rue Juliette Dodu; s €83, d €101-124, ste €195; P ❄ 🖥 🗻) Escape the plebeian hordes and live like a colonial administrator in this stylish Creole building dating from the early 19th century. Although the rooms are unextraordinary, there are still enough vintage touches in the reception area – period furnishings, plump armchairs and old-fashioned tiles – to satisfy the snob within, with the added lure of a pool. It's a two-minute strut south of the Barachois.

Mercure Créolia (☎ 0262 94 26 26; www.accor hotels.com; 14 Rue du Stade, Montgaillard; d €100-170; P ⊠ 🖳 🕱) Located some way south of the city centre in a tranquil neighbourhood, your efforts in getting up here are rewarded with splendid views over the coast. Rooms are functional and unflashy, but you'll be too busy lounging by the pool and drinking up the view to mind.

EATING

Oh to have a few more hours in the day to squeeze in more epicurean delights! Thanks to the French passion for gastronomy, St-Denis is a nirvana for food-lovers, with a smorgasbord of eateries to suit all palates and budgets. French or Creole? Chinese or Indian? Fusion or traditional? Throw budgetary caution to the wind and splurge. Most places accept credit cards.

Restaurants

Le Roland Garros (☎ 0262 41 44 37; 2 Pl Sarda Garriga; mains €11-25; ⊗ lunch & dinner) *Oh la la*, this heavenly place has the feel of a true Parisian bistro – packed, buzzing and full of attitude. You can't really go wrong – everything is pretty good – but if you want a recommendation, go for the *tartare de poisson* (fish tartare).

Le Castel Lounge Restaurant (☎ 0262 41 38 85; 81 Rue Jean Chatel; mains €12-22, menu €26; ⊗ lunch Tue-Sat, dinner Tue-Sun) When the owner of Le Castel Boulanger, chef Jerôme Brudhon, opened this place in 2006, it was an instant hit. Tastebuds are kept on the move at this ode to design – a sleek, loungey space with low-hanging table lights and cocoa-hued furnishings. It mostly serves up creative contemporary dishes.

Clos St-Jacques (☎ 0262 21 59 09; 5 Ruelle Édouard; mains €13-18, menus €20-24; ⊗ lunch Mon-Fri, dinner Tue-Sat) Subdued lighting, elegant furnishings and a smattering of fancy decorative touches, including quirky replicas of cicadas hanging on the walls, provide the perfect setting for a romantic dinner.

La Récré (☎ 0262 23 83 41; 21 Ave de la Victoire; mains €13-17; ⊗ lunch Mon-Sat, dinner Wed-Sat) Set in a courtyard that opens onto a busy street (but a hedge of tropical plants protects you from the hustle and bustle), La Récré is a popular joint for informal dining, with a wide-ranging menu focussing on fish and meat dishes. If you want to impress (or shock) your friends at home, order a *tartare de cheval* (horse tartare).

Reflets des Îles (☎ 0262 21 73 82; 27 Rue de l'Est; mains €13-21; ⊗ lunch & dinner daily except Wed & Sun) This much-lauded eatery specialising in Creole food is the perfect place to try out *cuisine lontan* (traditional dishes). Dip into one of 15 cracking *carris* (curries) and *civets* (stews). The menu is translated in English – a rarity in Réunion. The waiters play the tropical-island card with their snazzy shirts.

Le DCP (☎ 0262 20 10 14; 46 Rue Jules Auber; mains €16-17, menus €20-26; ⊗ lunch & dinner) If you have a weakness for ultrafresh fish, Le DCP is the place to indulge. The décor is another clincher: it occupies a restored Creole building with an agreeable terrace. Inside, aquatic murals and shades of blue and white create a 20,000-leagues-under-the-sea-like ambience.

Le Ness (☎ 0262 47 62 53; 52 Rue Victor Mac Auliffe; mains €18-29, menus €19-38; ⊗ lunch Mon-Fri, dinner Mon-Sat) Spice up your day or night at this refreshing fusion place. Le Ness serves lush menus of French fare with a tropical twist such as grilled duck in a fruit sauce.

L'Atelier de Ben (☎ 0262 41 85 73; 12 Rue de la Compagnie; mains €18-28; ⊗ lunch Tue-Fri, dinner Tue-Fri & Sat) A true alchemist, the French chef here fuses French with Asian to create a cuisine that stuns and seduces. The *filet de bœuf poêlé, pain perdu aux truffes, wok de légumes et noisettes torréfiées* (beef fillet served with a special truffle-scented bread, wok-fried vegetables and roasted hazelnuts) is even more delicious than its poetic name suggests. The décor? Best described as 'contemporary plain'.

Other temptations:

Le Cadre Noir (☎ 0262 21 44 88; 11 Rue de Paris; mains €10-12; ⊗ 11am-6pm Tue-Sat) Art-gallery setting ideal for a light lunch comprising a main course and dessert, all homemade. Also does great afternoon tea and cakes.

Kim Son (☎ 0262 21 75 00; 13 Rue du Maréchal Leclerc; mains €10-20; ⊗ lunch Tue-Sat) Offers well-prepared Vietnamese and Chinese fare in rustic surrounds.

Helios (☎ 0262 20 21 50; 88 Rue Pasteur; mains €13-25; ⊗ lunch & dinner Tue-Sat) This St-Denis icon has a good repertoire of flavoursome *métro* dishes, best enjoyed on the flowery terrace.

Le Labourdonnais (☎ 0262 21 44 26; 14 Rue L'Amiral Lacaze; mains €15-25, menus €22-35; 😋 lunch & dinner Mon-Sat) One of the town's top-drawer eateries, with prices to match. The décor blends rustic beams and stone walls with colonial-era elegance.

Quick Eats

Le Castel Boulanger (☎ 0262 21 27 66; 43 Rue de la Compagnie; 😋 6am-2pm & 3.30-7pm Mon-Sat, 7am-noon Sun) Hands-down the best bakery-deli in St-Denis, with such a tantalising array of brioches, croissants, *macatias* (a variety of buns) and sandwiches that we almost made ourselves a nuisance here. Excellent breakfasts too (from €7.50).

Le Castel Glacier (☎ 0262 41 38 85; www.lecastel.re; 81 Rue Jean Chatel; ice creams from €2; 😋 10am-11pm Mon-Sat, 2.30-11pm Sun) We also lost all self-control at this talismanic ice-cream parlour a short waddle away from Castel Boulanger (same management). Just thinking of chocolate makes us salivate; you don't want to know what happens when we recall the *fèves du Tonka* (a variety of cocoa). Also serves up snack options, including salads, at lunchtime.

Le Massalé (☎ 0262 21 75 06; 30 Rue Alexis de Villeneuve; 😋 10am-8.30pm Mon-Sat, 11am-8.30pm Sun) Another divine tooth-killer is this teeny outlet that tempts you with its colourful array of Indian snacks and sweets to eat in or take away. Perennial favourites include samosas as well as candy-pink or apple-green *balfi*. Wash it down with a glass of cardamom tea.

B@bookcafé (☎ 0262 90 90 65; 82-88 Rue Juliette Dodu; mains €7-12; 😋 lunch Mon-Sat) A snazzy spot upstairs in the Librairie Autrement. Good salads.

L'Igloo (☎ 0262 21 34 69; 67 Rue Jean Chatel; mains €8-12; 😋 11am-midnight) One day we were unfaithful to Le Castel Glacier and had an ice-creamy affair with L'Igloo, unable to resist the phenomenally creamy *fruits des bois* ice-cream concoction. It's equally adept at serving up omelettes, fish dishes and salads. True to its name, the refreshing décor screams 'Antarctica', with white-and-blue murals.

La Cardamome (☎ 0262 21 25 46; 48 Rue Pasteur; mains €10-14, buffet €8-11; 😋 lunch & dinner) With its dramatic pink-and-green interior (no chubby Buddha by the door!), this little Indian joint has to be St-Denis' kookiest spot. Nothing beats its buffet featuring about 10 Indian offerings, a steal at €8 at lunchtime. Takeaways available.

Self-catering

For fresh fruit and vegetables, there is a wide range of cheap produce at the **Petit Marché** (Rue Maréchal Leclerc; 😋 6am-6pm Mon-Sat, 6am-noon Sun).

DRINKING & ENTERTAINMENT

If it's Ibiza-style nightlife you're after, you're barking up the wrong tree here. Most of Réunion's action is down the coast at L'Hermitage-les-Bains (p187) and St-Pierre (p216). However, there's a handful of OK nightspots to keep you entertained in the centre of St-Denis.

Le Bar a Cas (☎ 0262 20 17 68; 19 Rue Pasteur; 😋 7am-midnight) A studenty in-the-know set favours this funky drinking spot with violet walls and a décor that distracts. Snag a seat on the buzzing street terrace or in the vivacious room. Feeling peckish? Keep up your strength with a beefsteak or an omelette.

Cyclone Café (☎ 0262 20 00 23; 24 Rue Jean Chatel; 😋 5pm-2am Mon-Sat) Like bees to Bacardi, students (and the odd grizzled geezer) swarm on this pub-like, beer-friendly watering hole when live bands perform certain evenings. Good blend of electro, *maloya* (traditional dance music of Réunion), hardtek and drum 'n' bass. A small *pression* (draft beer) will cost you €3.

Alternatives:

Jazzy Bar (☎ 0262 21 85 01; 20 Rue Labourdonnais; 😋 7pm-2am Tue-Sat) A jazz lounge and a great late-night haunt for aspiring insomniacs.

Le Boy's (☎ 0692 66 25 53; 108 Rue Pasteur; 😋 9pm-4am Fri & Sat) Gay friendly – you guessed it.

Le Rallye (☎ 0262 20 34 66; 3 Ave de la Victoire; 😋 6am-midnight) A trendily downbeat bar (with local DJs) and a café that's a popular hangout.

Le Zanzibar (☎ 0262 20 01 18; 41 Rue Pasteur; 😋 lunch Tue-Sat, bar & dinner 5pm-midnight) A bar and a restaurant. Gay friendly.

Moda Bar (☎ 0262 58 76 14; 75 Rue Pasteur; 😋 7pm-2am Thu-Sat) A formulaic but friendly place offering regular karaoke nights. Also features live bands.

SHOPPING

The main shopping streets are the semi-pedestrianised Rue Maréchal Leclerc and Rue Juliette Dodu.

Grand Marché (2 Rue Maréchal Leclerc; 😋 8am-6pm Mon-Sat) This place has a mishmash of items for sale, including Malagasy wooden handicrafts, fragrant spices, woven baskets, embroidery, T-shirts, furniture and a jumble of knick-knacks.

RÉUNION

Petit Marché (Rue Maréchal Leclerc) On the east side of town, this is mainly a fresh-produce market, but you can buy herbs and spices and local *rhums arrangés* (flavoured rums) here at competitive prices.

Soredisc (☎ 0262 21 68 29; 61 Rue Pasteur) For tapes and CDs of *maloya, séga* and other local music, this store has by far and away the biggest selection.

GETTING THERE & AWAY
Air
The vast majority of flights come in to **Roland Garros International Airport** (☎ 0262 28 16 16; www.reunion.aeroport.fr in French), about 10km east of St-Denis.

Airlines with offices in St-Denis:

Air Austral (☎ 0825 013 012; 4 Rue de Nice)
Air France (☎ 0820 820 820; 7 Ave de la Victoire)
Air Madagascar (☎ 0262 21 05 21; 31 Rue Jules Auber)
Air Mauritius (☎ 0262 41 23 26; 13 Rue Charles Gounod)
Corsairfly (☎ 0262 40 96 72; 37 Rue Juliette Dodu)

For further information regarding air travel see p253.

Bus
L'Océan bus terminal, the main long-distance bus station, is on the seafront. From here **Car Jaune** (☎ 0810 123 974) operates various services. Information for Car Jaune regarding all its routes and *horaires* (timetables) around the island and the airport bus service is available from the information counter at the bus terminal. You can also pick up timetables at the tourist office. Some of the more useful routes include the following:

Line A West to St-Pierre via Le Port, St-Paul, St-Gilles-les-Bains, St-Leu, Étang-Salé-les-Bains and St-Louis (€4.20, 1¾ hours, about 10 daily).
Lines F or G East to St-Benoît via Ste-Suzanne and St-André (€3, one hour, about 12 daily).
Z'éclair (express) East to St-Benoît via St-André (€3.50, one hour, about 10 daily).
Z'éclair (express) West to St-Pierre via St-Leu (€7, 1¼ hours).

For more information on buses around the island, see p254.

Car & Motorcycle
There's not much point in having a car in St-Denis unless you're using it as a base to explore the rest of the island. If that's the case, you can either pick a car up at the airport or avoid paying the airport surcharge (around €20) by having it delivered to your hotel. Multinational rental companies have booths at the airport. Several local companies also rent cars that are cheaper. Ask your hotel or the tourist office to suggest a company. For more information on car hire, see p254.

Ferry
St-Denis' ferry terminal is at Le Port located 20km west of St-Denis. For further information see p305.

GETTING AROUND
St-Denis is relatively small and getting around the centre on foot is a breeze.

To/From the Airport
Taxis between St-Denis and Roland Garros International Airport cost around €20 during the day and €30 at night. Cheaper and almost as convenient is the regular Navette Aéroport service, which runs from L'Océan bus terminal to the airport about once an hour between 7am and 7.45pm (between 7.30am and 7.15pm coming from the airport). The fare is €4 and the journey takes a minimum of 20 minutes.

To/From the Port
The terminal for passenger ferries to Mauritius is in Le Port, 20km west of St-Denis. There are no bus services direct to the terminal. All nonexpress buses between St-Denis and St-Pierre stop at the bus station in Le Port, from where locally operated buses depart roughly every 30 minutes for the Gare Maritime, Port Est. You're better off splashing out on a taxi (€40 from St-Denis).

There is a small information desk at the ferry terminal, open for arrivals, but no other facilities for tourists. Taxis wait on arrival.

Taxi
Taxis around town are generally expensive. The minimum fare is €2.50 and a trip across town will set you back at least €8.

During the day you should have no problem finding a taxi. It gets more difficult at night, when you might have to phone for one. A reliable company offering a 24-hour service is **Taxis Paille-en-Queue** (☎ 0262 29 20 29).

RÉUNION

THE WEST

Welcome to Réunion's Sunshine Coast, or Réunion's Riviera, or the leeward coast. However you label it, say hello to this 45km-long string of seaside resorts and suburbs running from St-Paul to St-Louis. Truth is, there's a bit of a Groundhog Day feel about this series of getaways along the RN1, and tourist development has got a little out of hand to the south of St-Paul. But this region does have a wealth of developed tourist facilities and attractions, including the best of the island's beaches (which is not saying a lot). It's an easy introduction to Réunion, but traffic jams on the coastal road go pretty far toward shattering any illusions of a tropical paradise.

Sea, sand and sun are not the only *raison d'être* on the west coast. There's also a super-fluity of activities on land and sea. Big surf breaks issue a siren's call to surfers, steep drop-offs tempt divers, spectacular slopes beckon mountain bikers, while paragliders soar over the lagoon.

But while the west is synonymous with beach culture and traffic snarls, it also contains the antithesis to these. In this most populous, most visited region there remain hidden corners of untouched wonder, where you can soothe your soul. Despite the new, monstrous Route des Tamarins that zips along the flanks of the mountains down to Étang-Salé-les-Bains (due to be completed in 2009), it's easy to leave behind the coastal hedonism and explore the glorious hinterland and its bucolic offerings – think sugar-cane fields, lush orchards, geranium plantations and cryptomeria forests swathing the slopes of the mountains, studded with character-filled villages that retain a palpable rural air. Oh, and charming *chambres d'hôtes* where you can retreat in homely comfort.

With the exception of St-Louis and the Hauts (hills), this region is predominantly Zoreilles (the name used in Réunion for people from France) territory and feels closer to mainland France than South Africa. Brush up on your French!

DOS D'ANE

After St-Denis' busy streets and before tackling the seaside resorts further south, a drive up to the isolated village of Dos d'Ane, in the hills above Le Port (take the D1), will give you a breath of fresh air. It's an excellent base for **hikes** in the interior; from here you can walk to the Plaine d'Affouches and La Roche Écrite, as well as into the Cirque de Mafate via the Rivière des Galets route. An easy day's walk from Dos d'Ane will get you to the *gîte* at Grand Place, while a magnificent but a more challenging route will take you up the beautiful Bras des Merles to Aurère. For a shorter ramble, there are superb views to be had from the Roche Verre Bouteille lookout, less than an hour's walk from the Cap Noir car park above Dos d'Ane. The beginning of the path is signed.

If you like peace, quiet and sigh-inducing views, you'll have few quibbles with **Chambre d'hôtes et Gîte Les Acacias – Chez Axel Nativel** (☎ 0262 32 02 34; Rue Germain Elisabeth, Dos d'Ane; dm/ r €15/40), which offers two *chambres d'hôtes* and three spick-and-span six-bed dorms. The hearty evening meals (dinner €18) go down well after a day's tramping and the views from the terrace are stupendous.

To get to Dos d'Ane by public transport you'll have to change buses in Le Port. All nonexpress and some express buses between St-Pierre and St-Denis stop at the Le Port bus station. From Le Port, there are six buses a day from Monday to Saturday but only three on Sunday.

ST-PAUL
pop 20,000

Lively if not jaw-dropping in beauty, Réunion's second-largest *commune* after St-Denis deserves a quick stop if you're into history. It's also an obvious transit point if you plan to reach Le Maïdo (p180) by public transport.

Most tourists who do come here visit the bright and well-kept **Cimetière Marin**, the cemetery at the southern end of town. It contains the remains of various famous Réunionnais, including the poet Leconte de Lisle (1818–94). The cemetery's star guest, however, is the pirate Olivier 'La Buse' Levasseur (The Buzzard), who was the scourge of the Indian Ocean from about 1720 to 1730, when he was captured, taken to St-Paul and hanged. People are still searching for the location of La Buse's treasure in Mauritius, Réunion and the Seychelles. The grave is marked by the pirates' trademark skull and crossbones.

Make sure you save energy for the animated **market** on the seafront promenade.

RÉUNION

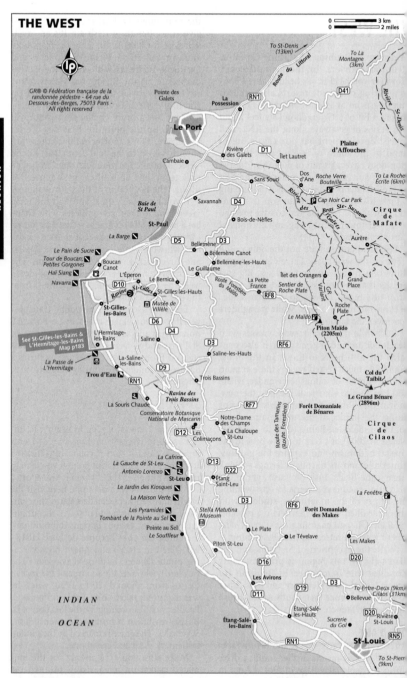

THE WEST

| 0 | 3 km |
| 0 | 2 miles |

GR® © Fédération française de la randonnée pédestre - 64 rue du Dessous-des-Berges, 75013 Paris - All rights reserved

To St-Denis (13km)
To La Montagne (3km)
Route du Littoral

Pointe des Galets
La Possession
RN1
D41
Rivière St-Denis

Le Port

Plaine d'Affouches

Rivière des Galets
D1
Îlet Lautret

Cambaie
Dos d'Âne
Roche Verre Bouteille
To La Roche Écrite (6km)

Sans Souci
Cap Noir Car Park

Baie de St Paul
Savannah
D4
Bras
Rivière des Galets
Cirque de Mafate

St-Paul
Bois-de-Nèfles

La Barge
Bellemène
D3
Aurère

Le Pain de Sucre
D5
Bellemène Canot
Bellemène-les-Hauts

Tour de Boucan; Petites Gorgones
Boucan Canot
Le Guillaume

Haï Siang
L'Éperon
Route Forestière du Maïdo
La Petite France
Îlet des Orangers
Grand Place

Navarra
Le Bernica
St-Gilles
RF8
Sentier de Roche Plate
GR Variante

Ravine
St-Gilles-les-Bains
St-Gilles-les-Hauts
Roche Plate

St-Gilles-les-Bains
Musée de Villèle
Le Maïdo
Piton Maïdo (2205m)

See St-Gilles-les-Bains & L'Hermitage-les-Bains Map p183
D6
L'Hermitage-les-Bains
D4
Saline
D3

La Passe de L'Hermitage
La-Saline-les-Bains
Saline-les-Hauts
RF6
Col du Taïbit

Trou d'Eau
RN1
D9
Trois Bassins
Le Grand Bénare (2896m)

La Souris Chaude
Ravine des Trois Bassins
RF7
Forêt Domaniale de Bénares
Cirque de Cilaos

Conservatoire Botanique National de Mascarin
Notre-Dame des Champs
Route des Tamarins (Route Forestière)

D12
Les Colimaçons
La Chaloupe St-Leu

La Cafrine
D13
La Gauche de St-Leu
Antonio Lorenzo
St-Leu
D22
Étang Saint-Leu
La Fenêtre

Le Jardin des Kiosques
D3
RF6
Forêt Domaniale des Makes

La Maison Verte
Stella Matutina Museum

Les Pyramides
Tombant de la Pointe au Sel
Le Plate
Le Tévelave
Les Makes

Pointe au Sel
Le Souffleur
Piton St-Leu

INDIAN
D16
D20

OCEAN
Les Avirons
D19
D3
To Entre-Deux (9km) Cilaos (31km)

D11
Bellevue

Étang-Salé-les-Hauts
D20
Rivière St-Louis

Étang-Salé-les-Bains
Sucrerie du Gol
St-Louis
RN5

RN1
To St-Pierr (9km)

s held all day on Friday and on Saturday morning. With its heaps of local veg-
tables, fruits and spices, it makes for a
olourful experience.

Sleeping & Eating

a Veranda (☎ 0692 69 70 23; d €32-34; ☒) This
very central place to stay was partially renovated and extended in 2007, with a series of
uncluttered but clean rooms with air-con
and private bathrooms. It's nothing fancy
but will do for a night's kip.

Snack La Bergère (☎ 0262 45 13 07; Place du Marché
orain; mains €6-10; ☽ lunch & dinner) This cheap
and cheerful *camion-snack* (snack van) on
the seafront market place is a good-value pit
stop. Fork out €8 for a plate of grilled fish or
voluminous salad and you'll leave patting
your tummy contentedly.

Cabane Bambou (☎ 0262 57 10 32; 93 Rue Marius
et Ary Leblond; mains €7.50-11; ☽ lunch daily, dinner Mon-
Fri) This cosy little eatery set in a restored
Creole home prepares delectable *métro*
fare with a creative twist served in a snug
décor, with bamboo sticks and colourful
fabrics adorning green walls. The *brochette
royale* (skewered swordfish and freshwater
prawns) certainly won our heart. It's opposite La Veranda.

Restaurant de l'Étang (☎ 0262 45 29 68; 1 Blvd
Jacob de la Haye; mains €12-17; ☽ lunch daily, dinner Tue-
Sat) North of the centre, this haven of peace
is blessed with a lush garden that's a perfect
spot for a relaxed feed or tipple. There's
nothing unorthodox on the menu, just the
usual Creole suspects cooked to perfection:
cabri massalé (goat *carri*) and *espadon combava* (tuna with a variety of aromatic citrus),
among others.

Getting There & Away

St-Paul lies on Car Jaune's bus route between
St-Denis (€2.70) and St-Pierre (€4.30). There
are express buses every one to two hours in
either direction (fewer on Sunday) and much
more frequent nonexpress services.

The local bus company **Réseau Éolis** (☎ 0262
42 54 65) operates fairly infrequent services
from the central bus station to villages up in
the hills such as Le Bernica, La Petite France,
Villèle, Le Guillaume and L'Éperon, among
others. Walkers, take note: there's also a special bus to Le Maïdo (that takes you to the
start of the Sentier du Maïdo) three times
daily except Sunday.

LES HAUTS DE ST-PAUL

A world away from the hurly-burly of the
coast, the verdant Hauts de St-Paul is wonderful country for exploring off the beaten
track, but unless you have a lot of time, you
need a vehicle. Buses serve most places from
St-Paul, but they aren't really convenient for
the Hauts. We won't suggest any set itinerary,
for this area lends itself to a DIY approach –
from St-Paul, use the D5 as a launchpad, then
follow your nose (but bring a good map).
You'll come across hamlets with such charming names as **Bellemène-les-Hauts**, **Bois-de-
Nèfles**, **Le Bernica**, **Le Guillaume**… It's as cute as
it sounds! Start early morning to get the best
views of the coast.

Sleeping & Eating

Chambre d'hôtes Chez Suzy et Gaia (☎ 0262 32 45
14, 0692 59 84 39; http://monsite.wanadoo.fr/chezgayaet
suzie in French; 197 Route Hubert-Delisle, Bellemène Canot;
d €37) This mellow *chambre d'hôte* run by
a hospitable Indian couple is manna from
heaven for vegetarians. No artery thickeners
at dinner (€24), but homegrown vegetables.
It has two rooms – be sure to ask for the '*vue
mer*' (room with a sea view). A few electric
wires in front of the panoramic terrace spoil
the overall look (and the views), but that's
just about it.

Chambre d'hôtes L'Alambic des Palmistes (☎ 0262
32 86 17; Chemin des Palmistes, Le Guillaume; s/d €40/50)
This quirky B&B is a winner, not least for the
marvellous sense of timelessness that is still
patent in this property – a converted geranium
distillery, with all the fixtures. The three dinky
wooden bungalows look like they've fallen off
a gypsy caravan train, and are decorated with
local flair. But the real draw is the setting –
total hush and seclusion, and lush vegetation. It's about 6km up from Le Guillaume
(it's signposted). Dinner (€20) is available for
those wanting a total retreat.

our pick Villa La Clé des Champs (☎ 0262 32 37 60,
0692 20 17 04; www.ilereunion.com/cledeschamps in French;
154 Chemin des Barrières, Bellemène-les-Hauts; d €120, ste
€150) Looking for a night at some place extra-
special? Make a beeline for this lovely *maison
d'hôtes*, the pride and joy of friendly owners
Martine and Léon. Set high in the hills above
Bellemène-les-Hauts, it has five rooms done
out in chic warm Provençal or oriental colours, with sensational views over the coast
thrown in for free. This author's choice:
the 'Rose', sporting *tadelakt* (Moroccan

stucco) walls. Food is a big thing here (dinner from €45); Martine is a real cordon bleu chef, mastering such gourmet dishes as *terrine d'espadon fumé au coriandre avec confit de poivron au miel* (smoked swordfish terrine with coriander, preserved green pepper and honey). If you're in the mood for it, Martine can arrange a candlelit dinner on the terrace. Oh, and there's a Jacuzzi in the garden for a spot of late-night nuzzling with your beloved.

LE MAÏDO & AROUND

Be prepared to fall on your knees in awe: far above St-Paul and St-Gilles-les-Bains on the rim of the Cirque de Mafate, Le Maïdo is one of the most impressive viewpoints in Réunion. The lookout is perched atop the mountain peak at 2205m and offers stunning views down into the Cirque and back to the coast. As with other viewpoints, you should arrive early in the day – by 7am if possible – if you want to see anything other than cloud.

Getting there is half the fun. The sealed Route Forestière du Maïdo winds all the way up to the viewpoint from Le Guillaume (14km) in the hills above St-Gilles-les-Bains, offering a scenic drive through majestic cryptomeria forests. You'll also find a smattering of attractions along the way to keep you entertained.

A word of warning: expect traffic snarls on Sunday when hundreds of picnicking families set up base in the shade of trees along the road.

Sights & Activities
MOUNTAIN BIKING

The Maïdo area, with its thrillingly steep descents and spectacular mountain scenery makes it a top two-wheel destination. The Megavalanche Mountain Race – the biggest downhill race in the Indian Ocean region – takes place here each year. It is a 2205m descent using a mass start and draws riders from across Réunion and the world.

Fancy a downhill ride at your own pace? See the boxed text, below.

HIKING

Hiking options abound near Le Maïdo. The peak is the starting point for the tough walk along the Cirque rim to the summit of **Le Grand Bénare** (2896m), another impressive lookout (allow at least six hours for the return trip). Hikers can also descend from Le Maïdo into the Cirque de Mafate via the Sentier de Roche-Plate, which meets the GR R2 variant that connects the villages of Roche-Plate and Îlet des Orangers (allow three hours to reach Roche-Plate). Ambitious walkers can head in the direction of Îlet des Orangers and down to the hamlet of Sans Souci near Le Port for a very long day's walk (at least eight hours). See p231 for more information on hiking in Mafate.

HORSE RIDING

The **Centre Équestre du Maïdo** (☎ 0692 67 54 47; Route du Maïdo, La Petite France; horse riding per hr €2?; poney rides €7-12; ☺ 9am-noon & 1.30-5pm Wed, Sat & Sun school term, daily school holidays) organises gentle

---

THRILLING DOWNHILLS

The spectacular flanks of Le Maïdo will prove a sort of nirvana for mountain bikers who prefer sitting back and letting gravity do the work. The 35km, 2205m descent follows trails that wind through tamarind and cryptomeria forests and sugar-cane fields. Throughout the ride you're presented with astounding views of the lagoon and the coast.

Rando Réunion Passion (Map p183; ☎ 0262 45 18 67, 0692 21 11 11; www.descente-vtt.com; 3 Rue Alexis) in St-Gilles-les-Bains is a professional and enthusiastic set-up that offers a range of mountain-bike trips for riders of all levels. The most popular ride is the 'Classique du Maïdo' descent, from the lookout to the coast. If you're a beginner, fear not! You won't ride at breakneck speed, and various stops are organised along the way, where the guide will give you the lowdown on flora and fauna. Half-day packages including bike hire, transport to the start (by minivan) and a guide cost around €45 per person (minimum four). Children over 12 are welcome.

If you want to open up the throttle a little more, opt for the 'Maïdo Sportif' (€52) or the 'Méga, Tête Dure' (€60) descents.

The ultimate is the 'Rando du Volcano' (Volcano Ride), which takes in the southern flank of the Piton de la Fournaise down to St-Joseph (€150). Memorable!

jaunts around La Petite France. Pony rides are available for children.

PARC AVENTURE

For Tarzan types, **La Forêt de L'Aventure** (☎ 0692 30 01 54; adult/child €20/15; Route Forestière des Cryptomérias, La Petite France; ☒ 9am-5pm daily school holidays, by reservation school term) has set up two wonderful adventure circuits in a 3-hectare perimeter, with a variety of fixtures, including tyrolean slides. There's a 'Mini Forêt' for the kiddies (over five). It's signposted, about 500m to the north of La Petite France, after L'Alambic Bègue (see below).

OTHER ATTRACTIONS

The hamlet of **La Petite France** (1000m) is famous for its traditional **distilleries** producing essential oils from geranium, cryptomeria and vetiver leaves (nice smell!). They run small shops where you can stock up on perfumes, soaps and other natural health products – if you're looking for an aphrodisiac concoction, this is your chance. Stop off at the following places, all scattered along the main road in La Petite France:

Distillerie du Maïdo – Chez Nanou Le Savoyard (☎ 0692 61 75 43; www.distilleriedumaido.com; La Petite France; ☒ 8.30am-6pm)
La Maison du Géranium Rosat (☎ 0692 82 15 00; La Petite France; ☒ 8.30am-5pm daily except Wed & Fri afternoon)
L'Alambic Bègue (☎ 0692 64 58 25; La Petite France; ☒ 8.30am-6pm)

Further up, at an altitude of 1500m, the **Relais du Maïdo** (☎ 0262 32 40 32; Route du Maïdo; ☒ Tue-Sun) is a kind of theme park, with a smattering of attractions, mostly geared to children, including pony rides (€5), quad bikes (€5 to €10) and archery (€6). There's also an onsite restaurant.

Sleeping & Eating

Why not escape the heat and stop overnight in La Petite France? It makes a convenient base for an early-morning start up to Le Maïdo. Choose from **Chambre d'hôtes Chez Rose Magdeleine** (☎ 0262 32 53 50; Chemin de l'École, La Petite France; d €34, dinner €18), a well-run B&B just off the main road, or nearby **L'És-Sens-Ciel** (☎ 0262 55 37 75; Route du Maïdo, La Petite France; d €60, dinner €25), another reputable B&B set in a massive blue house, with four neat rooms.

If hunger strikes, **Chez Doudou** (☎ 0262 32 55 87; Route de Maïdo, PK 3; mains €12-13; ☒ lunch Thu-Tue) and **Chez Ary et Lucette** (☎ 0262 32 40 69; Route du Maïdo, PK3; mains €10-13; ☒ lunch Wed-Mon), opposite Chez Doudou, whip up comforting Creole *carris* served with all the traditional accompaniments. With its barn-like surrounds, Chez Doudou boasts a kind of ramshackle charm while Chez Ary et Lucette enjoys the best views. Both are full to bursting at weekends.

Getting There & Around

Réseau Éolis (line 2) runs three buses a day (Monday to Saturday) taking walkers from St-Paul to the start of the Sentier du Maïdo, the footpath into the Cirque de Mafate, which strikes off the road about 4km below the summit. The first bus up the hill leaves at 6am and the last one down is at 5.20pm (€1.50, one hour).

BOUCAN CANOT
pop 2000

Some say Boucan Canot (the final 't' is pronounced), dubbed the Réunionnais St-Tropez, is *très branché* (very hip) and fashionable. We think it's parvenu and pretentious. But hey, after (or before) roughing it in the Cirques, a whiff of pose and glitz doesn't do any harm. Whatever your verdict, bring your designer sunglasses in this attitude-fuelled little resort town.

The obvious focus here is the beach. It's been listed as one of Réunion's best, and once you get a glimpse of the gentle curve of the bright white sand, lined with palms and casuarina trees and framed with basalt rocks and cliffs, you'll see why. It gets packed on weekends. Caveat: currents can be strong.

Sleeping

La Villa Du Soleil (☎ 0262 24 38 69; www.lavilladusoleil .com in French; 54 Route de Boucan Canot; s/d from €40/46; ☒ ☒) Wedged between the highway (noise!) and the beach, this family-run hotel is the most affordable establishment in Boucan Canot, with 12 ordinary rooms arranged around a courtyard. It feels a tad compact, but at this price we're not complaining.

Résidence Les Boucaniers (☎ 0262 24 23 89; www .les-boucaniers.com in French; 29 Route de Boucan Canot; d from €72; ☒ ☒) Rumbling with the heavyweight hotels in this neck of the woods, these fine-looking self-catering studios and apartments have lovely views of the beach. Breathe in

RÉUNION

the sea air and sun-splashed hedonism from the balcony.

If you want to do Boucan Canot in style, opt for **Le Saint-Alexis** (☎ 0262 24 42 04; www .hotelsaintalexis.com; 44 Route de Boucan Canot; d €140-310; ❂ ▣ ▨), a four-star venue with all the luxury trappings, or **Le Boucan Canot** (☎ 0262 33 44 44; www.boucancanot.com; 32 Route de Boucan Canot; d €137-274; ❂ ▨), another four-star bigwig (though ageing a bit) at the other end of the beach.

Eating

There's a clutch of snack stands and laid-back café-restaurants along the seafront promenade.

Ti Boucan (☎ 0262 24 85 08; Route de Boucan Canot; mains €7-15, menu €12; ❂ lunch daily) Punters are drawn to the civilised yet casual Ti Boucan for its choice of grills, salads and its brilliant-value *formule* (lunch set menu). In the afternoon, pinch a spot on the small terrace and enjoy a fresh fruit juice while watching the swagger of suntanned scenesters passing by.

Boucan Beach (Route de Boucan Canot; mains €8-17; ❂ lunch & dinner) Service is *casse-pas-la-tête* (unfussy) and the décor is unpretentious at this friendly stalwart set in a Creole house on the seafront. Fuel up with wholesome *carris*.

Bambou Bar (☎ 0262 24 59 29; Route de Boucan Canot; mains €10-30; ❂ lunch Wed-Sun, dinner Tue-Sun) An espadrille's throw from the beach, this perennial fave scores high on atmosphere, with a thatched roof and plenty of wood and greenery. Pounce on its good-value grills or *métro* mains. Pair any and all with a chilled Dodo beer or a bottle of wine and you'll be perfectly sated. Bounteous wood-fired pizzas are also available.

Getting There & Away

Car Jaune's (lines B and C) between St-Denis and St-Pierre run through the centre of Boucan-Canot.

ST-GILLES-LES-BAINS & L'HERMITAGE-LES-BAINS

pop 6000

Robinson Crusoe–style beaches and pristine wilderness, oh no no! The tourism machine shifts into overdrive in the large resort complex of St-Gilles and L'Hermitage (as they are usually known), with white sands, restaurants, nightclubs and a boisterous atmosphere on weekends. St-Gilles and L'Hermitage are where the real action is, if by 'action' you mean

pretty beaches, pretty people and pretty dreadful hangovers. During the week, however, the atmosphere is much more relaxed and you shouldn't have to fight for a space to lay your towel. There are numerous water activities on offer, from diving to deep-sea fishing. The surf here isn't bad either; many amateurs hone their skills in St-Gilles before attempting the more challenging swells at St-Leu.

Let's be frank: it's got that generic resort feel and there's no discernible Creole character. Those travellers seeking traditional Creole flavour might come away slightly disappointed.

Don't get us wrong, though: plenty of people do enjoy themselves in St-Gilles, and it's a great place to meet Zoreilles from every corner of, well, France. But if a beachfront full of Gallic passers-by isn't your thing, here's the antidote: clunk your safety belt, jump on a serpentine country road and drive up to some rustic and authentic villages in the Hauts!

Information

ATM-clad commercial banks are a dime a dozen along the main drag in St-Gilles.

Hotwave (☎ 0262 24 04 04; 37 Rue du Général de Gaulle, St-Gilles-les-Bains; per hr €7; ❂ 10am-7pm Mon-Sat) Internet café.

Office du tourisme (☎ 0810 797 797; www.saintpaul -lareunion.com; 1 Pl Paul-Julius Bénard, St-Gilles-les-Bains; ❂ 10am-6pm) Has helpful English-speaking staff.

Post office (Rue de la Poste; ❂ 8.15am-5pm Mon-Fri, 8am-noon Sat) Has an ATM.

Sights

The attractive **Plage des Roches Noires** (Les Roches Noires beach) is obviously the biggest pull at St-Gilles. Further south, **Plage de L'Hermitage** (L'Hermitage beach), lined with casuarina trees, is another alluring place to fry in the sun. Both are safe for swimming and extremely popular on weekends. Snorkelling is better at Plage de L'Hermitage.

In the modern Port de Plaisance complex the quite engaging **Aquarium de la Réunion** (☎ 0262 33 44 00; www.aquariumdelareunion.com in French; adult/child €8/5; ❂ 10am-5.30pm Tue-Sun) houses a series of excellent underwater displays, including tanks with lobsters, barracudas, groupers and small sharks.

Appealing to a wider audience than just plant lovers and gardeners, **Le Jardin d'Eden** (☎ 0262 33 83 16; RN1; adult/child €6/3; ❂ 10am-6pm Sat-Thu), across the main highway from

ST-GILLES-LES-BAINS & L'HERMITAGE-LES-BAINS

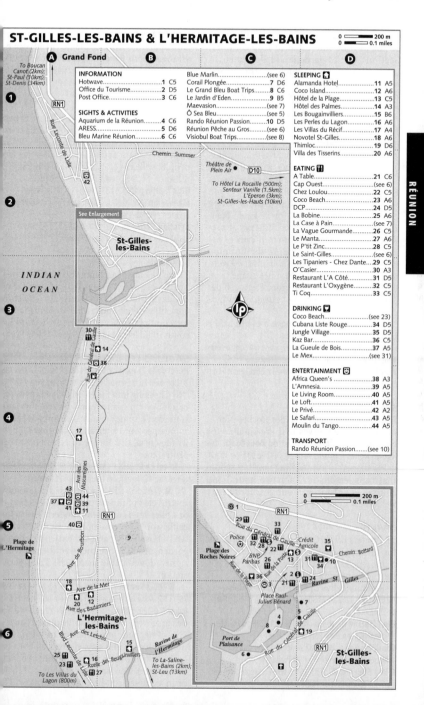

0 — 200 m
0 — 0.1 miles

INFORMATION
Hotwave.................................**1** C5
Office du Tourisme.............**2** D5
Post Office...........................**3** C6

SIGHTS & ACTIVITIES
Aquarium de la Réunion....**4** C6
ARESS...................................**5** D6
Bleu Marine Réunion.........**6** C6
Blue Marlin......................(see 6)
Corail Plongée....................**7** D6
Le Grand Bleu Boat Trips...**8** C6
Le Jardin d'Eden.................**9** B5
Maevasion........................(see 7)
Ô Sea Bleu.......................(see 5)
Rando Réunion Passion.....**10** D5
Réunion Pêche au Gros....(see 6)
Visiobul Boat Trips.........(see 8)

SLEEPING
Alamanda Hotel................**11** A5
Coco Island.......................**12** A6
Hôtel de la Plage..............**13** C5
Hôtel des Palmes..............**14** A3
Les Bougainvilliers............**15** B6
Les Perles du Lagon..........**16** A6
Les Villas du Récif............**17** A4
Novotel St-Gilles...............**18** A6
Thimloc.............................**19** D6
Villa des Tisserins.............**20** A6

EATING
A Table..............................**21** C6
Cap Ouest.......................(see 6)
Chez Loulou......................**22** C5
Coco Beach.......................**23** A6
DCP...................................**24** D5
La Bobine..........................**25** A6
La Case à Pain.................(see 7)
La Vague Gourmande.......**26** C5
Le Manta...........................**27** A6
Le P'tit Zinc......................**28** C5
Le Saint-Gilles................(see 6)
Les Tipaniers - Chez Dante....**29** C5
O'Casier.............................**30** A3
Restaurant L'A Côté..........**31** D5
Restaurant L'Oxygène........**32** C5
Ti Coq...............................**33** C5

DRINKING
Coco Beach....................(see 23)
Cubana Liste Rouge..........**34** D5
Jungle Village...................**35** D5
Kaz Bar.............................**36** C5
La Gueule de Bois............**37** A5
Le Mex...........................(see 31)

ENTERTAINMENT
Africa Queen's..................**38** A3
L'Amnesia.........................**39** A5
Le Living Room.................**40** A5
Le Loft..............................**41** A5
Le Privé............................**42** A2
Le Safari............................**43** A5
Moulin du Tango...............**44** A5

TRANSPORT
Rando Réunion Passion.......(see 10)

RÉUNION

L'Hermitage, is definitely worth an hour or so for anyone interested in tropical flora. Sections of the gardens are dedicated to interesting concepts such as the sacred plants of the Hindus, medicinal plants, edible tropical plants, spices and aphrodisiac plants.

Activities
BOAT EXCURSIONS
The best way to discover St-Gilles' iridescent lagoon is by joining a boat excursion. Various operators offer *promenades en mer* (boat excursions) and *observation sous-marine* (glass-bottomed tours) along the coast towards St-Leu or St-Paul. 'Safaris Dauphin' (dolphin encounters), sunset cruises and daylong catamaran cruises are also available. Depending on the duration of the cruise (the shortest tours last 30 minutes) and the type of boat, rates range from €10 to €90 per adult and from €5 to €50 per child. Tours go every day but are weather-dependent.

The following outfits have a booth at the jetty beside the aquarium:

Le Grand Bleu (☎ 0262 33 28 32; www.reunioncroisieres .com in French) Has the largest range of tours.
Visiobul (☎ 0262 24 37 04; www.visiobul-reunion.com in French)

SURFING
Hawaii it ain't, but Plage des Roches Noires has respectable waves that are suitable for beginners. **École de Surf et de Bodyboard des Roches Noires** (☎ 0262 24 63 28, 0692 86 00 59; bertrand. surf@wanadoo.fr) is a 'travelling' surfing school that runs lessons (€27 for two hours) and courses (€122 for 10 hours). Children are welcome.

DIVING
The waters off St-Gilles offer plenty of scope for diving (including the chance to explore a few wrecks), whatever your level. See p30 for more information about diving.

Reputable dive operators in St-Gilles:
ARESS (☎ 0262 24 23 30; www.aress.fr in French; Port de Plaisance)
Bleu Marine Réunion (☎ 0262 24 22 00; www.bleu -marine-reunion.com; Port de Plaisance)
Corail Plongée (☎ 0262 24 46 38; www.corail -plongee.com in French; Port de Plaisance)
Ô Sea Bleu (☎ 0262 33 16 15; www.reunion-plongee .com in French; Port de Plaisance)

MOUNTAIN BIKING
Downhill rides from Le Maïdo (p180) can be arranged with **Rando Réunion Passion** (☎ 0262 45 18 67, 0692 21 11 11; www.descente-vtt.com; 3 Rue St Alexis).

SPORTFISHING
St-Gilles is a good base for fans of Ernest Hemingway. The waters off the west coast are a pelagic playpen for schools of marlin, swordfish, shark and tuna. A fishing trip (six people) will set you back €400/600 per half-/full-day. Three recommended outfits:
Blue Marlin (☎ 0262 33 73 48; Port de Plaisance)
Maevasion (☎ 0262 33 38 04; www.maeva-fishing.com in French; Port de Plaisance)
Réunion Pêche au Gros (☎ 0262 33 33 99; www .reunionfishingclub.com; Port de Plaisance)

Sleeping
There's plenty of accommodation in the area but almost everything is booked out during holiday periods and on weekends. The more appealing hotels and *chambres d'hôtes* are in the countryside just north of town or to the south in L'Hermitage-les-Bains.

ST-GILLES-LES-BAINS
Hôtel de la Plage (☎ 0262 24 06 37; fax 0262 33 20 05; 20 Rue de la Poste; d with/without bathroom from €36/€32; 🖳) Checking into the Hôtel de la Plage is a bit of a lucky dip; some rooms have bathrooms, some don't, some are spacious, some are boxy, some open onto a terrace, some don't. Luckily they're all fine for the price you pay. Very central too.

Hôtel La Rocaille (☎ 0262 33 29 29; www.hotellar caille.com; 45 Chemin des Lantanas; d incl breakfast €77-85; 🖳 🖳) Accessed by a dirt road a few kilometres east of the centre (in the direction of St-Gilles-les-Hauts), the modernish La Rocaille won't disappoint, with spotless rooms, well-chosen tiles and an enticing tropical garden. And did we mention the pool? It's signed down a lane beside the Total petrol station.

ourpick **Senteur Vanille** (☎ 0262 24 04 88, 0692 78 13 05; www.senteurvanille.com; Route du Théâtre; bungalow €60-120, chalet €97-120; 🖳) A true find for peace seekers, Senteur Vanille makes you feel you've stepped into a Garden of Eden, with mango, lychee and papaya trees all over the grounds (the owner is a major fruit producer in Réunion). Curl up in a well-equipped chalet or in a cute-as-can-be Creole bungalow. The wonderful setting makes it easy to meet the three-night minimum stay. The nearest beach is a 15-minute walk down a path. Same direction as La Rocaille.

Other places to rest your head:

Thimloc (☎ 0262 24 23 24; 165 Rue du Général de Gaulle; d €47-54; 🏊) This place offers little to attract the eye inside, but does offer every possible convenience in terms of location. Has six adjoining rooms.

Hôtel des Palmes (☎ 0262 24 47 12; fax 0262 24 30 62; 205 Rue du Général de Gaulle; d €52) This two-star offers good-sized villas, but its location ain't so great – it's sandwiched between the highway and the main road to L'Hermitage.

L'HERMITAGE-LES-BAINS

Budget

Villa des Tisserins (☎ 0262 33 15 23; villa.des.tisserins@wanadoo.fr; 25 Ave de la Mer; d €35-50; 🏊) If you're looking to save and be close to the beach, this laid-back guesthouse in a distinctive Creole house is a bonanza. Mellow out in the garden or take a dip in the kidney-shaped pool. Excellent value.

Coco Island (☎ 0262 33 82 41; http://cocoisland france.com in French; 21 Ave de la Mer; d €33-54; 🏊) A few doors from Villa des Tisserins, this is another popular budget option, with 12 unimaginative rooms of varying size and shape – have a look before committing. Cheaper rooms share bathrooms. Guests can use the communal kitchen.

Midrange & Top End

Les Perles du Lagon (☎ 0262 33 83 45; www.location vacance-reunion.com in French; 1 Ruelle des Bougainvilliers; €49; 🏊) Clean, tiled rooms with self-catering facilities and a location a mere stone's throw away from the beach make this one of the best deals in town. There are only three studios, so book ahead if you can. A three-night minimum usually applies.

Les Bougainvilliers (☎ 0692 22 15 23; www.bou ainvillier.com; 27 Ruelle des Bougainvilliers; d €50-59; 🅿 🏊 🍴) A short stroll from Les Perles du Lagon, this well-run guesthouse offers eight simply furnished rooms. The catch? Some cop a bit of road noise from the highway, and privacy is almost nonexistent – the pool almost licks the terrace of the downstairs room.

Alamanda Hotel (☎ 0262 33 10 10; www.alamanda in French; 81 Ave de Bourbon; s €62-105, d €86-152; 🏊 🍴) With its Creole architecture, garden and bright, modern rooms, this two-star

provides for a very agreeable stay, though make sure you're overlooking the garden, not the car park.

Les Villas du Lagon (☎ 0262 70 00 00; www.villas -du-lagon.com; 28 Rue du Lagon; s €160-220, d €200-280; 🏊 💻 🍴) Simply stunning, Les Villas du Lagon pays elegant homage to luxurious colonial architecture, with a gaggle of Creole-style villas scattered amid a verdant property overlooking the beach. It attracts holidaymakers looking for comfortable rooms and plenty of resort amenities, including three restaurants, a big pool and a kids club. At the very south end of the beach at L'Hermitage.

Other options:

Novotel Saint-Gilles (☎ 0262 24 44 44; www .accorhotels.com; Ave de la Mer; s/d €140/180; 🏊 🍴) Accor's flagship Réunionnais resort is popular with airline crews, which is a good omen.

Les Villas du Récif (☎ 0262 70 01 00; www.villas-du -recif.fr; 50 Ave du Bourbon; s with half board €150-205, d with half board €200-260; 🏊 🍴) After a much-needed renovation, this three-star venue now flaunts its rejuvenated look with pride. Same ownership as Les Villas du Lagon.

Eating

St-Gilles is well endowed with eating places, and new restaurants are constantly opening up. As a result of the continuous flow of hungry tourists, standards tend to be more variable than elsewhere on the island.

ST-GILLES-LES-BAINS

La Case à Pain (☎ 0262 33 27 89; 27 Rue du Port; ⏱ 7am-7pm Tue-Sun) Hmm! We can still smell the scent of freshly baked *pain frotté à la vanille* (a variety of bread flavoured with vanilla) wafting from the door (available on weekends only). Its other offerings, including brioches, are worth the dental bills, too.

La Vague Gourmande (☎ 0262 24 53 06; 13 Rue de la Poste; ice creams from €1.60; ⏱ 8am-8pm Wed-Mon, 2-8pm Tue) Since the '80s Claude Jaminet has been satisfying ice-cream devotees in his refreshingly attitude-free den and we know why. There are lots of original flavours, such as *litchis* (lychee) and *cœur de boeuf* (custard apple).

Chez Loulou (☎ 0262 24 40 41; 86 Rue du Général de Gaulle; mains €6; ⏱ 7am-1pm & 3-7pm Mon-Sat, 7am-1pm Sun) The most iconic Creole *case* (house) for miles around, with a distinctive turquoise façade on the main drag. The belt-bustingly good *tartelettes* (fruit pies) and *macatias* (a variety of bun) continue to torment us! Good sandwiches and takeaway meals at lunchtime, too.

O'Casier (☎ 0262 33 17 38; 190 Rue du Général de Gaulle; mains €10-22; ☯ lunch & dinner Tue-Fri & Sun, dinner Sat) Get in early here as this sassy *bistrot chic* (gastropub) teems with punters anxious to wrap their lips around *tartines* and *métro* dishes. Since wine also features high here, get stuck into the list of well-chosen French tipples.

our pick Le P'tit Zinc (☎ 0262 24 07 50; 58 Rue du Général de Gaulle; mains €14-25, menus €10-15; ☯ dinner Mon-Sat) This venue has a tantalising menu showcasing all the classics of Creole cuisine, served in snug surrounds complete with wood beams, elegant furnishings and tropical plants. Feeling adventurous? Go for the *carri pat' cochon* (pig's trotter *carri*). The spiffing balcony on the 1st floor (two tables only) is a good place to linger over a meal.

DCP (☎ 0262 33 02 96; Place du Marché; mains €16-19, menus €20-26; ☯ lunch & dinner Tue-Sun) Fish lovers, you'll find nirvana here: the DCP has a wide assortment of fish delivered daily from the harbour. Order it grilled, *à la vapeur* (steamed) or raw, accompanied with a curcuma, pineapple or Roquefort sauce.

A Table (☎ 0262 20 00 24; Place du Marché; mains €18-20, menus €17-21; ☯ lunch & dinner Tue-Sat) This slick loungey place features parquet floors and wood furnishings and doubles as a teashop in the afternoon. Its forte? *Métro* fare with a sophisticated twist, such as *filet mignon au thé rouge* (tenderloin of beef flavoured with red tea). One minus: there's no view from the terrace.

Restaurant L'Oxygène (☎ 0692 03 40 34; 1 Rue de la Plage; mains €18-21, menu €36; ☯ lunch & dinner Tue-Fri, dinner Sat & Mon) L'Oxygène boasts contemporary furnishings, colourful paintings on the wall and elegantly presented concoctions, such as a succulent *caviar d'aubergine au curry* (puréed aubergine with curry). Pity about the dull location, though; it's on the ground floor of an unremarkable building.

Le Saint-Gilles (☎ 0262 24 51 27; www.lesaintgilles.net; Port de Plaisance; mains €18-45, menu €42; ☯ lunch & dinner Tue-Sat, lunch Sun) A bastion of *haute cuisine*, Le Saint-Gilles attracts gourmets keen to enjoy elaborate fish and meat dishes, such as *feuilleté de crevettes au gingembre* (flaky pastry stuffed with shrimp and ginger) or a seafood platter. The vanilla *crème brûlée* is a perfect coda to a delightful meal. Nab a seat

on the terrace and perve on boats you wish you owned.

Other recommendations:

Ti Coq (☎ 0262 33 22 98; 79bis Rue du Général de Gaulle; mains €10-24; ☯ lunch & dinner Mon-Sat) Dripping in tropical garb, Ti Coq is widely acclaimed for its hearty Creole dishes served on banana leaves. Good *métro* fare, too.

Les Tipaniers – Chez Dante (☎ 0262 24 28 84; 58bis Rue du Général de Gaulle; mains €10-26, menu €29; ☯ lunch & dinner Wed-Mon) A good choice for an intimate meal, with an enticing veranda and candles at night. Various preparations of *magret de canard* (duck) and Creole dishes compete for your attention.

Restaurant L'A Côté (☎ 0262 32 10 26; 122 Rue du Général de Gaulle; mains €12-25; ☯ dinner Mon-Sat) This newcomer is always bustling at dinner. It specialises in French cuisine and pastas.

Cap Ouest (☎ 0262 33 21 56; Port de Plaisance; mains €14-23, lunchtime menu €12; ☯ 8.30am-midnight except Wed) Light meals are available at this buzzing eatery.

L'HERMITAGE-LES-BAINS

Coco Beach (☎ 0262 33 81 43; Blvd Leconte de Lisle; mains €10-19; ☯ lunch & dinner) Brimming with good cheer, this eatery overlooking the beach has garnered high praise for its grills and ultrafresh fish, salads and pastas. It's also a good place to hang out and just enjoy the tropical atmosphere and fashionable buzz with a fresh Dodo beer in hand.

La Bobine (☎ 0262 33 94 36; Blvd Leconte de Lisle; mains €12-25; ☯ lunch & dinner) This sprightly restaurant slap bang on the beach woos diners from afar. Grab a seat on the breezy alfresco deck and tuck into delicious fish or meat dishes, such as *filet de voilier* (swordfish steak) or *assiette grand cru* (a combo platter of fish), which transcend their simple ingredients. Smart service too. In mid-2007 this place was closed following a mini-tsunami; the timing of its reopening was uncertain.

Le Manta (☎ 0262 33 82 44; Blvd Leconte de Lisle; mains €14-20; ☯ lunch & dinner) Specialities like kangaroo fillet and *filet de Saint-Pierre* (John Dory fillet) make a good argument on behalf of Le Manta, as does the lush garden. No, it's not right on the beach – it's just across the road.

Drinking

St-Gilles is one of the top places in Réunion (on an equal footing with St-Pierre) for bar hopping. The atmosphere is very *Zoreilles* – you could be mistaken for thinking you're in the French Côte d'Azur. Most places are scattered along Rue du Général de Gaulle and the chi-chi seafront. As the bars fade from about midnight on, the centre of pleasurable gravity shifts to L'Hermitage (see Entertainment).

Cubana Liste Rouge (☎ 0262 33 24 91; 122 Rue du Général de Gaulle; 🕑 6pm-2am) Kick off the night with a few shots at this salsa-inspired venue featuring bordello-red curtains.

Le Mex (☎ 0262 33 04 05; 122 Rue du Général de Gaulle; 🕑 6pm-2am) Slightly reminiscent of a Mexican hacienda, Le Mex is best experienced in the evening when a posse of inebriated bodies can be found dramatically propped at the bar. Skip the food.

Coco Beach (☎ 0262 33 81 43; Blvd Leconte de Lisle; 🕑 lunch & dinner) This beachside restaurant in L'Hermitage is packed on Sunday evening, when there's live music. There's also plenty of Dodo beer with which to lubricate your gullet.

Jungle Village (☎ 0262 33 21 93; Rue du Général de Gaulle; 🕑 7pm-2am Mon-Sat) Big, bold and cheesy – it's hard to miss the log-cabin exterior and the ugly monkey mannequin above the entrance – sums up this popular bar on St-Gilles' main drag.

Kaz Bar (☎ 0262 96 04 16; 49 Rue de la Plage; 🕑 5pm-midnight) This pleasant, open-air bar with lively tropical décor was *the* happening scene when we visited. It usually gets going around 9pm as casually fashionable young things gather for a pre-disco warm-up. Don't miss the *apéro-concert* (live band and an apéritif) on Thursday evening. You can also eat here. On the seafront.

La Gueule de Bois (☎ 0262 24 78 26; 5 Rue des Îles Éparses; 🕑 6pm-1am Tue-Sun) Was also in-vogue at the time of writing. The name of this cheerful den is a French expression meaning 'hangover' in French, which is pretty appropriate given the incendiary rums on offer. It hosts live bands certain evenings. Food is also served.

Entertainment

Party, party, party! L'Hermitage rocks on weekends. By far the capital of Réunion's club scene, it has the greatest density of discos on the island. The fun starts late – after 11pm – and places typically close around 5am. Cover charges vary between €10 and €15 at most venues (but some are free). You don't need to be completely dolled up but if you're wearing shorts or flip-flops you'll be turned away. Check the flyers posted around town or ask the locals to find out which clubs are the flavour of the month – it's constantly changing.

Le Privé (☎ 0262 24 04 17; www.le-prive.fr in French; 1 Rue du Général de Gaulle) St-Gilles' sole club (all others are in L'Hermitage). It's been around for a while, but it's still a big draw. Young, old, gay and straight pack into Le Privé for a wild night of fun. Famous for its ladies night on Thursday.

Moulin du Tango (☎ 0262 24 53 90; www.moulin-du-tango.fr; Ave Bourbon) Bump hips with a more mature crowd in this self-styled 'retro' dance club in L'Hermitage. Famous for its Bal des Célibataires ('singles' ball') on Wednesday.

Le Living Room (☎ 0262 33 15 00; 2 Mail Rodrigues) Ground zero for sexy young things shaking it up all weekend. Catch local DJs spinning a smorgasbord of deep house, dance, techno and funk.

Other staunch favourites:

Africa Queen's (☎ 0262 33 01 68; 205 Rue du Général de Gaulle) Weekend nights you can barely breathe for the crowds. Expect R&B, hip-hop and electro house.

L'Amnesia (☎ 0262 33 00 11; 71 Ave Bourbon) Another crowd-puller in L'Hermitage. Latin and dance music dominate the play list.

Le Loft (☎ 0262 24 81 06; 1 Rue des Îles Éparses) Another hot spot that's cookin' after 2am, with scantily clad clubbers posturing on podiums.

Le Safari (☎ 0262 25 99 13; 1 Rue des Îles Éparses) A local place that pulls in just about everybody on the island on weekends, when a DJ cranks up the salsa, R&B and other soundtracks.

Getting There & Away

Car Jaune's nonexpress buses between St-Denis and St-Pierre (lines B and C) run through the centre of St-Gilles down Rue du Général de Gaulle. Buses run about every half-hour in either direction from 5am to 6pm. The trip to St-Denis takes at least one hour and costs around €3.

Getting Around

CAR & MOTORCYCLE

There are also numerous local operators and a few international outlets in St-Gilles. Find them along Rue du Général de Gaulle.

BIKE

Rando Réunion Passion (☎ 262 45 18 67; www.descente-vtt.com; 3 Rue St Alexis) rents out mountain bikes (€12 for a half day).

ST-GILLES-LES-HAUTS & AROUND

pop 2000

If all these beaches start to overwhelm and if you need a break from the commercialism of the coast, a 20-minute drive from St-Gilles-les-Bains transports you to yet another world up in the hills, in St-Gilles-les-Hauts. For some cultural sustenance, head to the **musée de Villèle** (☎ 0262 55 64 10; admission €2; ☒ 9.30am-5.30pm Tue-Sun), south of St-Gilles-les-Hauts on the D6. It's set in the former home of a wealthy coffee- and sugar-baroness who, among other things, owned 300 slaves. Legend has it that she was a cruel woman and that her tormented screams can still be heard from the hellish fires whenever Piton de la Fournaise is erupting. She died in 1846 and her body lies in the **Chapelle Pointue**, on the D6 by the entrance to the museum. The house itself, which is only accessible on a guided tour (in French only), was built in 1787 and is full of elegant period furniture. After the tour, you're free to wander the outbuildings and the 10-hectare park, which contains the ruins of the sugar mill.

You could also stop off in the village of L'Éperon and visit the **Village Artisanal de L'Éperon**. Housed in a picturesque old grist, it's home to a small community of artists and artisans. There are also a number of boutiques selling ceramics, locally tanned leather and other *objets d'art*.

The villages of St-Gilles-les-Hauts, Villèle and L'Éperon can all be reached by fairly infrequent minibuses out of St-Paul (see p179).

Sleeping & Eating

There are several options for accommodation in the hamlets that dot the hillside above St-Gilles-les-Hauts.

Chambre d'hôtes Mme Edith Ramassamy (☎ 0262 55 55 06; ramassamy.anthony@wanadoo.fr; 100 Chemin des Roses, St-Gilles-les-Hauts; d €31, dinner €18) Your friendly hosts, an Indian couple, have built a reputation for warmth and savoury Indian cuisine. Guests return year after year to these five simple rooms in a modern house. It's signposted from opposite the Chapelle Pointue.

La Villa des Songes (☎ 0262 22 03 36; www.lavilla dessonges.fr in French; St-Gilles-les-Hauts; d €78; ☒ ☐) Don't be discouraged by the modest exterior and the unspectacular location, on the main road, opposite a petrol station. This newish, welcoming, traveller-savvy haven in a beautifully restored Creole house is best described as 'scrubbed-up rustic' – a rare species on

the island. It has 12 rooms, all decorated in classical local style – parquet flooring or tiles, colourwashed walls, wooden and wrought-iron furnishings – and an enticing restaurant, La Frigousse (see below).

L'Imprévu (☎ 0262 55 36 34; 72 Rue Joseph Hubert, St-Gilles-les-Hauts; mains €8-20; ☒ lunch Mon-Fri, dinner Mon-Sat) Chef Ludovic works his magic at this cheerful restaurant in a little Creole building on the main road. The menu has a split personality: it features ordinary pizzas and the usual *carris* as well as more refined preparations, such as *pavé de légine en croûte d'épice* (thick piece of *légine* fish encased in pastry).

La Frigousse (St-Gilles-les-Hauts; mains €12-25; ☒ lunch daily, dinner Mon-Sat) The restaurant of La Villa des Songes, La Frigousse tempts the foodies with *cuisine métro avec une touch créole* (French fare with a Creole twist). How about *espadon sauce gingembre* (swordfish with ginger sauce) for a meeting of culinary cultures? It also majors on vegetarian dishes (yes, vegetarian dishes).

LA SALINE-LES-BAINS & AROUND

pop 2750

If you find the scene in St-Gilles and L'Hermitage a little too much, head to La Saline-les-Bains. Though immediately to the south of L'Hermitage along the coast, it has a distinct atmosphere. Here it's more mellow, more alternative, more non-conformist, and the beach of **Trou d'Eau** is usually less crowded. Not a fan of tan-lines? Head further south and

---

PERFUMED ISLE

In keeping with the French love of perfume, Réunion has long been the garden of the great fragrance houses of Paris. Essential oils, which are used as a fixative in perfumes, are extracted from roots or leaves. The mainstays of the essential-oil business are vetiver (an Asian grass), geranium and the evocative ylang-ylang, which you can often smell in the night air all over the island. All are cultivated in the Hauts (hills), and the oils are extracted in traditional distilleries. It is still a cottage industry, concentrated mainly around Le Maïdo and St-Joseph. The cultivation of these plants is in slow decline, but certain Parisian perfumers still insist on the best oils from Réunion for their fragrances.

lay your towel on **Plage de la Souris Chaude**, a 'maverick beach', which is a favourite among nudists (only just tolerated) and gay men (head to the northern tip of the beach).

The area is also popular for **surfing**, especially for beginners. To the south of La Saline, surfers gather at the mouth of the **Ravine des Trois Bassins**, where the waves are generally easier and more consistent than around St-Leu. A number of operators park their vans on the clifftop and offer lessons for adults and children (see p190).

Sleeping
LA SALINE-LES-BAINS

Le Vacoa (☎ 0262 24 12 48; www.levacoa.com; 54 Rue Antoine de Bertin; d €50-52; 🅿 🖳 🖭) A five-minute stroll from the beach, this little two-storey *résidence hôtelière* (mini-resort) contains 15 modern, well-appointed (albeit hanky-sized) rooms arranged around a central courtyard. There's a kitchen for guests' use.

La Maison du Lagon (☎ 0262 24 30 14; www.la maisondulagon.com in French; 72 Rue Auguste Lacaussade; s €65-100, d €85-120, ste €190; 🅿 🖳 🖭) This villa has a compact but respectable collection of various-sized rooms – try to snaffle a seafacing one or, better yet, splurge for the suite. The real bonus here is the location – it's *les pieds dans l'eau* (right by the beach).

Hôtel Swalibo (☎ 0262 24 10 97; www.swalibo.com in French; 9 Rue des Salines; s €90-99, d €115-130; 🅿 🖳 🖭) This intimate two-storey hotel stands out as the most polished retreat in town. The rooms are well appointed and decorated with vivid frescoes. The gleaming pool is an instant elixir when it's swelteringly hot. There's an onsite restaurant. It's 200m away from the beach.

LA SOURIS CHAUDE

With your own wheels, you'll need a code to enter La Souris Chaude residential area – phone your accommodation ahead and they will give you the code.

Kitouni Guesthouse (☎ 0262 34 05 82, 0692 60 84 05; http://site.voila.fr/kitoony in French; s/d with shared bathroom €25/30) Kitouni means, er, 'naked bum' in Creole. Fear not, this is a respectable port of call on top of being a cast-iron bargain for budget travellers and surfies, with three tidy rooms, a kitchen for guests' use, a lounge with TV and a lovely garden to snooze under swaying palms. You're only steps from the beach.

Le Dalon Plage (☎ 0262 34 29 77, 0692 04 94 26; ledalon@wanadoo.fr; d €45; 🅿 🖭) It's *au naturel*

at this hedonistic, gay-friendly place almost next door to Kitouni. Guests are allowed (if not incited) to swim naked in the gleaming pool. Well, we were too prudish to get our kit off and instead preferred to slumber in the fully-equipped bungalow – a wonderful retreat.

Eating
LA SALINE-LES-BAINS

Planch'Alizé (☎ 0262 24 62 61; Rue des Mouettes; mains €12-18; 🕑 10am-dusk) For a decent beach munch, nothing can beat this casual eatery. It also rents canoes, kayaks and paddleboats.

Le Copacabana (☎ 0262 24 16 31; Rue Lacaussade; mains €13-21; 🕑 lunch daily, dinner Fri & Sat) Simple meals are the order of the day at this convivial little bar-restaurant right on the beach. It's also a laid-back spot to sip a *rhum arrangé* or a refreshing fruit juice any time of the day. You'll find it about 150m further south from La Maison du Lagon.

our pick **La Tomate** (☎ 0262 33 02 42; 25bis Rue des Argonautes; mains €19-24; 🕑 dinner Tue-Sat) Tucked away in a side street running parallel to the main road, this hip venture provides an enjoyable dining experience with innovative food. Whet your palate with tandoori-style *camarons* (freshwater prawns) salad and finish off your meal with, say, the *gratin de mangue au lait de coco* (mango gratin with coconut milk – more, please). It also scores high on atmosphere, with dark-wood parquet floors and red-accented walls highlighted by quirky-chic lighting and furnishings.

LA SOURIS CHAUDE

Attitude Kfé (☎ 0262 24 80 86; RN1; mains €19-30; 🕑 lunch & dinner Thu-Tue) Perched on a hill overlooking the main road, this hip restaurant will satisfy capricious gourmets, with particular emphasis on *métro* fare. Another highlight is the setting – there's a pool and a tropical garden.

ST-LEU
pop 25,000

Since the good old days of the sugar industry ended, forward-looking St-Leu has transformed itself into a mecca for outdoor enthusiasts. This is the place to get high – legally: no doubt you'll be tempted to join the paragliders who wheel down from the Hauts to the lagoon. Scuba divers swear that the drop-offs here are

RÉUNION

the best on the island and surfing fiends rave about the tremendous Gauche de St-Leu.

And culture? St-Leu has a smattering of handsome stone buildings dating from the French colonial era, such as the *mairie* (town hall) and the church opposite. Other attractions are the shady park along the seafront and a protected beach that is popular with families.

St-Leu is also optimally placed for explorations of the coast and forays into the Hauts.

Information

Cyber Cafi (☎ 0262 49 83 84; 82 Rue Haute; per hr €3.50; 🕒 9am-noon & 1-6pm Mon-Fri, noon-6pm Sat) Internet café.

Laverie Océane (5 Rue de L'Étang; 🕒 8am-6pm Mon-Sat) Same location as Palais d'Asie (see opposite).

Office du Tourisme de St-Leu (☎ 0262 34 63 40; ot.stleu@wanadoo.fr; 1 Rue Le Barrelier; 🕒 1.30-5.30pm Mon, 9am-noon & 1.30-5.30pm Tue-Fri, 9am-noon & 2-5pm Sat) At the north end of the main road passing through the centre of town. It has brochures galore and helpful, English-speaking staff.

Sights

Feeling superstitious? Head straight to the little white **chapel of Notre-Dame de la Salette**, perched on the side of the hill to the east of town. It was built in 1859 as a plea for protection against the cholera epidemic sweeping the entire island. Whether by luck or divine intervention, St-Leu was spared from the epidemic, and thousands of pilgrims come here each year on 19 September to offer their thanks.

About 2km north of St-Leu, **Kelonia** (☎ 0262 34 81 10; www.kelonia.org in French; adult/child €7/3; 🕒 9am-5pm) is a well-organised turtle farm, which has been redesigned recently to good effect. There's lots of information, and you get a close-up look at the five different varieties of turtle found in the waters around Réunion. The kids will love it!

On the cliffs at Pointe au Sel, between St-Leu and Étang-Salé-les-Bains, **Le Souffleur** (The Blowhole) is a rocky crevice that spurts up a tower of water as the waves crash against it. It's only worth making the journey, however, if the sea is pretty rough.

Activities

DIVING

The dive spots off Pointe au Sel to the south of St-Leu offer some of the best underwater landscapes in Réunion, while the lagoon closer to St-Leu is good for coral. See p27 for more information about diving.

Reputable dive centres:

Abyss Plongée (☎ 0262 34 79 79; www.abyss-plongee.com; 17 Blvd Bonnier)

Aqua Bulle (☎ 0262 34 88 58; www.aquabulle-plongee.com; 30 Rue des Cocotiers)

Bleu Océan (☎ 0262 34 97 49; www.bleuocean.fr; 25 Rue du Général Lambert)

Excelsus (☎ 0262 34 73 65; www.excelsus-plongee.com in French; Pointe des Châteaux)

Réunion Plongée (☎ 0262 34 77 77; www.reunionplongee.com; 13 Ave des Artisans)

PARAGLIDING

St-Leu is one of the world's top spots for paragliding, with excellent uplifting thermals year-round. If you're new to dangling yourself in the air, you can tandem paraglide with one of the many operators offering flights (from €65 for a 20-minute aerial buzz). They also run introductory courses from €150. The most popular launch pad is at an altitude of 800m, high above the town. There's another launch pad at 1500m. The descent from the mountain is amazing, with heart-stopping views over the lagoon and the coast. Children over six are welcome.

Operators with good credentials and professional staff:

Airanx (☎ 0692 68 81 81; www.airanx.com in French; 38 Rue du Général Lambert)

Azurtech (☎ 0262 34 91 89; www.azurtech.com in French; Pointe des Châteaux)

Bourbon Parapente (☎ 0262 34 18 34, 0692 87 58 74; www.bourbonparapente.com in French; Rue du Général Lambert)

Parapente Réunion (☎ 0262 24 87 84; www.parapente-reunion.fr in French; 1 Route des Colimaçons)

SURFING

One word: awesome. The surf break known as La Gauche de St-Leu ('the Left of St-Leu') has achieved cult status among surfies from all over the Indian Ocean. Certainly not for the faint-hearted, it instils profound respect (if not fear) even in the most seasoned surfers. The best season runs from May to October.

Beginners should make for a spot called La Cafrine, which is a bit more innocuous, or head to La Ravine de Trois Bassins (see p189) or St-Gilles-les-Bains (p184).

To brush up on your surfing skills or try a first lesson, contact **École de surf Cyril Theveneau** (☎ 0692 04 40 40; cyriltheveneau@yahoo.fr) or **École** de surf de St-Leu (☎ 0692 65 44 92). Both outfits offer tuition and courses for all levels (€15 per hour). They don't have shops – call ahead for an appointment.

Festivals & Events

If you plan a visit to St-Leu in August, try to make it coincide with the **Sakifo festival** (www .sakifo.com), the best music festival on the island and a definite must-see. Mouse-click your way to the website for more information.

Sleeping

Dodo Spot (☎ 0262 34 76 98; www.dodospot.com; 67 Rue du Général Lambert; d with shared bathroom €30-39, studios €45-55) On the northern edge of town, this is a good standby, if you can forgive some flagrant omissions in the brochure and on the website. Sure, it's almost 'two steps away from the lagoon', but there's no mention of the traffic-congested highway in between! Rooms vary in size and standards, but are functional and the plant-filled property is welcoming. The studios are well worth the few extra bucks.

Résidence des Alizés (☎ 0262 34 82 31; marie-josee .cornette@wanadoo.fr; 48bis Rue des Alizés; d €33-45; 🍴) If it's modern comforts you're after, this is one of St-Leu's best bargains, with four impeccable rooms and two bungalows. Ask for a room with a sea view. On the southern outskirts of town.

Iloha (☎ 0262 34 89 89; www.iloha.fr; Pointe des Châteaux; s €65-80, d €73-90; 🍴 🏊) It's not quite the upscale option it thinks it is, but the pool, the onsite restaurant and mature gardens do add a resort flavour. Views take in the lagoon. Good for families. It's on Route des Colimaçons, north of town.

Blue Margouillat (☎ 0262 34 64 00; www.blue-mar gouillat.com; Impasse Jean Albany; r €129-200; 🍴 🖥 🏊) This delightful, small hotel on the southern outskirts of St-Leu adds a welcoming touch of glam to the local hotel scene, with just 14 artfully designed and sensitively furnished rooms, a romantic restaurant that serves dinner (mains €25, menus €29 to €43) daily and smashing views.

Other places:

Ti Som (☎ 0692 24 18 12; 228 Rue du Général Lambert; dm €15) Far from flash, but this is the cheapest place to stay for miles. The shared kitchen is a plus.

Palais d'Asie (☎ 0262 34 80 41; 5 Rue de l'Étang; d €32-45; 🏊) The 'Palais' bit is a gross misnomer but it's a good pick for the thrifty traveller, comfortably central,

with functional rooms. And no, that icon's not a misprint – it really does have its own (small) swimming pool.

Repos Laleu (☎ 0262 34 93 84; http://perso.orange .fr/repos.laleu in French; 249 Rue du Général Lambert; d €41-55) Offers eight fully equipped apartments, smack dab in the centre.

Eating

Chez Lulu (☎ 0262 34 89 53; Rue Le Barrelier; mains €8-9; 🕒 closed lunch Sun) Blink and you'll miss the tiny entrance of this little eatery next to the tourist office. Long on character and short on frills, it whips up well-prepared Creole dishes at wallet-friendly prices. Its *rougail morue* (cod rougail) is especially good.

Villa Vanille (☎ 0262 34 03 15; 69 Rue du Lagon; mains €12-20; 🕒 lunch Wed-Mon, dinner Wed-Sun) This zinging spot was the flavour of the month when we visited. No plastic chairs (sweet mercy!), but teak furnishings and an agreeable terrace. Choose from frondy salads, meat and fish dishes – the *steak d'espadon à la vanille* (swordfish flavoured with vanilla) was delicious – and ice creams. Lounge on the beach across the road once you've finished your meal – this is the life!

O'Jacaré (☎ 0262 34 88 88; 55 Ave Général Lambert; mains €14-22; 🕒 Mon-Sat) After an adrenaline-pumping tandem paragliding flight, you're going to need to regain your equilibrium with some proteins, including a toothsome *tartare de thon* (tuna tartare). If you find the shady terrace too noisy – it's on the busy roundabout near the tourist office – retreat to the dining room, which boasts an odd Brazilian theme, with yellow-and-green walls.

Other recommendations:

Chez Stephanie (☎ 0262 34 89 30; 135 Rue Général Lambert; mains €10; 🕒 lunch & dinner) Prices are inflated at this longstanding institution but it's very central and open every day. Food-wise, expect mamma-style *carris* and *civets*.

Le Lagon (☎ 0262 34 79 13; 2 Rue du Lagon; mains €10-16; 🕒 lunch & dinner except Tue) This beachfront place won't start a revolution but the menu covers enough territory to please most palates.

Drinking & Entertainment

Le Comptoir 974 (☎ 0262 33 55 36; 228 Rue du Général Lambert; 🕒 6am-midnight Mon-Sat) St-Leu's best drinking spot (an easy distinction, given the lack of competitors). Take a seat in the room or join the happy din at the main bar, which also features a vibrant dance floor. Chances are

RÉUNION

RÉUNION

that you'll bump into your diving/paragliding/ surfing instructor. Live music on Thursday.

Le Séchoir – Le K (☎ 0262 34 79 69; le.sechoir@wanadoo .fr; 125 Rue du Général Lambert) One of Réunion's venues for contemporary theatre, dance and music, as well as puppet shows, circus acts and other cultural activities. The organisers also put on open-air concerts and film shows in the area. Contact the tourist office to find out about the latest shows.

Getting There & Away

Car Jaune buses between St-Denis and St-Pierre run through the centre of St-Leu (about 10 daily). The bus station is near the town hall. From there, Ti' Car Jaune minibuses have services for most villages in the Hauts.

AROUND ST-LEU

After all that exertion in St-Leu, there's no better way to wind down than by exploring the villages that cling to the sloping hills high above the town. The zigzagging roads are scenic to boot and the atmosphere wonderfully laid-back.

To the north of St-Leu, take the D12, known as Route des Colimaçons – a series of intestine-like S-curves – then veer due south on the D3 to **La Chaloupe St-Leu** before plunging back to the coast via **Piton St-Leu**. If you really want to get away from it all, you could continue to drive uphill from the village of **Les Colimaçons** until you reach the Route Forestière (forest road), also known as Route des Tamarins, which threads for 36km across the slopes from Le Tévelave and Le Maïdo – sensational. Whatever your itinerary, a good road map is essential for it's easy to get disorientated.

Aside from the scenery and the astounding vistas, there are a few not-to-be-missed attractions in the area. On the Route des Colimaçons, on the slopes north of St-Leu, you'll find the **Conservatoire Botanique National de Mascarin** (☎ 0262 24 92 27; 2 Rue du Père Georges, Les Colimaçons; adult/child €5/2; ☺ 9am-5pm Tue-Sun). This attractive garden is in the grounds of a 19th-century Creole mansion. You can easily spend half a day exploring the site, which spreads over 7 hectares and contains an impressive collection of native plant species, all neatly labelled, as well as many from around the Indian Ocean.

Another must-see is the well-organised **Stella Matutina museum** (☎ 0262 34 16 24; 10 Allée des Flamboyants; adult/child €7/2.50; ☺ 9.30am-4.45pm

Tue-Sun), which lies 4km south of St-Leu on the D11 to Piton St-Leu and Les Avirons. It's dedicated primarily to the sugar industry, but also provides insights into the history of the island and has exhibits on other products known and loved by the Réunionnais, such as vanilla, orchids, geraniums and vetiver.

Many of the villages in the hills above St-Leu, including Piton St-Leu and Les Colimaçons, lie on the Car Jaune bus route E from St-Pierre to La Chaloupe St-Leu. They can also be reached from the bus station in St-Leu.

Sleeping & Eating

There are several peaceful villages within 10km of St-Leu that offer accommodation in a relaxed, rural setting. All the places listed below boast bird's-eye views down to the coast (and the new expressway between St-Paul and Étang-Salé-les-Bains, alas).

Chambre d'hôtes Caz' Océane (☎ /fax 0262 54 89 40; 28 Chemin Mutel, Notre-Dame-des-Champs, La Chaloupe St-Leu; s/d €25/28, dinner €17) Run by a friendly Zoreilles couple, this B&B in the hamlet of Notre-Dame-des-Champs offers good value for money. No one would accuse the three rooms of being over-decorated but they are adequate and guests can use a terrace with million-dollar views – perfect for an *apéro* (apéritif) after a bout of sightseeing. Excellent breakfast too (the homemade fruit salad is a killer).

Chambre d'hôtes Chez François Huet (☎ 0262 54 76 70; 202 Chemin Potier, Les Colimaçons; www.lareunion .com/chezhuet; d €40, dinner €18) Delivering style and substance, rooms here are sparkling, fresh and colourful. Shell out for the Creole-style *gîte* (€45) in the flower-filled garden if you intend to stay more than three nights. When it comes to preparing fish dishes, François Huet knows his stuff. It's signposted, uphill from the botanical garden.

Chambre d'hôtes Bardzour – Chez Marie-Claire Vion (☎ 0262 34 13 97; www.bardzour.com in French; 22 Chemin Georges Thénor, Piton St-Leu; d €45-55, dinner €20; ☒ ☒) This is a lovely option if you're looking for a secluded, rural atmosphere. These well-equipped rooms set among orchards provide a very cushy landing after a hard day's driving. *Table d'hôtes* meals are available twice a week (usually on Tuesday and Thursday). To find it, take the D11 towards Stella Matutina and Piton St-Leu, then continue to the very end of the lane.

LES AVIRONS & LE TÉVELAVE

pop 1500

Les Avirons is nothing inspirational but Le Tévelave, about 10km up an impossibly twisty road in the hills above Les Avirons, is a gem of a village. It offers a real taste of rural life and is a great base for walkers. You can really feel a sense of wilderness and seclusion here, light years away from the bling and bustle of the coast. At the top of the village is the starting point for the Route Forestière, more poetically known as the Route des Tamarins. This road leads through a cryptomeria forest and emerges 36km later below Le Maïdo.

Sleeping & Eating

Ferme-Auberge L'Écorce Blanc (☎ 0262 38 31 52; 46 Rue Francis Rivière; d incl breakfast €30, meals €20) Aaargh, the 600m-long access road is dreadfully steep, but you'll be rewarded with sensational views over the coast. Perched on the side of a hill, way above town, this friendly *ferme auberge* (farm inn) is beloved by locals for its authentic home cooking (by reservation). Sadly, the indoor dining room is as atmospheric as a dentist's waiting room. There are also four simple rooms that open onto the dining room (noisy at meal times); toilets are shared.

ourpick Chambre d'hôtes Case Namasté (☎ 0262 38 35 89; namastedufayet@wanadoo.fr; 17 Rue Francis Rivière; s/d with shared bathroom €35/45) This B&B with an affable hostess will smooth away any stresses that the traffic jams on the coastal road might induce. The whole place is full of grace and a Zen-like ambience you won't find elsewhere. The large communal area, with an open fireplace and exposed beams, is cosy to boot, as are the three shiny-clean rooms, with wood-panelled walls and feminine touches. And mercifully, Maud Dufayet's cuisine is low on calories; here it's more easy-to-digest tofu than stodgy *carri*. It's near the *terrain de pétanque* (pétanque pitch). It's not signposted.

Les Fougères (☎ 0262 38 32 96; fax 0262 383026; 53 Route des Merles; s/d incl breakfast €50, mains €13-16; ☽ lunch & dinner Tue-Sat, lunch Sun) The panoramic views and the secluded location, right at the start of the forest road, are the biggest perks to staying in this rural hotel with Creole architecture. Otherwise, the atmosphere is a bit staid and the rooms are functional. Angle for a room at the back.

ÉTANG-SALÉ-LES-BAINS

pop 12,000

Miles away from the hullaballo around St-Gilles, Étang-Salé-les-Bains is more a low-key resort for locals than foreign tourists, and the black-sand **beach** is much quieter than the coast further north.

The **Office du Tourisme de l'Étang-Salé** (☎ 0262 26 67 32; otsi.run@wanadoo.fr; 74 Rue Octave Bénard; ☽ 9am-5pm Mon-Fri, 9am-noon Sat) is housed in the old train station on the roundabout that marks the town centre.

Very few visitors know that **diving** is available at Étang-Salé-les-Bains. And what diving! The owners of **Plongée Salée** (☎ 0262 91 71 23; www.plongeesaleereunion.com in French; Centre Carine) take only small groups. The sites are almost untouched.

If your idea of ocean activity is reeling in a big one, make a beeline for **La Reine Claude** (☎ 0692 17 02 39; Port de l'Étang Salé). This small, convivial outfit offers personalised service and organises **deep-sea fishing** trips for about €70 per person (maximum three people).

There aren't too many options for accommodation in or around Étang-Salé-les-Bains, although it does boast the island's only official camp site, **Camping Municipal de l'Étang-Salé-les-Bains** (☎ 0262 91 75 86; camping.letangsale@wanadoo.fr; Rue Guy Hoarau; camp site per night €10-13), in a shady spot a short walk back from the beach. If you don't want to spend your night under canvas, the three-star **Le Floralys – Caro Beach** (☎ 0262 91 79 79; www.carobeach.com; 2 Ave de l'Océan; s €72-120, d €150; ☒ ☒), set in a 3-hectare garden beside the roundabout in the middle of town, features serviceable rooms. A short walk south of the main roundabout, **L'Été Indien** (☎ 0262 26 67 33; 1 Rue des Salines; mains €8-15; ☽ lunch & dinner Tue-Sun) specialises in pizzas, grills and ice-cream concoctions.

ST-LOUIS

pop 44,000

If St-Gilles and L'Hermitage are very Westernised and touristy, St-Louis, by contrast, is very Indian and falls below many travellers' radars. This is the heart of Tamil culture on the west coast, and it won't take long to feel that the city exudes an undeniably exotic atmosphere. The town doesn't have anything fantastic to offer, but it is certainly worth a stop to soak up the ambience and admire a handful of religious buildings, including a Tamil temple, a splendid mosque and the biggest

RÉUNION

church on the island. St-Louis can also be a convenient springboard for the mystifying hinterland (Entre-Deux, Les Makes), St-Pierre and even Cilaos.

A highlight (and a major landmark, with its big chimneys) is the **Sucrerie du Gol** (☎ 0262 91 05 47; visitesucrerie@gqf.com; adult/child €5/3), about 1.5km west of St-Louis. You can tour this old sugar refinery, one of only two on the island still functioning, during the cane harvest (July to December). Visits take place daily (except Sunday and Monday) with prior reservation.

our pick **Chambre d'hôtes Case Tatave** (☎ 0262 39 72 54; www.location-gite-ile-reunion.com in French; 55 Rue Hubert Delisle, Rivière St Louis; s €38, €50-54, dinner €16; 🖭) is a peach of a place. Genuine locals, Veronique and Frédéric, are passionate about Creole culture and have renovated this lovely house with a happy respect for the spirit of the place. Curl up with your sweetie in one of the three oh-so-inviting suites complete with parquet flooring, period furniture, Creole ceilings and rich fabrics. Case Tatave would be a 'find' just on the strength of its character, but when you factor in the warm welcome, the affordable prices and the yummy meals, this charming B&B is a discovery. One minus: bathrooms are not ensuite in two of the suites. It's in Rivière St-Louis, about 6km from St-Louis.

Car Jaune buses between St-Denis and St-Pierre run through St-Louis (about 10 daily). Buses to Cilaos run from the bus station (€1.50, six daily).

LES MAKES
pop 2500
One of Réunion's best-kept secrets, Les Makes boasts a wonderful bucolic atmosphere and a lovely setting. Snuggled into the seams of the Hauts, it's accessible via a tortuous secondary road from St-Louis (12km). At almost 1200m, breathing in the fresh alpine air here is enough therapy for a lifetime.

The area is ideal for **stargazing**. The **Observatoire astronomique** (☎ 0262 37 86 83; www.ilereunion .com/observatoire-makes/ in French; 18 Rue Georges Bizet; adult/child €9/5) offers stargazing programmes from 9pm to midnight. It's best to call ahead to confirm the programme is on.

It's a sin to visit Les Makes and not take the forest road that leads to **La Fenêtre** (The Window), another 10km further uphill. Hold on to your hat and lift your jaw off the floor as you approach the viewpoint – the view over the entire Cirque de Cilaos and the surround-

ing craggy summits that jab the skyline will be etched in your memory forever. La Fenêtre is also a wonderful picnic spot. **Hiking** is another option, with a series of well-marked trails leading from the lookout. Hint: arrive early, before it gets cloudy.

Horse riding is also a terrific way of exploring the surrounding forests. It can be arranged through **Centre Équestre de la Fenêtre** (☎ 0262 37 88 74; Route de la Fenêtre, Les Makes; per hr €16; 🕐 Tue-Sat).

Should you fall under the spell of this charming village (no doubt you will!), you can bunk down at the **Chambre d'hôtes Le Vieil Alambic – Chez Jean-Luc d'Eurveilher** (☎ /fax 0262 37 82 77; 55 Rue Montplaisir, Les Makes; d €40, dinner €20), an adorable B&B on the road to La Fenêtre, with four tidy rooms (no views) and highly respected *table d'hôtes* meals. Rejoicing begins with, say, *beignets de papaye verte au fromage* (papaya fritters with cheese), followed by *carri canard maïs* (duck *carri*). Save room for desserts – the *mousse des cimes* (a homemade mousse with local fruits) is a victory for humanity. Self-caterers will opt for **Chalets des Makes** (☎ 0262 37 80 10; www.bungalowrun.com in French; 5 Rue Raisins Marrons, Les Makes; d €46), which comprises four chalet-like bungalows in flowering gardens. Meals are available on request.

ENTRE-DEUX
pop 5170
This sweet little village high in the hills 18km north of St-Pierre got its name (which means 'between two') because it is situated between two rivers – the Bras de Cilaos and the Bras de la Plaine, which join to form the Rivière St-Étienne. Entre-Deux is a delightful place to stay and get a taste of rural life. It boasts a wealth of *cases créoles*, traditional country cottages surrounded by well-tended and fertile gardens, many of which are being restored. There's also a strong tradition of local crafts, including natty slippers made from the leaves of an aloe-like plant called *choca*.

The **tourist office** (☎ 0262 39 69 80; ot.entredeux@ wanadoo.fr; 9 Rue Fortuné Hoareau; 🕐 8am-5pm Mon-Sat) occupies a pretty *case créole* on the road into the village. Staff give guided visits (usually in French) of the village (adult/child €9/5) and can provide leaflets on walks in the region (including climbing Le Dimitile) and on local artisans.

Opportunities for **hiking** abound. Many visitors come here for the tough hike up the slopes of iconic **Le Dimitile** (1837m) to a sensational view over the Cirque de Cilaos. If you leave at dawn, the ascent and descent can be done in a single day. You should plan on at least eight hours, however, and unless you're superhuman it's preferable to stay at one of the two *gîtes* near the summit. The tourist office can provide information and sketch maps detailing the various routes.

Feeling lazy? Join a 4WD tour. **Kreolie 4x4** (☎ 0262 39 50 87; www.kreolie4x4.com in French; 4 Impasse des Avocats) runs day trips that include Entre-Deux and the viewpoint at Le Dimitile (€92, including lunch). Guides are informative, providing interesting titbits on the area's flora and fauna (in French).

SLEEPING

Auberge de Jeunesse (☎ 0262 39 59 20; 120 Chemin Defaud, Ravine des Citrons; dm €14; **P**) The most obvious choice if funds are short, this youth hostel occupies an enticing villa in a tranquil neighbourhood, about 3km from the centre (follow the Ravine des Citrons sign). Inside, it's much less eye candy, with monastically plain two- to eight-person rooms. Evening meals are available for groups only.

Chambre d'hôtes Mirest – Lucienne Clain (☎ 0262 39 65 43; www.mirest-reunion.com in French; 1 Chemin Sources-Raisin; d €40, dinner €20) What sets this *chambre d'hôte* apart is the stunning architecture – no plain, concrete building, but a cheerful mix of wood and lava stones. Its three rooms are airy and comfortable and open onto a flourishing garden. The dining room serves up panoramic views along with *table d'hôtes*.

Chambre d'hôtes Les Durentas (☎ 0262 39 64 03, 0692 68 68 82; www.lesdurentas.com in French; 35 Chemin Defaud, Ravine des Citrons; d €42, dinner €18; **Ⓡ**) Lovely, clean *chambre d'hôte* with two plain but restful rooms, opposite the youth hostel. There's a pool in the flowering garden. Top that off with the affable welcome of Madame, who is a good cook too, and you have a *chambre d'hôte* that beckons you to stay for a few extra days.

our pick **Le Dimitile** (☎ 0262 39 20 00; www.dimitile.eu; 30 Rue Bras Long; d incl breakfast €130; **P** **Ⓧ** **▯** **Ⓡ**) A place of easy bliss, miles from the hustle and bustle of the coast. This beautifully manicured haven is run with flair and care by a couple from Alsace. Saffron yellows on the façade, cosy reds on the floors, attractive Creole furnishings and natural stones create a warmly authentic atmosphere in the 18 rooms. Flat-screen TVs, glistening bathrooms and a well-regarded onsite restaurant (mains €16 to €28;

open lunch and dinner) are also *de rigueur*. The cherry on the icing? A lovely pool for cooling dips.

Up on Le Dimitile, **Gîte Émile** (Map p218; ☎ 0262 39 66 42, 0262 57 43 03; dm with half board per person €31) run by M François Payet offers basic accommodation in five- to twelve-person dorms. You can also hunker down in the *gîte d'étape* run by **Mme Francia Bardil** (Map p218; ☎ 0262 39 60 84, 0262 57 64 29; dm with half board per person €33), which also has rustic dorms. Hearty meals are served at both *gîtes*.

EATING

Le Chocas (☎ 0262 69 56 06; 12 Rue de l'Église; mains €9-13; ☾ lunch Tue-Sun) Don't know what *chocas* is? It's time to get a hands-on education. Nestled in a lush garden, this reputable eatery specialises in this quirky-tasting vegetable, prepared in all its forms (with fish, shrimps etc). You can also pick up the usual Creole suspects. The fuchsia tablecloths add a touch of fancy.

Le Longanis (☎ 0262 39 70 56; 9bis Rue du Commerce; mains €8-13; ☾ lunch Mon-Sat, dinner Mon-Tue & Thu-Sat) This venue right in the centre boasts a happy buzz at lunchtime. The menu is a who's who of Creole specialities, with the odd salad and *suggestions* (daily specials) thrown in. It's more honest than refined, but at these prices you're unlikely to have much to complain about.

GETTING THERE & AWAY

Car Jaune operates a bus service between Entre-Deux and the *gare routière* in St-Pierre. There are five buses a day from Monday to Saturday and two on a Sunday.

THE CIRQUES

A trip to the Cirques is an iconic Réunion experience. No amount of hyperbole could ever communicate the astonishingly guileless beauty of the island's heart and soul, where the earth swells as mightily as an angry sea. Knitted together like a three-leaf clover, the Cirques of Cilaos, Salazie and Mafate are different in spirit from the rest of the island – more inward-looking, more secretive, more austere, less commercially minded. Quintessentially Réunionnais. The fast-paced and hedonistic coastal life seems light years away. The few roads daring to traverse the

RÉUNION

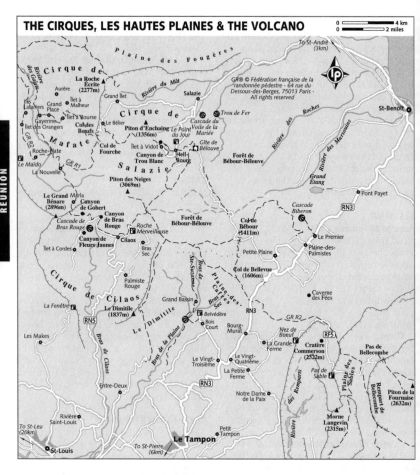

THE CIRQUES, LES HAUTES PLAINES & THE VOLCANO

gorges and ranges are more crooked than a politician, winding in and out of tortuous valleys.

The whole island was once the dome of a vast prehistoric shield volcano, centred on Piton des Neiges, but the collapse of subterranean lava chambers formed the starting point for the creation of the Cirques. Millions of years of rainfall and erosion did the rest, scouring out the amphitheatres that are visible today.

No prize for guessing that this rugged region is a fantastic playground for the stimulus-needy, with staggering mountain scenery, a mesh of well-marked trails and jaw-dropping canyons that beg to be explored. But if all you need is to decompress,

there are always epicurean delights, including a robust cuisine scene and welcoming accommodation options where you can rejuvenate mind and body. Nothing glam, just a good balance of warmth, hospitality and comfort.

Nature is not the only drawcard. The Cirques are also of strong historical interest. They first began to be settled by runaway slaves or *marrons* (see p157) in the 18th century, and their descendants still inhabit some of the wild remote villages of the Cirques. The people residing here are an independent and unhurried lot, adamantly tied to their *îlet* (village) and their traditions.

Each Cirque has its own personality – try to include the three of them in your itinerary.

IRQUE DE CILAOS

The setting couldn't be more grandiose. Think snaggle-toothed volcanic peaks, deep avines and forests that are straight out of a Brothers Grimm fairy tale. At times, swirling anks of cloud add a touch of the bizarre. A weet sprinkling of secluded hamlets top off his area's indisputable 'wow!' effect.

Thrill-seekers, rejoice: the Cirque de Cilaos is the mother of all canyoning experiences on the island, with three iconic canyons that are set in some of the most impressive scenery in Réunion. Hiking is also extraordinary (see p238). Another pull s the smattering of well-priced hotels and B&Bs.

To get here, clunk in your safety belt and take a deep breath: the RN5, which connects St-Louis with Cilaos, 37km to the north, is Réunion's premier drive (and that is saying a lot!). Snaking steeply around more than 400 twists and turns along the way up into the amphitheatre, it provides vista-point junkies with a steady fix. *Bon voyage*!

Cilaos

pop 6000

Cilaos is ensnared by scenery so mind-blowingly dramatic it's practically Alpine. One word says it all: Piton des Neiges (3069m). The iconic peak towers over the town of Cilaos, acting like a magnet to hiking fiends. But there's no obligation to overdo it: a smattering of museums, a slew of under-rated vineyards, regenerative thermal baths and plenty of short walks mean this incredible dose of natural magnificence can also be appreciated at a more relaxed pace.

The largest settlement in any of the Cirques, Cilaos sits 1200m above sea level. Developed as a spa resort at the end of the 19th century, the town's fortunes still rest on tourism, particularly hiking and canyoning, backed up by agriculture and the bottled mineral-water industry. The area is known for the production of lentils, embroidery and, increasingly, palatable red and white wines.

Cilaos fills up quickly on weekends. But despite its popularity it manages to stave off changes that would detract from its appeal as an 'ecotourism' destination – there are no massive hotels or blaring discos, only low-key, small-scale operations. Enjoy it to the hilt.

INFORMATION

There aren't any banks in Cilaos. There is an ATM at the post office that accepts Visa and MasterCard, but don't rely on it completely: it occasionally runs out of euros, especially on weekends.

Maison du Tourisme (☎ 0262 31 71 71; mmocilaos@wanadoo.fr; 2bis Rue Mac Auliffe; ☼ 8.30am-12.30pm & 1.30-5.30pm Mon-Sat, 9am-noon Sun) The tourism office is particularly helpful, with multilingual staff who provide reliable information about local and long-distance walks and dispense lists of accommodation, restaurants and activities. You can also book *gîtes de montagne* here.

Post office (76 Rue du Père Boiteau; ☼ 8am-4pm Mon-Fri, 8-11.30am Sat)

Vidéo Club 3 Salazes (40 Rue St-Louis; per hr €12; ☼ 9am-noon & 2-9pm Tue-Sun)

SIGHTS

Maison du Peuplement des Hauts

Close to Cilaos' church, the informative **Maison du Peuplement des Hauts** (☎ 0262 31 88 01; 5bis Chemin du Séminaire; adult/child €5.50/3.20; ☼ 10am-noon & 2.30-6pm Wed-Mon, 9.30-11.30am & 1.30-4.30pm Sun) is dedicated to the escaped slaves who first settled the hostile landscape of the Cirques. The displays are imaginative and provide a much-needed monument to the unsung Creole heroes of Réunion (see p157).

Maison de la Broderie

The originator of Cilaos' embroidery tradition was Angèle Mac Auliffe, the daughter of the town's first doctor of thermal medicine. Looking for a pastime to fill the long, damp days in the Cirque, Angèle established the first embroidery workshop with 20 women producing what later evolved into a distinctive Cilaos style of embroidery.

Nowadays, the **Maison de la Broderie** (☎ 0262 31 77 48; Rue des Écoles; admission €1; ☼ 9.30am-noon & 2-5pm Mon-Sat, 9.30am-noon Sun) is home to an association of 30 or so local women dedicated to keeping the craft alive. They embroider and sell children's clothes, serviettes, place settings and tablecloths. It's laborious work: a single placemat takes between 12 and 15 days to complete.

Sources Thermales

The *sources thermales* (thermal springs) of Cilaos were first brought to the attention of the outside world in 1815 by a goat hunter from St-Louis, Paulin Técher. A track into the Cirque was constructed in 1842, paving the

RÉUNION

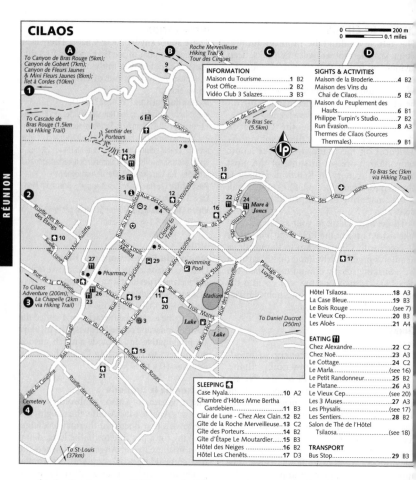

CILAOS

0 ____ 200 m
0 ____ 0.1 miles

INFORMATION
Maison du Tourisme.....................1 B2
Post Office.....................................2 B2
Vidéo Club 3 Salazes....................3 B3

SIGHTS & ACTIVITIES
Maison de la Broderie..................4 B2
Maison des Vins du
  Chai de Cilaos..........................5 B2
Maison du Peuplement des
  Hauts.......................................6 B1
Philippe Turpin's Studio...............7 B2
Run Évasion..................................8 A3
Thermes de Cilaos (Sources
  Thermales).................................9 B1

To Canyon de Bras Rouge (5km);
Canyon de Gobert (7km);
Canyon de Fleurs Jaunes
& Mini Fleurs Jaunes (8km);
Îlet à Cordes (10km)

To Cascade de
Bras Rouge (1.5km
via Hiking Trail)

Roche Merveilleuse
Hiking Trail &
Tour des Cirques

To Bras Sec
(5.5km)

To Bras Sec (3km
via Hiking Trail)

To Cilaos
Adventure (200m);
La Chapelle (2km
via Hiking Trail)

To Daniel Ducrot
(250m)

To St-Louis
(37km)

SLEEPING
Case Nyala...................................10 A2
Chambre d'Hôtes Mme Bertha
  Gardebien.................................11 B3
Clair de Lune - Chez Alex Clain..12 B2
Gîte de la Roche Merveilleuse...13 C2
Gîte des Porteurs.......................14 B2
Gîte d'Étape Le Moutardier.......15 B3
Hôtel des Neiges.......................16 B2
Hôtel Les Chenêts......................17 D3

Hôtel Tsilaosa.............................18 A3
La Case Bleue.............................19 B3
Le Bois Rouge ....(see 7)
Le Vieux Cep.............................20 B3
Les Aloès 21 A3

EATING
Chez Alexandre..........................22 C2
Chez Noë...................................23 A3
Le Cottage.................................24 C2
Le Marla...................................(see 16)
Le Petit Randonneur..................25 B2
Le Platane.................................26 A3
Le Vieux Cep............................(see 20)
Les 3 Muses...............................27 A3
Les Physalis..............................(see 17)
Les Sentiers..............................28 B2
Salon de Thé de l'Hôtel
  Tsilaosa..................................(see 18)

TRANSPORT
Bus Stop.....................................29 B3

way for the development of Cilaos as a health
spa for rich colonials. The spring is heated by
volcanic chambers far below the surface. It's
said to relieve rheumatic pain, among other
bone and muscular ailments.

The old thermal station was opened in
1896, but the spring became blocked in a
cyclone that occurred in 1948. The project
was revived in 1971, only to close in 1987
because of damage to the buildings caused
by the chemicals in the spa water. The latest
incarnation of the Cilaos spa is the **Thermes
de Cilaos** (☎ 0262 31 72 27; thermes-cilaos@cg974.fr; Route
de Bras-Sec; 🕙 9am-6pm Mon-Sat, 9am-5pm Sun) at the
north end of town. All manner of health
treatments are offered, including a 20-minute
hydromassage (€17). This is a perfect way

to rejuvenate tired and sore muscles after
your hike.

Maison des Vins

You can learn more about Cilaos wine at
the **Maison des Vins du Chai de Cilaos** (☎ 0262 31
79 69; 34 Rue des Glycines; 🕙 9am-noon & 2-5.30pm Mon-
Sat). A short film (in French) is followed by a
guided tour of the modern vinification plant
and a wine tasting. Take home a bottle from
about €10.

Philippe Turpin's Studio

The sculptor and printmaker Philippe Turpin,
who etches on copper and then rolls the prints
off the inky plates, has a **studio** (☎ 0262 31 73 64;
2 Route des Source; 🕙 9am-noon & 2-6pm) that is open

o the public. Turpin captures the wonder of Réunion in a fantastical, almost medieval way; his renditions of the Cirques resemble illustrations of fairy kingdoms.

ACTIVITIES

Canyoning

Of the stellar spots for canyoning in Réunion, the Cilaos area tops the list, with three major canyons that draw action-seekers like bees to a honey pot: Canyons de Gobert, Fleurs Jaunes and Bras Rouge. All are very atmospheric; you can expect various jumps, leaps into natural pools and jaw-dropping rappelling. Access to the canyons involves a preliminary 15-minute hike. The time spent in the canyon is about three hours. The most suitable canyons for beginners and families are Canyon de Gobert and Mini Fleurs Jaunes (which is a section of Fleurs Jaunes). Plan on €45 to €70 per person. All canyoning outings are led by a qualified instructor. The major operators include the following (some don't have offices but can be reached by phone):

Bouisset Fabrice (☎ 0692 66 22 73)

Canyon Ric a Ric (☎ 0692 86 54 85; www.canyon eunion.com)

Cilaos Aventure (☎ 0692 66 73 42; 12 Chemin de la Chapelle)

Daniel Ducrot (☎ 0262 31 76 33, 0692 65 90 67; www canyoning-cilaos.com; Chemin des Trois Mares)

Run Évasion (☎ 0262 31 83 57; www.runevasion.fr in French; 23 Rue du Père Boiteau)

Hiking

There are fabulous hiking options in the vicinity of Cilaos, with well-marked trails suitable for all levels of fitness. The tourist office produces a small leaflet that gives an overview of the walks in the Cirque. The most popular walks include Cascade de Bras Rouge (2½ hours), Roche Merveilleuse (two hours), Sen-

tier des Sources (a one-hour loop), Col du Taïbit (five hours) and the mind-boggling ascent of Piton des Neiges (about nine hours in all).

See p231 for more about hiking, and p238 for the ascent of Piton des Neiges.

SLEEPING

Cilaos has ample choice of accommodation options, but it can become crowded at weekends and during the tourist season.

Budget

La Case Bleue (☎ 0692 65 74 96; 15 Rue Alsace Corré; dm €14) An excellent choice, this *gîte d'étape* spreads into two attractive Creole houses painted in blue. Both boast an impeccable communal kitchen, pathogen-free bathrooms, new mattresses and crisp sheets. Breakfast costs €5.

Gîte de la Roche Merveilleuse (☎ 0262 31 82 42; 1 Rue des Platanes; dm €14.50, d €33-36) This all-wood *gîte* looks like a Canadian chalet transplanted to Cilaos. Its best asset is the panoramic view from the terrace. Meals can be arranged if there's a minimum of five persons.

Clair de Lune – Chez Alex Clain (☎ 0262 31 88 03; 10 Rue Wenceslas Rivière; dm incl breakfast €15) Run by Alex, who knows a thing or 50 about Cilaos and adopts all guests like stray kittens, this congenial spot has rooms of varying size and shape, with three- to nine-bed dorms and one double. Bathrooms are shared. The living area is a good place to swap tales with like-minded travellers.

Other options:

Gîte d'étape Le Moutardier (☎ 0262 31 76 06; Chemin des Roses; dm €14) This solid option in two Creole houses is brought to life with lashings of colourful paint on the façade. Rooms can sleep two to six, and there's a communal kitchen.

Chambre d'hôtes Mme Bertha Gardebien (☎ 0262 31 72 15; 50 Rue St-Louis; s/d €25/35, dinner

---

A TOAST IS IN ORDER

You mustn't leave Cilaos without sampling a glass (or three) of *vin de Cilaos* (Cilaos wine). Not to be deprived of their wine, the French brought vines with them to Réunion in the 17th century. They were originally grown along the west coast, but in the late 19th century settlers introduced vines into the Cirques, cultivating them on trellises outside their houses or on tiny terraces hacked out of the hillside. For years, the wines they produced were sugary sweet whites, reminiscent of sherry and tawny port. In the late 1970s, however, a few enterprising growers in Cilaos upgraded their vine stock and began producing something far more palatable. In addition to sweet and dry whites, growers now produce reds and rosés. They are not necessarily the most distinguished of wines but they're improving in quality.

€15) Perfect for travellers looking for budget tariffs without the hype, this unassuming B&B run by a retired couple provides three no-frills rooms (with shared bathroom).

Midrange & Top End

Gîte des Porteurs (☎ 0262 31 82 88; les.porteurs@wanadoo.fr; 1 Rue des Thermes; d €40) Next door to the restaurant Les Sentiers, this newish operation features four rooms in a gleaming white Creole villa.

Hôtel des Neiges (☎ 0262 31 72 33; www.hotel-des-neiges.com; 1 Rue de la Mare à Joncs; s €51-61, d €60-70; ☒) The candy-pink exterior is a bit migraine-inducing (and seems to have spilled over onto the website!) but otherwise this two-star hotel is a safe-bet pad, with well-maintained rooms and professional service. A neat garden, a smallish pool and a restaurant complete this rosy picture.

Case Nyala (☎ 0262 31 89 57, 0692 87 70 14; www.case-nyala.com; 8 Ruelle des Lianes; d incl breakfast €65-75; ☒) On a quiet backstreet close to the centre, this little Creole place is oh-so-sweet with its lemon-yellow walls and green shutters. Inside is a clutch of cosy, contemporary rooms and a well-appointed communal kitchen. Yes, the rum in the glass flasks on the shelves is complimentary (thanks, Monsieur Frossard!). Families will opt for the larger, self-contained bungalow at the rear.

Hôtel Tsilaosa (☎ 0262 37 39 39; su.dijoux@outremeronline.com; Rue du Père Boiteau; s €78-84, d €94-102, all incl breakfast) For discerning visitors with fatter wallets (and creakier joints), this three-star abode in a restored Creole home offers a smooth stay, with 15 rooms that are imaginatively decked out in local style; those upstairs boast mountain views.

Le Vieux Cep (☎ 0262 31 71 89; www.levieuxcep-reunion.com; 2 Rue des Trois Mares; s/d incl breakfast €79/86; ☒) Though slightly ageing, Cilaos' starlet hasn't lost its sheen, with an enviable location, flower-filled gardens, sunny rooms and solid amenities, including a small sauna, a Jacuzzi, a pool and an onsite restaurant. Rooms in the older block are more rustic; newer rooms have less character, but better bathrooms. All rooms peek out onto the Piton des Neiges. Mountain bikes are available for rent.

Hôtel Les Chenêts (☎ 0262 31 85 85; leschenets@ilereunion.com; Rue des Trois Mares; d incl breakfast €98; ☒) Cilaos' most luxurious hotel is a big, colourful place with a touch of a hunting lodge about its foyer. The rooms are spacious and come with gleaming bathrooms. There's a heated pool, a sauna, a bar and a good restaurant Les Physalis.

Other recommendations:

Le Bois Rouge (☎ 0262 31 73 64; 2 Route des Sources) This boutique-ish hotel with a handful of rooms artfully decorated by artist-owner Philippe Turpin had just closed when we visited, but the owner was planning to sell it to new management. Ask while you're there.

Les Aloès (☎ 0262 318100; www.hotel-aloes.com in French; 14 Rue St-Louis; s/d €51/65) Friendly two-star hotel on the edge of town. Bright blues, yellows and ochres colour the well-tended rooms. The upstairs ones have the best views. The owner is very knowledgeable about hiking.

EATING

We'll be honest: despite the choice of eateries on offer, don't expect gastronomic thrills in Cilaos. Most places tend to rest on their laurels, with rather stodgy fare served in generic surrounds. On the bright side, Cilaos holds a few surprises up its sleeves. It's noted for its lentils, grown mainly around Îlet à Cordes and its wines (see p199).

Self-caterers will find grocery stores and bakeries (croissants and *macatias* – delish! along the main street.

Salon de Thé de l'hôtel Tsilaosa (☎ 0262 37 39 39; Rue du Père Boiteau; cakes €3-4; ☒ 2-6pm) This delightfully peaceful venue in the hotel's tea room (see left) will torment the sweet-toothed and weak-willed with homemade cakes and pies, including a *tarte à la confiture de pêche* (tart with peach jam), and about 15 varieties of tea. Enough said, we're drooling on the keyboard!

Le Platane (☎ 0692 63 20 64; Rue du Père Boiteau; mains €6-14; ☒ lunch & dinner Tue-Sun) Here you can wrap your mandibles around omelettes, salads and *carris*, but skip the unexceptional pizzas – Cilaos is not Naples. Despite some splashes of colour on the walls and the attractive Creole architecture, Le Platane is lacking in atmosphere.

Les Sentiers (☎ 0262 31 71 54; 63 Rue du Père Boiteau; mains €10-13, menu €19; ☒ lunch daily except Wed, dinner daily except Tue & Wed) Come lunch and dinner this cute *case créole* is alive with action. Tables spill from inside out onto a breezy terrace. The food isn't the best, but it's filling and the rustic décor is easy on the eye, with exposed beams and flashing laminate floors. The only weak point on our visit was the flimsy service.

Chez Noë (☎ 0262 31 79 93; 40 Rue du Père Boiteau; mains €11-19, menus €22-27; ☒ lunch & dinner Tue-Sun) A longstanding institution, Chez Noë is almost a

ite of passage in Cilaos, but some say it rests
n its laurels – we agree. It churns out invig-
rating Creole favourites such as sausage with
entils and *gratin de chou chou* (choko; a green
quash-like vegetable that is served baked).

Les 3 Muses (☎ 0262 31 86 62; 25 Rue du Père Boiteau;
mains €14-19; ☽ lunch & dinner Sat-Wed) At this seeth-
ng place on the main drag, the menu runs the
;amut of *métro* and Creole standards.

Le Vieux Cep (☎ 0262 31 71 89; 2 Rue des Trois Mares;
mains €12-28; ☽ lunch & dinner) Don't eat here if you
want to remain on good terms with your diet-
cian! After sampling half of the *côte de porc
umée aux lentilles de Cilaos* (smoked pork
ib with Cilaos lentils), the signature dish,
ur bulging insides forced us get horizontal.
The service is old-fashioned and the décor
eriously rustic, with an open fireplace, stone
valls and exposed beams.

Other places to get your fill:

hez Alexandre (☎ 0692 48 86 25; 7 Rue de la Mare à
oncs; mains €7; ☽ lunch & dinner Wed-Mon) The paltry
ill, cool staff, copious Creole daily specials and hearty
andwiches here are sure to keep you feeling satisfied.

e Petit Randonneur (☎ 0262 31 79 55; Rue du Père
oiteau; mains €9-16; ☽ lunch & dinner Sat-Thu) The
uality isn't earth shattering at 'The Little Walker', but
either is the bill.

e Cottage (☎ 0262 31 70 38; 2 Chemin des Saules;
mains €11-16; ☽ lunch & dinner Sat-Thu) The all-wood
urrounds boast a kind of rustic charm and the dining
ooms overlook the Mare à Joncs. Has no-nonsense
aditional fare.

e Marla (☎ 0262 31 72 33; 1 Rue de la Mare à Joncs;
mains €15; ☽ lunch & dinner) The restaurant at the Hôtel
es Neiges (see opposite) offers homely Creole meals.

es Physalis (☎ 0262 31 85 85; Rue des Trois Mares;
mains €11-25; ☽ lunch & dinner) A well-regarded venue,
t the Hôtel Les Chenêts (see opposite). Sadly, the sterile
ining room seriously detracts from the atmosphere.

;ETTING THERE & AWAY
Cilaos is located 112km from St-Denis by
oad and 37km from the nearest coastal
own, St-Louis.

Buses to Cilaos depart from St-Louis.
There are about 10 buses daily, with eight
n Sunday (€1.50, 1½ hours). The last serv-
ce up to Cilaos leaves St-Pierre at 5.15pm;
;oing down again, the last bus leaves Cilaos
t 4pm, but this terminates at St-Louis.

There are nine buses a day (four on Sun-
ay) from Cilaos to Bras Sec (€1) between
.30am and 7pm. The tourist office in Cilaos
as timetables.

For Îlet à Cordes (€1) there are about
nine buses daily (only four on Sunday) from
7.20am to 7pm, with the last bus back just
after 3pm. Another option for Îlet à Cordes
is the minibus service offered by the **Société
Cilaosienne de Transport** (☎ 0262 31 85 87, 0692 66 13
30), which costs €28 for two people. The same
outfit provides transport from Cilaos to Le
Bloc on the GR R1 to Hell-Bourg (€15 for
two people) and to the trailhead for the Col
du Taïbit on the GR R1/GR R2 to Mafate (€15
for two people), saving you about an hour's
walking time in each case.

GETTING AROUND
Run Évasion (☎ 0262 31 83 57; 23 Rue du Père Boiteau)
rents out mountain bikes for about €16/20
for a half/full day.

Îlet à Cordes
Îlet à Cordes is a marvellous 'stop the world
and get off' place and you'll leave with reluc-
tance. The setting is truly photogenic: wherever you look, this tiny *écart* (settlement) is
cradled by soaring mountains, with major
peaks looming on the horizon.

SLEEPING & EATING
Gîte d'étape et Chambre d'hôtes de l'Îlet (☎ 0262
25 38 57, 0692 64 74 48; 27 Chemin Terre-Fine; dm/d €18/40,
dinner €18) This venue offers bog-standard dorm
beds in several wood-panelled rooms, which
are somewhat lacking in privacy. Solange
Grondin, your amenable hostess, prides herself on her farm cooking, which usually means
pork with cauliflower, *brèdes chou chou* (a
mix of local vegetables) and girth-expanding
gâteaux pays (homemade cakes).

Chambre d'hôtes Chez Carole Maillot (☎ 0262 25
74 57; 18bis Chemin Terre-Fine; s/d €34/38) Offers two
exceedingly clean rooms (aim for the upstairs one) in a modern house at the far end
of the village. The secluded location makes
for great stargazing and the views over Le
Grand Bénare and Piton des Neiges never fail
to impress. No meals are served but there's a
communal kitchen. You can also have dinner
at Chez Hélène Payet (by reservation), a five-
minute jog away.

Chambre d'hôtes Chez Hélène Payet (☎ 0262 35
18 13, 0692 68 49 68; 13 Chemin Terre-Fine; d €40, dinner
€18) Madame Payet has four reassuringly Air-
Wicked rooms in an alluring tropical garden.
The food is more poultry with homegrown
vegetables than creative concoctions.

RÉUNION

Le Reposoir (☎ 0262 25 14 36; Chemin Terre-Fine; ⏰ 7am-7pm Mon-Sat, 7am-1pm & 5-7pm Sun) Across the road from Gîte d'étape et Chambre d'hôtes de l'Îlet, this modest café-bar serves snacks and sandwiches, and has a limited selection of goods if you're fixing your own food.

GETTING THERE & AWAY
See p201 for buses to/from Îlet à Cordes.

Bras-Sec
As in Îlet à Cordes, you've reached *le bout du monde* (the end of the Earth) in Bras-Sec, about 12km from Cilaos. This is a place to just kick back and enjoy the get-away-from-it-all atmosphere.

SLEEPING & EATING
our pick Domaine des Fahams (☎ 0262 96 03 87; www .lesfahams.com in French; 3 Chemin Saül; bungalows per person €10, dinner €15) One of the area's best-kept secrets, this trippy venue in splendid isolation offers superb views over the surrounding peaks. Digs are in three all-wood bungalows and one quirky 'tepee'. Meals come in for warm praise, with an emphasis on produce from the farm (goose, duck); there's even a microbrewery – here's your chance to sample unique, homemade nectars, flavoured with *faham* (a local plant). And look at the rates!

Les Calumets (☎ 0262 35 40 63; http:calumets.neuf .fr; Chemin Saül; s/d with shared bathroom €15/30, dinner €17) The setting is bona fide wild: free-ranging geese foraging on the lush grounds, a fish pond and a pristine cryptomeria forest at the back. Bridging the gap between *gîte d'étape* and B&B, this quirky affair run by an empathetic Breton couple is a good deal. Angle for one of the two rooms in the all-wood building at the front; the two other rooms at the back of the main house feel rather claustrophobic. Good French-inspired cooking at dinner, *en famille* (with the family).

Gîte d'étape Les Mimosas (☎ 0262 96 72 73; 29 Chemin Saül; dm incl breakfast €16, s/d incl breakfast €25/33, dinner €18) This is an unflashy but friendly place with functional two- to seven-person dorms.

GETTING THERE & AWAY
See p201 for buses to/from Bras-Sec.

CIRQUE DE SALAZIE
If you need a break from beach-bumming and want to cool off in forested mountains, head to the Cirque de Salazie. Like the Cirque de Cilaos, the Cirque de Salazie has bags of natural panache, with soaring peaks, soul-stirring vistas, thundering waterfalls, tortuous roads and a spattering of rural hamlets thrown in for good measure.

The winding mountain road that slithers into the Cirque from St-André on the northeast coast offers awesome views and is reason enough to make the trip. Yet the prize at the end of it is golden too: with its Creole colour, Hell-Bourg is the crowning glory of the Cirque.

The Cirque de Salazie is a bit 'flatter' (although 'flat' is not the first word that will spring to mind when you see it!) than the Cirque de Cilaos, but the scenery as you approach is nearly as awesome. The vegetation is incredibly lush and waterfalls tumble down the mountains, even over the road in places – Salazie is the wettest of the three Cirques.

For detailed information on the Tour des Cirques, a hiking route that takes in the Cirque de Salazie, see p238.

Salazie
The town from which the Cirque de Salazie takes its name lies at the eastern entrance to the Cirque. There's not much to detain you here, and most visitors press on to Hell-Bourg. You'll have to change buses here if you're heading further up into the Cirque.

The post office, opposite the hotel, has an ATM (the only one in the Cirque). There's also an internet café, **Cyber Salazie** (☎ 0692 05 62 24; per hr €5; ⏰ 9am-10pm Tue-Sun), just up the road.

If everything is full in Hell-Bourg, the **Hôtel Salazien** (☎ 0262 47 57 05; fax 0262 47 51 65; 134 Rue Pompidou; s/d €35/45), on the main drag, is a good plan B, though atmosphere is not its strong suit. If you're a light sleeper, ask for a room at the back. The attached restaurant is nothing to write home about; instead head to **Le P'tit Bambou** (☎ 0262 47 51 51; mains €10-12; ⏰ lunch daily except Wed), further up, which serves hearty fare with a zesty Chinese twist in rustic surrounds.

GETTING THERE & AWAY
The road alongside the gorge of the Rivière du Mât from St-André to Salazie winds past superb waterfalls. The road to Grand Îlet turns off the Hell-Bourg road just south of Salazie.

There are seven buses daily from St-André to Salazie (€1.60) between 6.10am and 5.45pm (in the opposite direction, buses run from 5.30am to 4.40pm). On Sunday buses leave St-

RÉUNION

André at 8.40am, 1.30pm and 5.45pm (8am, 2.40pm and 2.40pm from Salazie).

Buses from Salazie to Hell-Bourg (€1.10) un about every two hours from 6.45am to .20pm. In the opposite direction, there are ervices from 6.15am to 5.45pm. There are our buses in each direction on Sunday.

Services to Grand Îlet (€2.20) run from .45am to 6.20pm (9.15am to 6.20pm on unday).

ell-Bourg

he town of Hell-Bourg emerges like a ham-et in a fairy tale after 9km of tight bends rom Salazie. You can't but be dazzled by the abulous backdrop – the majestic mountain valls that encase Hell-Bourg like a grandiose mphitheatre. No prize for guessing that this ugged terrain offers fantastic hiking opportu-ities. It offers plenty to more sedentary types s well. Culture aficionados will get their fill in his quintessential Réunionnais town with its nchanting centre, where old Creole mansions ine the streets.

Hell-Bourg takes its curious name from he former governor Amiral de Hell; the town tself is anything but! It served as a thermal esort until a landslide blocked the spring in 948. Visitors can still see the ruins of the ld baths.

The helpful **Maison du Tourisme** (☎ 0262 47 9 89; pat.salazie@wanadoo.fr; 47 Rue Général de Gaulle; 9am-noon & 1-5pm) is the local tourist infor-nation centre and can also arrange book-ngs at *gîtes de montagne*. There is also a post office on Rue Général de Gaulle, but no banks.

SIGHTS

First up, architecture and history buffs should take a look at the town's appealing **Creole build-ings**, which date back as far as the 1840s, when Hell-Bourg was a famous resort town that attracted a rather well-heeled crowd. You can go on a guided tour (in French) organised by the tourist office or the Écomusée (see below); it takes about an hour and costs €4.

One of the loveliest of Hell-Bourg's Creole houses is **Maison Folio** (☎ 0262 47 80 98; 20 Rue Amiral Lacaze; admission €4; 9am-11.30pm & 2-5pm), a typical 19th-century bourgeois villa almost engulfed by its densely planted garden. The owners show you around, pointing out the amaz-ing variety of aromatic, edible, medicinal and decorative plants, and give insights into local culture – unfortunately, only in French.

The small **Écomusée de Salazie** (☎ 0262 47 89 28; admission €2; 9am-4pm) on the north side of town encapsulates the history and culture of the Cirque.

The **thermal bath ruins** are found in the ravine a short walk west of town. There's not much left now, but it's a quiet and leafy spot.

A kilometre below Hell-Bourg on the road to Salazie is a superb viewpoint known as **Le Point du Jour**. From here you have a stunning view over the peaks of Salazie, or, alterna-tively, a view of dense cloud, depending on the weather. Further along the same route, just north of the turn-off to Grand Îlet, don't

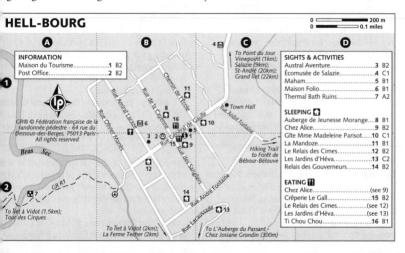

miss the **Cascade du Voile de la Mariée** (Bridal Veil Falls). These towering falls drop in several stages from the often cloud-obscured heights into the ravine at the roadside. You get an even better view from the Grand Îlet road.

ACTIVITIES

Not surprisingly, the Salazie area is an adventure playground for outdoor enthusiasts. Popular day **hikes** from Hell-Bourg include Forêt de Bébour-Bélouve (about four hours), Piton d'Enchaing (six hours) and Source Manouilh (about five hours). The town makes a pleasant alternative to Cilaos if you're planning to hike up to Piton des Neiges or into the Cirque de Mafate via Col des Bœufs. Hikers doing the Tour des Cirques route will have to pass through Hell-Bourg as they cross the Cirque de Salazie. For more information on all of these hiking possibilities, see p231.

Just thinking of the **canyoning** options available in the Cirque makes our spine tingle. Get wet at Trou Blanc, which is said to be the most 'aquatic' canyon in Réunion. Some sections are appropriately named 'The Washing Machine', 'The Bath', 'The Aquaplaning'… Other reputable canyons include Trois Cascades and Voile de la Mariée. Note that getting to the sensational canyon of Trou de Fer (see p212) is feasible from Hell-Bourg, but you have to be very fit – it's an exhausting 14-hour excursion. Count on €42/65 for a half-/full-day excursion.

Reliable operators:

Alpanes (☎ 0692 77 75 30; www.alpanes.com in French) Doesn't have an office in Hell-Bourg. Offers canyoning trips to Trou Blanc, Voile de la Mariée and Trou de Fer.

Austral Aventure (☎ 0262 32 40 29; www.creole .org/austral-aventure; Rue Amiral Lacaze, Hell-Bourg) Has canyoning trips to Trou Blanc, Voile de la Mariée, Trois Cascades et Trou de Fer (from Hell-Bourg), as well as guided hikes to Forêt de Bébour-Bélouve.

Maham (☎ 0262 47 87 87, 0692 86 50 67; www .randoneereunion.com in French; Rue Général de Gaulle, Hell-Bourg) Beside the tourist office. Can arrange guided hikes to Forêt de Bébour-Bélouve and canyoning outings to Trou Blanc.

SLEEPING

La Ferme Techer (☎ 0692 31 29 52; 21 Chemin Bras Sec, Îlet à Vidot; camp site per person €10) For that 'end-of-the-earth' feeling, you could head to this homely camp site, in the hamlet of Îlet à Vidot, about 2km northwest of Hell-Bourg. You'd be hard pressed to find a more peaceful setting to pitch your tent, within a grassy, manicured property. The ablution block is in top nick. Laurent, the sporty owner (he's the local fireman and has run the Grand Raid race) can take you to various scenic spots in the area and provide you with a wealth of information (alas, in French) about local plants and architecture (€10).

Auberge de Jeunesse Morange (☎ 0262 47 41 31; 2 Rue de la Cayenne; dm weekdays/weekends €14.50/16.50; ☽ 7.30-9am, 11am-2pm & 5-7.30pm daily) Backpacking in style. How can you not be blown away by this colonial mansion soothingly positioned in verdant grounds, with a majestic entrance, high ceilings, typically Creole reddish floor and million dollar views over the peaks? Beds are in two- to eight-person dorms.

La Mandoze (☎ 0262 47 89 65, 0692 65 65 28; Chemin de l'École; dm/d €14.50/36) This *gîte* set in a Creole house has all the hallmarks of a great deal: renovated, well-maintained (if a bit boxy) rooms that can sleep six people, well-scrubbed bathrooms, a tranquil location and a tab that won't burn a hole in your pocket. For those wanting more privacy, a few doubles, with wood-panelled walls, are available. The owner, Patrick Manoro, is a mine of local knowledge and occasionally plays guitar for his guests in the evening.

Gîte Mme Madeleine Parisot (☎ 02 62 47 83 44; 16 Rue Général de Gaulle; dm €16, dinner €16) The energetic Madame Parisot runs a homely *gîte d'étape* spread over several old Creole houses in the centre of town. Some rooms can charitably be termed 'compact', so ask to see a few before committing.

Chez Alice (☎ 0262 47 86 24; 1 Rue des Sangliers; s/d incl breakfast €25/35) Clad in more wood than a Swedish sauna, this is a good option if you're counting the pennies. The nine rooms feel a tad hanky-sized but are perfectly acceptable. Some of them have private bathrooms. It's behind the restaurant.

L'Auberge du Passant – Chez Josiane Grondin (☎ 0262 47 86 28; Rue du Stade; d €40, meals €16) Peacefully positioned on the outskirts of town, this *chambre d'hôte* is the perfect place to decompress, with two adjoining rooms occupying a neat bungalow surrounded by lots of greenery. Bail out if you're offered a darker room in the main house. *Table d'hôte* meals come in for warm praise, especially the duck with vanilla.

Relais des Gouverneurs (☎ 0262 47 76 21; 2bis Rue Amiral Lacaze; d €45-70, meals €18) If you have a so pot for romantic places, you need look no urther. Park your backpack (or your suitcase) n one of the two thoughtfully decorated Prestige rooms complete with four-poster beds, vooden floors and pastel-coloured walls. The heaper Standard and Familiale rooms are nore ordinary but excellent value.

Le Relais des Cimes (☎ 0262 47 81 58; www.relais lescimes.com in French; 67 Rue Général de Gaulle; s/d €55/68) One of the most reliable players in town, the Relais des Cimes has luminous rooms, prim athrooms and professional service and gets onsistently good reviews from visitors. It's a ad impersonal and we found the mattresses a bit saggy, though.

our pick **Les Jardins d'Héva** (☎ /fax 0262 47 87 87; 6 Rue Lacaussade; d incl breakfast €85) This recent entry hits all the right charm buttons. The five handsomely designed bungalows feel like cosy doll's houses; each has a theme and is decorated differently: the Indian has a pink-and-green colour theme, the Belle de France boasts Creole ceilings and exposed beams, the Creole features frescoes, the Malgache is all about earthy tones and the Chinoise combines grey-and-red hues. An added bonus is the spa, where you can reinvigorate weary feet after a busy day's walking. Alas, no views to speak of.

EATING
While Cilaos is known for its lentils, Hell-Bourg is synonymous with *chou chou* or choko, a green, pear-shaped vegetable imported from Brazil in 1834. It comes in salads, gratins and as *chou chou* gâteau to finish. You can stock up on basic provisions at the grocers and other food shops along the main road.

Crêperie Le Gall (☎ 0262 47 87 48; 55 Rue du Général de Gaulle; mains €3-9, menus €9-16; ☾ noon-6pm Sat-Thu) The only place for miles around that serves succulent pancakes. Yes, pancakes! Wash it all down with a *bolée de cidre* (bowl of cider). Lovely.

Chez Alice (☎ 0262 47 86 24; 1 Rue des Sangliers; mains €10-13, menus €17-20; ☾ lunch & dinner Tue-Sun) The fare at this family-run veteran is certainly not gourmet but has a temptingly pronounced regional flavour. Among the many winners are the Hell-Bourg trout, the *gratin de chou chou* (choko gratin) and the *carri porc aux pommes de terre* (pork with potatoes), all served at affordable prices in rustic surrounds. Portions are large enough to satisfy the most voracious hiker. It's often mobbed at weekends.

Ti Chou Chou (☎ 0262 47 80 93; 42 Rue Général de Gaulle; mains around €11, menus €14-22; ☾ lunch & dinner Sat-Wed, lunch Thu) This small restaurant with its appealing colourful façade on the main drag is run by a friendly young team. Herbivores will opt for the *assiette ti chou chou*, which offers a combination of *chou chou, cresson* and *capucine* (all local vegetables).

Le Relais des Cimes (☎ 0262 47 81 58; 67 Rue Général de Gaulle; mains €11-15, menus €14-22; ☾ lunch & dinner) Nothing mediocre will ever pass your lips at this Hell-Bourg classic, so order from the varied menu with abandon. If you want a recommendation, go for the trout with vanilla flambéed in rum, the house speciality. The setting is mildly rustic, with wooden ceilings and red-and-white chequered tablecloths.

Les Jardins d'Héva (☎ /fax 0262 47 87 87; 16 Rue Lacaussade; menus €15-22; ☾ lunch & dinner) No, you're not hallucinating, the view from the terrace is real. Central Hell-Bourg at your feet, the jagged peaks of the Cirques in the distance. Tuck into well-prepared *carris* and fish dishes.

GETTING THERE & AWAY
Buses run between Salazie and Hell-Bourg (€1.10) about every two hours from 6.45am to 6.20pm. In the opposite direction, there are services from 6.15am to 5.45pm. There are four buses in each direction on Sunday.

Grand Îlet & Around
This is a sweet, picturesque spot. About 17km west of Salazie, accessed by a scenic white-knuckle road, Grand Îlet really feels like the end of the line. The village sits at the base of the ridge separating the Cirque de Salazie and the Cirque de Mafate. Above the village are the mountain passes of Col des Bœufs and Col de Fourche, which form the main pedestrian routes between the two Cirques; access is via the village of Le Bélier, 3km above Grand Îlet, where you'll find the start of the *route forestière* that leads to Col des Bœufs. Toss aside that mobile phone, shed all the stresses nibbling your psyche and set about the serious business of relaxing or walking.

While there's nowhere to stay in Le Bélier, you'll find several *chambres d'hôtes* in Grand Îlet as well as a few shops selling basic foodstuffs.

SLEEPING & EATING
Chambre d'hôtes Liliane Bonnald (☎ 0262 41 71 62; fax 0262 47 73 34; Chemin Camp-Pierrot; d €38, meals €18) In

RÉUNION

a modernish house on the road to Le Bélier, the five rooms upstairs won't be selected for a *Wallpaper* photo shoot but are kept tickety-boo and boast a few fancy touches, such as Creole ceilings and wood panelling on the walls. Liliane Bonnald, your affable host, is a good cook too (ah, the *porc à la patate douce*; pork and sweet potato) and may well treat you with a wicked rum flavoured with wild orchid.

Chambre d'hôtes La Campierelle – Chez Christine Boyer (☎ 0262 47 70 87; Chemin du Camp-Pierrot; d €38, meals €18) Cross the road from Chambre d'hôtes Liliane Bonnald and you'll be greeted by an old lady wearing a straw hat, Madame Boyer, the mother of Liliane Bonnald. She rents out four humble rooms in a small Creole house just off the road. It's no great shakes and the bathrooms feel a bit dated, but it's OK and when it comes to concocting traditional *carris* at dinner, Madame Boyer knows her stuff.

Chambre d'hôtes Le Cimendef – Chez Noeline et Daniel Campton (☎ 0262 47 73 59; www.chambres dhotecimendef.com in French; Route du Bélier; s/d €33/40, ste €85, meals €18) All five rooms are pleasing and are graced with ravishing views over the Cimendef (2226m), but we were smitten by the darling Prestige suite, which features a Jacuzzi, timber floor, a luminous bathroom with well-chosen tiles, Creole ceilings, flat-screen TV, teak furniture, an enticing orange colour scheme and your own terrace – seventh heaven after

roughing it in the Cirque de Mafate. You'll also eat well here.

Snack Le Grand Îlet (☎ 0262 47 71 19; mains €8; lunch & dinner daily) Looks like nothing from the outside but this economical, neon-lit eatery is worth stopping at for its copious daily dishes (pork rib with mushrooms and chicken with *brèdes*). Find it just northwest of Grand Îlet's main square.

GETTING THERE & AROUND

There are seven buses a day (five on Sunday) from Salazie to Grand Îlet and Le Bélier (€2.20) between 6.45am (9.15am on Sunday) and 6.20pm. Heading back to Salazie services depart from Le Bélier between around 5.45am and 5pm (7am to 5.20pm on Sunday), calling at Grand Îlet 10 minutes later.

If you're coming here to hike and have your own car, you can leave it in the guarded **car park** (parking 1/2 days €2/10) at Le Petit Col, 6km up the *route forestière* and only 20 minutes' walk below the Col des Bœufs; the attendant also runs a 24-hour snack kiosk.

CIRQUE DE MAFATE

We only need to say one word: mesmerising. Nothing can prepare you for that first glimpse of this geologic wonder, with its dramatic scenery, shifting colours, blissful serenity (except for the occasional whirring of choppers) and unsurpassed grandeur. No cars, no

---

THE CIRQUES & THE VOLCANO FROM ABOVE

Helicopter tours of the magnificent Cirques and the volcano offer a sensational view of the tortured landscape of the interior. While they aren't cheap, most travellers rate such a trip as a highlight of their visit to Réunion – well worth the splurge.

Helilagon (☎ 0262 55 55 55; www.helilagon.com in French), based at L'Éperon, in the hills above St-Gilles-les-Bains, offers three different tours, including a 45-minute flight above all three Cirques and Piton de la Fournaise (€260 per person, or €220 without doing the volcano). Prices include transfers to the heliport from hotels in St-Gilles-les-Bains. **Corail Hélicoptère** (☎ 0262 22 22 66; www.corail-helicopteres.com) runs similar tours from Pierrefonds airport, near St-Pierre.

If you really want to feel the wind in your hair, several outfits offer tandem microlight flights with a qualified instructor. They run about 10 different tours around the island, starting at €30 for a gentle tour above the lagoon. It costs around €140 for a tour of the three Cirques. If the volcano is active, they usually run a Spécial Volcan tour, taking in the volcano in eruption – hair-raising, literally! Needless to say, all flights are dependent on the prevailing weather conditions. For more information, contact the following:

Felix ULM (☎ 0262 43 02 59; www.felixulm.com in French) Based in Cambaie, near St-Paul.
Les Passagers du Vent (☎ 0262 42 95 95; www.ulm-reunion.com in French) Based in Cambaie, near St-Paul.
Mascareignes Air Lines (☎ 0262 32 53 25; www.mascareignes.fr in French) Based in Pierrefonds, near St-Pierre.
Papangue ULM (☎ 0692 08 85 86; www.fransurf.com/papangue-ulm in French) Based near Ste-Marie.

owns, no stress. Just soaring mountains, jag-
ed peaks, giddily deep ravines, thick forests
nd a sprinkle of tiny *écarts* where time seems
o have stood still.

Apart from its grandiose topography, what
ets the Cirque de Mafate apart is its relative
naccessibility, despite being very close to the
oastal fleshpots. There are no roads that lead
nto the Cirque (although a *route forestière*
uns right up to the pass at Col des Bœufs),
o the villages that are scattered in this giant
xtinct volcano are accessible only by foot.

Unsurprisingly, the Cirque de Mafate is
walker's paradise, with a good network of
aths connecting the villages.

The Cirque was named after a runaway
lave, the chieftain and sorcerer Mafate, who
ook refuge among its ramparts. He was
unted down and killed in 1751 by a hunter
f runaway slaves.

Sights & Activities

Despite its remoteness and seclusion, the
Cirque de Mafate is populated. In the val-
eys, plateaus and spurs that slice up the
aw-dropping terrain are scattered discreet
ittle Creole settlements that retain a rough-
diamond rural edge. Not much happens in
these villages but it's hard not to fall under
the spell of their phenomenal setting. They
provide a few trappings of civilisation if you're
walking through the Cirque.

The southern part of the Cirque is called
Haut Mafate (Higher Mafate) and receives the
bulk of visitors. It comprises peaceful **Marla**,
the highest hamlet of the Cirque at an altitude
of 1621m; **La Nouvelle**, dubbed the 'capital of
Mafate' and one of the main gateways to the
Cirque, perched on a plateau at an altitude
of 1421m; and **Roche-Plate**, at the foot of the
grandiose Maïdo.

The northern part of the Cirque is called
Bas Mafate (Lower Mafate) and is consid-
ered even more secretive than Haut Mafate.
It comprises **Îlet à Bourse**, **Îlet à Malheur**, **Aurère**,
Grand Place, **Cayenne**, **Les Lataniers** and **Îlet des
Orangers**. Aurère is perched Machu-Picchu–
like above the precipitous canyon of the Bras
Bémale. The two tiny communities of Grand
Place and Cayenne lie above the rushing
Rivière des Galets near the Cirque's main
outlet.

Mafate offers some of the most inspirational **hiking** trails in Réunion, so pack your
sturdy shoes and delve into the Cirque (see

the chapter Hiking in Réunion, p231). If
you'd prefer to take it easy and see all this
fantasyland from the air, book a **helicopter** or
an **ultralight aircraft** tour (see opposite).

Sleeping & Eating

You don't need to carry depressing freeze-
dried food to visit Mafate. You'll find a slew
of decent *gîtes* (*privés* or belonging to the
Maison de la Montagne et de la Mer) that
offer *petit ravitaillement* (supplies), soft
drinks, alcohol (beer and wine) and meals.
Don't expect gastronomic ecstasy, though –
it's normally satisfying, wholesome *carris* and
homemade cakes. Plan on €13 to €15 for a
meal. Digs are in basic dorms but a few *gîtes*
also offer double rooms. You'll find water
at every *refuge*, but between stops there are
very few sources of drinking water.

Check out the website at http://runrando
.free.fr for more information about *gîtes*
in Mafate.

LA NOUVELLE

Gîte Joseph Cuvelier (☎ 0262 43 49 63; dm €13.50,
breakfast/meal €5/15)

Gîte M Oréo (☎ 0262 43 58 57; dm/d €14/31, break-
fast/meal €4/14)

Gîte Martial Gravina (☎ 0262 43 01 73; dm/d
€14/32, breakfast/meal €4/14) At Plaine aux Sables, a 45-
minute walk from La Nouvelle. Has two doubles.

Gîte Serge Paul Bègue (☎ 0262 43 51 74; dm €13)
Accommodation only.

Relais de Mafate (☎ 0262 43 61 77; dm/d €15/35,
breakfast/meal €6/16)

ROCHE-PLATE

Auberge du Bronchard (☎ 0262 43 83 66; dm/d
€4/35, breakfast/meal €5/15) Has two doubles.

Gîte M Thomas (☎ 0262 42 28 79; dm €12, breakfast/
meal €4/14)

MARLA

Gîte Expedit Hoareau (☎ 0262 43 78 31; dm €13,
breakfast/meal €5/15)

Gîte Giroday (☎ 0262 43 83 13; dm with half board €30)

Gîte Maison de la Montagne (☎ 0262 43 78 31; dm
€14, breakfast/meal €5/15)

ÎLET À MALHEUR

Gîte Guy Libelle (☎ 0262 43 56 96; dm €14, break-
fast/meal €5/14)

Gîte L'Arbre du Voyageur (☎ 0262 43 50 60; dm/d
with half board €35/70, camp site per person €10)

RÉUNION

AURÈRE

Auberge Piton Cabris (☎ 0262 43 36 83; dm €14, breakfast/meal €5/14)

Gîte Boyer (☎ 0262 55 02 33; d €32, dm with half board €32) Has a few double rooms.

Gîte François Libelle (☎ 0262 42 31 36; dm €14, breakfast/meal €5/14)

ÎLET À BOURSE

Gîte Maison de la Montagne (☎ 0262 43 43 93; dm €14, breakfast/meal €4/14)

GRAND PLACE & CAYENNE

Gîte Cœur de Mafate (☎ 0262 51 01 68; dm €14, breakfast/meal €4/14)

Gîte d'Ivrin Pause (☎ 0262 43 40 08; dm with half board €33)

Gîte Le Pavillon (☎ 0262 43 66 76, 0692 66 60 83; dm/d with half board €33/74) Has two doubles.

Gîte Maison de la Montagne de Cayenne (☎ 0262 43 85 42; dm €14.50, breakfast/meal €4/14) Down in the valley at Cayenne.

LES LATANIERS

Gîte Jean-Paul Cernot (☎ 0262 43 82 41; dm with half board €36)

Gîte M Yoland (☎ 0262 43 50 90; dm with half board €34)

LES HAUTES PLAINES & THE VOLCANO

Réunion's only cross-island road passes through the Plaine-des-Cafres and the Plaine-des-Palmistes, collectively known as Les Hautes Plaines (the High Plains; Map p196). At an altitude of about 1000m, the air is refreshingly crisp and often swathed in misty fog – a blessing if you're coming from the scorching coastal cities.

These relatively large open areas actually form the saddle that separates the massif (comprising the three Cirques) from the volcano, Piton de la Fournaise. And what a volcano! It ranks as one of the most active volcanoes on earth, playing in the same league as Hawaii. At the time of writing, it was erupting in spectacular fashion. It's also one of the most accessible ones – you can trek up and around the caldera (when it's not erupting, that is). For detailed information on hiking in the volcano area

and the Cirques, see the chapter Hiking i Réunion, p231.

Because there's a road from the Haute Plaines that approaches within a few kilo metres of the summit of the volcano, nearl all visitors approach it from this side.

PLAINE-DES-CAFRES & AROUND

Vast pastures where cattle graze. Velvet-gree hills undulating off into the horizon. Fres air. Mist. Conifers. Filled with iconic pastora landscapes, the Plaine-des-Cafres area bear an unexpected likeness to Bavaria. It is coo relaxing and oxygenated. Chalk that up to alti tude and attitude. It sits 1200m above sea leve and is regularly massaged by cool breezes Once a refuge for runaway slaves from th coast, the Plaine-des-Cafres is a vast, gentl rolling area that spreads between the Cirque and Piton de la Fournaise.

Approaching from the south (St-Pierre) the Plaine-des-Cafres begins shortly after th sprawling, nondescript town of Le Tampo and ends at Col de Bellevue, at the top of th winding road that plunges down to Plaine des-Palmistes. North of Le Tampon on RN (the cross-island road) are numerous smal settlements that are named for their distanc from the sea – Le Vingt-Quatrième (24th), fo example, is 24km from the ocean.

The most interesting place on the Plaine des-Cafres from a visitor's perspective is **Bourg Murat**, which is the obvious launch pad for th volcano. It's in this rural settlement where th Route Forestière du Volcan turns off to Piton de la Fournaise (see p210). The town and th surrounding area have a wealth of accommo dation and dining choices, making it a handy base. The perfect bucolic retreat, Bourg-Mura offers a real opportunity to sample authentic rural Réunionnais life.

Pick up some brochures at the well-organised **Office du Tourisme** (☎ 0262 59 09 82, www.sudreunion.com; cnr Rue des Genêts & Rue du Volcan Bourg-Murat; ☷ 9am-noon & 1.30-5pm Mon-Sat), which is located about 400m east of the Maison du Volcan in Bourg-Murat.

Sights & Activities

Everything you need to know about the Piton de la Fournaise and volcanoes in general should become clear at the excellent **Maison du Volcan** (☎ 0262 59 00 26; RN3, Bourg-Murat; adult/ child €6.50/3; ☷ 9.30am-5pm Tue-Sun). Unfortunately, most of the information is in French, but some nteractive displays are in English and the ideos of eruptions are self-explanatory.

Horse riding is a fun and ecofriendly way to ommune with the pastoral wilderness around ourg-Murat. The ultimate is a two- to three- ay excursion that takes in the eerie landscape round the volcano – highly recommended. ates range from €16 for a one-hour jaunt o about €110 per day for a multiday trek. among reputable operators:

entre Équestre Alti Merens (☎ 0262 59 18 84, 692 04 12 38; 120 Rue Maurice Kraft, PK26; ☒ closed lon morning & Fri morning) On the southern edge of ourg-Murat.

entre Équestre Notre-Dame de la Paix (☎ 0262 9 34 49, 0692 61 46 79; 41 Chemin de la Chapelle, otre-Dame de la Paix; ☒ daily by reservation) In the tiny amlet of Notre-Dame de la Paix (follow the signs from the N3 at Le Vingt-Troisième).

curies du Volcan (☎ 0692 66 62 90; 9bis Domaine ellevue, Bourg-Murat; ☒ daily by reservation) On the orthern edge of Bourg-Murat.

or information on **hiking** around the volcano, ee p231.

Sleeping

hez Dan's (☎ 0262 59 14 84, 0692 26 50 22; 40A, Route otre-Dame de la Paix, La Petite Ferme; r per person €15, dinner 12-15) Chez Dan's is as cosy as a bird's nest,

with three tidy rooms in a modern house with electric-blue shutters. Walking in you'll be shocked that rooms here don't cost double the price. On a clear day you get a glimpse of the glistening sea from the upstairs room. Good meals too.

our pick **Gîte Marmite Lontan** (☎ 0262 57 46 09, 0692 60 51 38; www.marmitelontan.com; s with half board €34) This little cracker is isolated on the Route du Volcan about 2km from the centre of Bourg-Murat. Entering the property, you feel as if you've stumbled onto the set of *Little House on the Prairie*. In the role of Charles Ingalls you have amiable Pilou, a *Zoréole* (a European who has totally embraced the Creole lifestyle). The neat dorms sleep two to four people and the whole place radiates a ramshackle air – from the quirky dining room, which is a Pandora's box of *objets lontan* (utensils and other knick-knacks from the old days), to the 450-odd types of aromatic rum fermenting in giant pirate-style glass flasks.

Chambre d'hôtes Piton de L'Eau (☎ 0262 59 28 07; Grande Ferme; d €42, dinner €20) There's nothing neutral about this B&B, and the yellow façade announces it's exotic. It has adventurously decorated doubles in 'Brazilian' colours (think appealing vanilla-and-green hues). The *table d'hôte* meals major on *cuisine au feu de bois* (wood-fired cooking). It's in Grande

RÉUNION

DETOUR TO GRAND BASSIN – THE LOST VALLEY

The utterly picturesque valley of Grand Bassin (Map p196), known as *la vallée perdue* (the lost valley) or *Mafate en miniature* (Mafate in miniature), can't go without mention because it's one of the few areas in Réunion that is only accessible on foot. Thanks to its splendid isolation, this little morsel of paradise is a dream come true for those seeking to get well and truly off the beaten track.

Grand Bassin is formed by the confluence of three rivers. Near to where they join is a lovely waterfall where you can dunk yourself (just blissful!) and a quiet hamlet with a handful of *gîtes*. The fast-paced coastal life seems a world away.

To get there, follow the road to Bois Court from Vingt-Troisième village. At the end of the road you can look down into the valley from the Belvédère viewpoint. The path down to Grand Bassin begins on Rue Thomas Payet, 800m south of the Belvédère. It plunges almost straight down to the river 600m below; allow 1½ hours for the descent and at least 2½ hours to get back up again.

Grand Bassin is a terrific place to kick off your shoes for a few days and relax. Digs are in rustic dorms, but that's part of the fun. Prices are the same at all *gîtes*: €26 per person with half board in dorm. Daytrippers will fork out €16 for a meal. Some *gîtes* have doubles (€30 per person with half board).

Auberge de Grand-Bassin (☎ 0262 59 21 99)
L'Oasis (☎ 0262 27 51 91)
La Vieille Tonnelle (☎ 0262 27 51 02) Has three doubles.
Les Orchidées (☎ 0262 38 02 73) Has one double.
Paille-en-Queue (☎ 0262 59 03 66)

Ferme, a hamlet about 3km from the centre of Bourg-Murat.

La Ferme du Pêcher Gourmand (☎ 0262 59 29 79; http://perso.wanadoo.fr/pecher.gourmand/in French; RN3, PK25; d €44) This modern *auberge* is run by a friendly couple and is surrounded by a pleasant garden. The six adjoining rooms are a bit of a squeeze, but the setting more than compensates.

Chambre d'hôtes Les Zakacias – Chez Madeleine Robert (☎ 0262 59 20 59; gite-les-zakacias@wanadoo.fr; La Petite Ferme; d €45, dinner €19) At the end of a long day's sightseeing, it's a joy to snuggle into the freshly pressed bed sheets of this B&B in La Petite Ferme, to the south of Bourg-Murat. There are two rooms, with a Barbie-esque colour scheme, and a *gîte*, all set in a lush garden. The owner is a fisherman, so expect fresh fish at dinner.

Hôtel l'Ecrin (☎ 0262 59 02 02; www.hotel-ecrin.fr.st; RN3, PK27, Bourg-Murat; s incl breakfast €60, d incl breakfast €82-100) The Ecrin would not be your ideal honeymoon hotel but the amenities are fine, the location very central and most rooms boast lovely views over the mountains.

Other options:

Gîte Chez Myris (☎ 0692 64 20 26; 8 Rue Josemont Lauret, Bourg-Murat; dm/d €14.50/32, dinner €16) This converted Art-Deco–inspired house has a few doubles and dorms that sleep six. The rooftop terrace has lovely views over, ahem, a few electric wires.

Gîte de la Fournaise (☎ 0262 59 29 75; gitedelafournaise@wanadoo.fr; RN3, Bourg-Murat; dm €15, d €32) Has two OK dorms downstairs. The double room upstairs is a bit dank.

Hôtel-Auberge Le Volcan (☎ 0262 27 50 91; fax 0262 59 17 21; RN3, PK27, Bourg-Murat; s/d €29/40) Features stock-standard rooms in two buildings smack-bang in the middle of Bourg-Murat.

Les Géraniums (☎ 0262 59 11 06; hotelgeranium@wanadoo.fr; RN3, PK24; s/d €57/66) The Géraniums is a tad overrated but nonetheless of a good standard. Avoid the rooms that overlook the parking lot. It's in Le Vingt-Quatrième on the main road south of Bourg-Murat.

Eating

Most lodging options offer half board.

Palais du Fromage (☎ 0262 59 27 15; Route du Volcan; cheese & pancakes €2-3; ☺ 10am-5.30pm Thu-Sun) This unassuming dairy farm past the Bourg-Murat tourist office on the Route du Volcan has a lot to answer for – namely our raging addiction to *fromage spécial de Sylvie*, the farm's signature product (fromage blanc laced with honey, caramel and cinnamon) – a feast for the tastebuds, best enjoyed at a picnic table i the cryptomeria forest nearby.

our pick **Le Vieux Bardeau** (☎ 0262 59 09 44; RN PK24; mains €10-20, menu €25; ☺ lunch & dinner dail Recapture the atmosphere of the colonia era in this gracefully ageing diva occupyin a lemon-yellow Creole mansion beside th main road in Le Vingt-Quatrième. This i an altar to *cuisine métro lontan* (traditiona French recipes) and *coin créole* (traditiona Creole specialities), but with an unusual deli cacy. Warmly recommended.

Hôtel-Auberge du Volcan (☎ 0262 27 50 91; RN PK27, Bourg-Murat; mains €11-13; ☺ lunch Tue-Sun, dinne Tue-Sat) You'll find all the usual Creole favour ites and a sprinkling of *métro* dishes serve in hearty portions in this country inn in th centre of Bourg-Murat.

Relais Commerson (☎ 0262 27 52 87; 37 Bois Joly Po tier, Bourg-Murat; mains €11-27, menus €15-32; ☺ lunch Thu Tue, dinner Sat) A rustic dining room and a men laden with inspired Creole fare, including *ca marons with morilles* (prawns with morels).

Le Panoramic (☎ 0262 59 36 12; RN3, PK27, Bourg Murat; mains €13-20, menus €14-27; ☺ lunch & dinne Do swordfish fillet, minced duck with guav sauce, and kangaroo fillet (!) tickle your fancy Enjoy a long list of well-prepared *métro* an Creole specialities in this modern abod behind Hôtel l'Ecrin.

La Ferme du Pêcher Gourmand (☎ 0262 59 2 79; RN3, PK25; menus €21-29; ☺ lunch Sat & Sun, dinne daily) Duck is king of the castle in this delight ful *ferme-auberge* (farm restaurant) on th main road south of Bourg-Murat. And it' no wonder: the owner's spouse is from Béar (southwest France). Bring an empty tum: th set menu is a culinary feast revolving aroun duck preparations and organic vegetables. A *moelleux au chocolat* (cake stuffed with melt ing chocolate) will finish you off sweetly.

Getting There & Away

There are three buses daily (two on Sunday each way between St-Benoît and St-Pierre vi Plaine-des-Cafres and Plaine-des-Palmistes From St-Pierre to Bourg-Murat, the fare i €2.70. Coming from St-Benoît, it's €5.40.

PITON DE LA FOURNAISE (THE VOLCANO)

The magnum opus of Mother Nature i Réunion, the Piton de la Fournaise is th island's most famous natural attraction Simply dubbed *le volcan* (the volcano) by éunionnais, the Piton de la Fournaise is not dormant monster, but an active geological onder that erupts with great regularity; at ie time of writing, the central, 900m-wide **olomieu Crater** had just collapsed by 300m (!), nd new lava fields had just been formed on s southeastern flanks, down to the coast. The naller **Bory Crater** is inactive. Other noticeable atures include the very photogenic **Formica o**, a small scoria cone. The good news is that 's one of the world's most accessible active olcanoes, and it's possible to hike up to the rater rim (though this is subject to change epending on current conditions, so ask while ou're there). See Hiking in Réunion (p241) r a detailed description of the hike. You n also fly over the volcano (see p206), or pproach the area from the saddle of a horse ee p209).

The main gateway to the volcano is Bourg-Iurat (p208), where you can visit the Maison u Volcan. From there, a scenic, zigzagging econdary road leads to **Pas de Bellecombe** 400m), the 'entrance' to the volcanic area, out 30km southeast of Bourg-Murat. The radual change of scenery is mind-boggling. he grassy meadows and cryptomeria forests pical of the Hautes Plaines progressively nange to scrubland and Martian landscape. e sure to pause at **Belvédère du Nez-de-Bœuf** iewpoint), blessed with unsurpassable views ver the valley gouged by the Rivière des Rem-arts. About 22km from Bourg-Murat, you'll lunge down to a wide windswept plain, made f ashes, **Plaine des Sables**. With its lunar land-cape, it's reminiscent of a *Mad Max* scene. here's a fabulous viewpoint at 2360m – Pas es Sables – that will leave you speechless.

If you wish to stop overnight to soak in this randiose scenery, the **Gîte du Volcan** (0262 51 3 29, 0692 85 20 91; dm €14.50, lunch €12-16, dinner €16) oasts a stunning location, a 15-minute walk om Pas de Bellecombe. Hot water is limited. ookings must be made through Maison de la Iontagne et de la Mer in St-Denis (see p172) r through any tourist office. The restaurant open at lunch for daytrippers.

LAINE-DES-PALMISTES

here were once large numbers of palm trees n the Plaine-des-Palmistes (hence the name), ut as a result of heavy consumption of palm-eart salad, few now remain. The town itself is pread out along the highway and is a pleasant scape from the coast. Its only specific sight is

the **Domaine des Tourelles**, a lovely 1920s Creole building just south of the town centre, which now houses a shop selling local crafts and produce, and a small tourist office (temporarily closed when we passed by).

For Tarzan types, **Forestia** (0262 49 69 20; Route de la Petite Plaine; adult/child €22/17; by reservation) has six adventure circuits of varying levels of difficulty, including a very safe one for the kiddies (over four). The setting, in a dense cryptomeria forest, is enchanting. It's on the road to Forêt de Bébour-Bélouve, about 3km from the highway (direction Petite Plaine).

Another great way to commune with nature is to walk to the **Cascade Biberon**, a 240m-high waterfall and natural swimming lake to the north of Plaine-des-Palmistes. It's situated a half-hour stroll away from the highway (it's signposted).

Sleeping
Gîte du Pic des Sables (0262 51 37 33, 0692 64 54 97; Route de la Petite Plaine; dm €15/50, breakfast/dinner €5/17) This cheery but cramped *gîte d'étape* in a peaceful setting is popular with walkers and canyoning groups. For more privacy, shell out for one of the newish *chambres d'hôtes*. Elian Jista, the affable owner, has mountain bikes for rent (€18 per day). It's on the road to Forêt de Bébour-Bélouve, about 4km from the highway (direction Petite Plaine). If you phone ahead, the owner will collect you from the bus stop in Plaine-des-Palmistes.

Chambre d'hôtes Le Conflore du Piton (0262 51 41 04, 0692 67 62 33; 91 Rue Dureau; d €48, dinner €22) Despite an overly exuberant deployment of greens and oranges in the two rooms, this smart Creole house located 1.5km south of the RN3 is a welcoming option, with soaring mountains forming the picture-perfect backdrop.

Chambre d'hôtes L'Échelle (0262 51 48 55, 0692 08 99 38; www.ilereunion.com/echelle; 16 Allée des Agapanthes; d €52, dinner €22) From your first glimpse of the virginal-white façade and spacious grounds, it's clear that this imposing Creole-style modern home is in top nick. The added bonus is that it's also relaxed and unpretentious, thanks to the friendly owners, a Breton couple. Watch out for their devilish *faham*-flavoured *rhum arrangé*!

Auberge Créoline (0262 51 30 36; www.auberge -creoline.com; 303 Rue de la République; s/d €45/60) Has four tidy rooms at the back of the restaurant (see p212).

La Ferme du Pommeau (☎ 0262 51 40 70; www .pommeau.fr; 10 Allée des Pois de Senteur; s/d €48/62) This rambling two-star hotel consists of several nicely maintained buildings in a quiet location on the eastern edge of town. Inside, it's a bit disappointing, with clean but unadventurous rooms and Ikea-minimalist décor. There's a reliable restaurant on site.

Eating

Les Platanes – Chez Jean-Paul (☎ 0262 51 31 69; 167 Rue de la République; mains €13-15; ♥ lunch Tue-Sun, dinner Thu-Sat) A fixture in Plaine-des-Palmistes. Chow down on Creole and Chinese mains served in rather dull surrounds.

Auberge Créoline (☎ 0262 51 30 36; 303 Rue de la République; mains €14-18; ♥ lunch Tue-Sun) Judging by the fish *carri*, this jolly café-restaurant set back from the main road doesn't concoct the best Creole dishes in the world but it'll do the job if you're feeling peckish.

Chez Céline (☎ 0262 51 16 30; 6 Rue du Vieux Clocher; mains €12-21, menus €10-15; ♥ 8.30am-5pm Wed-Mon) If you appreciate fine dining in cosy surrounds, this adorable Creole house surrounded by manicured gardens couldn't be more perfect. The menu centres around Creole specialities with a creative twist. Céline prides herself on her *Délice des Hauts* creation, which mixes seafood and salad. She also serves breakfast, including an 'Anglo-Saxon' breakfast, should you feel homesick.

La Ferme du Pommeau (☎ 0262 51 40 70; 10 Allée des Pois de Senteur; mains €14-22; ♥ lunch & dinner Mon-Sat, lunch Sun) This is the real deal, with friendly staff and generous servings. Creole cuisine is the forte, with everything from guinea fowl with *combava* (an aromatic citrus fruit) to duck with cider, though *métro* dishes also feature.

Getting There & Away

Plaine-des-Palmistes lies on the cross-island highway between St-Benoît and St-Pierre. There are three buses a day (two on Sunday) in each direction. The fare from St-Pierre is €4.90.

AROUND PLAINE-DES-PALMISTES

An absolute must-see, the majestic **Forêt de Bébour-Bélouve** could set the stage for a new version of *Jurassic Park*, with a mix of tamarind trees, huge *fanjan* (fern trees) and moss. It lies to the northwest of Plaine-des-Palmistes, and is accessible via a surfaced forest road which begins at La Petite Plaine,

just southwest of Plaine-des-Palmistes, an finishes 20km further on, 400m from th **Gîte de Bélouve** (☎ 0692 85 93 07; Forêt de Bébou Bélouve; dm/d €14.50/€33, breakfast/meal €5/€15), fro where there is a superb view over the Cirqu de Salazie. Digs are in six- to 12-bed dorm Bookings are essential.

The forest is crisscrossed by footpath of varying levels of difficulty, from a one hour *sentier botanique* (nature trail) to a easy 3.5km walk that leads to a look-ou from where you can marvel at horseshoe shaped falls known as the **Trou de Fer**, haile as one of the most spectacular natural sigh in Réunion – it has graced the covers o many books. The path to the falls is sig posted from the Gîte de Bélouve. Hint: re a mountain bike at Gîte du Pic des Sable (p211) and explore the area at your leisure

Note that the forest road is closed to tra fic 2.5km below the Gîte de Bélouve fro noon on Friday to 7am on Monday. Ju leave your car at the car park and walk t the *gîte*.

ST-PIERRE

pop 26,000

If you need to let off steam before (or afte heading off into the Cirques, you've com to the right place. St-Pierre pulses with a energy unknown elsewhere on the island, e pecially at weekends. Havana it ain't, but th vibrant, feisty, good-natured city knows wha really counts in life: having a good time.

If St-Denis is Réunion's administrativ and business capital, enchanting St-Pierre i its throbbing heart. Basking in the clear ligh of the southwest, the 'capital of the south has an entirely different feel from its north ern counterparts. It remains unmistakabl more Creole than cosmopolitan and rathe staid St-Denis.

When not tearing it up on the dance floc or recovering from a hangover on the beach make a beeline for St-Pierre's attractions, in cluding a slew of colonial-era edifices scat tered in the centre and an attractive seafron The picturesque Terre Sainte district is als worth a stroll.

Orientation

The centre of St-Pierre consists of a compac grid of streets. Most places are easily walk ble, though the bus station for the long-distance buses, at the junction of Rue de Presbytère and Rue Luc Lorion, is a bit of a hike.

Information

There are ATMs at the central post office and at most banks in the town centre.

Central post office (Rue des Bons Enfants; 7.30am-5.30pm Mon-Fri, 7.30am-noon Sat)

Centre Hospitalier de St-Pierre (02 62 35 90 00; RN2, Terre Sainte) St Pierre's main hospital.

Crédit Agricole (Rue du Four à Chaux; 8am-4.15pm Mon-Wed & Fri, 8am-3.30pm Thu) Has an ATM.

Jet Set Bar (32 Blvd Hubert-Delisle; per hr €4; 9am-11pm Mon-Thu, 9am-midnight Fri & Sat, 11am-midnight

Sun) Internet café. Fast, friendly, high-tech and reliably open late.

Laverie-Pressing (8 Rue Méziaire Guignard; per load €5; 8am-6pm Mon-Sat) Laundry.

Office du Tourisme de St-Pierre (0262 25 02 36; www.sudreunion.com; Place Napoléon Hoareau; 9am-noon & 1-4.45pm Mon-Fri, 9am-noon & 1-3.30pm Sat) Has English-speaking staff and can provide useful brochures and a town map. You can also book *gîtes de montagne* here.

Sights

Compact, colourful St-Pierre is easily seen in a day on foot. You'll find a scattering of colonial buildings in the centre, including the old **Hôtel de Ville**, which started life as a coffee warehouse for the French East India Company during the 18th century. The old

colonial-era train station is now occupied by a nightclub. Nearby is the **Bassin de Radout**, a dry dock dating from the 19th century. Another must-see is the **entrepôt Kervéguen**, which was used as a warehouse for the French East India Company. In the same area, keep your eyes peeled for the **médiathèque Raphaël Barquisseau**, another building dating from the thriving era of the French East India Company. There are many other Creole mansions and houses that beg to be admired, especially along Rue Marius et Ary Leblond. If you still have energy to burn, it's well worth exploring the **Terre Sainte** district, to the east of the centre. Though no longer the traditional fishing village it used to be, this area has its own peculiar appeal.

The **cemetery** at the western end of Blvd Hubert-Delisle is worth the wander. The grave of the African sorcerer, Le Sitarane, is still a popular pilgrimage spot for Réunionnais who believe in *gris gris* or black magic. It is covertly used for black magic rites by people looking to bring misfortune upon others. The grave is usually covered with offerings, from glasses of rum, candles and pieces of red cloth to neat and tidy rows of cigarettes and even the occasional beheaded rooster! The grave is on the right-hand side at the west end of the cemetery.

No trip to St-Pierre would be complete without a wander through the **main market**, which takes place on Saturday morning (7am to noon) and sprawls along the seafront at the west end of Blvd Hubert-Delisle. During the week (8am to 6pm Monday to Saturday) there's a smaller **covered market** (Rue Victor le Vigoureux) under a hall in the town centre. Alongside fresh fruit and vegetables, stalls sell souvenirs such as local spices and herbs, *vacoa* bags and the usual assortment of Malagasy crafts.

After having succumbed to all-night carousing and luscious cuisine in St-Pierre, you might want to repent your sins. Head straight to the charming **St-Pierre church** (Rue Auguste Babet) if you are Catholic, to the splendid **mosque** (Rue François de Mahy) if you're Muslim, to the impressive **Hindu temple** (Ravine Blanche) if you are Hindu, and to the discreet **Chinese temple** (Rue Marius et Ary Leblond) if you are Buddhist. But if, like us, you are a hedonist beyond redemption, you might rather lounge on the white-sand **beach**!

Activities

Kayaking and **sailing** can be arranged through **Base Nautique de St-Pierre** (☎ 0262 25 57 00; Blvd Hubert-Delisle), usually on Wednesday and Saturday. Guided trips cost about €15 per hour.

There's good **diving** off St-Pierre (see p3?? for more information). Contact **Base Nautique de St-Pierre** (☎ 0692 86 83 18; Blvd Hubert-Delisle) or **Plongée Océan Indien** (☎ 0262 31 03 91, 0692 69 41 57; Harbour) at the yacht harbour.

Sleeping

St-Pierre has a variety of hotels that cater for a range of budgets. Most are concentrated down towards the seafront.

Tropic Hotel (☎ 0262 25 90 70; www.tropic-hotel.com; 2 Rue Auguste Babet; d €28-36; ❄) Although the Tropic Hotel scores low on the charm scale, its competitive prices and central location make it a worthwhile option if you don't want to deplete your accommodation budget. Avoid the cheaper rooms – they share toilets and don't have air-con. If you have your own wheels, note that there's private parking.

Chez Papa Daya (☎ 0262 25 64 87, 0692 12 20 12; www.chezpapadaya.com in French; 27 Rue du Four à Chaux; s with/without bathroom €25/16, d with/without bathroom €35/25; P ❄ 💻) Papa Daya is something of an institution for bargain-hunters, but its standing has been challenged in recent years by two newcomers whose owners are members of the same family as Monsieur Daya. Overall it's more homely, if a bit more cramped than its competitors, with lots of greenery and jolly murals around, and facilities include a simple kitchen, a laundry room and a TV lounge.

Le Nathania (☎ 0262 25 04 57; www.hotelnathania.com in French; 12 Rue François de Mahy; s with shared bathroom €20, d with/without bathroom from €30/25; P ❄) Another traveller-friendly stalwart. What it lacks in style is made up for by an ace location and tidy rooms with TV. The cheapest have shared facilities. There's also a well-equipped kitchen and laundry area. Prices drop after two nights. Credit cards are accepted.

L'Escale Touristique (☎ 0262 35 20 95; 14 Rue Désiré Barquisseau; d with/without bathroom €35/25; P ❄) Almost a carbon copy of Le Nathania (same family, same ambience, and probably the same architect). For those who like the idea of being able to dip in and out of central St-Pierre at will, this is another attractive option. Rooms are well scrubbed, but a bit samey though it's hard to argue with the prices. Added perks include free parking, a kitchen for guests' use and a laundry room. Don't expect dollops of atmosphere.

Alizé Plage (☎ 0262 35 22 21; www.ilereunion.com /alizeplage; 17 bis Blvd Hubert-Delisle; d €75; 🍴) The Alizé thinks it is irresistible because its position right on the beach is peerless. Hubris: only three rooms come with sea views, and though they are nicely appointed, they won't contend for a design Oscar.

ourpick Villa Belle (☎ 0692 65 89 99; www.villabelle .net in French; 45 Rue Rodier; s/d €140/150; P 🍴 💻 🛁) If you could smell charm, this super smooth boutique B&B in a converted Creole mansion would reek of it to high heaven. It's the epitome of a refined cocoon, revelling quietly in minimalist lines, soothing colour accents and well thought-out decorative touches, including contemporary art works by the owner himself. Like the rest of the place, the communal areas are a sensory interplay of light, wood and stone. After a day of turf pounding, relax in the stress-melting pool. Gay friendly.

Villa Morgane (☎ 0262 25 82 77; www.villamor gane.re in French; 334 Rue de L'Amiral Lacaze; d €120-200; 🍴 💻 🛁) Style gurus will go giddy over this revamped, reworked and reinvigorated *maison d'hôte*. The tropical garden is easily surpassed by an opulent interior. No expense has been spared in dousing guests in sassy swank. The four themed rooms have been creatively designed, some with Italian flair, some with Asian touches. If you're willing to impress your sweetie, opt for the Pompéï suite, complete with frescoes, parquet floor and ornate stucco ceilings – it has to be believed (check out the website). Just one quibble: there's no private parking.

Other recommendations:

Les Chrysalides (☎ 0262 25 75 64; www.chrysalides -hotel.com in French; 6 Rue Caumont; d €45; P 🍴) Middle-of-the-road sums up this two-star venture with a handy location and unmemorable rooms.

Résidence Mers du Sud (☎ 0262 25 39 09, 0692 61 43 41; www.mers-du-sud.com in French; 27 Blvd Hubert-Delisle; d €50-91; 🍴) It's certainly not 'South Seas', but this set of well-scrubbed yet compact rooms makes this waterfront establishment a good-value choice. There's a bit of street noise but nothing to lose sleep over.

Eating

The excellent Creole, French, Italian and Asian restaurants make this town as pleas-

ing to the belly as it is to the eye; you won't want to be skipping any meals here.

Aloha (☎ 0262 35 53 53; 51 Rue François de Mahy; ice creams & pancakes from €2; 🕙 11am-6.30pm Mon-Wed & Fri, 10am-11pm Fri, 2-7pm Sun) There is an argument for skipping dessert wherever you lunch or dine and heading straight to this drool-inducing ice-cream parlour instead. Amid a mind-boggling array of flavours, the electric purple *pitaya* screams 'try me'. Lip-smackingly good pancakes too.

Kaz Vitamines (☎ 0262 25 30 86; 6 Rue François de Mahy; mains €4-5; 🕙 10am-6pm Mon-Sat) If you've reached your *carri*-eating limits, head down to this quirky den for a cold veggie soup (€4) or a salad, just off the main drag.

Belo Horizonte (☎ 0262 22 31 95; 10 Rue François de Mahy; mains €8-14; 🕙 lunch daily, dinner Fri & Sat) Walls saturated in cheery coloured accents – baby-pink, citrus, apple-green – and other fancy decorative touches set the tone of this zinging quick-eat joint where you can tuck into salads, hot tarts and other healthy dishes.

L'Osteria (☎ 0262 25 14 15; 16 Rue Marius et Ary Leblond; mains €8-26; 🕙 lunch & dinner Mon-Sat) *Mamma mia!* Italian food does not always suit the tropics but this Mediterranean redoubt set in a rustic stone house fits the bill. Pasta offerings span *carbonara* through to tasty spaghetti with smoked swordfish, as well as pizzas dense enough to drown grandpa's dentures. Satisfying grilled meats too.

Festi Viandes (☎ 0262 25 22 84; 12 Rue Augustin Archambaud; mains €9-17, menus €10-22; 🕙 lunch & dinner Mon-Sat) In a city where fish dishes are the norm, this meat-lover's paradise, discreetly located on the 1st floor of an unremarkable building, is a happy exception. Sink your teeth into a juicy beefsteak or a succulent *brochette* (skewered meat). Enough proteins? Wood-fired pizzas are also available.

Le Rétro (☎ 0262 25 33 06; 34 Blvd Hubert-Delisle; mains €9-23, menus €11-23; 🕙 lunch & dinner) Of all the things you might not expect to see on the seafront, an 'authentic' Parisian brasserie ranks quite highly. But that's exactly what this is, except that *serveurs* are less surly than in the City of Light. Pastas, salads, seafood and meat dishes grace the menu.

Le Flamboyant (☎ 0262 35 02 15; 11 Rue Désiré Barquisseau; mains €10-15, menus €16-35; 🕙 lunch Mon-Sat, dinner Mon, Tue & Thu-Sat) In this staunchly Creole classic, blow your tastebuds (and your arteries) with one of 15 hearty *carris*. Be brave and try the *carri pat' cochon* (pig's trotter *carri*). You might surprise yourself. Sample the whole thing on the terrace in the shade of a stately flamboyant tree.

Le Marin Bleu (☎ 0262 35 61 65; 45 Rue de L'Amiral Lacaze; mains €12-25; ☽ lunch & dinner Mon-Sat) This immutable seafood favourite in the Terre Sainte district gets the thumbs up for its choice of fish dishes cooked to crispy perfection. The loosely nautical décor, with a blue-and-white colour scheme, matches the menu.

Flagrant Délice (☎ 0692 87 28 03; 115 Rue François de Mahy; mains €13-25, lunch menus €14-18; ☽ lunch Tue-Fri, dinner Tue-Sat) *The* hippest eatery at the time of writing, Flagrant Délice is a gourmand's play-pen. Be good to yourself with kangaroo fillet with onion chutney, John Dory fillet, beef with morels and luscious wines. Try to nab a seat at the 'Petit Coin Exotique' (little exotic corner), complete with cushions, by the pool (yes, the pool is an integral part of the décor).

Alizé Plage (☎ 0262 25 80 63; 17bis Blvd Hubert-Delisle; mains €15-22, menus €25-40; ☽ lunch & dinner) We found the *célèbre tartare de thon rouge* (famed red tuna tartare) a bit disappointing on our visit. Hunker down à la carte with less pretentious dishes, such as the swordfish fillet with vanilla sauce. Bag a seat on the small terrace overlooking the beach.

Le Carpe Diem (☎ 0262 25 45 12; 47 Blvd Hubert-Delisle; mains €16-25; ☽ lunch Mon-Fri, dinner Mon-Sat) Another dash of culinary flair in cosy surrounds (parquet floors and teak furniture), the Carpe Diem offers ambitious French-inspired dishes with a twist, from *souris d'agneau au thym* (a choice piece of lamb flavoured with thyme) to skewered duck with banana.

Le Pétrel de Barau (☎ 0262 35 14 88; 16 Rue Augustin Archambaud; mains €24-35, menu €45; ☽ lunch & dinner Mon-Fri, dinner Sat) Cognoscenti saunter here for upper-crust French-inspired fare with a creative bent, a respectable wine list and smart service. The masterfully renovated Creole house provides the perfect setting in which to sample star-worthy dishes such as beef fillet with truffle vinegar. Room should be kept for desserts.

Other flavoursome feeds:

La Détente (☎ 0262 25 66 77; 4 Rue François Isautier; mains €10-15; ☽ lunch & dinner) No culinary acrobatics in this few-frills haunt overlooking a parking lot, just keep-the-faith Creole staples, including a very affordable *carri bichiques* (a curry made from tiny sprat-like fish; €15) in season.

Pot a G (☎ 0262 59 66 94; 7 Rue Auguste Babet; mains €10-17; ☽ lunch Tue-Fri, dinner Thu-Sat) Sick of stodgy

carris? Then head here for loveable *métro* fare served in a strong design-led interior.

L'Utopia (☎ 0262 35 15 83; 8 Rue Marius et Ary Leblond; mains €15-25, menus €10-39; ☽ lunch & dinner Mon-Sat) Good atmosphere and affordable prices were let down by some sketchy service and skimpy daily specials when we visited L'Utopia. Chef's day off perhaps? You be the judge.

Drinking & Entertainment

Night owls, rejoice: St-Pierre has a well-established party reputation. Nightlife swings until the morning hours at weekends. The best buzz can be found on the seafront and in the vicinity of the town hall. Most places open from 6pm and close at around 2am or later. Admission prices, when there are any, usually run from €5 to €12.

Kaz Vitamines (☎ 0262 25 30 86; 6 Rue François de Mahy; juices from €4; ☽ 10am-6pm Mon-Sat) This juice bar is perfect to recover from a hangover, with smoothies and vegetable and fruit concoctions. Try the explosively fruity (and eye-poppingly purple) *cocktail La Kaz*, which is a mix of *pitaya*, banana and lime.

Malone's (☎ 0262 25 02 22; 36 Blvd Hubert-Delisle; ☽ daily) St-Pierre's long-standing hip, hot (it gets congested) and happening spot on weekends. Swill a beer or two to imbibe the feel-good vibe before hitting the clubs.

Café de la Gare – Latina Café (☎ 0262 35 24 44; 17 Blvd Hubert-Delisle; ☽ Tue-Sun) One of the most atmospheric spots for a drink is the terrace of this café in the old train station. In the evening it transforms into a convivial bar. It's full of attitude and atmosphere; booze it up with new friends or spend a quiet hour by yourself, people-watching.

Le Bug (☎ 0262 43 87 78; 4 Rue des Bons Enfants; ☽ Tue-Sat) Techno reigns supreme here, with a fiery nod to rock 'n' roll once a week. Come evening, the oompah-pah music can rattle the brain into oblivion.

Kabarhum (☎ 0262 35 39 44; www.kabarhum.com in French; Blvd Hubert-Delisle; ☽ Tue-Sat) A beautifully rustic bar, the best rums in town, a friendly atmosphere, a mixed crowd and scattered tables – what more could you want?

L'Africa Queen (7 Blvd Hubert-Delisle; ☽ Fri & Sat) If there's a constant here, it's the promise that the music, whatever the style, will get you groovin'. DJs roll through salsa, hip-hop, house, electro and soul but always find a way to keep the dance floor filled. Heart-start the night with a few shots at Café de la Gare, in the same building.

Jet Set Bar (☎ 0262 32 83 86; 32 Blvd Hubert-Delisle; ☺ daily) The ultimate chill-out bar by day, this place is equally enjoyable by night on weekends when groovy DJs take over with deep and chill house, electronica and other beats, depending on their whim. It's cool, funky and low-key at the same time.

Khalif (7 Blvd Hubert-Delisle; ☺ Fri & Sat) One of the hottest spots in St-Pierre when we dropped by. If you're after *maloya, séga* or some sexy tropical sounds, look no further than Khalif. Same location as Café de la Gare.

Cherwaine's (☎ 0262 35 69 49; 6 Rue Auguste Babet; ☺ daily) This bar is a pillar of St-Pierre's gay scene. Sets aside certain nights for entertainment offerings, including karaoke.

Bato Fou (☎ 0262 25 65 61; 15 Rue de la République) To the west of town, this is one of Réunion's prime concert venues and a launch pad for local bands on the boil.

Other happening places include the club-like **Blue Cat** (☎ 0262 96 70 06; www.bluecat-bar com in French; 33 Blvd Hubert-Delisle; ☺ daily), which prides itself on its two bars and its pool; **Aquarhum** (☎ 0262 96 34 12; 18 Petit Blvd de la Plage; ☺ Tue-Sun); and **Piano Bar** (☎ 0262 25 85 17; 6 Rue des Bons Enfants; ☺ Tue-Sun), which caters for an older crowd with down-tempo jazz and soul beats.

Getting There & Away

AIR

Air Mauritius and Air Austral operate daily flights between **Pierrefonds Airport** (☎ 0262 96 77 66; www.grandsudreunion.org), 5km west of St-Pierre, and Mauritius. See p302 for more information.

Airlines with offices in St-Pierre:

Air Austral (☎ 0825 01 30 12; 14 Rue Augustin Archambaud)

Air France (☎ 0820 82 08 20; 72 Rue Luc Lorion)

Air Mauritius (☎ 0262 96 06 00; 7 Rue François de Mahy)

BUS

Car Jaune's long-haul buses stop at the long-distance bus station beside the junction of Rue Presbytère and Rue Luc Lorion, west of town. Regular and express buses to/from St-Denis (€7) run frequently along the west coast via St-Louis and St-Gilles-les-Bains. There are also two or three services a day to St-Benoît via Plaine-des-Palmistes (€7.50) and the same number around the south coast through St-Joseph and Ste-Philippe (€7). For Cilaos, change in St-Louis.

THE WILD SOUTH

Aaaah, the *Sud Sauvage* (Wild South), where the unhurried life is complemented by the splendid scenery of fecund volcanic slopes, occasional beaches, waves crashing on the rocky shoreline and country roads that twist like snakes into the Hauts. In both landscape and character, the south coast is where the real wilderness of Réunion begins to unfold. Once you've left St-Pierre, a gentle splendour and a sense of escapism become tangible. The change of scenery climaxes with the Grand Brûlé, where black lava fields slice through the forest and even reach the ocean at several points.

The Wild South has charming treasures and enough elbow room to make it special. A car is the ideal way to cover the region, but it's possible (if not expedient) to get from town to town by bus. It's a great area to sidle down for a few days, ditch your guidebook (but not your map) and poke around, but don't tell others where you'll be!

ST-PIERRE TO ST-JOSEPH

At last! No more traffic snarls (well, almost). Life – and travel – becomes more sedate as one heads west through some of the south coast's delicious scenery. With only a few exceptions urban life is left behind once the road traverses **Grand Bois** and snakes its way along the coastline.

Beach lovers should stop at **Plage de Grande Anse**, which is framed with basaltic cliffs and features a white-sand beach, a protected tide pool and picnic shelters (take the D30 that branches off the RN2 and winds down for about 2km to the beach). Alas, don't expect a Robinson Crusoe experience on weekends, when the beach is often swamped with visitors. Pick up some brochures at the small **tourist office** (☎ 0262 31 27 73; Plage de Grande Anse; ☺ 10am-5pm Mon-Sat), at the end of the parking lot.

Backtrack to the RN2 and drive east until you reach the turnoff for **Petite Île**. From Petite Île, a scenic road wobbles slowly up to some charming villages in the Hauts. Continue uphill until the junction with the D3. If you turn left, you'll reach **Mont-Vert-les-Hauts**, approximately 5km to the west (and from then it's an easy drive downhill to the coast via

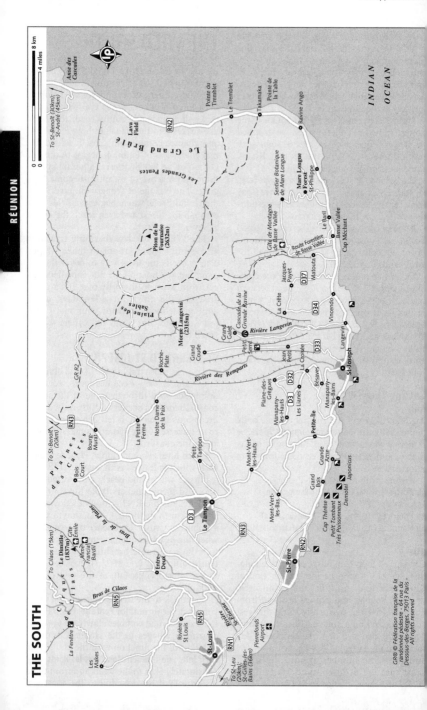

THE SOUTH

RÉUNION

Mont-Vert-les-Bas); if you turn right, you will
cross **Manapany-les-Hauts** before reaching Les
Lianes for St-Joseph.

Seeing the area from the saddle of a horse
is a fun way to experience the visual appeal of
the region, even if you're not an experienced
rider. **L'Écurie du Relais** (☎ 0262 56 78 67, 0692 00 42
78; http://monsite.wanadoo.fr/ecurie.du.relais in French; 75
Chemin Léopold Lebon, Manapany-les-Hauts; ☼ Tue-Sun
by reservation) has guided trips in the Hauts as
well as day tours to Grande Anse. Expect to
pay around €17 for an hour and €110 for a
day tour.

Back on the coastal road, head to **Manapany-
es-Bains**. This charming spot lies at the mouth
of an impressive ravine and boasts a protected
tide pool where you can splash about.

Sleeping & Eating

Despite some signs on the road, many places
are not easy to find, but that's part of the
charm. Check locations on the website (if
any) or call ahead. Of course, some words in
French for directions always help.

Gandalf Safari Camp (☎ 0692 40 78 39;
www.gandalfsafaricamp.de; 87 Blvd de l'Océan, Manapany-
es-Bains; r with shared toilets €25; ▯) Bargain! Chris-
tina and Claus, the German owners, have
long lived in Africa, hence the name. They
launched this venue in 2006 and brought a
refreshing dash of originality on the accommodation scene in the Wild South. The five
rooms are individually designed, with such
themes as Kreol, Malagasy, Arab, Chinese
and Indian. We fell for the Malagasy, complete with wooden masks, a fake baobab tree
and other delightful knick knacks. English
is spoken.

L'Eau Forte (☎ 0262 56 32 84; www.eau-forte.fr; 137bis
Blvd de l'Océan, Manapany-les-Bains; d €40) Another
bargain. Perfect for self-caterers, this fully
equipped, spick-and-span villa boasts an ace
location, right above Plage de Grande Anse.
If hunger beckons, Chez Jo is a coin's toss
down the road. There's a two-night minimum
stay.

Chambre d'hôtes Les Embruns (☎ 0262 56 76 16;
www.les-embruns974.com in French; 24 Chemin Neuf, Petite
le; d €43-46) Next door to Lé Gaillard, this is
another reassuring B&B with a manicured
garden and meticulously maintained rooms.
Oh yeah, and the ocean views are straight
from heaven.

Chambre d'hôtes Chez Maoul (☎ 0262 56 82 26;
5 Rue du Piton, Petite Île; d €45, dinner €17; ▯ ▯) The

four wood-clad rooms in this homely B&B
have a cabin-in-the-woods feel but offer a
fine sense of originality, as testified by the cute
Do-Myel room: walls are bedecked with newspapers (as in old Creole houses) and a copy of
the Universal Declaration of Human Rights
(translated into Creole). Maoul is a former
maloya musician and is known to break out
in song at dinner time.

Chambre d'hôtes Vérémer (☎ 0262 31 65 10; www
.chambre-gite-veremer.com; 40 Chemin Sylvain Vitry, Petite
Île; d €45-52; ▯ ▯) Three cocoon-like rooms
in a neat Creole building nestled in a well-
tended tropical garden, with superlative views
and a splendid pool that guests can use in the
morning and in the afternoon. Aim for the
Mer room, which opens onto the garden
and the pool. Coming from St-Pierre, it's
signposted off the main road just beyond the
turning for Petite-Île. Grande Anse beach is
3.5km away.

Chambre d'hôtes La Cour Mont Vert (☎ 0262 31
21 10; www.courmontvert.com; 18ter Chemin Roland Garros,
Mont-Vert-les-Bas; d €60, dinner from €20) Your heart
will lift at the dreamy views over the coast;
your body will rejuvenate with the Valatchy's
healthy meals; your soul will find peace in the
four button-cute Creole bungalows set in rural
grounds awash with mangoes and lychees.
Simply arrive, absorb and enjoy.

Chambre d'hôtes Lé Gaillard (☎ 0262 56 77 68;
www.le-gaillard.net; 26 Chemin Neuf, Petite Île; d €70; ▯)
An inviting B&B, despite the price tag. It's
obvious that great care has gone into decorat-
ing each room – not in an ostentatious way,
rather in a quirkily exotic manner that puts a
smile on your face. Add in a lovely pool and
jaw-dropping ocean views and you have a
winning formula.

Palm Hotel & Spa (☎ 0262 56 30 30; www.palm
.re; Grande Anse; d incl breakfast €80-200; ▯ ▯ ▯) If
you're really looking to push the boat out in
the Wild South, then to be honest there's only
one choice. Opened in April 2007, this new
temple of luxury was an instant hit. In an ambience of effortless sophistication, you'll find
all the trappings of a big-league player. These
include spacious villas and lodges on stilts
that are artfully decorated, two restaurants,
two pools and a luxurious spa. The sweeping views of the ocean below from the terraces make a sundowner taste all the sweeter.
Wholly delightful.

Restaurant Chez Jo (☎ 0262 31 48 83; 143 Blvd de
L'Océan, Manapany-les-Bains; mains €7-20; ☼ lunch Tue-Sun,

dinner Fri & Sat) In this buzzy eatery overlooking the tide pool in Manapany-les-Bains, you're bound to find something on the menu that takes your fancy. Whether you treat yourself to ostrich steak, salads or chicken with *pleurotes* (mushrooms), or just pop in for an exquisite fruit juice (from €2.50), Chez Jo is a rare treat with virtually zero guilt factor.

Le Vacoa (☎ 0262 56 95 17; 25 Route de Grande Anse; mains €10-15; ☺ lunch & dinner Tue-Sun) Strategically positioned on the road to Plage de Grande Anse, this modest eatery offers a full menu of familiar favourites, including Creole and Chinese dishes. Bag a seat on the breezy terrace and be wooed by the vistas over the cobalt-blue waters of the Baie de Grande Anse, or take away and eat on the beach.

ST-JOSEPH
pop 13,000

The Wild South's hub, modernish St-Joseph (say 'St-Jo' if you want to sound local) won't leap to the top of your list of preferred destinations in Réunion but it's a good place if you need to catch some urban vibes. It also offers useful services, including a tourist office and banks with ATMs, but no internet café. While it oozes the kind of sunny languor you'd associate with the tropics, the snarled traffic and bustling shopping streets at peak hours impart the energy (and stress) of a city. That, combined with the dearth of atmospheric accommodation options, makes it good for a pit stop but there are better places in the Hauts to really kick back and hang out.

If you can, plan to be in St-Jo on a Friday morning, when the streets spill over with numerous stalls.

The **Maison du Tourisme du Sud Sauvage** (☎ 0262 37 37 11; www.sudsauvage.com; 3 Rue Paul Demange; ☺ 9am-5pm Mon-Sat) is near the bus station in the centre. The centre's staff can tell you just about everything you need to know about travelling in the Wild South, and there are enough leaflets to paper your living room. English is spoken.

At the entrance of St-Joseph (it's signposted), the **Orchidarium** (☎ 0692 25 86 26; €4; ☺ by appointment) is worth a peek if you're into tropical flowers. The owner, Bertrand Hoareau, will be happy to explain everything you ever wanted to know about orchids (in French) but were too afraid to ask.

Psst! One of the best-kept secrets in the Wild South is a secluded cove with a splendid black-sand **beach**, at the entrance of St-Jo (coming from St-Pierre). Drive past the first roundabout (where the Quick lies), then take the first right on to Rue de la Station de Transit. Follow the road for about 300m until you reach a skate park. Leave your car here and walk for about five minutes down a path to the shore… Enjoy!

Sleeping & Eating

Accommodation options are thin on the ground in St-Jo. Frankly said, your best bet is to bunk down in a cosy *chambres d'hôtes* in the Hauts.

La Case (☎ 0262 56 07 50; www.case.fr; 2 Rue Jean Bart; d €40-47; [P] [X] [⚡]) La Case's zero personality compound and sterile rooms are balanced by self-catering facilities, pool, friendly staff, and the choice of air-con or fan, meaning you can sacrifice character for comfort. It's on the eastern edge of town, on the road to St-Philippe.

La Case (☎ 0262 56 41 66; 31 Rue Leconte Delisle; mains €13-30; ☺ lunch & dinner Mon-Sat) No misprint – same name as the previous venue. Don't miss this soulful restaurant right in the thick of things – it gets favourable word-of-mouth reviews along with our stamp of approval. Stepping through the Creole doorway is like zapping away a century; expect timber beams, darkwood parquet and old-fashioned paintings adorning the white walls. The perfect setting for an intimate *dîner à deux* (dinner for two). The snapper fillet with crab sauce and the *tarte tatin à la papaye* (a variety of papaya pie) are divine.

L'Ambroisie (☎ 0262 31 51 99; 306 Rue Raphaël Babet; mains €10-18, menu €18; ☺ lunch Tue-Sat, dinner Tue & Thu-Sat) After having fallen for La Case, L'Ambroisie pales in comparison, with its naive murals featuring Greek gods and a standard selection of *carris* and *métro* staples. That said, you can eat decently at a fraction of the price.

Getting There & Away

St-Joseph lies on Car Jaune's coastal bus route between St-Pierre and St-Benoît. In addition to the central bus station, buses stop in Petite-Île, Vincendo and Manapany-les-Bains.

LES HAUTS DE ST-JOSEPH

Lose yourself in the Hauts! Starting from St-Joseph you can cherry-pick an itinerary in the hinterland that takes in drowsy hamlets where locals all know each other, green velvet

---

BACKROADS: GRAND COUDE, THE END OF THE WORLD

The timeless hamlet of Grand Coude, perched on a plateau at an altitude of 1300m, boasts a marvellous setting, with the soaring Morne Langevin (2315m) as the backdrop. Here you'll be smitten by mellow tranquillity and laid-back lifestyle (whisper it softly).

From St-Joseph, take the narrow D33, which passes through **Jean Petit** and twists its way across splendidly rugged scenery of looming peaks and deep gorges. Pull over for a picnic at **Petit Serré**, where a narrow ridge divides two valleys, the valley of the Rivière Langevin on your right and the valley of the Rivière des Remparts on your left. At one point the ridge is little wider than the road itself – you have the feeling of driving on a razor's edge! The views over the valleys are awesome. At the end of the D33, about 20km north of St-Joseph, Grand Coude appears like a mirage.

Soak up the rural atmosphere and visit **Le Labyrinthe En Champ Thé** (☎ 0692 60 18 88; Grand Coude; adult/child €5/4, guided tour €8/4; ☼ 9am-noon & 1-5pm Tue-Sat, 9am-5pm Sun). It's definitely worth an hour or so for anyone interested in tropical flora, with an emphasis on tea.

You can stop overnight at **Chambre d'hôtes L'Eucalyptus** (☎ 0262 56 39 48; 24 Chemin de la Croizure, Grand Coude; s/d €32/40, dinner €18), where absolute peace and quiet prevail. Choose between the dinky all-wood bungalow or one of the two simple rooms in a white-and-yellow Creole building. Unwind in the generous garden, where coffee and geranium fill the air (ask for a cup of Bourbon Pointu coffee). Venison and wild boar feature prominently on the menu.

Another no-frills but authentic place is **Ferme Équestre Equi-Libre** (☎ 0262 56 25 90, 0692 08 06 63; Rue Théophile Gautier, Grand Coude; camp site per person €10, dm €25, bungalow €50-75, lunch & dinner from €16).

---

mountains cloaked in layers of wispy cloud, rolling sugar-cane fields, twisting roads and panoramas to make the heart beat faster.

Follow the picturesque D3 that cuts inland before swinging northwestwards to Manapany-Les-Hauts. You'll pass **Bésaves** and **Les Lianes**. You could also drive up to **Plaine-des-Grègues** (follow the D32, which branches off the D3 in La Croisée), the highest village of the area, which crouches in a bowl of mountains. This village is famed for its plantations of curcuma and vetiver, which are both used in perfumery. Learn more about the virtues (and fragrances) of these plants at the **Maison du Curcuma** (☎ 0262 47 54 66; 14 Chemin du Rond, Plaine-des-Grègues; admission free; ☼ 9am-noon & 1.30-5pm).

Les Hauts de St-Joseph are a source of inspiration for many artists and artisans who sell their *objets d'art* and crafts. Many of these artisans' workshops are open to the public. Pick up a brochure from the St-Joseph tourist office, which contains their contact details.

Indiana Jones–types will make a beeline for the **Rivière des Remparts**, an easily overlooked splendour immediately north of St-Joseph. This valley – one of the wildest in the south – is accessible on foot (or by 4WD). The classic hike is along the river, up to the hamlet of Roche-Plate, about 18km to the north, and on to Nez de Bœuf on the road that leads to Piton de la Fournaise (see p210). In Roche-Plate, you can break up your journey at the welcoming

Gîte de Roche Plate (☎ 0262 59 13 94; Roche-Plate; dm with half board €35). Allow about four hours to reach the *gîte* from St-Joseph, and another four hours to Nez de Bœuf. Unforgettable.

Sleeping & Eating

Chambre d'hôtes Chez Nathalie Hoareau (☎ 0262 37 61 92; 205 Rue Edmon Albius, Bésaves; d €40) A village address in the gently rolling Hauts de St-Joseph. There are two plain rooms at the back, but with one of the most delightful gardens you'll find in this price category. The owner, Didier Hoareau, is a sugar-cane producer and grows a high-quality variety of coffee and is happy to lead guests in this Garden of Eden.

Chambre d'hôtes L'Arpège Austral (☎ 0262 56 36 89; 53 Rue des Prunes, St-Joseph; d €48, bungalow €55, dinner €20) Wonderful to be so near St-Joseph (2.5km), yet in such a serene spot. Sylvie and Hary, your hosts, are musicians and their B&B is an ode to good taste, with two rooms with sloping ceilings and teak furniture. For more privacy, the adjoining bungalow, sheathed with soothing yellows and decked out with a private terrace, fits the bill. Book in for a *table d'hôtes* meal and you may feast on a *carri diététique* (a low-calorie *carri*) on the shady terrace overlooking a garden dotted with mature trees. It's on the road to Grand Coude (follow the D33).

Chambre d'hôtes La Plantation (☎ 0262 56 08 86; www.laplantation.net; 124 Chemin de Jean Petit; d €75,

RÉUNION

ste €95, dinner €25; 🖳) This B&B nestled amid sugar-cane fields boasts a small pool and lush tropical garden with staggering views of the coast. There are three rooms and one gleaming suite, all featuring handsomely designed bathrooms. Marie-Laure, your chirpy host, has applied all her flair to the décor, marrying vital colour harmonies and high-quality fabrics. At the end of the day, treat yourself to a sumptuous *table d'hôtes* meal on the veranda. Downsides: access to the pool is restricted (no dip by moonlight!), and only two of the rooms come with sea views. Monsieur is a serious hiker and a mine of local information. Rates drop for stays of more than two nights. Find La Plantation on the road to Grand Coude, about 5km from St-Joseph.

ST-JOSEPH TO ST-PHILIPPE

The coastline between St-Joseph and St-Philippe is definitely alluring: a string of rocky coves and dramatic cliffs pounded by crashing waves and backed by steep hills clad with dense forests and undulating sugar-cane fields, with a few black-sand beaches thrown in for good measure.

Inland, it's no less spectacular. Abandon your map and follow the sinuous *départementales* (secondary roads) that wiggle up to the Hauts and creep through beguiling settlements, which warrant scenic drives and boast killer views over the ocean and plunging canyons.

About 4km east of St-Joseph, you'll reach **Langevin**. From the coast, the **Rivière Langevin** valley slithers into the mountains. A narrow road follows the wide stony bed of the river and leads to **Cascade de la Grande Ravine**, an impressive waterfall about 9km from the junction with the coastal road. If you need to cool off, there are plenty of natural pools along the river where you can dunk yourself. Our favourites include Trou Noir (it's signposted) and a pool that lies about 200m before the Cascade de la Grande Ravine (you can't miss it). Come prepared: this valley is extremely popular with picnicking families on Sunday.

Further east, in **Vincendo**, follow the D34 that goes uphill to the north and takes you to the hamlet of **La Crête**. From there, the D37 leads due east to another peaceful settlement, **Jacques-Payet**, before zigzagging downhill until the junction with the coastal road. In Vincendo, few visitors get wind of the black-sand **beach** fringed by *vacoa* trees a few kilometres

south of the main road. There are some dangerous currents at certain times of the year, so ask around before diving in.

And now, **Basse-Vallée**. The area is known for its production of baskets, bags (called *bertels*), hats and other items from *vacoa* fronds. You can see them being made and learn more about this versatile palm at **Cass' le Coin** (☎ 0262 37 09 61; 57 Rue Labourdonnais; ⏰ 10am-noon & 1.30-4pm Mon-Sat) and **Association Vacoa Sud** (☎ 0262 37 16 96; RN2; ⏰ 9am-5pm). Then head to **Cap Méchant**, one of the eeriest landscapes in the Wild South, with huge lava fields, windswept black cliffs and rows of *vacoa* trees. There's an excellent coastal path along the sea cliffs (bring sturdy shoes).

Further east, **Le Baril** is the last settlement before St-Philippe.

Sleeping & Eating
RIVIÈRE LANGEVIN

If you haven't brought a picnic, there's a bevy of cheap and cheerful eateries along the river at the entrance of the valley. They're pretty much of a muchness and serve up Creole classics, which you can eat in or take away. Recommended options:

Le Benjoin (☎ 0262 56 23 90; Route de la Passerelle; mains €6-11; ⏰ lunch Tue-Sun) Famed for its *thé dansant* (tea dance) on Wednesday and Sunday afternoon.

Les Pieds dans L'Eau (☎ 0262 37 13 64; Route de la Passerelle; mains €6-11; ⏰ lunch daily) Cheap Creole staples.

VINCENDO & LES HAUTS

Rougail Mangue (☎ 0262 31 55 09; 12 Rue Marcel Pagnol, Vincendo; dm €13, s/d €20/39, dinner €12-20) You'd never guess it from the road but this unfussy abode is as welcoming as an old friend's hug thanks to its Italian owner, Cosimo. The ground floor is occupied by a smart communal room, two dorms that can accommodate two to eight persons and two squeaky-clean rooms; thumbs up for the cheery double blessed with addictive ocean views. After a long day's driving on twisty roads, nothing can beat a dip in the pool followed by a sundowner. Breakfast is extra (€5) and can be enjoyed alfresco under a gazebo. It's on the main road, between Langevin and Vincendo.

Gîte La Table des Randonneurs (☎ 0692 61 73 47; 17 Chemin des Barbadines, Jacques-Payet; dm incl breakfast €15, bungalow at weekends €200, dinner €20) Way up in the hills, 'The Hikers' Table' is a safe bet. Dorms and dining room are in no danger of appearing in *House Beautiful*, but everything is in immaculate shape and functional. The menu features local delicacies like smoked luck with *vacoa*. It's about 7km northeast of Vincendo (follow the D37).

Ferme-Auberge Desprairies (☎ 0262 37 39 45; www .ferme-auberge-desprairies.com in French; 44 Route de Matouta; d €34, meals €18) One of the best things about this inoffensive inn is the road to it, which travels through sugar-cane fields despite being only a couple of kilometres from the coast. The walls are decorated with shades of red not seen since mood rings went out of style – not to mention the bedspreads with floral designs. Corny? Yes, but rooms are clean and in this location for this price, you won't hear anyone complaining. Follow the D37 to the east to get here.

La Médina du Sud (☎ 0262 37 32 51; www.lamedina doc.com; 23 Chemin de la Marine, Vincendo; d €45; ☒) There's nothing Moorish in this modern building by the turn-off for the beach, except the owner's origins. The four rooms are characterless but fully equipped, well proportioned and perfectly serviceable, with the added bonus of a pool. There's a two-night minimum.

Le Tagine (☎ 0262 37 32 51; 23 Chemin de la Marine, Vincendo; mains €10-20; ☺ lunch daily, dinner Thu-Sat) Next door to La Médina du Sud (same owner), Le Tagine is a good place to give your tastebuds something new to sing about, with toothsome Moroccan couscous and tajines. Traditional Creole dishes and salads also feature on the menu.

BASSE-VALLÉE & CAP MÉCHANT

Gîte de Montagne de Basse Vallée (☎ 0262 37 36 25; Basse-Vallée; dm €14.50, dinner €16) This *gîte de montagne* is about 8km above the village of Basse Vallée, along the Route Forestière de Basse Vallée. Bookings must be made through the Maison de la Montagne et de la Mer (p172) or a tourist office.

Gîte de Théophane (☎ 0262 37 13 14, 0692 18 86 84; Route Forestière, Basse-Vallée; dm with half board €38, dinner €18) Another rural paradise, lost in the middle of the forest, and accessible on foot (about 30 minutes) via a scenic *sentier forestier* (forest dirt track) or by 4WD only from the Route Forestière (signed at the junction). It can't get more Wild South than this.

Ferme-Auberge Le Rond de Basse Vallée (☎ 0692 85 03 37, 0692 69 65 51; Basse-Vallée; d €40, meal €20) A recent addition in this superbly unspoilt area, this inn is a great place to commune with nature. There are four rooms with virginal-white walls and spick-and-span bathrooms in a Creole-style

building. The restaurant is across the road and features regional dishes with authentic flavours, including – you guessed it – *vacoa*. It's about 5.5km above the village of Basse-Vallée, along the Route Forestière de Basse-Vallée.

On the seafront in Cap Méchant, locals disagree about which outpost does the best *carris*, chop sueys and *porc au palmiste* (pork with palm hearts) – you'll just have to try them all for yourself: **L'Étoile de Mer** (☎ 0262 37 04 60; mains €10-17; Cap Méchant; ☺ lunch daily); **Le Pinpin** (☎ 0262 37 04 19; Cap Méchant; mains €12-17; ☺ lunch daily except Wed); and **Le Cap Méchant** (☎ 0692 85 39 28; Cap Méchant, Basse-Vallée; mains €10-13; ☺ lunch Tue-Sun). They are mobbed at weekends but almost deserted on weekdays.

LE BARIL

Chambre d'hôtes Le Pinpin d'Amour (☎ 0262 37 14 86; damour-marieclaude@wanadoo.fr; 56 Chemin Paul Hoareau, Le Baril; d €50, dinner €23) Spending a night at this original *chambre d'hôte* makes a good story to tell the folks back home. Your hosts have a passion for *vacoa* and pinpin (the palm's edible artichoke-like fruit), meaning you'll be guaranteed to taste them at dinner (and even at breakfast), prepared in all their forms. Accommodation-wise, the six appealing, if a bit itty-bitty rooms, sport pastel colour walls and honey-boarded floors. It's in the hills above Le Baril, about 2km from the coastal road. Alas, no sea views from the rooms.

Hôtel-Restaurant Le Baril (☎ 0262 37 01 04; www .anthurium.com in French; RN2, Le Baril; s/d €51/57; ☒) Despite its location above the rocky shoreline and its onsite restaurant, we can't help feeling the 13 units are a tad overpriced for what you get. If you're in one of the bungalows on the front your stay will be accompanied by the crash of waves right below, which can be either soothing or a little nerve-wracking.

Snack-Bar P'ti Lu (80 Puits-des-Anglais, Le Baril; mains €7-11; ☺ lunch Tue-Sun) Never short of rambunctious families at weekends, this no-fuss little restaurant beside the tidal swimming pool at Puits-des-Anglais is a good spot to carbo-load after a dip. Eat in or take away.

ST-PHILIPPE
pop 5000
Vegetarians will reach Shangri-la in St-Philippe, the self-proclaimed capital of *vacoa*. No joke – no less than 5000 visitors turn up to join St-Philippois townsfolk for the 10-day Fête du Vacoa in August.

The only town of consequence in the Wild South (along with St-Joseph), St-Philippe has a wonderfully down-to-earth, unfussy ambience. Although this friendly little town is devoid of overwhelming sights, it has a slew of (good) surprises up its sleeves and is optimally placed for explorations of the coast and forays into the Hauts. Oh, and St-Philippe lies in the shadow of the Piton de la Fournaise.

The small **Eco-Musée de St-Philippe – Au Bon Roi Louis** (☎ 0262 37 16 43; adult/child €5/2; ☑ 9am-noon & 2-4.30pm Mon-Sat), a few doors down from St-Philippe's town hall, makes for a perfect introduction to the area's history and culture. The little Creole house is stuffed with an eclectic assortment of antiques and agricultural equipment. Visitors receive a very detailed tour (in French) from the owners.

With its handful of colourful fishing boats, the teensy **fishing harbour** is also worth a peek.

Inland, don't miss the 3-hectare garden, **Le Jardin des Parfums et des Épices** (☎ 0262 37 06 36; www.jardin-parfums-epices.fr in French; adult/child €6.10/3.05; ☑ tours 10.30am & 2.30pm). It contains over 1500 species in a natural setting in the Mare Longue forest, 3km west of St-Philippe. Knowledgeable and enthusiastic guides present the island's history, economy and culture through the plants; tours (in French) must be booked at least one day ahead. Continue a few kilometres further up to the **Sentier Botanique de Mare Longue**. This pristine forest has an end-of-the-world feeling that will appeal to those in search of hush. From the car park you can tackle one of the three interpretative trails in the primary forest.

St-Philippe's **tourist office** (☎ 0262 37 10 43; Place de la Mairie; ☑ 10am-5pm Mon-Sat) is on the main road beside the town hall.

Sleeping & Eating

There are slim pickings in the eating and sleeping departments.

Chambre d'hôtes Au Domaine du Vacoa (☎ 0262 37 03 12, 0692 68 28 07; 11C Rue du Centre; d €50, dinner from €22) This newish B&B set in a pert little *case créole* features two spacious rooms enhanced with splashes of colour, back-friendly mattresses, crisply dressed beds and pathogen-free bathrooms. And sea views. At dinner warm your insides with duck (freshly slaughtered when we dropped by!), *vacoa* and other vegetables from the garden – all organic, of course.

Marmite du Pêcheur (☎ 0262 37 01 01; 18A Ravine Ango; mains €12-30, menu €17; ☑ lunch daily except Wed) Stuffed to the gills with *vacoa*? Can't stomach one more morsel of *carri poulet*? Then opt for this eatery where cuisine is predominantly fishy – crab, shrimps, fish, and mussels, climaxing with a gargantuan *marmite du pêcheur* (€30), a kind of seafood stew. Downside: the dining room doesn't register a mere blip on the charm radar. It's just off the main road.

LE GRAND BRÛLÉ

The crowning glory of the Wild South, the arid, eerie landscape of Le Grand Brûlé is 6km-wide volcanic plain formed by the main lava flow from the volcano. This is where the action goes when the volcano is erupting. The steep slopes above, known as Les Grandes Pentes, have funnelled lava down to the coast for thousands of years. Because of the lack of population, this area forms an important nature reserve for native birds.

In 1986, in one of the most violent eruptions in recent years, the lava unusually flowed south of Le Grand Brûlé to reach the sea between **Pointe du Tremblet** and **Pointe de la Table**. This eruption added over 30 hectares to the island's area, and more than 450 people had to be evacuated and several homes were lost. An interpretative trail has been set up at Pointe de la Table and makes for a lovely hike on the basaltic cliffs pounded by the ocean.

THE EAST

With competition like the rural idyll of the Wild South, the majestic landscapes in the Cirques, the magnetic power exerted by the Piton de la Fournaise and the sybaritic temptations to the West, the east coast from St-Denis to Ste-Rose is shamefully underrated, thus largely ignored by travellers. All the better for you: this gentle, less-visited part of the island remains something of a 'secret'.

The east coast is everything the west coast is not: low-key, unpretentious and luxuriant (yes, it *does* get much more rain). It has more soothing beauty. While this coast lacks the beaches of the west, the region makes up for it with spectacular waterfalls and lush tropical vegetation. The main produce of the area is sugar cane, but the region is also known for its vanilla plantations and fruit orchards, including lychees.

This coastal stretch is also considered to be 'other', partially as it's the bastion of Tamil culture in Réunion. Here you'll find

distinctive atmosphere, with numerous
emples and colourful religious festivals.
'or visitors it's an opportunity to discover
Réunion you never imagined.

Tourism in this area remains on a hum-
le scale, with no star attractions. However,
t's worth taking a few days to explore the
uiet recesses of this stretch of coast where
ou can experience Réunion from a different
erspective and soak up a gentle ambience.

TE-SUZANNE & AROUND
op 20,000

'he seaside town of Ste-Suzanne is usually
limpsed in passing by most tourists on the
oute down the coast, which is a shame be-
ause there are charming pockets in the area
lat beg discovery. Just beyond the church
wards the southern end of town is a road
gnposted inland to **Cascade Niagara**, a 60m
aterfall on the Rivière Ste-Suzanne. At the
id of the road, about 2km further on, you
ind up at the waterfall and attendant tropi-
il pool just ready for a refreshing dip. On
eekends it's a popular picnic site.

Garden fans and architecture buffs will
pecially enjoy a visit to the classic **Domaine
i Grand Hazier** (Map p226; ☎ 0262 52 32 81; tours €5;
'') daily by reservation), a superb 18th-century sugar
anter's residence 3km northwest of Ste-
izanne. It's an official French historical mon-
nent with a 2-hectare garden planted with a
riety of tropical flowers and fruit trees.

The nicest place to eat in Ste-Suzanne is
· **Bocage** (☎ 0262 52 21 54; mains €8-20; '' lunch
e-Sun, dinner Tue-Sat), in a tranquil park by
e river at the south end of Ste-Suzanne. It
rves mainly Chinese food plus a smatter-
g of *métro* and Creole dishes.

Ste-Suzanne is served by Car Jaune bus
utes F and G running between St-Denis
d St-Benoît.

T-ANDRÉ & AROUND
p 44,000

-André is the anti–St-Gilles. While St-Gilles
nd the northwestern coast) is appropriately
ibbed 'Zoreille-Land', St-André is the epi-
ntre of Tamil culture in Réunion, and you'll
e more women draped in vividly coloured
ris than Zoreilles wearing designer glasses
d trendy shirts. Busy streets transport you to
ity somewhere in India with curry houses,
ri shops and bric-a-brac traders. You'll defi-
tely feel closer to Bombay than Paris.

The mainly Tamil population is descended
from indentured labourers who were brought
from India to work in the sugar-cane fields and
factories after slavery was abolished in 1848.

Orientation & Information
St-André is very spread out – it's best to get
around by car.

You'll find banks with ATMs in the centre.
The **Office Municipal du Tourisme de St-André** (☎ 0262
46 91 63; omt.standre@wanadoo.fr; Parc du Colosse; '' 9am-5pm
Mon-Sat) is inconveniently located in the coastal
leisure park 3km north of the town centre.

Sights
St André's Indian atmosphere is most apparent in the Hindu temples dotted around the
town. The most imposing are the **Temple of
Colosse** (Chemin Champ-Borne) and **Kali Temple** (Ave de
l'Île de France); the latter is open to visitors (shoes
must be removed before entering).

Also worth a look are **Maison Valliamé** (Rue
Lagourgue), a handsome colonial villa a short
walk northeast of the centre. A huge seafront
leisure park, the **Parc du Colosse**, is being developed on the former sugar-cane fields on
St-André's eastern outskirts.

The **Sucrerie de Bois-Rouge** (Map p226; ☎ 0262 58
59 74; www.bois-rouge.fr in French; 2 Chemin du Bois Rouge;
guided tour adult/child €8/4, distillery €3.50/1.75; '' by reservation Mon-Fri, closed 20 Dec-20 Jan) is on the coast
3km north of St-André. During the cane harvest (July to December) visitors are shown
around the huge, high-tech plant, following
the process from the delivery of the cut cane
to the final glittering crystals. The two-hour
tour includes the neighbouring distillery,
where the by-products (cane juice and molasses) are made into rum. From January to
June, you can only visit the distillery. Children
under seven years aren't allowed into the refinery. English-language tours are available.

Sleeping & Eating
Chambre d'hôtes Au P'tit Coin Exotique (☎ 0262
46 46 07; 460 Rue Virapatrin; s/d €38/40, dinner €18) Run
by an affable retired Tamil couple, this 'little exotic corner' in a modern building surrounded by luxuriant gardens is a safe bet,
with three unadorned but well-kept rooms.
Madame Patou-Reverdy, who keeps the place
shipshape, is a great cook too – she'll probably prepare a *massalé* (Indian-style stew)
during your stay. Don't miss out on her *rum
tisane* (aromatic rum) – incendiary!

RÉUNION

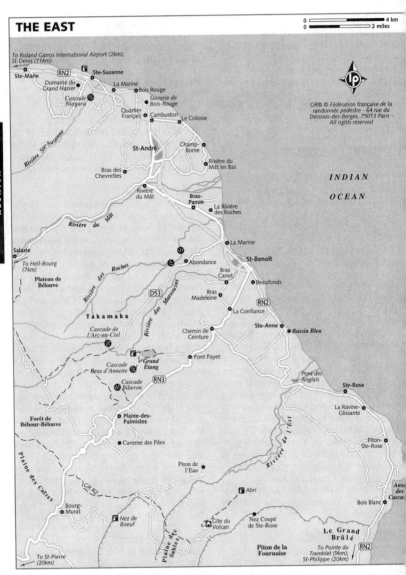

THE EAST

0 ─────── 4 km
0 ─────── 2 miles

GR® © Fédération française de la randonnée pédestre - 64 rue du Dessous-des-Berges, 75013 Paris - All rights reserved

Chambre d'hôtes Véronique Savriama (☎ 0262 46 69 84; 1084 Chemin Quatre-Vingt; d €38, dinner €17-20; ❄) This place is efficiently run but not as welcoming as the previous *chambre d'hôte*. The four upstairs rooms are a tad sombre and smallish but come with air-con and have their own entrance. Best asset is the tasty *table d'hôtes* meals, with an Indian emphasis.

Pity about the very ordinary dining roo̶ though. It's in the hamlet of Rivière du M̶ les Bas on the coast southeast of St-Andr̶

Chambre d'hôtes L'Auberge du Désert – C̶ Éric Bédier (☎ 0262 46 64 43; Bras-des-Chevret̶ d €40, dinner €18) Find this secluded B&B ab̶ 2.5km from the town centre (it's signposte̶ Featuring six comfy rooms in an impos̶

RÉUNION

LITTLE INDIA

Who said that Réunion was too Westernised? If you happen to be around Ste-Suzanne and St-André at certain periods of the year, you'll discover a very exotic side of the island, with lots of colourful festivals organised by the Tamil community. If you're about, be sure to join in the heady hype of these local festivals! In January, don't miss **Tamil fire-walking** ceremonies, when participants enter a meditative state and then walk over red-hot embers as a sign of devotion to various deities. Thousands of goats are slaughtered as offerings and are distributed among the participants. Another must-see is the **Cavadee** festival, which usually takes place in January or February. In October or November, make a beeline for **Divali** (aka Dipavali), the Festival of Light. Dancers and decorated floats parade through the town centre. Visitors are welcome. Contact the tourist office in St-André for specific dates.

---

building ensnared in a tropical garden, its standout feature is the large pool at the back – bliss after a long day's driving.

Le Beau Rivage (☎ 0262 46 08 66; Chemin Champ-Borne; mains €12-29; ☽ lunch Tue-Sun, dinner Tue-Wed & Thu-Sat) True to its name ('the beautiful shore'), Le Beau Rivage boasts a fantastic location – it's on the seafront, beside the church ruins in Champ-Borne (ask for a table near the windows). The cuisine flits between China, France and the Indian Ocean.

Le Champ Borne (☎ 0262 46 16 67; Chemin Champ-Borne; mains €12-28; ☽ lunch daily, dinner Thu-Sat) Another respected option, across the road from the seafront (read: no views). The mile-long menu roves from Creole dishes to Chinese specialities at prices that are more sweet than sour. One negative: the dining room is utterly functional. Call a designer, please!

Getting There & Away

Buses from St-Denis to St-Benoît pass through St-André. If you're travelling to Salazie by bus, you will have to change here; there are seven buses daily in each direction (three on Sunday). From Salazie there are connections to Hell-Bourg.

BRAS-PANON
pop 9800

Bras-Panon is Réunion's vanilla capital, and most visitors come here to see (and smell!) the fragrant vanilla-processing plant. The town is also associated with a rare sprat-like delicacy known as *bichiques*. In early summer (around November or December) these are caught at the mouth of the Rivière des Roches as they swim upriver to spawn.

The **Coopérative de Vanille** (☎ 0262 51 70 12; RN2; admission €5; ☽ 9am-noon & 2-4.15pm Mon-Sat),

a working vanilla-processing plant, offers an introduction to the process of producing Réunion's famous Vanille Bourbon. After the 40-minute guided tour, visitors are welcome to pick up a few samples in the factory shop. It's worth a visit just for the dreamy smell.

Car Jaune buses (lines F and G) stop outside the vanilla cooperative en route between St-André and St-Benoît.

Sleeping & Eating

There's not much in the way of accommodation in Bras-Panon. Restaurants are easier to find.

Ferme-Auberge Chez Éva Annibal (☎ 0262 51 53 76; fax 0262 51 52 01; Chemin Rivière du Mât; d with shared bathroom incl breakfast €30, dinner €20) Pack a hearty thirst and giant-sized appetite before venturing into this plain but feisty inn. The Full Monty feast comprises rum, *gratin de légumes* (baked vegetables), fish curry, duck with vanilla, and cakes, all clearly emblazoned with a Creole Mama stamp of approval. There are also three functional but clean rooms with sloping ceilings and communal facilities upstairs.

Chambre d'hôtes La Passiflore (☎ 0262 51 74 68; www.lapassiflore.re; 31 Rue des Baies-Roses; d €45, dinner €20) Run by a well-travelled *métro* couple, this B&B stands in a haven of tropical peace in a side street near the Coopérative. Monsieur has a friendly handshake, Madame is gentle and welcoming, and meals on the shady *varangue* may include *gigot flambé au whisky* (a piece of meat flambéed with whisky) or vitamin-loaded salads. The three clinically clean rooms are embellished with a few exotic bits and bobs. Float in the scintillating pool or bask in the sunny garden. Air-con is extra (€4).

Le Bec Fin (☎ 0262 51 52 24; 66 RN2; mains €10-13, menu €12-18; ☽ lunch daily, dinner Thu-Sat) Tickle your tastebuds with a slurp of *planteur* (aromatic rum), then continue your indulgence with a feisty portion of *sarcives* (a variety of sausage) or *porc sauce grand mère* (pork in grandma's sauce). On weekdays it lays on an excellent buffet lunch for just €12.

Le Beauvallon (☎ 0262 50 42 92; Rivière des Roches; mains €7-25; ☽ lunch daily) Le Beauvallon is well known to everyone in Bras-Panon, not least for its location beside the mouth of the Rivière des Roches and its seasonal, scrumptious *carri bichiques*. On the flipside, the vast dining room doesn't contain one whit of soul or character.

Le Vani-La (☎ 0262 51 56 58; 21 RN2; mains €10-15; ☽ lunch Mon-Fri) Vanilla is king of the castle in this little restaurant right beside the Coopérative de Vanille. It turns up in both savoury and sweet dishes.

ST-BENOÎT & AROUND

pop 31,500

Sugar-cane fields, lychee and mango orchards, rice, spices, coffee… Great carpets of deep-green felt seem to have been draped over the lower hills that surround St-Benoît, a major agricultural and fishing centre.

No one can accuse St-Benoît of being overburdened with tourist sights. The area's best features lie elsewhere; turn your attention from the coast and plant it firmly in the cooler recesses of the hills and valleys to the west. The Rivière des Marsouins valley in particular is a delight, with its plunging waterfalls and luxuriant vegetation. Small wonder that there is excellent white-water rafting here.

Sights & Activities

TAKAMAKA

North of St-Benoît the D53 strikes southwest, following the Rivière des Marsouin: 15km upstream to end beside the Takamaka viewpoint. Be prepared to fall on your knee in awe: despite a small power plant near the viewpoint, the overwhelming impression i of a wild, virtually untouched valley, its wall cloaked with impenetrable forests. Here an there the dense green is broken by a silve ribbon of cascading water.

Takamaka provides an incredible stage fo action-seekers in search of an adrenaline fix **Canyoning** trips in the valley can be arrange through **Alpanes** (☎ 0692 77 75 30; www.alpanes.com in French) as well as other outfitters (see p199 based elsewhere on the island, but it's not fo the faint-hearted – you'll have to be experi enced. But what a thrill!

GRAND ÉTANG

Around 12km southwest of St-Benoît alon the road towards Plaine-des-Palmistes, is th 3km road to Grand Étang (Big Pond). pretty picnic spot lies at the bottom of an al most vertical ridge separating it from the Riv ière des Marsouins valley. Most people simp walk around the lake. It's muddy in places, bu shouldn't take more than a couple of hours, in cluding a side-trip to an impressive waterfa

Our tip: saddle up! **Horse riding** is the be: way to soak up the drop-dead gorgeous scer ery. The **Ferme Équestre du Grand Étang** (☎ 026 50 90 03; www.ferme-equestre-grand-etang.fr in Frenc Pont Payet; half/full day €45/110; ☽ daily), just beyon

---

VANILLA UNVEILED

The vanilla orchid was introduced into Réunion from Mexico around 1820, but early attempts at cultivation failed because of the absence of the Mexican bee that pollinates the flower and triggers the development of the vanilla pod. Fortunately for custard lovers everywhere, a method of hand-pollination was discovered in Réunion in 1841 by a 12-year-old slave, Edmond Albius. Vanilla was highly prized in Europe at the time and Albius' discovery ushered in an economic boom, at least for the French 'vanilla barons'.

The vanilla bubble burst, however, when synthetic vanilla – made from coal – was invented in the late 19th century. Réunion's vanilla industry was almost wiped out, but in recent years the growing demand for natural products has led to something of a revival. You'll now find vanilla 'plantations' hidden in the forests from Ste-Suzanne south to St-Philippe.

The majority of Réunion's crop is exported (Coca Cola is the world's single biggest buyer), but vanilla is still a firm favourite in local cuisine. It crops up in all sorts of delicacies, from cakes and pastries to coffee, liqueurs, even vanilla duck and chicken. Best of all is the sublime flavour of a vanilla-steeped *rhum arrangé* (a mixture of rum, fruit juice, cane syrup and a blend of herbs and berries).

he turn-off to Grand Étang, arranges half-
lay treks to Grand Étang; the full-day trek
ncludes lunch. It's also possible to arrange
onger excursions to Bras Canot (two days),
Takamaka (three days) and around Piton de
a Fournaise (minimum three days). Ask for
Fanou, who can speak English.

WHITEWATER RAFTING
Réunion's best white water is found near St-
Benoît. The Rivière des Marsouins and the
Rivière du Mât offer magical white-water
experiences for both first-time runners and
easoned enthusiasts. A half-day excursion
will set you back €45.

Some companies specialising in rafting
rips in the area:
Cilaos Aventure (☎ 0692 66 73 42; www.cilaos
aventure.com in French)
Oasis Eaux Vives (☎ 0692 00 16 23; www.oasisev
.com in French)
Run Aventures (☎ 0262 64 08 22; www.runaventures
.com)

Sleeping & Eating
Hostellerie de la Confiance (☎ 0262 50 90 50; La Confiance; s/d €55/60; ❄ ⛺) The stables of this once
grand 18th-century Creole mansion surrounded by a 2-hectare garden of lush tropical vegetation have been converted into an
eight-room inn. Though the setting is superb,
he rooms are a tad long in the tooth. The restaurant (mains €13 to €19; open lunch Sunday
o Friday, dinner daily) overlooks the garden.
t's about 6km from St-Benoît along the road
owards Plaine-des-Palmistes.
Chambre d'hôtes L'Orangeraie (☎ 0262 50 97 60,
692 01 18 87; http://monsite.wanadoo.fr/orangeraie; d €47,
dinner €20) A good port of call if you want to
get away from it all. The rooms are ordinary
but the setting is fabulous – tropical plants
everywhere – and Madame is a good cook.
Much of the produce cooked up is straight
from the *potager* (veggie patch). At breakfast,
you can dip into six varieties of homemade
ams. Hmm, just thinking of the ginger jam
makes us lick our fingers! It's about 7km from
St-Benoît along the road towards Plaine-des-
Palmistes (take the RN3 in the direction of
Plaine-des-Palmistes and follow the signs
from the Ferme Équestre at Pont Payet).

Getting There & Away
From St-Benoît a scenic road (the RN3) cuts
across the Plaine-des-Palmistes to St-Pierre and
St-Louis on the far side of the island. Alternatively, you can continue south along the coast
road, passing through Ste-Anne, Ste-Rose, St-
Philippe and St-Joseph to reach St-Pierre.

St-Benoît is a major transport hub. Bus
services to and from St-Denis run approximately every half hour. There are also two
services linking St-Benoît and St-Pierre:
line H follows the RN3 over the Plaine-des-
Palmistes; line I takes the coast road via Ste-
Philippe and St-Joseph. In both cases there
are about four buses daily.

STE-ANNE
The village of Ste-Anne, about 5km south
along the coast from St-Benoît, is noted for
its surprisingly extravagant **church**. The façade
of the building is covered in stucco depic-
tions of fruit, flowers and angels. The overall
effect is flamboyant rather than tasteful, and
is reminiscent of the mestizo architecture of
the Andes in South America.

There's no beach in Ste-Anne, but if you
need to cool off, there's no better place than
Bassin Bleu, appropriately dubbed 'the lagoon
of the east', at the mouth of a river, on the
southern edge of town. It's a superb swimming spot, with crystal-clear water and big
boulders. Take a plunge! Take note that it's
mobbed at weekends.

If you need to recharge the batteries,
L'Auberge Créole (☎ 0262 51 10 10; 1 Chemin Case Ste-
Anne; mains €7-25; ✆ lunch daily except Wed, dinner daily
except Mon, Wed & Sun), not far from the church,
fits the bill, with an eclectic menu featuring
Creole, *métro* and Chinese dishes, as well as
wood-fired pizzas. Service is unpredictable.
Hint: take your order to go and eat under
vacoa trees at Bassin Bleu.

Between Ste-Anne and Ste-Rose is the
graceful **Pont des Anglais** suspension bridge
over the Rivière de l'Est, now bypassed by the
main highway but open to pedestrians. It was
claimed to be the longest suspension bridge
in the world at the time of its construction in
the late 19th century.

Ste-Anne is a stop on the coastal bus route
from St-Benoît to St-Pierre.

STE-ROSE & AROUND
pop 6600
South of St-Benoît, the landscape becomes
more open and less populated as the road
hugs the coast around Piton de la Fournaise,
the volcano which regularly spews lava down

its eastern flanks. The small fishing community of Ste-Rose has its harbour at the inlet of La Marine. There's a monument here to the young English commander Corbett, who was killed in 1809 during a naval battle against the French off the coast.

South of Ste-Rose the first tongues of lava from Piton de la Fournaise start to make their appearance.

Sights & Activities

Notre Dame des Laves is in **Piton Ste-Rose**, 4.5km south of Ste-Rose. The lava flow from a 1977 eruption went through the village, split when it came to the church and reformed again on the other side. Many people see the church's escape as a miracle of divine intervention. A wooden log 'washed up' by the lava now forms the lectern inside the church, while the stained-glass windows depict various stages of the eruption. Next to the church stands **La Vierge au Parasol**, a statue of the Virgin Mary optimistically holding an umbrella as protection against the volcano! A local planter set it up at the turn of the century in the hope of protecting his vanilla pods from volcanic hellfire and brimstone.

Anse des Cascades is beside the sea about 3km south of Piton Ste-Rose. The water from the hills drops dramatically into the sea near a traditional little fishing harbour. The coconut grove is splendid and is a hugely popular picnic spot.

Beyond Anse des Cascades, the main road continues south along the coast, climbs and then drops down to cross the 6km-wide volcanic plain known as Le Grand Brûlé (see p224).

Sleeping & Eating

STE-ROSE

Ferme-Auberge La Cayenne (☎ 0262 47 23 46; 317 Ravine Glissante; d incl breakfast €40-55, dinner €20) This well-run guesthouse scores points with its location – it's perched above the sea in La Ravine-Glissante, 1.5km south of Ste-Rose, which means lots of breeze and smashing views. Of the six rooms, the cheapest share communal toilets and have no views (not to mention the minuscule cubicle showers) – angle for a more expensive one. The owner, Madame Narayanin, cooks beautifully, using mostly home-grown ingredients. Let the breeze tickle your skin while you eat authentic cuisine alfresco on the covered terrace. The

only downside is the Roz d'Zil disco on the main road just behind La Cayenne; it can be a bit noisy on Friday and Saturday nights.

Chambre d'hôtes La Roseraye – Chez M Adam de Villiers (☎ 0262 47 21 33; 206 RN2, Ste-Rose; d €40-45 dinner €18) Another safe bet for the weary heat-drenched travellers: La Roseraye's most memorable features are the riot of greenery all round the sprawling property, the tastefully adorned rooms and the antiquated charm that wraps the place – it's a converted sugar-cane plantation. One weak point: some rooms are a bit close to the main road.

Hôtel-Restaurant La Fournaise (☎ 0262 47 03 40; www.hotellafournaise.fr; 154 RN2; s/d €40/65; 🅿 🚲) There's a fresh feel in this newish venture off the main road. Spruce rooms, shiny-clean toilets, colourful walls, air-con, an onsite restaurant and a pool are the order of the day here. The catch? It lacks charisma.

PITON STE-ROSE

Chambre d'hôtes Le Joyau des Laves (☎ 0262 47 34 00 www.joyaudeslaves.com in French; d €36-55; menus €11-25 🕑 lunch daily, dinner daily except Fri & Sun) On a headland 7km south of Ste-Rose, this is a comfortable *chambre d'hôte* run by a delightful young couple. Even if you're not staying, it's worth phoning ahead to eat in the restaurant and try local specialities such as palm hearts and *baba figues* (banana flowers) from the surrounding gardens.

Two pleasing eateries in the centre:

Les 2 Pitons de la Fournaise (☎ 0262 47 23 16; RN2; mains €8-16; 🕑 lunch & dinner) It's opposite the church – good to know if you feel guilty (of gluttony, that is).

Fleurs de Canne (☎ 0262 47 92 33; 43bis Lot Lacroix; mains €10-20; 🕑 lunch daily except Wed & Sat, dinner daily except Wed & Sun) A vast array of Creole and *métro* dishes await at this reputable eatery.

ANSE DES CASCADES

Restaurant des Cascades (☎ 0262 47 20 42; mains €10-20, menu €10; 🕑 9.30am-5.30pm daily except Fri) A local and tourist favourite, this ramshackle beach restaurant in a lovely coconut grove bursts to the seams on weekends. It serves fresh fish and Creole dishes as well as sandwiches. Nab a seat if it's not too busy, otherwise take your order to go and enjoy it in a quieter spot near the beach.

Getting There & Away

Buses running from St-Benoît to St-Pierre make handy stops near Notre Dame des Laves, Anse des Cascades and La Vierge au Parasol.

Hiking in Réunion

Now we're talking. Forget lounging on a white-sand beach on the west coast – hiking is *the* very best of what Réunion has to offer. The island is virtually unique in the Indian Ocean for offering both superb mountain scenery and excellent outdoor infrastructure, with more than a thousand kilometres of hiking trails, the best of which take you through an awe-inspiring landscape of jagged mountain crests, forested valleys, tumbling waterfalls and surreal volcanic tuff. Vast swathes of the interior of the island are accessible only by foot. As a result, the natural environment is remarkably intact, with a huge variety of flora, from tropical rainforest to gnarled thickets of giant heather. Formed from one mighty dead volcano (Piton des Neiges) and one very active volcano (Piton de la Fournaise), the island is a paradise for hikers, adventure-sports enthusiasts or indeed anyone who is receptive to the untamed beauty of a wilderness environment. The good news is you don't need to be a masochist to enjoy this walking wonderland. You needn't carry anything much heavier than a daypack; homely *gîtes* (lodges) and *chambres d'hôtes* (family-run B&Bs) are spaced at convenient distances along popular trails, offering simple accommodation and wholesome meals – sample a *rougail saucisses* (hearty sausage stew) in Cirque de Mafate and you'll know what we mean.

There are two major hiking trails, known as Grande Randonnée Route 1 (GR R1) and Grande Randonnée Route 2 (GR R2), with numerous offshoots. The GR R1 does a tour of Piton des Neiges, passing through Cilaos, the Forêt de Bébour-Bélouve, Hell-Bourg and the Cirque de Mafate. The GR R2 makes an epic traverse across the island all the way from St-Denis to St-Philippe via the three Cirques, the Plaine-des-Cafres and Piton de la Fournaise.

The trails are well maintained, but the tropical rainfall can eat through footpaths and wash away steps and handrails. Even experienced hikers should be prepared for tortuous ascents, slippery mud chutes, and narrow paths beside sheer precipices. The routes are well signposted on the whole, but it's essential to carry a good map and you should check locally on the current situation; trails are occasionally closed for maintenance, especially following severe storms.

The trails described in this section are popular hikes, though there are countless variations, and they should be well within the capabilities of any reasonably fit adult; children with a sense of adventure and a good head for heights should be able to do the walks with a little extra time.

If you don't have time for a multiday trek, there are also plenty of great day hikes that will give you a taste of life in rural Réunion – we've outlined some of them.

The hiking times given are for an average hiker carrying a light daypack and taking only brief breaks.

WHEN TO HIKE

The best time to hike is during the dry season, from around late April to the end of October; May and June, as well as September and October, are probably the best months of all. The weather is extremely changeable from one part of this small island to the other. For example, you can leave Col des Bœufs shrouded in mist and arrive at the village of La Nouvelle under a blazing sun.

The weather in Réunion has a tendency to become worse as the day goes on. As the hours pass, the island's uplands seem to delight in 'trapping' any cloud that happens to come their way. An early start is therefore one of the best defences against the vagaries of the elements.

The next day's weather forecast is shown on the two main TV channels after the evening news (generally around 8pm). You can also get the forecast by telephoning the **Météo France voice service** (☎ 0892 68 08 08; per min €0.30). Cyclone bulletins are available on ☎ 0897 65 01 01 (€0.51 per minute). Both these services are in French. Also check out the website www.meteo.fr/temps/domtom/La_Reunion (in French).

WHAT TO BRING

Good shoes are essential for hiking the trails of Réunion, which are made of gravel and stone and often very steep, muddy or slippery. Hiking shoes with good ankle support are better than sneakers. If you're overnighting, take a pair of sandals for the evening – your feet will thank you.

Be sure to carry water (at least 2L for a day's hiking), wet-weather gear, a warm top, a hat, sunscreen, sunglasses, insect repellent, a whistle, a torch and a basic medical kit including plasters (Band-Aids), elastic bandages and muscle balm for blisters and minor muscle injuries. If you intend sleeping out at altitude, you'll need a decent sleeping bag, as temperatures in the Cirques can fall rapidly at night. Although the *gîtes* provide sheets and blankets, a sheet sleeping bag (sleep sheet) wouldn't go amiss.

In most places to stay and places to eat, payment will be expected in cash, so bring a stash of euros with you. The only places to get euros in the Cirques are the ATMs at the post offices in Salazie and Cilaos, and these can't be depended on.

> **HIKING TIPS**
>
> Safety is basically a matter of common sense and being prepared. Remember to do the following:
>
> - use a detailed and up-to-date map
> - double-check the state of the paths before setting out
> - check the weather report before setting out
> - leave early enough to reach your destination before dark
> - take plenty of water and energy-rich snacks
> - wear comfortable hiking boots
> - take wet-weather gear
> - carry a basic medical kit
> - tell people where you're going if you are hiking alone

You will be able to buy most last-minute supplies at a sporting-goods store or one of the big supermarkets in Réunion as well as in Cilaos.

INFORMATION SOURCES

Hiking information is provided by the headquarters of the **Maison de la Montagne et de la Mer** (Map pp170-1; ☎ 0262 90 78 78; www.reunion-nature .com in French; 5 Rue Rontaunay; ☽ 9am-5pm Mon-Thu, 9am-4pm Fri) in St-Denis and by associated tourist offices, including those in Cilaos, Salazie, Hell-Bourg, St-Gilles-les-Bains, St-Pierre, St-Leu and Bourg-Murat. All these offices organise bookings for *gîtes de montagne* (mountain lodges) and can give advice as to which paths are currently closed. They also provide guides and arrange hiking tours.

By far the most useful website for hikers is that of the Maison de la Montagne et de la Mer (see above). It allows you to book *gîtes de montagne* online and buy maps and guides, and also has general information about hiking in Réunion, including brief details of the most popular walks, places to buy food in the Cirques and so forth. The information is not always up-to-date, however, so double-check on the ground.

The website http://runrando.free.fr (in French) is also useful.

For information on *état des sentiers* (closed trails), phone the voice service at ☎ 0262 37 38 39 (in French).

The **Fédération Française de la Randonnée Pédestre** (FFRP; www.ffrandonnee.fr) is responsible for the development and upkeep of the GR walking tracks.

MAPS

Réunion is covered by the six 1:25,000 scale maps published by the **Institut Géographique National** (IGN; www.ign.fr in French). These maps are reasonably up-to-date and show trails and *gîtes*. Map number 4402 RT is one of the most useful for hikers, since it covers Cirque de Mafate and Cirque de Salazie as well as the northern part of the Cirque de Cilaos. It also covers the whole of the GR R1. For Piton de la Fournaise (the volcano), use map number 4406 RT. The maps are sold all over the island, including at the Maison de la Montagne et de la Mer in St-Denis.

BOOKS

Several excellent route guides are available at the Maison de la Montagne et de la Mer. Though only in French, they are still useful for their maps.

The definitive guide to the GR R1 and GR R2 is the *Topo-guide GR* Grande randonnée L'île de la Réunion* (2006), published by the FFRP. It uses 1:25,000 scale IGN maps and includes eight one-day hikes of varying lengths and degrees of difficulty. The FFRP also publishes the *Topo-guide PR* Sentiers forestiers de L'île de la Réunion* (2007).

Published locally by Orphie, *52 Balades et Randonnées Faciles* is designed with children in mind and describes outings that can be covered in less than four hours. A broader range of walks is covered by *62 Randonnées Réunionnaises* (also by Orphie). The loose-leaf format, with one walk per page, is extremely practical.

For the volcano area and the Wild South, nothing can beat the excellent *Le Guide du Piton de la Fournaise* by Jean-Luc Allègre.

TOURS & GUIDES

Réunion's hiking trails are well established and reasonably well signposted, but you may get more information about the environment you are walking through if you go with a local guide. The Maison de la Montagne et de la Mer publishes *La Réunion: une*

Île Grandeur Nature, which lists organised adventure trips on the island. Alternatively, contact one of the following operators.

Fully qualified mountain guides can be contacted through the Maison de la Montagne et de la Mer and local tourist offices (see opposite). Rates are negotiable and vary according to the length and degree of difficulty of the hike; an undemanding one-day outing should start at around €120 for a group of five people.

Alpanes (☎ 0692 77 75 30; www.alpanes.com in French)

Austral Aventure (☎ 0262 32 40 29; www.creole.org /austral-aventure; Rue Amiral Lacaze, Hell-Bourg)

Maham (☎ 0262 47 87 87, 0692 86 50 67; www .randoneereunion.com in French; Rue Général de Gaulle, Hell-Bourg)

Rando Run (☎ 0262 26 31 31; www.randorun.com in French)

Run Évasion (☎ 0262 31 83 57; www.runevasion.fr in French; 23 Rue du Père Boiteau, Cilaos)

SLEEPING & EATING

Most of the accommodation for hikers consists of *gîtes de montagne* (mostly found in isolated locations on the trails themselves) or of privately run *gîtes d'étape* along the walking trails. Both offer dorm beds and meals. There's often very little to separate the two types of *gîte* in terms of comfort or facilities. Showers are often solar heated and are rarely piping hot; some places can be downright cold at night. A third option consists of small, family-run *chambres d'hôtes* (mostly found in the villages at the ends of the hiking trails). Your choice of where to stay will most likely be based on where you can find a room. There are also a few hotels in Hell-Bourg and Cilaos for that last night of luxury (and central heating) before you set out on your hike. See p245 for more information on accommodation and costs in Réunion.

Many visitors from mainland France book their accommodation before arriving in Réunion, so don't make the mistake of leaving it to the last minute. During July and August and around Christmas it's hard to find a bed in the Cirques for love or money. At other times it's best to book at least a couple of months in advance, particularly for popular places such as the *gîtes* at Caverne Dufour (for Piton des Neiges) and Piton de la Fournaise.

The *gîtes de montagne* are managed by the Maison de la Montagne et de la Mer and must be booked and paid for in advance. This can be done at the Maison de la Montagne et de la Mer in St-Denis (or through its website) and at certain tourist offices (see p232). Most of these offices accept credit cards, though check beforehand to be sure this is the case. When you pay, you will receive a voucher to be given to the manager of the *gîte* where you will be staying. You must call the *gîte* to book your meals at least two days in advance; this can be done at the same time as the original booking if you'd rather, but meals still have to paid for on the spot. For the privately owned *gîtes*, it is less restrictive in terms of logistics; you can book directly through the *gîte*.

If all this organisation doesn't fit in with your idea of adventure, you can camp for free in some areas in the Cirques, but only for one night at a time. Popular spots in the Cirque de Mafate include Trois Roches on the GR R2 between Marla and Roche-Plate; Le Grand Sable on the GR R1 near Le Bélier; Plaine des Tamarins on the GR R1 near La Nouvelle; and at the *gîte* at Bébour-Bélouve, on the Cirque de Salazie's rim. Setting up camp on Piton de la Fournaise (the volcano) is forbidden for obvious reasons.

Most *gîtes* offer Creole meals, which are normally hearty, though a little rustic for some palates. The standard fare is *carri poulet* (chicken curry), *boucané* (smoked pork) or *rougail saucisses*, often with local wine or *rhum arrangé* (rum punch) thrown in. Breakfast usually consists of just a cup of coffee with bread and jam.

If you plan to self-cater, you will need to bring plenty of carbohydrate-rich food. Instant noodles are light and filling, while chocolate and other sugary snacks can provide the energy necessary to make it up that last mountain ridge. There are cooking facilities at a few *gîtes*, but you are best off bringing a camping stove; note that you are not allowed to light fires anywhere in the forest areas. Some villages in the Cirques have shops where you can purchase a very limited variety of food; few places stock anything more wholesome than biscuits, processed cheese and canned sardines.

THE HAUT MAFATE

Duration	4 days
Distance	20.4km
Difficulty	moderate
Start/Finish	Col des Bœufs car park
Nearest Town	Grand Îlet (p205)

Surrounded by ramparts, crisscrossed with gullies and studded with narrow ridges, Cirque de Mafate (p206) is the wildest and most remote of Réunion's Cirques. The following itinerary takes you through some of the most scenic parts of the Cirque in four days. Cirque de Mafate is only accessible on foot, but a forestry road runs up to the pass at Col des Bœufs between Cirque de Mafate and the Cirque de Salazie. The other main routes into Mafate are from Cilaos via the Col du Taïbit (2082m); along the banks of the Rivière des Galets from Dos d'Ane or Sans Souci; and via Le Maïdo, which involves a precipitous descent into Roche-Plate. Most people take the easy option and hop over the ridge at Col des Bœufs.

This hike can also be combined with the Tour des Cirques (see p238).

GETTING TO/FROM THE HIKE

There is no regular public transport to the beginning of the hike. From Grand Îlet, you'll have to hitch a ride to Col des Bœufs car park. If you drive, take note that secure parking is available at the car park, but you'll have to fork out €10 per day.

Day 1: Col des Bœufs Car Park to La Nouvelle
2hr, 4.5km, 520m descent

The trail to La Nouvelle starts at the car park at **Col des Bœufs**, from where you'll get your first glimpse of the Cirque de Mafate (and what a glimpse!). Ahead, GR R1 plunges steeply to the forested **Plaine des Tamarins**. At the time of writing, the Col des Bœufs was temporarily closed; if it's still the case by the time your read this, you can use the **Col de Fourche**, about 15 minutes further south (a purpose-built path has been established between Col des Bœufs and Col de Fourche). The *tamarin des Hauts* (mountain tamarind trees) are cloaked in a yellowish lichen called *barbe de capucins* (monks' beard), and the low cloud often creates a slightly spooky

ECO-WALKING

To help preserve the ecology and beauty of Réunion, consider these tips when hiking.

Rubbish

- Carry out all your rubbish. Don't overlook easily forgotten items, such as silver paper, orange peel, cigarette butts and plastic wrappers. Empty packaging should be stored in a dedicated rubbish bag. Make an effort to carry out rubbish left by others.

- Never bury your rubbish: digging disturbs soil and ground cover and encourages erosion. Buried rubbish will likely be dug up by animals, who may be injured or poisoned by it. It may also take years to decompose.

- Minimise waste by taking minimal packaging and no more food than you will need. Take reusable containers or stuff sacks.

- Sanitary products, condoms and toilet paper should be carried out despite the inconvenience. They burn and decompose poorly.

Human Waste Disposal

- Contamination of water sources by human faeces can lead to the transmission of all sorts of nasties. Where there is a toilet, use it. Where there is none, bury your waste. Cover the waste with soil and a rock.

Erosion

- Hillsides and mountain slopes, especially at high altitudes, are prone to erosion. Stick to existing tracks and avoid short cuts.

- If a well-used track passes through a mud patch, walk through the mud so as not to increase the size of the patch.

- Avoid removing any plant life – it keeps the topsoil in place.

atmosphere like something from Tolkien's *The Lord of the Rings*.

Follow the path signposted to La Nouvelle (the other branch heads south to Marla), which meanders through the forest in a fairly leisurely fashion before dropping rapidly to the village of **La Nouvelle**. There are some fabulous views of **Le Grand Bénare** on the Cirque rim to the south as you descend.

La Nouvelle used to be a cattle-raising centre, but tourism has very much taken over as the village's main source of income. The village has several shops, a school, an interesting shingle-roofed chapel and, unique in the Cirque, a (solar-powered) payphone; you'll need a phonecard to use it.

La Nouvelle is well endowed with *gîtes d'étape* (see p207 for details). It also boasts a bakery and no fewer than three groceries where you can buy basic provisions.

Day 2: La Nouvelle to Roche-Plate via Le Bronchard

4½hr, 4.7km, 320m ascent, 730m descent

The trail to Grand Place, Cayenne and Roche-Plate via Le Bronchard turns downhill just after the La Nouvelle chapel and heads into the maize fields before plummeting into the valley of the **Rivière des Galets**. This steep and often treacherous descent is not for the fainthearted, though reassuring handrails are provided for some of the steeper sections.

To make up for the risk, the views are to die for (figuratively speaking!) and an exhilarating two hours or so will get you to the bottom of the Cirque, where you can take a well-deserved splash in the river. When you've recovered your energies, ford the river and start the arduous ascent up the far side of the valley.

When you reach the white metal cross at **Le Bronchard**, the worst is over. The final stretch descends not into the ravine as it first appears, but slowly down to the village of **Roche-Plate**. Ignore the turn-off to Marla, Trois Roches and La Nouvelle, which branches off to the left as you enter the village. The village of Roche-Plate sits at the foot of the majestic **Le Maïdo** (2205m). You'll find two *gîtes* in Roche-Plate (see p207 for details).

Day 3: Roche-Plate to Marla via Trois Roches

5½hr, 6.8km, 910m ascent, 330m descent

The trail to Marla via Trois Roches begins where the trail from La Nouvelle enters Roche-Plate. The first section rises steadily through a dry landscape with *choka* (an agave species). Towering overhead are the peaks of Le Grand Bénare and Le Gros Morne. Apart from one significant drop, the path stays fairly level before descending to the waterfall at **Trois Roches** (about 2¾ hours from Roche-Plate).

THE HAUT MAFATE & TOUR DES CIRQUES

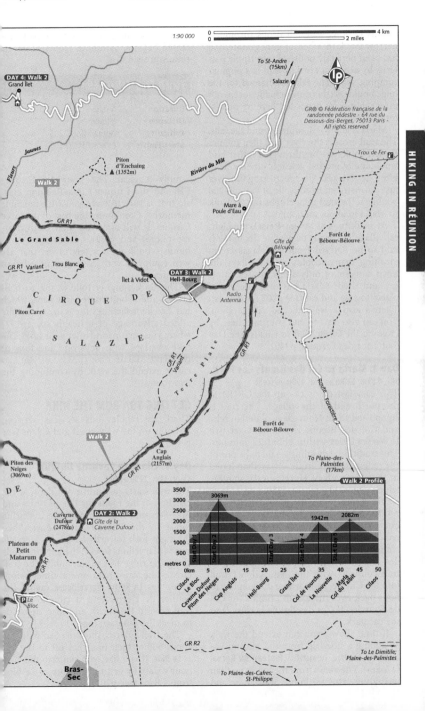

1:90 000

0   4 km
0   2 miles

To St-Andre (15km)

Salazie

Trou de Fer

DAY 4: Walk 2
Grand Îlet

Piton d'Enchaing
▲ (1352m)

Rivière du Mât

Fleurs Jaunes

Walk 2

Mare à Poule d'Eau

Forêt de Bébour-Bélouve

GR R1

Gîte de Bélouve

Le Grand Sable

GR R1 Variant   Trou Blanc

DAY 3: Walk 2
Hell-Bourg

Îlet à Vidot

Radio Antenna

CIRQUE DE

Piton Carré

SALAZIE

GR R1 Variant

GR R1

Terre Plate

Forêt de Bébour-Bélouve

Route Forestière 2

Walk 2

Cap Anglais (2157m)

To Plaine-des-Palmistes (17km)

▲ Piton des Neiges (3069m)

GR R1

Caverne Dufour (2478m)

DAY 2: Walk 2
Gîte de la Caverne Dufour

DE

Plateau du Petit Matarum

GR R1

Le Bloc

Walk 2 Profile

metres	
3500	
3000	3069m
2500	
2000	1942m 2082m
1500	
1000	
500	
0	

Start Day 2   Start Day 3   Start Day 4   Start Day 5

0km   5   10   15   20   25   30   35   40   45   50

Cilaos   Le Bloc   Caverne Dufour / Piton des Neiges   Cap Anglais   Hell-Bourg   Grand Îlet   Col de Fourche   La Nouvelle   Mafate / Col du Tabit   Cilaos

Bras-Sec

GR R2

To Le Dimitile; Plaine-des-Palmistes

To Plaine-des-Cafres; St-Philippe

This curious waterfall drops through a narrow crack in a bed of grey granite that has been perfectly polished into ripple patterns by aeons of erosion, and is a popular camping spot. The falls are named for the huge boulders (there are actually seven, not three) that were deposited here by prehistoric torrents.

Marla is about 2¾ hours beyond the falls. The trail crosses the river and then follows the left bank, passing through a rather arid landscape of eroded volcanic cinders from Piton des Neiges. After recrossing the river just downstream from a pile of vast alluvial boulders, the trail then climbs the far bank to Marla in about an hour.

At an altitude of 1640m, **Marla** is the highest village in Cirque de Mafate. Its name is said to be derived from a Malagasy term meaning 'many people', but these days, the town consists of only a few houses. Hungry and tired? Marla has a smattering of places to stay and eat (see p207 for details). There's also a well-stocked village shop. You can also elect to end your hike here by crossing the **Col du Taïbit** to Cilaos (see Day 5 of Tour des Cirques, p240).

Day 4: Marla to Col des Bœufs Car Park
3hr, 4.8km, 540m ascent, 190m descent
This easy last day picks up the GR R1 at the north end of the village. The trail is signposted to La Nouvelle, Col de Fourche and Col des Bœufs, and should get you to **Maison Laclos** within about 20 minutes. This traditional dwelling – said to be one of the oldest in the Cirque – was abandoned in the aftermath of Hurricane Hyacinthe, which came through in 1980, and is now a ruin. From there, the main GR R1 trail returns to La Nouvelle, but you can cut out some distance by taking the right-hand fork, a GR R1 variant, which cuts straight back up (northward) to the Plaine des Tamarins (allow about one hour). This trail connects with the main GR R1 trail into the Cirque, from where it's roughly an hour back over the Col des Bœufs (or Col de Fourche, if Col des Bœufs is closed) to the car park.

If time allows, you can extend the walk by adding a side trip from the Maison Laclos up to the beautiful **Plateau du Kerval** (1768m). The views from the top more than justify the extra 1½ hours' walk there and

back. At the time of writing the path wa closed but it should have reopened by the time you read this.

TOUR DES CIRQUES

Duration	5 days
Distance	51.5km
Difficulty	demanding
Start/Finish	Cilaos (p197)

Simply magical. The Tour des Cirques ('Round the Cirques') is a Réunion classic that is sure to leave you with indelible memories. Combining the best of the three Cirques, it will offer you three distinct atmospheres and various landscapes. As a bonus, you'll cross a few towns that are well equipped with cosy accommodation facilities.

The walk roughly follows the path of GR R1 and is best started in Cilaos, which has excellent facilities for walkers and the added advantage of a health spa (p197) where you can unwind after your hike. The hike overlaps with days one and four of the Haut Mafate hike (p234), so you can easily extend the walk by combining the two routes.

GETTING TO/FROM THE HIKE
There are regular bus services between St-Louis on the west coast and Cilaos (see p201).

Day 1: Cilaos to Caverne Dufour
4½hr, 5km, 1290 ascent
The trail starts just north of Cilaos, at the junction of the roads for Îlet à Cordes and Bras-Sec, and rises through the casuarina forest to the Plateau des Chênes. Take the right fork towards La Roche Merveilleuse (Marvellous Rock); the left fork leads along the ridge to Col du Taïbit. The trail crosses the forest road several times before it reaches **La Roche Merveilleuse** (avoid the Sentier de Découverte, a circular nature trail around the rock), and then descends to meet the Bras-Sec road.

The trail follows the Bras-Sec road for about 500m, then branches off to the left at **Le Bloc**. If you like, you can skip this first hour's walk by getting a bus up to Le Bloc from Cilaos (see p201).

From Le Bloc, the path climbs steadily through a forest of cryptomeria (a cedarlike tree) to the **Plateau du Petit Matarum**, where the forest changes to stunted giant heather bushes (known as *branles* or *brandes*), cloaked in wisps of lichen. It's uphill all the way from here to the *gîte*. Once you gain the saddle, there's a turn-off on the right to the Col de Bébour and Le Dimitile, and a short distance further on, you'll come to the **Gîte de la Caverne Dufour** (☎ 0262 21 15 26; dm €14.50, breakfast/dinner €5/14) at nearly 2500m. Though still pretty rustic, this *gîte de montagne* now boasts inside toilets and (cold) showers. You'll need to bring plenty of warm clothes and remember to book well in advance through Maison de la Montagne et de la Mer (p232); even with 48 beds, it's often packed out.

Day 2: Caverne Dufour to Hell-Bourg via Piton des Neiges
7hr, 11km, 600m ascent, 2140 descent

Because the summit of Piton des Neiges is usually cloaked in cloud by mid-morning, most people choose to stay overnight at the Gîte de la Caverne Dufour, starting out for the peak at, or even before, dawn. The path begins directly opposite the *gîte* and is clearly marked in white on the rock face, but you should bring a torch (flashlight) if you start out before dawn. The climb takes about three hours return.

The landscape becomes increasingly rocky the higher you climb, and the final section rises steeply over shifting cinders that make for slippery footing. At the summit there are few traces of vegetation, and the red, black and ochre rock leaves little doubt about the mountain's volcanic origins. On a clear day, the whole island is spread out beneath you. If you didn't beat the cloud to the summit, you may just be confronted by an enveloping cloak of white.

Back at the Caverne Dufour, the trail to Hell-Bourg (six hours) runs north across the saddle and skirts the rim of the Cirque de Salazie, passing through giant heather forest. It's a bit of a mud chute, so watch your footing. After 1½ hours you'll reach a white-painted cross at **Cap Anglais**, from where there are excellent views over the Cirque de Salazie. If you just want some creature comforts, you can take the GR R1

variant straight downhill from here to the southern end of Hell-Bourg (3½ hours), emerging near the stadium and the trout farm.

More interesting is the walk along the Cirque rim through the lush **Forêt de Bébour-Bélouve**. Just beyond the turn-off, the trail begins a series of slippery ascents and descents through a marshy area of heather forest. Anchored metal ladders and wooden boardwalks are provided to help you over the boggiest sections. Once you start to see ferns among the trees, the worst is over.

From here, the trail enters an enchanted tropical forest, with primordial ferns and huge trees draped in sheets of moss. The woods suddenly seem to come alive with the sound of birdsong. Walking is easier through this lush area, and plaques describe some of the wildlife you are seeing and hearing. Around four hours from Cap Anglais you'll reach a radio antenna on the lip of the Cirque. This point offers spectacular views over Hell-Bourg and plenty of photo opportunities.

Following the gravel forest road for another kilometre, you'll come to the comfortable and beautifully situated **Gîte de Bélouve** (see p212). If you've got the time, you could overnight here and the following day take a side trip to the Trou de Fer (p243) before hitting the bright lights of Hell-Bourg.

The final descent to **Hell-Bourg** from the Gîte de Bélouve takes around two hours. Cut through the garden of the *gîte* and bear left at the lookout. You emerge in Hell-Bourg by the park on Rue Général de Gaulle. Treat yourself to a meal and a hot shower when you arrive! (For information on places to stay and eat in Hell-Bourg, see p203.)

Day 3: Hell-Bourg to Grand Îlet
6hr, 11km

Start this day's walk by taking the track at the end of Rue Général de Gaulle in Hell-Bourg to the thermal-bath ruins (see Map p203); this track connects with the Îlet à Vidot road, which will take you to the car park in Îlet à Vidot.

From the car park, a dirt road descends into the valley, reaching a turn-off on the left to Trou Blanc after about 500m. Ignore this turn-off and continue straight ahead, passing a turning on the right to Piton d'Enchaing. The track ascends rather uneventfully for the next 1½ hours, crossing several ravines, before skirting along the edge of a large plantation of casuarina trees at Le Grand Sable. The trail then drops down to cross one of the tributaries of the Rivière des Fleurs Jaunes. There's an excellent bivouac on the far bank where the trail to Le Bélier (a GR R1 variant) strikes off to the right through the woods. Allow about three hours from Hell-Bourg to reach this point.

From there, take the GR R1 variant, following signs down to Le Bélier. You should reach the road at Le Bélier after 1½ to two hours. From there it's less than an hour's walk downhill to Grand Îlet, where you'll find grocers, a bread shop and overnight accommodation, including comfortable *chambre d'hôtes* (see p205).

Day 4: Grand Îlet to La Nouvelle
6hr, 12km, 900m ascent, 520 descent

The day begins with a slog back uphill to Le Bélier and then on up the *route forestière* (forest road) to the Col des Bœufs; allow around 3½ hours to the top. Alternatively, you can spare yourself the first hour's walk by taking the bus from Grand Îlet to Le Bélier, or even get a ride up to Col des Bœufs car park just below the summit (see p206). At the time of writing the Col des Bœufs was temporarily closed; if it's still the case by the time you read this, use the Col de Fourche (see The Haut Mafate, Day 1, p234).

From the Col des Bœufs it's an easy 2½-hour hike to **La Nouvelle**. This is the same as the first day of the Haut Mafate walk, crossing the atmospheric Plaine des Tamarins and descending on the far side to the village of La Nouvelle. (For more information on this part of the route, see p234.)

A more attractive, but also more demanding alternative to the hike from Le Bélier to the Col des Bœufs is to take the GR R1 variant signed to 'La Nouvelle via Col de Fourche'. The trail branches left off the *route forestière* about one hour's walk above Le Bélier. The ascent to the Col de Fourche takes about 2½ hours, and it's then another 20-minute walk to where you meet the path from the Col des Bœufs.

Day 5: La Nouvelle to Cilaos
6hr, 12.5km, 620m ascent, 870m descent

This final day will take you back to the modern comforts of Cilaos, passing through some stunning countryside on the way.

The first section is a fairly easy two-hour walk to Marla via **Maison Laclos** (a former Creole house, destroyed following a cyclone in 2002), beginning with a steep descent into the Ravine Gérien and passing some nice views of the Cirque. Be sure to ignore the trails signed off to 'Marla par passerelle' and to the 'Plaine aux Sables'.

Marla consists only of a few houses, but the village shop sells snacks and drinks (for more information on Marla, see p206). From here, ignore paths off to the right for Trois Roches and Roche-Plate, but keep heading south towards the reservoir. The trail ascends steadily towards the obvious low point on the ridge, reaching **Col du Taïbit** in about 1½ hours. If you reach this viewpoint early in the morning, there are magnificent views over the Cirque de Mafate, and down the Cirque de Cilaos to St-Louis and the coast.

The trail (GR R1/R2) descends slowly to the plateau at **Îlet des Salazes**, before dropping steeply through drier country to cross the Îlet à Cordes road after about two hours. You could always pick up a lift or a bus to Cilaos here, but die-hards should continue across the road and descend into the valley. The trail divides just beyond. The easier and prettier option is to take the right fork, following the GR R2 along the west bank of the Bras de Étangs. It crosses the river near the Cascade de Bras Rouge and then climbs gradually to come out at the Thermes de Cilaos. From there you can take a short-cut up the Sentier des Porteurs for the final ascent into town.

Depending on how you feel, you could stop off at the spa in Cilaos for a massage.

EMERGENCIES

In a real emergency out on the trail, lifting both arms to form a 'V' is a signal to helicopter pilots who fly over the island that you need help. If you have a mobile phone, call the emergency services on ☎ 112 or ☎ 0262 93 09 30. *Gîtes de montagne* (mountain lodges) have telephones with which you can contact emergency services.

r hit one of the restaurants in town for a
vell-earned Bourbon beer!

PITON DE LA FOURNAISE

Duration	5½ hours
Distance	10.5km
Difficulty	moderate
Ascent	1000m
Descent	250m
Start/Finish	Pas de Bellecombe
Nearest Town	Bourg-Murat (p208)

Now is your chance to get up close and
personal with one of the world's most
active volcanoes (it was erupting at the
time of writing) – Piton de la Fournaise
Map p196). Réunion's iconic feature, this
smouldering volcano is simply a must-do
for walkers. The scenery is eerily lunar,
and it could form a perfect backdrop for a
new version of *Mad Max*.

The walk to the summit can get very
busy, but the fascinating tortured landscape more than makes up for the crowds
of people. Most people simply walk up to
the two central craters, along their northern rims and back again (about three and
a half hours), but it's worth continuing all
the way round to appreciate the monster
in its full grandeur (allow an extra two
hours).

GETTING TO/FROM THE HIKE

For those with a vehicle, getting to the
volcano couldn't be easier because of the
all-weather Route Forestière du Volcan,
which climbs 30km from Bourg-Murat all
the way to Pas de Bellecombe on the crater's
outer rim. On the way it passes a superb
lookout over the Rivière des Remparts just
below Nez de Bœuf (2135m) and crosses
the eerie landscape of the Plaine des Sables
(see p211).

Without your own car, the 5½-hour
hike to the volcano from Bourg-Murat via
the Sentier Josémont (GR R2) is regarded
as something of a walk for masochists, as
it's easy to pick up a ride along the Route
Forestière du Volcan instead.

THE HIKE

While the volcano walk is popular, it
shouldn't be taken lightly. The landscape
here is harsh and arid, despite the mist that
can drench hikers to the skin. The chilly
wind whips away moisture, leaving walkers
dehydrated and breathless. At times it can
feel like you are walking on Mars, with only
the dry crunch of the cinders underfoot for
company.

Early morning is the best time to climb
the volcano, as you stand a better chance
of clear views, but this is when everyone
else hits the trail as well. The path from the
ridge across the lava plain can resemble a
trail of ants, with hundreds of walkers all
heading for the peak at the same time.

Many people get a head start by staying
at the **Gîte du Volcan** (see p211) and leave at
the crack of dawn, so be sure to book well
in advance.

The *gîte* is a 15-minute walk from the **Pas
de Bellecombe**, where the Sentier du Volcan
starts in earnest by plunging 527 steps to
the floor of the immense U-shaped outer
crater, known as **Enclos Foucqué**. The route
across the lava plain is marked with white
paint spots. The liquid origin of the rocks
is quite apparent here – it's like walking on
solidified cake-mix. As you make your way
across the lava formations, be mindful of
the endless snags.

On the way, you'll pass a small scoria
cone, **Formica Leo**, and a cavern in the lava
known as Chapelle de Rosemont. From
here, the right-hand path climbs steeply
and directly to the 2632m-high, 200m-wide
Bory Crater, while the left fork takes a more
gradual route up the northern wall of the
gaping 900m-wide **Dolomieu Crater**.

Once at the top, you can decide whether
to do the circuit around both craters or just
traverse the track that connects the Bory
and Dolomieu Craters along their northern
rims. While walking along the rim, watch
out for large fissures, holes and, most of all,
overhangs. Leave the way you came – there
are no safe routes across the lava flows to
the southeast.

Until 2007, all the action had taken place
in the smaller craters on the south and east
flanks of the volcano. But early 2007, the
Dolomieu Crater collapsed by 300m. Scientists keep a close watch on the volcano's
moods, and are poised to issue warnings if
things look to be gathering steam. At the first
sign of an eruption, the paths around the volcano and the road up to it will be closed.

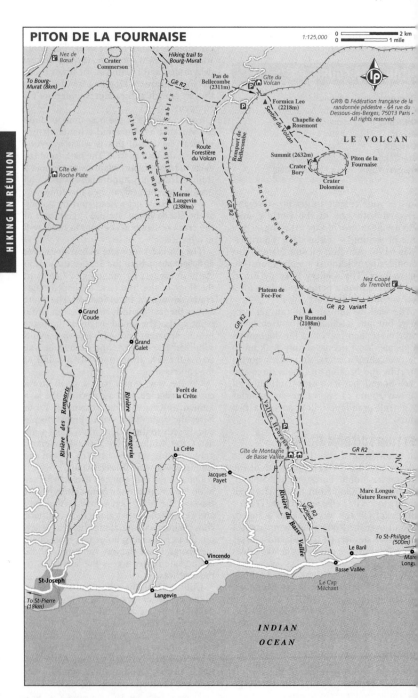

PITON DE LA FOURNAISE

1:125,000

MORE HIKES

For more suggestions of hikes on the island, see the Réunion chapter (p168).

TROU DE FER

This trail starts beside the Gîte de Bélouve (see p212) and takes you across a plateau covered in tamarind forests to a magnificent viewpoint overlooking the lost valley of Trou de Fer. It makes an easy three-hour return trip from the *gîte* or a more challenging hike from Hell-Bourg (allow 6½ hours total walking time). The path is well signed but after heavy rain it can get very muddy across the plateau. Carry IGN's 1:25,000 topographic map number 4402 RT.

PITON D'ENCHAING

This soaring 1356m peak is a popular but very challenging day hike from Hell-Bourg (see p203).

To get to the peak, follow the GR R1 through Îlet à Vidot and fork right when the trail divides (the left fork for Trou Blanc is currently closed). A short distance further on, the trail to Piton d'Enchaing branches off to the right. Allow about 2½ hours each way from Hell-Bourg. The IGN's 1:25,000 topographic map number 4402 RT shows the route.

LA ROCHE ÉCRITE

This 2277m peak offers a spectacular view of the Cirque de Mafate and it's conveniently close to St-Denis. Like the higher Piton des Neiges, it is often obscured by clouds by about 10am, so start very early – it would be a crime to miss out on the stupendous views.

There are several possible routes to the peak. The most popular option takes you along the GR R2 from the car park at the end of the forest road (RF1) 5.5km above Le Brûlé to the *gîte de montagne* at Plaine des Chicots (two hours), then on to Caverne des Soldats, through huge slabs of lava and limestone, and up the summit (1½ hours). You can then either return the same way or strike west from the *gîte de montagne* along the Cirque rim to Dos d'Ane (p177); allow four hours for the descent.

From the summit it's possible to drop down via a precipitous path to Grand Îlet in the Cirque de Salazie and cross over into Mafate via the Col des Bœufs.

IGN's 1:25,000 topographic map 4402 RT covers the area.

LE DIMITILE

We love Le Dimitile (1837m). The phenomenal views over the Cirque de Cilaos, the atmosphere and the varied vegetation lend to this summit a palpable aura. Or it could well be due to its historical significance; *marrons* (runaway slaves) took refuge in the area in the late 19th century. From Entre-Deux (p194), there are several options to reach the summit. The shortest route starts from the end of the D26, at an altitude of 1100m (about three hours return). There are two *gîtes* near the summit (p195). Carry IGN's 1:25,000 topographic map number 4405 RT.

THE BAS MAFATE (LOWER MAFATE)

After a loop in the Haut Mafate (see p234), you might want to explore the Bas Mafate, which is even more secluded (and this is saying a lot) and less 'touristy' than Haut Mafate. A three-day hike starting at Bord Martin on the Route Forestière leading up to Col des Bœufs car park takes in Îlet à Malheur, Aurère, Îlet à Bourse, Grand Place, Cayenne, Îlet des Orangers and Roche-Plate. From Roche-Plate, you can connect with the Haut Mafate itinerary.

THE RIVIÈRE DES REMPARTS

The stunning gorge of the Rivière des Remparts to St-Joseph is a magnet for walkers. The total walking time is about 10 hours, but you can break the journey halfway at the excellent Gîte de Roche Plate (see p221).

The trail starts just north of the Nez de Bœuf viewpoint on the road to the volcano (see p210), branching left off the GR R2 some 8km west of the Gîte du Volcan. The initial descent is precipitous, but once past Roche-Plate, it's a gentle hike along the river to the sea. Use IGN's 1:25,000 topographic map *Piton de la Fournaise* (map number 4406 RT).

THE DESCENT OF THE VOLCANO

The quickest hiking route down the volcano is the GR R2 to Bourg-Murat (five hours), but there are more challenging and interesting options that take two days and require another early start, so you may need to spend a second night in the Gîte du Volcan. For more information about these trails, consult the Maison de la Montagne et de la Mer (p232) or the tourist office at Bourg-Murat. The following option follows the Vallée Heureuse, one of the most spectacular valleys in southern Réunion.

Heading south from the Gîte du Volcan, the GR R2 runs along the west rim of the Enclos Foucqué and then veers due south through Plateau de Foc-Foc and skirts west of the Vallée Heureuse before dropping abruptly to the Rivière de Basse Vallée (6½ hours). From here it's only about an hour straight down the valley to the coast on a GR R2 variant. Alternatively, you can overnight at the Gîte de Montagne de Basse Vallée (p223) and follow the GR R2 eastwards to descend via the dense woods of the Mare Longue Nature Reserve (four hours). It brings you out a couple of kilometres west of St-Philippe. Then it's a 20-minute walk on the main road to the centre of St-Philippe.

The route is covered by IGN's 1:25,000 topographic map *Piton de la Fournaise* (map number 4406 RT).

Réunion Directory

CONTENTS

ACCOMMODATION

While accommodation in Réunion might not reach the stellar heights of Mauritius and Seychelles, there is still plenty of choice. The smarter hotels tend to be concentrated around the coast and in the attractive mountain towns of Cilaos and Hell-Bourg. In the midrange bracket, there's a smattering of small, family hotels and lots of *chambres d'hôtes* (B&Bs), the best of which offer excellent value for money. Budget travellers will find it hard to keep costs down in St-Denis and the coastal towns around St-Gilles-les-Bains, but elsewhere youth hostels, *gîtes* and the cheaper *chambres d'hôtes* fit the bill. Generally, for a double room you can expect to pay under €40 for budget accommodation, between €40 to €100 for midrange, and over €100 for top-end accommodation.

It is wise to book well in advance, particularly in high season (the mainland France and local school holidays, particularly July and August and around Christmas), when the best places fill up weeks, if not months, ahead.

Recommendations under Sleeping entries are in ascending order of price.

Camping

Bad news for those who want to spend their holiday under canvas: there's only one official camp site, on the southwest coast at Étang-Salé-les-Bains.

However, you can camp for free in some designated areas in the Cirques, but only for one night at a time. Setting up camp on Piton de la Fournaise (the volcano) is forbidden for obvious reasons.

Chambres d'Hôtes

Chambres d'hôtes are the French equivalent of B&Bs. They are normally tucked away in the hills or in scenic locations and offer a window into a more traditional way of life. Options include everything from restored Creole houses or modern buildings to rooms in family houses. On the whole standards are high, and rooms are generally excellent value. B&B rates are from around €40 for a double room. Breakfast is always included.

Many *chambres d'hôtes* also offer *table d'hôtes* (hearty evening meals) at around €17 to €25 per person (set menu), but this must be reserved in advance.

Many *chambres d'hôtes* are members of Gîtes de France, which is represented at the **Maison de la Montagne et de la Mer** (Map pp170-1; ☎ 0262 90 78 90; www.reunion-nature.com in French; 5 Rue Rontaunay, St-Denis). It has a brochure listing all the *chambres d'hôtes* in Réunion. They are also listed on the website. *Chambres d'hôtes* can be booked either through Gîtes de France or by phoning the owners directly.

Gîtes de Montagnes

Gîtes de montagnes are basic mountain cabins or lodges, operated by the government through the Maison de la Montagne et de la Mer. It is possible to organise a walking holiday using the *gîtes de montagnes* only.

PRACTICALITIES

- Réunion uses the metric system for weights and measures.
- Electric current is 220V, 50Hz AC; plugs have two round pins.
- Video recorders and players run on the PAL system.
- If your French is up to it, keep a finger on the pulse by reading the daily regional newspaper *Journal de l'Île de la Réunion* (JIR; www.clicanoo.com) and *Le Quotidien,* both good for features and events listings.
- TV viewers have the choice of two government channels, Télé Réunion and Tempo, as well as the independent Antenne Réunion. Most of the programming on the public channels comes from mainland France.
- Tune in to *RFO* (www.rfo.fr), *Kreol FM* (www.kreolfm.fr) or *Radio Free Dom* (www.radiofreedom .fr) for local news (in French and in Creole), reports and… gossip!

The *gîtes de montagnes* in Réunion are generally in pretty good condition. Thanks to solar power, they all now have electricity, although not all get as cushy as providing warm showers. The Gîte de la Caverne Dufour at Piton des Neiges is the most basic: it has no hot water, but there are now inside toilets.

Gîtes de montagnes must be booked and paid for in advance, and charges are not refundable unless a cyclone or a cyclone alert prevents your arrival. You can book through the **Maison de la Montagne et de la Mer** (Map pp170-1; ☎ 0262 90 78 78; www.reunion-nature.com in French; 5 Rue Rontaunay) in St-Denis or through affiliated tourist offices, including those in Cilaos, Salazie, Hell-Bourg, St-Gilles-les-Bains, St-Pierre, St-Leu and Bourg-Murat (see individual town entries for contact details). It's highly recommended that you book well in advance, especially during the busy tourist seasons. One night's accommodation without food costs around €14.50 per person.

When staying in a *gîte de montagne,* you have to call the *gîte* at least two days ahead to book your meals (or you can ask for this to be done for you when you make the original booking). Dinner costs from €14 to €16, and usually consists of hearty *carris* (curries). Breakfast costs around €5 and normally consists of coffee, bread and jam.

Sleeping arrangements usually consist of bunk beds in shared rooms, so be prepared for the communal living that this entails, although the newer *gîtes* usually have a few private rooms. Sheets and blankets are provided, though you might want to bring a sheet sleeping bag (a sleep sheet).

It's not a bad idea to also bring along toilet paper and a torch. It can get quite chilly at night, so warm clothing will be in order. Some places will let you cook, but many kitchens are so basic – and sometimes grimy – that you probably won't bother.

On arrival and departure you must 'book in and out with the manager, who will collect your voucher and payment for meals. In theory, you're not meant to occupy a *gîte* before 3pm or remain past 10am. For more information about these *gîtes* and for hiking-related information, see the chapter Hiking in Réunion (p231).

Gîtes d'Étape

Gîtes d'étape, sometimes simply called *gîtes* are privately owned and work in roughly the same way as the *gîtes de montagnes,* offering dorm beds and meals. One main difference is that you can book these places directly with the owners. There are numerous *gîtes d'étape* in the Cirque de Mafate, and others dotted around the island; most are in the vicinity of walking trails. The host will often offer meals or cooking facilities.

You'll find a number of *gîtes d'étape* listed in the Gîtes de France leaflet, *Île de la Réunion* (see Chambres d'Hôtes, p245). Local tourist offices should be able to provide lists of others in their area. Also check out the website www.reunion-nature.com (in French).

Rental Accommodation & Gîtes Ruraux

Gîtes ruraux are private houses and lodges that families and groups can rent for self catering holidays, normally by the week or weekend. There are dozens of *gîtes ruraux* scattered all over the island.

Most offer lodging for four or more people, with facilities of varying standards; you may have to bring your own bed sheets in some cases. Costs vary from around €300 to €400 per week and from €150 to €250 for a weekend (note that not all offer bookings for just a weekend).

Contact Gîtes de France, represented through **Maison de la Montagne et de la Mer** (Map pp170-1; ☎ 0262 90 78 90; www.reunion-nature .com in French; 5 Rue Rontaunay, St-Denis), local tourist offices or check out the website www .reunion-nature.com (in French). *Gîtes ruraux* can be booked either through Gîtes de France or by phoning the owners directly. A deposit of some sort is usually required in advance.

Youth Hostels

Réunion has four *auberges de jeunesse* (youth hostels), which are located in Bernica, Entre-Deux, Hell-Bourg and St-Denis. They are operated by the **Fédération Réunionnaise des Auberges de Jeunesse** (Map pp170-1; ☎ 0262 41 15 34; www.auberge-jeunesse-reunion.com; 2 Pl Étienne Regnault, St-Denis). Bookings can be made directly with the hostel.

Officially, the hostels are only open to Hostelling International (HI) card holders. In practice, you can stay at a hostel even if you're not a member, but you'll have to pay a small extra charge (about €2 per night).

Guests over 18 years of age pay €13 per night and an additional €3 for breakfast. Evening meals are usually available for €9.50 per person.

Hotels

If you're after serious cosseting and ultra-posh digs, you've opened this book on the wrong page. Most hotels on the island are rated as one-, two- or three-star, and lots are unclassified. There is only a sprinkling of four-star hotels.

Réunion isn't flush with hotels, so getting a room can sometimes be difficult. Primarily, they're found in St-Denis and around the beach resorts of the west coast, especially St-Gilles-les-Bains, though you'll also find some scattered in the interior.

Most room rates include breakfast, but check when booking to be sure.

ACTIVITIES

Want to get the heart pumping and the lungs gasping? You've come to the right place. Réunion offers a smorgasbord of activities for the adventure-seeker all over the island. Do you want to shoot down a river in a raft? Explore the countryside on horseback? No problem: it's all here, plus more; surfing, canyoning, paragliding, mountain biking and even Parcs Aventure are yours for the doing.

And if you need to recharge the batteries after all that exertion, rest easy: good restaurants serving wholesome *carris* are never far away.

High standards of professionalism are pretty uniform whatever the activity you choose. Just one quibble: the operators don't have much experience in dealing with English-speaking clients – brush up your French!

Canyoning

If walking, sliding, rappelling, diving, jumping and swimming down canyons is your thing, Réunion's canyoning hotspots are found in the Cirque de Salazie and Cirque de Cilaos, which are famous for their deep throats, torrents and narrow gorges. For seasoned canyoners, Takamaka, on the east coast, and Trou de Fer, accessible from the Hautes Plaines, are talismanic.

Deep-Sea Fishing

As elsewhere in the Indian Ocean region, the season for deep-sea fishing is tied to the feeding habits of bait-fish species; you stand the best chance of hooking a monster marlin from January to March. A boat with crew costs roughly €400/700 per half/full day (maximum of six people).

The main operators are based in St-Gilles-les-Bains (p184).

Diving

Réunion is certainly not a hardcore diver's destination, but that doesn't mean you should give it a wide berth. The west coast boasts its fair share of underwater wonders and deserves attention for its number of relaxed sites, with the added lure of a few wrecks and wall dives. You'll find professional dive centres in St-Gilles-les-Bains, St-Leu, Étang-Salé-les-Bains and St-Pierre.

For further information, see p29.

RÉUNION DIRECTORY

Hiking

Hiking is without a doubt the most rewarding activity in Réunion, with an excellent system of well-marked trails and an extraordinarily varied terrain. No visitor to the island should miss the superb rugged Cirques of Cilaos, Salazie and Mafate. For the less energetic, the volcano climb makes a manageable day trip and offers some of the most unusual and impressive scenery on the island.

For more information about hiking in Réunion, see p231.

Horse Riding

Saddling up is a fun and ecofriendly way to commune with the wilderness and enjoy the glorious hinterlands and lush forests. Horse riding is commonplace on the island. You don't need any riding experience, as riding centres cater to all levels of proficiency. Rides range from one-hour jaunts (from around €16) to multiday, fully catered treks. Particularly good areas include the Hautes Plaines, the Wild South and even the volcano.

Mountain Biking

In recent years Réunion has seen an explosion of interest in the *vélo tout terrain* (VTT) or mountain bike. More than 1400km of special biking trails winding through its forests and scooting down its mountainsides have been established. Sadly, maintenance is poor and most trails have now overgrown with weeds. Truth is, there's only one active hotspot: Le Maïdo. But what a hotspot! An outfitter based in St-Gilles-les-Bains (see the boxed text, p180) organises downhill runs from the upper reaches of Le Maïdo down to the coast.

Paragliding

On the west coast, the St-Leu area ranks as one of the best paragliding spots in the world, with consistently excellent upliftings throughout the year. Local companies offer everything from tandem flights over the lagoon for beginners to longer outings soaring over the Cirques. Prices range from €65 to €130 depending on the length of the flight. Children are welcome.

Parcs Aventure

Another thrilling way to see nature, this French-inspired activity allows you to swing through the forest à la *George of the Jungle*. There are two Parcs Aventure in Réunion, one near Le Maïdo (p181) and the other in Forêt de Bébour-Bélouve (p211). Each one consists of a series of fixtures built into the trees, at varying heights, usually including aerial platforms, walkways, 'Tarzan' swings, suspension bridges and steel-rope lines (also known as tyrolean slides), which are all connected. Visitors are strapped into harnesses and hooked onto a cable-and-pulley system that allows them to move safely from tree to tree. Children are welcome provided they are over 1m in height.

Rafting

The wealth of scenic rivers that decorate eastern Réunion make it a water-lover's dream destination. Rivière des Marsouins and Rivière du Mât offer top-class runs to get the blood racing.

The price for all these activities (with a guide and equipment) usually starts at around €50/70 per person for a half-/full day excursion.

RÉUNION FOR CRAZIES

If you want to work off any extra pounds gained in Réunion's fine restaurants, here's the solution: take part in the Grand Raid, one of the world's most challenging cross-country races. It's held every October or November. The route roughly follows the path of the GR R2 hiking trail, which traverses the island from St-Denis to Mare Longue, near St-Philippe, taking in parts of the Mafate and Cilaos Cirques, the Plaine-des-Cafres and the lunar landscape around Piton de la Fournaise.

Covering some 130km, the Grand Raid would be a challenging race over level ground, but runners also have to negotiate a total of some 7000m of altitude change, hence the race is nicknamed the 'Cross-Country for Crazies'! The pack leaders can complete this agonising run in 18 hours or less, but contestants are allowed up to 60 hours to finish.

Feel like entering? Contact the **Association Le Grand Raid** (☎ 0262 20 32 00; www.grandraid -reunion.com). We'd be curious to hear about your performance!

BEACHED DREAMS

Those who've come to Réunion buoyed by dreams of lounging on idyllic white-sand beaches with their beloved were badly advised by their travel agent. The island is quite lacking in those sandy excuses to laze about. Réunion is much more an outdoor and mountain destination than a beach destination. That said, there are a few good surprises on the west coast within the protective barrier of the lagoon. They include the beaches at St-Gilles-les-Bains, L'Hermitage-les-Bains, La Saline-les-Bains and Étang-Salé-les-Bains, all suitable for swimming. *The* beach as far as locals are concerned is Boucan Canot. All these beaches have lifeguards and designated safe swimming areas. There are also a few beaches in the south, including some black-sand ones. There are dangerous currents, so take advice before plunging in.

Surfing

Réunion has a good mix of quality waves perfect for beginners and experienced surfers. Reefs, rocky shelves and hollow sandy beach breaks can all be found – take your pick! Surfing has become increasingly popular in Réunion and some of the breaks are internationally known, especially the tricky Gauche de St-Leu. Today there are surf schools up and running at most premier surf beaches, including St-Gilles-les-Bains, La Saline-les-Bains and St-Leu.

In general, there are good conditions from May to November.

BUSINESS HOURS

As in mainland France, lunches are long, relaxed affairs in Réunion, and most shops and offices close for at least two hours at lunchtime.

Banks usually open 8am to 4pm, Monday to Friday or Tuesday to Saturday.

Government offices are open from 8.30am to noon and then 2pm to 5pm Monday to Thursday, 8.30am to noon and 2pm to 3pm Friday. Shops are open from 8.30am to noon and 2.30pm to 6pm Monday to Saturday (some close Monday).

Restaurants open for lunch between noon or 12.30pm and 2pm and for dinner from 7.30pm; they are often closed on one or two days of the week.

CHILDREN

Hire the baby-sitter and bring the kids: Réunion is an eminently suitable destination if you're travelling with the sticky-fingered set. With its abundance of beaches, picnic spots and outdoor activities, from paragliding to scuba diving, plus its healthy food, it offers plenty to do for travellers of all ages in a generally hazard-free setting.

Most locals have a number of children themselves and will not be troubled by a screaming child at the next table, should your little treasure throw a tantrum over dinner.

Few hotels offer kids clubs, but on the other hand many places provide cots for free and additional beds for children at a small extra cost. Most *chambres d'hôtes* welcome children.

Many restaurants will provide high chairs and have children's menus with significantly lower prices.

There are excellent medical facilities in the main cities.

Lonely Planet's *Travel with Children* is a great before-you-go resource containing general tips on vacationing with the kiddies.

CLIMATE CHARTS

For further information on choosing the best time of the year for visiting Réunion, see p169.

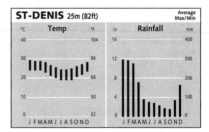

CUSTOMS

The following items can be brought into Réunion duty-free: 200 cigarettes, 50 cigars, 1L of strong liquor or 2L of liquor that is less than 22% alcohol by volume, 2L of wine, 50g of perfume and 0.25L of *eau de toilette* and other goods up to the value of €880. Anything over the limit must be declared on arrival.

There are restrictions on importing plants and animals, for which import permits are required.

With regards to currency, anyone entering or leaving the island must declare sums in excess of €7600.

DANGERS & ANNOYANCES

Attacks by *les dents de la mer* (sharks) occasionally happen, and most years see a shark attack on a surfer or spear fisherman. This is no reason to be paranoid, though; the risks are statistically very low. The locals know their ocean, so it's best to seek their advice before entering the water.

Swimmers should always be aware of currents and riptides. Drowning is a major cause of accidental death for visitors. If you're not familiar with water conditions, ask around. It's best not to swim alone in unfamiliar places.

Unfortunately Réunion has a bad record when it comes to road safety, which means that you must drive defensively at all times. Potential dangers include drunk drivers, excessive speed, twisting roads and blind bends.

Hikers setting out into the wilderness should be adequately prepared for their trips.

Overall, Réunion is relatively safe compared with most Western countries, but occasional robberies do occur. Don't leave anything of value in a rental car or on the beach.

Violence is rarely a problem, and muggings are almost unheard of. Intoxicated people are the most likely troublemakers.

EMBASSIES & CONSULATES
French Embassies & Consulates

Australia Canberra (☎ 02-6216 0100; www.ambafrance -au.org; 6 Perth Ave, Yarralumla, ACT 2600) Sydney Consulate (☎ 02-9261 5779; consulat@consulfrance-sydney .org; Level 26, St Martin's Tower, 31 Market St, Sydney, NSW 2000)
Canada Ottowa (☎ 613-789 1795; www.ambafrance -ca.org; 42 Sussex Dr, Ottawa, ON K1M 2C9) Toronto Consulate (☎ 416-925 8041; www.consulfrance-toronto.org; 2 Bloor St East, Suite 2200, Toronto, ON M4W 1A8)
Germany Berlin (☎ 030-590 039 000; www.botschaft -frankreich.de; Pariser Platz 5, 10117 Berlin)
Ireland (☎ 01-277 5000; www.ambafrance.ie.org; 36 Ailesbury Rd, Ballsbridge, Dublin 4)
Mauritius (☎ 202 0100; www.ambafrance-mu.org; 14 St-Georges St, Port-Louis)
Netherlands (☎ 020-530 6969; www.consulfrance-am sterdam.org; Vijzelgracht 2, 1000 HA Amsterdam)

New Zealand (☎ 04-384 2555; www.ambafrance -nz.org; 34-42 Manners St, Wellington)
UK London (☎ 020-7073 1000; www.ambafrance-uk.org 58 Knightsbridge, London SW1X 7JT) Consulate (☎ 020-7073 1200; www.consulfrance-londres.org; 21 Cromwell Rd, London SW7 2EN) Visa section (☎ 020-7073 1250; 6A Cromwell Place, London SW7 2EW) Edinburgh (☎ 0131-225 7954; 21 Randolph Cres, EH3 7TT)
USA Washington (☎ 202-944 6195; www.ambafrance -us.org; 4101 Reservoir Rd NW, Washington, DC 20007); New York Consulate (☎ 212-606 3600; www.consulfrance -newyork.org; 934 Fifth Ave, NY 10021); San Francisco Consulate (☎ 415-397 4330; www.consulfrance-sanfrancisco .org; 540 Bush St, CA 94108); other consulates are located in Atlanta, Boston, Chicago, Houston, Los Angeles, Miami and New Orleans.

Embassies & Consulates in Réunion

Since Réunion isn't independent, only a few countries have diplomatic representation:
Belgium (☎ 0262 97 99 10; chatel@runnet.com; 72 Av Eudoxie Nonge, BP 32, 97491 Ste-Clotilde)
Germany (☎ 0262 21 62 06; fax 0262 21 74 55; 9c Rue de Lorraine, 97400 St-Denis)
Madagascar (☎ 0262 72 07 30; consulat -madrun@wanadoo.fr; 29 Rue St Joseph Ouvrier, 97400 St-Denis)
Seychelles (☎ 0262 57 26 38; hrop@wanadoo.fr; 67 Rue de Kerveguen, 97430 Le Tampon)
Switzerland (☎ 0262 45 55 74; 107 Rue Crève Coeur, 97460 St-Paul)

FESTIVALS & EVENTS

Major festivals in Réunion involve street parties, exhibitions, sports events, music dancing and various other activities. Rural fairs are also hugely popular and usually celebrate local produce, which can be anything from *chou chou* (choko; a green squash-like vegetable) to sugar cane. For foreigners, they offer the chance to be immersed in local culture and to buy top quality regional specialities.

Abolition of Slavery Day (a national holiday) is taken very seriously, particularly among the Creole population, who still occupy a disadvantaged position in society.

The Indian community is principally made up of Tamil Hindus and they hold some amazing rites, including *cavadee* (in which pilgrims practise self-mutilation and impressive fire-walking ceremonies. The Hindu temple in St-André is the most popular location for these events. For more about these festivals, see p136.

To find out what's happening during your stay contact any of the tourist offices in the relevant town.

Main festivals in Réunion:

January
Fête du Miel Vert (Festival of Honey) Plaine-des-Cafres.
Fête des Vendanges (Wine Harvest Festival) Cilaos.
Fire-walking ceremonies Various locations.

February
Cavadee Tamil procession; St-André.
Chinese New Year Various locations.

March
Leu Tempo Theatre festival; St-Leu.

April
Tamil New Year Dance displays; various locations.

May
Fête du Chou Chou (Festival of Chou Chou) Hell-Bourg.
Fête du Choca (Festival of Choca) Crafts made from choca leaves; Entre-Deux.

June
Fête des Goyaviers (Festival of Guava) Plaine-les-Palmistes.

August
Fête du Vacoa (Festival of Vacoa) Crafts made from crew-pine fronds; St-Philippe.
Pèlerinage à la Vierge au Parasol (Pilgrimage to the Virgin with the Parasol) Ste-Rose.
Sakifo (Festival of Creole music) St-Leu.

September
Florchidées (flower show) St-André.
Fête de Notre Dame de la Salette (Festival of Notre Dame de la Salette) Fair and street events over 10 days; St-Leu.

October
Fête de l'Ail (Festival of Garlic) Petite Île.
Fête des Bichiques (Festival of Bichiques) Bras-Panon.
Fête du Safran (Festival of Saffron) Plaine-des-Grègues.
Semaine Créole (Creole Week) A week of cultural events; various locations.
Grand Raid Cross-country race in October or November from St-Philippe to St-Denis.
Divali (Dipavali) Tamil festival of light in late October or early November; St-André and other locations.

November
Fête du Curcuma (Festival of Curcuma) St-Joseph.
Fête des Lentilles (Festival of Lentils) Cilaos.

December
Mégavalanche Mountain-bike descent in early December; Maïdo to St-Paul.

FOOD

Eating reviews listed in the Réunion chapter usually indicate the price of mains, followed by the price of menus (two- or three-course set menus). Set menus include all courses but no wine, except in some *chambres d'hôtes*, where wine may be included. Within each eating section, restaurants appear in order of ascending prices.

You should be able to get a reasonable *plat du jour* (dish of the day) at lunchtime for between €8 and €12. For a full, midrange restaurant meal you should expect to pay €25 to €35 per person with wine.

For information on Réunionnais gastronomy, see p162.

GAY & LESBIAN TRAVELLERS

French laws concerning homosexuality prevail in Réunion, which means there is no legal discrimination against homosexual activity and homophobia is relatively uncommon.

Throughout the island, but particularly on the west coast, there are restaurants, bars, operators and accommodation places that make a point of welcoming gays and lesbians. Certain areas are the focus of the gay and lesbian communities, among them St-Denis, St-Pierre and La Saline-les-Bains. Tourist offices have a leaflet that lists gay-friendly venues in Réunion. The **Comité du Tourisme de la Réunion** (☎ 0262 21 00 41; www.la-reunion-tourisme.com in French; Place du 20 Décembre 1848, 97472 St-Denis Cedex) has a useful link on its website (see 'Gay Friendly' at the bottom of the home page).

HOLIDAYS

Most of Réunion's offices, museums and shops are closed during *jours fériés* (public holidays), which are as follows:
New Year's Day 1 January
Easter Monday March/April
Labour Day 1 May
Victory Day 1945 8 May
Ascension Day late May or June
Bastille Day (National Day) 14 July
Assumption Day 15 August
All Saints' Day 1 November
Armistice Day 1918 11 November
Abolition of Slavery Day 20 December
Christmas Day 25 December

INSURANCE

Insurance requirements for Réunion are the same as for Mauritius; see p138 for more information.

INTERNET ACCESS

Currently, internet cafés tend to be found only in bigger towns and resort areas such as Cilaos, Salazie, St-Denis, St-Gilles-les-Bains, St-Leu and St-Pierre, and consider yourself lucky if you can find more than one or two outlets in each city. Most hotel rooms are not really geared towards travellers seeking to connect to the internet and usually don't have the necessary plugs and sockets, and wi-fi access is still in its infancy.

The connection is generally good and rates are fairly standard at around €6 per hour.

MAPS

For most purposes the IGN Carte Touristique La Réunion map, at a scale of 1:100,000 (1cm = 1km), which covers the island in one sheet, is perfectly adequate. The most detailed and accurate maps for hiking are the six-sheet 1:25,000 series (see p233).

MONEY

As in France, the unit of currency is the euro (€), which is divided into 100 cents. Euro coins come in denominations of one, two, five, 10, 20 and 50 cents and one and two euros. Banknotes are issued in denominations of five, 10, 20, 50, 100, 200 and 500 euros.

For exchange rates, see the table inside the front cover. For information on costs, see p17.

ATMs

Most banks and post offices have an ATM (known as a *guichet automatique de banque* or *gabier*) which honours major international credit cards. Visa and MasterCard are the most widely accepted. They are the easiest way to access funds while in Réunion. If you're heading off into the Cirques, it's wise to stock up with euros beforehand. There is only one ATM in Cilaos and one in Salazie.

Credit Cards

Credit cards will prove the cheapest and easiest way to pay for major purchases in Réunion. Visa (Carte Bleue) and MasterCard (Eurocard) are the cards most widely accepted by hotels, restaurants, supermarkets, major petrol stations and stores. Credit cards are mandatory if you want to rent a car, as they'll be used as a form of *caution* (deposit). Smaller places, however, sometimes refuse cards for small amounts (typically under €16) and it's rare for *chambres d'hôtes* and *gîtes d'étape* to take credit cards.

Moneychangers

Changing money in Réunion? Dream on! The number of banks that have foreign-exchange facilities and do change cash has been dramatically reduced since the introduction of the euro. This service tends to be dropped in favour of ATMs. Therefore, consider yourself very lucky if you find a bank that changes foreign currencies on the island.

There are no exchange facilities at either Roland Garros International Airport or the ferry terminal in Le Port, though the airport does at least have an ATM.

As a general strategy, it's sensible to bring a fair supply of euros with you and to top it up from the ATMs.

Travellers Cheques

Travellers cheques are not widely accepted in Réunion; you'll find that most banks are reluctant to change them. Stash up on cash and rely on your credit card.

PHOTOGRAPHY

Print and slide film are widely available in Réunion and you'll find decent developing studios in major towns. For tips on how to take great photographs of the island's stunning scenery, see the boxed text, p140.

TELEPHONE

Réunion's telephone system is efficient. There are numerous public telephones scattered around the island and you can directly dial international numbers on them. They only accept *télécartes* (phonecards), not coins. Phone cards are available at post offices and shops.

Alternatively, there are various prepaid calling cards (available at newsagents) that require you to dial a free number and enter a personal identity number before you place your call.

When making a call to Réunion from abroad, you'll need to dial the international code for Réunion (262), followed by the local number minus the first 0. All mobile phone numbers start with the prefix 06. I calling a Réunion mobile number from over-seas, you would drop the first 0, that is dial 00 262 6, then six digits. There are no area codes in Réunion.

Mobile Phones

If you have a GSM phone, check with your service provider at home about using your mobile phone in Réunion and the charges involved.

If your GSM phone has been 'unlocked', it is also possible to buy a SIM card with either of the two local network operators: Orange (France Télécom) and SFR.

The network covers most towns and villages throughout the island, even in the interior.

TOURIST INFORMATION

There are generally *offices du tourisme* (tourist offices) in most main towns across the island. Most of them have at least one staff member who speaks English.

Tourist-office staff provide maps, brochures and the twice-yearly magazine *Guide RUN*, which is a useful directory of hotels, restaurants, discos and other places of interest to visitors.

The **Comité du Tourisme de la Réunion** (Map pp170-1; ☎ 0262 21 00 41; www.la-reunion-tourisme.com in French; Place du 20 Décembre 1848, 97472 St-Denis Cedex) is Réunion's regional tourist office.

You can also contact the French tourist office in your home country; these are listed on www.franceguide.com.

TOURS

Reputable tour operators in Réunion include **Bourbon Tourisme** (☎ 0262 33 08 70; www .bourbontourisme.com in French) and **Papangue Tour** (☎ 0262 41 61 92; papangueprod@wanadoo.fr). Both can organise tailor-made trips and provide English-speaking guides.

TRAVELLERS WITH DISABILITIES

Independent travel is difficult for anyone with mobility problems in Réunion. Only the newest of newly remodeled businesses have features specifically suited to wheelchair use.

Negotiating the streets of most towns in a wheelchair is frustrating given the lack of adequate equipment, and most outdoor attractions and historic places don't have trails suited to wheelchair use. One notable exception is the newly refurbished Kelonia, in St-Leu (see p190).

VISAS

Though Réunion is a French department, it's not part of the Schengen treaty. The visa requirements for entry to Réunion are almost the same as for France, bar a few exceptions. For EU nationals, a national ID or a passport suffices. Citizens of a number of other Western countries, including Australia, the USA, Canada and New Zealand do not need visas to visit Réunion as tourists for up to three months; they need only a passport.

Other nationals should check with the French embassy or consulate nearest your home address to find out if you need a visa. For example, Brazilian citizens do not need a visa to enter mainland France but do require a visa for Réunion.

Except for EU nationals, those who don't need a visa and wish to stay for longer than three months need to apply for a *carte de séjour* (residence permit). Contact the **Service des Étrangers** (☎ 0262 40 77 77; 4 Place de la Préfecture) at the Préfecture in St-Denis.

WOMEN TRAVELLERS

The sight of women travelling, be it in a group or alone, is not met with too much surprise or curiosity, and women travelling by themselves should encounter no difficulties, as long as sensible precautions observed in most Western countries are adhered to.

Women can enter most bars alone, but there are still a few places where this may attract unwanted attention – you'll get a pretty good idea when you enter.

It's not advisable to walk alone on the trails in the interior.

TRANSPORT AROUND RÉUNION

AIR

Réunion has two international airports. The vast majority of flights come into **Roland Garros International Airport** (☎ 0262 48 81 81; www .reunion.aeroport.fr) about 10km east of St-Denis. Coming from Mauritius, you have the option of landing at **Pierrefonds Airport** (☎ 0262 96 80 00; www.grandsudreunion.org in French), in the south of the island near St-Pierre.

For more information regarding air travel, see p302.

BICYCLE

The traffic, the haste of most motorists and the steep and precarious nature of the mountain roads means that those considering cycling as a form of transport in Réunion should be prepared for some hair-raising and potentially dangerous situations.

BUS

Réunion's major towns and many of the little ones in between are linked by bus. The island's bus service is knows as **Car Jaune** (☎ 0810 123 974) and has distinctive yellow buses. The main *gare routière* (bus station) is on Blvd Lancastel on the St-Denis seafront.

Buses on most routes run between about 6am and 7pm, with a limited number of services on Sunday. For a few sample fares, you'll pay €7 from St-Denis to St-Pierre, €3.50 from St-Denis to St-Benoît and €7 from St-Benoît to St-Pierre via Plaine-des-Cafres. You can pay the driver as you board. To get the bus to stop, you ring the bell or clap your hands twice loudly.

Car Jaune provides regional minibus services for several areas on the island; these services are known as Ti' Car Jaune (from *petit;* 'small'). Ti' Car Jaune buses run from St-Benoît, St-Joseph, Ste-Rose, St-Leu and St-Paul. These convoluted local routes can be fairly confusing, particularly if you don't speak much French. Of most use to travellers are the buses from St-André to Salazie, Salazie to Hell-Bourg, Grand Îlet and Le Bélier, and the buses from St-Louis to Cilaos, Îlet à Cordes and Bras-Sec.

CAR

With most attractions located in the hills, we strongly recommend hiring a vehicle. No other form of transport lets you explore the island's secret backwaters as a set of motorised wheels. There are some gorgeous runs, cruising along the island's dramatic roads; heading into the mountains via the Cirques roads is a magnificent experience. The superbly engineered roads snake through hairpin bends, up steep slopes and along sheer drops, surrounded all the while by glorious – and distracting – scenery.

The road system on the island is excellent and well signposted. Route Nationale 1 (RN1), the main road around the island, approaches international motorway standards in parts. *Routes départementales,* whose names begin with the letter D (or RD), are tertiary local roads, many of them very tortuous (use your horn!). By the time you read this, large chunks of the new Route des Tamarins, which will connect St-Paul to Étang-Salé-les-Bains (34km), will be completed. It will certainly reduce the horrendous traffic jams that plague the west coast.

The experience is likely to be marred somewhat by the local drivers, who insist on driving these roads at breakneck speeds.

Petrol stations are very easy to come by. A litre of unleaded costs about €1.25. Most stations accept credit cards.

Hire

Good news: *location de voitures* (car hire) is extremely popular in Réunion, and rates are very reasonable. Most companies stipulate that the driver must be at least 21 (sometimes 23) years of age, have held a driving licence for at least a year, and have a passport or some other form of identification. EU citizens can drive on their national driving licence; from elsewhere, you'll need an international driving licence.

Prices and regulations don't vary much between the main international rental companies. Rates start at €40 per day (including insurance and unlimited mileage) and can drop as low as €30 per day or €25 if you rent for several days. Most companies require a credit card, primarily so that you can leave a deposit. They'll probably ask you to leave a signed credit-card slip without a sum written on it as a deposit.

All major firms have a desk at the airports, and most offer delivery. They also have representatives in St-Gilles-les-Bains and St-Pierre. There are also plenty of cheaper independent operators around the island – tourist offices can give you details. Alternatively, **Autoescape** (☎ 0808 2341 362; www.autoescape.com) organises reliable car hire at favourable rates through partner firms.

Road Rules

Like mainland France, Réunion keeps to the right side of the road. Speed limits are clearly indicated and vary from 50km/h in towns to 110km/h on dual carriageways. Drivers and passengers are required to wear seat belts. The alcohol limit is 0.5g/L.

Seychelles

Seychelles Snapshots

Bel Ombre is one of several possible locations for the treasure trove of the legendary pirate Olivier Levasseur, known as 'La Buse' (the Buzzard).

The Seychelles were named in honour of the French finance minister to Louis XV, Jean Moreau de Séchelles.

The Seychelles is a paradise for tourists, no doubt about it, and most tourists leave with a very positive impression of the country, proclaiming to the world that the Seychelles is a 'haven of stability', and 'a very peaceful country'. Whether or not the Seychelles is heaven for its own population is another story. Politically, the situation has not evolved for more than 30 years. The ruling party, the Seychelles People's Progressive Front (SPPF), led by president James Michel, has been governing the country since 1977 and has been staunchly clinging to power ever since. Michel doesn't seem willing to cede his power to any of his opponents; he prematurely dissolved the National Assembly in March 2007, following the boycott of the assembly proceedings by the opposition party, and the general elections in May 2007 returned 18 SPPF members as against seven members of the SPF opposition party led by Wavel Ramkalawan (exactly the same numbers as before the dissolution). The leadership of the SPPF continues. It's a stalemate.

But, after all, these elections were held democratically. Well, almost. The methods the SPPF allegedly used to obtain votes are more than dubious. The SPPF has a firm grip on the media, and the freedom of the press is threatened, as testified by the closing down of the opposition newspaper, *Regar,* in 2006. Critics claimed that the government bought votes with Rs 500 notes (introduced in July 2005). There were also allegations of gerrymandering and threats.

Whatever the result of the 2007 election, it can't be denied that the situation is deteriorating. In October 2006, opposition protesters and security forces clashed outside the Seychelles parliament after MPs backed a bill restricting private radio-station ownership (which ended the opposition's hopes of running its own radio station) – this violent confrontation was condemned by press-freedom campaigners Reporters Without Borders. Wavel Ramkalawan himself was injured. As one of our contacts put it, 'The Seychellois are a very pacific, somewhat inhibited people. But when they feel a situation has gone too far, they really can go to great lengths to express their anger'. It's true that anger and frustration are simmering in the Seychelles. 'We want new perspectives. The ruling party has been controlling everything for ages. We live in a fake democracy.'

Meanwhile, tourism is picking up, which is good news for the budget of the country. The image of paradise hasn't been tainted – yet.

FAST FACTS

Population: 81,000

Territory size: 445 sq km

Languages: English, French, Creole

Capital: Victoria

Highest point: Morne Seychellois (907m)

Largest island: Mahé

Distance from Mahé to Mauritius: 1720km

Distance from Mahé to Bombay: 2800km

Average weight of a coco fesse: 10-15kg

HISTORY

Until the 18th century the Seychelles was uninhabited. The islands were first spotted by Portuguese explorers, but the first recorded landing was by a British East India Company ship in 1609. Pirates and privateers used the Seychelles as a temporary base during lulls in their maraudings.

THE COLONIAL PERIOD

In 1742, Mahé de Labourdonnais, the governor of what is now Mauritius, sent Captain Lazare Picault to investigate the islands. Picault named the main island after his employer (and the bay where he landed after himself) and laid the way for the French to claim possession of the islands 12 years later.

It took a while for the French to do anything with their possession. It wasn't until 1770 that the first batch of 21 settlers and seven slaves arrived on Ste Anne Island. After a few false starts, the settlers began growing spices, cassava, sugarcane and maize.

In the 18th century, the British began taking an interest in the Seychelles. The French were not willing to die for their colony and didn't resist British attacks, and the Seychelles became a British dependency in 1814. The British did little to develop the islands except increase the number of slaves. After abolition in 1835, freed slaves from around the region were also brought here. Because few British settled, however, the French language and culture remained dominant.

Over the years the islands have been used as a holding pen for numerous political prisoners and exiles – not a bad place to be exiled!

In 1903 the Seychelles became a crown colony administered from London. It promptly went into the political and economic doldrums until 1964, when two political parties were formed. France Albert René, a young lawyer, founded the Seychelles People's United Party (SPUP). A fellow lawyer, James Mancham, led the new Seychelles Democratic Party (SDP).

INDEPENDENCE

Mancham's SDP, made up of businesspeople and planters, won the elections in 1966 and 1970. René's SPUP fought on a socialist and independence ticket. In June 1975 a coalition of the two parties gave the appearance of unity in the lead-up to independence, which was granted a year later. Mancham became the first president of the Republic of Seychelles and René the prime minister.

The flamboyant Sir Jim (as James Mancham was known) – poet and playboy – placed all his eggs in one basket: tourism. He jet-setted around the world with a beautiful socialite on each arm, and he put the Seychelles on the map.

The rich and famous poured in for holidays and to party, party, party. Adnan Khashoggi and other Arab millionaires bought large tracts of land, while film stars and celebrities came to enhance their romantic, glamorous images.

According to René and the SPUP, however, the wealth was not being spread evenly and the country was no more than a rich person's playground. René stated that poor Creoles were little better off than slaves.

THE LONG ROAD TO DEMOCRACY

In June 1977, barely a year after independence, René and a team of Tanzanian-trained rebels carried out an almost bloodless coup while Mancham was in London attending a Commonwealth Conference. In the following years, René consolidated his position by deporting many supporters of the outlawed SDP. Opposed to René's one-party socialist state, these *grands blancs* (white landowners) set up 'resistance movements' in Britain, South Africa and Australia.

The country fell into disarray as the tourist trade dried to a trickle. The 1980s saw a campaign of civil disruption by supporters of the SDP, two army mutinies and more foiled coup attempts.

Finally, facing growing international criticism and the threatened withdrawal of foreign aid, René pulled a political about-face in the early 1990s; he abandoned one-party rule and announced the return to a multiparty democracy.

Elections were held in 1992 under the watchful eye of Commonwealth observers. René and his renamed Seychelles People's Progressive Front won

The Freedom Sq monument known to locals as Twa Zwazo (meaning 'three birds') is said to represent the continents of Africa, Europe and Asia, each of which has played a part in the development of the Seychellois.

William McAteer's *Rivals in Eden* and *Hard Times in Paradise* trace the islands' history from the first French landing in 1740 up to 1919. Deryck Scarr brings things up to date in *Seychelles since 1770*, which covers the 20th century.

58.4% of the votes; Mancham, who had returned to the Seychelles, fielded 33.7% for his SDP and claimed the results were rigged.

René maintained his grip on power, while the SDP's star continued to wane. Even Mancham himself abandoned the SDP in favour of the centrist Seychelles National Party (SNP) in 1999. In the 2002 elections, the SNP, led by Wavel Ramkalawan, an Anglican priest, confirmed its stand as the main opposition party by winning over 42% of the vote.

In April 2004, René finally relinquished the presidency to the former vice president, James Michel, who had stood by René through thick and thin. After a close race with Wavel Ramkalawan, the opposition leader, Michel won the 2006 presidential election, gaining 53.5% of the vote.

While René has been much criticised over the years, there's no denying that overall standards of health, education and housing have improved, and annual per capita income has grown from around US$1000 in 1976 to close on US$7000 today.

THE CULTURE

THE NATIONAL IDENTITY

Seychellois people may appear somewhat indifferent to strangers (at least by comparison with people in other African nations) at first meeting, but once the ice has broken you will find intense friendliness and warmth. There's not much anti-colonial feeling evident – it has long been replaced with a sense of national pride that developed after independence.

As in Mauritius and Réunion, it is the Creole language, cuisine and culture that helps bind the Seychelles society. Over 90% of the population speak Creole as their first language, though most also speak English – the language of government and business – and French.

The government has worked hard to promote social cohesion. As a result, racism is extremely rare, though there are concerns that the number of immigrant workers, particularly Indian labourers brought in to work on construction sites, may upset the balance.

On the whole, however, the Seychellois are pretty relaxed, and traditional work patterns are very different from Western ones.

Despite the apparently easy-going existence, the living standards of many Seychellois are lower than you might expect, mostly because of the disproportionately high cost of living. The islands may seem very westernised, but the minimum wage is around Rs 2000 (€325) per month. As prices creep up and more people struggle to make ends meet, burglaries and petty theft are on the rise. Crime levels are still extremely low, but it's a favourite topic of conversation among islanders.

Since 1982, when Creole was made the language of education, literacy rates have risen to nearly 90%.

LIFESTYLE

Thanks to the islands' close links with Europe, the contemporary face of the Seychelles is surprisingly modern. The main island of Mahé is a rather sophisticated place, characterised as much by Western-style clothing, brand-new cars, mobile phones and modern houses as by any overt signs of traditional Creole culture. But beneath this strongly Westernised veneer, many aspects of traditional Creole culture survive. They live on in dance, music, hospitality, ancient beliefs, the language, the carefree attitude, and in many other day-to-day ways of doing things.

The society continues to be largely male dominated. Fortunately for women, the tourism industry is regarded as an equal-opportunity employer.

Most Seychellois are Catholic, but marriage is an unpopular institution. The reasons cited are that not marrying is a relic of slavery, when marriages simply didn't take place, and that marriage is expensive. As a result an estimated 75% of children are born out of wedlock. There's no taboo about illegitimacy, however. Though the children tend to stay with the mother, fathers are legally obliged to support their offspring.

Since the age of consent is only 14 years, there are a large number of teen-age mothers. Pregnant girls are not allowed to attend school, and after the birth few bother to return. This obviously has a negative impact on education levels and job options for a certain number of women.

The Seychellois are generally tolerant of gay and lesbian relationships as long as couples don't flaunt their sexuality. Indeed, there are few rules and regulations to be followed, beyond respecting local attitudes towards nudity and visiting places of religious worship.

ECONOMY

The economy is heavily reliant on tourism, which now employs at least 20% of the labour force, with exclusive resorts replacing the spice and coconut plantations. Despite the worldwide downturn in tourism, the sector has been picking up in recent years and the number of arrivals to the Seychelles is on the increase, with more than 150,000 visitors per year at the time of writing.

The other mainstay of the economy is industrial fishing, which actually overtook tourism as the country's biggest foreign-exchange earner in 2002.

Nevertheless, the economy remains extremely vulnerable to external events. Despite attempts to strengthen its agricultural base and use more locally manufactured products, the Seychelles continues to import 90% of its needs. As a result, even a slight dip in export earnings causes major ructions in the economy.

The chronic foreign-exchange shortage has pushed the government to encourage foreign investments thanks to tax incentives and other benefits. Sectors targeted include offshore banking and insurance, trans-shipment and shipping registration.

The huge Indian Ocean Tuna plant in Victoria is the world's second-largest tuna cannery.

POPULATION

The population of the Seychelles is more strongly African than in Mauritius or Réunion, but even so you'll see almost every shade of skin and hair imaginable, arising from a mixture of largely French and African genes, together with infusions of Indian, Chinese and Arab blood. Distinct Indian and Chinese communities make up only a tiny proportion of the ethnic mix, however, the rest being Creole. As for the *grands blancs,* most were dispossessed in the wake of the 1977 coup.

About 90% of Seychellois live on Mahé and nearly a third of these are concentrated in and around the capital. Most of the remaining 10% live on Praslin and La Digue, while the other islands are either uninhabited or are home to tiny communities.

RELIGION

Nearly 90% of Seychellois are Roman Catholic, 7% are Anglican and 2.5% belong to the rapidly expanding evangelical churches. The remainder belong to the tiny Hindu, Muslim and Chinese communities largely based in Victoria.

Most people are avid churchgoers. On a Sunday, Victoria's Catholic and Anglican cathedrals as well as the smaller churches scattered around the main islands are full to bursting.

SEYCHELLES SNAPSHOTS

There is also a widespread belief in the supernatural and in the old magic of spirits known as *gris gris*. Sorcery was outlawed in 1958, but a few *bonhommes* and *bonnefemmes di bois* (medicine men and women) still practise their cures and curses and concoct potions for love, luck and revenge.

ARTS

Since these islands were originally uninhabited, the Creoles are the closest the country has to an indigenous population. Many aspects of their African origins survive, including the *séga* and *moutia* dances.

Did you know that the film *Goodbye Emmanuelle* was filmed on La Digue?

Literature

The Lenstiti Kreol (Creole Institute), near Anse aux Pins on Mahé, was set up to research and promote Creole language and literature. It publishes a few books each year in Creole by local authors as well as translations of foreign works; these are available at the Institute.

Among the most important local authors writing in Creole are the poet-playwright Christian Sevina, short-story author and playwright Marie-Thérèse Choppy, poet Antoine Abel and mystery writer Jean-Joseph Madeleine. Unfortunately, their works are not yet available in English.

In fact there is surprising little English-language fiction about these islands. Most authors go in for travelogues and autobiographies. The one exception is long-time resident Glynn Burridge, who mixes fact and fiction in his short stories. They are published locally in two volumes under the title of *Voices: Seychelles Short Stories* and are available in the bookshops in Victoria.

Music & Dance

The Indian, European, Chinese and Arabic backgrounds of the Seychellois are reflected in their music. The accordion, banjo and violin music brought to the islands by the early European settlers has blended with that of the *makalapo*, a stringed instrument with a tin soundbox; the *zez*, a monochord sitar; African skin drums; and the *bom*, a bowed instrument.

You may also come across roving *camtole* bands, which feature fiddle, banjo, accordion and drums. They sometimes accompany the *contredanse*, a dance similar to the quadrille. European influences are also evident in the *mazok*, which is reminiscent of the French waltz, and the *kotis*, which has its roots in Scottish country dancing.

It is the sombre *moutia*, however, with its strong African rhythms, that is the traditional dance of the Seychelles. The slow, repetitive dance routines were originally accompanied by prayers that the slaves turned into work chants, similar to the early black gospel music of the USA. The *moutia* is normally danced around an open fire and serves as the primary evening entertainment.

The Seychelles version of the *séga* differs little from that of Mauritius. Many of the large hotels hold *séga* dance displays at least one night a week.

Patrick Victor and Jean-Marc Volcy are two of the Seychelles' best-known musicians, playing Creole pop and folk music. Other local stars are Emmanuel Marie and the late Raymond Lebon, whose daughter Sheila Paul made it into the local charts with an updated rendering of her father's romantic ballads.

David André's *Esper Sa Sanson*, some of which is sung in English, and Jean Ally's *Welcome* (an entirely English-language recording of *séga*) are both good introductions to local music and should be available in music stores in Victoria.

Visual Arts

Over recent decades, more and more artists have settled in the Seychelles and spawned a local industry catering to souvenir-hungry tourists. While shops are full of stereotypical scenes of palm trees and sunsets, there are also some innovative and talented artists around.

Michael Adams is the best-known and most distinctive contemporary artist. He has a studio near Baie Lazare in South Mahé. George Camille is another highly regarded artist who takes his inspiration from nature. He has a gallery on Praslin. Other notable artists are Barbara Jenson, who has a studio on La Digue, Gerard Devoud at Baie Lazare and Nigel Henry at Beau Vallon.

Look out, too, for works by Leon Radegonde, who produces innovative abstract collages; Andrew Gee, who specialises in watercolours of fish and silk paintings; and the sun-drenched paintings of Christine Harter. The painter and sculptor Egbert Marday produces powerful sketches of fisherfolk and plantation workers, but is perhaps best known for the statue of a man with a walking cane, situated outside the courthouse on Victoria's Independence Ave. Lorenzo Appiani produced the sculptures on the roundabouts at each end of 5th June Ave in Victoria.

FOOD & DRINK

Meat lovers, come prepared: the cuisine of the Seychelles is heavily influenced by the surrounding ocean, with fish appearing as the main ingredient in many dishes. Cultural influences are also distinctive, with a blend of European (mostly French and Italian) and African gastronomic delights.

STAPLES & SPECIALITIES

Fish, fish, FISH! And rice. This is the most common combination (*pwason ek diri,* in Creole patois) in the Seychelles, and we won't complain – fish is guaranteed to be served ultrafresh and literally melts in your mouth. You'll devour *bourgeois, capitaine,* shark, *job,* parrotfish, caranx, grouper and tuna, among others. To bring variety, they are cooked in innumerable guises: grilled, steamed, minced, smoked, stewed, salted, baked, wrapped in a banana leaf; the list goes on and on.

Seafood lovers will have found their spiritual home in the Seychelles; lobster, crab, seashells (especially *trouloulou* and *teck teck,* two local varieties of shells) and octopus are widely available.

The Seychelles is dripping with tropical fruit, including mango, banana, breadfruit, papaya, coconut, grapefruit, pineapple and carambole. Mixed with spices, they make wonderful accompaniments, such as the flavourful *chatini* (chutney). Vanilla, cinammon and nutmeg are used to flavour stews and other preparations.

Gastronauts might consider trying *civet de chauve souris* (bat curry), which is considered a delicacy. You'll also find meat, but it's imported.

DRINKS

Freshly squeezed juices and coconut water are the most natural and thirst-quenching drinks around. If you want to put some wobble in your step, Seybrew, the local brand of beer, is sold everywhere. Eku, another locally produced beer, is a bit harder to find. Wine is available at most restaurants, but be aware that some bottles will have been exposed to the heat.

Feeling adventurous? Try the infamous *calou,* a kind of palm wine – devilish. It's not sold in restaurants, but most families prepare their own poison.

SEYCHELLES SNAPSHOTS

The Seychellois are said to be the biggest fish-eaters in the world, with an average annual consumption of 90kg per person.

Traditional Seychelles cuisine is the focus of *Dekouver Marmit,* compiled by the Ministry of Local Government, Sports & Culture.

SEYCHELLES' TOP FIVE

This is a quick selection of some of our favourite places to indulge in fine dining, chosen for palate pleasure over price considerations. Turn to the appropriate page to initiate salivation.

Coco Rouge (p287) Unfussy and laid-back. Killer smoked fish salad.
Le Corsaire (p275) Style meets substance here.
Lanbousir (p293) A beach shack near the most glamorous beach of the Seychelles.
Laurier Guest House (p287) Phenomenal Creole buffet.
Les Rochers (p287) Romantic to boot.

WHERE TO EAT & DRINK

There's a full gamut of restaurant types, from funky shacks and burger joints to ritzy restaurants. Larger hotels have a choice of restaurants, with one always serving buffets (usually Creole or seafood). There is not a vast selection of street snacks to choose from in the Seychelles, but street vendors sell fresh fruit and fish – a good option if you're self-catering. Grocery stores are also widely available in Mahé and in Praslin. The Victoria market is another good place to stock up on fresh food.

EATING WITH KIDS

If you're travelling with the tykes, you'll find that children's menus are not normally offered in restaurants. However, most local eateries will accommodate two children splitting a meal or can produce child-size portions on request. You can also ask for restaurant staff to bring you simple food.

VEGETARIANS & VEGANS

Restaurant menus in the Seychelles are dominated by fish, seafood and meat dishes, though there are actually a few salad and pasta dishes that are meat-free. If you're self-catering, you'll have much more choice, with a good selection of fruits and vegetables.

If you're staying somewhere where your meals are cooked for you (for example in a guesthouse), make sure you tell your hosts in advance you're vegetarian so that they can prepare something for you.

HABITS & CUSTOMS

Dining habits and customs in the Seychelles are similar to those elsewhere in the region, and in the home countries of most Western travellers. Lunch is usually the main meal of the day and is typically served at around noon. Dinner tends to be a lighter version of lunch and is eaten around 7pm. Meals are central to family life on weekends.

Arachnophobes may have a difficult time in the Seychelles. Almost every tree branch is draped in sheets of tough sticky silk belonging to the huge palm spider. Despite its size – up to 10cm – this obtrusive arachnid is harmless to humans.

ENVIRONMENT

The Seychelles is a haven for wildlife, particularly birds and tropical fish. Because of the islands' isolation and the comparatively late arrival of humans, many species are endemic to the Seychelles.

THE LAND

The Seychelles lies about 1600km off the east coast of Africa and just south of the equator. It is made up of 115 islands, of which the central islands (including Mahé, Praslin and La Digue) are granite and the outly ing islands are coral atolls. The granite islands, which do not share the volcanic nature of Réunion and Mauritius, appear to be peaks of a huge submerged plateau that was torn away from Africa when the continental plates shifted about 65 million years ago.

WILDLIFE
Animals
Common mammals and reptiles include the fruit bat or flying fox, the gecko, the skink and the tenrec (a hedgehoglike mammal imported from Madagascar). There are also some small snakes, but they are not dangerous.

More noteworthy is the fact that giant tortoises, which feature on the Seychelles coat of arms, are now found only in the Seychelles and the Galápagos Islands, off Ecuador. The French and English wiped out the giant tortoises from all the Seychelles islands except Aldabra, where happily more than 100,000 still survive. Many have been brought to the central islands, where they munch their way around hotel gardens, and there is a free-roaming colony on Curieuse Island.

Almost every island seems to have some rare species of bird: on Frégate, Cousin, Cousine and Aride there are magpie robins (known as *pie chanteuse* in Creole); on Cousin, Cousine and Aride you'll find the Seychelles warbler; La Digue has the *veuve* (paradise flycatcher); and Praslin has the black parrot. The bare-legged scops owl and the Seychelles kestrel live on Mahé, and Bird Island is home to millions of sooty terns.

For further information on marine life, see p33.

Plants
The coconut palm and the casuarina are the Seychelles' most common trees. There are a few banyans and you're also likely to see screw pines, bamboo and tortoise trees (so named because the fruit looks like the tortoises that eat it).

There are about 80 endemic plant species. Virgin forest now exists only on the higher parts of Silhouette Island and Mahé, and in the Vallée de Mai on Praslin, which is one of only two places in the world where the giant coco de mer palm grows wild. The other is nearby Curieuse Island.

Cousin and Aride Islands support huge colonies of lesser (black) noddies. During the birds' elaborate courtship, the male bird offers his mate leaves until he finds one to her satisfaction (she indicates her approval by defecating on it!).

Esmeralda is in *Guinness World Records* as the oldest tortoise in the world. She is actually a he, weighs more than 300kg and is believed to be over 200 years old. He lives on Bird Island.

SEYCHELLES SNAPSHOTS

PARADISE UNDER THREAT?
Brochures may continue to paint the Seychelles as an unspoilt, green-and-blue paradise, but the environmental impact of construction projects that were under way when we visited cannot be swept under the carpet. Every year, more resort hotels and lodges pop up, most notably on formerly pristine beaches or secluded islands. By the time you read this, there will be new tourist developments on Round Island, Eden Island, Long Island, Mahé (Port Launay and Petite Anse) and Praslin (Beau Vallon). Sure, they have nothing on the concrete-and-glass horrors of, say, Hawaii or Cancun, but they still necessitate additional support systems, including roads and numerous vehicle trips, not to mention cutting down vegetation. So far, the government has traditionally tried to balance tourist developments with the protection of the natural assets that attract the tourists (and therefore revenue) to the islands, but the rising population and the growing demands of tourism are putting a strain on that policy. How long will it resist the temptation of easy money?

Another problem is that many developers are foreigners, which means that the big money goes out of the country. It's of much greater benefit to locals when travellers stay in smaller hotels and guesthouses, rather than the large, foreign-controlled resorts.

In the high, remote parts of Mahé and Silhouette Island, you may com
across the insect-eating pitcher plant, which either clings to trees or bushe
or sprawls along the ground.

On the floral front, there are plenty of orchids, bougainvilleas, hibiscuses
gardenias and frangipanis.

The botanical gardens in Victoria provide a pleasant and interesting
walk. The Vallée de Mai on Praslin is a must. For chance discoveries, ge
away from the beach for a day and head into the hills on Mahé, Praslin
or La Digue.

The *Field Guide to the
Birds of Seychelles*, by
Adrian Skerrett, Ian
Bullock and Tony Disley,
offers the most compre-
hensive and informative
guide to local bird life.

NATIONAL PARKS

The Seychelles currently boasts two national parks and seven marine na
tional parks, as well as several other protected areas under government and
NGO (non-governmental organisation) management. In all, about 46% of
the country's total landmass is now protected as well as some 45 sq km
of ocean, providing an invaluable resource for scientific investigation and
species protection.

The most important protected areas include those listed in the table
on below.

ENVIRONMENTAL ISSUES

Overall the Seychelles has a pretty good record for protecting its natura
environment. As early as 1968, Birdlife International set the ball rolling
when it bought Cousin Island and began studying some of the country'
critically endangered species. This was followed in the 1970s with legislation
to establish national parks and marine reserves.

The Seychelles was also the first African country to draw up a 10-yea
environmental management plan, in 1990, which ushered in a more in
tegrated approach. Under the current plan the government wants 80% of

SEYCHELLES NATIONAL PARKS

Park	Features	Activities	Best time to visit	Page
Aldabra Marine Reserve	raised coral atoll, tidal lagoon, birdlife, marine turtles, giant tortoises	diving, snorkelling, scientific study	Nov, Dec & mid-Mar–mid-May	boxed text, p288
Aride Island Marine Nature Reserve	granite island, coral reef, seabirds, fish life, marine turtles	bird-watching, snorkelling	Sep-May	boxed text, p288
Cousin Island Special Reserve	granite island, natural vegetation, hawksbill turtles, seabirds, lizards	bird-watching	all year	p283
Curieuse Marine National Park	granite island, coral reefs, coco de mer palms, giant tortoises, mangrove swamps, marine turtles, fish life	diving, snorkelling, walking	all year	p283
Morne Seychellois National Park	forested peaks, mangroves, glacis habitats	hiking, botany, bird-watching	May-Sep	p275
Port Launay & Baie Ternay Marine National Park	mangrove swamps, fish life, coral reefs	diving, snorkelling	all year	p278
Praslin National Park (Vallée de Mai)	native forest, coco de mer, other endemic palms, black parrot	botany, bird-watching, walking	all year	p280
Ste Anne Marine National Park	forested islands, coral reef, varied marine ecosystems, marine turtles	glass-bottomed boat trips, snorkelling, diving	all year	p273

protected areas to be under private management by 2010. This is partly for financial reasons (someone else bears the cost) and partly to increase the involvement of local communities in decision-making and day-to-day management. The plan also sets strict guidelines for all new building and development projects.

Not that the government's record is entirely unblemished. In 1998 it authorised a vast land-reclamation project on Mahé's northeast coast to provide much-needed space for housing. This has caused widespread silting, marring the natural beauty of this coast indefinitely, though the alternative was to clear large tracts of forest. A difficult choice.

Tourism has had a similarly mixed impact. Hotels have been built on previously unspoilt beaches, causing problems with waste management and increased pressure on fragile ecosystems, not to mention more difficult access to public beaches. On the other hand, tourist dollars provide much-needed revenue for funding conservation projects. Local attitudes have also changed as people have learned to value their environment.

Further impetus for change is coming from NGOs operating at both community and government levels. They have notched up some spectacular successes, such as the Magpie Robin Recovery Program, funded by the Royal Society for the Protection of Birds and Birdlife International. From just 23 magpie robins languishing on Frégate Island in 1990, there are now nearly 200 living on Frégate, Cousin and Cousine Islands. Similar results have been achieved with the Seychelles warbler on Cousin, Cousine and Aride Islands.

As part of these projects, a number of islands have been painstakingly restored to their original habitat by replacing alien plant and animal species with native varieties. Several islands have also been developed for ecotourism, notably Frégate, Bird, Denis, North and Alphonse Islands, with the likelihood that Aldabra and other outer islands will follow. The visitors not only help fund conservation work, but it is also easier to protect the islands from poachers and predators if they are inhabited. With any luck, this marriage of conservation and tourism will point the way to the future.

Get to know more about the Seychelles' fabulous environment and conservation programmes at the Nature Seychelles site at www.natureseychelles.org.

SEYCHELLES SNAPSHOTS

Seychelles

You're planning a trip to the Seychelles? Lucky you! Mother Nature was very generous with these 115 islands scattered in the Indian Ocean and has spoiled them rotten. Undeniably, the beaches are the big attraction, and what beaches: exquisite ribbons of white sand lapped by topaz waters and backed by lush hills and big glacis boulders. And nary a crowd in sight.

With such a dreamlike setting, the Seychelles is unsurprisingly a choice place for a honeymoon. But there's much more to do than simply cracking open a bottle of champagne with the loved one in a luxurious hotel. Having earned a reputation as a paradigm of ecotourism, the Seychelles is a top spot to watch birds and giant tortoises in their natural habitat. And a vast living world lies just below the turquoise waters, beckoning divers of all levels. When you tire of beaches you can venture inland on jungle trails, indulge in fine dining or enjoy the sublime laid-back tempo.

And time has come to spread the word: yes, this paradise is accessible to us all. On top of ultraluxurious options, the Seychelles has plenty of quaint, affordable self-catering facilities and guesthouses, often situated on some of the best land. Though it remains an expensive destination, its tourist authorities are now targeting non-millionaires, promoting these economy options. But fear not: mass tourism it will never be.

Which island should you go to? Don't sweat the decision too much. Be it one of the three main islands of Mahé, Praslin or La Digue, or any outlying island, you'll strike gold.

Seduced? Push open your travel agent's door and book your ticket to paradise.

HIGHLIGHTS

- Scratching the leathery neck of a giant tortoise on **Curieuse Island** (p283)
- Splashing around in the jewelled waters of **Anse Source d'Argent** (p291), **Anse Soleil** (p278), **Petite Anse** (p278) or **Grande Anse** (p291) – absolute heaven
- Diving with toothy critters at **Shark Bank** (p31)
- Taking a guided walk in **Morne Seychellois National Park** (p275) to mug up on botany
- Living out that stranded-on-a-desert-island fantasy on secluded **Bird Island** (boxed text, p288)
- Hearing yourself screaming 'Oh, these coconuts are so sexy!' in the **Vallée de Mai** (p281)
- Devouring ultra fresh fish in one of **Praslin's restaurants** (p286)

SEYCHELLES

MAURITIUS

RÉUNION

| ■ TELEPHONE CODE: 248 | ■ POPULATION: 81,000 | ■ AREA: 455 SQ KM |

CLIMATE & WHEN TO GO

The seasons in the Seychelles are defined by the trade winds. These bring warmer, wetter airstreams from the northwest from October to April. From May to September the southeast trades usher in cooler, drier weather but the winds whip up the waves and you'll want to find protected beaches. The turnaround periods (March to April and October to November) are normally calm and windless.

The rain generally comes in sudden, heavy bursts. Mahé and Silhouette, the most mountainous islands, get the highest rainfall. January is the wettest month by far, and July and August the driest. Temperatures range between 24°C and 32°C throughout the year.

Although the Seychelles lies outside the cyclone zone, cyclone activity elsewhere in the Indian Ocean can still bring unseasonably grey, windy weather between December and March.

Hotel prices shoot up and accommodation can be hard to find during the peak seasons from December to January and July to August. Easter can also get busy.

See p297 for the climate chart for Victoria, the capital of Mahé.

MAHÉ

When it comes to wishing for the archetypal idyllic island, it's impossible to think past the glorious bays caressed by gorgeously multihued waters (the ones you see in travel mags) of Mahé. To the northeast, a range of granite peaks, including Mahé's highest point, Morne Seychellois (905m), adds to this vivid panorama.

By far the largest and most developed of the Seychelles islands, Mahé (named by the French in honour of the 18th-century governor of Mauritius, Mahé de Labourdonnais) is home to the country's capital, Victoria, and to about 90% of the Seychelles' population. Small wonder that it has excellent vacation and adventure opportunities. Best of all, most spots along the coast are easy to reach by bus or car, so travellers have no trouble sampling the full variety of options the area has to offer.

That said, Mahé has its fair share of the mundane, as testified by industrial devel-

opment on the northeast coast and a land-reclamation project that is marring the appearance of the island around Victoria. Yet paradise lies close at hand – a bus or car ride of no more than 20 minutes will bring you to fabulous natural attractions.

VICTORIA

pop 23,300

Victoria may be the country's main economic, political and commercial hub but peak hour here lasts an unbearable five minutes! It is home to about a third of the Seychelles' population, but even so Victoria retains the air of a provincial town. While it may not fulfil all fantasies about tropical paradises, the city still has a little charm and a little promise when you scratch beneath the surface. There's a bustling market, enviable-quality dining options for a place its size, manicured botanical gardens and a fistful of attractive old colonial buildings sidling up alongside modern structures and shopping plazas. It's also a good place to grab last-minute gifts before heading home.

Oh, and there's the setting. Victoria is set against an impressive backdrop of hills that seem to tumble into the turquoise sea.

Information
BOOKSHOPS

Antigone (☎ 225443; Victoria House, Francis Rachel St) Stocks a reasonable range of English-language novels and books on the Seychelles, plus a few imported newspapers and magazines.

Memorabilia (☎ 321190; Revolution Ave) Gift shop and art gallery with a selection of Seychelles titles.

EMERGENCY

Ambulance (☎ 999)

Central Police Station (☎ 288000; Revolution Ave)

Police (☎ 999)

INTERNET ACCESS

Double Click (☎ 610590; Palm St; per hr Rs 40; ⏰ 8am-9pm Mon-Sat, 9am-8pm Sun) Great little café open after hours.

Kokonet (☎ 322000; Pirates Arms bldg, Independence Ave; per hr Rs 20; ⏰ 8am-6pm Mon-Fri, 9am-noon Sat)

MEDICAL SERVICES

Behram's Pharmacy (☎ 225559; Victoria House, Francis Rachel St; ⏰ 8.30am-4.45pm Mon-Fri, 8.15am-12.30pm Sat)

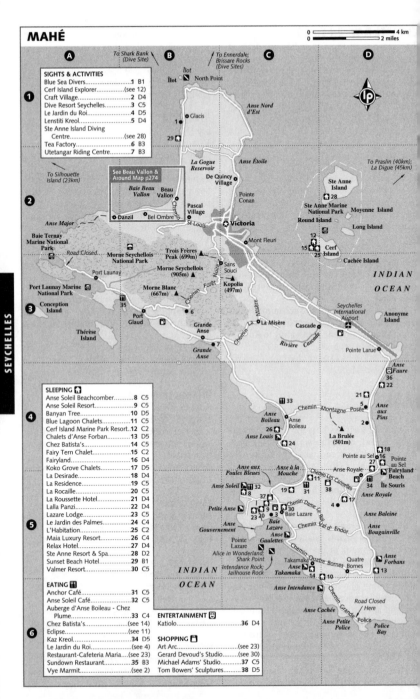

MAHÉ

0 — 4 km
0 — 2 miles

SIGHTS & ACTIVITIES

Blue Sea Divers	1	B1
Cerf Island Explorer	(see 12)	
Craft Village	2	D4
Dive Resort Seychelles	3	C5
Le Jardin du Roi	4	D5
Lenstiti Kreol	5	D4
Ste Anne Island Diving Centre	(see 28)	
Tea Factory	6	B3
Utetangar Riding Centre	7	B3

See Beau Vallon & Around Map p274

SLEEPING

Anse Soleil Beachcomber	8	C5
Anse Soleil Resort	9	C5
Banyan Tree	10	D5
Blue Lagoon Chalets	11	C5
Cerf Island Marine Park Resort	12	C2
Chalets d'Anse Forban	13	D5
Chez Batista's	14	C5
Fairy Tern Chalet	15	C2
Fairyland	16	D4
Koko Grove Chalets	17	D5
La Desirade	18	D4
La Residence	19	C5
La Rocaille	20	C5
La Roussette Hotel	21	D4
Lalla Panzi	22	D4
Lazare Lodge	23	C5
Le Jardin des Palmes	24	C4
L'Habitation	25	C2
Maia Luxury Resort	26	C4
Relax Hotel	27	D4
Ste Anne Resort & Spa	28	D2
Sunset Beach Hotel	29	B1
Valmer Resort	30	C5

EATING

Anchor Café	31	C5
Anse Soleil Café	32	C5
Auberge d'Anse Boileau - Chez Plume	33	C4
Chez Batista's	(see 14)	
Eclipse	(see 11)	
Kaz Kreol	34	D5
Le Jardin du Roi	(see 4)	
Restaurant-Cafeteria Maria	(see 23)	
Sundown Restaurant	35	B3
Vye Marmit	(see 2)	

ENTERTAINMENT

Katiolo	36	D4

SHOPPING

Art Arc	(see 23)	
Gerard Devoud's Studio	(see 30)	
Michael Adams' Studio	37	C5
Tom Bowers' Sculptures	38	D5

SEYCHELLES

Victoria Hospital (☎ 388000; Mont Fleuri) The country's main hospital has an emergency unit and outpatient and dental clinics.

MONEY
All the major banks have ATMs and exchange facilities.

Barclays Bank Independence Ave (☎ 383838; ☼ 8.30am-2.30pm, 8.30-11am Sat); Market (☎ 383838; Albert St; ☼ 8.30am-2.30pm, Sat 8.30-11am)

Nouvobanq (☎ 293000; Francis Rachel St; ☼ 8.30am-2pm Mon-Fri, 8.30-11.30am Sat)

Seychelles Savings Bank (☎ 225251; Kingsgate House, Independence Ave)

POST
Central post office (Independence Ave; ☼ 8am-5pm Mon-Fri, 8am-noon Sat)

TOURIST INFORMATION
Tourist office (☎ 610800; www.seychelles.travel; Independence Ave; ☼ 8am-5pm Mon-Fri, 9am-noon Sat) Competent staff hand out booklets detailing all the country's accommodation options and decent maps of Mahé, Praslin and La Digue.

TRAVEL AGENCIES
Victoria's three main travel agencies offer the full range of services, including ticketing, car hire, yacht charter and tours around Mahé and to other islands.

Créole Holidays (☎ 224900; www.creoleholidays.sc; Kingsgate House, Independence Ave)

Creole Travel Services (☎ 297000; www.creoletravelservices.com; Albert St)

Mason's Travel (☎ 322642; www.masonstravel.com; Revolution Ave)

Sights & Activities
The focal point of downtown is a downsized replica of the **clock tower** on London's Vauxhall Bridge. The replica was brought to Victoria in 1903 when the Seychelles became a crown colony. The **old courthouse** (Supreme Court; Francis Rachel St) beside the clock tower will appeal to fans of Creole architecture, as will the colonial buildings that are scattered along Francis Rachel St and Albert St. Make a beeline for **Kanti House** (Albert St), a decrepit yet atmospheric building.

When it first opened, the revamped covered **market** (Market St; ☼ 5.30am-5pm Mon-Fri, 5.30am-noon Sat) was something of a tourist gimmick, but over the years it's evolved into quite a lively, bustling place. Early morning is the best time to come, when fishmongers display an aston-

ishing variety of seafood, from parrot fish to barracuda.

The **Natural History Museum** (☎ 321333; admission Rs 10; Independence Ave; ☼ 8.30am-4.30pm Mon-Thu, 8.30am-noon Fri & Sat) is worth a quick visit to learn about the islands' curious creatures, such as the Seychelles crocodile and the giant tortoise, both now sadly vanished from the main islands.

Not to be confused with the Natural History Museum, the **National Museum of History** (☎ 225253; State House Ave; admission Rs 10; ☼ 8.30am-4.30pm Mon, Tue, Thu & Fri, 8.30am-noon Sat) contains a small but well-displayed collection of historical artefacts. Other exhibits also relate to the settlement of the islands and to local culture, including musical instruments, games and *gris gris* (black magic).

For respite, the manicured **botanical gardens** (☎ 224644; admission €5; ☼ 8am-5pm), full of streams and birdsong, are about 10 minutes' walk south of the centre. This is a good place to mug up on native plant life before venturing further afield. Star attractions are the coco de mer palms (see the boxed text, p283) lining the main alley. There's also a spice grove, a pen of giant tortoises and a patch of rainforest complete with fruit bats.

Sleeping
Victoria's range of accommodation is disappointingly slim, especially considering it's the capital, but it does make sense to stay elsewhere and visit the town on day trips.

Hotel Bel Air (☎ 224416; www.seychelles.net/belair; Bel Air Rd; s/d incl breakfast €65/86; ☼) On the road to Sans Souci, this affable address has a friendly homely feel and there's a well-established garden with tropical plants. While the modest furnishings and inoffensive fabrics won't snag any design awards, rooms are clean and well kept. It's an easy bus ride from the centre.

Mountain Rise (☎ 225308; mountainrise@seychelles .sc; Sans Souci Rd; s/d incl breakfast €105/130) High above the botanical gardens, this serene colonial bungalow has five immaculate suites equipped to a high standard. There's also a good restaurant.

Eating
Victoria is relatively well endowed with places to eat. In addition to the following, there are many takeaway outlets offering Creole staples such as grilled fish and chicken curry in the streets around the market.

SEYCHELLES

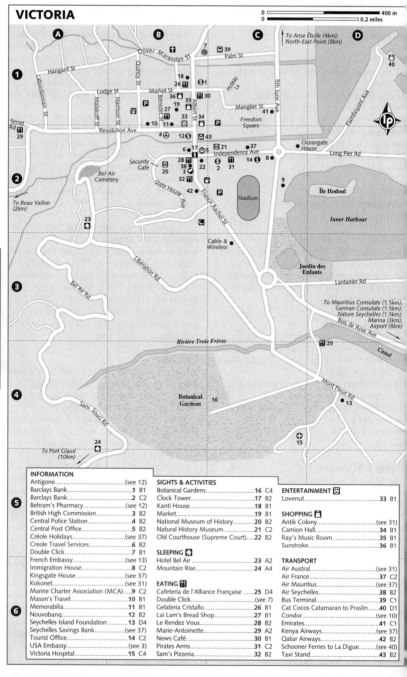

VICTORIA

Gelateria Cristallo (Market St; ice creams Rs 8-15; ☻ 8.30am-5pm Mon-Fri, 8.30am-2pm Sat) Cristallo's tempting ice creams will satisfy everyone, except your personal trainer.

Lai Lam's Bread Shop (Benezet St; ☻ 8am-5pm) If you're a carbo seeker, head straight to that lively island of yeasty goodness smack dab in the centre. You won't be able to resist the aroma of freshly baked bread and cakes!

ourpick **News Café** (☎ 322999; Trinity House, Albert St; mains Rs 20-40; ☻ breakfast & lunch) This cheerful café-bar overlooking the main drag is an excellent venue to devour a comforting breakfast (muesli!) and read the daily newspapers, or to take a lunchtime break from town. The generous sandwiches and satisfying salads are best enjoyed at the tables out front, allowing premium views of the people parade going past.

Double Click (☎ 610590; Palm St; mains Rs 25-55; ☻ 8am-9pm Mon-Sat, 9am-8pm Sun) This buzzy eatery popular with students rustles up light and healthy meals, including salads and soups. Sandwiches will quell greater hunger pangs. Keep your fluids up with a zesty smoothie or a juice concoction.

Cafeteria de l'Alliance Française (☎ 282424; Bois de Rose Ave; mains Rs 50-70; ☻ 9am-6pm Mon-Fri, 9am-2pm Sat) This *très* French outpost is handy for a bite at lunchtime if you're mooching around the botanical gardens.

Pirates Arms (☎ 225001; Independence Ave; mains Rs 50-130; ☻ 9am-11pm Mon-Sat, noon-11pm Sun) Legendary to the point where it has become *the* meeting point in Victoria, this central café-restaurant veritably thrums the minute it opens its doors for breakfast. The menu is as long as your arm and runs from salads and sandwiches to pizzas and meat or fish dishes.

Sam's Pizzeria (☎ 322499; Francis Rachel St; mains Rs 60-90; ☻ lunch & dinner) Step into this snazzy spot for an escape from the busy street. Walls are adorned with paintings by local artist George Camille, which gives the place a splash of style. Get things going with pizzas cooked in a wood-fired oven, or well-presented salads, including an excellent tandoori chicken salad.

Le Rendez Vous (☎ 323556; Francis Rachel St; mains Rs 75-175; ☻ 9am-10pm Mon-Sat) Is this breezy, 1st-floor eatery overlooking the main square suitable for a rendezvous? No idea, as we had dinner on our very own, but the food proves a worthy paramour; treat yourself to French-influenced dishes (but avoid the skimpy smoked fish and mango salad). An

oversized ice cream will finish you off sweetly. The Balinese-meets-Amazonian décor is easy on the eye, with darkwood furnishings, tropical plants and candlelit tables.

Marie-Antoinette (☎ 266222; Serret Rd, St Louis; menu Rs 130; ☻ lunch & dinner Mon-Sat) This atmospheric Creole restaurant is a good place to test your stomach capacity. The set menu includes fish and aubergine fritters, tuna steak grilled fish, chicken curry, rice and salad. It's set in a beautiful old colonial house on the road to Beau Vallon. One proviso: this venue is notorious for its ups and downs.

Entertainment

The most popular drinking hole is the Pirates Arms, which doubles as a bar and offers live music (a crooner with a guitar) several nights a week.

Need to let off steam and rub shoulders with local lovelies? Showcase your dance-floor repertoire at the **Lovenut** (☎ 596707; Revolution Ave; admission men/women Rs 100/50; ☻ Wed, Fri & Sat), slap bang in the centre. A cafeteria by day, Lovenut becomes a trendy discotheque at night. Earmark Friday 6.30pm for jazz sessions.

Shopping

The majority of craft and gift shops are concentrated in and around the market. **Camion Hall** (Albert St) is a crafts centre with a range of upmarket shops, including Caprice des Îles, which sells fabulous fabrics; Aphrodite Marine, a model-ship manufacturer; Pineapple Studio, which does a nice line in general souvenirs; and the jeweller Kreol'or.

Another souvenir shop worth browsing is **Antik Colony** (☎ 321700; Pirates Arms Bldg, Independence Ave). George Camille's lovely paintings can be found at **Sunstroke** (☎ 224767; Market St).

For a wide selection of Creole music, visit **Ray's Music Room** (☎ 322674; Premier Bldg, Albert St).

Getting There & Around

Victoria is the main transport hub for buses around Mahé and for boats to Praslin and La Digue. For information about these services and for flights around the islands, see p300. For further information regarding air travel see p302.

Coming from the airport, a taxi into town costs around Rs 75 plus Rs 5 per piece of luggage. Alternatively, cross the road and pick up any bus heading north. See p301 for more about local buses.

The following airlines have offices in Mahé.

Air Austral (☎ 323262; Independence Ave) Represented by Horizon Travel.

Air France (☎ 322414; Kingsgate House, Independence Ave)

Air Mauritius (☎ 322414; Kingsgate House, Independence Ave)

Air Seychelles (☎ 381000; Francis Rachel St)

Condor (☎ 322642; Revolution Ave)

Emirates (☎ 292700; 5th June Ave)

Kenya Airways (☎ 322989; Kingsgate House, Independence Ave)

Qatar Airways (☎ 224518; Francis Rachel St)

BEAU VALLON & THE NORTH COAST

A long, brilliant white arc of sands laced by palms and takamaka trees, Beau Vallon (Map p274; on Mahé's northwest coast, 3km from Victoria) is the most popular beach in Mahé, yet not the most appealing. It's one of the few beaches where the water is deep enough for swimming (watch out for large swells between June and November). It's overbuilt by Seychellois standards, but you'll find it remarkably low-key and quiet if you have experienced other tropical destinations. The seaside ambience, with fishermen selling fresh fish late in the afternoon in the shade of takamaka trees, adds a dash of real life to the area.

In Beau Vallon village (Map p274), where the road from Victoria forks west to Bel Ombre and northeast to Glacis, there is a petrol station, a Barclays Bank ATM, a Cable & Wireless internet café and the police station. You'll find convenience stores supplying basic foodstuffs and other necessities on the beach road and around the junction with the Bel Ombre road.

Beau Vallon is the main destination on the northwest coast because of its beach and tourist infrastructure, but there's also some great scenery north, up the coast to **Glacis** and **North Point**. With your own wheels, it's a scenic drive on a narrow road that hugs the coastline, with intermittent, lovely views over secluded coves at the foot of the cliffs. From North Point, you can head down to Victoria via **Anse Étoile**.

Activities

There's good snorkelling offshore and there's plenty of great diving within a 20-minute boat ride (see p31). Established dive shops include the following:

Big Blue Divers (Map p274; ☎ 261106; www.bigblue divers.net)

Blue Sea Divers (Map p268; ☎ 526051; www.bluesea divers.com) In Glacis.

Diable des Mers (Map p274; ☎ 248385; odream@ seychelles.net)

Seychelles Underwater Centre (Map p274; ☎ 247357; www.diveseychelles.com.sc) At the Coral Strand Hotel.

Sleeping

Beau Vallon and Bel Ombre offer the widest range of accommodation in north Mahé.

our pick Georgina's Cottage (Map p274; ☎ 247016; georgina@seychelles.net; Beau Vallon; s/d incl breakfast €45/60 ☒) An excellent option if you're working to a tight budget, Georgina's Cottage offers eight rooms, a communal kitchen, a lounge area and a leafy tropical garden for added appeal. Luxury it ain't – the old-fashioned décor could do with a little sprucing up – but at this price it would be churlish to quibble. A 20m Frisbee throw from the beach, it's also very close to dive centres, restaurants and shops. The copious breakfast is served on the veranda. Patrick, the owner's son, is full of local info. Air-con is extra (€5).

Panorama – Relais des Îles (Map p274; ☎ 247300; www.panorama-guesthouse.com; Beau Vallon; s €75, d €95-125, all incl breakfast) Just above the main coast road, the 10 modern units arranged in a quiet garden won't win any awards for originality and the furnishings are functional rather than luxurious (white walls, white tiles), but otherwise the Panorama delivers the goods perfectly adequately. Location is tiptop and owner Vesna Rakic is well clued-up on the island.

Beau Vallon Bungalows (Map p274; ☎ 247382; www .seychelles.net/bvbung; Beau Vallon; s/d incl breakfast €80/90 ☒) Another cluster of well-run cottages, tranquilly set in a well-manicured garden, on the same property as Romance Bungalows. The style of the units is modern and functional. It's set back from the main coast road, and is handy to everything.

Villa Gaia (Map p274; ☎ 710690; www.villagaia-seychelles .com; Bel Ombre; villas €95) This elegant villa with lots of personal touches is the pride and joy of Michou Walsh, your English hostess and a mine of local knowledge. Fab for families, the self-contained villa contains enough room to accommodate a small troupe. The only downside might be the coast road nearby, but a wall should seal you off from traffic noise. Fancy a dip? There's a little white-sand beach across the road.

ESCAPES TO STE ANNE MARINE NATIONAL PARK

A definite must-see, Ste Anne Marine National Park (Map p268) off Victoria consists of six islands. Of these, day-trippers are permitted to land on Cerf and Moyenne Islands. For a complete escape, you can stay on Cerf and Ste Anne (and on Round and Long by the time you read this). The park is fantastic for swimming and snorkelling. Sadly, the coral in the park is no longer as awesome as it was. Silting from construction works in the bay has led to significant coral damage, compounded by several episodes of coral 'bleaching'.

The park is primarily visited on glass-bottomed boat tours offered by the main travel agencies in Victoria (see p269). The cost of a full day's outing including snorkelling and lunch starts at €85/50 per adult/child. You can also contact the **Marine Charter Association** (MCA; Map p270; ☎ 322126; mca@seychelles.net; 5th June Ave, Victoria), which charges only €50/25 per adult/child, or **Cerf Island Explorer** (Map p268; ☎ 570043; pal@seychelles.net), based at the Ste Anne Resort & Spa (see below). And yes, there's diving in the park! There are about 10 dive sites, scattered off the various islands. Contact **Ste Anne Island Diving Centre** (Map p268; ☎ 570043; pal@seychelles.net; from €70) at the Ste Anne Resort & Spa.

Note that the park authorities charge a fee of €10 per person (free for children under 12 years) to enter the marine park. Tour operators usually include this in their prices.

Cerf Island

About 60 people live on Cerf Island, including Wilbur Smith, the South African novelist. As with Moyenne and Round Islands, there's good snorkelling and the beaches are seriously alluring.

You can stay at a comfortable little colonial-style hotel, **L'Habitation** (Map p268; ☎ 323111; habicerf@seychelles.net; s/d with half board €208/243; ❖ ✉), just a 10-minute boat ride from Victoria. Run by the friendly Delta, this 12-room charmer is right on the beach and welcomes families. If you're looking for a place for romance, head to the more exclusive **Cerf Island Marine Park Resort** (Map p268; ☎ 294500; www.cerf-resort.com; s/d with half board from €466/530; ❖), further south. Another recommended option is the newish **Fairy Tern Chalet** (Map p268; ☎ 321733; www.fairy ternchalet.sc; bungalows €125; ❖), approximately halfway between the two resorts. Digs are in two squeaky-clean bungalows overlooking the beach.

If there's enough demand the restaurants at L'Habitation and Cerf Island Marine Park Resort will usually offer a package including transport and lunch or dinner.

Moyenne Island

Moyenne is owned by Brendon Grimshaw, who has spent the last 40 years hacking back the jungle to create his own tropical paradise. The native fauna and flora have been carefully regenerated and everything is neatly labelled, giving it the air of a botanical garden.

Day tours are organised exclusively through **Creole Travel Services** (Map p270; ☎ 297000; www .creoletravelservices.com; Albert St).

Round Island

This island was once home to a leper colony, but these days it's better known for the offshore snorkelling. A 10-villa luxury resort was under construction at the time of writing. For more information check out www.enchantedseychelles.com.

Ste Anne Island

The largest of the six islands, and only 4km east of Victoria, Ste Anne boasts two ravishing beaches, along which spreads the super-swanky **Ste Anne Resort & Spa** (Map p268; ☎ 292000; www .sainteanne-resort.com; s/d from €682/974; ❖ ▢ ✉), with 87 glorious villas and top-notch amenities, including a spa, a dive centre and a kids club.

Long Island & Cachée Island

Long Island has long been home to the prison but should welcome a new type of inmate with the opening of a swish Shangri-la Hotel & Spa in 2008. Check out www.shangri-la.com. The smallest island of the lot, Cachée, lies southeast of Cerf. It's uninhabited.

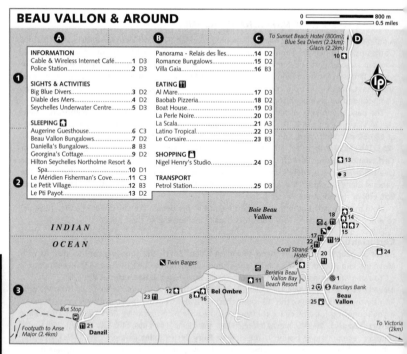

BEAU VALLON & AROUND

0 _____ 800 m
0 _____ 0.5 miles

INFORMATION
Cable & Wireless Internet Café..........1 D3
Police Station....................................2 D3

SIGHTS & ACTIVITIES
Big Blue Divers..................................3 D2
Diable des Mers.................................4 D2
Seychelles Underwater Centre...........5 D3

SLEEPING
Augerine Guesthouse.........................6 C3
Beau Vallon Bungalows......................7 D2
Daniella's Bungalows.........................8 B3
Georgina's Cottage............................9 D2
Hilton Seychelles Northolme Resort &
 Spa...10 D1
Le Méridien Fisherman's Cove.........11 C3
Le Petit Village...............................12 B3
Le Pti Payot...................................13 D2

Panorama - Relais des Îles...............14 D2
Romance Bungalows........................15 D2
Villa Gaia.......................................16 B3

EATING
Al Mare...17 D3
Baobab Pizzeria..............................18 D2
Boat House....................................19 D3
La Perle Noire................................20 D3
La Scala..21 A3
Latino Tropical...............................22 D3
Le Corsaire....................................23 B3

SHOPPING
Nigel Henry's Studio........................24 D3

TRANSPORT
Petrol Station.................................25 D3

To Sunset Beach Hotel (800m);
Blue Sea Divers (2.2km);
Glacis (2.2km)

INDIAN

OCEAN

*Baie Beau
Vallon*

Twin Barges

*Coral Strand
Hotel*

*Berjaya Beau
Vallon Bay
Beach Resort*

Bel Ombre

Barclays Bank

**Beau
Vallon**

Bus Stop

Footpath to Anse
Major (2.4km)

Danzil

To Victoria
(2km)

SEYCHELLES

Romance Bungalows (Map p274; ☎ 410382, 247732; www.romancebungalows.com; Beau Vallon; s/d incl breakfast €97/105; ☒) We could tell you that the 'Romance Bungalows' live up to their name and are suitable for a cuddle with your sweetheart, but we won't. At least they provide all the home comforts, assuming you live in a spacious, well-appointed flat with a spotless kitchen (but no maid). The beach is only steps away and all amenities are within easy reach.

our pick **Le Pti Payot** (Map p274; ☎ 261447; payot@ seychelles.net; Beau Vallon; d €98; ☒) Three immaculate and roomy chalets with bird's-eye views (No 3 is the best) in a lush garden. What more could you want?

Le Petit Village (Map p274; ☎ 284969; www.lepetitvillage .com; Bel Ombre; d €220; ☒) Luxury self-catering accommodation in log cabins overlooking the ocean in Bel Ombre. There's a choice between one-bedroom studios and two-bedroom apartments, all equipped to a very high standard. There were talks of changing ownership, so stay tuned.

Sunset Beach Hotel (Map p268; ☎ 261111; www.sunset -beach.com; Glacis; s €370-440, d €390-460, all incl breakfast; ☒ ☐ ☒) This sunset-friendly seducer boasts

an ace location on a little headland among rocks and trees. Its charm lies partly in its intimate scale, with only 29 cottages. The pool shows some signs of wear and tear, but after one sundowner in the bar overlooking the ocean all will be forgiven.

Also recommended:

Daniella's Bungalows (Map p274; ☎ 247914; www .daniellasbungalows.com; Bel Ombre; s/d incl breakfast €80/100; ☒) Has 10 clean but ordinary rooms in a well-tended garden. It's a five-minute walk to the beach. Air-con is extra (€10).

Augerine Guesthouse (Map p274; ☎ 247257; Beau Vallon; s €80-100, d €100-130, all incl breakfast; ☒) This reputable abode was undergoing a major revamp when we visited and should feature 16 spick-and-span rooms (including 13 rooms with sea views) and a restaurant by the time you pop in. On the beach next to the big Berjaya hotel.

Le Méridien Fisherman's Cove (Map p274; ☎ 677000; www.lemeridien.com/fishcove; Bel Ombre; d incl breakfast €545-775, ste from €815; ☒ ☐ ☒) A splendid resort with plush rooms, though not as glam as the Northolme. Be wowed by the staggering bow-shaped lobby.

Hilton Seychelles Northolme Resort & Spa (Map p274; ☎ 299000; www.hiltonworldresorts.com; Glacis; d incl breakfast €610-755; ☒ ☐ ☒) This ultraluxurious establishment has 40 stadium-sized villas blessed with swoony views over the bay. The pool deck alone looks like photo-shoot set for *Elle*, and the interior follows suit. A place for celebs, royal families and honeymooners. If (s)he takes you there, (s)he's serious.

ating

Whatever you think of this coastal stretch, you are sure to have memorable eating experiences here.

Baobab Pizzeria (Map p274; ☎ 247167; Beau Vallon; mains Rs 32-60; ☺ lunch & dinner) Madame Michel presides over this ramshackle, sand-floored eatery wedged between the coast road and the beach. After a morning spent in the waves, re-energise with a piping-hot pizza or fish and chips.

Latino Tropical (Map p274; ☎ 620101; Beau Vallon; mains Rs 40-70; ☺ lunch & dinner Tue-Thu) Paella? Chicken kebab with salad? The menu is a curious mishmash of Spanish and Seychellois, and the décor is enhanced by African touches, such as masks hanging on the walls, and earthy hues. A trendy place breathing new life into the Beau Vallon area, the Latino Tropical is also a great place for a tipple any time of the day (and night), best enjoyed on the alluring terrace overlooking the seafront.

Al Mare (Map p274; ☎ 620240; Beau Vallon; mains Rs 90-125; ☺ 1-10pm) Large, well-spaced tables, colourful tablecloths, potted plants and high ceilings put diners in the right mood to settle down for a big night sampling the ambitious dishes on offer – mostly seafood and pastas. Or you could simply park yourself with a cocktail (from Rs 40) outside to watch the sunset on Silhouette Island – soul-stirring. Sandwiches are also available in the afternoon.

La Scala (Map p274; ☎ 247535; Bel Ombre; mains Rs 95-135; ☺ dinner Mon-Sat) An old favourite of visitors and locals alike, this restaurant specialises in Italian cooking. It might feel weird to sit down for *lasagne al forno* and breaded veal on a tropical Indian Ocean island, but go with the flow – the fare is top-quality and the low-lit ambience on the breezy terrace suitably romantic. A respectable selection of wines stands at your beck and call. At the end of the coast road near Danzil.

La Perle Noire (Map p274; ☎ 620220; Bel Ombre; mains Rs 60-150; ☺ dinner Mon-Sat) The 'Black Pearl' scores high on atmosphere, with an eye-catching nautical theme and seafaring paraphernalia liberally scattered around the dining rooms (can we borrow your superb model

ships?). The eclectic menu features fish, meat and pasta dishes, but the food doesn't quite live up to the promise of the surrounds.

ourpick Le Corsaire (Map p274; ☎ 247171; Bel Ombre; mains Rs 65-200; ☺ dinner Tue-Sun) North Mahé's most prestigious address, Le Corsaire is an atmospheric place just perfect for that special meal. You could lose yourself just in the homemade tiramisu that arrives at the end of the meal. Judging by the *tournedos de bœuf sauce Bearnaise* (a choice piece of steak in a Béarnaise sauce) the beautifully presented mains are just as yummy though, so don't worry *too* much about saving room for dessert. Gastronauts could opt for bat in white-wine sauce. Le Corsaire occupies a half-timbered mansion that seems to have come straight out from rural Normandy. Strong wine list too.

Boat House (Map p274; ☎ 247898; Beau Vallon; buffet Rs 145; ☺ dinner Mon-Sat) If you want to push the boat out, this perennial favourite fits the bill. Bring an empty tum and dive face first into its massive buffet displayed on an outrigger. With 20 different dishes on offer, it's bound to appeal to both carnivores and vegivores. The front walls are left open to the breeze (very welcome on a hot night).

Shopping
Nigel Henry's studio (Map p274; ☎ 715353; Beau Vallon; ☺ 10am-5pm Mon-Sat) Henry's acrylics capture all the life and colour of the local markets.

Getting There & Away
Buses leave regularly from Victoria for Beau Vallon, either straight over the hill via St Louis, or the long way round via Glacis. The last bus to Victoria leaves around 7.30pm; it's a Rs 70 taxi ride if you miss it.

MORNE SEYCHELLOIS NATIONAL PARK
While the dazzling coastline of Mahé is undoubtedly the main attraction, it's crucial that you take the time to explore the island's mountainous interior. One of Mahé's highlights, the splendid Morne Seychellois National Park (Map p268) encompasses an impressive 20% of the land area of Mahé and contains a wide variety of habitats, from coastal mangrove forests up to the country's highest peak, the Morne Seychellois (905m). Choked in thick forest formation, the enigmatic, central part of the park is virtually deserted and can only be reached by walking

trails; you don't have to go very far before the outside world starts to feel a long, long way away. Without a doubt, the best way to appreciate the area is a guided walk; see the boxed text, below for more information.

The road over the mountains from Victoria to Port Glaud, which cuts through the Morne Seychellois National Park, is a stunning scenic drive.

EAST COAST

Let's face it: much of the east coast is given over to housing, so there are only a few spots that fit the picture-postcard ideal.

And swimming is not *that* tempting, with very shallow waters and a profusion of algae – hardcore beach-hounds may be disappointed. This is not to say the east coast isn't a worthwhile place to visit. South of the airport are a number of small enclaves and undeveloped areas, where travellers looking for peace and isolation will find both in no short supply. Take the oft-overlooked, little known **Fairyland beach**: this gem of a beach offers great snorkelling and shimmering waters. Other good strips of sand are found at **Anse Royale**, **Anse Bougainville** and **Anse Forbans** further south.

WALKING IN THE MORNE SEYCHELLOIS NATIONAL PARK

Unleash your inner Indiana Jones! There's more to do in the Seychelles than simply laze the days away on gorgeous beaches with a Seybrew in hand. If you've got itchy feet, there are excellent walks in the Morne Seychellois National Park, with a number of footpaths and hiking trails through the jungle-clad hills. These are detailed in a series of leaflets that are available at the botanical gardens (p269) or the tourist office (p269) in Victoria. The trails are reasonably well signed and are marked by intermittent yellow splotches of paint on the trees and rocks, but it's not a bad idea to hire a guide, who will also provide natural and cultural insights. **Basil Beaudoin** (☎ /fax 241790, 514972) leads hiking and bird-watching trips into the Mahé back country and charges €80 for an informative day's walk with lunch and transport (€50 for a half day). Bring plenty of water. Following is a selection of inspirational hikes.

Danzil to Anse Major

The walk to this lovely and secluded beach takes you along a coast fringed by impressive glacis rock formations. The path starts at the end of the road heading west from Beau Vallon. Though the last stretch down to the beach is a bit of a scramble, it's a fairly easy romp. The beach is blissfully quiet, and is good for swimming, though there can be strong currents. You'll have to return by the same route, a total of roughly 5km.

Tea Factory to Morne Blanc

The imposing white bulk of Morne Blanc and its almost sheer 500m face make a great hiking destination. Although the track is only 600m long, it is quite steep – climbing 250m from start to finish. Unless you're pretty fit, plan on roughly an hour for the ascent. The reward is a tremendous view over the northwest coast and the sight of tropical birds circling below you. The path starts 250m up the road from the tea factory on the cross-island road from Victoria to Port Glaud. You have to descend the same way.

Kopolia Peak

This is the easier of two walks to the peaks overlooking Victoria and the Ste Anne Marine National Park. The trail starts on the cross-island Chemin Forêt Noire about 5km above Victoria. It's only just over 1km to the top of Kopolia (497m), but the final section is quite steep; allow roughly two hours there and back.

Trois Frères Peak

It's a long, steep climb to the top of Trois Frères Peak (699m), behind Victoria, but worth it for panoramic views. The path is well signed from the Sans Souci forest station on the Chemin Forêt Noire, about 4km from Victoria, although the final leg is tricky to follow. Allow four hours in total.

Once you've got your fill of working your tan, head to **Le Jardin du Roi** (Map p268; ☎ 371313; admission Rs 25; ☽ 10am-5.30pm), located 2km up in the hills above Anse Royale. This lush spice garden owes its existence to Pierre Poivre, the French spice entrepreneur. There is a self-guided walk around the 35-hectare orchard-crossed-with-forest, and you can help yourself to star fruit and other tropical delights as you wander around. The planter's house contains a one-room **museum** and there's a pleasant café-restaurant (right) with smashing views down to the coast.

The rather fancy-pants **Craft Village** (Map p268; ☎ 376100; admission free; ☽ 9.30am-5.30pm) at Anse aux Pins consists of a cluster of craft shops grouped around the Domaine de Val des Près, an old plantation house with a few bits of memorabilia. The rather motley assortment of crafts on offer includes model boats, pottery and products fashioned from the hugely versatile coconut tree. You can also eat here in the Vye Marmit restaurant (right). A two-minute drive from the craft village, you can take a peek at **Lenstiti Kreol** (Creole Institute; Map p268; see p260), which is set in a lovely colonial building.

Sleeping

Lalla Panzi (Map p268; ☎ 376411; fax 375633; Anse aux Pins; s/d incl breakfast €45/60; ☒) Lalla Panzi is not the beachfront paradise you were dreaming of, but it's a neat property leading down to the sea. This friendly guesthouse offers four scrupulously clean rooms arranged around a cosy lounge – room 3 is our favourite, despite the rosy colour scheme in the bathroom. Though on the main road, it's quiet enough at night. The only downside is the resident dogs, which are a bit intimidating at first sight. Cash only.

Koko Grove Chalets (Map p268; ☎ 371538, 712102; Anse Royale; d €95-150) We love this place, in a hilly setting with boggling views of the coast. If you're not desperate to stay within earshot of the sea, then these two timbered chalets, set in a secluded garden with fruit trees and flowers blossoming, represent perhaps the best value anywhere this side of Mahé. The two units are self-contained, with spacious living areas and large private verandas overlooking the swimming pool. If you're preparing your own food, there's a store 400m down the road.

Fairyland (Map p268; ☎ 371700; www.fairyland.net tc; Pointe au Sel; s/d incl breakfast €95/115; ☒) Though 'Fairyland' is an exaggerated description, it's a good-value option if you're looking for a comfortable base on the east coast. Run by a Seychellois-Swedish couple, it exudes low-key vibes and features six bright, capacious and uncluttered rooms with big balconies; three rooms open onto the lagoon, occupying a beautiful stretch of white sand. It's cruel that the water's not deep enough for swimming – although the proximity of Fairyland beach is adequate compensation. When the sea air piques your hunger, succumb to fish and chips at the downstairs restaurant.

ᴏᴜʀ ᴘɪᴄᴋ Chalets d'Anse Forban (Map p268; ☎ 366111; www.forbans.com; Anse Forbans; d €115; ☒) 'Tranquillity; 12 sparklingly clean, fully equipped bungalows with newly tiled bathrooms; expansive lawns; family-friendly; lovely beach with good swimming' – this is what we scribbled on our notepad when we visited. Add a few sunloungers and the proximity of a store, and you have a fantastic deal.

Other solid options:

La Desirade (Map p268; ☎ 373873; Anse aux Pins; r €70; ☒) Three light-filled, self-contained bungalows with an excellent beachfront setting.

Relax Hotel (Map p268; ☎ 382900; www.lerelaxhotel .com; Anse Royale; s €60-105, d €75-115, all incl breakfast; ☒ ☒) This attractive 10-room hotel is outstandingly positioned atop a hill overlooking Fairyland beach. Get a load of that cracking view from your terrace (aim for rooms 4 and 5).

La Roussette Hotel (Map p268; ☎ 376245; www.seych elles.net/larousse; d incl breakfast €115-140; ☒) Opposite the Lalla Panzi and set back from the road in gardens, this is a well-managed complex of immaculate yet impersonal bungalows. Three-night minimum stays are preferred.

Eating

ᴏᴜʀ ᴘɪᴄᴋ Le Jardin du Roi (Map p268; ☎ 371313; Anse Royale; mains Rs 50-135; ☽ 10am-4.30pm) The setting is wonderful at this café-restaurant way up the hills at the spice garden (see opposite), and it puts you in the mood for a fruit juice or a crunchy salad as soon as you sit down. Fish dishes and sandwiches also feature on the menu. Save a cranny for ice creams; they are confected fresh on the premises. Utterly superlative is the cinnamon, nutmeg and lime combo (Rs 55). The Sunday *planteur* buffet (Rs 125) is a popular weekly event.

Kaz Kreol (Map p268; ☎ 371680; Anse Royale; mains Rs 60-100; ☽ lunch & dinner Tue-Sun) This family-run address sits right on the beach at Anse Royale. The menu strikes a good balance between

SEYCHELLES

seafood, pizzas and meat, not to mention a few Chinese specialities. Dining space is gaily decorated with fish and palm-tree murals, which matches the tropical atmosphere.

Vye Marmit (Map p268; ☎ 376155; Anse aux Pins; mains Rs 75-150; ☻ 11am-9pm Mon-Sat) Here's a suave number with an atmospheric setting – it occupies a planter's house in the Craft Village. The menu is appropriately traditional Creole, with such savoury classics as crab, octopus and ray curries, fish fillet in a banana leaf or *chèvre braisé au vin rouge* (goat cooked in a red-wine sauce). If you want to travel your tastebuds, order the *civet de chauve souris* (bat stew).

Entertainment
Katiolo (Map p268; ☎ 375453; Anse Faure; men/women Rs 100/50; ☻ Wed, Fri & Sat) If you still have some energy to burn, the east coast is home to Mahé's currently most popular nightclub. It's worth checking out ladies night on Wednesday. It's a fairly hip venue, so dress up rather than down.

Getting There & Away
Buses leave regularly from Victoria for the east coast. The last bus to Victoria leaves around 7.30pm.

WEST COAST
The west coast is exquisite on the eyes. There are one or two sights to aim for, but it's the beaches and coastal scenery that are the star attractions. Wilder than the east, this is the part of Mahé where green hills tumble past coconut-strewn jungles before sliding gently into translucent waters.

The coastal drive between Anse Takamaka to the southwest up to Port Launay to the northwest provides tantalising glimpses of a number of beautiful spots. Throw away the guidebook for a day and go looking for your own slice of paradise.

The west coast is easily accessed from the east coast via several scenic roads that cut through the mountainous interior. Starting from Anse Forbans to the southeast, the road wiggles up through the mountain before reaching Quatre Bornes, from where a road leads to **Police Bay**, a splendid spot at the southern tip of the island. Sadly, the currents are too dangerous for swimming, but the beaches are great places to watch the surf (bring a picnic). Another road leads to

the Banyan Tree hotel and the high-profile beach at **Anse Intendance** (from the police station at Quatre Bornes, take the 1.7km concrete road that leads down to the beach).

Coming up the west coast, **Anse Takamaka**, **Anse Gaulettes** and **Anse à la Mouche** all vie for the 'best beach' accolade, though most people plump for the idyllic little beach of **Anse Soleil**, a pocket-sized paradise where you can pause for lunch. It's accessible via a secondary road (it's signposted). Beach-hounds will make a beeline for **Petite Anse**, another top spot accessible after a 20-minute walk. As the sun-low sky deepens to orange, this beach just might be heaven (though a new five-star hotel, the Four Seasons, the construction of which should be completed by 2009, will probably mar the experience).

To the north of Anse à la Mouche the coast is a bit less glam but appealing nonetheless. If you can find access to **Anse Louis** (where the super-swish Maia resort lies) you'll be rewarded with a superlative beach you never knew existed. You'll then go past **Grande Anse** before reaching **Port Glaud**, a laid-back town which lazily spreads itself along the coast. Further north you'll find **Port Launay** and **Port Launay Marine National Park**, Mahé's forgotten corner (which is reason enough to go there), where the road comes to an end. Mangrove swamps. Seclusion. Birdsong. Deserted beaches. You've reached the end of the earth. It's all yours.

Tea-lovers will pause at the working **tea factory** (Map p268; ☎ 378221; admission with/without guided tour Rs 20/10; ☻ 10am-4pm Mon-Fri) on the Sans Souci road about 3km above Port Glaud. It's best to visit before noon, when you can see the whole process from drying to packing. The estate produces about 45 tonnes of organic tea per year for export.

There are excellent dive sites off the southwestern coast (see p27). Diving can be arranged through the reputable **Dive Resort Seychelles** (Map p268; ☎ 361813, 717272; www.seychelles.net/divereso), based at the Plantation Club Hotel.

We also recommend taking a one-hour horse-riding excursion with **Utetangar Riding Centre** (Map p268; ☎ 712355; Grande Anse; 1hr ride €40). There's nothing quite like galloping on Grande Anse beach with the wind in your hair. You'll also traverse some rainforest. Book one day in advance.

Sleeping

Accommodation in west Mahé ranges from modest but charming guesthouses and self-catering apartments to big resort hotels with everything laid on.

La Rocaille (Map p268; ☎ 524238; Anse Gouvernement Rd, Anse Soleil; d €60) This is a pleasant find, on the hill that separates Anse Gouvernement from Anse Soleil. The grounds are nice enough, with lots of vegetation and birdsong. The friendly owners offer fruits to guests and are happy to drive them to the nearest village to stock up on food supplies. Too bad there's just one room. The nearest beach is at Anse Gouvernement, about 400m down the hill, but Anse Soleil is not that far either – about 1.5km to the north.

Lazare Lodge (Map p268; ☎ 361915, 633006; www .lazarelodge.com; Anse Gouvernement Rd, Anse Soleil; s/d €65/100, ste €12, all incl breakfast) Opposite La Rocaille, this all-wood, lodgelike venue (the owner is South African) has five neat rooms, including one suite. Meals are available on request and are served on the splendid terrace overlooking Baie Lazare and the jungle-clad hills – very *Out of Africa*.

Anse Soleil Resort (Map p268; ☎ 361090; fax 361435; Anse Soleil; d €70; ✷) Just four self-catering apartments; the Kitouz is the best, but all are well equipped and spacious. It's on the road to Anse Soleil in a great location, with wonderful views over Anse à la Mouche (if you can ignore the power lines).

Chez Batista's (Map p268; ☎ 366300; www.chez batista.com; Anse Takamaka; s €76-94, d €135-170, villas €350; ✷) Your only concern here: whether to frolick on the beach *now* or first sip a cocktail at the restaurant. This stress-melting venue boasts an idyllic location on Takamaka beach and features six tidy rooms enlivened with murals as well as three luxurious villas, not to mention a pen with giant tortoises. All in all, it's a bit compact but excellent value. All prices include breakfast.

La Residence (Map p268; ☎ 371733; Anse à la Mouche; d €90; ✷) Perched on a hillside, the six fully equipped apartments and three villas are fresh and light-drenched yet simply furnished. The buildings are functional rather than whimsical but there are good views from the terrace despite the odd power line).

Anse Soleil Beachcomber (Map p268; ☎ 361461; www.beachcomber.sc; Anse Soleil; s €105-140, d €120-180, incl breakfast; ✷) Among rocks on the secluded cove of Anse Soleil, this small, family-run hotel

with only 14 rooms is a perfect hideaway. The rooms are clean and simple with private terraces. Room 10 has the best setting – it offers more seclusion amid boulders and opens onto the sea shore, but the recent Premier rooms are not bad either. Half board is available. Anse Soleil Café is almost next door.

Blue Lagoon Chalets (Map p268; ☎ 371197; www.seych elles.net/bluelagoon; Anse à la Mouche; d €120; ✷) The friendly owner here offers four well-cared-for holiday units that sleep up to four people and are fully equipped, a hop from the sea shore.

ourpick Valmer Resort (Map p268; ☎ 381555; www.valmerresort; Baie Lazare; d €150-380; ✷ 🖳 🖭) No, you're not hallucinating, the view is real. Topaz waters in the distance, tropical foliage in the garden. This well-run venue seduces those who stay with tastefully done-out chalets (the standard apartments are more ordinary). If not lounging by the pool, a dazzling mirage that seems to melt into the sea on the horizon, lock the door of your room, draw the curtains and crack open a bottle of champagne. There's an onsite restaurant, run by the brother of local painter Gerard Devoud.

Le Jardin des Palmes (Map p268; ☎ 389100; www .seychelles.net/thepalmresort; Anse à la Mouche; s €153-180, d €230-250, all incl breakfast; ✷ 🖭) Perched on a hillside overlooking Anse à la Mouche, this discreet number is a picturesque oasis with a gleaming pool, 10 all-wood rooms and an onsite restaurant.

Banyan Tree (Map p268; ☎ 383500; www.banyan tree.com; Anse Intendance; d incl breakfast from €1100; ✷ 🖳 🖭) A member of the Leading Small Hotels of the World, this is Maia's main competitor. Privacy is paramount at this ultraluxurious, creatively designed resort in an exceptional setting. The villas are enormous, many-roomed affairs complete with personal pools. Nestled in a grove overlooking Anse Intendance, the spa will make you go 'aaah'.

Maia Luxury Resort (Map p268; ☎ 390000; www .maia.com.sc; Anse Louis; d incl breakfast €1610-2230; ✷ 🖳 🖭) There is so much to love in this five-star masterpiece – the absolutely sumptuous villas, the 'zero stress' ambience (as one employee put it), the best clifftop views in Mahé, the glorious porcelain sand beaches, the sense of privacy, the spectacular infinity pool and wow-factor spa – that it defies description. Next time you get married, book your honeymoon here!

Eating

Eclipse (Map p268; ☎ 372106; Anse à la Mouche; mains Rs 50-80; ☯ 11am-8.30pm) Across the road from the beach, this lively eatery is high on atmosphere, with well-designed wooden tables and chairs. Alas, no views to speak of. How about the food? Beef fillet in wine sauce, grilled chicken in mango sauce, and tuna steak in coconut milk are examples of the innovative fare on offer.

Restaurant-Cafeteria Maria (Map p268; ☎ 361812; Anse Gouvernement Rd, Anse Soleil; mains Rs 50-90; ☯ 10am-9pm) Maria, the Seychellois spouse of artist Antonio Filippin (see right), had just opened this quirky restaurant beside her husband's studio when we passed through. The cavernous interior is discombobulating, with granite tabletops and concrete walls sprayed with paint. Food-wise, it majors on tried-and-true Creole recipes, such as grilled fish, chicken curry in coconut milk, and pancakes.

Anchor Café (Map p268; ☎ 371289; Anse à la Mouche; mains Rs 50-115; ☯ 11am-9pm Mon-Sat) Cafeteria-style eating is what you'll get at this locale. Tuck into standard dishes such as burgers, salads, pork chops or grilled fish. Eat alfresco, near a huge anchor in the garden.

ourpick Anse Soleil Café (Map p268; ☎ 361700; Anse Soleil; mains Rs 60-100; ☯ noon-6pm) This unfussy little eatery could hardly be better situated: it's right on the beach at Anse Soleil. The menu is short and concentrates on simply prepared seafood served in generous portions; the shark steak is superb. Digest all this over a drink afterwards.

Sundown Restaurant (Map p268; ☎ 378352; Port Glaud; mains Rs 60-140; ☯ noon-9pm Mon, Wed & Fri, noon-6pm Tue, Thu & Sat) Well-prepared local seafood, a reggae soundtrack and a laid-back atmosphere make this a heart-stealer. Light years away from the glitz usually associated with the Seychelles, it can't get more mellow than this.

Auberge d'Anse Boileau – Chez Plume (Map p268; ☎ 355050; www.seychelles.net/auberge-plume; Anse Boileau; mains Rs 65-160; ☯ dinner Mon-Sat) It's worth crossing the island for the crafty food at this perennial fave, dressed with white furnishings. A *capitaine* (threadfin) sounds innocuous, but it will arrive slathered with a passionfruit sauce. Bookings essential.

Chez Batista's (Map p268; ☎ 366300; Anse Takamaka; mains Rs 100-300; ☯ lunch & dinner Mon-Sat) Location, location, location. From the impressive thatched canopy, the picture-perfect beach and the endless turquoise bay spread out in front of you. This is a great place for seafood including lobster and ginger crab. Good juices too. The eclectic lunch buffet (Rs 150) is the best option on the island on Sunday. It's wise to book on weekends – it's a snug eatery with a big reputation.

Shopping

The glorious southwest seems to be an endless source of inspiration for a number of artists. Visit **Michael Adams' studio** (Map p268; ☎ 361006; www.seychelles.net/adams; Anse à la Mouche; ☯ 10am-4pm Mon-Fri, 10am-noon Sat), where silkscreen prints burst with the vivid life of the forests. They are irresistible and highly collectable, so bring plenty of rupees if you're thinking of buying. Keep some cash for **Tow Bowers' sculptures** (Map p268; ☎ 371518; Anse à la Mouche) and for Antonio Filippin's somewhat risqué woodcarvings. Antonio's quirky studio, **Art Arc** (Map p268; ☎ 510977; Baie Lazare) is perched on a hill between Anse Gouvernement and Anse Soleil. Gerard Devoud's eye-goggling paintings are also sure to enliven your bedroom. **Gerard Devoud's studio** (Map p268; ☎ 381313; Baie Lazare) is at Valmer Resort.

Getting There & Away

Buses leave regularly from Victoria for the west coast. The last bus to Victoria leaves around 7.30pm.

PRASLIN

A wicked seductress, Praslin has lots of temptations: stylish lodgings, high-quality restaurants serving the freshest of fish, tangled velvet jungle, curving hills dropping down to gin-clear seas, gorgeous stretches of silky sand edged with palm trees and a slow-motion ambience. No, you're not dreaming!

Lying about 45km northeast of Mahé, the second-largest island in the Seychelles falls somewhere between the relative hustle and bustle of Mahé and the sleepiness of La Digue. Like Mahé, Praslin is a granite island with a ridge of mountains running east-west along the centre. The island is 12km long and 5km across at its widest point. The 5000 inhabitants of Praslin are scattered around the coast in a series of small settlements. The most important from a visitor's perspective are **Anse Volbert** (also known as Côte d'Or

SEYCHELLES' BEST BEACHES

It's gruelling work investigating which beaches qualify as the best of Seychelles. Here's a few of our favourites:

- Beau Vallon (Mahé; p272) – Mahé's longest and most popular beach, sweeping blond sand backed by takamaka trees
- Fairyland (Mahé; p276) – easily overlooked but has good snorkelling
- Anse Soleil (Mahé; p278) – an intimate paradise, killer sunsets
- Anse Takamaka (Mahé; p278) – Mahé's most elegant beach is the perfect place for a romantic stroll
- Anse Lazio (Praslin; below) – excellent for sunbathing and snorkelling, and famous for its beach restaurants
- Anse Source d'Argent (La Digue; p291) – crystalline, glossy, and framed with glacis boulders, this is the most photogenic of all the Seychelles' beaches
- Grand Anse (La Digue; p291) – idyllic stretch of sand, excellent for frolicking in the crashing surf

If you're looking for something ultra-exclusive, you can mark your footprints in pristine sand at Denis, Silhouette, Desroches and Bird Islands (see p288).

and **Grande Anse**. At the southeast tip of the island is **Baie Ste Anne**, Praslin's main port.

Praslin has all you need to decompress and throw your cares to the wind. Prepare yourself for soggy fingers and toes: here you'll probably spend as much time in the water as out of it. But if playing sardines on the strand ceases to do it for you, there are a few walks, boat excursions to nearby islands famed for their birdlife, scuba diving and snorkelling that will keep you buzzing.

INFORMATION

All the major banks have ATMs and exchange facilities. Praslin's two tourist offices can provide maps and basic information and help with accommodation and excursion bookings. Praslin's travel agents all offer similar excursions at similar prices and can organise car hire, boat charters, boat excursions, water activities, air tickets and the like.

Airport tourist office (☎ 233346; stbpraslin@ seychelles.sc; Praslin Airport; ☻ 8am-1pm & 2-4pm Mon-Fri, 8am-noon Sat)

Baie Ste Anne tourist office (☎ 232669; stbpraslin@seychelles.sc; Baie Ste Anne; ☻ 8am-1pm & 2-4pm Mon-Fri, 8am-noon Sat)

Barclays Bank Baie Ste Anne (☎ 232218); Grand Anse (☎ 233344)

Central post office (☎ 233212; Grand Anse; ☻ 8am-noon & 1-4pm Mon-Fri) Next to the police station in Grand Anse.

Creole Travel Services (☎ 294294; Grand Anse) Travel agency.

Mason's Travel (☎ 288750; Grand Anse) Travel agency.

Mauritius Commercial Bank (MCB) Anse Volbert (☎ 232602); Grand Anse (☎ 233940)

Nadia's Internet Café (☎ 233478; Grand Anse; per hr Rs 30; ☻ 8.30am-8pm Mon-Thu, 8.30am-5.30pm Fri, 6.30-8pm Sat, 9am-noon Sun) Inside Ocean Plaza Building.

Seychelles Savings Bank (☎ 233810; Grand Anse)

SIGHTS & ACTIVITIES
Vallée de Mai

Praslin's World Heritage–listed **Vallée de Mai** (adult/under 12yr €15/free; ☻ 8am-5.30pm) is one of only two places in the world where you can see the rare coco de mer palms growing in their natural state (the other being nearby Curieuse Island). If the entry price seems steep, remember this is a unique chance to experience a slice of Eden. Three trails lead through the park, of which the longest takes around three hours. Signs indicate some of the other endemic trees to look out for, including several varieties of pandanus (screw pine) and latanier palms.

Beaches

Is **Anse Lazio**, on the northwest tip of the island, the most enticing beach in the Indian Ocean? It's picture postcard everywhere you look. Here, the long, broad pale-sand beach has lapis lazuli waters on one side and a thick fringe of palm and takamaka trees on the

SEYCHELLES

PRASLIN

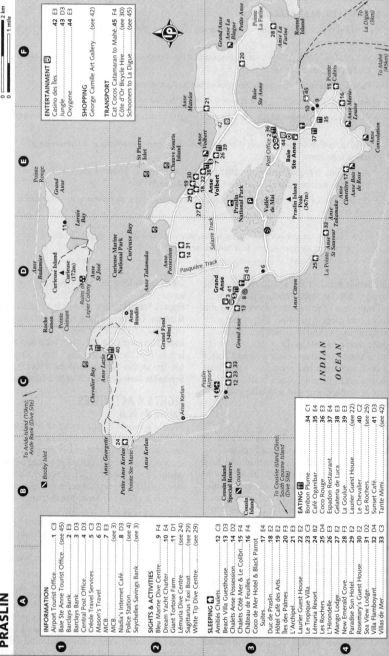

SEXY COCONUTS

This must be the sexiest fruit on earth, and it could be mistaken for some kind of erotic gadgetry in a sex shop. The *coco fesse* (the fruit of the coco de mer palm) looks like, ahem, buttocks with a female sex. Now you can understand why these strange, sensual fruits excited the 17th-century sailors who first stumbled upon them after months at sea. This rare palm grows naturally only in the Seychelles.

Only female trees produce the erotically shaped nuts, which can weigh over 30kg. The male tree possesses a decidedly phallic flower stem of 1m or longer, adding to the coco de mer's steamy reputation.

Harvesting the nuts is strictly controlled by the **Seychelles Island Foundation** (SIF; Map p270; www.sif.sc; Mont Fleuri Rd, Victoria), an NGO which manages the Vallée de Mai on behalf of the government. Money from the sale of nuts goes towards SIF's conservation work in the Vallée de Mai and on Aldabra.

If you want to lug one of these nuts home, be prepared to pay at least €200. They come in a husky state and will need to be polished; beware of ready-polished nuts, which are often fakes. The safest place to buy is directly from SIF, which will issue you with the required export permit.

---

other, and it's framed by a series of granite boulders at each extremity. You won't find a better place for sunbathing and snorkelling.

Don't get too excited, though. Come here on a cloudy day (yes, that might happen!) and the wow factor vanishes altogether.

There is another lovely, long stretch of sand at **Anse Volbert**, while right at the island's southern tip, **Anse Consolation** and **Anse Marie-Louise** are also pretty spots.

Sadly, **Anse Georgette**, which is an indescribably lovely stretch of white sand at the north-western tip of the island, has been engulfed by the Lémuria Resort. In theory, it's a public beach that is accessible to anybody. In practice, you might be turned back at the gate of the Lémuria.

Boat Excursions to Nearby Islands

Curieuse Island is a granite island 1km off Praslin's north coast and was a leper colony from 1833 until 1965. Curieuse is used as a breeding centre for giant Aldabra tortoises. The wardens at the **giant tortoise farm** show visitors round the pens, after which you're free to explore the rest of the island. Most visitors to Curieuse Island arrive on an organised tour arranged through their hotel or any tour operator. Day trips cost around €95/50 for an adult/child including lunch, snorkelling at St Pierre Islet and the marine-park entry fee of €10.

The alternative is to charter your own boat from Anse Volbert. **Sagittarius Taxi Boat** (☎ 232234, 512137), on the beach beside the Paradise Sun Hotel, charges €25 for Curieuse;

Curieuse with St Pierre costs €30. You can also contact Edwin at Laurier Guest House (see p285), whose tours get rave reviews from travellers.

About 2km southwest of Praslin, **Cousin Island** is run as a nature reserve by **Nature Seychelles** (www.nature.org.sc). The bird population is estimated to exceed 300,000 on an island measuring just 1km in diameter. It's an amazing experience to walk through thick forest with birds seemingly nesting on every branch.

The island is also an important nesting ground for hawksbill turtles. As many as 100 turtles nest here between September and February. At any time of year you're bound to see lizards; Cousin boasts one of the highest densities of lizards in the world.

Cousin can only be visited as part of an organised tour from Tuesday to Friday. Half-day tours of Cousin can be arranged through Praslin's hotels and tour operators for around €70/35 per adult/child. The adult price includes a €25 landing fee, which goes towards conservation efforts.

The waters around **St Pierre Islet**, off Anse Volbert, are excellent for snorkelling and sloshing around. Boat trips to St Pierre organised by hotels and private operators cost upwards of €20 per person.

Diving

There is some great diving off Praslin. See p32 for more information on dive sites.
Bleu Marine Dive Centre (☎ 513518; Baie Ste Anne) At the jetty.

Lémuria Dive Centre (☎ 281281; Anse Kerlan) At the Lémuria Resort.

Octopus Dive Centre (☎ 232350, 512350; Anse Volbert)

White Tip Dive Centre (☎ 232282, 514282; Anse Volbert) Based at Paradise Sun Hotel.

Kayaking

It's not a bad idea to rent a kayak and explore Anse Volbert at your leisure and paddle round Chauve Souris Island. **Sagittarius Taxi Boat** (☎ 232234, 512137) handles rentals (from €10 per hour).

SLEEPING

Demand for accommodation is high in Praslin. To avoid disappointment, particularly in high season, book your accommodation well in advance.

Truly budget options are nonexistent, but a number of guesthouses offer perfectly comfortable double rooms with private bathroom for under €100.

Anse Volbert, with its restaurants and other tourist facilities, makes a good base. Grand Anse is busier and less attractive, but less touristy, and there are some decent options within walking distance of the Baie Ste Anne jetty. If you're looking for a real hideaway, head for the wild and empty promontories to either side of Baie Ste Anne.

Most places offer their guests a free shuttle to Anse Lazio.

Grand Anse & Anse Kerlan Area

Beach Villa Guesthouse (☎ 233445; martin@seychelles .net; Grand Anse; d incl breakfast €90; ❄) With tempting sunloungers, grassy garden areas and a lovely beachfront location, this is one of the most dependable venues in the area. Rooms are impeccably kept with tiled floors, the service is personable and the ambience unfussy. Air-con is extra (€8). Run by the same family as Amitiés Chalets.

Villas de Mer (☎ 233972; www.seychelles-holidays.com Grand Anse; d incl breakfast €152; ❄ ▣) This relaxed operation is recommended for its cheerfully appointed, spick-and-span rooms with terracotta tiles, plump bedding and partial ocean views. A well-tended pool and an excellent beachside restaurant round off the offerings José, the bartender, concocts a wicked *calou*.

Lémuria Resort (☎ 281281; www.lemuriaresort.com Anse Kerlan; d incl breakfast €626-1246; ❄ ▣ ▣) Praslin's top-drawer establishment occupies the whole northwest tip of the island. If you're not bowled over by features such as the voluminous foyer and the soothing spa, you certainly will be by the three-tiered infinity pool the three gorgeous beaches and the expansive grounds in which the villas blend in among the rocks and water features. Facilities include three restaurants, a kids club and an 18-hole golf course. One blemish: the property has engulfed the idyllic Anse Georgette, which is now a de facto part of the hotel, though it's a public beach by law.

Other recommendations:

Amitiés Chalets (☎ 233445; martin@seychelles.net; Grand Anse; d incl breakfast €90-110; ❄) Four neat rooms, a well-tended property and a beachfront location make this a good all-round bet. The beautiful little thatched cottage at the back (called 'Round') is our fave. Near the airstrip.

Le Tropique Villa (☎ 233805, 513027; www.seychelles .net/tropic-villa; Grand Anse; d incl breakfast €117-130; ❄ ▣) Offers six fully equipped bungalows (four of which have sea views) in top nick in a beachside setting near the airstrip.

IT'S A WILD, WILD WORLD

Robbie Bression is a conservationist who works on Bird Island. After years of supervising numerous conservation projects, such as turtle and bird monitoring, and studying the behaviour of various species in the Indian Ocean, he still thinks the Seychelles is an unmatched haunt for wildlife enthusiasts. 'The Seychelles is a kind of Noah's ark. Take Bird Island: it's predator-free, and hundreds of thousands of birds come each year to nest. You just have to sit on your veranda and birds just land on your head. Not to mention giant turtles; come here and you'll meet Esmeralda, the oldest living tortoise in the world. He (yes, he!) likes being stroked under the neck. And despite his age, he's still sexually active.' A hot tip? 'If you can, try to include Cousin, Cousine, Aride and Frégate islands in your itinerary – they all boast prodigious bird life and turtle populations. But the ultimate in ecotourism and wildlife viewing is Aldabra Atoll. It's absolutely unbelievable. If you can afford to go there, do it, you'll never regret it. There is talk of opening up a few facilities for ecotourists on Aldabra, but it's still too early to trumpet it.'

Anse Volbert Area

Rosemary's Guest House (☎ /fax 232176; Anse Volbert; s/d €45/70) Yes, you read those prices right (we asked twice). Relaxed and friendly, this homey place offers quality accommodation at wallet-friendly prices. The three fan-cooled rooms are simply furnished yet tidy and boast bouncy beds and crisp sheets. Location is ace; you can bask lizardlike in the garden within earshot of the waves. Meals are available to guests on request (€15). There are plans to build four new rooms. Our favourite for budget travellers.

Mango Lodge (☎ 232077; www.mangolodge.com; Anse Volbert; s €88-116, d €116-136, incl breakfast) These digs offer something different, with a cluster of well-appointed bungalows and offbeat, stilt-raised A-framed chalets precariously perched on a greenery-cloaked hillside. What a hallucinogenic view! It's only 600m from Anse Volbert, but the access road is very steep – you definitely need wheels to stay here.

Laurier Guest House (☎ 232241; www.lauriersey chelles.com; Anse Volbert; s/d incl breakfast €90/110) One of the best deals at Anse Volbert. Run by friendly Edwin and Sybille, it features four (more to come) uncomplicated and smallish but neat rooms. The woodcarved posts on the terrace are a nice touch.

L'Hirondelle (☎ 232243; www.seychelles.net/hiron delle; Anse Volbert; r €95) The four rooms, although they won't knock your socks off, are comfortable and come fully equipped, and each has a balcony or a terrace that commands a blue-green lagoon vista. Downside: it's not shielded from the noise of the coast road.

Duc de Praslin (☎ 232252; www.leduc-seychelles.com; Anse Volbert; s €160-215, d €180-250, all incl breakfast; ❄) Spacious and well-run, clean and comfortable, friendly and serviceable. Yes, all the key words apply here, just as you would expect at a hotel of this kind on an island like Praslin. There's a nicely laid out garden. The owners have plans to redesign the whole place in 2008 to 2009 – stay tuned.

our pick **Hôtel Café des Arts** (☎ 232170; www.cafe .sc; Anse Volbert; d incl breakfast €180-225) A pleasant oasis. Personable and homely, the digs are not ultraposh (there's no air-con), but inside they are tastefully designed with natural materials, including bamboo, coconut and takamaka wood. Hot tip: angle for the more expensive beach bungalow – a better deal than the garden digs. The place has an artistic vibe – there's a small art gallery at reception.

L'Archipel (☎ 284700; www.larchipel.com; Anse Gouvernement; d incl breakfast €370-670; ❄ ▢ ▣) Serious swank. This resort occupies a large, nicely landscaped plot by the beach, at Anse Gouvernement (the eastern tip of Anse Volbert). Squeezed in between the spacious, stand-alone, split-level units are a swimming pool and a restaurant. The walk up to the highest bungalows may leave the terminally unfit short of breath. Naturally, you'll find all the usual resort facilities onsite.

Paradise Sun Hotel (☎ 293293; www.paradisesun .com; Anse Volbert; s/d with half board €385/546; ❄ ▢) If you're looking for the classic Seychelles setting, complete with shady palms, lagoon views and a splendid china-white stretch of sand just steps from your door, then this Praslin classic won't disappoint. After a massive post-tsunami refurbishment, this resort-style operation now offers 80 smartly finished bungalows with dark wood fixtures and granite bricks, ample space and heaps of amenities, including a dive centre, a pool and a restaurant. It's kid-friendly.

Anse Possession

Chalets Anse Possession (☎ /fax 232180; Anse Possession; r €80-110) Three two-bedroom villas are set in lush greenery off the coast road. Although not the height of luxury, rooms are clean, comfy, roomy…and bland – perfect for the traveller who's not fussy. Good value.

Sea View Lodge (☎ 711965, 780001; www.kokonet.sc /seaviewlodge; Anse Possession; r €100-120) This place has three newly built bungalows, two of which are perched on a hillside. Needless to say the verandas have stunning views over the bay and Curieuse Island. All are fully equipped and very spacious. For self-caterers, there's a small shop just down the road. No beach.

Baie Ste Anne & Pointe Cabris Area

Chalets Côté Mer & Le Colibri (☎ 294200; www.chez .com/jmc/seychelles; Baie Ste Anne; d incl breakfast €85-125; ❄) An excellent deal at the southeastern tip of Baie Ste Anne. Features a clutch of A-framed bungalows and comfy rooms perched on a hillside overlooking the sea. The Colibri bungalows are slightly hipper than the Chalets Côté Mer. Some units are lovingly built from hardwoods and decked out with granite floors and takamaka furnishings, and most offer glorious views over La Digue. Lovers of fine food will enjoy the cooking here – the French owner, René Parmentier, has made a name as an adept chef. There's no beach but snorkelling is excellent.

Îles des Palmes (☎ 711051; www.beachbungalow.sc; Baie Ste Anne; bungalows €135-180) Has 18 purpose-built, roomy, self-contained villas strung out along a gentle beach. Hire a kayak (€10) to explore offshore, take a midday snooze in a hammock under the swaying palms, or scratch the leathery necks of resident giant tortoises. Bikes are available (€10).

New Emerald Cove (☎ 232323; www.emerald.sc; Anse La Farine; s with half board €325-377, d with half board €383-474; 🏊 🛥) If you're looking for the perfect compromise between style, atmosphere and seclusion, then look no further than this little slice of heaven nestled in Anse La Farine, and accessible by boat only (from Baie Ste Anne jetty). Facing Round Island, the 42 units are stylishly decorated, the beach is ravishing, and the shimmering pool seems to disappear into the ocean and horizon.

ourpick Château de Feuilles (☎ 290000; www.chateaudefeuilles.com; Pointe Cabris; d incl breakfast €365-545; 🏊 🖥 🛥) Paradise awaits you here. This bijou hideaway sits on an unfathomably beautiful headland near Baie Ste Anne. The proprietors have made the most of the exquisite landscape, with nine luxurious villas ingeniously deployed over several acres of tropical gardens. A serene symphony of earth tones and natural textures, elegant furnishings, sensational views, high-class amenities (including a complimentary car and a hilltop Jacuzzi), an uber-romantic poolside restaurant – every detail is spot-on. There's a three-night minimum stay. Go on, you know you deserve it.

Anse St-Sauveur Area

Villa Flamboyant (☎ 233036; rosycob18@yahoo.com; Anse St Sauveur; d €90, bungalows €140, all incl breakfast) A true charmer. You'll be impressed by the large building (a converted planter's house) that merges effortlessly with a surrounding panoply of stately flamboyant trees. Much of the heritage structure and charm of its former life remains, but the six rooms have been renovated extensively and are comfortable, and come with parquet floors and exposed beams. Rooms 2 and 3 overlook the beach but are not the most intimate. Also available are two modern, fully equipped bungalows. Rosemary, your charming host, is a good cook. Meals are served in a snug dining room, furnished with Creole chairs and ceilings. Great stuff.

ourpick Les Rochers (☎ 233034; magda@seychelle.net; Anse St Sauveur; d €100-200; 🏊) Who knows why this staggeringly beautiful family-run hideaway will be able to handle all this publicity but it can't go without mention because it's simply seventh heaven. We can't gush enough about the three fully equipped beachfront villas, all decorated with flair and imaginatively laid out. We recommend booking the Kutia with takamaka furnishings and rooms cut into the rock face, or the Grande Case, ideal for families, with a vast lounge area carved into a big boulder opening onto the beach. As if this wasn't enough, there's excellent swimming and snorkelling at the front, and if you don't fancy cooking, Les Rochers boasts a high-quality restaurant. Joël Confait, the son, can organise any boat trips. Picture-perfect in practically every way. It's in very, very high demand (word of mouth, my friends) so book early.

Coco de Mer Hotel & Black Parrot Suites (☎ 233900; www.cocodemer.com, www.blackparrot.com; s €195-205, d €260-280, ste €318; 🏊 🛥) Choose the Black Parrot Suites if you want some serious cosseting; the Coco de Mer, with 40 rooms, has more of a resort feel. There's no beach (bar an unimpressive artificial one) but you can cool off in the pool in the shape of a *coco fesse* (yes, they dared) or prop up the quirky Mango Bar and marvel at the mango tree that goes through the roof. All prices include breakfast.

EATING

Since most people eat in their hotels or guesthouses, there are relatively few independent restaurants on Praslin. You'll find takeaways at Grand Anse, Baie Ste Anne and Anse Volbert, and a clutch of smarter places scattered around the coast.

Most hotels have excellent restaurants that are open to all comers. You'll eat very well at Lémuria Resort. Others hotels with restaurants that merit a visit for their own sake include Duc de Praslin and L'Archipel.

Anse Volbert Area

ourpick Gelateria de Luca (Anse Volbert; mains Rs 40-70; 🕐 11am-8pm) Praslin's prime ice-cream parlour will leave you a drooling mess. Order a coppa tropicale (Rs 40), and you'll see why. It also whips up pasta dishes and various snacks, and the vitamin-packed passionfruit juice is killer. Two minuses: the décor is unimaginative and there's no view.

La Goulue (☎ 232223; Anse Volbert; mains Rs 60-140; ☺ lunch & dinner Mon-Sat) This little eatery doesn't have beach frontage but the terrace catches some breeze and the menu should please most palates. It features Creole staples with a French twist, such as *steak au poivre crème cognac* (steak with pepper in cognac cream sauce), and various filling snacks.

Tante Mimi (☎ 232500; Anse Volbert; mains Rs 100-200; ☺ lunch Sun, dinner daily) Tante Mimi is a real heartbreaker. At the casino in Anse Volbert, you couldn't ask for a more atmospheric setting – think a lovely old colonial house, creaky parquet flooring, Creole furnishings throughout, candlelit tables, silver cutlery, chandeliers and a wide-ranging menu featuring Creole classics. Unfortunately we found the food only average and the service utterly amateurish. Give it a second chance, perhaps. Free pick-up.

our pick Laurier Guest House (☎ 232241; Anse Volbert; buffet Rs 250; ☺ dinner Thu-Tue) Charismatic Edwin and his Belgian spouse prepare a spectacular buffet at dinner – we walked out belly first. Rejoicing begins with lip-smacking hors d'oeuvre displayed on a boat-shaped table, followed by sizzling meat and fish morsels expertly grilled by Edwin, who is hardly visible from a smoke cloud behind the barbecue. The dining room is atmospheric, especially the new wing, with wrought-iron furnishings. You may be serenaded by a local crooner on certain evenings (we had 'No Woman No Cry'; and you?). Make sure you reserve.

Grand Anse

Sunset Café (☎ 233383; Grand Anse; mains Rs 60-200; ☺ lunch & dinner Mon-Sat) Lobster for less than Rs 250? Yes, it's possible. This small, pleasantly informal number is worth visiting for the good, cheap and wholesome food created from quality ingredients. It has a few outdoor tables.

Baie Ste Anne

our pick Coco Rouge (☎ 232228; Baie Ste Anne; mains Rs 60, dinner menu Rs 125; ☺ lunch & dinner Mon-Sat) Everyone loves an insider's tip, and Coco Rouge is that easy-to-miss 'secret spot' that locals like to recommend. Run by Tony, a teacher, it serves up a sensational-value set menu at dinner, with the best smoked fish salad (mixed with avocado and veggies) we've had in the Seychelles. The *poisson à la créole* (Creole-style fish), the Chinese noo-

dles and the salad were delectable too. The setting is refreshingly simple, with sturdy takamaka tables. We'll be back – see you there.

Espadon Restaurant (☎ 770453; Baie Ste Anne; mains Rs 65, menu Rs 150; ☺ lunch & dinner Mon-Sat) This tiny, typically Creole joint is a great place for a cheap and fast meal at lunchtime, or for a fixed menu come the evening. The naive fresco sporting colourful fish is amusing.

Café Oganibar (☎ 23211; Baie Ste Anne; mains Rs 75-140; ☺ breakfast, lunch & dinner) Under new management, the Oganibar is big in ambitions, with such concoctions as fish fillet baked in banana leaves, braised chicken with honey, and grilled prawns with garlic butter. There's a Creole buffet on Thursday evening and a Chinese buffet on Saturday evening.

Anse Lazio

Le Chevalier (☎ 560488; Anse Lazio; mains Rs 75-180; ☺ lunch) Can't get a table at Bonbon Plume? Don't despair. Here's an acceptable plan B. OK, it's not right on the beach and the setting is frustratingly bland, but the octopus curry and the tuna steak go down a treat. Steer clear of the tuna salad (Rs 75), made with canned tuna.

Bonbon Plume (☎ 232136; Anse Lazio; mains Rs 115-180, menu Rs 180; ☺ lunch) Is it a tourist trap or a seafood mecca? Both, perhaps. With such a location – the palm-thatched canopy is right on the beach – tables are unsurprisingly in high demand. Anything from *moules à la seychelloise* (Seychellois-style mussels) to the catch of the day, this is a simple seafood delight. Your choice of critter will have a huge influence on the fiscal outlay. For grilled lobster or *cigale de mer* (squill fish), you'll be looking at Rs 350.

Anse St Sauveur

our pick Les Rochers (☎ 233034; Anse St Sauveur; mains Rs 220-450; ☺ dinner Wed-Sat) Pray for a table at this suave venue set in a wonderfully secluded property by the sea. Flickering candles, soft music, swaying palms, a thatched terrace and the sound of waves washing the beach make it a real date-pleaser. Order cocktails, clink glasses and fall in love. No alchemy? There's always the delicious food, such as lobster with garlic, and the magical atmosphere at night. It has a can't-go-wrong wine list – treat yourself to a glass of Chateauneuf du Pape (a French

SEYCHELLES

red). Vegetarian options too. Reservations are essential.

ENTERTAINMENT

Nightlife in Praslin? No, really? It usually comes as a surprise to many visitors that the island rocks (by Seychellois standards) on Friday and Saturday evenings. Shakers and movers head en masse to the **Jungle** (Grand Anse; admission Rs 50; ⏰ 10pm-4am Fri & Sat) or to **Oxygene** (Baie Ste Anne; admission Rs 50; ⏰ 10pm-4am Fri & Sat).

Other than that, most large hotels put on their own entertainment programmes, or you can try your luck at the **Casino des Îles** (☎ 232500; Anse Volbert; ⏰ slot machines noon-2am, gaming tables 7.30pm-3am). Call ahead and you will be picked up from your hotel.

SHOPPING

George Camille Art Gallery (Casino des Îles, Anse Volbert) Camille's work is inspired by the beauty and nature around him, incorporating stylised fish, geckos and coco de mer palms in his works, as well as more conventional scenes of rural life.

GETTING THERE & AWAY

Praslin Airport (☎ 284666) is 3km from Grand Anse and has flights every hour or so from Mahé. For further information, see p300.

It's almost as quick to take the Cat Cocos catamaran from Victoria, or you can save money by hopping on a cargo boat from Mahé to La Digue and then getting a schooner on to Praslin. See p300 for routes, times and prices.

GETTING AROUND

Praslin has a decent bus service as well as the usual taxis. A taxi ride from the airport to Anse Volbert will set you back Rs 125. For more information, see p301.

THE BEST OF THE REST

If you want to live out that stranded-on-a-deserted-island fantasy, take your pick from the following menu.

Aride Island

The most northerly of the granite islands, Aride lies 10km north of Praslin and supports the greatest concentration of sea birds in the area. Aride can be reached by boat between September and May only. Tours can be arranged through travel agencies, hotels and guesthouses in Praslin. A day trip costs about €100/50 per adult/child. Volunteer programmes are available (see www.arideisland.net).

Félicité

This mountainous island, 3km northeast of La Digue, is run as an extremely luxurious resort by **La Digue Island Lodge** (☎ 292525; www.ladigue.sc; island package €1000; ✷ ✷) on La Digue. There are some excellent snorkelling sites around the island.

Bird Island

Now is your chance to relive a scene from Alfred Hitchcock's *The Birds*! Hundreds of thousands of sooty terns, fairy terns and common noddies descend en masse between May and October on this tiny coral island 96km north of Mahé. Hawksbill turtles breed on the island's beaches between October and February, while their land-bound relatives lumber around the interior. It is also good for snorkelling, swimming and simply lazing around.

The only place to stay is the ecologically friendly **Bird Island Lodge** (☎ 323322, 224925; www .birdislandseychelles.com; s/d with full board from €335/430) – the quintessential island sanctuary and the stuff of castaway dreams. Reservations can be made in person at the office in **Kingsgate House** (Map p270; Independence Ave, Victoria).

Denis Island

The privately owned Denis Island, 85km north of Mahé, is similar to Bird Island, but is even more exclusive. Live like a prince(ss) at the superswish **Taj Denis Island** (☎ 295999; www.denisisland.com; d with half board €770-1700; ✷). Famous for sportfishing and diving.

A car is a great way to see the island. Most travel agents and hotels will assist you in organising car hire.

You can hire bikes through your accommodation or from **Côte d'Or Bicycle Hire** (☎ 232071) in Anse Volbert for Rs 50 per day.

Hopping around the small islands off Praslin is done by chartered boat; trips are usually organised through the hotels or tour operators.

LA DIGUE

Ah, La Digue. Remember that tropical paradise that appears in countless adverts and glossy travel brochures? Here it's the real thing, with jade-green waters, lovely bays studded with heart-palpitatingly gorgeous beaches, and green hills cloaked with tan-

gled jungle and tall trees. The *coup de grâce* (though a bit overhyped for some tastes) is Anse Source d'Argent on the west coast, with its picture-perfect, sea-smoothed glacis rocks. As if that wasn't enough, La Digue is ideally situated as a springboard to surrounding islands, including Félicité, Grande Sœur and the fairy-tale Île Cocos.

Despite its lush beauty, La Digue has managed to escape the somewhat rampant tourist development that affects Mahé and Praslin, and there's only one settlement on the island, La Passe. Sure, it's certainly not undiscovered, and the recent small casino has brought some protest from locals anxious to preserve the island's traditional way of life. But La Digue has a more laid-back feel than the other main islands, with only one surfaced road and virtually no cars, just the odd ox cart. Time moves at a crawl, the atmosphere is chilled out to

Silhouette Island

This imposing island 20km from Mahé is named for an 18th-century French minister. With steep forested mountain peaks rising from the ocean above stunning palm-shaded beaches, Silhouette is a truly magnificent island hideaway. The romance is reserved for guests of the exclusive **Labriz Silhouette** (☎ 293949; www.labriz-seychelles.com; d incl breakfast €350-1050; 🍴 💻 🏊). Diving is available.

Frégate Island & North Island

Another paradise awaits you at tiny Frégate, about 55km east of Mahé, where lies the superlative **Frégate Island Private** (☎ 224925; www.fregate.com; d with full board €2200; 🍴 💻 🏊). North Island, about 25km north of Mahé, boasts the ultra-exclusive **North Island Resort** (☎ 293100; www.north-island.com; d full board from €1520; 🍴 💻 🏊). Diving is available on both islands.

Outer Islands

The majority of the Seychelles islands are scattered over hundreds of kilometres to the southwest of the main Mahé group. Sadly, most of these islands are accessible only to yachtsmen and those who can afford to stay at the extremely exclusive resorts.

The **Amirantes Group** lies about 250km southwest of Mahé. Its main island is **Desroches**, which is reserved for guests of the luxury **Desroches Island Resort** (☎ 229003; www.naiaderesort.com; d with full board €750; 🍴 🏊). Diving can be arranged through its onsite dive centre.

Another 200km further south, the **Alphonse Group** is another cluster of coral islands that provides some of the best saltwater fly-fishing in the world. The largest of the group, the 1.2km-wide **Alphonse Island**, is home to the **Alphonse Island Resort** (☎ 229030; www.alphonse-resort.com), which was closed for renovation at the time of writing.

The **Aldabra Group** is the most remote and most interesting of the outer island groups. It includes **Aldabra Atoll**, the world's largest raised coral atoll, which is a Unesco World Heritage Site and nature reserve and lies more than 1000km from Mahé. Aldabra Atoll is home to about 150,000 giant tortoises, and flocks of migratory birds fly in and out in their thousands. Aldabra is managed by the **Seychelles Island Foundation** (SIF; Map p270; www.sif.sc; Mont Fleuri Rd, Victoria) in Victoria. Until now the islands have only really been accessible to scientists, volunteers and a very small number of tourists. However, SIF is considering tapping into the lucrative ecotourism market in order to raise funds. Contact SIF for more information.

SEYCHELLES

the max, and the place is definitely more a back-to-nature than a jet-set-tourist kind of haven, making it possible to find a deserted *anse* (bay) to commune with your quest for inner peace.

Transport to La Digue is absurdly easy. It's only about 5km from Praslin, and getting by boat from one island to the other is simplicity itself, so you've no excuse not to spend a day or two at the very least on this island.

If money's any object, La Digue has a growing number of quaint family guesthouses and self-catering apartments in which to rest your head. While hardly glitzy, they usually boast loads of gracious charm.

INFORMATION

All venues are in La Passe.

Barclays Bank (☎ 234148; ☒ 10am-2.30pm Mon-Fri)

Creole Travel Services (☎ 234411; ☒ 8am-noon & 1-4pm Mon-Fri, 8am-noon Sat) An agent for Cat Cocos. Can arrange tours and boat excursions.

Explorer Internet Café (per hr Rs 60; ☒ 9am-noon, 1.30-7pm Mon-Fri, 9am-6pm Sat) Same building as Mason's Travel.

La Digue Video & Internet Café (per hr Rs 60; ☒ 9am-9pm Mon-Sat, 3-8pm Sun)

Mauritius Commercial Bank (MCB; ☎ 234560; ☒ 8.30am-12.15pm & 1-3pm Mon-Fri)

Mason's Travel (☎ 234227; ☒ 8am-4.30pm Mon-Fri, 8am-noon Sat) Can organise tours and boat excursions.

Post office (☒ 8am-noon & 1-4pm Mon-Fri)

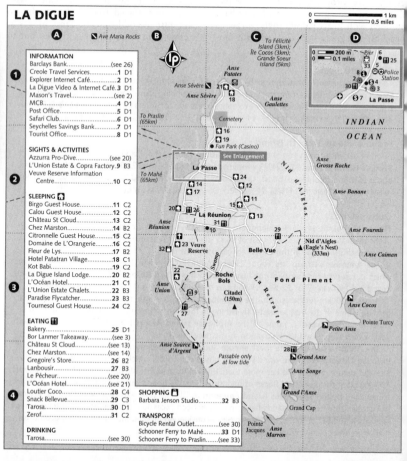

LA DIGUE

Safari Club (☎ 234575; ⌚ 9am-7pm) Can organise tours and boat excursions.

Seychelles Savings Bank (☎ 234135; ⌚ 8.30am-2.30pm Mon-Sat, 9am-11pm Sat)

Tourist office (☎ 234393; ⌚ 8am-4.30pm Mon-Fri, 8.30am-1pm Sat) Provides basic information and helps organise tours.

SIGHTS & ACTIVITIES
La Passe
A visit to tiny La Passe almost feels like stepping back in time, so perfectly does it capture the image of a sleepy tropical port. Virtually no cars clog the streets. Men and women talk shop on the jetty while waiting for the schooner to arrive. Children ride bicycles on the tree-lined roads. Youngsters flirt and hang around the Fun Park casino. Come Saturday night, most islanders head to Tarosa for some serious dancing and drinking.

Check out the few souvenir shops near the jetty, sign up for a boat excursion or hire a bicycle and just peddle around a bit.

Beaches
Most new arrivals head straight for the beach at **Anse Source d'Argent**, and we don't blame them. *This* is the tropical paradise we've all been daydreaming about all winter: a dazzling white-sand beach backed by naturally sculpted granite boulders that would have made Henry Moore proud.

Alas, don't expect a Robinson Crusoe experience – it can get pretty crowded here, especially at high tide when the beach virtually disappears. If possible, it's best to come in the late afternoon when the crowds begin to thin out and the colours are at their most intense. Another downside: Anse Source d'Argent is scenic to boot, but not that great for swimming due to the shallow water. Is Anse Source d'Argent overhyped? You be the judge.

Take note that the path down to Anse Source d'Argent runs through the old L'Union Estate coconut plantation. In other words, you'll have to pay the €4 entry fee (valid for a day) to access the beach.

On the southeast coast, **Grand Anse** is a stunning beach to sun yourself on, and it sees fewer visitors because of the effort required to get there (though you can easily walk or cycle the 4km or so from La Passe). One caveat: swimming may be dangerous because of the strong offshore currents during the southeast monsoon, from April to October.

Beyond Grand Anse, two of the island's quietest beaches are **Petite Anse** and **Anse Cocos**. To reach them, take the path heading northeast from Grand Anse. Petite Anse is palm-fringed and idyllic, though there are strong currents here too. Anse Cocos is reached by a rather vague track at the north end of Petite Anse.

On the north coast, **Anse Sévère** is good for snorkelling when the sea is not too rough. Closer to La Passe, **Anse Réunion** is another alluring beach but there are usually many algae drifting along the shore.

Nid d'Aigle
Ready to huff and puff? Tackle Nid d'Aigle (Eagle's Nest), the highest point on La Digue (333m). It commands such spectacular views of La Digue and neighbouring islands that you'll think you're watching a movie.

From La Passe, follow the inland concrete road that leads up to Snack Bellevue (it's signposted). The last section is very steep. After a mood-lifting refreshment at the bar, follow the narrow path that starts behind the Snack. After about 15 minutes, you'll reach an intersection on a ridge; turn right and follow the path until you reach Nid d'Aigle (no sign) after another 10 minutes.

L'Union Estate & Copra Factory
At one time, the main industry on La Digue was coconut farming, centred on L'Union Estate coconut plantation south of La Passe. These days **L'Union Estate** (admission €4) is run as an informal 'theme park', with demonstrations of extracting oil from copra (dried coconut flesh). Also in the grounds are the Old Plantation House, a colonial-era graveyard, a boatyard and the obligatory pen of giant tortoises. **Horse-riding** (per hr Rs 100) is also available on the estate (by reservation only).

Veuve Reserve
La Digue is the last refuge of the black paradise flycatcher, which locals call the *veuve* (widow). This small forest reserve has been set aside to protect its natural habitat, but you're just as likely to see the birds elsewhere on the island. Entry to the reserve is free. There's a small **information centre** (☎ 234353; ⌚ 8am-4pm).

Boat Excursions to Nearby Islands
Taking a boat excursion to nearby **Île Cocos**, **Félicité** and **Grande Sœur** will be one of the main highlights of your visit to the Seychelles and

292 LA DIGUE •• Sleeping

Book accommodation online at lonelyplanet.com

it's well worth the expense. Full-day tours typically stop to snorkel off Île Cocos and Félicité and picnic on Grande Sœur. The best snorkelling spots can be found off the iconic Île Cocos.

Most lodgings and travel agencies on La Digue can arrange such trips. Prices are about €80, including a barbecued fish lunch. Half-day tours can also be organised (€50).

Diving

La Digue has much to offer under the surface. **Azzura Pro-Dive** (☎ 292525; www.ladigue.sc) at La Digue Island Lodge organises dive trips in the area. See p32 for information on dive sites.

SLEEPING

As more guesthouses and hotels open on La Digue it is becoming easier to find accommodation. Prices are usually negotiable if it's slack and if you pay cash. Most places offer half-board options. The cheapest ones don't accept credit cards.

Citronnelle Guest House (☎/fax 234230; s/d incl breakfast €30/60; 🏠) If you've been looking high and low for a decent €30 room, you've found it. On the inland road in La Passe is this brilliantly priced guesthouse with five well-kept rooms arranged around a courtyard. Ambience is not this place's forte, but its convenient location and very affordable prices make amends for this.

Chez Marston (☎ 234023; mars@seychelles.sc; s/d incl breakfast €50/80; 🏠) Features a row of five anodyne rooms. For the price we'd expect a better view than the back kitchen of the restaurant.

our pick **Calou Guest House** (☎ 234083; www.calou .de; s/d with half board €80/123) Everything about this place is calming (except, maybe, the occasional barking dog). The five fan-cooled bungalows with private terrace are simple but agreeably designed and rest in a leafy plot; stunning, jungle-clad hills soar as the backdrop. And yes, you can order *calou* wine (devilish!). Recommended.

Kot Babi (☎ 234747; www.kokonet.sc/babi2; d incl breakfast €100; 🏠) In a mammoth white colonial mansion, this immaculately kept place has four sparklingly clean rooms. The owner, Robert Labiche, is a former chef at luxury resorts and will whip up delicious Creole meals. The only impediment: its location near the casino is not *that* exceptional.

Fleur de Lys (☎ 234459; www.fleurdelysey.com; d €115-125; 🏠) A chilled universe is created here by a lazy-day garden and a clutch of trim, Creole-style bungalows with spotless bathrooms and kitchenettes. Flake out in the serene setting or chatter with the knowledgeable Scottish owner. Breakfast is extra (€10).

Château St Cloud (☎ 234346; www.seychelles.net /stcloud; s €120-250, d €160-350, all incl breakfast; 🏠 🏊) An agreeable place set in a former colonial estate. One of the most reliable bases on the island, it has well-appointed rooms of varying sizes and shapes, a restaurant and a pool surrounded by a tropical Garden of Eden. If you're flush, book in to one of the deluxe rooms, which marry modern and Creole design influences.

our pick **L'Océan Hotel** (☎ 234180; hocean@seychelles .net; d incl breakfast €175; 🏠) One of our favourites for original character and oceanfront location, L'Océan has been creatively decorated, providing visual flair as well as a good range of facilities, including a restaurant. Every bedroom boasts stupendous views of the sea and is decorated with driftwood, shells and paintings by local artist George Camille. Hint: aim for the Petite Sœur and Grande Sœur rooms (competition from honeymooners will be fierce, though).

Domaine de L'Orangerie (☎ 248444; reservations@ orangerie.sc; d incl breakfast €198; 🏠) A quietly stylish place at the northern end of La Passe. Dotted in manicured gardens, the 10 villas are dressed up in a Creole-Balinese fusion with hardwood furnishings, four-poster beds and rich textiles. Step inside and let the Zen-like tranquillity envelop you. The owner has plans to build a pool and additional villas at the back of the property. If only it was on the beach!

La Digue Island Lodge (☎ 292525; www.ladigue.sc; s with half board €170-350, d with half board €230-510; 🏠 🏊) La Digue's one truly upmarket resort satisfies fantasies of a palm-fringed, white-sand beach overlooking emerald waters (but expect algae at certain times of the year). It comprises A-frame chalets packed rather close together, though the garden setting is attractive, as well as an atmospheric plantation house and standard bungalows. Amenities are solid, with two restaurants, a dive centre, three bars and boat excursions to Félicité Island.

Other options:

Tournesol Guest House (☎ 234155; tournesol@ seychelles.sc; s/d incl breakfast €40/80; 🏠) This no-frills option in a verdant property tricks its otherwise nondescript rooms out with kitschy bedspreads and curtains (read: '70s-inspired floral motifs).

Birgo Guest House (☎ 234518; www.birgo.sc; d incl breakfast €110; ❄) A commendable guesthouse in a balmy garden setting.

Hotel Patatran Village (☎ 234333; www.patatran seychelles.com; s €118-138, d €151-178, all incl breakfast; ❄ ⌨) Rooms here are serviceable and blessed with lovely views of Anse Patates but hardly fuel the imagination. Lacks the charm of nearby L'Océan.

Paradise Flycatcher (☎ 234015; mcdurup@seychelles .net; s/d with half board €131/191) Four capacious villas on a grassy property.

L'Union Estate Chalets (☎ 234240; www.ladigue .sc; chalets €425) Four spacious bungalows overlooking the beach at L'Union Estate.

EATING

If eating out in the evening, remember to take a torch with you as there are few street lights, and note that most restaurants close around 9.30pm.

Bor Lanmer Takeaway (mains Rs 25; ☽ lunch & dinner) If you're looking for a quick food fix, check out the options at this cheap-and-cheerful eatery near the jetty.

Snack Bellevue (mains Rs 40-80; ☽ 11am-6pm) It's a hell of a hike or ride to get to this eagle's eyrie, but you'll be amply rewarded with cardiac-arresting views from the terrace. It serves up the usual suspects at very reasonable prices (not a mean feat, given the location).

Tarosa (☎ 234407; mains €45-90; ☽ breakfast, lunch & dinner) This is La Digue's social hub, on the jetty. There's a little of everything for everyone, from satisfying breakfasts to sandwiches and smoked fish salad. It features a live band on Friday evening.

Chez Marston (☎ 234023; mains Rs 45-95; ☽ lunch & dinner) This institution serves some of the best food on the island. The wide-ranging menu features salads, sandwiches, prawns, fish or crab curries, pizzas and burgers, among others. The ambience is so chilled, you could kick your feet up on the chair and pull out a novel and no one would bat an eyelid. Or you could discuss the hardships of island life with Marston, the blue-eyed owner, who is a local character.

our pick **Lanbousir** (mains Rs 50-90; ☽ 10am-4pm daily) This sand-floored eatery run by three affable ladies is an ideal spot for a filling lunch after (or before) working your tan at nearby Anse Source d'Argent. Start things off with smoked fish salad, move on to a meltingly tender *job* fillet, then finish off with a rich banana pancake. Wash it all down with a lemon juice or a chilled coconut. A tourist's life is hard, isn't it?

Zerof (☎ 234439; mains Rs 60-85, menu Rs 125; ☽ lunch & dinner) Only your mum could fix a more comforting meal than you'll find at this cosy spot in a garden setting. The menu is a bargain, and the smoked fish salad truly palate-pleasing.

L'Océan Hotel (☎ 234180; mains Rs 60-120; ☽ lunch & dinner) The terrace restaurant of this hotel has killer views to the turquoise sea and even better views on the plate. '*Très bon*' (very good) was the verdict of a French couple sitting next to us, after wolfing down a plate of prawns. Judging by the spicy fish cooked traditional-style in a banana leaf, we agree. But avoid the banana cake – too dry. Enchanting setting, with tropical shells encased under the glass table.

Loutier Coco (☎ 514762; buffet Rs 125; ☽ 10am-4pm) Feel the sand in your toes at this oasis of a place on Grand Anse beach, but be prepared to share the experience with a raft of day-trippers here to enjoy the lavish buffet at lunchtime. The spread on offer includes grilled fish, traditional Creole curries and salads, fruit and coffee.

Château St Cloud (☎ 234346; mains Rs 60-135; ☽ lunch & dinner) The inhouse restaurant at Château St Cloud is worth considering for its eclectic menu but the food's not fantastically exciting and the atmosphere is a bit staid.

Le Pécheur (☎ 292525; menu Rs 200; ☽ dinner) Candles, French wines and a table on a palm-ruffled beach are all you need for a romantic night out with your significant other at this attractive restaurant at La Digue Island Lodge. Diners are serenaded by a local guitarist three times a week.

For self-caterers, **Gregoire's Store** (☎ 234024; ☽ 8am-7.45pm Mon-Sat, 8am-1pm Sun) near La Digue Island Lodge is the best-stocked supermarket on the island. There's also a small **bakery** (☽ 8am-6pm Mon-Sat) near the pier where you can gnaw your way to carbo bliss with fresh bread and cakes.

DRINKING

The restaurant-meets-bar Tarosa is the most 'happening' spot in town and transforms itself into an open-air club on Saturday evening. This is your chance to rub shoulders with La Digue's movers and shakers and relive *Saturday Night Fever* island-style!

SHOPPING

Barbara Jenson Studio (☎ 234406; www.barbarajen
sonstudio.com; Anse Réunion; ☺ 9am-6pm Mon-Sat)
Barbara's work reflects the unique landscape and ethnically diverse people of
the Seychelles.

GETTING THERE & AROUND

La Digue is easily reached by boat and
helicopter from both Mahé and Praslin. See
p300 for details.

Although there's now a stretch of surfaced road running through La Passe on
the west coast, elsewhere on La Digue the
'roads' are still just sandy tracks. This, coupled with the fact that the island is less
than 5km from north to south, means by
far the best – and most enjoyable – way to
get around is on foot or bicycle. There are
loads of bikes to rent. Operators have outlets near the pier, or you can book through
your hotel. Most places charge around Rs 50
per day.

Ox carts used to be a popular mode of
transport but are gradually being replaced by
open-sided lorries.

There are only a handful of taxis on La
Digue, as most people get around on bicycle
or on foot. A one-way ride from the pier to
Grand Anse costs around Rs 80.

Seychelles Directory

CONTENTS

ACCOMMODATION

Glossy brochures focus on ultraswish resorts but the Seychelles actually has a pretty wide range of accommodation options. Sure, you could easily whittle away your life savings on private island resorts, which are as sumptuous as the hype leads you to believe, but you can also benefit from the cheaper guesthouses and self-catering apartments that have sprung up over the last decade (and are still largely ignored by most first-time visitors).

All accommodation in the Seychelles is registered and regulated by the Ministry of Tourism. This ensures a certain standard of service and facilities. Camping is forbidden anywhere on the islands.

For a double room, you can expect to pay under €100 for budget accommodation, €100 to €250 for midrange and over €250 for top-end rooms. Rates include all government taxes, and often include breakfast. Recommendations in our Sleeping entries are in ascending order of price.

Even in the cheapest guesthouse you can expect to get a room with a private bathroom and a fan. Moving up the scale, there are now some very attractive family-run guesthouses and small hotels offering local colour; it's these that arguably represent the best value for money in the islands. If you want the full range of services, though, you'll need to opt for one of the larger hotels, which generally provide tour desks and a range of sports facilities. Standards have improved dramatically at the top end and some of the newer hotels now put those in Mauritius to shame for levels of service and all-round luxury. Best of all are the private island resorts, where you really are buying into the dream.

Virtually all the hotels and a few guesthouses charge higher rates during peak periods: Christmas to New Year, Easter, and July and August.

You are strongly advised to book well ahead, particularly during peak periods and at any time of year on Praslin and La Digue, where accommodation is more limited. You can contact the hotels direct, or make online bookings through **Seychelles European Reservations** (www.seychelles-resa.com), which specialises in the 'cheaper' end of the market. **Seychelles Secrets** (www.seychellessecrets.com) focuses on charming options.

ACTIVITIES
Cruises

The best months for cruising are April and October; the worst are January, July and August. You can charter schooners, yachts and motor cruisers through tour agents or the **Marine Charter Association** (MCA; ☎ 322126; mca@seychelles.net) in Victoria. Prices start at around €600 for a day trip. Tours to islands should include landing fees – make sure you ask when booking.

For the romantics, **Silhouette Cruises** (☎ 324026; www.seychelles-cruises.com), based near Victoria's

---

PRACTICALITIES

■ The Seychelles uses the metric system for weights and measures; kilometres, kilograms, litres and degrees in Celsius.

■ Electric current is 220V, 50Hz AC. The plugs in general use have square pins and three points.

■ The only daily paper is the government-controlled *Seychelles Nation* (www.nation.sc) which contains international and local news in English, French and Creole. Other newspapers include the weekly *People* (www.thepeople.sc), also government backed, and *Le Nouveau Seychelles Weekly* (www.seychellesweekly.com), the sole opposition paper.

■ The *Seychelles Broadcasting Corporation* (SBC; www.sbc.com) provides TV broadcasts from 6am to around midnight in English, French and Creole. The news in English is at 6pm. Many programmes are imported from England, America or France.

■ SBC also runs the main radio station, which broadcasts daily from 6am to 10pm in three languages, as well as a 24-hour music station, Paradise FM. The frequencies of these stations vary depending on where you are on the islands.

---

interisland ferry terminal, owns the delightful SV *Sea Shell* and SV *Sea Pearl*, a pair of old Dutch schooners that offer live-aboard cruises around the inner islands with activities such as deep-sea fishing and scuba diving thrown in.

Some other charter companies:

Angel Fish Ltd (☎ 344644; www.seychelles-charter.com; PO Box 1079, Victoria)

Dream Yacht Charters (Map p282; ☎ 232681; www.dream-yacht-seychelles.com; Baie St Anne, Praslin)

Sunsail (☎ 225700; www.sunsail.com; PO Box 1076, Victoria)

VPM Yacht Charters (☎ 347719; www.vpm-boats.com; PO Box 960, Victoria)

Water World (☎ 514735; www.seychelles.net/wworld; PO Box 735, Victoria)

Fishing

The Seychelles supports extremely rich fisheries for big game fish such as giant barracuda, sailfish and marlin. There is also excellent saltwater fly-fishing around the Alphonse islands for the dedicated – and wealthy – angler.

A number of operators have jumped on the boat, so to speak, offering all-inclusive trips where they do everything for you but put the fish on the hook. They can be contacted through the **Marine Charter Association** (☎ 322126; fax 224679) in Victoria. Alternatively, most yacht charter companies (see p295) and tour companies also offer fishing expeditions. Expect to pay in the region of €600/800 for a half/full day's outing. 'Tag and release' is widely practised.

Hiking

Because the islands are relatively small and the roads little travelled (away from north Mahé), walking is a pleasurable activity just about anywhere in the Seychelles. There are still lots of wild, hilly and mountainous areas where you can escape the crowds, appreciate the islands' natural scenery and enjoy some of the many alternatives to beach-oriented activities.

The Ministry of Environment produces a good set of leaflets (with maps) detailing individual hiking routes in Mahé's Morne Seychellois National Park (p275). They are available for between Rs 5 and Rs 10 each from the botanical gardens (p269) or the tourist office (p269) in Victoria.

Water Sports

The main draw is undoubtedly the water activities – snorkelling, diving, windsurfing, sailing and the like. Big hotels usually offer at least some water sports to their guests for free. Otherwise, there are plenty of independent operators around; the main centres are Beau Vallon on Mahé and Anse Volbert on Praslin. For detailed information on diving in the Seychelles, see p31.

BUSINESS HOURS

In general banks are open only from 8.30am to 2pm Monday to Friday, and 8.30am to 11am on Saturday. Government offices usually open from 8am to 4pm Monday to Friday. Restaurants are generally open from 11am to

3pm and 6pm to 9pm daily. Shop hours are typically 8am to 5pm Monday to Friday, and 8am to noon on Saturday.

CHILDREN

The Seychelles is a very child-friendly place. The big hotels cater for all age groups, offering baby-sitting services, kids clubs and activities laid on especially for teenagers. While children will happily spend all day splashing around in the lagoon, boat trips around the islands should also appeal. Communing with giant tortoises is a sure-fire hit and, with a bit of creativity, visiting some of the nature reserves can be fun. Finding special foods and other baby products can be difficult, especially outside Victoria, so you might want to bring your favourite brands with you.

Lonely Planet's *Travel with Children*, by Cathy Lanigan, gives you the lowdown on preparing for family travel.

CLIMATE CHARTS

For more information on the best time of the year for visiting Seychelles, see p267.

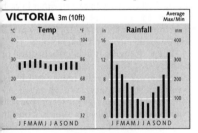

VICTORIA 3m (10ft)

EMBASSIES & CONSULATES

Seychelles Embassies & Consulates

The Seychelles has diplomatic representation in the following countries:

Australia (☎ 03-9796 9412; mazino@iprimus.com.au; 51 Belgrave Hallam Rd, Narre Warren, Victoria 3804)

Canada (☎ 514-2843 322; connsey@cam.org; 67 Rue Ste Catherine Ouest, Montreal, Québec H2X1Z7)

France (☎ 01 42 30 57 47; ambsey@aol.com; 51 Ave Mozart, 75016 Paris)

Germany (☎ 30-8909 0844; rasudhoff@t-online.de; Humboldtstrasse 47, D-14193 Berlin)

Mauritius (☎ 211 1688; gfok@intnet.mu; 616 St James Court, St Denis St, Port Louis)

UK (☎ 020-7935 7770; seyhclon@aol.com; 111 Baker St, London W1U 6RR)

USA (☎ 212-972 1785; seychelles@un.int; 800 Second Ave, Suite 400C, New York, NY 10017)

VOLUNTEERING IN THE SEYCHELLES

Wanna get involved in turtle-tagging, whale-shark monitoring or researching certain animal species? **Nature Protection Trust of Seychelles** (http://members.aol.com/jstgerlach), **Nature Seychelles** (www.natureseychelles.org), **Seychelles Island Foundation** (www.sif.sc) and **Marine Conservation Society Seychelles** (www.mcss.sc) all have volunteer programmes.

Embassies & Consulates in the Seychelles

Countries with embassies and consulates in the Seychelles include the following:

British High Commission (Map p270; ☎ 283666; www.bhcvictoria.sc; PO Box 161, Oliaji Trade Centre, Francis Rachel St, Victoria)

France (Map p270; ☎ 382500; www.ambafrance-sc.org; BP478, La Ciotat, Mont Fleuri, Victoria)

Germany (☎ 601100; Conservation Centre, Roche Caiman, PO Box 1310, Mahé)

Mauritius (☎ 601100; birdlife@seychelles.net; Conservation Centre, Roche Caiman, PO Box 1310, Mahé)

Netherlands (☎ 261200; consulgeers@hotmail.com; PO Box 372, Sunset Beach Hotel, Glacis, Mahé)

USA (Map p270; ☎ 222256; usoffice@seychelles.net; PO Box 251, Oliaji Trade Centre, Francis Rachel St, Victoria)

FESTIVALS & EVENTS

The Seychelles may lack the range of festivals found in Mauritius and Réunion, but there are some lively cultural bashes during the year and a whole raft of fishing competitions and other sporting events. The local newspapers usually have details of what's on, or you can ask at the tourist office.

JANUARY

Seychelles Sailing Cup (www.seychellescup.com) A seven-day regatta in the last week of January.

MARCH

Semaine de la Francophonie French culture takes over Mahé for a week of song recitals, films and art exhibitions in mid-March.

SUBIOS Underwater Festival (www.subios.com) Week-long underwater photography competition at Beau Vallon held in mid-March.

MAY

FetAfrik The Seychelles celebrates its African origins with a weekend of music and dance in late May.

FESTIVAL KREOL

Held every year during the last week of October, the vibrant **Festival Kreol** is an explosion of Creole cuisine, theatre, art, music and dance. Creole artists from other countries are invited to participate, and the festival provides young artists with a platform on which to unleash their creative talents. There are various Creole handicrafts and foodstuffs on sale. Events take place on Mahé, Praslin and La Digue.

OCTOBER
Festival Kreol (www.seychelles.net/festivalkreol) Week-long festival of Creole culture; last week of October.

FOOD

For a full explanation of local cuisine and drinks, refer to the Food & Drink section (p261). We usually indicate the price of mains, followed by the price of menus (two- or three-course set menus). Within each eating section, restaurants appear in ascending order of prices. For a full, midrange restaurant meal you should expect to pay €20 to €25 per person with wine.

GAY & LESBIAN TRAVELLERS

There is no open gay or lesbian scene in the Seychelles. The Seychellois are tolerant, but open displays of affection between gay of lesbian couples are best avoided.

HOLIDAYS

Public holidays in the Seychelles are observed as follows:
New Year 1 & 2 January
Good Friday March/April
Easter Day March/April
Labour Day 1 May
Liberation Day 5 June
Corpus Christi 10 June
National Day 18 June
Independence Day 29 June
Assumption 15 August
All Saints' Day 1 November
Immaculate Conception 8 December
Christmas Day 25 December

INSURANCE

A travel-insurance policy to cover theft, loss and medical problems is a good idea. Some policies specifically exclude dangerous activities, which can include scuba diving. See also p138.

INTERNET ACCESS

In Victoria, you'll never be far from an internet café. Fees are usually around Rs 40 per hour. Outside the capital, internet access is harder to find. At the time of writing, there was only one outlet with internet access in Praslin and two in La Digue.

Most upmarket hotels offer internet access to their guests.

MONEY

The unit of currency is the Seychelles rupee (Rs), which is divided into 100 cents (¢). Bank notes come in denominations of Rs 10, Rs 25, Rs 50, Rs 100 and Rs 500; there are coins of Rs 1, Rs 5, 1¢, 5¢, 10¢ and 25¢.

There are some complex rules governing foreign exchange in the Seychelles. By law visitors must pay for all accommodation (including meals and drinks at hotels), excursions, marine park fees, diving, car hire and transport in a major foreign currency (euros are the best currency to carry), either in cash or by credit card. Prices for these services are therefore nearly always quoted in euros (and less frequently in US dollars).

When changing travellers cheques or withdrawing money from an ATM, however, you will receive the money in rupees, not in foreign currency. Even when you pay for something in foreign currency, you will often receive the change in rupees. You can use rupees in shops, cafés and restaurants outside the hotels and for taxi and bus fares, but they can be quite hard to spend otherwise, so only change small amounts at a time.

If you pay cash in euros at guesthouses, small hotels or for car rentals, you'll be in a position to negotiate a discount (up to 20% if it's slack). Our tip: bring plenty of cash with you, and use a credit card as a backup.

If you want to change rupees back into foreign currency at the end of your stay, you must go back to the same bank (not necessarily the same branch, but it doesn't hurt) with the original exchange receipt or ATM slip. The maximum you can convert is Rs 800 and it is illegal to take more than Rs 2000 out of the country. If possible, do it in Victoria rather than at the airport.

ATMs

There are ATMs, which accept major international cards, at the airport and at all the major banks in Victoria. You'll also find ATMs at Beau Vallon on Mahé and on Praslin and La Digue.

Credit Cards

Major credit cards, including Visa and MasterCard, are accepted in most hotels, guesthouses, restaurants and tourist shops.

Moneychangers

The four main banks are Barclays Bank, Seychelles Savings Bank, Nouvobanq and Mauritius Commercial Bank (MCB). All have branches in Victoria while Barclays Bank and Nouvobanq have desks at the airport that are open for all flights – in theory at least. There are also banks on Praslin and La Digue. None of the banks charges commission for changing cash but some do so for travellers cheques, generally a flat rate of Rs 25.

PHOTOGRAPHY

The Seychelles is a photographer's dreams and there are myriad opportunities for still and video photography. Bring your own films and supplies. See the boxed text p140 for tips on taking pictures.

SOLO TRAVELLERS

Solo travellers will have an easy time of it in the Seychelles; there are no specific dangers, worries or scams associated with travelling on you own. The only disadvantage solo travellers will face is accommodation costs – quite often single room prices are in fact only marginally cheaper than doubles, and if you're renting an apartment you'll be charged by the unit as a whole in most cases.

When eating out, be prepared to be the only single in the midst of honeymooners!

TELEPHONE

The telephone system is efficient and reliable. There are public payphones (both coin and cardphones) on the three main islands from which you can make local and international calls. Telephone cards are available from Cable & Wireless and Airtel offices and from most retail outlets.

Local calls within and between the main islands cost around Rs 0.90 for up to three minutes. For an idea of international rates, calls to America, Australia and the UK with Cable & Wireless cost roughly Rs 8 per minute.

If you have a GSM phone and it has been 'unlocked', you can use a local SIM card purchased from either Cable & Wireless or Airtel.

TOURIST INFORMATION

The very well organised **Seychelles Tourism Bureau** (STB; www.seychelles.travel) is the only tourist information body in the Seychelles. The head office is in Victoria. It has two offices on Praslin and one office on La Digue.

TRAVELLERS WITH DISABILITIES

Most luxury hotels conform to international standards for disabled access, and it's usually possible to hire an assistant if you want to take an excursion.

Apart from that, special facilities for travellers with disabilities are few and far between in the Seychelles, and no beach is equipped with wheelchair access.

VISAS

You don't need a visa to enter the Seychelles, just a valid passport, an onward ticket, booked accommodation and sufficient

---

BLACK MARKET TEMPTATIONS

Oops, this is a bit of a taboo issue, but it's our duty to inform you: there is a black market in the Seychelles. It's illegal (but tempting) to change money on the black market because official rates massively overvalue the rupee (one euro bought 12 rupees on the black market when we were here, as against one euro buying eight rupees at official rates). Of course we could never recommend an illegal activity, but we hear that if you do indulge you should conduct your transaction very discreetly, with somebody you trust. Euros are the hot favourites.

You won't save that much, though. Rupees are only useful for restaurants, cafés and internet cafés, as well as bus and taxi fares. But if you're a serious foodie, it could amount to, er, a few hundred euros at the end of your trip (wine can also be paid for in rupees).

funds for your stay. On arrival at the airport, you will be given a visitor's visa for up to a month, depending on the departure date printed on your onward ticket.

If you wish to extend your visa or change your departure date, apply with proof of funds and your onward ticket at the **Immigration Office** (Map p270; ☎ 611100; immig@seychelles.net; Independence House, Independence Ave, Victoria; ⊗ 8am-noon & 1-4pm Mon-Fri). Processing takes about a week. The first three-month extension is free of charge.

WOMEN TRAVELLERS

Generally speaking, women travellers should have few problems getting around solo in the Seychelles. As in any country, however, women should use their common sense and remain conscious of their surroundings. Be wary of going to isolated stretches of beach alone.

TRANSPORT AROUND SEYCHELLES

AIR

The **Seychelles International Airport** (☎ 384400), about 8km south of Victoria, is the only international airport in the Seychelles.

Air Seychelles (☎ 381000; www.airseychelles.net) takes care of all interisland flights, whether scheduled or charter. The only scheduled services are between Mahé and Praslin, with around 20 flights per day in each direction. The fare for the 15-minute hop is €61 (€122 return). The luggage limit is only 20kg (€1 per kilo for excess luggage). Air Seychelles also flies to Alphonse, Bird, Denis, Desroches, Frégate and North Islands, but on a charter basis – these flights are handled directly by the hotel on the island.

Note that Mahé is the only hub for flights within the Seychelles.

Helicopter Seychelles (☎ 385858; www.helicopter seychelles.com), based at Seychelles International Airport, operates shuttle flights between Mahé and Praslin (€174 per person one way), Mahé and La Digue (€174), and Praslin and La Digue (€87). It also offers transfers to resort islands (bookings should be made through the hotel) and scenic flights.

BICYCLE

Bicycles are the principal form of transport on La Digue. On Praslin you can rent bikes at Anse Volbert or through your accommodation. Mahé is a bit hilly for casual cyclists and most visitors rent cars, so bike hire is hard to find there.

BOAT

Travel by boat is very easy between Mahé, Praslin and La Digue, with regular and efficient ferry services. For all other islands you have to charter a boat or take a tour.

Mahé to Praslin

The **Cat Cocos catamaran** (☎ 324843, 324844; www.catcocos.com) makes two to three return trips daily between Mahé and Praslin. Departing from Victoria, the journey takes about 50 minutes (not that much longer than the plane, if you include check-in time) and the fare is €40 one way (€45 in the upper, air-con lounge); children under twelve pay half fare. In high season, it's advisable to book your ticket at least a day in advance with the ferry company or through a travel agent.

Mahé to La Digue

Want to get off the beaten trail? Not afraid of seasickness? The schooner **La Belle Seraphina** (☎ 234254, 511345) is for you. This cargo boat runs between Mahé and La Digue from Monday to Friday and carries passengers if there is room. If you don't mind a bit of discomfort it's a fun and cheap way to travel. The boat generally departs around 11.30am from Mahé, and around 5am from La Digue, but check when making the booking. The three-hour crossing costs just €15/7 per adult/child.

Praslin to La Digue

The **Inter-Island Ferry Co** (☎ 232329) operates a schooner service between Praslin and La Digue. There are about seven departures daily between 7am and 5.15pm (5.45pm on Sunday) from Praslin and between 7.30am and 5.45pm (6.15pm on Sunday) from La Digue. The 30-minute trip can be a rocky one, sometimes spraying unsuspecting passengers with water. There are plans to add a faster and more comfortable catamaran service in the near future.

The one-way/return fare is €10/20 per adult and €5/10 per child under eight. It's a good idea to book ahead – most hotels will do this for you.

BUS

Good news: if you've got time, you don't really need to rent a car to visit the islands.

Mahé

An extensive bus service operates throughout Mahé. Destinations and routes are usually marked on the front of the bus. There is a flat rate of Rs 3 whatever the length of journey; pay the driver as you board. Bus stops have signs and shelters and there are also markings on the road.

Timetables and maps of each route are posted at the terminus in Victoria, where you can also pick up photocopied timetables at the **information office** (☎ 518339; ⊙ 8am-4pm Mon-Fri). All parts of the island are serviced. There's a bus roughly each hour on most routes from around 6am until 7pm (slightly later heading into Victoria).

Praslin

Praslin also boasts an efficient bus service. The basic route is from Anse Boudin to Mont Plaisir via Anse Volbert, Baie Ste Anne, Vallée de Mai, Grand Anse and the airport. Buses run in each direction every hour (every half-hour between Baie St Anne and Mont Plaisir) from 6am to 6.30pm. Anse Consolation and Anse La Blague are also serviced. For Anse Lazio, get off at Anse Boudin and walk to the beach (about 15 minutes). Timetables are available at the two tourist offices. There is a flat fare of Rs 3.

CAR

If you want to be controller of your own destiny, your best bet is to rent a car. Most of the road network on Mahé and Praslin is sealed and in good shape. More of a worry are the narrow bends and the speed at which some drivers, especially bus drivers, take them.

Drive on the left, and beware of drivers with fast cars and drowsy brains – especially late on Friday and Saturday nights. The speed limit is supposed to be 40kmh in built-up areas, 65kmh outside towns and 80kmh on the dual carriageway between Victoria and the airport. On Praslin the limit is 40kmh throughout the island.

Rental

There are any number of car-hire companies on Mahé and quite a few on Praslin, but little to choose between them as regards prices. The cheapest you're likely to get on Mahé is around €50 a day for a small hatchback (slightly less for longer periods). Rates on Praslin are about €10 to €15 more expensive. The tourist office in Victoria has a list of car rental outlets, or you can book through your hotel or guesthouse. The major companies also have offices at the airport. Note that payment must be made in hard currency (preferably euros).

Drivers must be over 23 years old and have held a driving licence for at least a year. Though it's wise to bring an international driver's licence, most companies accept a national licence.

TAXI

Taxis operate on Mahé and Praslin and there are even a handful on La Digue. Though taxis are metered you often have to insist pretty hard to get the driver to use it. In most cases you'll have to negotiate; make sure you fix a price before setting off.

SEYCHELLES DIRECTORY

Regional Transport

CONTENTS

GETTING THERE & AWAY

ENTERING THE COUNTRY
Mauritius

When entering Mauritius you must have a passport valid for at least six months from the date of entry, a visa for Mauritius (if necessary; see p150) and a ticket out of the country (together with a visa if necessary for your next port of call). If you don't have an onward ticket, you could be invited to buy one on the spot.

Immigration authorities will also want to know where you are staying in Mauritius (if you don't know just give them the name of any large hotel in this book) and may cause problems if you leave this answer blank. They may also grill you on your finances, especially if you are staying more than the standard two weeks; possession of a valid credit card is usually fine.

Réunion

As Réunion is a department of France, the formalities for entering the country are almost the same as those for entering mainland France, bar a few exceptions (see p253 for details on visa requirements). All visitors must possess a passport valid for at least three months from the date of entry, a visa (if required) and a return or onward ticket (plus a visa if necessary for your next destination).

Seychelles

'Titres de séjour' (a kind of tourist card/visa) of up to one month are issued free for all tourists on arrival. You just need to present a passport valid for at least six months from the date of entry, a return or onward ticket (with a visa for your next destination if required) and evidence of booked accommodation at least for your first few nights (mentioning the name of a hotel usually suffices). You may also be asked for evidence of sufficient funds to cover you during your stay; possession of a valid credit card is usually fine. For more information on visas, see p299.

AIR

Expensive flights have always been the biggest deterrent to travellers interested in visiting this region, and the sheer distance of the islands from most countries will never allow this to be a particularly cheap destination, despite prices having fallen in recent years.

By far the cheapest way to get here is to buy a package deal that includes flight and hotel accommodation. This can actually work out cheaper than just buying a return scheduled flight, and as you're totally free to ditch the hotel after a few days and travel around yourself, this is an option you should consider, even if you can't stand the idea of package holidays. A vast number of travel agents offer tour packages to these destinations; shop around online for the best bargains.

The principal hubs for airlines flying to this region are Paris and London. In general, prices are overall lowest on the Paris–Réunion route, although only just; London–Mauritius may be cheaper in high season. Depending on where you are coming from, it may work out cheaper to fly via Paris and Réunion and then take an onward flight to Mauritius or the Seychelles.

THINGS CHANGE...

The information in this chapter is particularly vulnerable to change. Check directly with the airline or a travel agent to make sure you understand how a fare (and ticket you may buy) works and be aware of the security requirements for international travel. Shop carefully. The details given in this chapter should be regarded as pointers and are not a substitute for your own careful, up-to-date research.

Airlines

Air Austral (airline code UU; ☎ in Mauritius 202 6677, in Réunion 0262 90 90 91, in Seychelles 323129; www.air-austral.com)

Air France (airline code AF; ☎ in Mauritius 202 6747, in Réunion 0820 82 08 20, in Seychelles 297180; www.airfrance.com)

Air Madagascar (airline code MD; ☎ in Mauritius 203 2150, in Réunion 0262 21 05 21; www.airmadagascar.com)

Air Mauritius (airline code MK; ☎ in Mauritius 207 7070, in Réunion 0262 94 83 83, in Seychelles 322414; www.airmauritius.com)

Air Seychelles (airline code HM; ☎ in Mauritius 202 6655, in Seychelles 381000; www.airseychelles.net)

British Airways (airline code BA; ☎ in Mauritius 202 8000, in Seychelles 224910; www.britishairways.com)

Condor (airline code DE; ☎ in Mauritius 213 4141, in Seychelles 288888; www.condor.com)

Corsair (airline code SS; ☎ in Réunion 0262 94 82 82; www.corsairfly.com)

Emirates (airline code EK; ☎ in Mauritius 213 9100, in Seychelles 292700; www.emirates.com)

Kenya Airways (airline code KQ; ☎ in Seychelles 322989; www.kenya-airways.com)

Qatar Airways (airline code QR; ☎ in Seychelles 224518; www.qatarairways.com)

South African Airways (airline code SA; ☎ in Mauritius 202 6737; www.flysaa.com)

Virgin Atlantic (airline code VS; Mauritius only; www.virginatlantic.com)

Tickets

The main point to remember when buying your air ticket is to start early. Mauritius, Réunion and the Seychelles are popular destinations and some flights are booked months in advance. Somewhat paradoxically, it's also worth looking last minute as that's when other good bargains sometimes become available; however, this can never be guaranteed of course.

If you are after a simple return ticket within fairly fixed dates, then it's easy to book online. Some of the better international online ticket sites include the following:

Ebookers (www.ebookers.com)
Expedia (www.expedia.com)
Flight Centre International (www.flightcentre.com)
Flights.com (www.flights.com)
STA (www.sta.com)
Travelocity (www.travelocity.com)

INTERCONTINENTAL TICKETS

It is possible to include Mauritius, Réunion and the Seychelles as part of a Round-the-World (RTW) ticket. These can be bought through one of the three big airline alliances (Oneworld Alliance, Sky Team and Star Alliance) or through a travel agent. RTW tickets put together by travel agents tend to be more expensive but allow you to devise your own itinerary. In general RTW tickets are valid for up to one year and are calculated on the basis of either the number of continents or the distance covered.

Oneworld Alliance also offers a Visit Africa pass, which covers eight African countries including the Seychelles. Fares are calculated according to the number of flights taken and you must fly to and from Africa with one of the alliance members.

Another option is to fly from A to Z with as many stopovers as you want going in one direction, rather than buying individual tickets; this is especially worth investigating for the Seychelles. If you choose this option, always do it through a knowledgeable travel agent and not the airlines. That way, the fare may be calculated on the basis of mileage rather than the sum of your journey's parts.

Online ticket sites for intercontinental tickets:

Airbrokers (www.airbrokers.com)
Airtreks.com (www.airtreks.com)
Oneworld Alliance (www.oneworldalliance.com)
Sky Team (www.skyteam.com)
Star Alliance (www.staralliance.com)

Africa

You can fly to Mauritius direct from a number of cities in Africa, including Johannesburg, Cape Town and Durban (South Africa), Antananarivo (Madagascar), Moroni (Comoros) and Nairobi (Kenya). Airlines serving these routes include Air Mauritius, Air Madagascar and South African Airways (SAA).

The Seychelles is not particularly well connected with Africa. The only direct flights are to and from Johannesburg and Nairobi with Air Seychelles and Kenya Airways.

Réunion can be reached direct from Johannesburg, Madagascar, Comoros and Mayotte with Air Austral and Air Madagascar.

Rennies Travel (www.renniestravel.com) and **STA Travel** (www.statravel.co.za) have offices throughout southern Africa. Check their websites for branch locations.

Australia

The cheapest flights from Australia to this region are usually via Singapore. Another option

CLIMATE CHANGE & TRAVEL

Climate change is a serious threat to the ecosystems that humans rely upon, and air travel is the fastest-growing contributor to the problem. Lonely Planet regards travel, overall, as a global benefit, but believes we all have a responsibility to limit our personal impact on global warming.

Flying & Climate Change

Pretty much every form of motor travel generates CO_2 (the main cause of human-induced climate change) but planes are far and away the worst offenders, not just because of the sheer distances they allow us to travel, but because they release greenhouse gases high into the atmosphere. The statistics are frightening: two people taking a return flight between Europe and the US will contribute as much to climate change as an average household's gas and electricity consumption over a whole year.

Carbon Offset Schemes

Climatecare.org and other websites use 'carbon calculators' that allow jetsetters to offset the greenhouse gases they are responsible for with contributions to energy-saving projects and other climate-friendly initiatives in the developing world – including projects in India, Honduras, Kazakhstan and Uganda.

Lonely Planet, together with Rough Guides and other concerned partners in the travel industry, supports the carbon offset scheme run by climatecare.org. Lonely Planet offsets all of its staff and author travel.

For more information check out our website: lonelyplanet.com.

---

is to fly via Africa. Two well-known agencies for discount fares with offices nationwide are **STA Travel** (☎ 1300 733 035; www.statravel.com.au) and **Flight Centre** (☎ 133 133; www.flightcentre.com.au). For online bookings, try www.travel.com.au.

Air Mauritius operates reasonably competitively priced direct flights from Sydney, Melbourne and Perth to Mauritius.

The cheapest way to get to Réunion is to fly to Mauritius and pick up the boat for St-Denis. A quicker alternative would obviously be to fly from Mauritius to St-Denis.

Return flights to the Seychelles from Melbourne and Sydney via Singapore are offered by both Air Seychelles (flying via Singapore) and Air Mauritius (flying via Mauritius).

Continental Europe

Most visitors from Europe arrive in Mauritius and Seychelles on hotel-flight package holidays, although this is much less the case for Réunion. Air Mauritius and Air Seychelles fly to a number of European destinations, including London, Paris, Zürich, Geneva, Rome, Munich, Frankfurt, Brussels and Vienna. Because of the French colonial connection, however, fares are generally cheaper from Paris than from other European cities. All flights from Europe to Réunion go via Paris. Note that prices shoot up during July and August and over the Christmas and New Year holidays. However, flights to Mauritius and Seychelles on Emirates via Dubai (and on Qatar Airways to Seychelles via Doha) are both very competitively priced and worth investigating, with connections from all over Europe.

FRANCE

Air Mauritius and Air France operate frequent flights from Paris to Mauritius. Another alternative is to look for special offers between Paris and Réunion and then take the boat or a return flight to Mauritius from Réunion.

There's more competition – and consequently lower fares – on the Paris–Réunion route. Air France, Air Austral, and Corsair (belonging to tour operator Nouvelle Frontières) all fly to St-Denis. Air Seychelles and Air France cover the Paris–Seychelles route.

Recommended agencies:

Anyway (☎ 0892 302 301; www.anyway.fr)
Lastminute (☎ 0899 785 000; www.lastminute.com)
Nouvelles Frontières (☎ 0825 000 747; www.nouvelles-frontieres.fr)
OTU Voyages (☎ 01 55 82 32 32; www.otu.fr) This agency specialises in student and youth travellers.
Voyageurs du Monde (☎ 0892 237 373; www.vdm.com)

GERMANY

Condor flies direct from Frankfurt to Mauritius and the Seychelles, and from Munich to Mauritius. Prices are not cheap to either destination, although a cheaper option for Mauritius is to fly via Paris on Air France; Air Seychelles operates direct flights from Frankfurt which can be quite reasonable. As with almost any country, you're often best off buying a package deal and taking advantage of the flight cost savings.

Recommended agencies:

Expedia (☎ 01805 007143; www.expedia.de)
Just Travel (☎ 089 747 3330; www.justtravel.de)
Lastminute (☎ 01805 284 366; www.lastminute.de)
STA Travel (☎ 069 743 032 92; www.statravel.de)

UK & Ireland

Both Air Mauritius and British Airways operate direct flights between London and Mauritius. A cheaper option, especially off-season, is to fly Air France via Paris.

Flights for Réunion generally connect through Paris. The return London–Réunion fare with Air France is no bargain, but you can sometimes get a cheaper deal by flying with one of the discount airlines on the London–Paris leg and buying a separate Paris–Réunion return.

Air Seychelles covers the London to Seychelles route and sometimes special deals make this route good value. Emirates via Dubai and Air France via Paris offer other good connections to Seychelles. All Irish travellers will need to connect through London or Paris.

Recommended travel agencies in the UK:

Flight Centre (☎ 0870 499 0040; www.flightcentre.co.uk)
Flightbookers (☎ 0871 223 5000; www.ebookers.com)
North-South Travel (☎ 01245 608 291; www.north-southtravel.co.uk) North-South Travel donates part of its profit to projects in the developing world.
Quest Travel (☎ 0871 423 0135; www.questtravel.com)
STA Travel (☎ 0871 230 0040; www.statravel.co.uk)
Trailfinders (☎ 0845 058 5858; www.trailfinders.com)
Travel Bag (☎ 0800 082 5000; www.travelbag.co.uk)

USA

Given the huge distance involved in travelling from North America to the Indian Ocean, you'll be paying a handsome sum to travel this route. Nearly all flights to the Indian Ocean from the US and Canada connect through London or Paris.

Rather than getting a through ticket, however, it's usually cheaper to take a discount flight to London or Paris and buy the onward ticket separately.

Discount travel agents in America are known as consolidators (although you won't see a sign on the door saying 'Consolidator'). San Francisco is the US ticket consolidator capital, although good deals can be found in Los Angeles, New York and other big cities.

SEA

Opportunities for sea travel to Mauritius, Réunion and the Seychelles are limited. The luxury cruise liner *MS Mauritius Trochetia* leaves Toamasina in Madagascar for Réunion and Mauritius approximately every two weeks. One-way fares to Réunion (28 hours) are €210/177 for a 1st/2nd-class cabin (based on two people sharing), and €247/227 to Mauritius (47 hours). More expensive deluxe cabins are also available. For tickets, go to **Tropical Service** (☎ 53 336 79; 23 Blvd Joffre), near the Hotel Joffre in Toamasina.

The only other alternatives are passing cruise liners, yachts and the occasional cargo-passenger ship. The cost is high, unless you can work your way as a crewmember. Cruise liners usually only stop for a day or two in each destination, but cruises do offer the opportunity of seeing the outer islands in the Seychelles group.

Companies offering Indian Ocean cruises:

African Safari Club (www.africansafariclub.com)
La Compagnie des Alizés (www.voile-reunion.com)
MS Royal Star (www.msroyalstar.com)
P&O (www.pocruises.com)
Seabourn (www.seabourn.com)
Silversea (www.silversea.com)

TRANSPORT AROUND THE REGION

The following section covers transport between Réunion, Mauritius and the Seychelles. Be aware that if you're planning to travel to both Mauritius and Réunion, it makes much better financial sense to visit Mauritius first and fly on to Réunion, as return flights work out around €120 cheaper when originating in Mauritius. The flat fare system of flights from Réunion to Mauritius hikes the fare by 40%.

AIR
Air Passes
There are currently no air passes of significance relating to the region, unless you manage to combine one or more of the islands within a RTW ticket (see p303). The Indian Ocean Pass, available for some time for people travelling between the islands of the Indian Ocean, has been discontinued.

Mauritius to Réunion
Air Mauritius and Air Austral between them operate several flights a day from Réunion to Mauritius. Return fares start at around €164 in low season if you fly Mauritius–Réunion–Mauritius, but are a far less reasonable €280 if you fly Réunion–Mauritius–Réunion. As well as the flights to St-Denis, there is a daily flight from Mauritius' Sir Seewoosagur Ramgoolam Airport to Pierrefonds Airport, Réunion's second airport in the south of the island near to St-Pierre. Return fares start at around €160 for a round trip from Mauritius, and, again are priced less competitively at €280 for a round trip when flying from Réunion. At the time of writing there were again no direct flights between Rodrigues and Réunion, although this may change (they have been introduced and cancelled due to heavy losses in the past), so you currently have to fly via Mauritius.

Mauritius to Seychelles
From the Seychelles, there's a choice between Air Mauritius and Air Seychelles, which between them operate four to five flights a week. Tickets cost from €305 for a return in low season.

Réunion to Seychelles
There was no direct air connection between Réunion and the Seychelles at the time of research. Those wishing to make this trip normally change planes in Mauritius, through which there are the best connections. Tickets are not cheap – the combination of the two return flights is around €550, although on the plus side you're able to break the trip and visit Mauritius.

In December and January (during the school holidays in Réunion) Air Austral operates one weekly flight from Réunion to Seychelles.

SEA
The **Mauritius Shipping Corporation** (www.mauritius shipping.intnet.mu) operates two boats between Réunion and Mauritius, with several sailings each month. The one-way journey takes about 11 hours. The newer and more comfortable boat is the *Mauritius Trochetia*. The return fare from Réunion in low/high season starts at roughly €160/230 for a berth in a 2nd-class cabin. From Mauritius, the price is Rs 4800/6700.

The sister ship, *Mauritius Pride* is slightly cheaper. For a reclining seat in low/high season, you'll pay around €135/160 return from Réunion and Rs 3000/3600 from Mauritius. The equivalent fares for a berth in a two-person cabin are €220/245 and Rs 5650/6900.

Tickets and information are available through travel agents or direct from the Mauritius Shipping Corporation representative **Coraline Shipping Agency** (Map pp58-9; ☎ 217 2285 msc@coraline.intnet.mu; Nova Bldg, Military Rd, Port Louis).

Health

CONTENTS

As long as you stay up to date with your vaccinations and take some basic preventive measures, you'd have to be pretty unlucky to succumb to most of the health hazards covered in this chapter. Mauritius, and to a lesser extent Réunion and the Seychelles, certainly have a fair selection of tropical diseases on offer, but you're much more likely to get a bout of diarrhoea or a sprained ankle than an exotic disease. One recent subject of concern in Mauritius and Réunion has been the Chikungunya epidemic of early 2006, which, while having returned to normal at the time of writing, is still something you should be aware of and a situation you should monitor.

BEFORE YOU GO

A little planning before departure, particularly for pre-existing illnesses, will save you a lot of trouble later. Before a long trip, get a check-up from your dentist and from your doctor if you have any regular medication or chronic illness, eg high blood pressure or asthma. You should also organise spare contact lenses and glasses (and take your optical prescription with you); get a first-aid and medical kit together; and arrange necessary vaccinations.

Travellers can register with the **International Association for Medical Advice to Travellers** (IAMAT; www.iamat.org). Its website can help travellers to find a doctor who has recognised training. You might also like to consider doing a first-aid course (contact the Red Cross or St John's Ambulance) or attending a remote medicine first-aid course, such as that offered by the **Royal Geographical Society** (www.wildernessmedicaltraining.co.uk).

If you are bringing medications with you, carry them in their original containers, clearly labelled. A signed and dated letter from your physician describing all medical conditions and medications, including generic names, is also a good idea. If carrying syringes or needles be sure to have a physician's letter documenting their medical necessity.

INSURANCE

Find out in advance whether your insurance plan will make payments directly to providers or will reimburse you later for overseas health expenditures (in many countries doctors expect payment in cash). It is vital to ensure that your travel insurance will cover the emergency transport required to get you to a good hospital, or all the way home, by air and with a medical attendant if necessary. Not all insurance policies cover this, so be sure to check the contract carefully. If you need medical help, your insurance company might be able to help locate the nearest hospital or clinic, or you can ask at your hotel. In an emergency, contact your embassy or consulate.

RECOMMENDED VACCINATIONS

The **World Health Organization** (www.who.int/en/) recommends that all travellers be adequately covered for diphtheria, tetanus, measles, mumps, rubella and polio, as well as for hepatitis B, regardless of their travel destination.

Although no vaccinations are officially required, many doctors recommend hepatitis A and B immunisations just to be sure; a yellow fever certificate is an entry requirement if travelling from an infected region (see p311).

Membership of the **African Medical and Research Foundation** (AMREF; www.amref.org) provides an air-evacuation service in medical emergencies in some African countries, sometimes including Mauritius, Réunion and the Seychelles, as well as air-ambulance transfers between medical facilities. Money paid by members for this service goes toward providing grass-roots medical assistance for local people.

MEDICAL CHECKLIST

It is a very good idea to carry a medical and first-aid kit with you, to help yourself in the case of minor illness or injury. Following is a list of items you should consider packing.

- antidiarrhoeal drugs (eg loperamide)
- acetaminophen (paracetamol) or aspirin
- anti-inflammatory drugs (eg ibuprofen)
- antihistamines (for hayfever and allergic reactions)
- antibacterial ointment (eg Bactroban) for cuts and abrasions (prescription only)
- steroid cream or hydrocortisone cream (for allergic rashes)
- bandages, gauze, gauze rolls
- adhesive or paper tape
- scissors, safety pins, tweezers
- thermometer
- pocket knife
- DEET-containing insect repellent for the skin
- sunblock
- oral rehydration salts
- iodine tablets (for water purification)
- syringes and sterile needles (if travelling to remote areas)

INTERNET RESOURCES

There is a wealth of travel-health advice available on the internet. **Lonelyplanet.com** (www.lonelyplanet.com) is a good place to start. The World Health Organization publishes a superb book called *International Travel and Health*, which is revised annually and is available online at no cost at www.who.int/ith/. Other health-related websites of general interest are **MD Travel Health** (www.mdtravelhealth.com), the **Centers for Disease Control and Prevention** (www.cdc.gov) and **Fit for Travel** (www.fitfortravel.scot.nhs.uk).

You may also like to consult your government's travel-health website, if one is available:

Australia (www.dfat.gov.au/travel/)
Canada (www.hc-sc.gc.ca/pphb-dgspsp/tmp-pmv/pub_e.html)
UK (www.doh.gov.uk/traveladvice/index.htm)
USA (www.cdc.gov/travel/)

FURTHER READING

A Comprehensive Guide to Wilderness and Travel Medicine b Eric A Weiss (1998)
Healthy Travel by Jane Wilson-Howarth (1999)
Healthy Travel Africa by Isabelle Young (2000)
How to Stay Healthy Abroad by Richard Dawood (2002)
Travel in Health by Graham Fry (1994)
Travel with Children by Cathy Lanigan (2004)

IN TRANSIT

DEEP VEIN THROMBOSIS (DVT)

Blood clots can form in the legs durin flights, chiefly because of prolonged immo bility. This formation of clots is known a deep vein thrombosis (DVT). Although mos blood clots are reabsorbed uneventfully some might break off and travel through th blood vessels to the lungs, where they coul cause life-threatening complications.

The chief symptom of DVT is swelling o pain of the foot, ankle or calf. When a bloo clot travels to the lungs, it may cause ches pain and breathing difficulty. Travellers wit any of these symptoms should immediatel seek medical attention.

To prevent the development of DVT dur ing flights, walk about the cabin, perform isometric compressions of the leg muscle (ie contract the leg muscles while sitting) drink plenty of fluids, and avoid alcohol.

JET LAG & MOTION SICKNESS

If you're crossing more than five time zone you could suffer jet lag, resulting in insom nia, fatigue, malaise or nausea. To avoid je lag, try drinking plenty of fluids (nonalco holic) and eating light meals. Upon arriva get exposure to natural sunlight and readjus your schedule (for meals, sleep, etc) as soo as possible.

Antihistamines such as dimenhydrinat (Dramamine) and meclizine (Antivert, Bon ine) are usually the first choice for treatin motion sickness. The main side effect of thes drugs is drowsiness. A herbal alternative i ginger (ginger tea, biscuits or crystallise ginger).

IN MAURITIUS, RÉUNION & SEYCHELLES

AVAILABILITY & COST OF HEALTH CARE

Health care in Mauritius and Réunion is generally excellent; the Seychelles is pretty good by African standards, but some travellers have been critical of the standard of the public health system. Generally, public hospitals offer the cheapest service, but may not have the most up-to-date equipment and medications; private hospitals and clinics are more expensive but tend to have more advanced drugs and equipment and better trained medical staff.

INFECTIOUS DISEASES

It's a formidable list but, as we say, a few precautions go a long way…

Chikungunya

This viral infection transmitted by certain mosquito bites was traditionally rare in the Indian Ocean until 2005 when an epidemic hit Réunion, Mauritius and Seychelles. Chikungunya (the unusual name means 'that which bends up' in the East African language of Makonde, a reference to the joint pain and physical distortions it creates in sufferers) is rarely fatal, but it can be, and it's always unpleasant. Symptoms are often flu-like, with joint pain, high fever and body rashes being the most common. It's important not to confuse it with dengue fever, but if diagnosed with Chikungunya then expect to be down for at least a week, possibly longer. The joint pain can be horrendous and there is no treatment, those infected need simply to rest inside (preferably under a mosquito net to prevent reinfection), taking gentle exercise to avoid joints stiffening unbearably. Over 200 people died in Réunion from Chikungunya in 2005 to 2006, but at the time of writing the epidemic was over and should not be considered a major threat. Still, the best way to avoid it is to avoid mosquito bites, so bring plenty of repellent, use the anti-mosquito plug-ins wherever you can and bring a mosquito net if you're really thorough.

Cholera

Cholera is usually only a problem during natural or artificial disasters, eg war, floods or earthquakes, although small outbreaks can also occur at other times. Travellers are rarely affected. It is caused by a bacteria and is spread via contaminated drinking water. The main symptom is profuse watery diarrhoea, which causes debilitation if fluids are not replaced quickly. Most cases of cholera can be avoided by paying close attention to the drinking water available and by avoiding potentially contaminated food. Treatment is by fluid replacement (orally or via a drip), but sometimes antibiotics are needed. Self-treatment is not advised.

Diphtheria

Diphtheria is spread through close respiratory contact. It usually results in a temperature and a severe sore throat. It is more of a problem for long stays than for short-term trips. The vaccine is given as an injection alone or with tetanus, and lasts 10 years.

Hepatitis A

Hepatitis A is spread through contaminated food (particularly shellfish) and water. It causes jaundice and, although it is rarely fatal, it can cause prolonged lethargy and delayed recovery. If you've had hepatitis A, you shouldn't drink alcohol for up to six months afterwards, but once you've recovered, there won't be any long-term problems. The first symptoms include dark urine and a yellow colour to the whites of the eyes. Sometimes a fever and abdominal pain might be present. Hepatitis A vaccine (Avaxim, VAQTA, Havrix) is given as an injection: a single dose will give protection for up to a year, and a booster after a year gives 10-year protection. Hepatitis A and typhoid vaccines can also be given as a single dose vaccine (Hepatyrix or Viatim).

Hepatitis B

Hepatitis B is spread through infected blood, contaminated needles and sexual intercourse. It can also be passed from an infected mother to the baby during childbirth. It affects the liver, causing jaundice and occasionally liver failure. Most people recover completely, but some people might be chronic carriers of the virus, which could lead eventually to cirrhosis or liver cancer. Those visiting high-risk areas for extended periods or those with increased social or occupational risk should be immunised. Many countries now routinely give hepatitis B as part of the routine childhood vaccination. It is given singly or can be given at the same time as hepatitis A (Hepatyrix).

A course will give protection for at least five years. It can be given over four weeks or six months.

HIV

Human immunodeficiency virus (HIV), the virus that causes acquired immune deficiency syndrome (AIDS), is an enormous problem throughout Africa, but is most acutely felt in sub-Saharan Africa. The impact of the virus on South Africa's health system is devastating. The virus is spread through infected blood and blood products, by sexual intercourse with an infected partner and from an infected mother to her baby during childbirth and breast-feeding. It can be spread through 'blood to blood' contacts, such as with contaminated instruments during medical, dental, acupuncture and other body-piercing procedures, and through sharing used intravenous needles. At present there is no cure; medication that might keep the disease under control is available, but these drugs are too expensive for the overwhelming majority of Africans, and are not readily available for travellers either. If you think you might have been infected with HIV, a blood test is necessary; a three-month gap after exposure and before testing is required to allow antibodies to appear in the blood.

Malaria

The risk of malaria in Mauritius and Réunion is extremely low; there is no risk in the Seychelles. The disease is caused by a parasite in the bloodstream spread via the bite of the female *Anopheles* mosquito. The early stages of malaria include headaches, fevers, generalised aches and pains, and malaise, which could be mistaken for flu. Other symptoms can include abdominal pain, diarrhoea and a cough. Several different drugs are used to prevent malaria, and new ones are in the pipeline – up-to-date advice is essential as some medication is more suitable for some travellers than others. There are antimalaria pills available and it is best to ask your doctor for further advice.

Meningococcal Meningitis

Meningococcal infection is spread through close respiratory contact and is more likely in crowded situations, such as dormitories, buses and clubs. Infection is uncommon in travellers. Vaccination is recommended for long stays and is especially important towards the end of the dry season. Symptoms include a fever, severe headache, neck stiffness and a red rash. Immediate medical treatment is necessary.

Poliomyelitis

Poliomyelitis is generally spread through contaminated food and water. It is one of the vaccines given in childhood and should be boosted every 10 years, either orally (a drop on the tongue) or as an injection. Polio can be carried asymptomatically (ie showing no symptoms) and could cause a transient fever. In rare cases it causes weakness or paralysis of one or more muscles, which might be permanent.

Rabies

Rabies is spread by receiving the bites or licks of an infected animal on broken skin. It is always fatal once the clinical symptoms start (which might be up to several months after an infected bite), so post-bite vaccination should be given as soon as possible. Post-bite vaccination (whether or not you've been vaccinated before the bite) prevents the virus from spreading to the central nervous system. Three preventive injections are needed over a month. If you have not been vaccinated you will need a course of five injections starting 24 hours after being bitten or as soon as possible after the injury. If you have been vaccinated, you will need fewer post-bite injections, and have more time to seek medical help.

Tuberculosis (TB)

TB is spread through close respiratory contact and occasionally by infected milk or milk products. BCG vaccination is a live vaccine and should not be given to pregnant women or immunocompromised individuals.

TB can be asymptomatic, only being picked up on a routine chest X-ray. Alternatively, it can cause a cough, weight loss or fever, sometimes months or even years after exposure.

Typhoid

Typhoid is spread through food or water contaminated by infected human faeces. The first symptom is usually a fever or a pink rash on the abdomen. Sometimes septicaemia (blood poisoning) can occur. A typhoid vaccine (Typhim Vi, Typherix) will give protection for three years. In some countries, the oral vaccine Vivotif is also available. Antibiotics are usually given as treatment, and death is rare unless septicaemia occurs.

Yellow Fever

Although not a problem in Mauritius, Réunion or the Seychelles, travellers should still carry a certificate as evidence of vaccination if they have recently been in an infected country. For a list of these countries visit the **World Health Organization website** (www.who.int/wer/) or the **Centers for Disease Control and Prevention website** (www.cdc.gov/travel/blusheet.htm). A traveller without a legally required, up-to-date certificate may be vaccinated and detained in isolation at the port of arrival for up to 10 days or possibly repatriated.

TRAVELLERS' DIARRHOEA

Although it's not inevitable that you will get diarrhoea while travelling in the region, it's certainly possible. Sometimes dietary changes, such as increased spices or oils, are the cause. To avoid diarrhoea, only eat fresh fruits or vegetables if cooked or peeled, and be wary of dairy products that might contain unpasteurised milk. Although freshly cooked food can often be a safe option, plates or serving utensils might be dirty, so you should be highly selective when eating food from street vendors (make sure that cooked food is piping hot all the way through). If you develop diarrhoea, be sure to drink plenty of fluids, preferably an oral rehydration solution containing water (lots), and some salt and sugar. A few loose stools don't require treatment, but if you start having more than four or five stools a day, you should start taking an antibiotic (usually a quinoline drug, such as ciprofloxacin or norfloxacin) and an antidiarrhoeal agent (such as loperamide) if you are not within easy reach of a toilet. However, if diarrhoea is bloody, persists for more than 72 hours or is accompanied by fever, shaking chills or severe abdominal pain, you should seek medical attention.

Amoebic Dysentery

Contracted by eating contaminated food and water, amoebic dysentery causes blood and mucus in the faeces. It can be relatively mild and tends to come on gradually, but seek medical advice if you think you have the illness, as it won't clear up without treatment (which is with specific antibiotics).

Giardiasis

Giardiasis, like amoebic dysentery, is also caused by ingesting contaminated food or water. The illness usually appears a week or more after you have been exposed to the offending parasite. Giardiasis might cause only a short-lived bout of typical travellers' diarrhoea, but it can also cause persistent diarrhoea. Ideally, seek medical advice if you suspect you have giardiasis, but if you are in a remote area you could start a course of antibiotics.

ENVIRONMENTAL HAZARDS
Heat Exhaustion

This condition occurs following heavy sweating and excessive fluid loss with inadequate replacement of fluids and salt, and is particularly common in hot climates when taking unaccustomed exercise before full acclimatisation. Symptoms include headache, dizziness and tiredness. Dehydration is already happening by the time you feel thirsty – aim to drink sufficient water to produce pale, diluted urine. Self-treatment is by fluid replacement with water and/or fruit juice, and cooling by cold water and fans. The treatment of the salt-loss component consists of consuming salty fluids as in soup, and adding a little more table salt to foods than usual.

Heatstroke

Heat exhaustion is a precursor to the much more serious condition of heatstroke. In this case there is damage to the sweating mechanism, with an excessive rise in body temperature; irrational and hyperactive behaviour; and eventually loss of consciousness and death. Rapid cooling by spraying the body with water and fanning is ideal. Emergency fluid and electrolyte replacement is usually also required by intravenous drip.

Insect Bites & Stings

Mosquitoes in the region rarely carry malaria, Chikungunya and dengue fever, but they (and

HEALTH

other insects) can cause irritation and infected bites. To avoid these, take the same precautions as you would for avoiding malaria, including wearing long pants and long-sleeved shirts, using mosquito repellents, avoiding highly scented perfumes or aftershaves etc. Bee and wasp stings cause major problems only to those who have a severe allergy to the stings (anaphylaxis), in which case carry an adrenaline (epinephrine) injection.

Leeches may be present in damp rainforest conditions; they attach themselves to your skin to suck your blood. Salt or a lighted cigarette end will make them fall off. Ticks can cause skin infections and other more serious diseases. If a tick is found attached, press down around the tick's head with tweezers, grab the head and gently pull upwards.

Marine Life

A number of Indian Ocean species are poisonous or may sting or bite. Watch out above all for sea urchins – while most hotel swimming areas have been carefully cleansed of these nasties, never take that for granted, and always

check using a diving mask. Be extremely careful of urchins when swimming outside of roped-off areas – they can be very numerous where they exist and dwell in shallow as well as deep water. Other far rarer creatures to look out for include the gaudy lion fish with its poisonous spined fins, and for the cleverly camouflaged – and exceptionally poisonous – stonefish. Some shells, such as the cone shell, can fire out a deadly poisonous barb. The species of fire coral (in fact a type of jellyfish) packs a powerful sting if touched. Shark attacks are almost totally unheard of but very occasionally sharks do come into these waters, and while most are harmless, don't take that for granted.

Water

As a general rule, tap water in Mauritius, Réunion and the Seychelles is safe to drink, but always take care immediately after a cyclone or cyclonic storm as mains water supplies can become contaminated by dead animals and other debris washed into the system. Never drink from streams as it might put you at risk of waterborne diseases.

Language

CONTENTS

MAURITIUS

It's said that when Mauritians have a community meeting, the people speak Creole, take minutes in English and discuss the outcome with government officials in French.

The official languages of the country are English and French. English is used mainly in government and business. French is the spoken language in educated and cultural circles, and is used in newspapers and magazines. You'll probably find that most people will first speak to you in French and only switch to English once they realise you don't understand a word they're saying.

Creole, the common bond, derives from French and has similarities with creoles spoken elsewhere. Ironically, the Creole spoken in Mauritius and Seychelles is more comprehensible to French people than the patois of Réunion, even though Réunion itself is thoroughly French. Most Indo-Mauritians speak Bhojpuri, derived from a Bihari dialect of Hindi.

There are major differences between the pronunciation and usage of Creole and standard French, but if you don't speak any French at all, you're doubly disadvantaged. *Parlez créole/Speak creole*, by Rose Hill (Mauritius: Editions de l'océan Indien) is a phrasebook in French and English.

For Mauritian Creole starters, you might like to try the following phrases:

How are you?	*Ki manière?*
Fine, thanks.	*Mon byen, mersi.*
I don't understand.	*Mo pas comprend.*
OK.	*Correc.*
Not OK.	*Pas correc.*
he, she, it	*li*
Do you have ...?	*Ou éna ...?*
I'd like ...	*Mo oulé ...*
I'm thirsty.	*Mo soif.*
Phoenix beer	*la bière zarnier* (literally 'spider beer' – the label looks like one)
Cheers!	*Tapeta!*
Great!	*Formidabe!*

RÉUNION

French is the official language of Réunion, but Creole is the most widely spoken one. Few people speak English.

The Creole of Réunion is beyond the comprehension even of most French people. A word that means one thing in French can mean something completely different in Creole, and where a word does have the same meaning, it's usually pronounced differently in Creole.

Creole has quite a number of *bons mots* and charming idioms, which are often the result of Hindi, Arab and Malagasy influences or misinterpretations of the original French word. *Bonbon la fesse* (bum toffee) is a suppository, *conserves* (preserves) are sunglasses, the *bazaar* is the market, and *cœur d'amant* (lover's heart) is a cardamom seed. *Coco* is your head, *caze* is your house, *marmaille* is your child, *baba* is your baby, *band* means 'family', *le fait noir* means 'night', and, if the stars are out, remember that *mi aime jou* means 'I love you'.

In Creole pronunciation there are two basic rules: **r** is generally not pronounced (when it is, it's pronounced lightly); and the

LANGUAGE

soft **j** and **ch** sounds of French are pronounced as 'z' and 's' respectively. For example, *manzay* for 'manger' (to eat), *zamais* for 'jamais' (never) and *sontay* for 'chanter' (to sing).

There are French-Creole dictionaries for sale in Réunion, but unfortunately there are no English-Creole dictionaries.

SEYCHELLES
English and French are the official languages of the Seychelles. Most people speak both, although French Creole (known as Kreol Seselwa) is the lingua franca. Kreol Seselwa was 'rehabilitated' and made semi-official in 1981, and is increasingly used in newspapers and literature. These days, most Seychellois will use English when speaking to tourists, French when conducting business, and Creole in the home.

Seychelles Creole is similar to that of Mauritius and Martinique, but differs remarkably from that of Réunion. In the local patois, the soft pronunciation of certain French consonants is hardened and some syllables are dropped completely. The soft **j** becomes 'z', for example. The following Creole phrases may help get you started:

Good morning/	*Bonzour.*
Good afternoon.	
How are you?	*Comman sava?*
Fine, thanks.	*Mon byen, mersi.*
What's your name?	*Ki mannyer ou apel?*
My name is ...	*Mon appel ...*
Where do you live?	*Koté ou resté?*
I don't understand.	*Mon pas konpran.*
I like it.	*Mon kontan.*
Where is ...?	*Ol i ...?*
How much is that?	*Kombyen sa?*
I'm thirsty.	*Mon soif.*
Can I have a beer,	*Mon kapa ganny en labyer*
please?	*silvouplé?*

WHAT'S A CREOLE?
When people of differing native languages come into contact and develop a simple mode of communication that is based in both languages, the product is known as a pidgin. Once this 'neo-language' has become established to the point where it possesses a defined grammatical structure and writing system, and children learn it as a first language, it becomes a creole.

The creoles of Mauritius, Réunion and Seychelles are a blend of French and an assortment of African languages, with regional variations; Seychelles Creole is similar to that of Mauritius, but differs significantly from the Creole spoken in Réunion.

FRENCH

Along with the local creoles, French is spoken in all three destinations. You'll find that menus on the islands are mostly in French with English variations in some cases.

For a more comprehensive guide to the French language, pick up a copy of Lonely Planet's *French Phrasebook*.

PRONUNCIATION
Most letters in French are pronounced more or less the same as their English counterparts. Here are a few that may cause confusion:

j	as the 's' in 'leisure', eg jour (day) written as 'zh' in our pronunciation guides
c	before **e** and **i**, as the 's' in 'sit'; before **a**, **o** and **u**, it's pronounced as English 'k'. When underscored with a 'cedilla (**ç**), it's always pronounced as the 's in 'sit'.
r	pronounced from the back of the throat while constricting the muscles to restrict the flow of air
n, m	where a syllable ends in a single **n** or **m**, these letters are not pronounced but the preceding vowel is given a nasal pronunciation

BE POLITE!
An important distinction is made in French between *tu* and *vous*, which both mean 'you'; *tu* is only used when addressing people you know well, children or animals. If you're addressing an adult who isn't a personal friend, *vous* should be used unless the person invites you to use *tu*. In general, younger people insist less on this distinction between polite and informal, and you will find that in many cases they use *tu* from the beginning of an acquaintance.

The polite form is used in all instances in this guide unless indicated by 'inf' (meaning 'informal') in brackets.

GENDER

All nouns in French are either masculine or feminine and adjectives reflect the gender of the noun they modify. The feminine form of many nouns and adjectives is indicated by a silent **e** added to the masculine form, as in *ami* and *amie* (the masculine and feminine for 'friend').

In the following phrases both masculine and feminine forms have been indicated where necessary. The masculine form comes first and is separated from the feminine by a slash. The gender of a noun is often indicated by a preceding article: 'the/a/some', *le/un/du* (m), *la/une/de la* (f); or one of the possessive adjectives, 'my/your/his/her', *mon/ton/son* (m), *ma/ta/sa* (f). With French, unlike English, the possessive adjective agrees in number and gender with the thing in question: 'his/her mother', *sa mère*.

ACCOMMODATION

I'm looking for a ...	*Je cherche ...*	zher shersh ...
camping ground	*un camping*	un kom·peeng
guesthouse	*une pension (de famille)*	ewn pon·syon (der fa·mee·ler)
hotel	*un hôtel*	un o·tel
youth hostel	*une auberge de jeunesse*	ewn o·berzh der zher·nes

Where is a cheap hotel?
Où est-ce qu'on peut trouver un hôtel pas cher?
oo es·kon per troo·vay un o·tel pa shair

What is the address?
Quelle est l'adresse?
kel e la·dres

Could you write it down, please?
Est-ce que vous pourriez l'écrire, s'il vous plaît?
e·sker voo poo·ryay lay·kreer seel voo play

Do you have any rooms available?
Est-ce que vous avez des chambres libres?
e·sker voo·za·vay day shom·brer lee·brer

I'd like (a) ...	*Je voudrais ...*	zher voo·dray ...
single room	*une chambre à un lit*	ewn shom·brer a un lee
double-bed room	*une chambre avec un grand lit*	ewn shom·brer a·vek un gron lee
twin room (with two beds)	*une chambre avec des lits jumeaux*	ewn shom·brer a·vek day lee zhew·mo

---

MAKING A RESERVATION
(for phone or written requests)

To ...	*A l'attention de ...*
From ...	*De la part de ...*
Date	*Date*
I'd like to book ...	*Je voudrais réserver ...* (see the list under 'Accommodation' for bed and room options)
in the name of ...	*au nom de ...*
from ... (date) **to ...**	*du ... au ...*
credit card	*carte de crédit*
number	*numéro*
expiry date	*date d'expiration*
Please confirm availability and price.	*Veuillez confirmer la disponibilité et le prix.*

---

room with a bathroom	*une chambre avec une salle de bains*	ewn shom·brer a·vek ewn sal der bun
to share a dorm	*coucher dans un dortoir*	koo·sher don zun dor·twa

How much is it ...?	*Quel est le prix ...?*	kel e ler pree ...
per night	*par nuit*	par nwee
per person	*par personne*	par per·son

May I see the room?
Est-ce que je peux voir la chambre?
es·ker zher per vwa la shom·brer

Where is the bathroom?
Où est la salle de bains? oo e la sal der bun

Where is the toilet?
Où sont les toilettes? oo·son lay twa·let

I'm leaving today.
Je pars aujourd'hui. zher par o·zhoor·dwee

We're leaving today.
Nous partons aujourd'hui. noo par·ton o·zhoor·dwee

air-conditioned	*climatisée*	klee ma·tee zay
a shower	*une douche*	oon doosh
a washbasin	*un lavabo*	un la·va·bo
hot water	*eau chaude*	o shod
a window	*une fenêtre*	oon fe·netr

a terrace
une terrace — oon tay·ras
a sea view
une vue sur la mer — oon vue sewr la mair
full board
pension complète — pon·syon kom·plet
half board
demi-pension — day·mee pon·syon
dining room
la salle à manger — la sal a mon·zhair
kitchen
la cuisine — la kwee·zeen
television
une télévision — ewn tay·lay·vee·zyon
swimming pool
une piscine — ewn pee·seen
towel
une serviette — ewn sair·vyet
(not) included
(non) compris — (non) kom·pree
on request
sur demande — sewr der·mond
price/tariff
le prix/tarif — ler pree/ta·reef

CONVERSATION & ESSENTIALS

Hello.	*Bonjour.*	bon·zhoor
Goodbye.	*Au revoir.*	o·rer·vwa
Yes.	*Oui.*	wee
No.	*Non.*	no
Please.	*S'il vous plaît.*	seel voo play
Thank you.	*Merci.*	mair·see
You're welcome.	*Je vous en prie.*	zher voo·zon pree
	De rien. (inf)	der ree·en
Excuse me.	*Excuse-moi.*	ek·skew·zay·mwa
Sorry. (forgive me)	*Pardon.*	par·don

What's your name?
Comment vous appelez-vous? — ko·mon voo·za·pay·lay voo
Comment tu t'appelles? (inf) — ko·mon tew ta·pel
My name is ...
Je m'appelle ... — zher ma·pel ...
Where are you from?
De quel pays êtes-vous? — der kel pay·ee et·voo
De quel pays es-tu? (inf) — der kel pay·ee e·tew
I'm from ...
Je viens de ... — zher vyen der ...
I like ...
J'aime ... — zhem ...
I don't like ...
Je n'aime pas ... — zher nem pa ...
Just a minute.
Une minute. — ewn mee·newt

SIGNS

Entrée	Entrance
Sortie	Exit
Renseignements	Information
Ouvert	Open
Fermé	Closed
Interdit	Prohibited
Chambres Libres	Rooms Available
(Commissariat de) Police	Police Station
Toilettes/WC	Toilets
Hommes	Men
Femmes	Women

DIRECTIONS

Where is ...?
Où est ...? — oo e ...
Go straight ahead.
Continuez tout droit. — kon·teen·way too drwa
Turn left.
Tournez à gauche. — toor·nay a gosh
Turn right.
Tournez à droite. — toor·nay a drwat
at the corner
au coin — o kwun
at the traffic lights
aux feux — o fer

behind	*derrière*	dair·ryair
in front of	*devant*	der·von
far (from)	*loin (de)*	lwun (der)
near (to)	*près (de)*	pray (der)
opposite	*en face de*	on fas der

beach	*la plage*	la plazh
bridge	*le pont*	ler pon
church	*l'église*	lay·gleez
island	*l'île*	leel
lake	*le lac*	ler lak
museum	*le musée*	ler mew·zay
sea	*la mer*	la mair
tourist office	*l'office de tourisme*	lo·fees der too·rees·mer

FOOD & DRINK
Useful Phrases

I'd like to reserve a table.
J'aimerais resérver une table. — zhay·mer·ray ray·zair·vay ewn ta·bler
A table for two, please.
Une table pour deux, s'il vous plaît. — oon ta·bler poor der seel voo play

Is service included in the bill?
  Est-ce que le service est inclu?
  es·ker ler sair·vees et un·klew
Do you have a menu in English?
  Est-ce que vous avez la carte en anglais?
  es·ker voo a·vay la kart on ong·glay
What's the speciality here?
  Quelle est la spécialité ici?
  kel ay la spay·sya·lee·tay ees·ee
I'd like a local speciality.
  J'aimerais une spécialité régionale.
  zhay·mer·ray ewn spay·sya·lee·tay ray·zhyo·nal
Could you recommend something?
  Est-ce que vous pouvez recommender quelque chose?
  es·ker voo poo·vay re·ko·mon·day kel·ker shoz
I'd like the dish of the day.
  Je voudrais avoir le plat du jour.
  zher voo·dray a·vwar ler pla doo zhoor
I'd like the set menu.
  Je prends le menu.
  zher pron ler mer·new
I'd like to order the ...
  Je voudrais commander ...
  zher voo·dray ko·mon·day
The bill, please.
  La note, s'il vous plaît.
  la not seel voo play
I'm a vegetarian.
  Je suis végétarien/végétarienne.(m/f)
  zher swee vay·zhay·ta·ryun/vay·zhay·ta·ryen

I don't eat ...
Je ne mange pas de ...   zher ner monzh pa de ...
  meat
  viande   vyond
  fish
  poisson   pwa·son
  seafood
  fruits de mer   frwee der mair

Food Glossary
BASICS

beurre	ber	butter
céréale	say·ray·al	cereal
gâteau	ga·to	cake
piment	pee·mon	chilli
sel	sel	salt

MEAT

agneau	a·nyo	lamb
bœuf	burf	beef
calamar	ka·la·mar	squid
camarons	ka·ma·ron	prawns
crevettes	krer·vet	shrimps

fruit de mer	frwee ded mair	seafood
langouste	long·goost	lobster
mourgatte	moor·gat	squid
poisson	pwa·son	fish
porc	por	pork
poulet	poo·lay	chicken
poulpe	poolp	octopus
truite	trweet	trout

FRUITS & VEGETABLES

ananas	a·na·nas	pineapple
banane	ba·nan	banana
chou chou	shoo shoo	choko (squash)
combava	kom·ba·va	knobbly lime
goyave	go·yav	guava
noix de coco	nwa der ko·ko	coconut
pomme	pom	apple
pomme de terre	pom der tair	potato

COOKING TERMS

bouilli	boo·yee	boiled
frit/frite (m/f)	free/freet	fried
fumé	few·may	smoked
grillé	gree·yay	grilled
rôti	ro·tee	roasted

DRINKS

bière	bee·yair	beer
café	ka·fay	coffee
jus de fruit	zhew der fwee	fruit juice
pression	pre·syon	draft beer
thé	tay	tea
vin (rouge/blanc)	vun (roozh/blong)	wine (red/white)

MENU DECODER

achards (a·shar) – pickled vegetable salad
alouda (a·loo·da) – sweet, milky drink, popular in Mauritius
baie rose (bey roz) – pink pepper
bhajas (bha·yas) – fried balls of besan dough with herbs or onions
bibasse (bee·bas) – medlar fruit
bichiques (bee·sheek) – sprat-like seafood delicacy
biryani (beer·ya·nee) – curried rice; sometimes called *briani*
bois de songe (bwa der sonzh) – local vegetable
bol renversé (bol ron·vair·say) – rice with various toppings, such as chicken, beef or mixed vegetables
bonbons piments (bon·bon pee·mon) – see *dhal puris*
boucané (boo·ka·nay) – smoked pork
bouillon brêdes (boo·yon bred) – green vegetables cooked in a lightly spiced broth
bouillon crabes (boo·yon kraab) – crabs cooked in broth
brêdes (bred) – leafy green vegetables similar to Chinese cabbage
cabri massalé (ka·bree ma·sa·lay) – goat curry

LANGUAGE

caca pigeon (ka·ka pee·zhon) – Indian nibbles (literally 'pigeon droppings')

camarons d'eau douce (ka·ma·ron daw doos) – freshwater shrimps

carri coco (ka·ree ko·ko) – mild meat curry with coconut cream

carri poulet/poulpe/poisson (ka·ree poo·lay/poolp/pwa·son) – chicken/octopus/fish curry

carri sauve souris (ka·ree sawv soo·ree) – bat curry

cassoulet (ka·soo·lay) – thick stew of duck meat and haricot beans

catless (kat·les) – Indian snack (cutlet in breadcrumbs)

char siu (char·syoo) – barbecue pork

chatini (cha·tee·nee) – finely chopped tomato, onion, chilli and coriander appetiser

confit de canard (kon·fee der ka·nar) – duck meat preserved in its own fat

dhal puris (dal poo·ree) – Indian snack (thin pancakes served with beans and chilli sauce)

dosa masala (do·sa ma·sa·la) – Indian snack (thin bread with spicy potato filling)

faratta (fa·ra·ta) – unleavened flaky flour pancakes

foie gras (fwa gra) – fattened duck liver

gajacks (ga·jaks) – predinner snacks

Gâteau Napolitaine (ga·to na·po·lee·ten) – butter biscuits with jam and icing

gâteaux piments (ga·to pee·mon) – Indian snack (deep-fried balls of lentils and chilli)

jalebies (ja·le·bee) – fried batter spirals in syrup

lassi (la·see) – Indian yoghurt drink

mazavaroo (ma·za·va·roo) – chilli and prawn paste cooked in oil

mine frit (min freet) – fried Chinese noodles

mojito (mo·khee·to) – refreshing alcoholic drink made with mint, lemon, sugar and rum

murg dopiaza (murg do·pya·za) – chicken in an onion and tomato sauce

murg makhani (murg ma·ka·nee) – chicken with a tomato and cream sauce

octopus vindaloo (ok·to·poos vin·da·loo) – octopus in turmeric and mustard seed sauce

pain fouré (pun foo·ray) – filled bread rolls

pasanda (pa·san·da) – curry laced with almonds and sesame seeds

phad thai (paad tai) – mixed fried noodles

porc à la sauce grand-mère (por a la sos gron·mair) – dish of pork with chilli sauce (literally 'pork in grandma's sauce')

rhum arrangés (room a·ran·zhay) – mixture of rum, fruit juice, cane syrup and a blend of herbs and berries

riz renversé (ree ron·vair·say) – see *bol renversé*

rogan josh (ro·gan josh) – spiced lamb

rosenberghis (ro·zen·bur·gis) – tiger prawns

rougail (roo·gay) – spicy chutney popular in Réunion

rougail saucisses (roo·gay so·sees) – sausages in tomato and onion sauce

salade ourite (sa·laad oo·reet) – octopus salad, with seasoning including oil, vinegar and sliced onions

samosa – Indian snack (pastry triangle with various fillings)

sauce rouge (sos roozh) – brandy sauce

tarte tatin (tart tar·tan) – apple tart

tom yum thalay (tom yum ta·lay) – lemongrass-laced seafood soup

vindaye (vin·day) – turmeric-flavoured sauce with mustard seeds and vinegar

waaria (waa·ree·ya) – spicy vegetable snack

HEALTH

| I'm ill. | *Je suis malade.* | zher swee ma·lad |
| It hurts here. | *J'ai une douleur ici.* | zhay ewn doo·ler ee·see |

I'm ...	*Je suis ...*	zher swee ...
asthmatic	*asthmatique*	(z)as·ma·teek
diabetic	*diabétique*	dee·a·bay·teek
epileptic	*épileptique*	(z)ay·pee·lep·teek

I'm allergic to ...	*Je suis allergique ...*	zher swee za·lair·zheek ...
antibiotics	*aux antibiotiques*	o zon·tee·byo·teek
nuts	*aux noix*	o nwa
peanuts	*aux cacahuètes*	o ka·ka·wet
penicillin	*à la pénicilline*	a la pay·nee·see·leen

antiseptic	*l'antiseptique*	lon·tee·sep·teek
aspirin	*l'aspirine*	las·pee·reen
condoms	*des préservatifs*	day pray·zair·va·teef
contraceptive	*le contraceptif*	ler kon·tra·sep·teef
diarrhoea	*la diarrhée*	la dya·ray
medicine	*le médicament*	ler may·dee·ka·mon
nausea	*la nausée*	la no·zay
sunblock cream	*la crème solaire*	la krem so·lair
tampons	*des tampons hygiéniques*	day tom·pon ee·zhen·eek

LANGUAGE DIFFICULTIES

Do you speak English?
Parlez-vous anglais?   par·lay·voo ong·lay

Does anyone here speak English?
Y a-t-il quelqu'un qui parle anglais?   ya·teel kel·kung kee par long·glay

How do you say ... in French?
Comment est-ce qu'on dit ... en français?   ko·mon es·kon dee ... on fron·say

What does ... mean?
Que veut dire ...?   ker ver deer ...

I understand.
Je comprends.   zher kom·pron

I don't understand.
Je ne comprends pas.   zher ner kom·pron pa

EMERGENCIES

Help!
   Au secours!   o skoor
There's been an accident!
   Il y a eu un accident!   eel ya ew un ak·see·don
I'm lost.
   Je me suis égaré/e. (m/f)   zhe me swee·zay·ga·ray
Leave me alone!
   Fichez-moi la paix!   fee·shay·mwa la pay

Call ...!   Appelez ...!   a·play ...
   a doctor   un médecin   un mayd·sun
   the police   la police   la po·lees

Could you write it down, please?
   Est-ce que vous pouvez   es·ker voo poo·vay
   l'écrire?   lay·kreer
Can you show me (on the map)?
   Pouvez-vous m'indiquer   poo·vay·voo mun·dee·kay
   (sur la carte)?   (sewr la kart)

NUMBERS

0	zero	zay·ro
1	un	un
2	deux	der
3	trois	trwa
4	quatre	ka·trer
5	cinq	sungk
6	six	sees
7	sept	set
8	huit	weet
9	neuf	nerf
10	dix	dees
11	onze	onz
12	douze	dooz
13	treize	trez
14	quatorze	ka·torz
15	quinze	kunz
16	seize	sez
17	dix-sept	dee·set
18	dix-huit	dee·zweet
19	dix-neuf	deez·nerf
20	vingt	vung
21	vingt et un	vung tay un
22	vingt-deux	vung·der
30	trente	tront
40	quarante	ka·ront
50	cinquante	sung·kont
60	soixante	swa·sont
70	soixante-dix	swa·son·dees
80	quatre-vingts	ka·trer·vung
90	quatre-vingt-dix	ka·trer·vung·dees
100	cent	son
1000	mille	meel

PAPERWORK

name	nom	nom
nationality	nationalité	na·syo·na·lee·tay
date/place	date/place	dat/plas
of birth	de naissance	der nay·sons
sex/gender	sexe	seks
passport	passeport	pas·por
visa	visa	vee·za

QUESTION WORDS

Who?	Qui?	kee
What?	Quoi?	kwa
What is it?	Qu'est-ce que	kes·ker
	c'est?	say
When?	Quand?	kon
Where?	Où?	oo
Which?	Quel/Quelle?	kel (m/f)
Why?	Pourquoi?	poor·kwa
How?	Comment?	ko·mon

SHOPPING & SERVICES

I'd like to buy ...
   Je voudrais acheter ...   zher voo·dray ash·tay ...
How much is it?
   C'est combien?   say kom·byun
I don't like it.
   Cela ne me plaît pas.   ser·la ner mer play pa
May I look at it?
   Est-ce que je peux le voir? es·ker zher per ler vwar
I'm just looking.
   Je regarde.   zher rer·gard
It's cheap.
   Ce n'est pas cher.   ser nay pa shair
It's too expensive.
   C'est trop cher.   say tro shair
I'll take it.
   Je le prends.   zher ler pron

Can I pay by ...?	Est-ce que je peux	es·ker zher per
	payer avec ...?	pay·yay a·vek ...
credit card	ma carte de	ma kart der
	crédit	kray·dee
travellers	des chèques	day shek
cheques	de voyage	der vwa·yazh

more	plus	plew
less	moins	mwa
smaller	plus petit	plew per·tee
bigger	plus grand	plew gron

I'm looking	Je cherche ...	zhe shersh ...
for ...		
a bank	une banque	ewn bonk
the hospital	l'hôpital	lo·pee·tal

the market	le marché	ler mar·shay
the police	la police	la po·lees
the post office	le bureau de poste	ler bew·ro der post
a public phone	une cabine téléphonique	ewn ka·been tay·lay·fo·neek
a public toilet	les toilettes	lay twa·let

TIME & DATES
What time is it?
Quelle heure est-il?   kel er e til
It's (8) o'clock.
Il est (huit) heures.   il e (weet) er
It's half past ...
Il est (...) heures et demie.   il e (...) er e day·mee
in the morning
du matin   dew ma·tun
in the afternoon
de l'après-midi   der la·pray·mee·dee
in the evening
du soir   dew swar

today	aujourd'hui	o·zhoor·dwee
tomorrow	demain	der·mun
yesterday	hier	yair

Monday	lundi	lun·dee
Tuesday	mardi	mar·dee
Wednesday	mercredi	mair·krer·dee
Thursday	jeudi	zher·dee
Friday	vendredi	von·drer·dee
Saturday	samedi	sam·dee
Sunday	dimanche	dee·monsh

January	janvier	zhon·vyay
February	février	fayv·ryay
March	mars	mars
April	avril	a·vreel
May	mai	may
June	juin	zhwun
July	juillet	zhwee·yay
August	août	oot
September	septembre	sep·tom·brer
October	octobre	ok·to·brer
November	novembre	no·vom·brer
December	décembre	day·som·brer

TRANSPORT
Public Transport
What time does ... leave/arrive?
À quelle heure part/arrive ...?   a kel er par/a·reev ...
boat	le bateau	ler ba·to
bus	le bus	ler bews
plane	l'avion	la·vyon

I'd like a ...	Je voudrais	zher voo·dray
ticket.	un billet ...	un bee·yay ...
one-way	simple	sum·pler
return	aller et retour	a·lay ay rer·toor

I want to go to ...
Je voudrais aller à ...   zher voo·dray a·lay a ...
The bus has been delayed.
Le bus est en retard.   ler bews et on rer·tar
The bus has been cancelled.
Le bus a été annulé.   ler bews a ay·tay a·new·lay

the first	le premier (m)	ler prer·myay
	la première (f)	la prer·myair
the last	le dernier (m)	ler dair·nyay
	la dernière (f)	la dair·nyair
ticket office	le guichet	ler gee·shay
timetable	l'horaire	lo·rair

Private Transport
I'd like to hire a/an...	Je voudrais louer ...	zher voo·dray loo·way ...
car	une voiture	ewn vwa·tewr
4WD	un quatre-quatre	un kat·kat
motorbike	une moto	ewn mo·to
bicycle	un vélo	un vay·lo

Is this the road to ...?
C'est la route pour ...?   say la root poor ...
Where's a service station?
Où est-ce qu'il y a une station-service?   oo es·keel ya ewn sta·syon·ser·vees
Please fill it up.
Le plein, s'il vous plaît.   ler plun seel voo play
I'd like ... litres.
Je voudrais ... litres.   zher voo·dray ... lee·trer

petrol/gas	essence	ay·sons
unleaded	sans plomb	son plom
leaded	au plomb	o plom
diesel	diesel	dyay·zel

I need a mechanic.
J'ai besoin d'un mécanicien.   zhay ber·zwun dun may·ka·nee·syun
The car/motorbike has broken down at ...
La voiture/moto est tombée en panne à ...   la vwa·tewr/mo·to ay tom·bay on pan a ...
The car/motorbike won't start.
La voiture/moto ne veut pas démarrer.   la vwa·tewr/mo·to ner ver pa day·ma·ray

I have a flat tyre.
 Mon pneu est à plat.
 mom pner ay ta pla
I've run out of petrol.
 Je suis en panne d'essence.
 zher swee zon pan day·sons
I had an accident.
 J'ai eu un accident.
 zhay ew un ak·see·don

TRAVEL WITH CHILDREN
Is there (a) ...?
Y a-t-il ...?   ya teel ...
I need (a) ...
J'ai besoin ...   zhay ber·zwun ...
  car baby seat
  d'un siège-enfant   dun syezh·on·fon
  disposable nappies/diapers
  de couches-culottes   der koosh·kew·lot
  formula (infant milk)
  de lait maternisé   de lay ma·ter·nee·zay
  highchair
  d'une chaise haute   dewn shay zot
  potty
  d'un pot de bébé   dun po der bay·bay
  stroller
  d'une poussette   dewn poo·set

Are children allowed?
 Les enfants sont permis? lay zon·fon son pair·mee

Glossary

auberge – farm inn
auberge de jeunesse – youth hostel

baba figue – the blossom of the banana tree
bassins – small lakes
bibliothèque – library
bom – stringed instrument with a bulbous gourd-shaped body
bonhommes/bonfemmes di bois – medicine men/women
branles, **brandes** – giant heather bushes

camtole – in the Seychelles, a traditional roving band featuring fiddle, banjo, drums and accordion
carte de séjour – residence permit
case créole – traditional Creole house
cavadee – Hindu festival featuring self-mutilating devotees
cerfs – stags
chambre d'hôte – family-run B&B
colons – colonial settlers
commune – administrative district
Compagnie des Indes Orientales – French East India Company
contredanse – dance similar to the quadrille

dentelles – decorative frieze on Creole houses

écart – settlement
ferme-auberge – farm restaurant
filaos – casuarina trees

gare routière – bus station
gendarmerie – police station
gîte – self-catering accommodation
gîte d'étape – walkers lodge
gîte de montagne – mountain lodge
grands blancs – rich whites
gris gris – black magic
guichet automatique de banque (GAB) – automated teller machine (ATM)

hauts – highlands
hôtel de ville – town hall; see also *mairie*

kanvar – light wooden frame or arch decorated with paper flowers
kotis – dance similar to Scottish dancing

la malaise Creole – Creole people's anger at their impoverished status
lambrequins – ornamental window and door borders

la métropole – mainland France as known in Réunion
le sud sauvage – wild south (southern part of Réunion island)
librairie – bookshop
location de voitures – car hire

mairie – town hall; whether a town has a mairie or a *hôtel de ville* depends on the local-government status of the town
makalapo – stringed instrument with a tin sound-box
maloya – traditional dance music of Réunion
marmite – traditional cooking pot
marrons – slaves who escaped from their owners
Mascarene Islands – the collective term for the group of volcanic islands in the West Indian Ocean consisting of Réunion, Mauritius and Rodrigues
massalé – Indian spice mix
mazok – dance reminiscent of the French waltz
menu du jour – set menu of the day
merle blanc – cuckoo shrike; Réunion's rarest bird
métro cuisine – cuisine of mainland France
moutia – sombre, traditional dance of the Seychelles
MWF – Mauritian Wildlife Foundation

office du tourisme – tourist office

paille-en-queue – white-tailed tropicbird
papangue – Maillardi buzzard, a protected hawklike bird
plat du jour – dish of the day
pétanque – game similar to bowls
pie chanteuse – magpie robins
puja – the burning of incense and camphor at the lake shore and offering of food and flowers

ragga – blend of reggae, house music and Indian music, popular in Mauritius
ravanne – primitive goatskin drum which traditionally accompanies the *séga* dance
route forestière – forestry road

séga – dance of African origin
seggae – combination of reggae and traditional *séga* music
sentier botanique – nature trail
sentier forestier – forest dirt track
sentiers marmailles – footpath suitable for children
source thermale – hot spring

table d'hôte – meal served at a *chambre d'hôte*
tamarin des Hauts – mountain tamarind tree
tec-tec – bird native to Réunion's highlands; also known as Réunion stonechat

télécarte – telephone card
teemeedee – Hindu/Tamil fire-walking ceremony honouring the gods
ti' cases – homes of the common folk

vacoa – screw pines; also known as pandanus
varangue – veranda

vélo tout terrain (VTT) – mountain bike
veuve – widow (Seychellois name for the paradise flycatcher)

zez – monochord sitar
Zoreilles – name used in Réunion for people from mainland France (literally 'the ears')

The Authors

TOM MASTERS
Coordinating Author

Tom got addicted to the Indian Ocean after writing the *Maldives* guidebook for Lonely Planet in 2006. He jumped at the chance to discover Mauritius next and was amazed to find how different it was, spending a culturally fascinating time exploring the island by bus, bike, car and on foot. Favourite moments included the endless romantic sunsets, a particularly special stay at Eureka in Moka, the diving at Pointe d'Esny and Flic-en-Flac and an utterly blissful week on the tiny, mountainous island of Rodrigues. Tom works as a freelance writer and documentary producer based in London. More of his work can be seen at www.mastersmafia.com. For this title Tom wrote the Getting Started, Itineraries, Mauritius and Regional Transport chapters.

JEAN-BERNARD CARILLET

A Paris-based journalist and photographer, Jean-Bernard has clocked up numerous trips to the Indian Ocean, including several extended stays in Réunion, where he tested his mettle driving along the twisting roads of the Hauts, hiking in the Cirques, paragliding over the lagoon, diving steep drop-offs, canyoning in the interior and flying over the volcano – a much-needed action-packed programme after gorging on the irresistible but calorie-busting Creole and *métro* cuisines.

For this edition he was all too happy to complement his Réunion trip with a more hedonistic journey in the Seychelles, where he milled about searching for the perfect beach and the best grilled fish.

Jean-Bernard has contributed to many Lonely Planet titles, both in French and English. For this title he wrote the Diving, Réunion and Seychelles chapters.

Behind the Scenes

THIS BOOK

This is the 6th edition of *Mauritius, Réunion & Seychelles*. The 1st edition was researched and written by Robert Willox. The 2nd edition was updated by Robert Strauss and Deanna Swaney, and the 3rd edition was updated by Sarina Singh. Joe Bindloss updated the 4th edition and Jann Dodd the 5th edition. This edition was researched and written by Tom Masters (Mauritius and coordinating author) and Jean-Bernard Carillet (Réunion, Seychelles and Diving). Dr Caroline Evans wrote the Health chapter.

This guidebook was commissioned in Lonely Planet's Melbourne office, and produced by the following:

Commissioning Editor Marg Toohey, Tashi Wheeler
Coordinating Editor Rosie Nicholson
Coordinating Cartographer Anthony Phelan

Coordinating Layout Designer Yvonne Bischofberger
Managing Editor Bruce Evans
Managing Cartographer Shahara Ahmed
Managing Layout Designer Celia Wood
Assisting Editors Yvonne Byron, Andrea Dobbin, Kate James, Maryanne Netto, Averil Robertson, Phillip Tang
Assisting Cartographers Barbara Benson, Andrew Smith
Assisting Layout Designers David Kemp, Wibowo Rusli
Cover Designer Marika Kozak
Project Manager Glenn van der Knijff
Language Content Coordinator Quentin Frayne

Thanks to Adam McCrow, Joshua Geoghegan, Emma Gilmour, Suyin Ng, Raphael Richards, Lyahna Spencer

THANKS
TOM MASTERS
Thanks to James for making my job feel like a holiday when he's around and for so excellently

---

LONELY PLANET: TRAVEL WIDELY, TREAD LIGHTLY, GIVE SUSTAINABLY

The Lonely Planet Story
The story begins with a classic travel adventure: Tony and Maureen Wheeler's 1972 journey across Europe and Asia to Australia. There was no useful information about the overland trail then, so Tony and Maureen published the first Lonely Planet guidebook to meet a growing need.

From a kitchen table, Lonely Planet has grown to become the largest independent travel publisher in the world, with offices in Melbourne (Australia), Oakland (USA) and London (UK). Today Lonely Planet guidebooks cover the globe. There is an ever-growing list of books and information in a variety of media. Some things haven't changed. The main aim is still to make it possible for adventurous individuals to get out there – to explore and better understand the world.

The Lonely Planet Foundation
The Lonely Planet Foundation proudly supports nimble nonprofit institutions working for change in the world. Each year the foundation donates 5% of Lonely Planet company profits to projects selected by staff and authors. Our partners range from Kabissa, which provides small nonprofits across Africa with access to technology, to the Foundation for Developing Cambodian Orphans, which supports girls at risk of falling victim to sex traffickers.

Our nonprofit partners are linked by a grass-roots approach to the areas of health, education or sustainable tourism. Many projects we support – such as one with BaAka (Pygmy) children in the forested areas of Central African Republic – choose to focus on women and children as one of the most effective ways to support the whole community.

Sometimes foundation assistance is as simple as helping to preserve a local ruin like the Minaret of Jam in Afghanistan; this incredible monument now draws intrepid tourists to the area and its restoration has greatly improved options for local people.

Just as travel is often about learning to see with new eyes, so many of the groups we work with aim to change the way people see themselves and the future for their children and communities.

preparing the sundowners. Huge thanks to José Savrimootoo of Exodus Car Hire for all his help and advice, to the MTPA, to the staff of the St Georges Hotel in Port Louis for always making me welcome, to the charming Baptiste family in Rodrigues, the Vexlard family in Grande Rivière Noire and in general to the many Mauritians who helped me along the way. Thanks also to Lonely Planet's venerable Marg Toohey for sending me back to paradise for the second time in a year and to Jean-Bernard Carillet, my co-author, for doing all the tough bits!

JEAN-BERNARD CARILLET
A huge thanks to Tom Masters, Marg Toohey, Emma Gilmour, Rosie Nicholson and the carto team for their patience, understanding and support throughout this challenging process.

While researching this guidebook I was lucky enough to encounter plenty of helpful Réunionnais and Seychellois, including Jean-Paul Diana, Axelle, Nadine, Kalou, Jasmine, Steph, Jean-Philippe, Alain Courbis, Christine Salem, Sharen Venus, Bernadette Willemin, Severine, Michel Gardette, Robbie Bresson and Jean-Michel Furia. Their assistance was invaluable, as were the countless pointers and tips I enjoyed from the travellers I met along the way.

OUR READERS
Many thanks to the travellers who used the last edition and wrote to us with helpful hints, useful advice and interesting anecdotes:

Hagar Abramson, Karolina Adamkiewicz, Katie Allen, Marcio Aloisio De Oliveira, S Appannah, Naomi Axford, Kim Seela Ballentyne-Dannau, Justin Blomeley, Uta Botterbrod, Lynda & Cameron Bremner, Melissa Brown, Adrian Burger, Gordon Burrows, Victoria Cameron, Bobby Collins, John Connell, Neil Cork, Judy Cove, G Cumberpatch, Nolan De Chalain, Dorothy De St Jorre, Julia Devore, Mausi Digel, Michael Dittenbach, Ronnie Dooley, Derek Drinkwater, Sara & Yonatan Eyal, Guido Faes, Ferdinand Fellinger, Dario Frigo, Jonathan Gill, Justin Giorgetti, Hazel Grant, Joris Habraken, S Harris, Glen Hart, Irene Hartmann, Kaori Hashimoto, Kaori Hashimoto, Corien Hiddink-Van Der Poel, Jon Holden, Denis Humbert, Trygve & Karen Inda, Lucy James, Piotr Janecki, Julie Kenyon, Boris Kester, Alan Kirsner, Leonard Kreuzer, Annette Kwan-Terry, Rachel Larson, Elaine Lee, Gay Lee, Nerissa Levy, Veronique Louis, Christiane Lux, Magali Malherbe, Graham

Mash, Markella Mikkelsen, Alissa Morris, Anita Newcourt, Finn Arup Nielsen, Bonnie Persons, Ronit Piso, Rebecca Quinlan, Marie Reynolds, Marcia Rooker, Walter Russell, Meara Sullivan-Thomas Jean-Pascal Schaefer, Liz Sexon, Manuela Siegert, Graham Slessar, Andreas Stangl, Uli Steinbrenner, Elisabeth Stocker, Jodi Stokol Eric Su, Heiko Suess, Katalin Szilagyi, Istvan Szucs, Martin Taylor, Stefanie Toussain, Emma Ulmer, Gordon Vaeth, Karine Van Malderen, Suzanne Van Skike, Barbara Waldis, Phil Ward, Caroline & Simon Webster, Hans Wiederroder, Danielle Wolbers, Pascale De Souza Dromund, Bert Van Den Berg

ACKNOWLEDGMENTS
Many thanks to the following for the use of their content:

Globe on title page ©Mountain High Maps 1993 Digital Wisdom, Inc.

GR®, GRP®, their way markings (white/red and yellow/red), and PR® are the Fédération française de la Randonnée pédestre's registered trademarks. GR®R1, GR®R2, GR®R3 Copyrights belong to the Fédération française de la Randonnée pédestre, reproduced with its kind permission.

SEND US YOUR FEEDBACK
We love to hear from travellers – your comments keep us on our toes and help make our books better. Our well-travelled team reads every word on what you loved or loathed about this book. Although we cannot reply individually to postal submissions, we always guarantee that your feedback goes straight to the appropriate authors, in time for the next edition. Each person who sends us information is thanked in the next edition – and the most useful submissions are rewarded with a free book.

To send us your updates – and find out about Lonely Planet events, newsletters and travel news – visit our award-winning website: **www.lonelyplanet.com/contact**.

Note: we may edit, reproduce and incorporate your comments in Lonely Planet products such as guidebooks, websites and digital products, so let us know if you don't want your comments reproduced or your name acknowledged. For a copy of our privacy policy visit www.lonelyplanet.com/privacy.

Index

12am	1am	2am	3am	4am	5am	6am	7am	8am	9am	10am	11am	12pm

Mon
Sun

International Date Line

ARCTIC OCEAN

CHUKCHI SEA

Russia

Alaska (US)
3am

BEAUFORT SEA

Queen Elizabeth Is (Can)

Banks Is (Can)

Victoria Is (Can)

5am

Ellesmere Is (Can)

BAFFIN BAY

Baffin Is (Can)

9am
Greenland (Denmark)

11am

GREENLAND SEA

NORWEGIAN SEA

Iceland

BERING SEA

4am

GULF OF ALASKA

2am

HUDSON BAY

Canada
6am

LABRADOR SEA

8am

8.30am

7am

NORTH ATLANTIC OCEAN

NORTH SEA

United Kingdom

Ireland

NORTH PACIFIC OCEAN

1am
Midway Is (US)

Hawaii (US)

United States

Mexico

GULF OF MEXICO

The Bahamas

Cuba

Haiti

CARIBBEAN SEA

Guatemala
Nicaragua

Eastern Caribbean Islands

Bermuda (UK)

Azores (Port)

Portugal

Canary Is (Sp)

Spain

Morocco

Mauritania
12pm

Cape Verde

Senegal
Guinea

Mali

Burkina Faso

Liberia

Ghana

GULF OF GUINEA

EQUATOR

Samoa

Kiribati

Tonga
12am

Cook Is (NZ)
1am

Tahiti
2am

French Polynesia (Fr)

2.30am

Pitcairn Is 3.30am (UK)

Easter Is (Chile)

Galapagos Is (Ecuador)

Panama

Ecuador

Colombia

Venezuela

Guyana

Suriname

Peru
7am

8am

Brazil 9am

Bolivia

Paraguay

Ascension (UK)

SOUTH ATLANTIC OCEAN

New Zealand

12.45am
Chatham Is (NZ)

SOUTH PACIFIC OCEAN

Chile

Uruguay

Argentina

Tristan da Cunha (UK)

Gough Is (UK)

Falkland Is (UK)

South Georgia & South Sandwich Is (UK)

Bouvet Is (Norway)

12am	1am	2am	3am	4am	5am	6am	7am	8am	9am	10am	11am	12pm

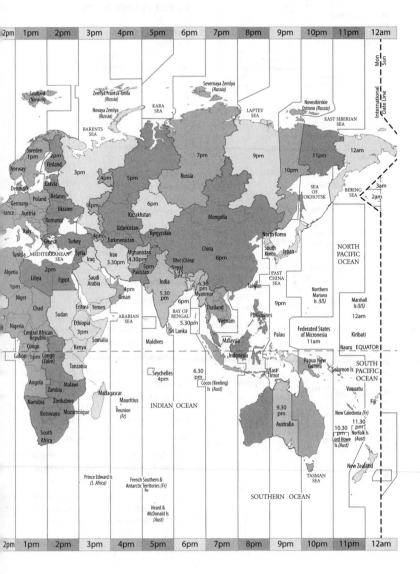

MAP LEGEND

ROUTES

M2 ... Motorway	...... Mall/Steps
A5 ... Primary	...... Tunnel
...... Secondary	...... Pedestrian Overpass
...... Tertiary	...... Walking Tour
...... Lane	...... Walking Tour Detour
...... Unsealed Road	...... Walking Trail
...... One-Way Street	...... Walking Path

TRANSPORT

...... Ferry	...... Rail

HYDROGRAPHY

...... River, Creek	...... Water
...... Reef	

BOUNDARIES

...... International	...... Regional, Suburb
...... State, Provincial	...... Cliff
...... Marine Park	

AREA FEATURES

...... Airport	...... Land
...... Area of Interest	...... Park
...... Beach, Desert	...... Rocks
...... Building	...... Sports
+ + + ... Cemetery, Christian	...... Urban

POPULATION

☉ CAPITAL (NATIONAL)	◉ CAPITAL (STATE)
● Large City	● Medium City
● Small City	● Town, Village

SYMBOLS

Sights/Activities
- Beach
- Castle, Fortress
- Christian
- Confucian
- Diving, Snorkeling
- Hindu
- Islamic
- Monument
- Museum, Gallery
- Point of Interest
- Pool
- Ruin
- Snorkelling
- Surfing, Surf Beach
- Zoo, Bird Sanctuary

Eating
- Eating

Drinking
- Drinking
- Café

Entertainment
- Entertainment

Shopping
- Shopping

Sleeping
- Sleeping

Transport
- Airport, Airfield
- Bus Station
- Parking Area
- Petrol Station
- Taxi Rank

Information
- Bank, ATM
- Embassy/Consulate
- Hospital, Medical
- Information
- Internet Facilities
- Police Station
- Post Office, GPO
- Telephone

Geographic
- Lighthouse
- Lookout
- Mountain, Volcano
- National Park
- Pass, Canyon
- Shelter, Hut
- Spot Height
- Waterfall

LONELY PLANET OFFICES

Australia
Head Office
Locked Bag 1, Footscray, Victoria 3011
☎ 03 8379 8000, fax 03 8379 8111
talk2us@lonelyplanet.com.au

USA
150 Linden St, Oakland, CA 94607
☎ 510 893 8555, toll free 800 275 8555
fax 510 893 8572
info@lonelyplanet.com

UK
72–82 Rosebery Ave,
Clerkenwell, London EC1R 4RW
☎ 020 7841 9000, fax 020 7841 9001
go@lonelyplanet.co.uk

Published by Lonely Planet Publications Pty Ltd
ABN 36 005 607 983

© Lonely Planet Publications Pty Ltd 2007

© photographers as indicated 2007

Cover photograph: Fishing in the Indian Ocean off Mahébourg, Mauritius, Peter Adams/Alamy. Many of the images in this guide are available for licensing from Lonely Planet Images: www.lonelyplanetimages.com.

Printed by SNP Security Printing Pte Ltd, Singapore